SPECIAL FEATURES IN *BRIDGING THE GAP*, TWE

Bridging the Gap

College Reading

TWELFTH EDITION

Brenda D. Smith
Professor Emerita, Georgia State University

LeeAnn Morris
Professor Emerita, San Jacinto College

Boston   Columbus   Indianapolis   New York   San Francisco
Amsterdam   Cape Town   Dubai   London   Madrid   Milan   Munich   Paris   Montréal   Toronto
Delhi   Mexico City   São Paulo   Sydney   Hong Kong   Seoul   Singapore   Taipei   Tokyo

In memory of my mother and father—B.D.S

To Tim, who loved to read—L.M.

Executive Editor: Matthew Wright
Program Manager: Eric Jorgensen
Development Editor: Janice Wiggins
Product Marketing Manager: Jennifer Edwards
Executive Field Marketing Manager: Joyce Nilsen
Media Producer: Marisa Massaro
Content Specialist: Julia Pomann
Media Editor: Tracy Cunningham
Project Manager: Donna Campion

Text Design, Project Coordination, and Electronic Page
 Makeup: Cenveo Publishing Services
Program Design Lead: Barbara Atkinson
Cover Designer: Cenveo® Publishing Services
Cover Illustration: DaBarti CGI/Shutterstock
Senior Manufacturing Buyer: Roy L. Pickering, Jr.
Printer/Binder: RR Donnelley / Willard
Cover Printer: Phoenix Color/Hagerstown

Acknowledgments of third-party content appear on pages 563-565, which constitute an extension of this copyright page.

PEARSON, ALWAYS LEARNING, and MYREADINGLAB are exclusive trademarks owned by Pearson Education, Inc. or its affiliates in the United States and/or other countries.

Unless otherwise indicated herein, any third-party trademarks that may appear in this work are the property of their respective owners and any references to third-party trademarks, logos, or other trade dress are for demonstrative or descriptive purposes only. Such references are not intended to imply any sponsorship, endorsement, authorization, or promotion of Pearson's products by the owners of such marks, or any relationship between the owner and Pearson Education, Inc., or its affiliates, authors, licensees, or distributors.

Library of Congress Cataloging-in-Publication Data
Names: Smith, Brenda D., date- author. | Morris, LeeAnn, author.
Title: Bridging the gap : college reading / Brenda D. Smith, LeeAnn Morris.
Description: Twelfth edition. | Boston : Pearson, [2016] | ?2017 | Includes
   index.
Identifiers: LCCN 2015040922| ISBN 9780134072760 (student edition) | ISBN
   9780134064918 (annotated instructor's edition)
Subjects: LCSH: Reading (Higher education) |Study skills.
Classification: LCC LB2395.3 .S64 2016 | DDC808/.0427—dc23
LCrecord available at http://lccn.loc.gov/2015040922

2   16

Student Edition ISBN 10:   0-13-407276-6
Student Edition ISBN 13:   978-0-13-407276-0
À la Carte Edition ISBN 10:   0-13-406482-8
A la Carte Edition ISBN 13: 978-0-13-406482-6

www.pearsonhighered.com

MyReadingLab™: Improving Reading Through Personalized Learning Experiences

In an ideal world, an instructor would work with each student to help improve reading skills with consistent challenges and rewards. Without that luxury, MyReadingLab offers a way to keep students focused and accelerate their progress using comprehensive pre-assignments and a powerful, adaptive study plan.

Flexible Enough to Fit Every Course Need

MyReadingLab can be set up to fit your specific course needs, whether you seek reading support to complement what you do in class, a way to administer many sections easily, or a self-paced environment for independent study.

Learning in Context

In addition to distinct pre-loaded learning paths for reading/writing skills practice and reading level practice, MyReadingLab incorporates numerous activities for practice and readings from the accompanying textbook. This makes the connection between what's done in and out of the classroom more relevant to students.

NEW! Learning Tools for Student Engagement

Create an Engaging Classroom

Learning Catalytics is an interactive, student-response tool in MyReadingLab that uses students' smartphones, tablets, or laptops, allowing instructors to generate class discussion easily, guide lectures, and promote peer-to-peer learning with real-time analytics.

Build Multimedia Assignments

MediaShare allows students to easily post multimodal assignments for peer review and instructor feedback. In both face-to-face and online courses, MediaShare enriches the student learning experience by enabling contextual feedback to be provided quickly and easily.

Direct Access to MyLab

Users can link from any Learning Management System (LMS) to Pearson's MyReadingLab. Access MyLab assignments, rosters and resources, and synchronize MyLab grades with the LMS gradebook.

Visit www.myreadinglab.com for more information.

BRIEF CONTENTS

DETAILED CONTENTS

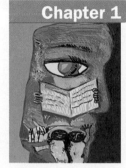

Chapter 2   Strategic Reading and Study 71

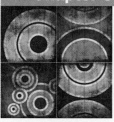

Chapter 4 Vocabulary 175

Chapter 6   Patterns of Organization   287

Chapter 7 Inference   341

Chapter 8   Point of View   405

PREFACE

Educators ground teaching on their beliefs about how learning occurs. Although teachers might not articulate their philosophy, classroom observers would see it in the resources, activities, policies, and daily routines that encompass the educational experience. Likewise, textbooks reflect but don't necessarily state authors' pedagogical principles. Musing on this notion, a conference speaker recently commented that textbooks rarely, if ever, contain an explanation of their undergirding philosophy. He went on to say that their authors may not even be guided by any particular theory or research but only by their personal experience and beliefs about how people learn. In its very title, though, *Bridging the Gap* is clear about the principles that guided the first edition, this twelfth edition, and every edition between them. Bridging—making connections—is the focus of this text.

The structure, materials, and activities throughout this book rest on the constructivist view that learning works best when connections are made between new ideas and what the learner already knows. *Bridging the Gap* challenges students to build on their previous reading experiences to develop strategies for the independence and challenge of college reading and learning. The longer selections, as well as the shorter textbook excerpts, also build schemata that are needed to absorb new concepts in criminal justice, health, history, philosophy, psychology, science, technology, and other academic disciplines. Likewise, video clips accompany longer reading selections to link academic topics to current events and place academic ideas in the context of the real world. Writing activities recognize the implicit connection between writing and reading. Perhaps more important than ever is the bridge to a career, job advancement, and a better quality of life—the goal that most college students are seeking. Instructors will recognize the theories of Jerome Bruner and Lev Vygotsky in the structure of this textbook, but providing bridges to effective reading strategies, new knowledge, the real world, careers, and college success is at the heart of *Bridging the Gap*.

NEW TO THE TWELFTH EDITION

The twelfth edition of *Bridging the Gap* holds true to the long tradition of solid instruction supported with fresh, new readings and features to connect with students.

- **NEW Readings Throughout. Twelve new, major reading selections plus brand new versions of two popular readings from the eleventh edition** provide high-interest topics, such as battling procrastination, conservation of earth's resources, managing stress in college, technology and health, a famous study on obedience, dealing with interpersonal conflict, the story of an inspiring student activist during the civil rights movement of the 1960s, climate change, and native American philosophy expressed in a "Coyote" myth. In response to reviewers' suggestions, a long reading selection now accompanies the vocabulary chapter. **New, short excerpts** freshen many of the practice exercises.

- **NEW Stronger emphasis on critical thinking.** Two new features in the twelfth edition of *Bridging the Gap* **focus on critical thinking.** A debut **collection of themed readings** concludes Chapter 10: Critical Thinking. The introduction and readings in the collection explore the interwoven threads of **technology, crime, and ethics,** and challenge students to analyze, synthesize, and respond. In addition, **Think Critically About the Selection** follows each of the 28 long reading selections to encourage extended thinking about topics that are raised in the readings. In some cases, this feature connects with the **Write About the Selection** feature that also follows each reading.

- **NEW Reorganization of chapters.** Long-time *Bridging the Gap* users will notice a **major reorganization of chapters.** Due to the widespread offering of student success courses that orient students to topics such as time management, cognitive styles, and routines of college life, **Chapter 1** of the twelfth edition emphasizes concerns that are common to college readers: **causes and cures for poor concentration while reading, reading rate and efficiency, and strategies for reading comprehension tests.** In response to reviewers' suggestions, topics that students need early in the course now appear closer to the beginning of the text. The **three stages of reading comprise Chapter 2; note taking and the study process appear in Chapter 3. A reading selection added to Chapter 4** provides authentic practice of **vocabulary strategies.** The main body of the twelfth edition includes Chapter 5: Main Idea and Supporting Details, Chapter 6: Patterns of Organization, Chapter 7: Inference, and Chapter 8: Point of View. The text concludes with coverage of **graphic illustrations (Chapter 9)** and **critical thinking (Chapter 10).** For the convenience of instructors and students, a new **chart, the Features Chart,** provides a **quick reference to topics and page numbers for the Vocabulary Boosters and Concept Preps.** It can be found on the first page of the book, facing the front cover.

- **NEW Build Background Knowledge—Video (in MyReadingLab).** A new feature, Build Background Knowledge, accompanies each of the longer readings in the text and offers links to engaging videos and apparatus in MyReadingLab that stimulate interest, develop background knowledge, and enrich understanding.

CONTENT AND ORGANIZATION

The twelfth edition continues another tradition of previous editions by using actual college textbook material for instruction and practice. Designed for an upper-level course in college reading, each chapter introduces a new strategy, provides short practice exercises to teach it, and then offers practice through longer textbook selections.

A new sequencing of topics begins with subjects that are critical to college reading success and then moves from lower to the higher levels of Bloom's Taxonomy to present students with gradually more challenging and sophisticated reading skills. Initial chapters discuss active academic learning, reading efficiency, and comprehension test-taking skills (Chapter 1), strategic reading and study (Chapter 2), organizing textbook material for study (Chapter 3), vocabulary (Chapter 4), main ideas and supporting details (Chapter 5), and patterns of organization (Chapter 6), Later chapters teach inference (Chapter 7), point of view (Chapter 8), graphic illustrations (Chapter 9), and critical thinking (Chapter 10). The reading and study strategies discussions that appear early in the book stress the need to construct the main idea of a passage and to select significant supporting details. Exercises throughout the text reinforce and encourage "engaged thinking" with specific strategies to use before, during, and after reading. Annotating during reading and three different methods of organizing textbook notes for later study are explained and then reinforced in the remaining chapters. The critical thinking chapter brings all of the reading skills to bear on the essential ability to analyze and evaluate reading material.

FEATURES

- Actual **textbook selections** are used for practice exercises.
- **Many academic disciplines** are represented throughout, including psychology, history, communications, business, health, sociology, criminal justice, philosophy, science, and literature; the latter includes the essay, short story, poetry, and narrative forms, and persuasive and expository nonfiction forms.
- **Vocabulary is presented in context;** vocabulary exercises follow each of the longer textbook reading selections. In addition to the end-of-chapter **Vocabulary Booster** lessons, a broad range of **vocabulary development** topics and corresponding exercises are presented in Chapter 4.
- **Reader's Tip** boxes give easy-to-access advice for readers, condensing strategies for improving reading into practical hints for quick reference.
- Each longer textbook reading selection has both **explicit and inferential questions.** Multiple-choice items are labeled as *main idea, inference,* or *detail questions.*
- Some reading selections include essay questions that elicit an organized **written response.**
- Although skills build and overlap, **each chapter can be taught as a separate unit** to fit individual class or student needs.
- Discussion and practice **exercises on barriers to critical thinking**—including cultural conditioning, self-deception, and oversimplification—appear throughout the book.
- Practice is offered in **identifying fallacies** in critical thinking and in **evaluating arguments.**

Additional features include:

- A list of **Learning Objectives** introduces each chapter and provides clear direction and purpose for reading. The objectives then appear next to the related content, and they are summarized at the end of the chapter in the **Summary Points.**
- **Brain Boosters** add brief, well-researched conclusions from neuroscientific research. They offer insights about how human brains learn and how to make the most of the brain's power.
- **QR codes** accompany the end-of-chapter reading selections. Scanning the code with a smartphone opens an audio presentation of the selection to access auditory learning modalities.

- **Video clips in Build Background Knowledge features** enhance the longer readings. These engaging videos, found in MyReadingLab, present the student with another perspective on some aspect or theme of the reading selection and encourage real-world connections.
- References with each of the longer reading selections at the end of each chapter refer students to the appropriate section of **MyReadingLab** for further practice.
- In **Concept Prep,** key concepts in a variety of academic disciplines are matched with the subjects in many of the longer reading selections. These selected concepts, reflecting common knowledge that lies at the core of each academic discipline, are also an important part of the shared cultural heritage of educated thinkers. Careers related to the discipline are included.

  The purpose of this innovative feature is to develop schematic and prior knowledge for students' later academic success. For example, the Concept Preps for Psychology discuss people and ideas at the heart of every introductory psychology course, including Sigmund Freud's and Carl Jung's theories, Ivan Pavlov's discovery of, and experiments with, classical conditioning, and B. F. Skinner's behaviorism.
- **Establish a Purpose for Reading** preview activities have been enriched to connect text-to-self by recalling prior knowledge and experiences, to encourage predictions, and to state a purpose.
- **Think Critically About the Reading** challenges readers to extend and deepen their thinking about ideas that are raised in the long reading selections.
- **Write About the Selection** questions encourage text-to-self and text-to-world connections by asking students to make a personal link to the textbook selection or a link to larger global issues.
- **Vocabulary Booster** activities at the end of each chapter focus on linking and learning words through word parts or word families. The lessons can be assigned weekly, and student progress can be measured using the assessment quizzes in the Instructor's Manual. In addition, the twelfth edition includes more than 160 vocabulary words in context after the longer reading selections.
- **Many new photos** have been carefully chosen to amplify the exposition.
- A **Progress Chart** is located on the inside back cover of the book so that students can record their progress in understanding the longer reading selections.
- Chapter-by-chapter **Reader's Journal** activities now appear in the Activities: Your Textbook section of MyReadingLab. With these reflective activities, students can learn about themselves, consider their strengths and weaknesses, and monitor their progress. After these activities are completed, they can either be e-mailed to the instructor or printed out and handed in.

THE TEACHING AND LEARNING PACKAGE

Text-Specific Ancillaries

- **MyReadingLab** In an ideal world, an instructor would work with each student to help improve reading skills with consistent challenges and rewards. Without that luxury, MyReadingLab offers a way to keep students focused and accelerate their progress using comprehensive pre-assignments and a powerful, adaptive study plan. MyReadingLab can be set up to fit your specific course needs, whether you seek reading support to complement what you do in class, a way to administer many sections easily, or a self-paced environment for independent study.

- **Annotated Instructor's Edition** (9780134064918). This is an exact replica of the student edition but includes all answers printed directly on the fill-in lines that are provided in the text. The Annotated Instructor's Edition now includes grade level equivalents for each of the longer reading selections.
- **Instructor's Manual** (9780134064901). This manual contains Vocabulary-in-context exercises to reinforce the words in the longer textbook selections. In addition, it includes four appendixes that further support student reading skills: 1. Making Sense of Figurative Language and Idioms for Native & Non-Native English Speakers; 2. Practice for Reading Efficiency; 3. Test-Taking Preparation; and, 4. The Reading Workshop: Topics and Formats for Book Discussions. Available for download.
- **Test Bank** (9780134064840). This supplement contains additional vocabulary and comprehension questions for each reading selection. The true-false, vocabulary, and comprehension quizzes can be used as pre-reading quizzes to stimulate interest or as evaluation quizzes after reading. Available for download.
- **MyTest** (9780134064864). This electronic test bank includes chapter tests and vocabulary tests in a web-based format.
- **Power Point Presentations** (9780134064871). Classroom presentations for each chapter. Available for download.
- **Answer Key** (9780134064833). The Answer Key contains the solutions to the exercises in the student edition of the text. Available for download.

ACKNOWLEDGMENTS

We want to recognize the expertise and dedication of the many people who contributed to the completion of the twelfth edition of *Bridging the Gap*. Special thanks go to Janice Wiggins, development editor, whose experienced hand skillfully guided this and several previous editions. Her expertise and wisdom promoted calm and clarity of purpose during the inevitable crises. We appreciate the leadership of Eric Stano, Vice President and Editorial Director for English, who kept the project moving from start to finish. Thanks go as well to the many other skilled professionals who gave careful attention to the thousands of details of accuracy, design, and production. Together—and with respect for the tradition of quality that this book represents—we made a good team.

A textbook is only as good as it is effective in the hands of students and instructors. We are especially grateful for the contributions of our colleagues in college reading. Their practical suggestions have lent important insights into the development of *Bridging the Gap* through its many revisions. We appreciate the reviewers of the eleventh edition from across the United States, whose suggestions shaped this twelfth edition:

Jennifer Avila
South Mountain Community College

Jacqueline Barry
Bristol Community College

Elaine Jolayemi
Ivy Technical Community College

Marjorie Ader Kerbel
Reading Area Community College

Dwight Rinehart
Reading Area Community College

Charoline Simmons
Motlow State Community College

Tricia Yamauchi
Glendale Community College

BRENDA D. SMITH
LEEANN MORRIS

1 Active Academic Reading

Learning Objectives

In this chapter, you will learn to:

1 Use active academic reading techniques
2 Improve concentration
3 Increase reading efficiency
4 Prepare for success on reading comprehension tests
5 Take control of your learning

Vocabulary Booster: Over, Under, Around, and Through

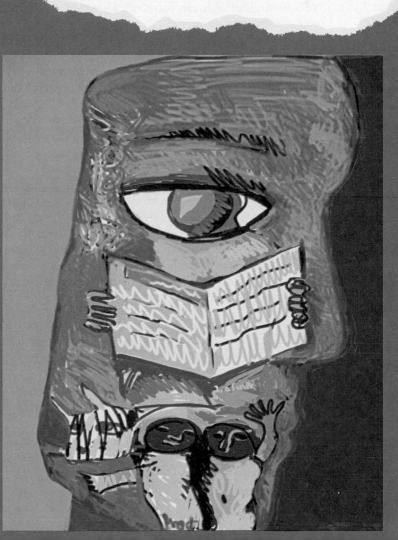

Diane Ong/Getty Images

WHAT IS ACTIVE ACADEMIC READING?

Active academic reading is the purposeful use of attention, effort, strategies, and resources to learn through reading. Developing active reading habits is one of the best things that you can do to smooth your path through college. Professors expect students to read for background and depth to understand the information that they provide during class time. Whether you read on a screen or a printed page, active reading will help you absorb ideas more thoroughly and more quickly.

In this chapter, we will discuss many factors that contribute to your ability to become an effective, active academic reader. First, however, let's consider what psychologists have to say about focusing your attention, thinking, and learning.

What Can We Learn From Cognitive Psychology and Neuroscience?

Cognitive psychology is the body of knowledge that describes how the mind works or, at least, how researchers think the mind works. Cognitive psychologists study how people process information from their five senses and how they think, learn, remember, express ideas, and solve problems. The information-processing model, which compares the human brain to a computer, has been useful to our understanding of brain function. However, as research continues, new concepts are also being developed.

Neuroscience is the scientific study of the molecular and cellular levels of the nervous system and of the systems within the brain. It includes the study of behavior produced by the brain. With the development of sophisticated medical imaging techniques, scientists can now view the changes that take place in the brain during cognitive, emotional, and physical activity. They can actually see what happens in the brain when people learn. Research in neuroscience is providing increasing information about the biological aspects of learning. The better we understand the process of learning, the more control we have over it.

How Does the Brain Screen Messages?   Cognitive psychologists use the word *attention* to describe a student's uninterrupted mental focus. Thinking and learning, they say, begin with attention. During every minute of the day, millions of sensory messages bombard the brain. How does the brain decide which messages to pay attention to and which to overlook? At this moment, are you thinking about the temperature of the room, outdoor noises, or what you are reading? With all this information available to you at the same time, how can your brain choose what's most important?

BRAIN BOOSTER

Medical imaging techniques, such as PET scans, fMRI technology, EEGs, and newly developing methods, allow neuroscientists to "see" the brain as it works. These instruments have created an explosion of knowledge that helps us understand how we can make better use of our brains to attain our learning goals. Scattered throughout this book you will notice a feature called "Brain Booster." In these short pieces, you will find practical ways to keep your brain working at its best—all thanks to research in neuroscience. Look for boxes like this one for brain-boosting tips.

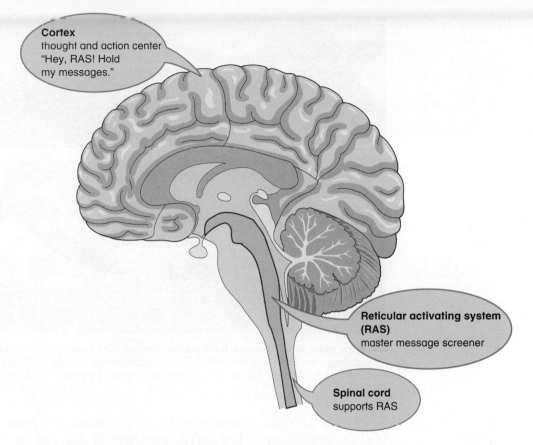

The brain relies on a dual command center to screen out one message and attend to another. Receptor cells send millions of messages per minute to your brain. Your reticular activating system (RAS)—a network of cells at the top of the spinal cord that runs to the brain—tells the cortex of the brain—the wrinkled outer layer that handles sensory processing, motor control, and memory storage—not to bother with most of the sensory input. For example, you are probably not aware at this moment of your back pressing against your chair or your clothes pulling on your body. Your RAS has decided not to clutter your brain with such irrelevant information and to alert the cortex only when there is an extreme problem, such as your foot going to sleep because you have been sitting on it.

The cortex can also make attention decisions and tell your RAS to hold some messages while you concentrate on others. How well are your RAS and cortex cooperating in blocking out distractions so that you can concentrate on learning?

Is Divided Attention Effective? Is it possible to do two things at once, such as watching television and doing homework? Is it safe to drive and talk on a cell phone? In a study on divided attention, researchers Rodriguez, Valdes-Sosa, and Freiwald[1] found that dividing your attention usually has a cost. You are more likely to perform one or both tasks less efficiently than if you were to concentrate on a

---

[1]V. Rodriguez, M. Valdes-Sosa, and W. Freiwald, "Dividing Attention Between Form and Motion During Transparent Surface Perception," *Cognitive Brain Research* 13 (2002): 187–93.

Dividing your attention can have a cost. Researchers have found that the auto accident rate among people who drive while talking on the phone (including those texting or using headsets) is four times that of drivers who do not use the phone while they drive.

Nito/Fotolia

single task. Likewise, extensive studies on cell phone use while driving seem to confirm the old adage, "You can't do two things at once and do them well."

Can Tasks Become Automatic?   Can you walk and chew gum at the same time? Does every simple activity require your undivided attention? Many tasks—walking, tying shoelaces, and driving a car, for example—begin under controlled processing, which means that they are deliberate and require concentrated mental effort to learn them. After much practice, however, such tasks become automatic. Driving

---

BRAIN BOOSTER

Are You Paying Attention?

Of course you are! Human brains are always attending to something. Perhaps the question should be, "What are you paying attention to?" Keeping our focus on a classroom lecture, a reading assignment, or a project is sometimes a struggle, but paying attention is critical to learning. Research tells us that two factors are most important to paying attention: meaning and emotion. So, think of a way to connect new information to something that you already know. Recognizing your crazy Uncle Charlie in something you studied in psychology class will help you understand and remember it. Think of how you can apply a new concept at work or in your personal life. These are ways to give real meaning to what you're learning. Likewise, link emotion to new concepts with a funny story, an interesting case study, or a real-life concern. Studying or sharing a new idea with a friend also lends emotional energy to learning. Meaning + Emotion = Attention. Make the equation work for you!

—Adapted from Patricia Wolfe, Brain Matters. © 2001 Association for Supervision and Curriculum Development: Alexandria, VA

a car is a learned behavior that researchers would say becomes an automatic process after thousands of hours of experience. You can probably drive and listen to the radio or a CD at the same time, but it may not be a good idea to drive and talk on a cell phone. Similarly, a skilled athlete can dribble a basketball automatically while also attending to strategy and position. Attention is actually not divided because it can shift away from tasks that have become automatic.

Automatic Aspects of Reading.   The idea of doing certain things automatically is especially significant in reading. As a first-grade reader, you had to concentrate on recognizing letters, words, and sentences, as well as trying to construct meaning. After years of practice and overlearning, much of the recognition aspect of reading has become automatic. You no longer stop laboriously to decode each word or each letter. For example, when you look at the word *child*, you automatically think of the meaning. Thus, you can focus your mental resources on understanding the message in which the word appears, rather than on understanding the word itself.

Help Your Brain Absorb New Information

Academic reading can be frustrating because it is not as automatic as everyday reading. For example, you may read through the sports section of your local newspaper with ease but stumble through a textbook chapter on human physiology. College textbooks often contain many unfamiliar words, new ideas, and complex concepts that the brain cannot automatically process. However, using the four strategies explained here can prepare your brain to accept, understand, and remember what you read.

Strategy #1: Preview Your Textbooks.   Give yourself a head start on understanding the organization and content of your college textbooks with just a few quick steps: (1) Notice the cover and title. (2) Glance at the title page. What can you learn about the authors from the information on this page? (3) Do the flip: Quickly rifle the pages from the back to the front. What pops out? Are there pictures, exercises to complete, repeated features? (4) Examine the table of contents. What are the major topics? Is there a pattern to their order or content? Notice the features at the end of the book. Is there an index, a glossary of terms, an answer key?

EXERCISE 1.1

Preview This Textbook for the Big Picture

Preview this textbook to get an overview of its scope and its sequence of topics. Think about how the chapter topics fit the goals of college reading. Glance at the chapters to get a sense of the organization and then answer the following questions:

1. How many chapters are in this text? Which ones do you think will be especially useful for you? _____

2. What seems to be the purpose of the Reader's Tip boxes throughout the text?

   _____

3. Does the text have specific exercises to help build vocabulary? Where are they located? _____

   _____

4. Which chapter provides information about determining main ideas?

_____

5. What is the purpose of the Brain Booster feature in the blue boxes?

_____

_____

6. Where do reading selections from history, science, and a variety of college subjects appear? _____

_____

7. What is on the inside of the back cover? _____

_____

Strategy #2: Learn New Vocabulary Early.   Your attention to a book's message can be interrupted by the need to attend to unknown words, creating the dilemma of trying to do two things at once—trying to figure out word meaning as well as trying to understand the message. After the break in concentration, you can regain your focus, and little harm is done if such breaks are infrequent. However, frequent interruptions in the automatic aspect of reading can undermine your ability to concentrate on the message. Thus, mastering the jargon or vocabulary of a new course early on can improve your concentration. Make a list of terms that are repeated in your textbooks and by your professors. Use either printed or online flash cards to learn their meanings.

Strategy #3: Read Assignments Before Class.   Activate your knowledge on the subject before class by reading homework assignments. Look at the illustrations and read the captions. Jot down several questions that you would like to ask the professor about the reading so that the lecture and class discussion can enhance your newly created knowledge network. Be aware that professors may not give a specific reading assignment, but they still expect you to read the textbook and other required materials for the course.

Strategy #4: Review Lecture Notes Before Class.   *Always, always*, review your notes before the next class period. Review them with a classmate during a break, on the phone, or via e-mail. Fill in gaps and make notations to ask questions and resolve confusion. This habit helps to consolidate the information. That is, it unites new and existing information to expand knowledge networks in your brain.

POOR CONCENTRATION: CAUSES AND CURES

Learning Objective 0

Improve concentration

Knowing how to concentrate is critical to college success. Concentration is a skill that is developed through self-discipline and practice. It is a **habit** that requires time and effort to develop for consistent success. Athletes must have it, surgeons must have it, and successful college students must have it. *Concentration is essential for active academic reading and learning.*

Concentration can be defined as the process of *paying attention*—that is, focusing full attention on the task at hand. Someone once said that the mark of a genius is the ability to concentrate completely on one thing at a time. This is easy if the task is fun and exciting, but it becomes more difficult when you are required to read something that is not very interesting to you. In such cases, you may find yourself looking from word to word and spacing out.

Students frequently ask, "How can I keep my mind on what I'm doing?" Or they say, "I finished the assignment, but I don't understand a thing I read!" The best way to increase concentration is to first identify external and internal distractions and then use a series of practical short- and long-range planning strategies to address these distractions.

External Distractions

External distractions are the temptations of the physical world that divert your attention away from your work. They are the people in the room, the noise in the background, the time of day, electronic distractions such as texts, e-mails, and social media, or your place for studying. To control these external distractions, you must create an environment that says, "This is the place and the time for me to get my work done."

Create a Place for Studying.   Start by establishing a private study cubicle; it may be in the library or learning center, at the kitchen table, or in your bedroom. Wherever your study place is, choose a straight chair and face the wall. Get rid of electronics and other temptations that trigger the mind to think of play. Stay away from your bed because it triggers sleep. Spread out your papers, books, and other symbols of studying, and create an atmosphere in which the visual stimuli signal work. Be consistent by trying to study in the same place at the same time.

Use a Calendar, Assignment Book, or Smartphone.   At the beginning of the term, record dates for tests, papers, and special projects on some kind of planner, such as a print or electronic calendar, assignment book, or smartphone. Use your planner to organize all of your course assignments. The mere sight of your planner will remind you of the need for both short- and long-term planning. Your first job is to devise a plan for being ready.

Schedule Weekly Activities.   Successful people do not let their time slip away; they manage time, rather than letting time manage them. Plan realistically and then follow your plan. After calculating the total study hours needed using the formula below, complete the weekly activity chart shown on page 8:

1. Enter your classes and all other fixed commitments such as work hours into the chart.

2. Calculate the number of study hours you should plan.

    Number of classes I'm taking: _____

    Number of hours each class meets each week: X _____

       Total hours in class each week   = _____

    Two study hours for each hour in class (some experts
    recommend three hours of study for each hour in class)   X ___2___

       Total number of study hours I should plan each week   = [____]

3. Distribute your total recommended study hours in reasonable places during the week. Make good use of time between classes as well as the longer blocks of time.

4. When you have a workable schedule, make copies of it.

Each week, make a list of the class assignments, divide them into small tasks, and write them into the schedule during the study hours that you have already planned. Be specific about each task (e.g., "read first half of Ch. 8 in psychology, brainstorm research paper topic for English"). Always include time for a regular review of your lecture notes.

WEEKLY ACTIVITY CHART

Time	Monday	Tuesday	Wednesday	Thursday	Friday	Saturday	Sunday
7:00–8:00							
8:00–9:00							
9:00–10:00							
10:00–11:00							
11:00–12:00							
12:00–1:00							
1:00–2:00							
2:00–3:00							
3:00–4:00							
4:00–5:00							
5:00–6:00							
6:00–7:00							
7:00–8:00							
8:00–9:00							
9:00–10:00							
10:00–11:00							
11:00–12:00							

Examinations require special planning. Many students do not realize how much time it takes to study for a major exam. Spread out your studying over several days and avoid last-minute cramming sessions late at night. Plan additional time for special projects and papers to avoid deadline crises.

Even though it is not necessary to write this on the chart, remember that you need short breaks. Research shows that studying in chunks rather than long spans is most efficient. Try the 50:10 ratio—study hard for 50 minutes, take a 10-minute break, and then promptly go back to studying for another 50 minutes.

Internal Distractions

Internal distractions are the concerns that come repeatedly into your mind as you try to keep your attention focused on an assignment. You have to run errands, do laundry, send e-mails, make telephone calls, and pay bills. How do you stop worrying about getting an inspection sticker for the car or about picking up tickets for Saturday's ball game when you need to be concentrating completely on your class assignment?

Make a "Worry" List. To gain control over mental disruptions, make a list of what is on your mind and is keeping you from concentrating on your studies. Jot down on paper your mental distractions and then analyze each one to determine if immediate action is necessary or possible. If you decide that you must do something right away, get up and do it. It will have been worthwhile if the quality of your study time—your concentration power—has improved.

For a big problem that you can't tackle immediately, ask yourself, "Is it worth the amount of brain time that I'm dedicating to it?" Take a few minutes to think and make notes on possible solutions. Jotting down necessary future action and forming a plan of attack will help relieve the worry and clear your mind for studying.

Make a "To Do" List. Right now, list five things that are on your mind that you need to remember to do. Many successful people start each day with such a **To Do List** (and some make a list before they go to sleep at night). Rank the activities on your list in order of priority and then do the most important things first.

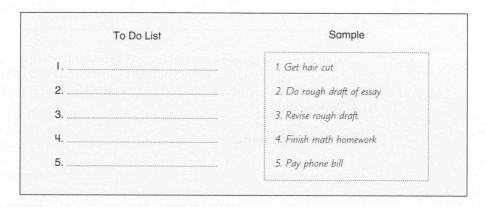

To Do List	Sample
1.	1. Get hair cut
2.	2. Do rough draft of essay
3.	3. Revise rough draft
4.	4. Finish math homework
5.	5. Pay phone bill

Increase Your Self-Confidence. Saying "I'll never pass this course" or "I can't get in the mood to study" is a huge internal distraction and the first step to failure.

Concentration requires self-confidence. Your enrollment in college indicates that you have made a commitment to a long-term goal. Ask yourself, "Who do I want to be in five years?" In the following space, describe how you view yourself, both professionally and personally, five years from now:

Five years from now I hope to be _____

_____

_____

Sometimes, identifying the traits that you admire in others can give you insight into your own values and desires. Think about the traits that you respect in others and about your own definition of success. Answer the two questions that follow and consider how your responses mirror your own aspirations and goals:

Who is the person you admire the most? _____

Why do you admire this person? _____

_____

Believe in yourself and in your ability to be what you want to be. Turn your negative feelings into a positive attitude. What are some of your positive traits? Are you a hard worker, an honest person, a loyal friend? Take a few minutes to pat yourself on the back. Think about your good points and, in the following spaces, list five positive traits that you believe you possess:

Positive Traits

1. _____

2. _____

3. _____

4. _____

5. _____

What have you already accomplished? Did you participate in athletics in high school, win any contests, or master any difficult skills? Recall your previous achievements and, in the following spaces, list three accomplishments that you view with pride:

Accomplishments

1. _____

2. _____

3. _____

BRAIN BOOSTER

Are you curious?

Think about how babies learn that they can make a toy squeak or that a kitten might bite. Is there a quiz or a flash card involved? Human brains are wired to explore and learn from the results. As you pursue this adventure called a college education, remember that curiosity about new ideas can be one of your best assets. In every class, find something that you want to know more about and go for it! The spark that ignites your interest might lie waiting in the textbook, in a lecture, or in an assignment. Fan that spark by going to the Internet, asking your professor, reading a book, doing an experiment, or talking to other students. Your natural curiosity may lead to a college major, a career, a lifelong hobby, or an A in the class.

—*Adapted from* Brain Rules: 12 Principles for Surviving and Thriving at Work, Home, and School, *by John Medina*

Reduce Anxiety.   Have you ever heard people say, "I work better under pressure"? This statement contains a degree of truth. A small amount of tension can help you direct your full attention on an immediate task. Yet, too much anxiety can cause nervous tension and discomfort, which interfere with the ability to concentrate. The causes of high anxiety can range from fear of failure to lack of organization and preparation. The problem is not easily solved, but some people like to go for a run or a brisk walk to relieve anxiety. Sustained physical activity can change the blood chemistry, bring oxygen to the brain, and improve mood, increasing the odds of focusing successfully on what needs to be done.

Another immediate, short-term fix for tension is muscle relaxation exercises and visualization. Use your imagination to visualize a peaceful setting in which you are calm and relaxed; then focus on this image as you breathe deeply to help relax your muscles and regain control. Take several deep breaths and allow your body to release the tension so that you can resume reading and concentrate on your work. Try that right now.

Spark an Interest.   Make a conscious effort to stimulate your curiosity before reading, even if it feels contrived. First, look over the assigned reading for words or phrases that attract your attention, glance at the pictures, check the number of pages, and then ask yourself the following questions: "What do I already know about this topic?" and "What do I want to learn about it?"

With practice, this method of thinking before reading can create a spark of enthusiasm that will make the actual reading more purposeful and make concentration more direct and intense. We will cover this in greater depth in Chapter 2.

Set a Time Goal.   An additional trick to spark your enthusiasm is to set a time goal. Short-term goals create a self-imposed pressure to pay attention, speed up, and get the job done. After looking over the material, predict the amount of time that you will need to finish it. Estimate a reasonable completion time and then push yourself to meet the goal. The purpose of a time goal is not to "speed read" the assignment but to be realistic about the amount of time to spend on a task and to learn how to estimate future study time.

The Reader's Tips below summarize how you can raise your level of concentration while studying and offer strategies for managing electronic distractions.

Reader's TIP Improving Concentration

- Create an environment that says, "Study."
- Use a calendar, assignment book, or smartphone calendar for short- and long-term planning.
- Make a list of distracting "worries."
- Keep a daily To Do List.
- Increase your self-confidence with positive self-talk.
- Reduce anxiety.
- Spark an interest by previewing class assignments.
- Set time goals for completing daily assignments.

Reader's TIP Managing Electronic Communication

College, work, and personal communication are most often done by e-mail, text message, or through social media platforms such as Twitter. And, while electronic communication is efficient, it sometimes provides yet another distraction for students. Follow these guidelines to manage electronic communication.

- Turn off or reduce notifications that you receive from social media such as Facebook and Twitter. (Is it necessary to know each time someone likes your latest post?)
- When sending and receiving text messages, set ground rules for yourself. Turn off your cell phone when you are studying or set strict times for checking text messages.
- Turn off your cell phone when you go to bed. The "ping" and/or vibration of an incoming text message interrupts sleep. Turn off your phone while you are sleeping or at least move it to another room. Developing good sleep habits increases concentration and academic performance.
- Control how much time you spend on e-mails.
- Don't feel that you have to reply to everything.
- If you are pressed for time, save the message as "new" or "unread" and reply later.
- Discourage back-and-forth e-mail chains by addressing issues with a phone or video call.
- Organize and delete e-mails often. Organize incoming e-mails into separate folders and delete unnecessary e-mails.
- Decrease the number of e-mails that you receive by using a spam filter to weed out useless e-mails.
- Unsubscribe to unwanted advertisements. There is usually a way to unsubscribe noted at the very bottom of the e-mail.

IS READING RATE IMPORTANT?

Learning Objective 3

Increase reading efficiency

Professors of college reading are more concerned with comprehension than with a student's **rate** of reading. They would say that students should not attempt to "speed read" textbooks, and they would be right. However, when students are asked what they would like to change about their reading, many will say, "I read too slowly. I would like to improve my reading speed." Whether or not this perception is accurate, rate is definitely a concern of college students.

Varying Rate and Technique to Fit Purpose

Reading efficiently is a much more helpful concept than reading fast. **Reading efficiently** means adjusting your reading rate to the material and the purpose for reading it. The most important outcome of reading is achieving your purpose. Mature readers take several factors into account before they begin to read. First, they identify what they want to get out of the material. Most of the reading that college students do is in textbooks, and textbooks usually demand complete comprehension and long-term recall. No matter what your *baseline* reading rate is (see page 14 for an explanation of baseline reading rates and to determine your rate), this purpose requires a slow rate and a thorough *study reading* technique. (Refer to Chapter 3, page 125 for an explanation of study reading.) If your purpose is pleasure, read at your normal, baseline rate using your standard method. However, if all you need from the material are the main ideas and major details, your rate will be fast, and skimming is the most efficient method. Faster yet is the rate used to locate small details, such as a date, a name, or a definition, within a large quantity of information. Scanning is the best technique for this purpose. (Skimming and scanning are explained briefly in the Reader's Tip on page 14.)

Use the Reader's Tip on page 14 to connect typical purposes and materials with the most efficient reading rates and techniques.

Rate Variations and Prior Knowledge

In addition to the reader's purpose, other reasons that textbooks usually require a slower reading rate than other materials are that the sentences are longer, the language is more formal, the vocabulary and ideas are new, and your prior knowledge may be limited. If you already have a lot of knowledge on a topic, you can usually read about it at a faster rate than if you are exploring a totally new subject. For example, a student who has some experience in the field of advertising will probably be able to read through the advertising chapter in a business textbook at a faster rate than a chapter on a less familiar topic, like supply-side economics. The student may need to slow to a crawl at the beginning of the economics chapter to understand the new concepts, but as the new ideas become more familiar, he or she may be able to read at a faster rate toward the end of the chapter.

Now, let's return to the question posed in the beginning of this section: Is reading rate important? While achieving your reading purpose with the intended level of comprehension is the ultimate goal, doing this faster is still worthwhile. Most college students would probably like to spend less time achieving the desired result. By acquiring certain reading habits, readers can increase their rate in every

Reader's TIP — Efficient Reading: Adjusting Rate and Technique to Material and Purpose

Material	Purpose for Reading	Technique	Rate
Textbooks	Complete comprehension and long-term recall	Study reading (thorough, careful, note taking). Refer to Chapter 3 (page 125).	Slow
Novels	Pleasure, short-term recall	Standard (usual, personal method)	Medium
News and magazine articles, Internet pages	General information, main ideas, and major details	Skimming (reading titles, headings, and first sentences only).	Fast
Television schedule, Internet surfing, Googling, dictionary, reference books, etc.	Specific information	Scanning (focusing only on needed information).	Fastest

reading situation. Practice the suggestions in the following section to become aware of efficient reading habits. Begin by determining your baseline reading rate.

What Is Your Baseline Reading Rate?

How many words do you read on the average each minute? To find out, read the following selection at your usual reading rate, just as you would have read it before you started thinking about speed. Time your reading of the selection so that you can calculate your rate. Read carefully enough to answer the ten comprehension questions that follow the selection. When you have determined your baseline rate, you can work to increase it.

EXERCISE 1.2

Assessing Baseline Rate

Time your reading of this selection so that you can compute your words-per-minute rate. To make the calculations easier, try to begin reading on an exact minute, with zero seconds. Record your starting and finishing times in minutes and seconds, and then determine your rate from the rate chart at the end of the passage. Answer the ten questions that follow and determine your comprehension rate by calculating the percentage of correct answers. Remember, read the selection at your normal rate.

Starting time: _____ minutes _____ seconds

THE PSYCHOLOGY OF LOVE

Many romantics believe there is only one true love awaiting them. Considering that there are 6½ billion people on the planet, the odds of finding said person are a bit daunting. What if you're in Omaha or Winnipeg and your true love is in Dubrovnik or Kankakee? You could wander for years and never cross paths.

Fortunately, evolution has made it possible to form deep and lasting attachments without traveling the world. In fact, the first major predictor of whom we love is plain *proximity:* We choose our friends and lovers from the set of people who live close by, or who study or work near us. The people who are nearest to you are most likely to be dearest to you, too. The second major predictor is *similarity*—in looks, attitudes, beliefs, values, personality, and interests. Although it is commonly believed that opposites attract, the fact is that we tend to choose friends and loved ones who are most like us. Many students use Facebook or Internet match sites to find romantic prospects who share their love of poker and action movies, their religious beliefs, or anything else they care about.

The Internet has made similarity-matching possible on all kinds of dimensions. There are nearly 1,000 dating Websites in the U.S., matching couples by age, political attitudes, religion or secularism, sexual orientation, and many other criteria. There are sites for people with disabilities, preferences for particular sexual activities, and even beloved pets. Some prominent matchmaking sites administer questionnaires and personality inventories, claiming to use scientific principles to pair up potential soul mates. These efforts vary in effectiveness. Can you think why? One reason is that many people think they know exactly what they "must have" in a partner, and then they meet someone who has few of those qualities but a whole bunch of others that suddenly become essential. (A woman we know thought she must have a man who was taller than she, until she met the love of her life, who is three inches shorter.) Another reason, though, is that the premises of some of these sciency-sounding matchmaking sites may be faulty, especially those based on unvalidated personality types and anecdotal testimonials. But one underlying premise of most Internet-matching sites is basically right—like attracts like.

The Ingredients of Love.   When people are asked to define the key ingredients of love, most agree that love is a mix of passion, intimacy, and commitment. Intimacy is based on deep knowledge of the other person, which accumulates gradually, but passion is based on emotion, which is generated by novelty and change. That is why passion is usually highest at the beginning of a relationship, when two people begin to disclose things about themselves to each other, and lowest when knowledge of the other person's beliefs and habits is at its maximum, when it seems that there is nothing left to learn about the beloved. Nonetheless, according to an analysis of a large number of adult couples and a meta-analysis of 25 studies of couples in long- and short-term relationships, romantic love can persist for many years and is strongly associated with a couple's happiness. What diminishes among these happy couples is that part of romantic love we might call *obsessiveness,* constant thinking and worrying about the loved one and the relationship.

Biological factors such as the brain's opiate system may contribute to early passion, as we noted, but most psychologists believe that the ability to sustain a long and intimate love relationship has more to do with a couple's attitudes, values, and balance of power than with genes or hormones. One of the most important psychological predictors of satisfaction in long-term relationships is the perception, by both partners, that the relationship is fair, rewarding, and balanced. Partners who feel overbenefited (getting more than they are giving) tend to feel guilty; those who feel underbenefited (not getting what they feel they deserve) tend to feel resentful and angry. A couple may tootle along comfortably until a stressful event—such as the arrival of children, serious illness, unemployment, or retirement—evokes simmering displeasure over issues of "what's fair."

Another key psychological factor in couples' ability to sustain love is the nature of their primary motivation to maintain the relationship: Is it positive (to enjoy affection and intimacy) or negative (to avoid feeling insecure and lonely)? Couples motivated by the former goal tend to report more satisfaction with their partners. We will see that this difference in motivation—positive or negative—affects happiness and satisfaction in many different domains of life.

The critical-thinking guideline, "define your terms," may never be more important than in matters of love. The way we define love deeply affects our satisfaction with relationships and whether or not our relationships last. After all, if you believe that the only real love is the kind defined by obsession, sexual passion, and hot emotion, then you may decide you are out of love when the initial phase of attraction fades, as it eventually must—and you will be repeatedly disappointed. Robert Solomon argued that "We conceive of [love] falsely. . . . We expect an explosion at the beginning powerful enough to fuel love through all of its ups and downs instead of viewing love as a process over which we have control, a process that tends to increase with time rather than wane."

Researchers themselves have often made this mistake. They have tended to define "falling in love" in the romantic thunderbolt mode: You are standing there, minding your own business, when Perfect Person strolls by and you are hopelessly smitten at first sight; you "fall"; your brain (and your soul) light up. However, people fall in love in different ways: Some couples do so gradually, over time, after "falling in friendship" first; and couples in arranged marriages may come to love each other long after the wedding. All the fMRIs in the world can't capture that.

(889 words)

—Carole Wade and Carol Tavris,
Psychology, 11th ed.

Time (Min)	Words per minute	Time (Min)	Words per Minute
2:00	445	4:40	191
2:10	411	4:50	184
2:20	381	5:00	178
2:30	356	5:10	172
2:40	334	5:20	167
2:50	314	5:30	162
3:00	296	5:40	157
3:10	281	5:50	153
3:20	267	6:00	148
3:30	254	6:10	144
3:40	242	6:20	141
3:50	232	6:30	137
4:00	223	6:40	134
4:10	214	6:50	130
4:20	205	7:00	127
4:30	197		

Finishing time: _____ minutes _____ seconds

Reading time in minutes and seconds: _____ : _____

Words per minute: _____

Mark each statement with *T* (true) or *F* (false).

_____ 1. According to this article, we're most likely to find true love far from where we live and work.

_____ 2. This article supports the idea that we're most attracted to people who are different from ourselves.

_____ 3. One reason that Internet matchmaking sites don't always work is that many people don't really know what kind of person will make them happy.

_____ 4. Most people agree that love is a mixture of passion, intimacy, and commitment.

_____ 5. Commitment is usually at its peak at the beginning of a relationship.

_____ 6. Passion usually, but not always, declines over time in a relationship.

_____ 7. Over time, couples in happy, long-term relationships worry more about the loved one and the relationship.

_____ 8. One of the best predictors of happiness in a relationship is the belief by both partners that the relationship is fair and rewarding.

_____ 9. A person's definition of love affects his or her satisfaction in relationships.

_____ 10.   According to this article, being friends first cannot result in a successful, long-term love relationship.

Comprehension rate (percentage of correct answers) _____ %

BRAIN BOOSTER

Music to Our Ears and to Our Brains

Music is experienced in many parts of the brain and can have several effects on the mind and body. For example, our pulse rates tend to synchronize with the beat of the music we hear. Certain music, then, causes us to be more alert and to learn better. Linking music with studying can help encode information into long-term memory. Music can also stimulate creativity, relieve fatigue, reduce pain and stress, and influence our emotional state. The specific effects vary from person to person, depending partly on culture, personality, and type of music, but researchers have little doubt that music is a helpful tool for improving reasoning, memory, and intelligence. Try playing something in the background with a quick, even beat while you practice the rate improvement habits in this chapter. See if this helps you read faster and concentrate better.

—*Adapted from Eric Jensen,* Brain-Based Learning: The New Paradigm of Teaching, *2nd edition*

Habits for Faster Reading

Regardless of your purpose and the reading technique that you select (see the Reader's Tip on page 14), you can improve your reading rate by developing efficient habits and dropping habits that interfere with speed and comprehension. All of the methods described on the next few pages require conscious effort at first, but with practice they will eventually become automatic.

Concentrate.   Fast readers, like fast race-car drivers, concentrate on what they are doing; they try to think quickly while they take in the important aspects of the course before them. Although we use our eyes, we actually read with our minds. If our attention is veering off course, we lose some of that cutting-edge quickness that is necessary for success. Slow readers tend to become bored because ideas are coming too slowly to keep their minds alert. Fast readers are curious to learn, mentally alert, and motivated to achieve.

Distractions that interfere with concentration, as mentioned earlier in this chapter, fall into two categories: external and internal. Take action to control the distractions that keep you from concentrating fully.

Stop Regressing.   While reading, have you ever realized halfway down the page that you have no idea what you have read? Your eyes were engaged, but your mind was wandering. Do you ever go back and reread sentences or paragraphs? Do you reread because the material was difficult to understand or because you were not concentrating? The second type of rereading is called **regression**—a habit that wastes time and causes confusion.

If regression is a problem for you, analyze when and why you are regressing. If you discern that your regression is due to distracting thoughts, start denying yourself this privilege in order to break the habit. Be demanding on yourself and expect 100 percent attention to the task. Visualize the incoming ideas and relate the new material to what you already know. Don't just read the words; think the ideas. Until they have eliminated the habit of regressing, some readers use an index card to cover lines that they have already read.

Rereading because you did not understand is a legitimate correction strategy used by good readers who monitor their own comprehension. Rereading because your mind was asleep is a waste of time and a habit of many slow readers.

Expand Fixations.   Your eyes must stop in order to read. These stops, called **fixations**, last a fraction of a second. On the average, 5 to 10 percent of reading time is spent on fixations. Thus, reading more than one word per fixation will reduce your total reading time.

Research on vision shows that the eye is able to see about one-half inch on either side of a fixation point. This means that a reader can see two, three, or possibly four words per fixation. To illustrate, read the following phrase:

in the car

Did you make three fixations, two, or one? Now read the following word:

entertainment

You can read this word automatically with one fixation. As a beginning reader, however, you probably stopped for each syllable for a total of four fixations. If you can read *entertainment,* which has 13 letters, with one fixation, you can certainly read the 8-letter phrase *in the car* with only one fixation.

Use your peripheral vision on either side of the fixation point to help you read two or three words per fixation. When expanding your fixations, take in phrases or thought units that seem to go together automatically. To illustrate, the following sentence has been grouped into thought units with fixation points:

After lunch,   I studied   in the library   at a table.
        •   •   •   •

By expanding your fixations, the sentence can easily be read with four fixations rather than ten and thus reduce your total reading time.

Stop Vocalizing.   Vocalizers move their lips while reading to pronounce each word. **Vocalization** is an immature habit that should be stopped. Putting a slip of paper or a pencil in your mouth while reading will alert you to lip movement and inspire you to stop.

Subvocalization, on the other hand, is the little voice in your head that reads for you. Some experts say that subvocalization is necessary for difficult material, and others say that fast readers are totally visual and do not need to hear the words. Good college readers will probably experience some of both. With easy reading tasks, you may find yourself speeding up to the point that you are not hearing every word, particularly the unimportant "filler" phrases. However, with more difficult textbook readings, your inner voice may speak every word. The voice seems to add another sensory dimension to help you comprehend. Because experts say that the inner voice can read up to about 400 words per minute, many college students can make a considerable improvement in speed while still experiencing the inner voice.

Preview.   Size up your reading assignment before you get started. If it is a chapter, glance through the pages and read the subheadings. Look at the pictures and notice the italicized words and boldface print. Make predictions about what you think the chapter will cover. Activate your schema, or prior knowledge, on the subject and prepare to learn something new.

Use Your Pen as a Pacer.   The technique of using your pen or fingers as a pacer means pointing under each line in a smooth, flowing motion, moving back and forth from line to line. Although as a child you were probably told never to point to words, guiding your eyes with a pen is a very effective technique for improving reading speed. The physical act of pointing tends to improve concentration by drawing your attention directly to the words. The forward motion of your pen tends to keep you from regressing because rereading would interrupt your established rhythm. By pulling your eyes down the page, the pen movement helps set a rapid, steady pace for reading and tends to shift you out of word-by-word reading and move you automatically into phrase reading.

The technique is demonstrated by the dotted lines in the passage in Exercise 1.3. Your pen moves in a *Z* pattern from one side of the central column to the other, allowing peripheral vision to take in the words to the left and right ends of the lines of print. Because you are trying to read several words at each fixation, your pen does not have to go to the extreme end of either side of the column.

> Rapid reading requires quick thinking
> and intense concentration. The reader
> must be alert and aggressive. Being
> interested in the subject helps improve speed.

As you begin to read faster and become more proficient with the *Z* pattern, you will notice the corners starting to round into an *S*. The *Z* pattern is turning into a more relaxed *S* swirl. When you get to the point of using the *S* swirl, you will be reading for ideas and not reading every word. You will be reading actively and aggressively, with good concentration. Use the *Z* pattern until you find your pen or hand movement has automatically turned into an *S*. The following illustration compares the two patterns.

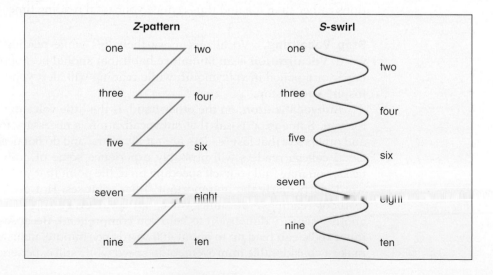

Push and Pace: Set a Time Goal.   Be alert and aggressive, and try to read faster. Sit up straight and read the text. Get uncomfortable and force yourself to concentrate. Changing old habits is difficult, but you will never read faster unless you try to read faster.

Set a time goal and pace yourself. Count the number of pages in your homework assignments and estimate according to your reading rate how many pages you can read in 30 minutes. Use a paper clip or a sticky note to mark the page you are trying to reach. Push yourself to achieve your goal.

EXERCISE 1.3

Pacing

Apply the methods for faster reading that are presented in this section to the passage and then calculate your reading rate. (The vertical lines in the passage help guide your reading in the *Z* pattern. Focus in the center of each line and use your peripheral vision to absorb the words at the left and right ends.)

COCA-COLA

Although not as important as textiles or tobacco in 1900, a soft drink developed by an Atlanta pharmacist, Dr. John Pemberton, eventually became the most renowned southern product in the world. Pemberton developed the drink—a mixture of oils, caffeine, coca leaves, and cola nuts—in his backyard in an effort to find a good-tasting cure for headaches. He called his concoction Coca-Cola. It was not an overnight success, and Pemberton, short of cash, sold the rights to it to another Atlantan, Asa Candler, in 1889. Candler tinkered with the formula to improve the taste and marketed the product heavily. By the mid-1890s, Coca-Cola enjoyed a national market. Southerners were such heavy consumers that the Georgia Baptist Association felt compelled to warn its members "the more you drink, the more you want to drink. We fear great harm will grow out of this sooner or later, to our young people in particular." The Baptists may have been onto something, as Coca-Cola's original formula did, in fact, include chemically active coca leaves.

—David Goldfield et al.,
The American Journey, 3rd ed.

(171 words)

Time (Min)	Words per Minute	Time (Min)	Words per Minute
0:30	346	1:00	173
0:40	260	1:10	94
0:50	208	1:20	86

Finishing time: _____ minutes _____ seconds

Words per minute: _____

Mark each statement with *T* (true) or *F* (false).

_____ 1. Coca-Cola was initially developed by a southern pharmacist to soothe ordinary headaches.

_____ 2. Dr. Pemberton made a fortune from his soft drink once it became a nationally marketed product.

STRATEGIES FOR READING COMPREHENSION TESTS

Throughout your school life, you have probably taken many tests that assess your understanding of reading material. Your college experience will be no exception. Professors in any course might give a test to determine how well you read and understand a reading assignment. In a reading course, you might have a comprehension test to measure your progress or how well you apply reading strategies. Comprehension tests differ from **content tests**, such as a final exam or unit test, that measure your knowledge of a subject that you have been studying. **Standardized reading tests**, such as the SAT or ACT, also measure comprehension, but they are designed for a very large population and are carefully constructed, administered, and scored in a consistent, or "standard," manner. Standardized test scores often help you qualify to enter or exit specific college programs. Sometimes they are used to screen job applicants.

The purpose of this section is to highlight strategies that will help you perform at your best on any reading comprehension test. Some of the suggestions may repeat what you already know, but take them seriously. Sadly, many students neglect to use methods that might seem to be common sense. As you read, use a highlighter or pen to mark the key tips for taking reading comprehension tests.

PLAN FOR SUCCESS

Successful students recognize that some of the best learning experiences arise from reflection on their preparation and performance on tests. Take advantage of this opportunity to perfect your test-taking skills. Consider the following advice that involves specific actions before, during, and after taking a reading comprehension test.

Before Taking a Test

Get Plenty of Sleep the Night Before.   The mental alertness that you derive from a good night's sleep can add as much as six points to your score and mean the difference between passing or failing. Why gamble by staying up late? Prioritize tasks and budget your time during the day so that you can go to bed on time.

Arrive Five or Ten Minutes Early and Get Settled.   If you run into class flustered at the last second, you will spend the first five minutes of the test calming yourself rather than getting immediately to work. Avoid unnecessary stress by arriving for the test early.

Know What to Expect on the Test.   Ask beforehand what will be expected on the test. Reading comprehension tests often present reading selections and predictable question types. Explanations and practice answering such questions begin in this chapter on page 25. You might also be expected to write a brief summary or to respond to an essay question about something that you have read outside of class or on the test itself. Know how the test will be scored so that you can plan your strategy accordingly. Is it better to guess or to leave a question unanswered?

(Almost always, leaving an answer blank counts as an error.) Also, know how your test results will be used.

Have Confidence in Your Abilities.   Achieve self-confidence and avoid anxiety by being well prepared. Be optimistic and approach the test with a positive mental attitude.

During the Test

Read to Comprehend Each Passage as a Whole.   Most experts recommend reading a selection before attempting to answer the questions about it. The reasoning is convincingly logical. Examining the questions first burdens the reader with a confusing collection of key words and phrases. Trying to remember many bits of information interferes with comprehending the author's message. Few people are capable of reading with five or six purposes in mind. Not only is the reading-of-questions-first method confusing, but also, because it is detail-oriented, it does not prepare you for more general questions concerning the main idea and implied meanings.

Instead, think about the main point. If you understand the central theme or main idea, the rest of the ideas will fall into place. Attempt to understand what each paragraph contributes to the central theme. Don't fret over remembering details but attempt to see how they contribute to the main point. If you find later that a minor detail is needed to answer a question, you can quickly use a key word to locate and reread to find the answer.

Anticipate What Is Coming Next.   Most test passages are untitled and thus offer no initial clue for content. Before reading, glance at the passage for a repeated word, name, or date. In other words, look for any quick clue to let you know whether the passage is about Queen Victoria, pit bulls, or chromosome reproduction. Do not rush through the first sentence. The first sentence further activates your schemata and sets the stage for what is to come. In some cases, the first sentence may give an overview or even state the central theme. In other cases, it may simply pique your curiosity or stimulate your imagination. You may begin to guess what will come next and how it will be stated.

Read Rapidly but Don't Allow Yourself to Feel Rushed.   Use your pen as a pacer to direct your attention both mentally and physically to the printed page. Using your pen will help you focus your attention, particularly at the times during the test when you feel more rushed. Ignore students who finish early and remind yourself that the goal is to do your best, not to win a race. Continue working with control and confidence.

Read to Learn and Enjoy.   Reading a passage to answer five or six questions is reading with an artificial purpose. Usually, you read to learn and enjoy, not for the sole purpose of answering questions. Most test passages can be fairly interesting to a receptive reader. Use the thinking strategies of a good reader to become involved in the material. Picture what you read and relate the ideas to what you already know.

Self-Test for the Main Idea.   Pull it together before pulling it apart. At the end of a passage, self-test for the main idea. Take 10 or 15 seconds to review the point that the author is trying to make. Again, if you understand the main point, the rest of the passage will fall into place.

Consider All Alternatives Before Choosing an Answer.   In fact, a good strategy is to answer the question mentally before looking at the answer choices. Then, read all of the options and select the one that best meshes with yours. Do not rush to record an answer without considering all of the alternatives. Multiple-choice test items usually ask for the best answer choice rather than merely any choice that is reasonable.

After the Test

Analyze Your Preparation.   Were you ready for the test? Did you prepare appropriately? Were you mentally and physically alert enough to function at your full capacity? How will you prepare for the next comprehension test?

Analyze the Test.   Was the test what you expected? If not, what was unexpected? Use your memory of the test to predict the patterns of future tests.

Analyze Your Performance.   Take note of the kinds of questions that caused you trouble. Take time to review the strategies and allow time for more practice. Standardized tests are not usually returned, but you do receive scores and subscores. What do your scores tell you about your strengths and weaknesses? What can you do to improve? Meet with your professor if you are confused or disappointed and ask for suggestions for improvement. Find out if tutorial sessions or study groups are available for you to join.

Read the Practice Passage on the next page and pretend it is part of a reading comprehension test. Read it using the suggestions just discussed. Note the handwritten reminders to make you aware of a few aspects of your thinking. When you

> **BRAIN BOOSTER**
>
> **Turn Mistakes into Successes**
>
> Mistaken information exists in neuronal networks just like correct information. Unless you do something about them, mistakes will persist. This is why the "after-test" analysis is so important. To change the erroneous information in neuronal networks, uncover the reasons for the mistake. Ask for help understanding the correct answer and connect it to what you already know. Build this understanding into a new or expanded neuronal network by repeating the correct information and using it. Instead of focusing on the mistake, focus on the new learning that you have created and reinforce it.

finish reading the Practice Passage, return to finish reading the paragraphs and section below.

Certainly, your reading of the passage contained many more thoughts than the notes on the page. The gossip at the beginning of the passage humanizes the empress and makes it easier for the reader to relate emotionally to the historic figure. Did you anticipate Peter's downfall and Catherine's subsequent relationships? Did you note the shift from gossip to accomplishments, both national and international? The shift signals the alert reader to a change in style, purpose, and structure.

Before proceeding to the questions that follow the passage, take a few seconds to regroup and think about what you have read. Self-test by pulling the material together before you tear it apart. Think about the focus of the passage and then work through the section about the types of questions that you will find on comprehension tests. Look for clues to recognizing the question type, strategies for determining the best answers, and examples based on the Practice Passage.

RECOGNIZE THE MAJOR TYPES OF COMPREHENSION QUESTIONS

Learn to recognize the types of questions that are often asked on reading comprehension tests. Although the wording might vary slightly, most tests will include one or more questions on the main idea, details, inference, the author's purpose, and vocabulary. Take note of the strategies for finding the best answers. The example questions are based on the Practice Passage.

Main Idea Questions

Main idea questions test your ability to find the central theme, central focus, gist, controlling idea, main point, or thesis of a passage. These terms are largely interchangeable in asking the reader to identify the main point of the passage. Main idea items are stated in any of the following forms:

The best statement of the main idea is . . .
The author's main point is . . .
The central theme of the passage is . . .
The best title for this passage is . . . (This wording is asking for the topic of the passage but is sometimes, confusingly, called a main idea question.)

Practice Passage

No title, so glance for key words. Dates? Names?

Great image

In January 1744 a coach from Berlin bumped its way eastward over ditches and mud toward Russia. It carried Sophia, a young German princess, on a bridal journey. At the Russian border she was met with pomp, appropriate for one chosen to be married to Peter, heir to the Russian throne. The wedding was celebrated in August 1745 with gaiety and ceremony. *Why wait 1½ years?*

Surprise!

Will he be tsar?

What is she planning?

For Sophia the marriage was anything but happy because the seventeen-year-old heir was "physically less than a man and mentally little more than a child." The "moronic booby" played with dolls and toy soldiers in his leisure time. He neglected his wife and was constantly in a drunken stupor. Moreover, Peter was strongly pro-German and made no secret of his contempt for the Russian people, intensifying the unhappiness of his ambitious young wife. This dreary period lasted for seventeen years, but Sophia used the time wisely. She set about "russifying" herself. She mastered the Russian language and avidly embraced the Russian faith; on joining the Orthodox church, she was renamed Catherine. She devoted herself to study, reading widely the works of Montesquieu, Voltaire, and other Western intellectuals. *What is that?   How?*

Did she kill him?

Ironic, since she's not Russian

When Peter became tsar in January 1762, Catherine immediately began plotting his downfall. Supported by the army, she seized power in July 1762 and tacitly consented to Peter's murder. It was announced that he died of "hemorrhoidal colic." Quickly taking over the conduct of governmental affairs, Catherine reveled in her new power. For the next thirty-four years the Russian people were dazzled by their ruler's political skill and cunning and her superb conduct of tortuous diplomacy. Perhaps even more, they were intrigued by gossip concerning her private life. *What gossip? Lovers?*

Unusual term

Did she kill them?

Long before she became empress, Catherine was involved with a number of male favorites referred to as her house pets. At first her affairs were clandestine, but soon she displayed her lovers as French kings paraded their mistresses. Once a young man was chosen, he was showered with lavish gifts; when the empress tired of him, he was given a lavish going-away present.

Now moving from personal into to accomplishments

Catherine is usually regarded as an enlightened despot. She formed the Imperial Academy of Art, began the first college of pharmacy, and imported foreign physicians. Her interest in architecture led to the construction of a number of fine palaces, villas, and public buildings and the first part of the Hermitage in Saint Petersburg. Attracted to Western culture, she carried on correspondence with the French *philosophes* and sought their flattery by seeming to champion liberal causes. The empress played especially on Voltaire's vanity, sending him copious praise about his literary endeavors. In turn this *philosophe* became her most ardent admirer. Yet while Catherine discussed liberty and equality before the law, her liberalism and dalliance with the Enlightenment was largely a pose—eloquent in theory, lacking in practice. The lot of serfs actually worsened, leading to a bloody uprising in 1773. This revolt brought an end to all talk of reform. And after the French Revolution, strict censorship was imposed. *Changes to foreign policy accomplishments*

Double-check years — not long

So, she did little toward human progress

In her conduct of foreign policy, the empress was ruthless and successful. She annexed a large part of Poland and, realizing that Turkey was in decline, waged two wars against this ailing power. As a result of force and diplomacy, Russian frontiers reached the Black Sea, the Caspian, and the Baltic. Well could this shrewd practitioner of power tell her adopted people, "I came to Russia a poor girl. Russia has dowered me richly, but I have paid her back with Azov, the Crimea, and Poland." *What was the point?*

—T. Walter Wallbank et al.,
Civilization Past and Present

Incorrect responses to items about the main idea and topic tend to fall into two categories. Some responses will be too general and express more ideas than are actually included in the passage. Other incorrect items will be details within the passage that support the main idea. The details may be interesting and grab your attention, but they do not describe the central focus of the passage. If you are having difficulty with the main idea, reread the first and last sentences of the passage. Sometimes, though not always, one of the two sentences will give you an overview or focus.

The following items apply to the Practice Passage on Catherine the Great.

EXAMPLE   Read the following main idea items. The italicized parenthetical remarks reflect the thinking involved in judging a correct or incorrect response.

_____ Which is the best statement of the main idea of this passage?

  a. Peter lost his country through ignorance and drink. (*Important detail, but focus is on her.*)
  b. Gossip of Catherine's affairs intrigued the Russian people. (*Very interesting, but a detail.*)
  c. Progress for the Russian people was slow to come. (*Too broad and general, or not really covered.*)
  d. Catherine came to Russia as a poor girl but emerged as a powerful empress and a shrewd politician. (*Yes, sounds great.*)

_____ The best title for this passage is

  a. Catherine Changes Her Name. (*Detail.*)
  b. Peter Against Catherine. (*Only part of the story, so detail.*)
  c. Catherine the Great, Empress of Russia. (*Sounds best.*)
  d. Success of Women in Russia. (*Too broad—this is only about one woman.*)

Detail Questions

Detail questions check your ability to locate and understand explicitly stated material. Frequently, such items can be answered correctly without a thorough understanding of the passage. To find the answer to such an item, note a key word in the question and then scan the passage for the word or a synonym. When you locate the term, reread the sentence to double-check your answer. Lead-ins for detail questions fall into the following patterns:

The author states that . . .
According to the author . . .
According to the passage . . .
All of the following are true except . . .
A person, term, or place is . . .

Incorrect answers to detail questions tend to be false statements. Sometimes, the test maker will trick the unsophisticated reader by using a pompous or catchy phrase from the passage as a **distractor**—a word that is meant to divert your attention away from the correct response. The phrase might indeed appear in the passage and sound authoritative, but on close inspection, it means nothing.

EXAMPLE   Read the following detail questions on Catherine the Great and note the remarks in parentheses:

_____ Catherine changed all the following *except* (*look for the only false item to be the answer*)

    a. her religion. (*True, she joined the Orthodox church.*)
    b. her name. (*True, from Sophia to Catherine.*)
    c. Russia's borders. (*True, she gained seaports.*)
    d. the poverty of the serfs. (*The serfs were worse off and still in poverty, so this is the best answer.*)

Inference Questions

Questions concerning inference test your ability to look beyond what is directly stated and your understanding of the suggested meaning. Items testing inference deal with the writer's attitudes, feelings, or the motivation of characters. They may appear in the form of sarcastic comments, snide remarks, favorable and unfavorable descriptions, and a host of other hints and clues. Lead-ins for such items include the following:

The author believes (or feels or implies) . . .
It can be inferred from the passage . . .
The passage or author suggests . . .
It can be concluded from the passage that . . .

To answer inference items correctly, look for clues to help you develop logical assumptions. Base your conclusions on what is known and what is suggested. Incorrect inference items tend to be false statements.

EXAMPLE   Study the following inference question. The parenthetical italicized remarks reflect the thought process involved in selecting the correct answer.

_____ The author implies that Catherine

    a. did not practice the enlightenment that she professed. (*Yes, "eloquent in theory but lacking practice."*)
    b. preferred French over Russian architecture. (*Not suggested.*)
    c. took Voltaire as her lover. (*Not suggested.*)
    d. came to Russia knowing her marriage would be unhappy. (*Not suggested.*)

Author's Purpose Questions

The purpose of a reading passage is not usually stated; it is implied. In a sense, the purpose is part of the main idea; you probably need to understand the main idea to understand the purpose. Generally however, reading comprehension tests include three basic types of passages, and each type tends to dictate its own purpose. Study the following three types of passages.

1. Factual
   Identification: gives the facts about science, history, or other subjects.

Strategy: if complex, do not try to understand each detail before going to the questions. Remember, you can look back.
Example: textbook.
Purposes: to inform, to explain, to describe, or to enlighten.

2. Opinion
   Identification: puts forth a particular point of view.
   Strategy: the author states opinions and then refutes them. Sort out the opinions of the author and the opinions of the opposition.
   Example: newspaper editorial.
   Purposes: to argue, to persuade, to condemn, or to ridicule.

3. Fiction
   Identification: tells a story.
   Strategy: read slowly to understand the motivation and interrelationships of characters.
   Example: novel or short story.
   Purposes: to entertain, narrate, describe, or shock.

EXAMPLE Read the following test item and identify the purpose:

_____ The purpose of the passage on Catherine is

    a. to argue. (*No side is taken.*)
    b. to explain. (*Yes, because it is factual material.*)
    c. to condemn. (*Not judgmental.*)
    d. to persuade. (*No opinion is pushed.*)

Vocabulary Questions

Vocabulary items test your general word knowledge as well as your ability to use context to figure out word meaning. The typical form for vocabulary items on reading comprehension tests is as follows:

As used in the passage, the best definition of _____ is _____ .

Note that both word knowledge and context are necessary for a correct response. The item is qualified by "As used in the passage," so you must go back and reread the sentence (context) in which the word appears to be sure you are not misled by multiple meanings. To illustrate, the word *pool* means *a body of water* as well as *a group of people* as in *the shrinking pool of job applicants.* As a test taker, you need to double-check the context to see which meaning appears in your test passage. In addition, if you know only one definition of the word *pool*, rereading the sentence perhaps will suggest the alternate meaning to you and will help you answer the item correctly.

EXAMPLE Read the following vocabulary test item and note the reader's thought process in the parenthetical statements:

_____ As used in the passage, the best definition of *dreary* (see the second paragraph) is

    a. sad. (*Yes, unhappiness is used in the previous sentence.*)

    b. commonplace. (*Possible, but not right in the sentence.*)
    c. stupid. (*Not right in the sentence.*)
    d. neglected. (*True, but not the definition of the word.*)

Essay Questions

Essay answers demand more effort and energy from the test taker than multiple-choice items. On a multiple-choice test, all of the correct answers are before you. On an essay exam, however, the only thing in front of you is a question and a blank sheet of paper. This blank sheet can be intimidating to many students. Your job is to organize ideas relating to the question and create a response in your own words. The following suggestions can help you respond effectively.

Translate the Question.   Frequently, an essay "question" is not a question at all but a statement that you are asked to support. When you see this type of question on a test, your first step is to read it and then reread it to be sure you understand it. Next, reword it into a question. Even if it begins with a question, translate it into your own words. Simplify the question into terms that you can understand. Break the question into its parts.

    Convert the translated parts of the question into the approach that you will use to answer each part. Will you define, describe, explain, or compare? State what you will do to answer the question.

EXAMPLE   The following example demonstrates the translation process:

- **Test item:** It is both appropriate and ironic to refer to Catherine as one of the great rulers of Russia.
- **Question.** Why is it both appropriate and ironic to refer to Catherine as one of the great rulers of Russia?
- **Translation:** The question has two parts:
  1. What did Catherine do that was great?
  2. What did she do that was the opposite of what you would expect (irony) of a great Russian ruler?
- **Response approach.** List what Catherine did that was great and then list what she did that was the opposite of what you would expect of a great Russian ruler. Relate her actions to the question. (See page 31.)

Answer the Question.   Make sure that your answer is a response to the question that is asked rather than a summary of everything that you know about the subject. Padding your answer by repeating the same idea or including irrelevant information is obvious to graders and seldom is appreciated. Refer to the Reader's Tip on page 32 for guidance to the meaning of key action words that are often used in essay questions.

EXAMPLE   The following is an inappropriate answer to the question, "Why is it both appropriate and ironic to refer to Catherine as one of the great rulers of Russia?"

> Catherine was born in Germany and came to Russia as a young girl to marry Peter. It was an unhappy marriage that lasted 17 years. She . . .

EXPLANATION   This response does not answer the question; rather, it is a summary.

Organize Your Response.   Do not write the first thing that pops into your head. Take a few minutes to brainstorm and jot down ideas. Number the ideas in the order in which you wish to present them and use the plan as your outline for writing.

In your first sentence, establish the purpose and direction of your response. Then list specific details that support, explain, prove, and develop your point. Reemphasize the points in a concluding sentence and restate your purpose. Whenever possible, use numbers or subheadings to simplify your message for the reader. If time runs short, use an outline or a diagram to express your remaining ideas.

EXAMPLE   To answer the previous question, think about the selection on Catherine and jot down the ideas that you would include in a response.

I. Appropriate	II. Ironic (opposite)
1. Acquired land	1. Not Russian
2. Art, medicine, buildings	2. Killed Peter
3. 34 years	3. Serfs very poor
4. Political skill & foreign diplomacy	4. Revolt against her

Use an Appropriate Style.   Your audience for this response is not your best friend but your learned professor who is giving you a grade. Be respectful and formal. Do not use slang. Do not use phrases like "as you know," "like," or "well." They may be appropriate in conversation, but they are not appropriate in academic writing.

Avoid empty words and thoughts. Words like *good*, *interesting*, and *nice* say very little. Be more direct and descriptive in your writing.

State your thesis, supply proof, and use transitional phrases to tie your ideas together. Words like *first*, *second*, and *finally* help to organize details. Terms like *however* and *on the other hand* show a shift in thought. Remember, you are pulling ideas together, so use phrases and words to help the reader see relationships.

EXAMPLE   Study the following response to the question for organization, transition, and style:

Catherine was a very good ruler of Russia. She tried to be Russian but she was from Germany. Catherine was a good politician and got Russia seaports on the Baltic, Caspian, and Black Sea. She had many boyfriends and there was gossip about her. She did very little for the serfs because they remained very poor for a long time. She built nice buildings and got doctors to help people. She was not as awesome as she pretended to be.

EXPLANATION   Notice the response's lack of organization, weak language, inappropriate phrases, and failure to use transitional words.

Be Aware of Appearance.   An essay written in a clear, legible hand is likely to receive a higher grade than one that is hard to read. Be particular about appearance and be considerate of the reader. Proofread for correct grammar, punctuation, and spelling.

View Your Response Objectively for Evaluation Points.   Respond in order to earn points. Some students feel that simply filling up the page deserves a passing grade. They do not understand how a whole page written on the subject of Catherine could receive no points.

Although essay exams seem totally subjective, they cannot be. Students need to know that a professor who gives an essay exam grades answers according to an objective scoring system. The professor examines the paper for certain relevant points that should be made. The student's grade reflects the quantity, quality, and clarity of these relevant points.

Reader's TIP) Key Words in Essay Questions

The following key words of instruction appear in essay questions.

- **Compare:** List the similarities between things.
- **Contrast:** Note the differences between things.
- **Criticize:** State your opinion and stress the weaknesses.
- **Define:** State the meaning so that the term is understood and use examples.
- **Describe:** State the characteristics so that the image is vivid.
- **Diagram:** Make a drawing that demonstrates relationships.
- **Discuss:** Define the issue and elaborate on the advantages and disadvantages.
- **Evaluate:** State positive and negative views and make a judgment.
- **Explain:** Show cause and effect and give reasons.
- **Illustrate:** Provide examples.
- **Interpret:** Explain your own understanding of a topic that includes your opinions.
- **Justify:** Give proof or reasons to support an opinion.
- **List:** Record a series of numbered items.
- **Outline:** Sketch out the main points with their significant supporting details.
- **Prove:** Use facts as evidence in support of an opinion.
- **Relate:** Connect items and show how one influences another.
- **Review:** Write an overview with a summary.
- **Summarize:** Retell the main points.
- **Trace:** Move sequentially from one event to another.

Do not add personal experiences or extraneous examples unless they are requested. Stick to the subject and the material. Demonstrate to the professor that you understand the selection by including only the relevant ideas in your response.

The professor scoring the response to the question about Catherine used the following checklist for evaluation:

Appropriate	Ironic
1. Acquired land	1. Not Russian
2. Art, medicine, buildings	2. Killed Peter
3. 34 years	3. Serfs very poor
4. Political skill and foreign diplomacy	4. Revolt against her

The professor determined that an A answer should contain all of the items. To pass, a student should include five of the eight categories covered. Listing and explaining fewer than five would not produce enough points to pass. Naturally, the professor would expect clarity and elaboration in each category.

After the Test, Read an A Answer.   Maybe the A answer will be yours. If so, share it with others. If not, ask to read an A answer so that you will have a model from which to learn. Ask your classmates or ask the professor.

EXAMPLE   Study the following response to the previous question. The answer received an A.

> To call Catherine one of the great rulers of Russia is both appropriate and ironic. It is appropriate because she expanded the borders of Russia. Through her cunning, Russia annexed part of Poland and expanded the frontier to the Black, Caspian, and Baltic seas. Catherine professed to be enlightened and formed an art academy and a college of pharmacy, and she imported foreign physicians. She built many architecturally significant buildings, including the Hermitage. For thirty-four years, she amazed the Russian people with her political skill and diplomacy.
>
> On the other hand, Catherine was not a great Russian, nor was she an enlightened leader of all the people. First, she was not Russian; she was German, but she had worked hard to "Russify" herself during the early years of her unhappy marriage. Second, and ironically, she murdered the legitimate ruler of Russia. When she seized power, she made sure the tsar quickly died of "hemorrhoidal colic." Third, she did nothing to improve the lot of the poor serfs, and after a bloody uprising in 1773, she became even more despotic. Yet, Catherine was an engaging character who, through her cunning and intellect, has become known to the world in history books as "Catherine the Great."

EXPLANATION   Note the organization, logical thinking, and effective use of transitions in this response.

LOCUS OF CONTROL

Learning Objective 5

Take control of your learning

Have you ever heard students say, "I do better when I don't study" or "No matter how much I study, I still get a C"? Learning theory psychologists agree that people develop attitudes about control of their lives and that such comments reflect an *external locus of control* regarding test taking, academic success, and life in general. People with an external **locus of control**, called "externalizers," feel that fate, luck, or other people control what happens to them. Because they feel that they can do little to avoid what befalls them, they do not face matters directly and thus do not take responsibility for failure or credit for success.

On the other hand, people who have an *internal locus of control* feel that they, not "fate," have control over what happens to them. Such students might evaluate test performance by saying, "I didn't study enough" or "I should have spent more time organizing my essay response." "Internalizers" feel that their rewards are due to their own actions, and they take steps to be sure that they receive those rewards. When it comes to college, be an internalizer: Take responsibility, take control, and accept credit for your success.

SUMMARY POINTS

1 What does it mean to use active academic reading techniques? (page 2)
- Manage attention, effort, learning strategies, and resources effectively.
- Develop an understanding of how the brain pays attention and work on the automatic aspects of reading.
- Develop habits that help your brain absorb new information.

2 How can I improve my ability to concentrate? (page 6)
- Identify common distractions: external and internal.
- Take control of distractions by creating a place to study, organizing time, making a list of distracting worries, making a daily To Do List, increasing self-confidence, reducing anxiety, sparking an interest in the subject, and setting a time goal for reading assignments.

3 How can I read more efficiently? (page 13)
- Vary your reading rate and technique to fit the purpose for reading; recognize that prior knowledge of the subject influences reading rate.
- Determine your baseline rate.
- Develop habits for faster reading, such as steady concentration, eliminating regressions and vocalizations, expanding fixations, previewing, using a pen as a pacer, and pushing to meet a time goal.

4 How can I improve my performance on reading comprehension tests? (page 22)
- Plan for success by using specific tactics before, during, and after the test.
- Recognize the major types of comprehension test questions (main idea, detail, inference, author's purpose, vocabulary, essay), apply the appropriate strategies, and practice.

5 What does it mean to develop an internal locus of control? (page 34)
- Take responsibility for your own learning rather than attributing success or failure to luck or an external situation.
- Read and listen actively, ask questions, seek help, complete assignments, prepare effectively for tests, and take any other steps necessary to learn.

| **SELECTION 1** | Psychology | MyReadingLab |

Visit Chapter 1: Active Academic Reading in MyReadingLab to complete the
Selection 1 activities and the Build Background Knowledge video activity.

Before reading the following selection, take a few minutes to analyze your
active reading potential and answer the following questions:

1. **External Distractions**   Consider your physical environment. Where are
   you, and what time is it? _My room, 7:11 k_

   What are your external distractions? _Yes I am_

2. **Internal Distractions**   What is popping into your mind and interfering with
   your concentration? _Day dreaming_

3. **Spark Interest**   Glance at the selection and predict what it will cover. What
   do you already know about this topic? What about the selection will be of
   interest to you? _____

4. **Set Time Goals**   How long will it take you to read the selection?
   _60_ minutes. To answer the questions? _45_ minutes.

Build Background Knowledge — VIDEO

Multitasking and Meditation: Stay Productive and Peaceful

To prepare for reading Selection 1, answer the
questions below. Then, watch this video on the relationship between meditation and productivity.

What do you know about meditation and its
benefits?

Do you think that meditation courses should be required in colleges and universities? Why or why not?

What benefit do you think meditation could have in your life?

This video helped me: _____

Increase Word Knowledge

What do you know about these words?

procrastination   gratification   modification   systematically   habitually
distractors   reinforcers   adhering   visualization   rationalization

Your instructor may give a brief vocabulary review before or after reading.

Time Goal

Record your starting time for reading. ___6___ : ___00___

ARE YOU STALLING? WIN THE BATTLE AGAINST PROCRASTINATION

Have you often thought that you could get better grades if only you had more time?
Do you often find yourself studying for an exam or completing a term paper at the
last minute? If so, it makes sense for you to learn how to overcome the greatest time
waster of all—procrastination. Research indicates that academic procrastination
5   arises partly out of a lack of confidence in one's ability to meet expectations. Other
studies suggest that a preference for short-term over long-term gratification is sometimes to blame. In other words, when students procrastinate, they may be choosing
the immediate pleasures of activities such as watching television or chatting with
friends over the sense of satisfaction that they will experience in the future by meet-
10   ing academic goals. Once procrastination has become established as a behavior pattern, it often persists for years.

Nevertheless, anyone can overcome procrastination, and gain self-confidence
in the process, by using behavior modification techniques. Systematically apply the
following suggestions to keep procrastination from interfering with your studying:

Gordon Swanson/Shutterstock

15   • Identify the environmental cues that habitually interfere with your studying.
Television, computer or video games, and even food can be powerful distractors that consume hours of valuable study time. However, these distractors
can be useful positive reinforcers to enjoy after you've finished studying.

20 • Schedule your study time and reinforce yourself for adhering to your schedule. Once you've scheduled it, be just as faithful to your schedule as you would be to a work schedule set by an employer. And be sure to schedule something you enjoy to immediately follow the study time.

• Get started. The most difficult part is getting started. Give yourself an extra reward for starting on time and, perhaps, a penalty for starting late.

25 • Use visualization. Much procrastination results from the failure to consider its negative consequences. Visualizing the consequences of not studying, such as trying to get through an exam you haven't adequately prepared for, can be an effective tool for combating procrastination.

30 • Beware of jumping to another task when you reach a difficult part of an assignment. This procrastination tactic gives you the feeling that you are busy and accomplishing something, but it is, nevertheless, an avoidance mechanism.

• Beware of preparation overkill. Procrastinators may actually spend hours preparing for a task rather than working on the task itself. For example, they

35 may gather enough library materials to write a book rather than a five-page term paper. This enables them to postpone writing the paper.

• Keep a record of the reasons you give yourself for postponing studying or completing important assignments. If a favorite rationalization is "I'll wait until I'm in the mood to do this," count the number of times in a week you

40 are seized with the desire to study. The mood to study typically arrives after you begin, not before.

Don't procrastinate! Begin now! Apply the steps outlined here to gain more control over your behavior and win the battle against procrastination.

(488 words)

—From Samuel E. Wood, Ellen Green Wood,
and Denise G. Boyd, *Mastering the World of Psychology*, 5th ed.

Time Goals

Record your finishing time: _____7___ : ___18___ .

Calculate your total reading time: _____1___ : ___13___ .

Rate your concentration as high _____ medium _____ or low ___✓___ .

Recall what you have read and review what you have learned.

Your instructor may choose to give a brief comprehension review.

THINK CRITICALLY ABOUT THE SELECTION

How can one activity, such as playing video games, be both a negative and a positive factor?

Bibliographic references to specific research studies were removed from this article. Would including the citations make the ideas more convincing? Why?

WRITE ABOUT THE SELECTION

Is procrastination a problem for you?

Response suggestion: If so, briefly describe your most irresistible distractors. Next, select two of the suggestions in the article that you think would work best for you. Write a paragraph in the form of a pledge that details the steps you will take to begin changing your procrastination habit.

If procrastination is not a problem for you, write a paragraph that explains the benefits that you will gain from working in a timely manner. Include specific examples.

SELECTION

1

CHECK YOUR COMPREHENSION

After reading the selection, answer the following questions with *a*, *b*, *c*, or *d*. To help you analyze your strengths and weaknesses, the question types are indicated.

Main Idea _____ 1. What is the best statement of the selection's main point?

    a. Many college students procrastinate.

    b. Procrastination is sometimes caused by a lack of confidence.

    c. Procrastination can cause students to fail academically.

    d. Procrastination can be overcome with behavior modification techniques.

Detail _____ 2. According to this article, which is the best action to take when you reach a difficult part of an assignment?

    a. Move on to an easier part of the assignment and come back to the hard part later.

    b. Take a break from the assignment to relax and regroup.

    c. Tackle it right away.

    d. Do another task on your To Do List so that you accomplish something.

Inference _____ 3. Based on the article, which of the following represents long-term gratification?

    a. spending several hours playing a video game

    b. earning an A in a difficult course

    c. having a quick snack

    d. binge watching a season of your favorite television show.

Main Idea _____ 4. Which sentence best states the main idea of the first paragraph?

    a. You could get better grades if you didn't procrastinate.

    b. Procrastination is the greatest time waster of all.

    c. There are several root causes of procrastination, and, with effort, they can be conquered.

    d. The procrastination habit can last for years.

Author's Purpose _____ 5. The source of the selection and its details suggest that its primary purpose is to

    a. inform readers of the causes and solutions for procrastination.

    b. convince readers to stop procrastinating.

    c. amuse readers with examples in which they might recognize themselves.

    d. impress readers with research-based information.

Detail _____ C _____ 6. Which of the following is NOT mentioned as a way to tackle procrastination?

   a. Create a schedule for study time.
   b. Visualize the consequences of not studying for a test.
   c. Record your reasons for procrastinating.
   d. Ask successful students how they manage procrastination.

Detail _____ C _____ 7. According to the selection, being in the mood to study usually
occurs

   a. after you begin to study.
   b. when you are well rested.
   c. when the assignment is first given.
   d. when the due date is near and time pressure is greatest.

Inference _____ A _____ 8. The selection implies that

   a. procrastination is an easy habit to break.
   b. using one or two of the techniques should be enough to break the
      habit.
   c. students might need outside help or coaching to break a long
      held procrastination habit.
   d. overcoming procrastination could take a long time and a lot of
      effort.

Main Idea _____ C _____ 9. The main point of the bulleted paragraphs is that

   a. there are several reasons for procrastination.
   b. several methods can help to break the procrastination habit.
   c. it is easy to break the procrastination habit.
   d. creating a schedule for accomplishing tasks is a helpful method.

Inference _____ D _____ 10. The phrase "seized with the desire to study" suggests that the author

   a. expects the number of times per week will be high.
   b. believes the desire is rewarding enough to happen often.
   c. assumes the desire occurs regularly for most students.
   d. thinks the desire doesn't strike students very often.

Answer the following questions with (*T*) true or (*F*) false.

Inference _____ T _____ 11. Although the selection only recommends visualizing negative
consequences of procrastinating, it is logical to infer that visualizing
positive results of getting things done early or on time would also be
a good motivator.

Inference _____ T _____ 12. The environmental distractions mentioned in the selection could
also be considered internal distractions, as discussed in the section
on concentration in this chapter.

Detail _____ 13. According to this selection, overpreparing to begin an assignment is a helpful behavior.

Detail _____ 14. According to the selection, conquering procrastination, in itself, can boost self-confidence.

Detail _____ 15. The selection mentions rewards for avoiding procrastination more often than punishments for engaging in it.

BUILD YOUR VOCABULARY

According to the way the italicized word was used in the selection, indicate *a, b, c,* or *d* for the word or phrase that gives the best definition. The number in parentheses indicates the line of the passage in which the word is located. Use a dictionary in addition to the context clues to more precisely define the terms.

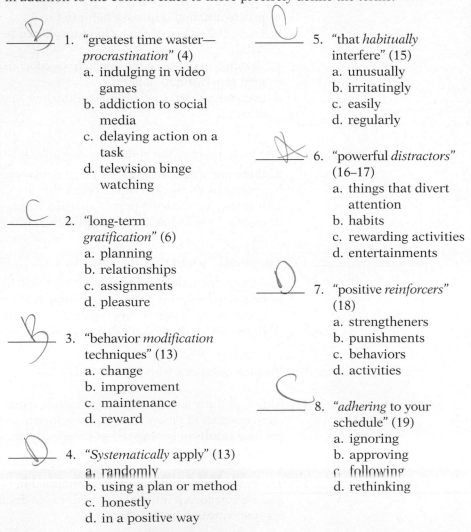

_____ 1. "greatest time waster— *procrastination*" (4)
a. indulging in video games
b. addiction to social media
c. delaying action on a task
d. television binge watching

_____ 2. "long-term *gratification*" (6)
a. planning
b. relationships
c. assignments
d. pleasure

_____ 3. "behavior *modification* techniques" (13)
a. change
b. improvement
c. maintenance
d. reward

_____ 4. "*Systematically* apply" (13)
a. randomly
b. using a plan or method
c. honestly
d. in a positive way

_____ 5. "that *habitually* interfere" (15)
a. unusually
b. irritatingly
c. easily
d. regularly

_____ 6. "powerful *distractors*" (16–17)
a. things that divert attention
b. habits
c. rewarding activities
d. entertainments

_____ 7. "positive *reinforcers*" (18)
a. strengtheners
b. punishments
c. behaviors
d. activities

_____ 8. "*adhering* to your schedule" (19)
a. ignoring
b. approving
c. following
d. rethinking

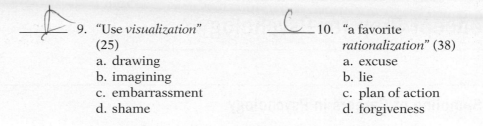

_____ 9. *"Use visualization"*
       (25)
       a. drawing
       b. imagining
       c. embarrassment
       d. shame

_____ 10. *"a favorite*
       rationalization" (38)
       a. excuse
       b. lie
       c. plan of action
       d. forgiveness

Time Goals

Record your time for answering the questions: ___8___ : ___0 0___.

Calculate your total reading time for reading and answering the questions:
___45_____.

What changes would you make to enhance your concentration on the next selection?

Concept Prep for Psychology

A Sampling of Careers in Psychology

Most careers in psychology require at least a Bachelor's degree. Many require a Master's degree or doctorate.

- Therapist
- Psychiatrist
- Professor
- School counselor or diagnostician

- Sports psychologist
- Researcher
- Adviser to businesses and other professionals
- Community health worker

What does psychology cover?

Psychology is the scientific study of behavior and the mind. Behavior is observed, studied, and measured with the ultimate objective of explaining why people act and think as they do. Special areas of study in psychology focus on the following questions:

- **Biological psychology:** How do your genes, brain, and hormones affect your behavior?
- **Behavioral psychology:** What stimulus in the environment triggers your response?
- **Cognitive psychology:** How do you think and remember?
- **Life span psychology:** How do thoughts, desires, and actions differ in infancy, childhood, adolescence, adulthood, and old age?

Why is Freud so important?

Sigmund Freud was a physician in Vienna, Austria, who formulated a theory of personality and a form of psychotherapy called *psychoanalysis*. Freud emerged as a leader in modern psychology and wrote 24 books popularizing his theories. After Freud's death in 1939, psychologists questioned many of his ideas and criticized him because of his focus on sexual desires. Still, Freud has contributed many ideas to our culture and words to our vocabulary.

Freud's theories evolved from observing and treating patients who suffered ailments without any visible physical basis but who responded favorably to hypnosis. He believed in treating their problems by tracing their difficulties back to childhood experiences. Freud also believed in *dream interpretation*, a process in which the unconscious mind provides clues to psychological problems.

Freud's basic theories suggest that people are driven from early childhood by three principal unconscious forces: the *id* (an animal instinct and desire for pleasure), the *ego* (the sense of self that fights the id for reasonable compromises), and the *superego* (the social feeling of right and wrong and community values). Other terms that Freud established include *pleasure principle,* which refers to an instinctive need to satisfy the id, regardless of the consequences; *libido,* which refers to sexual drive; and *egotism,* which refers to a sense of self-importance and conceit.

Other words that we use today emerge from Freud's five stages of personality development: *oral, anal, phallic, latency,* and *genital.* An *oral*

Sigmund Freud theorized that mundane behavior has underlying psychological causes.
Mary Evans Picture Library/Alamy

personality is fixated in the first stage of sucking and is satisfied by the pleasures of the mouth—for example, talking, smoking, eating, and chewing gum excessively. An *anal personality* is associated with the childhood period that involves bowel control and toilet training, and as an adult is excessively focused on details and orderliness. Another term that Freud popularized is *Oedipus complex*, which suggests that a young boy has a sexual desire for his mother. Finally, Freud was the originator of the term, *Freudian slip*, which refers to a misspoken word—such as *sex* for *six*—that reveals unconscious thoughts.

Who was Carl Jung?

Carl Jung was a Swiss psychologist who classified people as *introverts* (shy) or *extroverts* (outgoing). Jung was one of the original followers of Freud but later broke with him. Adding to Freud's theory of repressed personal experiences, Jung believed that we also inherit the memories and symbols of ancestors in an *inherited collective unconscious*. He believed that this was exhibited in an inborn fear of snakes or spiders. Jung also developed theories about concrete and abstract learning stages. Many of his theories are used as a basis for the Myers-Briggs Type Indicator.

REVIEW QUESTIONS

After studying the material, answer the following questions:

1. Using visual images on note cards to improve memory of vocabulary words suggests what area of psychology? _____

2. Desiring a rocky road ice cream cone after passing a Baskin-Robbins store suggests what area of psychology? _____

3. Mapping physical activity in different areas of the brain as people read or listen to music suggests what area of psychology? _____

4. Exploring stages of adolescence suggests what area of psychology? _____

5. What is psychoanalysis? _____

6. What are the goals of the id, ego, and superego? _____

7. How does Freud relate dreams to reality? _____

8. Why did some psychologists break with Freud? _____

9. How do the theories of Jung and Freud differ? _____

10. What is Jung's inherited collective unconscious? _____

Your instructor may choose to give a brief review of these psychology concepts.

Visit Chapter 1: Active Academic Reading in MyReadingLab to complete the Selection 2 activities and to complete the Build Background Knowledge video activity.

BEFORE reading the following selection, take a few minutes to analyze your active reading potential and answer the following questions.

1. **External Distractions**   Consider your physical environment. Where are you, and what time is it? _____

_____

What are your external distractions? _____

_____

2. **Internal Distractions**   What is popping into your mind and interfering with your concentration? _____

3. **Spark Interest**   Glance at the selection and predict what it will cover. What do you already know about the topic? What about the selection will be of interest to you? _____

4. **Set Time Goals**   How long will it take you to read the selection?

_____ minutes. To answer the questions? _____ minutes.

Build Background Knowledge — VIDEO

Obama, Biden Honor WWII Female War Heroes

To prepare for reading Selection 2, answer the questions below. Then, watch this video that features a very special visit to the White House by several women who played a critical role in World War II.

What do you know about U.S. women's roles in World War II?

Should women and men have the same duties and responsibilities in combat? Why or why not?

How do you think women's roles have changed in military action since World War II?

This video helped me: _____

_____

_____

Increase Word Knowledge

What do you know about these words?

competence	unprecedented	scarcities	incentives	barred
drafted	enlisted	camaraderie	prosperity	topsy-turvy

Your instructor may give a brief vocabulary review before or after reading.

Time Goal

Record your starting time for reading. ____9____:__00____

HOME FRONT WORKERS, ROSIE THE RIVETER, AND VICTORY GIRLS

War affects more than the soldiers who fight it and the people whose homelands are the battle sites. For those left at home in the United States during World War II, life was very different—perhaps in unexpected ways—from before the war. In some ways it was better.

CHANGES ON THE HOME FRONT

World War II opened up new possibilities for jobs, income, and labor organizing, for women as well as for men, and for new groups of workers. Disabled workers entered jobs previously considered beyond their abilities, fulfilling their tasks with skill and competence. For example, deaf people streamed into Akron, Ohio, to work in the
5 tire factories that became defense plants, making more money than they ever made before.

Along with new employment opportunities, workers' earnings rose nearly 70 percent. Income doubled for farmers and then doubled again. Labor union membership grew 50 percent, reaching an all-time high by the end of the war. In spite of
10 no-strike pledges, strikes pressured the aircraft industry in Detroit and elsewhere. A major strike of the United Mine Workers Union erupted in 1943. Congress responded with the Smith-Connally Act of 1943, which gave the president power to seize plants or mines wherever strikes interrupted war production.

Women and people of color joined unions in unprecedented numbers. Some
15 organized unions of their own. Energetic labor organizers like Luisa Moreno and Dorothy Ray Healy organized Mexican and Russian Jewish workers at the California Sanitary Canning Company into a powerful CIO cannery union that achieved wage increases and union recognition. Unions with white male leadership, however, admitted women and people of color reluctantly and tolerated them only during the
20 war emergency. Some unions required women to quit their jobs after the war.

NEW OPPORTUNITIES FOR WOMEN

World War II ushered in dramatic changes for American women. Wartime scarcities led to increased domestic labor as homemakers made do with rationed goods, mended

clothing, collected and saved scraps and metals, and planted "victory gardens" to help feed their families. Employment opportunities for women also increased. As a result
25 of the combined incentives of patriotism and good wages, women streamed into the paid labor force. Many women took "men's jobs" while the men went off to fight.

Rosie the Riveter became the heroic symbol of the woman war worker. Pictures of attractive "Rosies" building planes or constructing ships graced magazine covers and posters. Future Hollywood star Marilyn Monroe first gained attention when her
30 photograph appeared in *Yank,* a magazine for soldiers. The magazine pictured her not as the sex goddess she later became but as a typical Rosie the Riveter clad in overalls, working at her job in a defense plant.

Until 1943, black women were barred from work in defense industries. Poet Maya Angelou recalled that African Americans had to fight for the jobs they wanted.
35 She became the first black streetcar conductor in San Francisco during the war, but not without a struggle. She made herself a promise that "made my veins stand out, and my mouth tighten into a prune: I WOULD HAVE THE JOB. I WOULD BE A CONDUCTORETTE AND SLING A FULL MONEY CHANGER FROM MY BELT. I WOULD." And she did.

40 For the first time, married women joined the paid labor force in droves and public opinion supported them. During the Great Depression of the 1930s, 80 percent of Americans had objected to the idea of wives working outside the home; by 1942, only 13 percent still objected. However, mothers of young children found very little help. In 1943, the federal government finally responded to the needs of work-
45 ing mothers by funding day care centers. More than 3,000 centers enrolled 130,000 children. Still, the program served only a small proportion of working mothers. Most women relied on family members to care for their children. A Women's Bureau

This famous poster of "Rosie the Riveter" represents American women who worked in factories during World War II.
Stocktrek Images, Inc./Alamy

survey in 1944 found that 16 percent of mothers working in war industries had no child care arrangements. Meager to begin with and conceived as an emergency mea-
50 sure, government funding for child care would end after the war.

Before the war, most jobs for women were low-paying, nonunion positions that paid an average of $24.50 a week. Wartime manufacturing jobs paid almost twice that—$40.35 a week. During the conflict, 300,000 women worked in the aircraft industry alone. Almira Bondelid recalled that when her husband went overseas, "I
55 decided to stay in San Diego and went to work in a dime store. That was a terrible place to work, and as soon as I could I got a job at Convair [an aircraft manufacturer]. . . . I worked in the tool department as a draftsman, and by the time I left there two years later I was designing long drill jigs for parts of the wing and hull of B-24 bombers."

New opportunities for women also opened up in the armed services. All sectors
60 of the armed forces had dwindled in the years between the two wars and needed to gain size and strength. Along with the 10 million men age 21 to 35 drafted into the armed services and the 6 million who enlisted, 100,000 women volunteered for the Navy WAVES (Women Accepted for Voluntary Emergency Service) and 140,000 for the Women's Army Auxiliary Corps (WAAC). In 1943, the WAAC became the
65 Women's Army Corps (WAC), dropping "Auxiliary" from the name.

CHANGES IN MARRIAGE AND FAMILY LIFE

Most female enlistees and war workers enjoyed their work and wanted to continue after the war. The extra pay, independence, camaraderie, and satisfaction that their jobs provided had opened their eyes to new possibilities. Although most of the well-paying positions for women disappeared after the war as the returning veterans
70 reclaimed their jobs, women did not disappear from the paid labor force. The numbers of employed women continued to rise in the postwar years. Edith Speert, like many others, was never again content as a full-time housewife and mother. Edith's husband, Victor, was sent overseas in 1944. During the eighteen months of their separation, they penned 1,300 letters to each other, sometimes two or three times a
75 day. The letters revealed the love and affection they felt for one another, but Edith did not hesitate to tell Victor how she had changed. In a letter from Cleveland, dated November 9, 1945, she wrote:

Sweetie, I want to make sure I make myself clear about how I've changed. I want you to know *now* that you are not married to a girl that's interested
80 solely in a home—I shall definitely have to work all my life—I get emotional satisfaction out of working; and I don't doubt that many a night you will cook the supper while I'm at a meeting. Also, dearest—I shall never wash and iron—there are laundries for that! Do you think you'll be able to bear living with me? . . . I love you, Edith

85 Despite the shifting priorities of women, the war reversed the declining marriage and fertility rates of the 1930s. Between 1941 and 1945, the birthrate climbed from 19.4 to 24.5 per 1,000 population. The reversal stemmed, in part, from economic prosperity as well as the possibility of draft deferments for married men in the early war years. However, the desire to solidify relationships and establish con-
90 nections to the future during a time of great uncertainty perhaps served as the more powerful motivation. Thus, a curious paradox marked the war years: a widespread disruption of domestic life accompanied by a rush into marriage and parenthood.

CHANGES IN SEXUAL CONDUCT

At the same time that the war prompted family formation, wartime upheaval sent the sexual order topsy-turvy. For many young women, moving to a new city or tak-
95 ing a wartime job opened up new possibilities for independence, excitement, and sexual adventure. One young worker recalled:

> Chicago was just humming, no matter where I went. The bars were jammed . . . you could pick up anyone you wanted to. . . . There were service-men of all varieties roaming the streets all the time. There was never, never a
> 100 shortage of young, healthy bucks. . . . We never thought of getting tired. Two or three hours of sleep was normal. . . . I'd go down to the office every morn-ing half dead, but with a smile on my face, and report for work.

Some young women, known as "victory girls," believed that it was an act of patriotism to have a fling with a man in uniform before he went overseas. The inde-
105 pendence of these women raised fears of female sexuality as a dangerous, ungov-erned force. The worry extended beyond the traditional concern about prostitutes and "loose women" to include "good girls" whose sexual standards might relax during wartime. Public health campaigns warned enlisted men that victory girls would have their fun with a soldier and then leave him with a venereal disease,
110 incapable of fighting for his country.

Wartime also intensified concerns about homosexuality. Urban centers and the military provided new opportunities for gay men and lesbians to form relationships and build communities. Although the military officially banned homosexuals, many served by keeping their orientation secret. If discovered, gay men faced severe pun-
115 ishment, including confinement in cages called "queer stockades" or in psychiatric wards. Lesbians faced similar sanctions, although the women's corps, in an effort to assure the civilian world of their recruits' femininity, often looked the other way.

(1500 words)

—From Jacqueline Jones et al., *Created Equal*, 3rd ed.

Time Goals

Record your finishing time: _____ 9 _____ : _____ 九13 _____ .

Calculate your total reading time: _____ : _____ .

Rate your concentration as high _____ medium _____ or low ✓_____ .

Recall what you have read and review what you have learned.

Your instructor may choose to give a brief comprehension review.

THINK CRITICALLY ABOUT THE SELECTION

What labor conditions and opportunities that we enjoy today appear to have had their roots in World War II?

Ironically, war creates horrific effects in terms of human suffering and loss. On the other hand, it can also create economic growth and social change. What peaceful means can generate positive results without the negatives?

WRITE ABOUT THE SELECTION

Was there something in this selection that surprised you? For example, had you thought about the effect of a global war such as World War II on those at home in the United States? If you had, perhaps you had not considered that any effects might be positive. Think about the effects on women's roles and sexual standards described in this selection and how they compare to today's American society.

Response Suggestion: Make a two-column list. On the left side, list the changes in women's roles and sexual standards during World War II. On the right side, list today's conditions. Use these notes to write a four-paragraph essay in which you compare the two lists. Begin with a brief introductory paragraph. The second and third paragraphs should discuss the comparisons in the two areas of women's roles and sexual standards. In the fourth paragraph, briefly summarize and speculate on whether experiences during the war might have eventually led to the standards that we live with today.

CHECK YOUR COMPREHENSION

After reading the selection, answer the following questions with *a, b, c,* or *d*. To help you analyze your strengths and weaknesses, the question types are indicated.

Main Idea _____ B   1. Which phrase best describes the topic of this selection?

    a. changes in women's roles during World War II
    b. changes on the home front during World War II
    c. the effects of war on marriage and family life
    d. the effects of war

Main Idea _____ A   2. Which is the best statement describing the main point of the entire selection?

    a. War is difficult for everyone.
    b. Many women filled jobs that were once held by the men who went to fight.
    c. World War II had significant effects on the roles of women and others at home, which changed family life and sexual standards.
    d. Sexual standards were relaxed for some during World War II.

Inference _____ C   3. Based on the information in this selection, Rosie the Riveter was

    a. a symbol that represented the new roles women were filling during World War II.
    b. an actual person named Rosie who worked in an airplane manufacturing plant.
    c. the first role Marilyn Monroe had in the movies.
    d. also known as a victory girl.

Inference _____ A   4. One can logically infer that the B-24s Amelia Bondelid worked on were

    a. airplanes.
    b. aircraft carriers.
    c. submarines.
    d. landing crafts.

Detail _____ B   5. According to the article, Maya Angelou worked as a _____ during the war.

    a. streetcar conductor
    b. poet
    c. draftsman in an aircraft manufacturing plant
    d. riveter building airplanes

Main Idea _____ D   6. The main point of the section titled "Changes on the Home Front" is that

    a. many deaf people were hired in tire factories in Akron, Ohio.
    b. life was easier for some people during World War II.

SELECTION 2

c. World War II opened jobs and other opportunities for several groups of people who would not have been considered qualified before the war.

d. women and people of color joined and organized labor unions in California during World War II but were denied membership when the war ended.

Inference _____ 7. What is the most likely reason that the author included examples and quotes from women who lived during World War II?

a. to highlight famous historical individuals
b. to emphasize the large number of people whose lives were affected by the war
c. to show that women enjoyed their new roles
d. to personalize the facts so that readers can better understand their significance.

Detail _____ 8. The portion of Americans who believed that women should not work outside the home changed from _____ to _____.

a. 80% in the 1930s; 13% in 1942
b. 100,000; 140,000
c. 140,000; 100,000
d. 13% in the 1930s; 80% in 1942

Detail _____ 9. Which of the following were among the reasons cited for rising marriage and birth rates during World War II?

a. a poor economy and a desire to solidify relationships
b. economic prosperity and possible draft deferments for married men
c. changing sexual standards and disruption of domestic life
d. greater acceptance of gay and lesbian lifestyles

Detail _____ 10. Child care for women working outside their homes

a. was not provided by the government during World War II.
b. was provided entirely by family members of working mothers during World War II.
c. was reluctantly funded by the government but discontinued after the war.
d. was immediately recognized and generously funded by the government during the war.

Answer the following questions with (*T*) true or (*F*) false.

Inference _____ 11. Many women as well as men wanted to do military service during World War II.

Inference _____ 12. Many women experienced fulfillment and satisfaction from working outside their homes and wanted to continue to work after the war.

Detail _____ 13. Victory girls considered it patriotic to have a fling with a soldier before he went to war.

Detail _____ 14. Although good jobs were less available for women after the war, the number of women working outside their homes continued to rise.

Author's purpose _____ 15. The primary purpose of this selection is to inform readers.

BUILD YOUR VOCABULARY

According to the way the italicized word was used in the selection, indicate *a, b, c,* or *d* for the word or phrase that gives the best definition. The number in parentheses indicates the line of the passage in which the word is located. Use a dictionary in addition to the context clues to more precisely define the terms.

_____ 1. "skill and *competence*" (4)
  a. pride
  b. capability
  c. disability
  d. energy

_____ 2. "*unprecedented* numbers" (14)
  a. unheard-of
  b. established
  c. unsurprising
  d. familiar

_____ 3. "Wartime *scarcities*" (21)
  a. changes
  b. surpluses
  c. fears
  d. shortages

_____ 4. "combined *incentives*" (25)
  a. burdens
  b. encouragements
  c. requirements
  d. needs

_____ 5. "*barred* from work" (33)
  a. punished
  b. permitted
  c. fired
  d. forbidden

_____ 6. "*drafted* into the armed services" (61)
  a. volunteered
  b. accepted
  c. forced
  d. denied entrance

_____ 7. "6 million who *enlisted*" (62)
  a. volunteered
  b. refused
  c. enrolled in college
  d. worked on the home front

_____ 8. "*camaraderie*, and satisfaction" (67)
  a. loneliness
  b. hostility
  c. friendship
  d. nervousness

A   9. "from economic
prosperity" (88)
a. poverty
b. wealth
c. bankruptcy
d. statistics

B   10. "sent the sexual order
topsy-turvy" (94)
a. into confusion
b. into perfection
c. into perspective
d. into playfulness

Time Goals

Record your time for answering the questions: ___10_ : _00_____

Calculate your total time for reading and answering the questions:
_____ : _____

What changes would you make to enhance your concentration on the next
selection?

What events led up to World War II?

After Germany was defeated in World War I, which supposedly was the "war to end all wars," the *Allies* (United States, Britain, France, and Russia) expected Germany to pay for the war that they helped start. The Allies also changed the world map by taking away much of the German empire. The German people were stunned at their defeat, angry over the demands of the victors, and eventually unable to meet their debt payments. *Adolf Hitler*, a skillful and charismatic leader, seized this opportunity and tapped into the country's anger. He promised to restore national pride, and consequently many Germans were drawn to him. He became the leader of the *Nazi* Party, adopted the *swastika* as its symbol, and eventually became dictator of Germany.

Hitler strengthened the military, forged an alliance with Japan and Italy, and attacked and conquered much of continental Europe. When Britain, under the leadership of Prime Minister *Winston Churchill*, refused to bargain with Germany, Hitler ordered the *Luftwaffe*, the German air force, to destroy Britain from the air. The air raids, known as the *blitz*, failed in their purpose when the Royal Air Force (RAF) won the Battle of Britain. Hitler then attacked Russia.

What was the role of the United States in the war?

The United States, under *Franklin D. Roosevelt*, remained neutral. *Isolationists* opposed foreign involvement. That changed, however, on December 7, 1941, at 7:02 A.M., when the Japanese bombed *Pearl Harbor*, an American naval base in Hawaii. America declared war that same day. *General Douglas MacArthur* and *Admiral Chester Nimitz* were put in charge of forces in the Pacific, and *General Dwight D. Eisenhower* led the Allied soldiers in Europe.

What was D-Day?

Allied forces planned the liberation of Europe, and on June 6, 1944—on what came to be known as *D-Day*—thousands of brave soldiers secretly left England and stormed the beaches of Normandy, France. After two weeks of desperate fighting, the troops moved inland and liberated Paris by August. The Allied armies drove toward *Berlin*, the capital

Prime Minister Winston Churchill, President Franklin D. Roosevelt, and Soviet leader Joseph Stalin pose for pictures at the Yalta Conference in 1945.
Keystone/Getty

of Germany, and on April 30, Hitler committed suicide to avoid capture. The Germans surrendered one week later, and the European part of the war was over. Hitler, driven by his anti-Semitic hatred, had ordered the killing of more than 6 million innocent Jews. Many were taken by trains to concentration camps for extermination in gas chambers. This horrible carnage was called the *Holocaust*.

How did the war with Japan end?

The American forces in the Pacific were moving from island to island against fierce Japanese resistance. Victories were won with great loss of life. Upon FDR's death, Harry Truman had become president and was told of the *Manhattan Project*, a top-secret plan to develop an atomic bomb. On August 6, 1945, the *Enola Gay* flew over *Hiroshima, Japan*, and dropped an atomic bomb that obliterated the city. Three days later, a second bomb was dropped over *Nagasaki*. Within a few days, the Japanese asked for peace, and a month later they officially surrendered to General MacArthur aboard the battleship *U.S.S. Missouri* in Tokyo Bay. World War II had come to an end.

REVIEW QUESTIONS

After studying the material, answer the following questions:

1. How did the end of World War I affect the beginning of World War II?
   _____

2. Why were the Germans drawn to Hitler's message? _____
   _____

3. Who were Germany's allies in World War II? _____

4. Why did the Luftwaffe strike England? _____
   _____

5. Who were the isolationists? _____
   _____

6. What prompted the United States to enter the war? _____
   _____

7. What was the Holocaust? _____

8. What was D-Day? _____
   _____

9. What ended the war in Europe? _____
   _____

10. What ended the war in Japan? _____
    _____

Your instructor may choose to give a brief review of these history concepts.

SELECTION 3   Science   MyReadingLab

Visit Chapter 1: Active Academic Reading in MyReadingLab to complete the Selection 3 activities and to complete the Build Background Knowledge video activity.

BEFORE reading the following selection, take a few minutes to analyze your active learning potential and answer the following questions:

1. **External Distractions**   Consider your physical environment. Where are you, and what time is it? _____ My Room, 10:15 _____

   What are your external distractions? _____ My TV _____

2. **Internal Distractions**   What is popping into your mind and interfering with your concentration? _____ Sleeping _____

3. **Spark Interest**   Glance at the selection and predict what it will cover. What do you already know about this topic? What about the selection will be of interest to you? _____ Not really _____

4. **Set Time Goals**   How long will it take you to read the selection? _____ 45 _____ minutes. To answer the questions? _____ 30 _____ minutes.

Build Background Knowledge — VIDEO

Global Milestone

To prepare for reading Selection 3, answer the questions below. Then, watch this video from 2011 announcing that human population on the earth has hit 7 billion. (The human population on earth is expected to hit 8 billion by 2021.)

How do you think the earth is impacted by holding over 7 billion people?

Do you think world governments should take measures to address population growth? Why or why not?

Which of the earth's resources do you think is most impacted by increased human population?

This video helped me: _____

_____

_____

Increase Word Knowledge

What do you know about these words?

squatters	exemplify	finite	sustain	biosphere
endowment	collective	unprecedented	depleted	compensate

Your instructor may give a brief vocabulary review before or after reading.

Time Goal

Record your starting time for reading: ____10____ : ____00____

IS THERE ENOUGH EARTH FOR EVERYONE?

In Côte d'Ivoire, a country in western Africa, the government is waging a battle to protect some of its rapidly dwindling tropical rain forest from illegal hunters, farmers, and loggers. Officials destroy the shelters of the squatters, who immediately return and rebuild. One such squatter, Sep Djekoule, explained: "I have ten children
5 and we must eat. The forest is where I can provide for my family, and everybody has that right." His words exemplify the conflict between population growth and environmental protection, between the human drive to have many children and Earth's finite resources. How many people can Earth sustain?

The Global Footprint Network, consisting of an international group of scientists
10 and professionals from many fields, is attempting to assess humanity's ecological footprint. This project compares human demand for resources to Earth's capacity to supply these resources in a sustainable manner. "Sustainable" means that the resources could be renewed indefinitely, and the ability of the biosphere to supply them would not be diminished over time. Their question boils down to: "Is human-
15 ity living on the 'interest' produced by our global endowment, or are we eating into the 'principal' and so reducing its ability to support us?" The group concluded that, in 2007, humanity was already consuming 150% of the resources that were sustainably available. In other words, to avoid damaging Earth's resources (thus reducing Earth's carrying capacity), our population in 2007 required 1.5 Earths. But by 2012,
20 we had added well over 300 million more people.

A population that exceeds carrying capacity damages its ecosystem, reducing its future ability to sustain that population. Since humans began populating the earth, they have made advances in clothing, shelter, agriculture, medicine, and all other areas of human need to overcome environmental challenges. These technological developments
25 have allowed us to expand to previously uninhabited parts of the earth, to increase our population, and to use more of our natural resources. The result is that our collective ecological footprint now tramples Earth's sustainable resource base, reducing Earth's future capacity to support us. For example, each year, overgrazing and deforestation decrease the productivity of land, especially in developing countries where average
30 living standards, educational levels, and life expectancy are relatively low.

Overgrazing can lead to the loss of productive land. Human activities, including overgrazing, deforestation, and poor agricultural practices, reduce the productivity of the land. (Inset) An expanding human population, coupled with a loss of productive land, can lead to tragedy.

(Inset/top) Finbarr O'Reilly/Reuters Picture; (bottom) Images of Africa Photobank/Alamy

The human population now uses more than 37% of Earth's total land area to grow crops and livestock. Despite this, the United Nations estimates that more than 900 million people are undernourished, including an estimated 30% of the population of sub-Saharan Africa. Erosion reduces the ability of land to support both crops
35 and grazing livestock. The quest for farmland drives people to clear cut forests in places where the soil is poorly suited for agriculture. The demand for wood also causes large areas to be deforested annually, causing the runoff of much-needed fresh water, the erosion of precious topsoil, the pollution of rivers and oceans, and an overall reduction in the ability of the land and water to support future crops and
40 livestock, and to support the fish and other wild animals that people harvest for food. Our consumption of food, wood, and—more recently—biofuels (crops that provide fuel) drives the destruction of tens of millions of acres of rain forest annually, causing the extinction of species on an unprecedented scale.

The United Nations estimates that more than 30% of commercial ocean fish popu-
45 lations are being harvested unsustainably, and more than 50% more are being harvested at their maximum sustainable yield. In parts of India, China, Africa, and the United States, underground water stores are being depleted to irrigate cropland far faster than they are being refilled by natural processes. Because irrigated land supplies about 40% of human food crops, water shortages can rapidly lead to food shortages.
50 Our present population, at its present level of technology, is clearly "overgrazing" the biosphere. As the 5.7 billion people in less-developed countries strive to increase their standard of living, the damage to Earth's ecosystems accelerates. We all want to enjoy luxuries far beyond bare survival, but unfortunately, the resources currently demanded to support the high standard of living in developed countries
55 are unattainable for most of Earth's inhabitants. For example, supporting the world

population sustainably at the average standard of living in the United States would require 4.7 Earths. Technology can help us improve agricultural efficiency, conserve energy and water, reduce pollutants, and recycle far more of what we use. But tech-
60 nological advances are expensive to develop and difficult for many developing countries to implement. In the long run, no amount of technological innovation will compensate for our potential population growth, which we must restrain if we expect Earth to continue to support us.

Inevitably, the human population will stop growing. Either we must voluntarily reduce our birth rate, or various forms of environmental resistance, including disease
65 and starvation, will dramatically increase human death rates. Hope for the future lies in recognizing the signs of human overgrazing and responding by reducing our population before we cause further damage to the biosphere, diminishing its ability to support people and the other precious and irreplaceable forms of life on Earth.

(875 words)

—From Teresa Audesirk, Gerald Audesirk, and Bruce E. Byers, *Biology: Life on Earth With Physiology*, 10th ed.

SELECTION 3

Time Goals

Record your finishing time: ___10___ : ___50___.

Calculate your total reading time: _____ : _____.

Rate your concentration as high _____ medium ___✓___ or low _____.

Recall what you have read, and review what you have learned.

Your instructor may choose to give a brief comprehension review.

THINK CRITCALLY ABOUT THE SELECTION

The selection compares humans' use of Earth's resources to "interest" and "principal" in a savings account or an investment. In this context, "interest" refers to the money earned from an investment and "principal" refers to the amount of the original investment. Explain why this is a useful way to think of Earth's natural resources.

How have technological advances in food production or medicine, for instance, contributed to overpopulation and, consequently, to loss of natural resources?

WRITE ABOUT THE SELECTION

The selection presents a dire picture of Earth's future. The last paragraph offers a dramatic solution. However, until that solution is achieved, what can individuals do to slow the overconsumption of Earth's resources?

Response suggestion: Jot down a list of actions that individuals can take immediately. Write a letter that could be submitted to your college's newspaper, which encourages students to take part in "saving the planet." Be sure to give specific suggestions. Your ideas might go beyond individual actions to ways that your college or city can contribute.

CHECK YOUR COMPREHENSION

After reading the selection, answer the following questions with *a, b, c,* or *d.* To help you analyze your strengths and weaknesses, the question types are indicated. Use a dictionary in addition to the context clues to more precisely define the terms.

Main Idea _____ a 1. What is the topic of this selection?

   a. depletion of Earth's resources due to overpopulation
   b. the destruction of the planet
   c. the work of the Global Footprint Network
   d. saving Earth

Main Idea _____ c 2. What is the best statement of the selection's main point?

   a. Technology has increased food production.
   b. Earth is in danger.
   c. Overpopulation and overuse of resources are endangering the capacity of Earth to support life.
   d. Overgrazing and deforestation decrease productivity of land, especially in developing countries.

Detail _____ b 3. According to this article, more than _____ are undernourished.

   a. 900 million people
   b. 300 million people
   c. 37% of the world's people
   d. 30% of the world's people

Inference _____ b 4. In paragraph 2, the authors use the term *humanity's ecological footprint.* It is reasonable to infer that the term means

   a. the size of the human population.
   b. the effects of human activity on the natural environment.
   c. Earth's natural resources.
   d. the rapid loss of Earth's natural resources.

Detail _____ a 5. According to the selection, the total world population is _____ .

   a. 5.7 billion
   b. about 300 billion
   c. close to 900 million
   d. not stated in the article

Author's Purpose _____ a 6. Why did the authors use the story of Sep Djekoule to introduce the selection?

   a. to put an understandable personal perspective on a difficult global problem
   b. to show that Earth's resources are being poorly managed
   c. to create resentment against people who misuse resources for their own purposes
   d. to cause the reader to sympathize with Sep Djekoule's challenges

Main Idea _____ 7. Which of the following best expresses the main idea of paragraph 4?

    a. Clear-cutting forests causes water to run off, erode the topsoil, and pollute rivers and oceans.

    b. Destruction of rain forests is causing the rapid extinction of animal species.

    c. Hunger is a devastating problem in sub-Saharan Africa.

    d. Fulfillment of basic human needs has destructive effects on the environment.

Detail _____ 8. The selection concludes that the best solution for Earth's diminishing natural resources is to _____.

    a. develop better conservation measures

    b. reduce the birth rate

    c. reduce water pollutants

    d. increase the death rate

Inference _____ 9. The details in the selection suggest that today it would take _____ to avoid damaging the planet's existing resources.

    a. 4.7 Earths

    b. more than 1.5 Earths

    c. about the same resources as in 2007

    d. 300 million fewer people

Author's Purpose _____ 10. The primary purpose of this selection is to

    a. discourage readers from conserving resources.

    b. convince readers that climate change is inevitable.

    c. present facts that demonstrate the need for population control.

    d. inform readers of the status of Earth's natural resources.

Answer the following questions with (*T*) true or (*F*) false.

Inference _____ 11. The authors believe that technological advances can reverse the depletion of Earth's resources.

Inference _____ 12. It can be inferred from the passage that disease and starvation are natural forms of population control.

Detail _____ 13. Many people go hungry even though more than one-third of the earth's surface is used to grow crops and technology has increased crop yield.

Detail _____ 14. According to the selection, it would take 4.7 Earths to supply everyone with an average U.S. citizen's standard of living.

Inference _____ 15. The authors believe that the human population will eventually stop growing whether we take action to control it or not.

BUILD YOUR VOCABULARY

According to the way the italicized word was used in the selection, indicate *a, b, c,* or *d* for the word or phrase that gives the best definition. The number in parentheses indicates the line of the passage in which the word is located. Use a dictionary in addition to the context clues to more precisely define the terms.

_____ 1. "shelters of the *squatters*" (3)
   a. unlawful residents
   b. exercisers
   c. hunters
   d. loggers

_____ 2. "His words *exemplify*" (6)
   a. defy
   b. contrast
   c. illustrate
   d. heighten

_____ 3. "Earth's *finite* resources" (8)
   a. delicate
   b. natural
   c. abundant
   d. limited

_____ 4. "can Earth *sustain?*"(8)
   a. feed
   b. support
   c. create
   d. survive

_____ 5. "ability of the *biosphere*" (13)
   a. drinkable water
   b. Earth, its moon and oceans
   c. fertile land on Earth
   d. life-supporting layer of Earth's surface and atmosphere

_____ 6. "our global *endowment*" (15)
   a. gift
   b. system
   c. technology
   d. investments

_____ 7. "*collective* ecological footprint" (26)
   a. large
   b. shared
   c. worldly
   d. harmful

_____ 8. "an *unprecedented* scale" (43)
   a. unmatched
   b. dangerous
   c. rapidly moving
   d. immeasurable

_____ 9. "water stores are being *depleted*" (47)
   a. mobbed
   b. diverted
   c. changed
   d. used up

_____ 10. "will *compensate* for" (61)
   a. substitute
   b. stand
   c. pay
   d. stop

Time Goals

Record your time for answering the questions: ____10____ : ____45____ .

Calculate your total reading time for reading and answering the questions: _____ : _____ .

What changes would you make to enhance your concentration on the next selection?

VOCABULARY BOOSTER

Over, Under, Around, and Through

This is the first of ten end-of-chapter vocabulary lessons in this textbook that are designed to expand your vocabulary. Each lesson links words through shared prefixes, roots, and suffixes. The words are organized into different clusters or families to enhance your memory, to organize your learning, and to emphasize that many new words are made up of familiar parts. Strengthen your vocabulary by identifying your old friends in the new words. Then apply your knowledge of word parts to unlock and remember the meanings of the new words. You will learn more than 200 words through this easy word family approach.

Your instructor may choose to use these as weekly lessons by introducing the words at the beginning of the week, assigning review items for practice, and quizzing your knowledge of the words at the end of the week. All lessons follow the same format, except for slight variations in the lesson on doctors and the one on foreign terms. Following is the first one.

Study the following prefixes, words, and sentences:

Prefixes and	*sur-:* over, above, more	*sub-:* under, beneath
Their Meanings	*amb-, ambi-:* around, about, both	*dia-:* through

Words with *sur-:* "over, above, more"

The fugitive *surrendered* himself to the police when he could no longer avoid capture.

- *surcharge*: an additional charge, tax, or cost

  The *surcharge* on an item such as cigarettes or alcohol is sometimes called a "sin tax" because these items are considered by some to be vices rather than necessities.

- *surface*: uppermost or outermost area; top layer

  When the deep-sea diver reached the *surface,* he saw that he had drifted far from his boat.

- *surfeit*: overindulgence in eating or drinking; an excessive amount

  Thanksgiving dinner usually means a *surfeit* of foods far beyond the usual amount served for an everyday meal.

- *surmise*: to guess, to infer without certain evidence

  At the point that Cindy and Gary were 30 minutes late to the ball game, I *surmised* that they probably were not coming.

- *surveillance*: a watch kept over someone or something

  The United States flies *surveillance* missions all over the world to collect information that is vital to our security.

- **surplus**: an amount greater than needed

  The government had collected more taxes than needed, so the *surplus* was returned to the taxpayers.

Words with *sub-:* "under, beneath"

Jorge's *subconscious* belief that he wasn't a good athlete probably contributed to his poor performance during basketball tryouts.

- **subsequent**: occurring later, following

  Ill health usually occurs *subsequent* to long periods of ignoring good nutrition and getting little sleep.

- **subservient**: excessively submissive

  Victorian husbands expected their wives to be *subservient*.

- **subsidiary**: subordinate or secondary

  The food products corporation decided to sell its *subsidiary* clothing company and to remain focused on foods.

- **substantiate**: to establish by proof

  A witness was able to *substantiate* Linda's story that the auto accident was not her fault.

- **subvert**: to overthrow something, such as a government; to cause the ruin of

  Castro's regime came to power in Cuba by *subverting* Batista's presidency.

- **subsistence**: a means of supporting life

  Her small *subsistence* check from the government was all that the octogenarian had for living expenses after her husband died.

Words with *amb-* or *ambi-:* "around, about, both"

The horse's gait was kept to an *amble* as the jockey slowly walked it into the winner's circle.

- **ambience** or **ambiance**: the mood or atmosphere of a place or situation

  The day spa's low lighting, comfortable furnishings, and quiet music produced an *ambience* of soothing relaxation.

- **ambidextrous**: able to use both hands equally well; unusually skillful

  Being *ambidextrous* allows Keisha to write for long periods of time by switching hands when she gets tired.

- **ambiguous**: having two or more possible meanings

  Rosa was *ambiguous* when she said that she fell on the ski trip. We expected to see a cast on her leg, not a new boyfriend on her arm.

- **ambivalent**: fluctuating between two choices; having opposing feelings

  Jealousy and tremendous familial pride were the two *ambivalent* feelings that Juan was experiencing over his brother's acceptance at a prestigious school.

- *ambulatory*: capable of walking

  Doctors didn't think that Nora would be *ambulatory* again after the accident damaged her spinal cord.

- *ambition*: strong desire for fame or power

  His *ambition* to climb the corporate ladder drove Jim to work long hours to accomplish his goal.

Words with *dia-*: "through"

If you know the *diameter* of a circle, it is easy to find the circumference.

- *diagnosis*: a determination of the cause of medical symptoms; analysis of the cause of a situation

  The doctor's *diagnosis* of strep throat was proved correct by the lab report.

- *dialogue*: a conversation between two or more persons

  The three actors practiced the scenes in which they had a humorous *dialogue* together.

- *diametrical*: pertaining to a diameter; at opposite extremes

  Susan was pro-life and *diametrically* opposed to any pro-choice legislation in Congress.

- *diatribe*: bitter, abusive criticism

  After listening to a *diatribe* from her possessive boyfriend because she spent time with her girlfriends, Angelina decided to end the unhealthy relationship.

- *dialect*: a distinct variety of a language that differs from the standard

  Parts of rural England have *dialects* that differ from the English that is spoken in London.

- *diagonal*: an oblique or slanting line connecting opposite corners or angles

  Rather than being laid square, the floor tiles were laid on the *diagonal* for an additional decorative effect.

Review Questions

Part I

Choose the best word from the list to complete each sentence.

surcharge	surveillance	subsidiary	subsistence	ambience
ambivalent	ambulatory	diagnosis	surrender	subconscious

1. The mechanic was unable to make a thorough _____ of the engine trouble, as his computer system was temporarily out of order.

2. _____ feelings of not knowing which choices to make can delay a decision.

3. During the Depression, many unemployed Americans survived at barely a
   _____ level.

4. _____ cameras were used in a traffic study of the intersection to
   determine the need for a stoplight.

5. Frequently, states gain revenue by imposing a hefty _____ on luxury
   items such as alcohol and cigarettes.

6. _____ businesses are generally formed as offshoots of the parent
   company.

7. _____ patients are less likely to develop complications from surgery,
   such as blood clots and pneumonia, because they are mobile.

8. Shoppers tend to spend more in stores equipped with a pleasant
   _____; relaxing music, attractive displays, peaceful lighting, and
   tables with sample items encourage the customer to buy.

9. Freud believed that the _____ mind has a powerful influence on
   behavior.

10. After a week of very little rest, she was finally forced to _____ to her
    need for a good night's sleep.

Part II

Choose the best synonym from the list for each word.

| diametrical | dialogue | ambition | ambiguous | subvert |
| Substantiate | subsequent | amble | surfeit | diagonal |

11. opposite _____   16. excess _____

12. overthrow _____   17. walk _____

13. following _____   18. prove _____

14. discussion _____   19. desire _____

15. unclear _____   20. slanted _____

Your instructor may choose to give you a brief review.

2 Strategic Reading and Study

Learning Objectives

In this chapter, you will learn to:

1 Read strategically
2 Preview before reading
3 Use thinking strategies during reading
4 Apply active strategies for recall after reading

Vocabulary Booster: The Good, the Bad, and the Ugly

WHAT IS STRATEGIC READING?

**Learning
Objective 1**

Read strategically

In college, you can expect a demanding course load and, most likely, a greater volume of difficult material than you have been assigned in the past. How can you meet the challenge and become a more effective reader? The answer is to have an arsenal of techniques, or strategies, to help you navigate through the required reading in your courses. For example, mastering the decoding, or sounding out, of words is one strategy. It is an initial and essential one, but college readers must go far beyond this level into the realm of associating and remembering.

Reading strategically means using specific techniques for understanding, studying, and learning. Research studies find that students who systematically learn such techniques score higher on reading comprehension tests. These strategies—previewing, questioning, connecting, recalling, determining the main idea, recognizing significant supporting details, drawing inferences, and others—will be presented throughout the various chapters in this text. Keep in mind, though, that for greatest success, you must do more than understand the strategies. You must also know when, why, and how to use them.

Four Types of Readers

Just as not all types of reading are the same, not all readers are the same. To understand how readers differ, read the following description of the four levels of reading and learning:[1]

1. **Tacit learners/readers.** These readers lack awareness of how they think when reading.
2. **Aware learners/readers.** These readers realize when meaning has broken down or confusion has set in but may not have sufficient strategies for fixing the problem.
3. **Strategic learners/readers.** These readers use the thinking and comprehension strategies described in this text to enhance understanding and acquire knowledge. They are able to monitor and repair meaning when it is disrupted.
4. **Reflective learners/readers.** These readers are strategic about their thinking and apply strategies flexibly, depending on their goals or purposes for reading. In addition, they reflect on their thinking strategies and how they might be used and revised.

Which type describes your reading now? With this textbook, you are on your way to becoming a strategic and reflective learner and reader! The dynamic process of reading and learning can be broken down into manageable pieces. Master the parts and see how they contribute to the whole. We begin by breaking down reading into three stages and explaining the strategies to use for each.

The Stages of Reading

In 1946, after years of working with college students at Ohio State University, Francis P. Robinson developed a textbook **study system** that was designed to help

---

[1]S. Harvey and A. Goudvis, *Strategies That Work* (Portland, ME: Stenhouse Publishers, 2000), p. 17.

Thinking Processes of the Stages of Reading

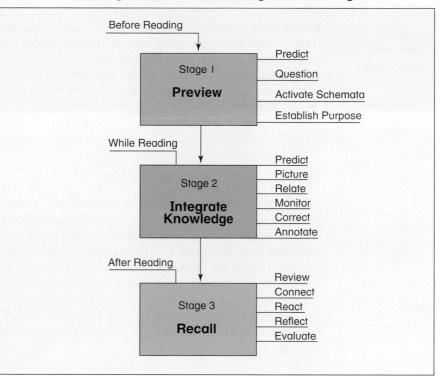

students efficiently read and learn from textbooks and effectively recall information for exams. The system was called SQ3R, with the letters standing for the following five steps: S̲urvey, Q̲uestion, R̲ead, R̲ecite, and R̲eview.

Numerous variations have been developed since SQ3R was introduced. One researcher, Norman Stahl, analyzed 65 textbook reading and learning systems and concluded that they have more similarities than differences.[2] The common elements in the systems include a previewing stage, a reading stage, and a final self-testing stage.

In the *previewing* stage, which occurs before reading, students make predictions, ask questions, activate schemata (past knowledge), and establish a purpose for reading. In the *knowledge integration* stage, which occurs during reading, students make predictions, picture images, answer questions, continually relate and integrate old and new knowledge, monitor understanding to clarify confusing points, use correction strategies, and annotate the text. The *recall* stage, which occurs after reading, involves reviewing to self-test and improve recall, making connections to blend new information with existing knowledge networks, and reacting and reflecting to evaluate and accept or reject ideas.

---

[2]N. A. Stahl, "Historical Analysis of Textbook Study Systems" (Ph.D. dissertation, University of Pittsburgh, 1983).

STAGE 1: STRATEGIES FOR PREVIEWING

Learning Objective 2

Preview before reading

Previewing is a method of personally connecting with the material before you start to read. When you preview, you look over the material, predict what the material is about, ask yourself what you already know about the topic, decide what you will probably know after you read, and make a plan for reading. See the Reader's Tip below for useful questions to ask before reading.

To preview, look over the material, think, and ask questions. The focus is on "What do I already know, what do I need to know, and how do I go about finding it out?"

Signposts for Previewing

Like public speakers, textbook authors follow this rule: "Tell them what you are going to tell them, tell them, and then tell them what you told them." Typically, a chapter begins with a brief overview of the topic, an outline, or questions. The ideas are then developed in clearly marked sections. Concluding statements at the end summarize the important points. These features are like signposts. They mark the key ideas. Although this pattern does not apply in every case, use it when available as a guide in determining what to read when previewing textbook material.

Because of differences in writing styles, no one set of rules for previewing will work for all materials. Read the following signposts when previewing a textbook chapter.

1 Title.   A title attracts attention, suggests content, and is the first and most obvious clue. Think about the title and turn it into a question. For an article entitled "Acupuncture," ask, "What is acupuncture?" For other questions, use the "five-*W* technique" of journalists to find out who, what, when, where, and why.

Reader's TIP   Ask Questions While Previewing

- **What is the topic of the material?** What does the title suggest? What do the subheadings, italics, and summaries suggest?
- **What do I already know?** What do I already know about this topic or a related topic? Is this new topic a small part of a larger idea or issue that I have thought about before?
- **What is my purpose for reading?** What will I need to know when I finish?
- **How is the material organized?** What is the general outline or framework of the material? Is the author listing reasons, explaining a process, or comparing a trend?
- **What will be my plan of attack?** What parts of the textbook seem most important? Do I need to read everything with equal care? Can I skim some parts? Can I skip some sections completely?

2 Introductory Material. To get an overview of an entire book, refer to the table of contents and preface. Sophisticated students use the table of contents as a study guide, turning the chapter headings into possible exam items. Many textbook chapters open with an outline, preview questions, or an interesting anecdote that sets the stage for learning. Italicized inserts, decorative symbols, and colored type are also used to highlight key concepts. The first paragraph frequently sets expectations.

3 Headings and Subheadings. Headings and subheadings are titles for sections within chapters. Headings are larger or closer to the edge of the page. They announce major ideas in the chapter. They outline the main points of the author's message and thus give the reader an overview of the organization and the content. Subheadings indicate important ideas within the topic of their heading. Turn headings and subheadings into questions to answer as you read.

4 Italics, Boldface Print, and Numbers. Italics and boldface print highlight words that merit special attention. These are usually new words or key words that you should be prepared to define and remember. For example, an explanation of sterilization in a biology text might emphasize the words *vasectomy* and *tubal ligation* in italics or boldface print. Numbers can also be used to signal a list of important details, like this: (1) vasectomy and (2) tubal ligation.

5 Visual Aids. Photographs with their captions, charts, graphs, and maps emphasize important points and sometimes condense text. Reviewing visuals provides clues to what information will be significant.

6 Concluding Summary. Many textbooks include a summary at the end of each chapter to highlight the important points. The summary can serve not only as a review to follow reading but also as an overview of the chapter prior to reading.

EXERCISE 2.1

Previewing This Chapter

To get an overview of this chapter and activate your schemata on the topic, read the signposts. Begin with the title and the numbered learning objectives on the opening page. The list of learning objectives serves as a good introduction to the chapter. Also, read the headings, subheadings, and special print as you turn the pages. Notice pictures and special features, such as the Reader's Tips, as you page through the chapter. Lastly, read the Summary Points. This shouldn't take more than a few minutes. Remember, your purpose is to see what ideas the chapter contains, identify what you already know, and plan your reading time. Use your preview to answer the following questions:

1. What are the four types of readers? _____

   _____

2. Name the three stages of reading. _____

   _____

3. How many touch points should you read during a preview? _____

_____

4. One purpose of a preview is to activate what? _____

5. What are the six thinking strategies that good readers use during reading?

_____

_____

6. The term _____ seems to be an important element of Stage 2.

7. What are three major recall methods suggested for Stage 3? _____

_____

8. What did you know about strategic reading before beginning this chapter?

_____

9. How much time are you allotting to read this chapter thoroughly? _____

_____

Use your answers to these questions to help establish a purpose or a learning strategy goal for reading the chapter. Why is this chapter important, and what do you hope to gain from reading it?

Preview to Activate Schemata

What do you bring to the printed page? As a reader, you are thinking and interacting before, during, and after reading. Your previewing of material first helps you predict the topic. Then, as a further part of the prereading stage, you need to activate your schema for what you perceive the topic to be.

A **schema** (plural, *schemata*) is like a computer file in your brain that holds all you know on a subject. Each time you learn something new, you pull out the computer file on that subject, add the new information, and return the file to storage. The depth of the schema or the amount of information contained in the file varies according to previous experience. For example, a scientist would have a larger, more detailed file for DNA than would most freshman biology students.

The richness of your background determines the amount you can activate. In general, the more schemata you are able to activate, the more meaningful your reading will be. In fact, most experts agree that the single best predictor of your reading comprehension is what you already know. In other words, the rich get richer. Why is that good news for you?

Once you have struggled with and learned about a subject, the next time you encounter the subject, reading and learning will be easier. You will have greatly expanded your schema for the subject. Does this help explain why some say that the freshman year is the hardest? Some students who barely make C's in introductory courses end up making A's and B's in their junior and senior years. They profited from previous hard work to establish the frameworks of knowledge in building schemata. Comfort yourself during the early struggles by saying, "The smart get smarter, and I'm getting smart!"

BRAIN BOOSTER

Schemata and Your Brain

Did you know that every time you learn something, visible growth occurs in your brain? Picture a thin tree trunk with a few branches. That is very much what a **dendrite** looks like. A dendrite growing from a brain cell (a **neuron**) is the physical evidence of a **schema** or piece of knowledge on a very specific subject. When you learn something new about that subject, its dendrite sprouts new branches. If the new learning also relates to another subject, then the dendrites connect to each other with a synapse to form a neural network. Before you know it, your brain is a mass of billions of intertwined dendrites, sparking their synapses with an electrical current. This is why relating what we already know to new information is so powerful.

Adapted from Learning and Memory: The Brain in Action, *by Marilee Sprenger*

STAGE 2: STRATEGIES FOR INTEGRATING KNOWLEDGE WHILE READING

Learning Objective 3

Use thinking strategies during reading

What are you thinking about when you read? Do you visualize? Do you make comparisons? If you don't understand, do you *notice* that you don't understand?

EXAMPLE

Read the following passage to answer the question, "What are echinoderms?" Are your thoughts similar to the inserted thoughts of the reader?

— What are they?

Echinoderms

Is this a shell?

Echinoderms have protective skeletal elements embedded in their body

Does this pump water?

walls. They also have an unusual feature called a water vascular system,

which is used as a kind of hydraulic pump to extend the soft, pouchlike

Feet have suckers?

tube feet, with their terminal suckers. They are sluggish creatures with

This means fierce searchers for food

poorly developed nervous systems. However, they are tenacious foragers.

Some species feed on shellfish, such as oysters. They wrap around their

Visualize. Oysters are very hard to open.

Are they turned inside out?

prey and pull relentlessly until the shells open just a bit. Then they evert

their stomachs, squeezing them between the shells, and digest the flesh

Is the stomach inside the oyster shell?

of the oysters on the spot.

Help! I still don't know what an echinoderm is.

Robert Wallace, *Biology: The Science of Life*

Were you able to follow the reader's inserted thoughts? Do you know what an echinoderm is? Can you guess? If you had known before reading that starfish are echinoderms, the passage would have been more entertaining and less challenging. If you have opened an oyster, you know the tenacity needed to open its shell. Reread the passage with this knowledge and visualize the gruesome drama. Later in this chapter, be ready to pull out your now enlarged schema on echinoderms and network of knowledge on a new passage.

Integrating Ideas: How Do Good Readers Think?

Understanding and remembering complex material requires both thinking and reading. As illustrated in the previous passage, the good reader is always predicting, visualizing, and drawing comparisons to **integrate knowledge,** both new and existing. Beth Davey, a reading researcher, broke these thoughts down into manageable and teachable strategies. The Reader's Tip on the next page lists six thinking strategies of good readers. Study them and visualize how you can use each one of them.

The first three thinking strategies that are used by good readers are perhaps the easiest to understand and the quickest to develop. From short stories as a young reader, you quickly learned to **predict** actions and outcomes. You would see the characters and scenes in your head. Such **visualizing** increased your level of involvement and enjoyment. You **related** the character's reactions and adventures to your own experiences.

When ideas get more complicated and reading becomes more difficult, however, the last three thinking strategies become essential elements in the pursuit of meaning. College textbooks are tough, requiring constant use of the **monitoring** strategy, frequent use of the **correction** strategy, and **annotating** to emphasize information for future study.

The final strategies involve a higher level of thinking than just picturing an oyster or a starfish. They reflect a deeper understanding of the process of obtaining meaning, and they require a reader who both understands and controls the thinking process. This ability to know and control is called *metacognition* (knowing about knowing).

Metacognition

When you look at the following words, what is your reaction?

feeet   thankz   supplyyied

Your reaction is probably, "The words don't look right. They are misspelled." The reason you realize the errors so quickly is that you have a global understanding of the manner in which letters can and cannot occur in the English language. You instantly recognize the errors through an immediate scan of your knowledge of words and the rules of ordering letters. Through your efficient recognition and correction, you have used information that goes beyond knowing about each of the three individual words. You have demonstrated a metacognitive awareness and understanding of spelling in the English language [3]

---

[3]The authors are grateful to Professor Jane Thielemann, University of Houston (Downtown), for inspiring this paragraph.

Reader's TIP — Using Thinking Strategies While Reading

- **Predict.** Develop hypotheses.
  "From the title, I predict that this section will give another example of a critical time for rats to learn a behavior."
  "In this next part, I think we'll find out why the ancient Greeks used mnemonic devices."
  "I think this is a description of an acupuncture treatment."
- **Picture.** Develop visual images during reading.
  "I have a picture of this scene in my mind. My pet is lying on the table with acupuncture needles sticking out of its fur."
- **Relate.** Share an analogy. Link prior knowledge with new information in the text. We call this the *"like-a" step*.
  "This is like my remembering, 'In 1492, Columbus sailed the ocean blue.'"
- **Monitor your ongoing comprehension.** Be aware of whether you understand the material.
  "This is confusing."
  "This just doesn't make sense. How can redwoods and cypress trees both be part of the same family?"
  "This is different from what I had expected."
- **Correct gaps in comprehension.** Use fix-up correction strategies.
  "I'd better reread."
  "Maybe I'll read ahead to see if it gets clearer."
  "I'd better change my picture of the story."
  "This is a new word to me. I'd better check the context to figure it out."
- **Annotate.** Mark the text by circling major details, underlining minor ones, and making brief notes in the margin. Annotating like this sorts the information now for study later.

The term **metacognition** is your own awareness and understanding of your thinking processes and your ability to regulate and direct these processes. *Cognition* refers to knowledge or thinking skills that you possess. The Greek prefix *meta-* suggests an abstract level of understanding, as if it were viewed from the outside. Thus, *metacognition* not only means having the knowledge but also refers to your own awareness and understanding of the thinking processes involved and your ability to regulate and direct these processes. If you know how to read, you are operating on a cognitive level. To operate on a metacognitive level, you must know the processes involved in reading—predicting, visualizing, relating new knowledge to old, clarifying points to monitor comprehension, using correction strategies, and annotating—and be able to regulate them.

The Strategies of Metacognition

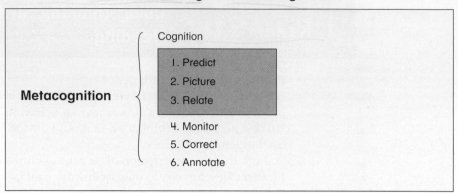

Let's take a real-life example. If you are reading a biology assignment and you are failing to understand it, you must first recognize that you are not comprehending. Next you must identify what and why you don't understand. Maybe you don't have enough background knowledge, your focus is overshadowed by details, you are relying on misconceptions that are not valid, or your attention is waning. Once you figure out the reason for your confusion, you can attempt a correction strategy. If your strategy does not work, try another and remain confident that you will succeed. The point of metacognition is to understand how to get meaning, to recognize when you don't have it, and to know what to do to straighten things out.

Here is another example: Do you know when you are really studying? In other words, what is the difference between really studying and simply going through the motions of studying? Sometimes, you can study intensely for an hour and accomplish a phenomenal amount. At other times, you can put in twice the time with books and notes but learn practically nothing. Do you know the difference, and do you know what to do about it?

Stay Focused.   Some students know the difference, whereas others do not. If you occasionally find yourself in the "going through the motions" frame of mind, think of your attention lapse not as lack of ability but as a wake-up call to reanalyze the task in front of you. Ask yourself, "What is my goal today? What can I do to focus more successfully on what needs to be done?" Picture yourself as an athlete who must keep an eye on the ball to win the game. Be your own coach by telling yourself that you can correct your problems and be more productive.

The Reader's Tip on the next page describes how you can improve your reading using metacognition.

Gain Insight Through Think-Alouds.   Experts say that the best way for instructors to teach comprehension strategies is not by just telling students what to do but by showing them what to do. Students seem to get the message best *when instructors demonstrate how they themselves actually think while reading*. How can that be done? Some instructors read a short passage out loud and verbalize internal thinking, similar to the thoughts inserted in the previous passage on echinoderms. Such modeling activities are called think-alouds. They will be inserted throughout this book to heighten your awareness of how good readers think.

Reader's TIP — Developing Metacognition for Reading

With instruction and practice, you can improve your reading performance.

- **Know about reading.** Are you aware of the many strategies that you use to comprehend? These include knowledge about words, main ideas, supporting details, and implied ideas. Also, think about the organization of the text and where meaning can be found.
- **Know how to monitor.** Monitor as an ongoing process throughout your reading. Use predicting and questioning to corroborate or discard ideas. Continually clarify and self-test to reinforce learning and pinpoint gaps in comprehension.
- **Know how to correct confusion.** Reread to reprocess a complex idea. Unravel a confusing writing style on a sentence level. Read ahead for ideas that unfold slowly. Consult a dictionary or other sources to fill in any background knowledge that you lack.

EXAMPLE Apply both your cognitive and metacognitive knowledge to answer the following test item. Interact with the material, monitor, and predict the ending phrase before reading the options. The inserted handwriting simulates a think-aloud by modeling the thinking of a good reader.

picture the comparison

pollutes and kills

What is euphemistically called an "oil spill" can very well become an oil disaster

for marine life. This is particularly true when refined or semirefined products are

wants to make more money

being transported. As the tankers get bigger, so do the accidents, yet we continue to

key word

a. fight for clean water   c. use profits for cleanup

b. search for more oil   d. build larger vessels

shows a parallel idea

Biology: The Science of Life

EXPLANATION Because you were an engaged thinker, you probably predicted the correct answer *d,* even before reading the four options.

In this test item as well as in the passage on Technology Addictions below, the inserted comments may be confusing to read because involvement differs and many thoughts occur on the subconscious level rather than on the conscious level. Stopping to consciously analyze these reactions may seem artificial and disruptive. It is important, however, to be aware of how you are incorporating the thinking strategies into your reading.

EXAMPLE   The following passage illustrates how Stage 2 thinking strategies can be used when you are reading longer textbook material. Modeled thoughts of the reader are again inserted for a simulated think-aloud. Again, keep in mind that each reader reacts differently to material depending on background knowledge and individual differences.

Exercise 2.2 will heighten your awareness of the process of interacting analytically with a piece of writing.

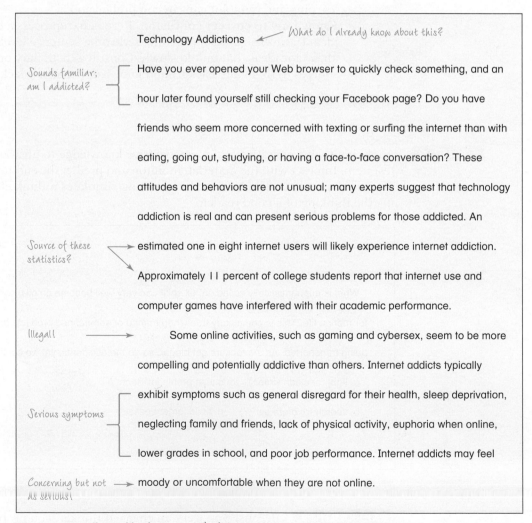

Technology Addictions   *← What do I already know about this?*

Sounds familiar; am I addicted?

Have you ever opened your Web browser to quickly check something, and an hour later found yourself still checking your Facebook page? Do you have friends who seem more concerned with texting or surfing the internet than with eating, going out, studying, or having a face-to-face conversation? These attitudes and behaviors are not unusual; many experts suggest that technology addiction is real and can present serious problems for those addicted. An

Source of these statistics?

estimated one in eight internet users will likely experience internet addiction. Approximately 11 percent of college students report that internet use and computer games have interfered with their academic performance.

Illegal!

Some online activities, such as gaming and cybersex, seem to be more compelling and potentially addictive than others. Internet addicts typically

Serious symptoms

exhibit symptoms such as general disregard for their health, sleep deprivation, neglecting family and friends, lack of physical activity, euphoria when online, lower grades in school, and poor job performance. Internet addicts may feel

Concerning but not as serious!

moody or uncomfortable when they are not online.

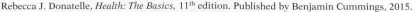

Rebecca J. Donatelle, *Health: The Basics,* 11th edition. Published by Benjamin Cummings, 2015.

EXERCISE 2.2 **Integrating Knowledge While Reading**

For the following passage, demonstrate with written notes the way you use the six thinking strategies as you read. The passage is double-spaced so that you can insert your thoughts and reactions between the lines. Begin by looking at the title and pulling out your recently enhanced mental computer file. Make a conscious effort to implement all of the following strategies as you read:

1. Predict (develop hypotheses).

2. Picture (develop images during reading).

3. Relate (link prior knowledge with new ideas).

4. Monitor your ongoing comprehension (clarify confusing points).

5. Correct gaps in comprehension (use correction strategies).

6. Annotate (mark the text).

SEA STARS

Let's take a look at one class of echinoderms—the sea stars. Sea stars (starfish) are well known for their voracious appetite when it comes to gourmet foods, such as oysters and clams. Obviously, they are the sworn enemy of oystermen. But these same oystermen may have inadvertently helped the spread of the sea stars. At one time, when they caught a starfish, they chopped it apart and vengefully kicked the pieces overboard. But they were unfamiliar with the regenerative powers of the starfish. The central disk merely grows new arms, and a single arm can form a new animal.

Stars are slow-moving predators, so their prey, obviously, are even slower-moving or immobile. Their ability to open an oyster shell is a testimony to their persistence. When a sea star finds an oyster or clam, the prey clamps its shell together tightly, a tactic that discourages most would-be predators, but not the starfish. It bends its body over the oyster and attaches its tube feet to the shell, and then begins to pull. Tiring is no problem since it uses tube feet in relays. Finally, the oyster can no longer hold itself shut, and it opens gradually—only a tiny bit, but it is enough. The star then protrudes its stomach out through its mouth. The soft stomach slips into the slightly opened

shell, surrounds the oyster, and digests it in its own shell.

—Robert Wallace,
Biology: The Science of Life

At first glance, you recognized the echinoderm as an old friend and activated your newly acquired schema. The description of the starfish lends itself to a vivid visualization. Were some of your predictions corroborated as you read the passage? Did you find yourself monitoring to reconcile new facts with old ideas? Did you need to use a correction strategy? Did you jot down some notes on the passage as you read? Did you guess about the regenerative powers? Has your schema for echinoderms been expanded?

STAGE 3: STRATEGIES FOR RECALLING

Learning Objective 4

Apply active strategies for recall after reading

To **recall,** you tell yourself what you have learned, relate it to what you already know, react, and evaluate. Actually, you do all of this before and during reading, but a deliberate recall is necessary when you finish reading to consolidate knowledge and improve learning. Call it a short conversation with yourself to debrief and digest. You need to be sure that you know the content, make connections, and update your schemata or computer files.

Recalling Through Writing

Answering multiple-choice questions after reading requires one type of mental processing, but writing about the reading requires another type of processing. Experts define writing as a "mode of learning," which means that writing is a process that helps students blend, reconcile, and gain personal ownership of new knowledge. When you write about a subject, you not only discover how much you know and don't know but also begin to unfold meaningful personal connections.

A humorous adage about the power of writing says, "How do I know what I think until I see what I say?" Writing can be hard work, but it helps you clarify and crystallize what you have learned. You discover your own thinking as you write. Use the power of this valuable tool to take your recall to a higher level. For the longer reading selections in this text, both multiple-choice and writing questions are offered to help you learn.

The Three Steps of Recalling

Recall can be broken down into three manageable strategies: Talk, write, and think about the reading. All are powerful, active methods to set ideas into memory. However, the most potent tool is writing.

Talk about it.

- Tell yourself or someone else what you learned.
- Review each section and say the main point aloud. Elaborate with as much detail as you can. Look back at the text only when necessary to confirm your recollections.

- Discuss confusing or especially interesting ideas with a classmate or with your instructor.

Write about it.

- Tackle the exercises and write answers to questions provided by the author.
- Use your annotations to make notes on a separate sheet of paper.
- Make flash cards to remember small pieces of information.
- Write a summary if you are reading a short story or other literary selection.

Think about it.

- React: Do you agree with the facts, opinions, and conclusions? Is the information well researched and believable? Did the author do a good job?
- Reflect on the ideas and how you can apply them.
- Consider how the material relates to another subject you're studying, to what you already knew about the topic, or to bigger issues, world events, or social concerns.

EXAMPLE   Today, many dead people receive some form of autopsy or postmortem examination. At least two main reasons for this are (1) the desire of the family to know the exact cause of death, and (2) the fact that increased medical knowledge results. Because of the important moral and legal restrictions on human experimentation, much of our knowledge of pathology comes from autopsies. This fact prompts many people to donate their bodies to medical schools and/or donate certain organs for possible transplantation.

—John Cunningham, *Human Biology*, 2nd ed.

EXPLANATION   A **recall diagram** (see below) is a quick format that can help you solidify ideas in the recall stage. The diagram graphically demonstrates a process that you will learn to do in your head. Using the diagram will help you learn to organize and visualize your reading.

(Topic)	*Why autopsies are done*
(Significant details — examples, facts, or phrases)	*To know exact cause of death* *To increase medical knowledge* *— thus donations*
(Relate)	*Do I want medical students studying my body?*
(React)	*I would donate my organs but not my body to medical school.*

Reader's TIP Thinking After Reading

- **Pinpoint the topic.** Get focused on the subject. Use the title and the subheadings to help you recognize and narrow down the topic.
- **Write the most important points.** Review the annotations that you made during reading and use them to make notes. Poor readers want to remember everything, thinking that all facts have equal importance. Good readers pull out the important issues and identify significant supporting information.
- **Relate the information.** Facts are difficult to learn in isolation. In history, events should not be seen as isolated happenings but, rather, as results of previous occurrences. Network your new knowledge to enhance memory. Relate new knowledge to yourself, to other written material, and to global issues.
- **React.** Form opinions and evaluate the material and the author. Decide what you wish to accept and what you will reject. Blend old and new knowledge, and write about what you have read.

BRAIN BOOSTER

Use It to Remember It!

The dendrites created in our brains when we learn need tending. Although experts think that they never go away completely, the synapses that connect our dendrites in neural networks have to be fired electrically to flourish. Dendrites that are not used shrink to make room and energy for others, but those we use often grow stronger. What does this mean to learning? It's why the recall stage is so important. Review, repeat, and use what you've learned to keep it. Talk about what you've read, write about it, think about it, read more, and REPEAT!

Adapted from Learning and Memory: The Brain in Action, *by Marilee Sprenger*

EXERCISE 2.3

Using Recall Diagrams

After reading and annotating each of the following passages, stop to recall what the passage contained. Use recall diagrams to record what the passage seems to be mainly about. List significant supporting details; identify a related idea, issue, or concern to which you feel the information is connected; and react.

Passage 1

ELEPHANTS IN ANCIENT WARFARE

Elephants were the most spectacular, extravagant, and unpredictable element in ancient warfare. Since the time of Alexander the Great, Hellenistic kings and commanders had tried to use the great strength, size, and relative invulnerability of the animals to throw opposing infantry into confusion and flight. Elephants' unusual smell and loud trumpeting also panicked horses not accustomed to the strange beasts, wreaking havoc with cavalry units. Mahouts, or drivers, who were usually Indians, controlled and directed the animal from a seat on the elephant's neck. Normally each elephant carried a small, towerlike structure from which archers could shoot down on the massed infantry. However, as with modern tanks, the primary importance of the beasts was the enormous shock effect created by a charge of massed war elephants.

—Mark Kishlansky et al.,
Civilization in the West, 6th ed.

(Topic) ——————————————————————

(Significant details)

(Relate) -

(React) ——————————————————————

Passage 2

UNDERSTANDING DROUGHT

Drought is different from other natural hazards in several ways. First, it occurs in a gradual, "creeping" way, making its onset and end difficult to determine. The effects of drought accumulate slowly over an extended time span and sometimes linger for years after the drought has ended. Second, there is not a precise and universally accepted definition of drought. This adds to the confusion about whether or not a drought is actually occurring and, if it is, its severity. Third, drought seldom produces structural damages, so its social and economic effects are less obvious than damages from other natural disasters.

—Frederick K. Lutgens and Edward J. Tarbuck,
*The Atmosphere: An Introduction
to Meteorology*, 9th ed.

(Topic) ——————————————————————

(Significant details)

(Relate) -

(React) ——————————————————————

SUMMARY POINTS

1 What does it mean to read strategically? (page 72)
Strategic reading is knowing and using techniques for understanding, studying, and learning. Improve your ability to read efficiently and learn from textbooks by previewing before reading, integrating knowledge during reading, and using recall strategies after reading.

2 What are the strategies for previewing? (page 74)
Previewing is a way to activate your schemata, to assess your needs before you start to read, and to provide an overview of the key concepts in the material. Read the signposts used in the selection: title, introduction, heading and subheadings, special print, visual aids, and concluding summary. Adjust as necessary to the format of the material.

3 What are the thinking strategies for integrating knowledge during reading? (page 77)
Good readers think metacognitively; they are aware of their understanding and take control of it. They use six thinking strategies to integrate their schemata with the new material: Predict, picture, relate, monitor, correct, and annotate.

4 What are the active strategies for recalling after reading? (page 84)
Recalling what you have read immediately after reading forces you to select the most important points, to identify the supporting details, to reflect and react to the new ideas, and ultimately to consolidate the ideas into memory. Active recall strategies include talking, writing, and thinking about what you have read. Writing is the most powerful of the three.

| **SELECTION 1** | History | MyReadingLab |

Visit Chapter 2: Strategic Reading and Study in MyReadingLab to complete the Selection 1 activities and the Build Background Knowledge video activity.

P‌REVIEW the next selection to predict its purpose and organization and to formulate your learning plan.

Activate Schemata

What business opportunities were available for women in the late 1800s?

Why is hard work an important key to success? What else does it take?

Establish a Purpose for Reading

As a widowed mother with a child, she was working as a washerwoman and seemed destined to poverty. Read to find out how Madam C. J. Walker overcame obstacles, achieved success, and offered opportunities to others.

Build Background Knowledge — VIDEO

How to Succeed As An Alpha Female Entrepreneur

To prepare for reading Selection 1, answer the questions below. Then, watch this video that offers tips on being a successful entrepreneur.

What experience do you (or someone you know) have in starting a business?

What types of obstacles do you think women face when starting a business?

Describe three ideas you have for starting a business.

This video helped me: _____

_____

_____

Increase Word Knowledge

What do you know about these words?

| entrepreneur | philanthropist | menial | regimen | salves |
| bolstered | undaunted | affluent | bequeathing | legacy |

Your instructor may give a brief vocabulary review before or after reading.

Integrate Knowledge While Reading

Questions have been inserted in the margins to stimulate your thinking while reading. Remember to

Predict	Picture	Relate	Monitor	Correct	Annotate

MADAM C. J. WALKER: BUSINESS SAVVY TO GENEROUS PHILANTHROPY

Is her name familiar?

Little more than a century ago, when entrepreneur Madam C. J. Walker founded her hair care and cosmetics empire, few women dared to imagine owning a business. During an era when American women were denied the right to vote and most African Americans were excluded—by law and by custom—from the nation's most prestigious
5   universities, corporations, professions and government positions, Madam Walker transformed herself from an uneducated laundress into a corporate executive—and one of the country's earliest self-made female millionaires. At a time when most American women who worked outside the home were factory or domestic workers, Walker led an international sales force of thousands of financially independent
10   African-American women. Her unlikely journey as a daughter of slaves, businesswoman, philanthropist and political activist remains an inspiration and an example of what one woman with courage, perseverance and a generous spirit can accomplish.

DAUGHTER OF SLAVES

What were her chances of success?

Born Sarah Breedlove in Delta, Louisiana, in December 1867, she was the first of her five siblings to begin life as a free person. As a young child Sarah worked beside her
15   parents, Owen and Minerva Breedlove, in the same cotton plantation fields where

Madam C. J. Walker sits proudly in the driver's seat of her own electric car.
A'Lelia Bundles/Madam Walker Family Collection

they had been enslaved until the end of the American Civil War. Sadly, when Sarah was seven years old, both her parents died. With no schools for black children in her community and no job prospects, she married a man named Moses McWilliams when she was just 14 years old. By the age of 20, Sarah was a widow with a young child.

20   Unable to support herself and her daughter, Lelia, she joined her older brothers in St. Louis, Missouri. Sarah obtained a job as a laundress, earning barely over a dollar a week, but she was determined that her daughter receive more formal education than she had. While many people looked down on washerwomen like Sarah, she refused to be ashamed of menial, but honest, work. She did admit, however, that she

25   was embarrassed by one aspect of her personal appearance: the severe scalp disease that was causing her to lose her hair. During the early 1900s, when most Americans lacked indoor plumbing and electricity, bathing was a luxury. As a result, Sarah and many other women were going bald because they washed their hair so infrequently, leaving it vulnerable to environmental hazards such as pollution, bacteria, and lice.

30   To cure her condition, she experimented with formulas until she discovered an ointment and a cleansing regimen that healed her scalp and allowed her hair to grow. She began selling her salves and teaching other women to groom and style their hair.

Was this the start of her success?

SUCCESSFUL BUSINESSWOMAN

Around this time Sarah met and married Charles Joseph Walker, a newspaper salesman, who helped her market and advertise her products. It was after their marriage

35   in 1906 that Sarah Breedlove began calling herself "Madam" C. J. Walker, a title of dignity and respect borrowed from the women who had created the French cosmetics and fashion industries. In 1910 Walker moved to Indianapolis, Indiana, where she built a factory, hair salon and beauty school to train her sales agents. She also became involved in the city's civic, cultural and political activities. Learning of a

40   campaign to construct a YMCA (Young Men's Christian Association) in the black community, she pledged $1,000 to the building fund. Her donation shocked her new neighbors because no black woman ever had contributed such a large sum to an organization like the YMCA. The laundress who once had made just a little more than a dollar a week now was earning enough money to help others.

45   Bolstered by the positive response to her gift, she set another goal for herself: to address the delegates of the 1912 National Negro Business League (NNBL) convention. Arriving in Chicago with soaring confidence, she tried to share her rags-to-riches story with NNBL founder Booker T. Washington. Washington was by that time a figure of national stature and arguably the most powerful African-American

50   leader of the era. For two days of the convention, he ignored her overture. Undaunted, Walker waited patiently until the final day of the conference, at which point she stood from her seat and addressed Washington as he presided at the podium: "Surely you are not going to shut the door in my face. I am a woman who came from the cotton fields of the South," Walker said. "I was promoted to the washtub. From

55   there I was promoted to the kitchen. And from there I promoted myself into the business of manufacturing hair goods and preparations. I have built my own factory on my own ground!"

I can picture this!

Washington was so shocked and annoyed that he still did not invite Walker to the stage, but he could no longer ignore her. The following year, Washington

60   accepted Walker's invitation to be a guest in her Indianapolis home during the dedication of the new YMCA. Walker also contributed to the Tuskegee Institute (a school founded by Washington in 1881 for the advancement of African Americans), funding

Was there a large population of African descendants there?

scholarships she created for African students there, which helped her further earn Washington's respect. At the 1913 NNBL convention, Washington graciously wel-
65 comed Walker as a keynote speaker.

Walker continued to expand her market and ventured beyond the United States to Cuba, Jamaica, Haiti, Panama, and Costa Rica. She hoped that—through the principles of entrepreneurship that had made her wealthy—her products could provide prosperity for women of African descent all over the world. While
70 she traveled, her daughter, Lelia, set to work opening another school and salon in an expensively decorated townhouse in New York City's predominantly African-American Harlem neighborhood. As the Madam C. J. Walker Manufacturing Company continued to grow, Walker and her daughter organized their sales force into local and state clubs. Her Walker Hair Culturists Union of America conven-
75 tion in Philadelphia in 1917 drew 200 agents and became one of the first national meetings of American women gathered to discuss business and commerce. At the convention, Walker happily listened to stories from former maids, cooks, share-croppers, and school teachers who now made more money than their former employers. As a reward, she gave prizes not only to the women who had sold the
80 most products, but to the women who had contributed the most to charity in their communities.

POLITICAL ACTIVIST AND PHILANTHROPIST

The next year, Walker moved into Villa Lewaro, a lavish estate in affluent Irvington-on-Hudson, New York, not far from the homes of oil mogul cum philanthropist John D. Rockefeller and railroad baron Jay Gould (two of the richest men in U.S.
85 history). With New York as her base, she became even more involved in political matters, joining the executive committee of the Silent Protest Parade, a July 1917 public demonstration in which more than 8,000 African Americans marched up Fifth Avenue to protest an East St. Louis riot that had left 39 black men, women, and children dead. A few days later, she and a group of Harlem leaders visited the White
90 House to urge President Woodrow Wilson to support legislation to make lynching a federal crime.

Was lynching common at that time?

Just before she died in May 1919, Walker pledged $5,000—equivalent to about $65,000 in today's dollars—to the National Association for the Advancement of Col-ored People's anti-lynching fund. At the time, it was the largest gift that the civil
95 rights organization ever had received. She also revised her will to reflect her passion for education, children, and the elderly by directing two-thirds of future net profits of her estate to charity and bequeathing nearly $100,000 to individuals, educational institutions, and orphanages.

LEGACY OF SUCCESS

Can I think of other African American women who have been successful in business?

Today her legacy is best preserved in the aspirations of those who are inspired by
100 her entrepreneurial success and philanthropic generosity, like billionaire business-woman Oprah Winfrey and U.S. Small Business Administration Deputy Director Marie Johns. In 1992 Walker was one of only 21 women inducted into the National Business Hall of Fame at the Museum of Science and Industry in Chicago.

Whenever people asked Madam Walker the secret to her success, she would
105 proudly tell them: "There is no royal flower-strewn path to success, and if there is, I have not found it, for whatever success I have attained has been the result of much hard work and many sleepless nights. I got my start by giving myself a start. So

don't sit down and wait for the opportunities to come. You have to get up and make them for yourselves!"

(1,407 words)

—From America.gov Archive, March 1, 2010,
Bureau of International Information Programs,
U.S. Department of State
by A'Lelia Bundles

A'Lelia Bundles, a former ABC News producer and executive, is Madam Walker's biographer and great-great-granddaughter. Bundles's book, On Her Own Ground: The Life and Times of Madam C. J. Walker *(Scribner), was a 2001 New York Times Notable Book. She lives in Washington, D.C.*

Recall

Stop to talk, write, and think about the selection.

Your instructor may choose to give you a brief comprehension review.

THINK CRITICALLY ABOUT THE SELECTION

Examine and describe the details in this selection. Are they facts, opinions, or examples?

What other information might have enhanced the selection?

Notice the author of this selection. What is her purpose in writing this selection?

After reading this selection, what is your view of Madam C. J. Walker? Why?

WRITE ABOUT THE SELECTION

What aspects of Walker's life show that she was a clever business strategist as well as an energetic, persistent, and ambitious woman?

Response suggestion: List the details from this selection that demonstrate these character traits. Use your list to write a description of Madam C. J. Walker's character.

CHECK YOUR COMPREHENSION

After reading the selection, answer the following questions with *a*, *b*, *c*, or *d*. To help you analyze your strengths and weaknesses, the question types are indicated.

Main Idea _____ 1. What is the best statement of the entire selection's main point?

    a. Madam C. J. Walker's parents were slaves.

    b. Madam C. J. Walker rose from poverty to become a role model as a successful businesswoman, political activist, and philanthropist.

    c. Anyone with courage and perseverance can become a wealthy business owner.

    d. She gave money to help children, the elderly, and others in the community.

Inference _____ 2. From this selection, we can conclude that

    a. Madam Walker's business grew out of a personal need for specialized beauty products.

    b. Sarah Breedlove's parents died of old age.

    c. Sarah Breedlove's life was difficult in Louisiana and also when she moved to St. Louis.

    d. Madam Walker was embarrassed by Booker T. Washington's refusal to acknowledge her in 1912.

Inference _____ 3. From the details given in the passage, we can infer that

    a. Walker was born before slavery was abolished in the United States.

    b. Walker's family was ill treated by their owners.

    c. Walker was born shortly after slavery was abolished in the United States.

    d. Walker and her family were forced to leave the plantation on which they worked.

Detail _____ 4. Which is a true statement about Madam Walker's business success?

    a. Walker built a fortune selling beauty products for African-American women.

    b. Walker started her business while she lived in Louisiana.

    c. Walker's business never expanded beyond the United States.

    d. Walker's husband, Charles J. Walker, was not helpful to her business.

Inference _____ 5. The details of Madam Walker's donations to charity in the section titled "Successful Businesswoman" suggest that

    a. many people came to her asking for donations.

    b. her only reason for giving was to help others.

    c. she favored charities that helped women.

    d. her donations were designed to build her business as well as to help others.

Main Idea ———— 6. The main point of the section titled "Political Activist and Philan-thropist" is that
   a. Madam Walker gave generously of her time, influence, and wealth to support causes of social justice and to help others.
   b. Madam Walker gave the equivalent of $65,000 in today's dollars to the National Association for the Advancement of Colored People's antilynching fund.
   c. Madam Walker's estate was near the homes of other wealthy people, such as John D. Rockefeller and Jay Gould.
   d. Madam Walker was a caring individual.

Detail ———— 7. Many women in the early 1900s experienced hair loss because
   a. they were malnourished.
   b. they brushed and combed their hair too roughly.
   c. they used dangerous products in their hair.
   d. it was difficult to keep their hair and scalps clean.

Main Idea ———— 8. What is the main point of the section titled "Successful Business-woman"?
   a. Madam Walker's success was due to smart business decisions as well as to her support of the African-American community and her desire to provide meaningful jobs for women of African descent.
   b. Calling herself "Madam" was a turning point in Madam Walker's success.
   c. Booker T. Washington's support was an important factor in Madam Walker's success.
   d. Madam Walker's business grew entirely because there was a high demand for her products.

Detail ———— 9. Madam Walker's business was named
   a. Madam Walker's House of Beauty.
   b. Madam C. J. Walker's Beauty Products.
   c. Madam C. J. Walker Manufacturing Company.
   d. The Madam Walker Company.

Inference ———— 10. From Walker's quote at the end of the selection, we can conclude that
   a. she believed her success was largely the result of the help that she received from her husband.
   b. she believed she was successful because of lucky circumstances.
   c. she credited her success to her own hard work and determination.
   d. she thought her success was due to her formal education.

Answer the following with *T* (true) or *F* (false).

Author's Purpose　————11. The primary purpose of this selection is to entertain the reader with an inspiring story.

Detail　————12. As a young mother, Breedlove received support from her brothers.

Detail　————13. Sarah Breedlove began calling herself "Madam" to mimic women who started French cosmetics and fashion companies.

Inference　————14. It was important to Walker to gain the respect of Booker T. Washington.

Inference　————15. Walker's company hired African-American women to sell its beauty products.

BUILD YOUR VOCABULARY

According to the way the italicized word was used in the selection, select *a, b, c,* or *d* for the word or phrase that gives the best definition. The number in parentheses indicates the line of the passage in which the word is located. Use a dictionary in addition to the context clues to more precisely define the terms.

———— 1. "*entrepreneur* Madam C. J. Walker" (1)
　　a. business owner
　　b. celebrity
　　c. risk taker
　　d. restauranteur

———— 2. "*philanthropist* and" (11)
　　a. a very wealthy person
　　b. a person who enjoys beauty
　　c. one who studies anthropology
　　d. one who promotes human welfare

———— 3. "ashamed of *menial*" (24)
　　a. superior
　　b. humble
　　c. dirty
　　d. difficult

———— 4. "a cleansing *regimen*" (31)
　　a. product
　　b. cream
　　c. soap
　　d. a system or plan

———— 5. "selling her *salves*" (32)
　　a. shampoos
　　b. hair sprays
　　c. cosmetics
　　d. ointments

———— 6. "*Bolstered* by" (45)
　　a. supported
　　b. discouraged
　　c. weakened
　　d. criticized

———— 7. "*Undaunted*, Walker waited" (50)
　　a. fearless
　　b. timid
　　c. shocked
　　d. angry

———— 8. "estate in *affluent*" (82)
　　a. average
　　b. beautiful
　　c. wealthy
　　d. suburban

_____ 9. "*bequeathing* nearly
$100,000" (97)
a. earning
b. giving in a will
c. saving
d. holding

_____ 10. "Today her *legacy*" (99)
a. something given from
the past
b. a successful company
c. a lesson
d. spirit

SELECTION 2	Health	MyReadingLab

Visit Chapter 2: Strategic Reading and Study in MyReadingLab to complete the Selection 2 activities and the Build Background Knowledge video activity.

PREVIEW the next selection to predict its purpose and organization and to formulate your learning plan.

Activate Schemata

Do you have a friend or a relative who has been hurt or killed because of alcohol?

Do you believe that heavy drinking is common among college students?

What are the reasons for drinking among college students?

What measures do you think effectively reduce the problem?

Establish a Purpose for Reading

Heavy drinking may not be as common among college students as you think, but the risks are still high. Read to learn the facts and what colleges are doing to address the problem.

Build Background Knowledge — VIDEO

Teenage Girls and Binge Drinking

To prepare for reading Selection 2, answer the questions below. Then, watch this video that looks at teen girls and binge drinking.

In what situations do you think college students—both male and female—are most likely to drink excessively?

What differences do you think there are between male and female binge drinking?

How should colleges address binge drinking?

This video helped me: _____

_____

_____

Increase Word Knowledge

What do you know about these words?

unintentional	binge	vulnerable	intoxicated	hazing
vandalism	curb	nonjudgmental	misperception	episodic

Your instructor may give a brief vocabulary review before or after reading.

Integrate Knowledge While Reading

Questions have been inserted in the margins to stimulate your thinking while reading. Remember to

Predict   Picture   Relate   Monitor   Correct   Annotate

HIGH-RISK DRINKING AND COLLEGE STUDENTS

Despite repeated warnings and tragic examples, some college students still fail to drink responsibly. The stakes for doing so are high because of the high risk for alcohol-related injuries and death. According to a recent study 1,825 college students die each year because of alcohol-related, unintentional injuries including car acci-
5 dents. Unintentional injuries are the leading cause of death in the 18- to 24-year-old age group and alcohol is the leading contributing factor in those deaths. Consumption of alcohol is the number one cause of preventable death among undergraduate college students in the United States today.

Who are the students who drink heavily? Why are these students drinking so
10 much, and what are their typical drinking behaviors? What impact does their drinking have, and what are college campuses doing to prevent this behavior? These are the questions we'll discuss in this section.

The Facts

WHO DRINKS?

It's likely that students who enter college will drink at some point, but there are groups of students who are more likely to drink more and more often. For example,

What is the source of the facts?

15 students who believe that their parents approve of their drinking are more likely to drink and to report a drinking-related problem. Students who drank heavily in high school are also at risk for heavy drinking in college. Most students have tried alcohol in high school. By twelfth grade, 26 percent of high school students report engaging in binge drinking, and 55 percent report having been drunk, while another 12 per-
20 cent report having had at least one full drink.

WHY DO COLLEGE STUDENTS DRINK SO MUCH?

Although everyone is at some risk for alcohol-related problems, college students seem to be particularly vulnerable. The college years bring more freedom, fewer restrictions, and many more opportunities to party with friends. In addition to *this* newfound college freedom, there are several other factors that encourage students to drink in college:

25 • Many college and university students' customs (e.g., Greek rush or initiations), norms (e.g., reputation as party schools, tailgate parties at football games), and traditional celebrations (e.g., St. Patrick's Day, Mardi Gras) encourage alcohol use.

SELECTION 2

30 • Advertising and promotions from the alcoholic beverage industry target students.

• College students are particularly vulnerable to peer influence and have a strong need to be accepted by their peers.

 Do men make similar assumptions?

• College women tend to care how much men want them to drink, and they tend to overestimate how much men prefer they consume. In a recent study, 35 26 percent of women stated that men would most likely want to be friends with a woman who drinks five or more drinks; 17 percent thought that men would be most attracted to that woman. Both estimates were almost double what men actually said.

• Students believe that alcohol will make them feel better, less stressed, more 40 sociable, and less self-conscious. The behaviors most commonly reported by students reflect these expectations: dancing, flirting, telling jokes, and laughing more frequently. The primary expectations of students going to bars and nightclubs are becoming intoxicated, socializing with friends, seeking romance or sex, and relieving problems or stress.

45 • More than 80 percent of college students drink alcohol to celebrate their twenty-first birthday, and they consume an average of nearly 13 drinks, with estimated blood alcohol concentrations (BACs) of 19 percent and higher.

• Students drink as part of hazing rituals. The use of alcohol in hazing is most prevalent in Greek and varsity athletics organizations, with more than 50 50 percent of students involved in these activities reporting participation in a drinking game as a hazing activity.

• The low price of alcohol, whether it is beer or liquor, is strongly related to higher rates of drinking and binging. In a recent study, students who paid the most money per gram of alcohol consumed the least amount of alcohol. 55 The least intoxicated students paid $4.44 for 14 grams of alcohol (one 12-ounce beer, one 5-ounce glass of wine, or 1 ounce of liquor), whereas those students who were found to be the drunkest paid $1.81 for the same amount of alcohol. All-you-can-drink specials attract students who want to drink and get drunk.

60 • Easy access to alcohol, often referred to as *density of alcohol outlets,* contributes to higher rates of binge drinking. Campus communities with a large number of bars and alcohol outlets have a higher rate of binge drinking than those with few bars and alcohol outlets in close vicinity to campus.

COLLEGE STUDENT DRINKING BEHAVIOR

College students are more likely than their noncollegiate peers to drink recklessly 65 and to engage in drinking games and other dangerous drinking practices. One such practice is **pre-gaming** (also called pre-loading or front-loading). Pre-gaming has become increasingly common on college campuses, and involves planned heavy drinking, usually in someone's home, apartment, or residence hall, prior to going out to a bar, nightclub, or sporting event. Sometimes it occurs prior to attending an 70 event where alcohol is not available. In a recent study of pre-gaming, 66 percent of college men and 68 percent of college women drank before going to a bar or nightclub. The goal of many pre-gamers is to get drunk. Some of the motivations for pre-gaming are to avoid paying for high-cost drinks, to socialize with friends, to reduce social anxiety, and to enhance male bonding. Pre-gamers have higher alcohol

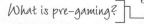 *What is pre-gaming?*

75 consumption during the evening and more negative consequences such as black
outs, hangover, passing out, and alcohol poisoning.

WHAT IS THE IMPACT OF STUDENT DRINKING?

Unfortunately, recent studies confirm what students have been experiencing for a
long time—drinking and binge drinkers cause problems not only for themselves,
but also for those around them. One study indicated that over 696,000 students be-
80 tween the ages of 18 and 24 were assaulted by another student who had been drinking. There is significant evidence that campus rape is linked to binge drinking.
Women from colleges with medium to high binge drinking rates are 1.5 times more
at risk of being raped than those from schools with a low binge drinking rate.
Although exact numbers are hard to find, estimates are that more than 97,000 stu-
85 dents between the ages of 18 and 24 experience alcohol-related sexual assault or date
rape each year in the United States. The laws regarding sexual consent are clear: A
person who is drunk or passed out cannot consent to sex. If you have sex with someone who is drunk or unconscious (passed out), you are committing rape. Claiming

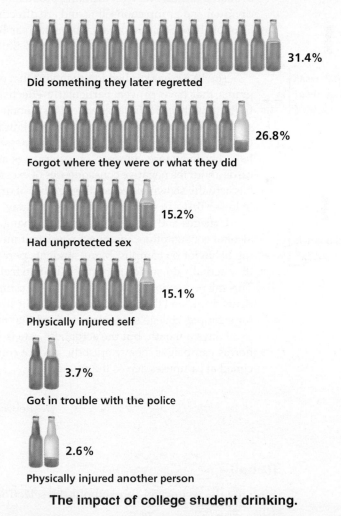

31.4%

Did something they later regretted

26.8%

Forgot where they were or what they did

15.2%

Had unprotected sex

15.1%

Physically injured self

3.7%

Got in trouble with the police

2.6%

Physically injured another person

The impact of college student drinking.

Source: Donatelle, *Access to Health*, 12e (Pearson-Benjamin Cummings), p. 353.

you were also drunk when you had sex with someone who is intoxicated or uncon-
90   scious will not absolve you of your legal and moral responsibility for this crime.

Other students report sleep and study disruptions and vandalism of personal
property. Approximately 25 percent of college students report negative academic
consequences because of their drinking. About 30 percent of students who drink
and 68 percent of binge drinkers say they have missed a class because of alcohol use.
95   The more students drink, the more likely they are to miss class, do poorly on tests
and papers, have lower grade point averages (GPAs), and fall behind on their
schoolwork. Some students may even drop out of school as a result of their drinking. The figure gives some examples of alcohol-related problems.

COLLEGES' EFFORTS TO REDUCE STUDENT DRINKING

Some colleges are taking action to curb binge drinking and alcohol abuse by institut-
100   ing strong policies against drinking. For example, university presidents have formed
a leadership group to help control the problem of alcohol abuse. Many fraternities
have elected to have "dry" houses. At the same time, schools are making more help
available to students with drinking problems. Today, most campuses offer both individual and group counseling and are directing more attention toward preventing
105   alcohol abuse. Student organizations such as BACCHUS (Boost Alcohol Consciousness Concerning the Health of University Students) promote responsible drinking
and party hosting.

The IAAA has studied interventions that effectively deal with the problem. Programs that have proven particularly effective include cognitive-behavioral skills
110   training with *motivational interviewing*, a nonjudgmental approach to working with
students to change behavior, and e-Interventions, which are electronically based alcohol education interventions using text messages. Preventive podcasts and e-mails
have become more common on campus. Sending electronic twenty-first birthday
cards about the negative consequences of excess drinking on that milestone birthday
115   has actually shown to reduce the number of drinks taken and consequently resulted
in lower BACs in women celebrating that day.

Colleges and universities are also trying a *social norms* approach to reducing
alcohol consumption, sending a consistent message to students about actual drinking behavior on campus. Many students perceive that their peers drink more than
120   they actually do, which may cause them to feel pressured to drink more themselves.
This misperception includes inaccurately estimating how much and how often students drink, and the actual consequences of students' drinking. In a national survey,
for example, college students perceived that 60 percent of students used alcohol 10
to 30 days a month, but the actual use rate is 16 percent. As a result of these social
125   norms campaigns, heavy episodic alcohol consumption—binge drinking—has declined at campuses across the country.

(1,474 words)

—Rebecca J. Donatelle and Patricia Ketchum,
Access to Health, 12th ed.

Which methods do I think would work best?

Does that mean thinking about results of behavior?

Students think it is more common?

Recall

Stop to talk, write, and think about the selection.

Your instructor may choose to give you a brief comprehension review.

THINK CRITICALLY ABOUT THE SELECTION

How do you think living at home during college might influence students' alcohol use?

Examine the bar graph. Would awareness of these facts help to curb alcohol abuse among college students?

Which of the efforts that colleges are making to reduce alcohol abuse do you think is likely to be the most effective? Why?

WRITE ABOUT THE SELECTION

Did any of the facts in this selection surprise you? What do you think would convince a college student to avoid reckless drinking?

Response Suggestion: Make a list of the prevention methods discussed in the selection and add ideas of your own. Build a convincing argument that might be published in a college newspaper or blog to persuade college students to exercise responsibility and good judgment about drinking. Include facts from the selection to support your position.

Your instructor may choose to give you a brief comprehension review.

CHECK YOUR COMPREHENSION

After reading the selection, answer the following questions with *a, b, c,* or *d*. To help you analyze your strengths and weaknesses, the question types are indicated.

Main Idea _____ 1. What is the best statement of the entire selection's main point?

  a. Excessive drinking can have several very harmful effects.
  b. High-risk drinking is a problem among college students, and college leaders are developing effective preventions.
  c. College students have more drinking problems than other people, and the consequences can be very severe.
  d. Colleges are trying various methods to reduce the problem of high-risk drinking.

Detail _____ 2. According to this article, who is most likely to drink irresponsibly?

  a. Students who think their parents approve of drinking.
  b. Students whose parents have been very strict about restricting alcohol.
  c. Students who did not drink in high school.
  d. Students who are physically active.

Inference _____ 3. The article implies that

  a. drinking before age 21 is legal.
  b. colleges are emphasizing responsible drinking instead of trying to stop students from drinking altogether.
  c. all college students drink alcohol.
  d. most colleges will prosecute students who drink if they are under age 21.

Detail _____ 4. Which of the following is NOT mentioned as a reason that college students are likely to drink excessively?

  a. greater freedom and more opportunities
  b. low price and easy availability of alcohol
  c. relief from stress and desire to be more at ease in social situations
  d. a genetic tendency to alcoholism

Main Idea _____ 5. The main point of the section titled "College Student Drinking Behavior" is that

  a. pre-gamers have a higher risk of negative consequences than others.
  b. one reason for pre-gaming is to avoid paying for high-cost drinks
  c. pre-gaming is an example of college student drinking behavior.
  d. pre-gaming usually occurs in someone's home or dorm.

Inference _____ 6. Based on the reasons for college drinking given in the article, which of the following is most likely to be true?

    a. Binge drinking would probably be less of a problem at a residential college that was far from a town or a city.

    b. Heavy drinking would be less of a problem in schools with a strong fraternity and sorority culture.

    c. Schools with strong athletic programs are less likely to have problems with excessive drinking.

    d. College students would be less likely to drink if they were brought up in homes where they were allowed to have occasional drinks.

Inference _____ 7. According to the bar graph about the negative consequences of drinking among college students,

    a. drinkers are more likely to injure someone else than to injure themselves.

    b. less than a quarter of drinkers forgot where they were or what they did.

    c. about 15% of drinkers engaged in sex.

    d. about 70% of drinkers did not do something that they later regretted.

Main Idea _____ 8. Which sentence best states the main idea of the section titled "Colleges' Efforts to Reduce Student Drinking"?

    a. Colleges are using several methods to reduce student drinking.

    b. Colleges should do something about student drinking.

    c. Student drinking is a common problem on college campuses.

    d. Most campuses offer counseling services to students with drinking problems.

Detail _____ 9. Which approach to reducing student drinking focuses on encouraging students in a nonjudgmental way to change their behavior?

    a. encouraging "dry" fraternity houses

    b. individual and group counseling

    c. cognitive-behavioral skills training and motivational interviewing

    d. BACCHUS

Detail _____ 10. The social norms approach focuses on which of the following methods?

    a. sending preventive podcasts and e-mails

    b. promoting responsible drinking and party hosting

    c. educating students as to the actual extent of student drinking

    d. sending electronic twenty-first birthday cards warning of the negative effects of excessive drinking

Answer the following with *T* (true) or *F* (false)

Inference   ————— 11. The article implies that almost all college students drink irresponsibly at some point.

Inference   ————— 12. Efforts on college campuses seem to be aimed more toward reducing high-risk drinking than to stopping drinking among college students.

Author's Purpose   ————— 13. The primary purpose of this selection is to inform readers about drinking among college students.

Detail   ————— 14. Having sex with a person who is drunk is rape in the eyes of the law.

Detail   ————— 15. Students believe that 60% of college students drink often, but the actual number is 16%.

BUILD YOUR VOCABULARY

According to the way the italicized word was used in the selection, indicate *a, b, c,* or *d* for the word or phrase that gives the best definition. The number in parentheses indicates the line of the passage in which the word is located. Use a dictionary in addition to the context clues to more precisely define the terms.

————— 1. "*unintentional* injuries" (4)
    a. thoughtful
    b. knowing
    c. unplanned
    d. deliberate

————— 2. "in *binge* drinking" (19)
    a. measured
    b. restrained
    c. social
    d. excessive

————— 3. "particularly *vulnerable*" (22)
    a. open
    b. unexposed
    c. unlikely
    d. knowledgeable

————— 4. "becoming *intoxicated*" (43)
    a. clear-headed
    b. drunk
    c. cool
    d. steady

————— 5. "a *hazing* activity" (51)
    a. social
    b. entertainment
    c. academic
    d. initiation into a club or organization

————— 6. "*vandalism* of personal property" (91)
    a. destruction
    b. stealing
    c. replacement
    d. removal

————— 7. "to *curb* binge drinking" (99)
    a. limit
    b. encourage
    c. educate
    d. describe

————— 8. "a *nonjudgmental* approach" (110)
    a. harsh
    b. intense
    c. uncritical
    d. merciless

_____ 9. "This *misperception* includes" (121)
a. clear understanding
b. error
c. appreciation
d. estimate

_____ 10. "heavy *episodic* alcohol consumption" (125)
a. occasional
b. constant
c. unchanging
d. damaging

SELECTION 3   Business   MyReadingLab

Visit Chapter 2: Strategic Reading and Study in MyReadingLab to complete the Selection 3 activities and the Build Background Knowledge video activity.

P REVIEW the next selection to predict its purpose and organization and to formulate your learning plan.

Activate Schemata

How can a company stay in business by giving away its products?

Would you be more likely to buy from a company if you knew that by doing so you would also be helping a needy child?

Establish a Purpose for Reading

TOMS Shoes is in the business of making shoes and giving half of them away. Read to find out how this company makes a profit while doing good around the world.

Build Background Knowledge — VIDEO

TOMS Shoes CEO Gives A Pair Away For Every Sale

To prepare for reading Selection 3, answer the questions below. Then, watch this video about TOMS Shoes and its president, Blake Mycoskie.

What obligations, if any, do businesses have to help economically disadvantaged people?

What type of support do businesses in your area provide to the local community?

Should all for-profit businesses be required to give back to the community? Why or why not?

This video helped me: _____

_____

_____

Increase Word Knowledge

What do you know about these words?

tango	founding	eco-consciousness	intern	fledgling
silica	disciples	chronicle	exponentially	deemed

Your instructor may give a brief vocabulary review before or after reading.

Integrate Knowledge While Reading

Questions have been inserted in the margins to stimulate your thinking while reading. Remember to

Predict   Picture   Relate   Monitor   Correct   Annotate

SELECTION
3

TOMS Shoes: *"Be the Change You Want to See in the World"*

If the world were a village of 100 people, 14 of the 100 would be illiterate, 20 would be malnourished. 23 would drink polluted water, 25 would have no shelter, 33 would have no electricity, and 40 would have *no shoes*. In 2006, these stark facts, especially the last one, struck Blake Mycoskie up close and personally as he visited
5   Argentina to learn how to play polo, practice his tango, and do some community service work. While there, the sight of barefoot children, too poor to have shoes, stunned him.

THE COMPANY IS BORN

Could they stay in business?

So in May 2006, Mycoskie launched TOMS Shoes (named from the concept of "Tomorrow's Shoes") with $300,000 of his own money. The founding concept was this:
10   For every pair of TOMS shoes that customers bought, the company would donate another pair of shoes to a child in need around the world. Mycoskie had previously started five successful strictly for-profit businesses. "But I was ready to do something more meaningful," says Mycoskie. "I always knew I wanted to help others. Now, it was time to do something that wasn't just for profit." Mycoskie remembered
15   Mahatma Gandhi's saying, *"Be* the change you want to see in the world."

DOING WELL BY DOING GOOD

"Doing good" is an important part of TOMS's mission. But so is "doing well." The company is very much a for-profit venture. However, at TOMS Shoes, the two missions go hand in hand. Beyond being socially admirable, the buy-one-give-one-away concept is also a good business proposition. In addition to scratching
20   Mycoskie's itch to help people, "the timing was perfect for the American consumer, too," he says. "With the rise of social- and eco-consciousness and the economy in a downturn, people were looking for innovative and affordable ways to make the world a better place."

With all of these "do good" and "do well" goals swirling in his head, Mycoskie
25   returned home from his Argentina trip, hired an intern, and set about making 250 pairs of shoes in the loft of his Santa Monica, California, home. Stuffing the shoes into three duffel bags, he made the fledgling company's first "Shoe Drop" tour, returning to the Argentine village and giving one pair of shoes to each child. Mycoskie arrived back home to find an article about his project on the front page of the *Los*
30   *Angeles Times* Calendar section. TOMS had been in business for only two weeks, but by that very afternoon, he had orders for 2,200 pairs of shoes on his Web site.

WORLD SHOE DROPS

By October 2006, TOMS had sold 10,000 pairs of shoes. True to the company's one-for-one promise, Mycoskie undertook a second TOMS Shoe Drop tour. Consistent with his new title, Chief Shoe Giver of TOMS Shoes, he led 15 employees and volun-
35 teers back to Argentina, where they went from school to school, village to village, and gave away another 10,000 pairs of shoes.

"We don't just drop the shoes off, as the name might imply," says Mycoskie. "We place the shoes on each child's feet so that we can establish a connection, which is such an important part of our brand. We want to give the children the feeling of
40 love, and warmth, and experience. But *we* also get those feelings as we give the shoes."

The One for One® idea caught fire. As word spread about TOMS, a nonprofit organization called "Friends of TOMS" formed to "create avenues for individuals to volunteer and experience [the TOMS] mission," participate in Shoe Drops, and "per-
45 form good works in their own communities and their own lives." *Vogue* magazine and other major publications ran stories on the company's philosophy and good works. In November 2007, 40 TOMS employees and volunteers embarked on the third Shoe Drop, travelling to South Africa to place shoes on the feet of 50,000 more children.

50 Next, TOMS Shoes turned its attention to Ethiopia, where 11 million people are at risk for podoconiosis, a disease often caused by silica in volcanic soils. Children's bare feet absorb the silica, which can cause elephantitis, severe swelling of the legs and feet. The disease progresses until surgery is required. The simple preventative cure? Shoes. As part of the Christmas season 2008, TOMS offered gift card packages,

A simple solution to a serious problem

Blake Mycoskie, founder of **TOMS** shoes. In addition to shoes, Mycoskie has started One for One®, in which every pair of **TOMS** eyewear purchased will help give sight to a person in need.
Michael Kovac/Getty Images for TOMS

55 which included a certificate for a pair of shoes and a DVD telling the TOMS story. The goal was to give 30,000 pairs of shoes to Ethiopian children in 30 days.

TOMS has also focused on needy children in the United States, stepping in to help children whose families were still recovering from Hurricane Katrina in Loui-siana. Also in the United States, TOMS started a grassroots marketing movement
60 called "TOMS Vagabonds." These traveling groups of TOMS disciples hit the road in vans full of TOMS shoes and help to organize events on college and school cam-puses and in communities all around the country. The Vagabonds' goal is to raise awareness about TOMS, sell shoes, and inspire more people to get involved with the company's movement. The Vagabonds chronicle the travels on TOMS Facebook
65 page (www.facebook.com, TOMSVagabonds), blog (www.tomsshoesblog.com), and Twitter site (http://twitter.com/tomsshoes).

GIVING: A SUCCESSFUL BUSINESS STRATEGY

By mid-2009, TOMS had sold (and therefore given away) more than 150,000 pairs of shoes. With sales in excess of $8 million, the company is profitable and growing exponentially. Mycoskie expected to sell and give away more than 300,000 pairs in
70 2009. Retailers such as Nordstrom, Urban Outfitters, and even Whole Foods are now offering TOMS in more than 400 U.S. outlets. In fact, Whole Foods is the company's biggest customer.

TOMS's rapid growth is the result of purchases by caring customers who then tell the TOMS story to their friends. Where the typical shoe company spends about
75 20 percent of sales on traditional advertising and promotion, TOMS hasn't spent a single dollar on it. It hasn't had to. "Ultimately, it is our customers who drive our success," says Mycoskie. "Giving not only makes you feel good, but it actually is a very good business strategy especially in this day and age. Your customers become your marketers."
80 Moreover, as TOMS's success shows, consumers like to feel good. A recent global study found that 71 percent of consumers said that despite the recession, they had given just as much time and money to causes they deemed worthy. Fifty-five percent of respondents also indicated they would pay more for a brand if it sup-ported a good cause.

85 TOMS Shoes is a great example of cause-related marketing—of "doing well by doing *good*." Mycoskie hopes that his company will inspire people to think differ-ently about business. "My thinking was that TOMS would show that entrepreneurs no longer had to choose between earning money or making a difference in the world," he says. "Business and charity or public service don't have to be mutually
90 exclusive. In fact, when they come together, they can be very powerful."

(1,133 words)

—Gary Armstrong and Philip Kotler,
Marketing: An Introduction, 10th ed.

It's possible to do both!

Recall

Stop to talk, write, and think about the selection. Use the headings and subhead-ings in the recall diagram that follows to guide your thinking. For each heading, jot down a key idea that you feel is important to remember:

(Topic) _____

(Significant
details)

_____

_____

_____

_____

_____

_____

_____

_____

_____

_____

(Relate) -

(React) _____

Your instructor may choose to give you a brief comprehension review.

THINK CRITICALLY ABOUT THE SELECTION

What similarities and differences do you see between the ways that Blake Mycoskie and Madam C. J. Walker (refer to Selection 1 in this chapter) used philanthropy to build their businesses?

Which do you think is more important to business success—excellent quality or social consciousness? Why?

In what ways are social media contributing to the way TOMS and other companies do business?

WRITE ABOUT THE SELECTION

Would you consider starting a business based on the principle of "Doing well by doing good"? What factors have made TOMS Shoes so successful? *Writing Suggestion:* Use your recall diagram to write a feature article that might be used in a business journal. Include a one-paragraph summary of the selection and a one-paragraph reaction that would interest people who own businesses or are thinking of starting a business.

CHECK YOUR COMPREHENSION

After reading the selection, answer the following questions with *a, b, c,* or *d.* To help you analyze your strengths and weaknesses, the question types are indicated.

Main Idea ———— 1. What is the best statement of the entire selection's main point?

  a. Succeeding in business is very difficult.
  b. TOMS Shoes was founded by Blake Mycoskie in 2006.
  c. TOMS Shoes gives away a pair of shoes for every pair sold.
  d. TOMS Shoes is a successful business based on cause-related marketing—"doing well by doing good."

Detail ———— 2. According to this selection, Blake Mycoskie

  a. had considerable business success before starting TOMS Shoes.
  b. borrowed money to start TOMS Shoes.
  c. had a college degree in business.
  d. had experience in manufacturing shoes.

Inference ———— 3. The article suggests that

  a. Mycoskie had business partners who helped him start TOMS.
  b. Mycoskie was active in humanitarian work before starting TOMS Shoes.
  c. Mycoskie had the idea to start TOMS before he went to Argentina.
  d. Mycoskie travels personally on all Shoe Drop tours.

Detail ———— 4. The first 250 pairs of shoes were made

  a. in the loft of Mycoskie's home.
  b. in the company's factory.
  c. in a rented shoe factory.
  d. by a crew of Mycoskie's friends.

Main Idea ———— 5. The main point of the section titled "World Shoe Drops" is that

  a. TOMS Shoes provided shoes for children recovering from Hurricane Katrina.
  b. TOMS messengers actually place shoes on children's feet personally.
  c. TOMS Shoes has provided shoes for needy children all over the world, including the United States.
  d. TOMS is filling an important humanitarian need.

Inference ———— 6. Which of the following was probably most influential in selling the first 2,200 pairs of TOMS shoes?

  a. Mycoskie's enthusiasm about the project
  b. a prominent article about the company in the *Los Angeles Times*
  c. the efforts of "TOMS Vagabonds"
  d. the "Friends of TOMS"

SELECTION **3**

Inference _____ 7. Why do the TOMS messengers place the donated shoes directly on children's feet?

    a. to be sure that the children get the correct size

    b. so that kids will get the styles that they like best

    c. to be sure that the shoes actually get to the children who need them most

    d. to give the children and themselves the satisfaction of a very personal connection

Main Idea _____ 8. Which sentence best states the main idea of the section titled "Giving: A Successful Business Strategy"?

    a. TOMS success shows that it is possible to earn money and help others, too.

    b. Consumers like to do good.

    c. Caring customers tell their friends about TOMS.

    d. TOMS is a great company.

Inference _____ 9. Which factor probably was most influential in the success of the Ethiopian Shoe Drop project?

    a. It occurred at Christmastime.

    b. People want to help others.

    c. The clear incentive to purchase immediately, the specific sales goal, and its appeal to buyers' desire to help others.

    d. Children in Ethiopia needed shoes.

Detail _____ 10. How are the "Friends of TOMS" involved in the company?

    a. They help to package shoes for delivery.

    b. They travel around the United States selling TOMS shoes.

    c. They participate in Shoe Drops and community service projects.

    d. They help to manufacture the shoes.

Answer the following with *T* (true) or *F* (false).

Author's Purpose _____ 11. The purpose of this selection is to encourage other companies to "do well by doing good."

Inference _____ 12. The TOMS business model is likely to work for any company.

Detail _____ 13. TOMS spends no money on traditional advertising.

Detail _____ 14. TOMS Vagabonds are volunteers who spread the word about the company at college campuses, sell shoes, and recruit others to get involved.

Detail _____ 15. Podoconiosis is a disease caused by absorption of silica through bare feet.

BUILD YOUR VOCABULARY

According to the way the italicized word was used in the selection, indicate *a, b, c,* or *d* for the word or phrase that gives the best definition. The number in parentheses indicates the line of the passage in which the word is located. Use a dictionary in addition to the context clues to more precisely define the terms.

_____ 1. "practice his *tango*" (5)
    a. language skills
    b. a Latin dance
    c. a musical instrument
    d. a South American game

_____ 2. "The *founding* concept" (9)
    a. final
    b. best
    c. surprising
    d. beginning

_____ 3. "social and *eco-consciousness*" (21)
    a. awareness of environmental concerns
    b. lack of money
    c. understanding of political issues
    d. poverty

_____ 4. "hired an *intern*" (25)
    a. professional
    b. a doctor
    c. a volunteer
    d. a student gaining work experience

_____ 5. "the *fledgling* company's first" (27)
    a. veteran
    b. established
    c. historic
    d. newcomer

_____ 6. "caused by *silica*" (51)
    a. compound found in sand and volcanic dust
    b. insects
    c. poisons
    d. bacteria

_____ 7. "TOMS *disciples*" (60)
    a. people who believe and spread the ideas of another
    b. leaders
    c. employees
    d. friends

_____ 8. "*chronicle* the travels" (64)
    a. enjoy
    b. read
    c. report
    d. understand

_____ 9. "growing *exponentially*" (69)
    a. slowly
    b. quietly
    c. very rapidly
    d. carefully

_____ 10. "they *deemed* worthy" (82)
    a. distrusted
    b. judged
    c. rejected
    d. criticized

Concept Prep for Business

What is a CD?

When you put money into a *CD (certificate of deposit)* through a bank, you are essentially lending the bank money for a fixed interest rate and for a designated period, called the *maturity*. The CD matures for one month or up to five years, and the interest rate is higher for the longer maturities. Banks then lend out the money at a higher rate for people to buy cars or houses. With a CD, the return of your *principal* (original money) is guaranteed. You do not have to worry about losing your money.

What is a bond?

A *bond* is a loan to a government or a corporation. For example, many cities sell *municipal bonds* to finance infrastructure improvements or schools. When you buy bonds, you are lending the city money, and the taxpayers will pay you interest. The interest rate on bonds is usually higher than that on CDs, but the risk is greater. You have a promise that you will be paid back at *maturity* (a specified period), and you hope the city will be able to fulfill this promise. If you buy a *U.S. Treasury Bill* or a *savings bond*, you are lending money to the federal government, which uses the money to pay down the national debt. Because U.S. Treasury bills are backed by the federal government, they are safer investments than municipal bonds.

What is a mutual fund?

A *mutual fund* is a company that pools the investment money of many individuals and purchases a *portfolio* (array of holdings) of stocks, bonds, and other securities. Each investor then shares accordingly in the profits or losses. Investors also pay a fee for professionals to manage the portfolio, which includes bookkeeping, researching, buying, and selling. All fees for management come out of profits before they are shared.

An advantage of mutual funds is that they offer instant *diversification*. With a $1,000 purchase, you can have a part ownership in many different stocks or bonds. Also, if you do not have the expertise to research individual stocks, you can rely on the judgment of the professional money managers. Different mutual funds specialize in different areas, such as large companies, small companies, or even *IPOs*, which are initial public offerings of stock. You would want to find one that matches your investment interests and that also has a positive track record of growth.

According to *U.S. News & World Report*, key careers in the field of business in 2015 include marketing manager, accountant, financial adviser, insurance agent, bookkeeping, accounting or audit clerk, and loan officer.
Pressmaster/Fotolia

What is a capital gain?

A capital gain is a profit on the sale of a property or a security. A *short-term capital gain* is a profit made on stocks or bonds that have been owned for less than one year. This profit is taxed as ordinary income and may be as high as 40 percent for people in upper tax brackets. A *long-term capital gain*, on the other hand, is a profit on a property or security that has been owned for over a year. On this, investors are taxed at a maximum of 15 percent.

REVIEW QUESTIONS

After studying the material, answer the following questions:

1. Are CD rates better for a month or a year? _____

_____

2. What does the bank do with your CD money? _____

_____

3. What is your principal? _____

_____

_____

4. What is municipal bond? _____

_____

_____

5. What are the advantages of a mutual fund? _____

_____

6. Is tax greater on a short- or long-term capital gain? _____

_____

7. How long must you hold a property before selling to achieve a long-term capital gain? _____

8. What is a portfolio? _____

_____

9. For the safest choice, should you pick bonds, CDs, or a mutual fund? _____

_____

10. What does *diversification* mean? _____

_____

_____

Your instructor may choose to give a brief review of these business concepts.

- *malfeasance*: misconduct or wrongdoing, especially by a public official

  Citizens demanded that the mayor resign for his *malfeasance*; he had used taxpayers' money for lavish meals and entertainment.

- *malfunction*: fail to function properly

  Although it worked well at the store, the computer *malfunctioned* when we got it home and set it up.

Words with *kakos- (caco-)*: "harsh, bad, ugly"

At a Halloween party, Franco enjoyed explaining that he was dressed as a *cacodemon*—an evil spirit.

- *cacophony*: a harsh, jarring sound; a discordant and meaningless mixture of sound

  The toddler's attempt to play an improvised drum set of pots, pans, and spoons created such a *cacophony* that her father required earplugs.

- *cacography*: bad handwriting; poor spelling

  Jo's beautiful calligraphy was in stark contrast to Mark's messy *cacography*.

Review Questions

Part I

Indicate whether the italicized word in each of the following sentences is used correctly (*C*) or incorrectly (*I*):

_____ 1. Some smokers consider a proposed law banning all smoking in public places to be pressure from nonsmoking *malcontents*.

_____ 2. Upper-class women of past centuries were often referred to as *malady* by members of lower social classes.

_____ 3. Runners frequently claim to experience a state of *euphoria* in what is known as a "runner's high."

_____ 4. Repeated *benevolent* acts may need to be corrected by counseling or behavior modification.

_____ 5. Belonging to a campus organization can be *beneficial* for students who would like to expand their circle of friends.

Part II

Choose the best synonym from the boxed list for the words below.

eulogy	maladroit	malaise	cacophony	malfeasance
malign	euthanasia	eureka	euphemism	malevolent

6. evil _____

7. harsh sound _____

8. substitute expression _____

9. wrongdoing _____

10. exclamation of discovery _____

11. awkward _____

12. death out of mercy _____

13. weakness _____

14. tribute _____

15. slander _____

3 Organizing Textbook Information for Study

Learning Objectives

In this chapter, you will learn to:

1 Organize for academic study
2 Annotate while reading
3 Make notes from textbook reading

Vocabulary Booster: Who's Who in Medicine?

Nik_Merkulov/Fotolia

GET ORGANIZED FOR COLLEGE STUDY

Learning Objective 1

Organize for academic study

If you are like most students, you have already confronted new challenges in college. Your courses may cover a great deal of information more rapidly than you are used to, and the study techniques you used in high school may not be as effective in college. In a sense, college textbook assignments are like the Olympics of reading. Can you train like an athlete to meet the challenge?

EXERCISE 3.1

Discovering Your Fitness as a Reader

Take the following inventory to see how you already measure up. Check *Yes* or *No* for your response.

What Kind of Reader Are You?

1. Do you mark your text while reading?   Yes _____ No _____

2. Do you make marginal notes while reading?   Yes _____ No _____

3. Do you take notes after reading?   Yes _____ No _____

4. Do you differentiate between details and main ideas?   Yes _____ No _____

5. Do you stop to summarize while reading?   Yes _____ No _____

6. Do you have a purpose behind note taking?   Yes _____ No _____

7. Do you review your textbook notes?   Yes _____ No _____

8. Do you review your class lecture notes within 24 hours?   Yes _____ No _____

9. Do you link old and new information to remember it?   Yes _____ No _____

10. Do you use maps or charts to condense your notes for study? Yes _____ No _____

If all of your answers were yes, you are well on your way to becoming an Olympic champ in the college reading arena! If some of your answers were no, you will want to start training now.

Your first assignment in most college courses will be to read the first chapter in the assigned textbook. At that time, you will immediately discover that a textbook chapter contains an amazing amount of information. Your instructor will continue to assign the remaining chapters in rapid succession. Don't panic! Your task is to select the information that you need to remember, learn it, and organize it for future study for a midterm or a final exam that is weeks or months away.

In a study of the demands on students in introductory college history courses during a ten-week term, professors analyzed the actual reading demands of classes that they observed and found that students were asked to read an average of 825 pages during each course. The average length of weekly assignments was more than 80 pages, but the amount varied both with the professor and the topic. In one class, students had to read 287 pages in only ten days.

Students were expected to grasp relationships between parts and wholes, place people and events in historical context, and retain facts. Professors spent 85 percent of class time lecturing and 6 percent of class time giving tests, which often totaled to 100 percent of the final grade. In short, the demands were high and students were expected to work independently to organize textbook material efficiently and effectively to prepare for that crucial 6 percent of test-taking time.

The task is difficult, but you have seen many others succeed—and even earn A's. Train for the challenge by using the skills of a successful learner. Consciously build knowledge networks (your foundation for thought interaction), use an active study process, and organize your materials for learning.

Building Knowledge Networks

The old notion of studying and learning is that studying is an information-gathering activity. Knowledge is the "product" that you can acquire by transferring information from the text to your memory. According to this view, good learners locate important information, review it, and then transfer the information to long-term memory. The problem with this model is that review does not always guarantee recall, and rehearsal is not always enough to ensure that information is encoded into long-term memory.

Experts now know that studying and learning involve more than review, rehearsal, and memorization; they require making meaningful connections. Cognitive psychologists focus on schemata, or prior knowledge, and the learner's own goals. To understand and remember, you must link new information to already existing schemata, creating networks of knowledge. As your personal knowledge expands, you create new networks. As the learner, you—not your professor—decide how much effort you need to expend, and you adjust your studying according to your answers to questions such as "How much do I need to know?" "Will the test be multiple-choice or essay?" and "Do I want to remember this forever?" In this way, you make judgments and select the material to remember and integrate into knowledge networks.

The Study Process

As you can see, studying in college requires more than memorizing facts the night before a test. An effective **study process**, or **study system**, begins by reading the textbook material thoroughly and then using active methods to prepare for tests and discussions. Reading thoroughly means using the three stages of reading, proceeding slowly enough to absorb meaning, actively sorting the more important from the less important details, and making notes during the recall stage. This is a reading technique known as **study reading**. Effort spent using study reading will save study time later because you are learning while reading. The steps in the study process and some ideas for studying your notes are shown below. Notice that the first three steps are the stages of reading that you learned in Chapter 2. The fourth step solidifies the material in memory so that you can do more than just know it; you can use it.

The Study Process

Preview

Integrate knowledge (read thoroughly)
- Use the five thinking strategies
- Annotate*

Recall
- Think about it
- Talk about it
- Write about it (make notes)*
    Cornell method
    Outlining
    Mapping

Study the notes
- Self-quiz; partner quiz
- Flash cards (for facts and small pieces of information)
- Jigsaw puzzle (Make a copy of your notes, cut it apart, and put it back together from memory.)
- Rewrite notes from memory
- Predict exam questions; practice answering them

*The steps marked with an asterisk are especially effective for setting material in long-term memory. If you annotate well, it is easy to organize the annotations into separate notes, and good notes provide all you need for test preparation.

Organizing Textbook Information

In this chapter, we discuss four methods of organizing textbook information for future study: (1) annotating, (2) Cornell-style note taking, (3) outlining, and (4) mapping. Why four methods? In a review of more than 500 research studies on organizing textbook information, two college reading professors concluded that "no one study strategy is appropriate for all students in all study situations." On the basis of these findings, they established guidelines encouraging students to develop a repertoire of skills in study reading. They felt that students need to know, for example, that underlining takes less time than note taking but that note taking can result in better test scores.

BRAIN BOOSTER

Exercise to Boost Brain Power

Sometimes studying for a long stretch is not the best use of our brains. After a period of intense concentration our minds wander, and our thinking slows down. One solution is exercise. Physical movement increases the amount of blood in the brain and thus the amount of oxygen and other nutrients the brain needs to function well. The greater blood supply also carries away waste materials more efficiently. If that isn't enough to convince us to get up and move, there's more. Exercise also produces BDNF, brain-derived neurotrophic factor, a protein that helps to keep existing brain cells healthy and generate new brain cells. How much exercise is enough? An aerobic workout 2 to 3 times a week plus strengthening exercises produces the best results, but just taking a walk helps boost thinking power.

—*Adapted from John J. Medina,* Brain Rules. *© 2008 John J. Medina. Pear Press: Seattle, WA*

Your selection of a study-reading strategy for organizing textbook material will vary based on the announced testing demands, the nature of the material, the amount of time that you have to devote to study, and your preference for a particular strategy. Being familiar with all four methods affords a repertoire of choices.

ANNOTATING

Learning Objective 2

Annotate while reading

Which of the following would seem to indicate the most effective use of the textbook as a learning tool?

1. A text without a single mark—not even the owner's name has spoiled the sacred pages
2. A text ablaze with color—almost every line is adorned with a red, blue, yellow, or green colored marker
3. A text with a scattered variety of markings—highlighting, underlines, numbers, and stars are interspersed with circles, arrows, and short, written notes

Naturally, option three is the best. The rationale for the first option is probably for a better book resale value, but usually used books resell for the same price whether they are marked or unmarked. The reason for the second option is probably procrastination in decision making. Students who highlight everything—the "yellow book disease"—rely on coming back later to figure out what is *really* important. Although selective highlighting in a light color such as yellow is a helpful strategy, highlighting everything is inefficient. The variety of markings in the third strategy enables you to pinpoint ideas for later study.

Why Annotate?

The textbook is a learning tool and should be used as such; it should not be preserved as a treasure. A college professor requires a particular text because it contains information that is vital to your understanding of the course material. The text places a vast body of knowledge in your hands—much more material than the professor could possibly give in class. It is your job to cull through this information, make some sense out of it, and select the important points that need to be remembered.

Annotating is a method of emphasizing main ideas, major supporting details, and key terms. The word *annotate* means "to add marks." By using a system of symbols and notations rather than just colored stripes, you mark the text during the first reading so that a complete rereading will not be necessary. The markings indicate pertinent points to review for an exam. If your time is short, however, highlighting with a colored marker is better than not making any marks at all. The "How to Annotate" Reader's Tip on page 126 offers an example of annotation.

When you finish reading, use your annotations to make a list of key terms and ideas on your own paper to have a reduced form of the information for review and self-testing. Making notes on separate paper not only makes studying more efficient but also further solidifies the information in memory.

Reader's TIP) How to Annotate

Develop a system of notations. Use circles, stars, numbers, and whatever else helps you put the material visually into perspective. *Anything that makes sense to you is a correct notation.* Just be consistent. Here is an example of one student's marking system:

Main idea	( )
Circle major details	⬯
Underline minor details	_____
Major trend or possible essay exam question	*
Important smaller point to know for multiple-choice item	✓
Word that you must be able to define	▭
Section of material to reread for review	{ }
Numbering of important details under a major issue	(1), (2), (3)
Didn't understand and must seek advice	?
Notes in the margin	Ex., Def., Topic
Questions in the margin	Why signif.?
Indicating relationships	～
Related issue or idea	← R

When to Annotate

Plan to annotate after a unit of thought has been presented and you can view the information as a whole. This may mean marking after a single paragraph or after three pages; your marking will vary with the material.

When you are first reading, every sentence seems of major importance as each new idea unfolds, and you may be tempted to annotate too much. Resist this tendency, as overmarking wastes both reading time and review time. Instead, be patient and read through a paragraph or a section until the end, at which point the author's complete thought will have been fully developed and the major points will have emerged from a background of lesser details. With all of the facts at your fingertips, you can decide what you want to remember. At the end of the course, your textbook should have that worn but well-organized look.

EXAMPLE   The following passage is taken from a biology textbook. Notice how the annotations have been used to highlight main ideas and significant supporting details. This same passage will be used throughout this chapter to demonstrate each of the four methods of organizing textbook material.

Circulatory Systems

When we examine the systems by which blood reaches all the cells of an animal, we find (two general types,) known as open and closed circulatory systems.

2 types

Def. I

Open Circulatory Systems

Open 1

The essential feature of the (**open circulatory system**) is that the blood moves through a body cavity—such as the abdominal cavity—and bathes the cells directly. The open circulatory system is particularly characteristic of insects and other arthropods, although it is also found in some other organisms.

2

Ex

Ex

In most insects the blood does not take a major part in oxygen transport. Oxygen enters the animal's body through a separate network of branching tubes that open to the atmosphere on the outside of the animal. (This type of respiratory system will be discussed in more detail in the next chapter.) Blood in an open circulatory system moves somewhat more slowly than in the average closed system. The slower system is adequate for insects because it does not have to supply the cells with oxygen.

3

4

5

Def. II

Closed Circulatory Systems

Closed

In a (**closed circulatory system,**) the blood flows through a well-defined system of vessels with many branches. In the majority of closed systems the blood is responsible for oxygen transport. To supply all the body cells with sufficient oxygen, the blood must move quickly through the blood vessels. A closed circulatory system must therefore have an efficient pumping mechanism, or heart, to set the blood in motion and keep it moving briskly through the body.

1

2

3

4

All vertebrates possess closed circulatory systems. Simple closed systems are also found in some invertebrates, including annelid worms. A good example of such a simple closed circulatory system can be seen in the earthworm.

Ex

Ex

Annotating

Using a variety of markings, annotate the following selection as if you were preparing for a quiz on the material. Remember, do not underscore immediately as you read but wait until you finish a paragraph or a section, and then mark the important points and add marginal notes.

WORK SCHEDULES

Several work-scheduling trends are evident in the new millennium: flextime, job sharing, job splitting, permanent part-time workers, telecommuting, and employee leasing. Companies are increasing their use of these flexible approaches to work. For example, Merck has reported increased use of flextime, telecommuting, and job sharing. The composition of Merck's workforce is also illustrative of trends for the future, as women make up 52 percent of its U.S. employees while minorities account for 24 percent. More significantly, in its U.S. operations 32 percent of the company's managerial positions are held by women while minorities account for 16 percent. All of these trends present unique challenges and opportunities for supervisors.

Flextime allows people to vary their starting and ending times. A company may specify a core time, requiring all employees to be on the job from 10:00 A.M. until 1:00 P.M., but some may start as early as 6:00 A.M. or as late as 10:00 A.M. Some may go home as early as 1:00 P.M. Flexible scheduling appeals to working parents with school-age children and to a growing number of self-managing information workers. But such work schedules make it difficult for one supervisor to manage people who work over a span of 10 or more hours. **Compressed workweeks** of four 10-hour days also help organizations meet the needs of employees.

The Bechtel Group, a construction and engineering firm, has 27,800 employees worldwide. It offers a flexible schedule to its employees in Houston, Texas. Under the plan, employees work nine-hour days, Monday through Thursday each week. Each Friday, about half the employees work eight hours, and the other half have the day off. All employees work 80 hours in nine days. Management initially feared that longer work days would mean lower productivity, but productivity has improved. Employees seemed to be scheduling more of their personal business for their off time.

Job sharing allows two or more people to work at one full-time job. A growing number of people want to work part time, and a growing number of businesses want more part-time employees. The employer benefits in several ways. It gets double the creativity for each shared job. It may also cut benefit costs, which often add 30 to 40 percent to an employee's salary. People come to work refreshed and eager to perform and experience less fatigue and stress. Boring jobs can be more attractive when performed for fewer than 40 hours each week.

Permanent part-time workers usually work for small companies that do not have enough work for a full-timer to perform. Part-time work may be for any number of hours and days per week, up to 35 hours. Older individuals, such as those who may have retired from other jobs, provide a source of reliable employees who may be interested in permanent part-time work.

Temporary workers or contingent workers fill millions of jobs in the United States each year. The U.S. Bureau of Labor has estimated, using a broad definition of "contingent workers," that 4.4 percent of the employed population consists of contingent workers. A somewhat lower estimate is provided by the CEO of Manpower Inc., who has estimated that 2.5 percent of the U.S. workforce is made up of temporary workers.

Temporary work agencies provide people to work part time for clients who need temporary help. Most come well trained for their jobs and work in skilled areas such as computer services, secretarial services, manufacturing, and accounting. Another view of the broad presence of temporary workers in the workforce is provided by the president of a temporary help firm that provides temporary employees to such employers as Sun Microsystems and Silicon Graphics: "There's not a single major company in the United States that doesn't have a substantial percentage of the workforce as contingent workers."

Telecommuting allows a full- or part-time employee to work at home while remaining connected to the employer by telecommunications devices such as computers, e-mail, the Internet, and fax machines. Estimates of the number of telecommuters in the United States vary widely, with numbers ranging from 9 million to 24 million. More than half of the Fortune 500 companies reported that 1 to 5 percent of their employees are involved in telecommuting, and some companies have large numbers of telecommuters. For example, Merrill Lynch has 3,500 telecommuters. Nortel, one of the pioneers in this area, had 3,600 telecommuters at one point. In addition, AT&T has announced a telecommuting day, encouraging and making arrangements for any worker who can to telecommute. Telecommuters can increase their quality of life by living in geographic areas that are long distances from their offices and combining work at home with child care arrangements. In addition, major disasters quickly isolate people from their jobs and places of employment. The terrorist attack on the World Trade Center on September 11, 2001, earthquakes, floods, and hurricanes have highlighted the value of telecommuting—within hours, companies whose physical plants were in ruins were making alternative arrangements to meet their customers' needs, thanks to cellular communications.

—Charles R. Greer and Warren Richard Plunkett,
Supervision: Diversity and Teams in the Workplace, 10th ed.

Review your annotations. Have you sufficiently emphasized the main idea and the significant supporting details? Use this checklist to evaluate your annotations:

Annotations Checklist

- ❏ I circled *major details* and underlined *minor ones*.
- ❏ I wrote brief labels or notes in the margins.
- ❏ I used abbreviations like *"def"* and *"ex"* in the margins.
- ❏ Where I saw lists of items, I numbered them.
- ❏ I used a consistent set of symbols such as *, ?, and *T* when they were appropriate.
- ❏ My annotations make sense when I reread them.
- ❏ I marked the right amount, not too much nor too little.
- ❏ My annotations tell me everything that I need to remember from the text.

Suggestions for improvement:

_____

_____

_____

_____

_____

NOTE TAKING

Learning Objective 3

Make notes from textbook reading

Note taking involves using your own words and separate paper to record information that you want and need to remember. Many students are in the habit of simply writing one line after another, but organizing notes into a visually clear form enhances their value for study purposes. Three common note-taking forms—the Cornell method, outlining, and mapping—are presented in the following pages.

When and How to Take Notes

Take notes from textbooks in the "Recall" stage of study reading, after reading and annotating in the "Integrating Knowledge" stage. Of course, taking notes from lectures is also important. The forms discussed here can be used then, too, but you might need to revise your notes after a lecture to be sure they make sense and contain all of the important information.

Whether your notes are from textbooks or lectures, record major topics, supporting details, and a few examples, but avoid trying to write everything. Record only what you need to remember—not too much or too little! The best notes have these characteristics:

- Organized clearly
- Show levels of importance
- Contain only necessary information

The Cornell Method

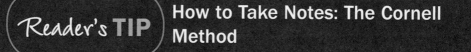

Reader's TIP — How to Take Notes: The Cornell Method

One of the most popular systems of note taking is called the Cornell method. The steps are as follows:

1. Draw a line down your paper two and one-half inches from the left side to create a two-and-one-half-inch margin for noting key words and a six-inch area on the right for phrases or sentence summaries.
2. After you have finished reading a section, tell yourself what you have read and jot down phrases or sentence summaries in the six-inch area on the right side of your paper. Use your own words and make sure that you have included the main ideas and significant supporting details. Be brief but use complete sentences.
3. Review your summary phrases or sentences. Write key words, categories, or labels in the column on the left side of your paper. These words can be used to stimulate your memory of the material for later study.

When to use Cornell-style notes. You can use the **Cornell method** to take notes from textbooks or from classroom lectures. The chart shown below, developed by Norman Stahl and James King, explains the procedure for lecture notes and gives a visual display of the results. Simply adapt the form for book notes.

Taking Class Notes: The Cornell Method	
← 2 1/2 INCHES →	← 6 INCHES →
REDUCE IDEAS TO CONCISE JOTTINGS AND SUMMARIES AS CUES FOR RECITING.	RECORD THE LECTURE AS FULLY AND AS MEANINGFULLY AS POSSIBLE.
Cornell method	This sheet demonstrates the Cornell method of taking classroom notes. It is recommended by experts from the Learning Center at Cornell University.
Line drawn down paper	You should draw a line down your note page about 2 1/2 inches from the left side. On the right side of the line, simply record your classroom notes as you usually do. Be sure that you write legibly.
After the lecture	After the lecture, you should read the notes, fill in materials that you missed, make your writing legible, and underline any important materials. Ask another classmate for help if you missed something during the lecture.
Use the recall column for key phrases	The recall column on the left will help you when you study for your tests. Jot down any important words or key phrases in the recall column. This activity forces you to rethink and summarize your notes. The key words should stick in your mind.
Five Rs	The Five Rs will help you take better notes based on the Cornell method.
Record	1. Record any information given during the lecture that you believe will be important.
Reduce	2. When you reduce your information, you are summarizing and listing key words/phrases in the recall column.
Recite	3. Cover the notes that you took for your class. Test yourself on the words in the recall section. This is what we mean by recite.
Reflect	4. You should reflect on the information that you received during the lecture. Determine how your ideas fit in with the information.
Review	5. If you review your notes, you will remember a great deal more when you take your exam.
Binder & paper	Remember, it is a good idea to keep your notes in a standard-sized binder. Also, you should use only full-sized binder paper. You will be able to add photocopied materials easily to your binder.
Hints	Abbreviations and symbols should be used when possible. Abbrev. & sym. give you time when used automatically.

The example below applies the Cornell method of note taking to the biology passage on the circulatory system that you have already read (see page 127). Although the creators of this method recommend the writing of sentence summaries, you may find that short phrases can sometimes be as or more efficient and still adequately communicate the message for later study.

Circulatory Systems	
<u>2 types</u>	For transporting blood to cells
• Open	Blood moves through body cavity
	Bathes cells directly
EX:	insects, other arthropods, some other organisms
	Oxygen enters body through network of branching tubes open to atmosphere on outside of animal
	Blood moves more slowly
	Blood does not supply cells with oxygen
• Closed	Blood flows through vessels with many branches
	Blood responsible for oxygen transport
	Blood moves quickly
	Has pumping mechanism (heart)
EX:	All vertebrates, some invertebrates (annelid worms, earthworm)

Advantages of Cornell-style notes.   This method clearly lines up the major ideas on the left with the supporting details on the right. It is easy to use and flexible for a variety of materials, whether in textbooks or lectures. Self- and partner quizzes are easy when the labels on the left are used as questions and the answers on the right are covered.

EXERCISE 3.3   ## Taking Cornell-Style Notes

Using a variety of markings, annotate the following selection as if you were preparing for a quiz on the material. Remember, do not underscore as you read but wait until you finish a paragraph or a section, and then mark the important points and add marginal notes. Prepare a two-column sheet and take notes using the Cornell method.

WHY THE FOOD PYRAMID HAS BEEN REVISED

The limitations of the USDA Food Guide Pyramid have resulted in serious criticisms about the effectiveness of the Pyramid as a tool and led nutrition experts to question its usefulness in designing a healthful diet. One major criticism is that it is overly simple and does not help consumers make appropriate food selections within each food group. For example, all the grains and cereals are grouped into one category with no distinction made between whole and refined grains or carbohydrates. A serving of Fruit Loops "counts" the same as a serving of oatmeal.

Yet nutritionists know that whole-grain foods contain important nutrients, such as fiber, vitamins, and minerals—nutrients that are typically lost when grains are refined. To help make up for this loss, some of these nutrients, but not all, are added back through a process called enrichment (or fortification). Whole grains are also high in fiber, increase the feeling of fullness, and are typically digested more slowly than refined grains, gradually releasing glucose into the blood. In contrast, refined-grain foods are low in fiber and typically high in simple sugars, causing a spike in blood glucose and contributing to increased hunger shortly after their consumption.

A second criticism is that the Pyramid makes a poor distinction between healthful and unhealthful fats. All the fats are lumped together at the tip of the Pyramid, and consumers are told to use them "sparingly." Not all fats have the same effect on health so they cannot be easily grouped together. We want to limit our intake of saturated and trans fats, while making sure our diets are adequate in the monounsaturated and polyunsaturated fats that are essential for good health and may protect against disease.

A third criticism is that the serving sizes suggested in the Food Guide Pyramid are unrealistic or do not coincide with typical serving sizes of foods listed on food labels. For instance, one serving of a muffin as defined in the Food Guide Pyramid is 1.5 ounces, but most muffins available to consumers range from 2 ounces to 8 ounces! The way that foods are packaged is also confusing to consumers. Unless people read food labels carefully, it is easy to consume an entire package of a food that contains multiple servings and assume that the entire package is equal to one serving. For example, it is common to find soft drinks sold in 20 fluid ounce bottles. Although the serving size listed on the label is 8 fluid ounces, and total servings per bottle is listed as 2.5, most people just drink the entire bottle in one sitting and assume they had one soft drink.

—Janice Thompson and Melinda Manore,
Nutrition: An Applied Approach

Review your annotations using the Annotation Checklist on page 129. Have you sufficiently marked the main idea and the significant supporting details?

EXERCISE 3.4   **Taking Cornell-Style Notes**

In college courses, you will usually take notes on lengthy chapters or entire books. For practice with note taking here, use the passage "Work Schedules" in Exercise 3.2, which you have already annotated (see pages 128–129). Prepare a two-column sheet and take notes using the Cornell method.

Outlining

Outlining enables you to organize and highlight major points and subordinate items of lesser importance. At a glance, the indentations, Roman numerals, numbers, and letters quickly show how one idea relates to another and how all aspects relate to the whole. The layout of the outline is simply a graphic display of main ideas and significant supporting details.

The following example is a picture-perfect version of the basic outline form. In practice, your "working outline" would probably not be as detailed or as formal as this one is. Use the tools of the outline format, *especially the indentations and numbers,* to devise your own system for organizing information.

I. First main idea
   A. Supporting idea
      1. Detail
      2. Detail
      3. Detail
        a. Minor detail
        b. Minor detail
   B. Supporting idea
      1. Detail
      2. Detail
   C. Supporting idea
II. Second main idea
   A. Supporting idea
   B. Supporting idea

Why Outline?   Students who outline usually drop the precision of picture-perfect outlines but still make good use of numbers, letters, indentations, and a mixture of topics and phrases to show levels of importance. A quick look to the far left of an outline indicates the main ideas or major details, with subordinate ideas indented underneath. The letters, numbers, and indentations form a visual display of the parts that make up the whole. Good outliners use plenty of paper so that the levels of importance are evident at a glance.

How to Outline.   While listening to a class lecture, you must almost instantly receive, synthesize, and select material and, at the same time, record something for future reference. The difficulty of the task demands order and decision making. Do not be so eager to copy down every detail so that you miss the big picture. One of the most efficient methods of taking lecture notes is to use a modified outline form—a version that adds stars, circles, and underlines to emphasize further the levels of importance. After a lecture, it can be helpful to reorganize notes into a more formal outline form. The Reader's Tip, "Guidelines for Successful Outlining," provides more details about how to outline.

Advantages of Outline Notes.   Outlines are highly organized and immediately reveal levels of importance. They are good for studying because they form a mental picture that is easy to remember. Outline notes can also be photocopied, cut apart, and reassembled for active studying.

Reader's TIP   Guidelines for Successful Outlining

The most important thing to remember when you are outlining is to ask yourself, *"What is my purpose?"* You don't need to include everything, and you don't need a picture-perfect version for study notes. Include only what you believe you will need to remember later and use a numbering system and indentations to show how one item relates to another. There are several other important guidelines to remember:

- **Get a general overview before you start.**
  How many main topics do there seem to be?
- **Use phrases rather than sentences.**
  Can you state it in a few short words?
- **Put it in your own words.**
  If you cannot paraphrase it, do you really understand it?
- **Be selective.**
  Are you recording key points or completely rewriting?
- **After outlining, indicate key terms with a yellow highlighter.**
  Highlighting makes key terms highly visible for later review and self-testing.

EXAMPLE   Notice how numbers, letters, and indentations are used in the following outline to show levels of importance.

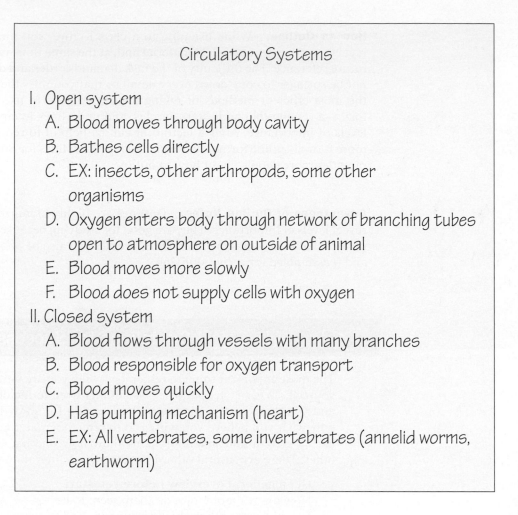

Circulatory Systems

I. Open system
   A. Blood moves through body cavity
   B. Bathes cells directly
   C. EX: insects, other arthropods, some other organisms
   D. Oxygen enters body through network of branching tubes open to atmosphere on outside of animal
   E. Blood moves more slowly
   F. Blood does not supply cells with oxygen
II. Closed system
   A. Blood flows through vessels with many branches
   B. Blood responsible for oxygen transport
   C. Blood moves quickly
   D. Has pumping mechanism (heart)
   E. EX: All vertebrates, some invertebrates (annelid worms, earthworm)

EXERCISE 3.5   **Taking Outline Notes**

Outline the key ideas in the following selection as if you were planning to use your notes to study for a quiz. Annotate as you read and then outline.

REACTING TO STRESS WITH DEFENSE MECHANISMS

Stress may occasionally promote positive outcomes. Motivated to overcome stress and the situations that produce it, we may learn new and adaptive responses. It is also clear, however, that stress involves a very unpleasant emotional component. Anxiety is a general feeling of tension or apprehension that often accompanies a perceived threat to one's well-being. It is this unpleasant emotional component that often prompts us to learn new responses to rid ourselves of stress.

There are a number of techniques, essentially self-deception, that we may employ to keep from feeling the unpleasantness associated with stress. These techniques, or tricks we play on ourselves, are not adaptive in the sense of helping us to get rid of anxiety by getting rid of the source of stress. Rather, they are mechanisms that we can and do use to defend ourselves against the *feelings* of stress. They are called **defense mechanisms**. Freud believed defense mechanisms to be the work of the unconscious mind. He claimed that they are ploys that our unconscious mind uses to protect us (our *self* or *ego*) from stress and anxiety. Many psychologists take issue with Freud's interpretation of defense mechanisms and consider defense mechanisms in more general terms than did Freud, but few will deny that defense mechanisms exist. It *is* true that they are generally ineffective if consciously or purposively employed. The list of defense mechanisms is a long one. Here, we'll review some of the more common defense mechanisms, providing an example of each, to give you an idea of how they might serve as a reaction to stress.

Repression. The notion of **repression** is the most basic of all the defense mechanisms. It is sometimes referred to as *motivated forgetting,* which gives us a good idea of what is involved. Repression is a matter of conveniently forgetting about some stressful, anxiety-producing event, conflict, or frustration. Paul had a teacher in high school he did not get along with at all. After spending an entire semester trying his best to do whatever was asked, Paul failed the course. The following summer, while walking with his girlfriend, Paul encountered this teacher. When he tried to introduce his girlfriend, Paul could not remember his teacher's name. He had repressed it. As a long-term reaction to stress, repressing the names of people we don't like or that we associate with unpleasant, stressful experiences is certainly not a very adaptive reaction. But at least it can protect us from dwelling on such unpleasantness.

Denial. **Denial** is a very basic mechanism of defense against stress. In denial, a person simply refuses to acknowledge the realities of a stressful situation. When a physician first tells a patient that he or she has a terminal illness, a common reaction is denial; the patient refuses to believe that there is anything seriously wrong.

Other less stressful events than serious illness sometimes evoke denial. Many smokers are intelligent individuals who are well aware of the data and the statistics that can readily convince them that they are slowly (or rapidly) killing themselves by continuing to smoke. But they deny the evidence. Somehow they are able to convince themselves that they aren't going to die from smoking; that's something that happens to other people, and besides, they *could* stop whenever they wanted.

Rationalization. **Rationalization** amounts to making excuses for our behaviors when facing the real reasons for our behaviors would be stressful. The real reason Kevin failed his psychology midterm is that he didn't study for it and has missed a number of classes. Kevin hates to admit, even to himself, that he could have been so stupid as to flunk that exam because of his own actions. As a result, he rationalizes: "It wasn't really *my* fault. I had a lousy instructor. We used a rotten text. The tests were grossly unfair. I've been fighting the darn flu all semester. And Marjorie had that big party the night before the exam." Now Susan, on the other hand, really did want to go to Marjorie's party, but she decided that she wouldn't go unless somebody asked her. As it happens, no one did. In short order, Susan rationalized that she "didn't want to go to that dumb party anyway"; she needed to "stay home and study."

Compensation. We might best think of **compensation** in the context of personal frustration. This defense mechanism is a matter of overemphasizing some positive trait or ability to counterbalance a shortcoming in some other trait or ability. If some particular goal-directed behavior becomes blocked, a person may compensate by putting extra effort and attention into some other aspect of behavior. For example, Karen, a seventh grader, wants to be popular. She's a reasonably bright and pleasant teenager, but isn't—in the judgment of her classmates—very pretty. Karen *may* compensate for her lack of good looks by studying very hard to be a good student, or by memorizing jokes and funny stories, or by becoming a good musician. Compensation is not just an attempt to be a well-rounded individual. It is a matter of expending *extra* energy and resources in one direction to offset shortcomings in other directions.

Fantasy. **Fantasy** is one of the more common defense mechanisms used by college students. It is often quite useful. Particularly after a hard day when stress levels are high, isn't it pleasant to sit in a comfortable chair, kick off your shoes, lie back, close your eyes, and daydream, perhaps about graduation day, picturing yourself walking across the stage to pick up your diploma—with honors?

When things are not going well for us, we may retreat into a world of fantasy where everything always goes well. Remember that to engage from time to time in fantasizing is a normal and acceptable response to stress. You should not get worried if you fantasize occasionally. On the other hand, you should realize that there are some potential dangers here. You need to be able to keep separate those activities that are real and those that occur in your fantasies. And you should realize that fantasy in itself will not solve whatever problem is causing you stress. Fantasizing about academic successes may help you feel better for a while, but it is not likely to make you a better student. . . .

The list of defense mechanisms provided above is not an exhaustive one. These are among the most common, and this list gives you an idea of what defense mechanisms are like.

—Josh R. Gerow, *Psychology: An Introduction,* 2nd ed., pp. 393–395.
Reprinted by permission of Pearson Education, Inc., Upper Saddle River, NJ

EXERCISE 3.6

Taking Outline Notes

For additional practice, outline the selection on "Work Schedules" beginning on page 128. Use your annotations and notes to help.

EXERCISE 3.7

Taking Outline Notes

For further practice, outline the selection "Why the Food Pyramid Has Been Revised" beginning on page 133. Use your annotations and notes to help.

BRAIN BOOSTER

Sleep and Problem Solving

Math students were taught a way to solve a set of problems but were told that there was also an easier method. Twelve hours after the math lesson, 20% discovered the easier method on their own. If the learners had 8 hours of sleep during the 12 hours, 60% discovered the trick! The experiment was done many times with the same results. It appears that our brains use time when the rest of the body is sleeping to consolidate the information it has processed earlier. Although just putting a book under the pillow while you sleep won't help, reading, studying the material, and then sleeping will.

—*Adapted from John J. Medina,* Brain Rules. © 2008
John J. Medina. Pear Press: Seattle, WA

Reader's TIP) How to Map

Use the following steps for mapping:

- **Draw a circle or a box** in the middle of a page. In it write the subject or topic of the material.
- **Determine the main ideas** that support the subject and write them on lines radiating from the central circle or box.
- **Determine the significant details** and write them on lines attached to each main idea. The number of details that you include will depend on the material and your purpose.

Mapping

Mapping is a visual system of condensing material to show relationships and levels of importance. A map is a diagram of the major points, with their significant subpoints, that support a topic. The purpose of mapping as an organizing strategy is to improve memory by grouping material in a highly visual way.

Why Map?   Proponents of popular learning-style theories would say that mapping offers a visual organization that appeals to learners with a preference for spatial representation, as opposed to the linear mode offered by outlining and Cornell-style note taking. A map provides a quick reference to overview an article or a chapter and can be used to reduce notes for later study. The Reader's Tip, "How to Map," shows the steps in mapping.

Maps are not restricted to any one pattern but can be formed in a variety of creative shapes, as the diagrams illustrate below.

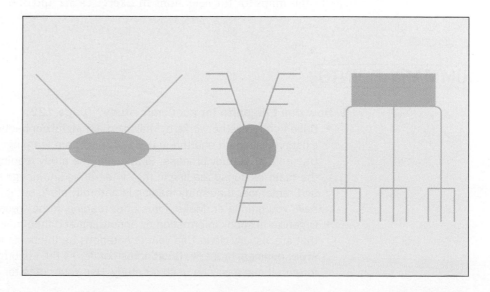

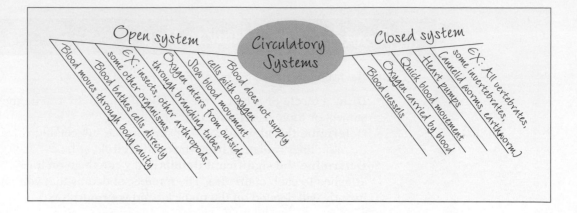

Advantages of Map Notes.   Map notes that are neatly done have the greatest visual impact of the three methods described in this chapter. They should be reserved for relatively small amounts of information. Otherwise, they become very crowded and resemble the web of a very disturbed spider! Like outline notes, maps lend themselves well to a jigsaw puzzle study activity. Cut up a photocopy of your map notes and arrange the elements to re-create the proper relationships.

The map above highlights the biology passage on the circulatory system (see page 127). Notice how the visual display emphasizes the groups of ideas supporting the topic.

EXERCISE 3.8   **Taking Map Notes**

Return to Exercise 3.5 on page 136 and design a map for the selection entitled "Reacting to Stress with Defense Mechanisms," which you previously outlined. Use your outline to help you design the map. Experiment with several different shapes for your map patterns on notebook or unlined paper. For additional practice, design maps for the selections in Exercises 3.2 and 3.3.

SUMMARY POINTS

1   **How can I organize for academic study? (page 122)**
   - Build knowledge networks by making meaningful connections between your existing schemata and the material that you are learning.
   - Use an active study process. Read using the study reading technique. Annotate the material during reading in the "integrating knowledge" stage. Be patient and remember that study reading is naturally slow, but it is thorough and will save you time later. Make notes after reading in the "recall" stage.
   - Organize textbook information by annotating and then making separate notes that are visually clear. Use your annotations as the basis for notes in the Cornell style, outlines, or maps. Good notes condense the important information into a form that can easily be used for study. Use your notes for active study.

2 How should I annotate textbooks? (page 125)
- Actively sort major ideas from supporting information and mark them differently. Circling major details and underlining minor ones works well.
- Use a consistent system of symbols and abbreviations.
- Make brief notes in the margin that relate to the markings in the text.
- Annotate *after* reading a unit of thought, such as a paragraph or a section.

3 How can I make notes from textbook reading? (page 130)
- Use the Cornell method (page 130). Divide your paper with a vertical line about two and one-half inches from the left side of the page. Write the topic at the top. Use the space on the left to write major ideas and labels—usually, the marginal notes that you wrote while you were annotating and sometimes the items that you circled. Use the column on the right side for the explanatory details that you need to remember—usually, the items that you underlined while you were annotating.
- Use outline form (page 134). Write the topic at the top. Then, use the standard system of Roman numerals, capital letters, numbers, and lowercase letters to illustrate the levels of importance of the information. Usually, the marginal notes of your annotations form the Roman numerals, circled ideas form the capital letters, and underlined items form the numbers and lowercase letters.
- Use map notes (page 139). Organize the topic and your annotations within a pattern of rectangles, circles, or other shapes, and connect the shapes to illustrate their relationships. Be sure that major details connect to the topic and that minor details connect to the major details.

SELECTION 1   # Business Communications MyReadingLab

Visit Chapter 3: Organizing Textbook Information for Study in MyReadingLab to complete the Selection 1 activities and the Build Background Knowledge video activity.

PREVIEW the next selection to predict its purpose and organization and to formulate your learning plan.

Activate Schemata

How important is the brand name of a product?
Would you buy a car whose name means "It doesn't go" in your language?

Establish a Purpose for Reading

Read the following excerpt from a marketing text to learn the importance of careful language in the advertising business.

Build Background Knowledge — VIDEO

Google Takes On Translation

To prepare for reading Selection 1, answer the questions below. Then, watch this video on the difficulties and misunderstandings that arise when translating language.

Why do you think it is so difficult to translate the meaning behind sayings such as: "Blood is thicker than water" to someone who does not speak English?

How do you think U.S. companies that have overseas business contacts can best address language translation issues?

How difficult would it be for you to translate the figure of speech: "It's raining cats and dogs" to someone who does not speak English?

This video helped me: _____

_____

_____

Increase Word Knowledge

What do you know about these words?

innocuous	marketer	blunders	characters	disparaging
frumpy	provocative	adapting	nuances	phonetic

Your instructor may give a brief vocabulary review before or after reading.

Integrate Knowledge While Reading

Questions have been inserted in the margin to stimulate your thinking while reading. Remember to

Predict   Picture   Relate   Monitor   Correct   Annotate

Skill Development: Note Taking

Annotate this selection and then make Cornell-style notes of the key ideas as if you were planning to use your notes to study for a quiz.

WATCH YOUR LANGUAGE!

Many global companies have had difficulty crossing the language barrier, with results ranging from mild embarrassment to outright failure. Seemingly innocuous brand names and advertising phrases can take on unintended or hidden meanings when translated into other languages. Careless translations can make a marketer
5 look downright foolish to foreign consumers.

The classic language blunders involve standardized brand names that do not translate well. When Coca-Cola first marketed Coke in China in the 1920s, it developed a group of Chinese characters that, when pronounced, sounded like the product name. Unfortunately, the characters actually translated as "bite the wax tadpole."
10 Now, the characters on Chinese Coke bottles translate as "happiness in the mouth."

Several modern-day marketers have had similar problems when their brand names crashed into the language barrier. Chevy's Nova translated into Spanish as *no va*—"it doesn't go." GM changed the name to Caribe (Spanish for Caribbean) and sales increased. Microsoft's operating system, Vista, turned out to be a disparaging
15 term for a frumpy old woman in Latvia. Rolls-Royce avoided the name Silver Mist in German markets, where *mist* means "manure." Sunbeam, however, entered the German market with its Mist Stick hair-curling iron. As should have been expected, the Germans had little use for a "manure wand." IKEA marketed a children's workbench named FARTFULL (the word means "speedy" in Swedish)—it soon discon-
20 tinued the product.

What would be a good heading for paragraphs 2, 3, & 4?

Interbrand of London, the firm that created household names such as Prozac and Acura, recently developed a brand-name "hall of shame" list, which contained these and other foreign brand names you're never likely to see inside the local Safeway: Krapp toilet paper (Denmark), Crapsy Fruit cereal (France), Poo curry powder
25 (Argentina), and Pschitt lemonade (France).

Is this paragraph about a different topic than paragraphs 2, 3, & 4?

Travelers often encounter well-intentioned advice from service firms that takes on meanings very different from those intended. The menu in one Swiss restaurant proudly stated, "Our wines leave you nothing to hope for." Signs in a Japanese hotel pronounced, "You are invited to take advantage of the chambermaid." At a laundry
30 in Rome, it was, "Ladies, leave your clothes here and spend the afternoon having a good time."

Advertising themes often lose—or gain—something in the translation. The Coors beer slogan "get loose with Coors" in Spanish came out as "get the runs with Coors." Coca-Cola's "Coke adds life" theme in Japanese translated into "Coke brings

Some standardized brand names do not translate well globally.
Francois Le Diascorn/Getty Images

35 your ancestors back from the dead." The milk industry learned too late that its American advertising question "Got Milk?" translated in Mexico as a more provocative "Are you lactating?" In Chinese, the KFC slogan "finger-lickin' good" came out as "eat your finger off." And Motorola's Hellomoto ring tone sounds like "Hello Fatty" in India. Even when the language is the same, word usage may differ from country to 40 country. Thus, the British ad line for Electrolux vacuum cleaners—"Nothing sucks like an Electrolux"—would capture few customers in the United States.

This paragraph is different than all the rest. What would be a good heading?

Thus, crossing the language barrier involves much more than simply translating names and slogans into other languages. "You can't uproot a concept and just translate it and put it into another market," says one translation consultant. "It's not 45 really about translating word for word, but actually adapting a certain meaning." Beyond just word meanings and nuances, international marketers must also consider things such as phonetic appeal and even associations with historical figures, legends, and other factors. The consultant points to the Chinese adaptation of the name for eBay's online free classified ads service—Kijiji (which means "village" in 50 Swahili)—as a localization success story. "In Chinese, the three characters used to phonetically represent the Kijiji name map almost exactly to the English pronunciation," she says. "Plus, they have the meaning of people pulling together to share things, which is totally descriptive of the business and brand."

(624 words)

—From Gary Armstrong and Philip Kotler,
Marketing: An Introduction, 9th ed., © 2009, p. 469.
Reprinted by permission of Pearson Education, Inc., Upper Saddle River, NJ.

Sources: Quotes from Randall Frost, "Lost in Translation," *Brandchannel.com*, November 13, 2006. For the above and other examples, see David A. Ricks, "Perspectives: Translation Blunders in International Business," *Journal of Language for International Business* 7, no. 2, 1996, pp. 50–55; Thomas T. Sermon, "Cutting Corners in Language Risky Business," *Marketing News*, April 23, 2001, p. 9; Martin Croft, "Mind Your Language," *Marketing*, June 19, 2003, pp. 35–39; Mark Lasswell, "Lost in Translation," *Business 2.0*, August 2004, pp. 68–70; "Lost in Translation," *Hispanic*, May 2005, p. 12; and Ross Thomson, "Lost in Translation," *Medical Marketing and Media*, March 2005, p. 82.

Recall

Review your notes. Stop to talk, write, and think about the selection.

Your instructor may choose to give you a brief comprehension review.

THINK CRITICALLY ABOUT THE SELECTION

If you, as a marketing manager for your company, were charged with creating a brand name for a new product, what factors would you have to consider?

How might you design a marketing campaign to recover from a branding mistake like those mentioned in the selection?

WRITE ABOUT THE SELECTION

Considering how easy it is to make a critical mistake when promoting a product or service in a foreign language and culture, how would you avoid such errors?

Response Suggestion: Imagine that you want to sell a product in a foreign country. How will you design a brand name and an advertising slogan that will appeal to the target audience? Whom will you consult? How will you learn about the language and the culture?

CHECK YOUR COMPREHENSION

After reading the selection, answer the following questions with *a, b, c,* or *d*. To help you analyze your strengths and weaknesses, the question types are indicated.

Main Idea ———— 1. Which is the best statement of the main idea of this selection?

  a. Advertising is a complicated business.
  b. Inattention to the language and customs of the target audience can be the downfall of an advertising campaign.
  c. Appealing brand names are important to sales.
  d. Advertising phrases that are designed to convince customers to pay for a service do not always translate well into a foreign language.

Detail ———— 2. Rolls-Royce changed the name of its Silver Mist model for the German car market because

  a. *mist* means manure in German.
  b. people associated the name with gray hair and aging.
  c. the sound of the name in German was offensive.
  d. The English word *silver* has an offensive meaning in German.

Main Idea ———— 3. Which statement best describes the point made by the details in paragraphs 2–4?

  a. American marketers often make foolish mistakes.
  b. Descriptions of the services that businesses offer do not always mean what is intended when they are translated into foreign languages.
  c. Brand names do not always translate appropriately into foreign languages.
  d. Sales of GM's Nova model increased when its name was changed to Caribe for the Spanish-speaking market.

Inference ———— 4. We can infer from the selection that

  a. Rolls-Royce researched the appropriateness of using the Silver Mist model name before marketing its car in Germany.
  b. the "Got Milk?" slogan translates very well into other languages.
  c. Krapp toilet paper would probably sell well in the United States because of the humorous brand name.
  d. Microsoft likely kept the name Vista when it marketed that product in Latvia.

Main Idea ———— 5. The main point made in paragraphs 5 and 6 is that

  a. direct translations of brand names into a foreign language do not always work.
  b. advertising slogans do not necessarily translate well into foreign languages.
  c. Coors's slogan translated into Spanish as "Get loose with Coors."
  d. Coca-Cola's unfortunate slogan meant "Coke brings your ancestors back from the dead" in Japanese.

Inference _____ 6. "Household names" as used in paragraph 4 means

  a. the names of famous interior designers.
  b. model names of popular cars.
  c. brands of household cleaning products.
  d. names that are commonly recognized.

Detail _____ 7. Which of the following examples illustrates successful market research?

  a. Motorola's Hellomoto ring tone for the Indian market
  b. The Chinese name for eBay's free online classifieds service
  c. For English speakers, the name of IKEA's workbench for children
  d. KFC's Chinese translation of "finger-lickin' good"

Inference _____ 8. In paragraph 3, the phrase "crashed into the language barrier" means that

  a. companies encountered problems with government regulations.
  b. marketers found that their brand names would not translate well into the languages of the target audiences.
  c. sales exceeded expectations because of the public attention created by poor brand name translations.
  d. products were banned in certain countries because of their offensive brand names.

Detail _____ 9. The author of this selection advises doing all of the following *except*

  a. testing the sound of the product name in the target language.
  b. directly translating the brand name or slogan to preserve brand recognition.
  c. researching associations with historical figures.
  d. finding a name that conveys the meaning of the English brand name.

Detail _____ 10. The examples in this selection

  a. were created by the author to illustrate the point.
  b. came from several business-related publications.
  c. came from the author's personal experience.
  d. all illustrated critical marketing mistakes.

Answer the following with *T* (true) or *F* (false):

Author's Purpose _____ 11. The author's purpose was to inform the reader of the importance of market research by giving humorous examples.

Detail _____ 12. Coca-Cola kept the labeling on its soft drink even though the direct translation into Chinese was "bite the wax tadpole."

Inference _____ 13. The purpose of the last paragraph is to illustrate foolish marketing mistakes.

Detail _____ 14. Rolls-Royce changed the name of its Silver Mist model before marketing the car in Germany.

Inference _____ 15. Sunbeam failed to test the name of its Mist Stick hair-curling iron in the German market before introducing the product.

BUILD YOUR VOCABULARY

According to the way the italicized word was used in the selection, indicate *a, b, c,* or *d* for the word or phrase that gives the best definition. The number in parentheses indicates the line of the passage in which the word is located. Use a dictionary in addition to the context clues to more precisely define the terms.

_____ 1. *"innocuous* brand names" (2)
  a. disastrous
  b. inappropriate
  c. harmless, inoffensive
  d. humorous

_____ 2. "a *marketer* look downright foolish" (4)
  a. seller
  b. product
  c. company executive
  d. buyer

_____ 3. "classic language *blunders*" (6)
  a. jokes
  b. translations
  c. parts of speech
  d. mistakes

_____ 4. "Chinese *characters*" (9)
  a. celebrities
  b. officials
  c. symbols representing words or ideas
  d. names of cartoon personalities

_____ 5. "a *disparaging* term" (14)
  a. flattering
  b. honorable
  c. angry
  d. insulting

_____ 6. "a *frumpy* old woman" (15)
  a. well-dressed
  b. unattractive, old-fashioned
  c. stylish
  d. poor

_____ 7. "a more *provocative*" (36)
  a. formal
  b. suggestive
  c. complicated
  d. acceptable

_____ 8. *"adapting* a certain meaning" (45)
  a. accepting as one's own
  b. understanding
  c. making suitable for a purpose
  d. explaining

_____ 9. "word meanings and *nuances*" (46)
  a. definitions
  b. spellings
  c. subtle shades of meaning
  d. uses of language

_____ 10. *"phonetic* appeal" (47)
  a. having to do with spelling
  b. pertaining to the meaning
  c. cultural
  d. relating to the sound of words or letters

Concept Prep for Communications and Language

A Sampling of Careers in Communications and Language

A bachelor's degree in communications or languages prepares students for many careers, some of which might require additional degrees or training.

- Advertising executive
- Public relations manager
- Speech, drama, journalism teacher
- Sales representative
- Lawyer
- Reporter
- Translator
- Diplomat
- Student tour coordinator

What is communications?

It is not unusual that, given the importance of mass communication in our daily lives, *communications* is one of the fastest growing departments in many colleges. The courses that focus on technologically based means of communicating examine the role of mass media in educating the public and influencing cultural, social, and economic change. Popular courses include mass media, journalism, film, and video. Other communications courses, which you are more likely to take as introductory courses, focus on interpersonal and intrapersonal communications. The courses are usually interactive and stress group and team performance by learning leadership and responsible group membership skills.

What are the important elements of communications?

- Public speakers and others in leadership roles usually have *charisma*, a magnetically charming personality and an extraordinary power to inspire loyalty and enthusiasm in others. Leaders such as John F. Kennedy and Martin Luther King, Jr. are described as charismatic.
- *Ethics* is another significant aspect of sound leadership, team performance, and business. Ethical decision making and behavior are aimed at distinguishing between right and wrong and acting in a manner that is morally correct and virtuous.
- When you are speaking formally, use fresh and concise language. Avoid using *clichés* such as "Don't let the cat out of the bag" and "Let's get down to brass tacks." These hackneyed, overused expressions were probably humorous when they were first used but are now considered to be tiresome. If they are interpreted literally, exactly word for word, the phrases do not make sense. The words are intentionally designed to take on a new descriptive or figurative meaning. In the previous phrases, the "cat in the bag" is a secret, and the "brass tacks" are the real issues. Such phrases are also called *idioms*, and they are especially confusing to people who are not native English speakers.
- Use appropriate *diction* for your audience. Diction refers to your choice of words. It can also refer to the quality of your pronunciation. Use clear and effective words, and enunciate them correctly.
- If you don't want giggles in the audience, avoid *double entendres*—expressions that have a double meaning. The second meaning is usually a mischievous and sexual interpretation of an innocent expression, such as "The athletes were hanging out in the locker room."
- More giggles may occur if you make a *malapropism*, a humorous confusion of two words that sound alike. Saying "a blue tarpon was spread over the building under repair" will have your audience envisioning a huge blue fish covering the structure rather than a large plastic tarp.
- Give credit when you use the words or ideas of another person. To steal the thoughts of others and use them as your own is *plagiarism*. Acknowledging credit to others does not detract from your work but, rather, enhances your status as a researcher.

American civil rights activist Dr. Martin Luther King, Jr. delivers his "I Have a Dream" speech at the Lincoln Memorial for the March on Washington on August 28, 1963.

Agence France Presse/Getty Images

- If you are duplicating published materials for distribution to a group, obtain *copyright* permission so that you are not acting illegally. A copy-right is legal protection that is granted to an author or a publishing company to prevent others from pirating a body of work. To obtain reprint permission, you will probably need to pay a fee.

- When you receive constructive criticism, don't be a *prima donna*. The words are derived from Latin and refer to the "first lady" in an opera. The connotation, however, is that the person is overly sensitive and difficult to work with. If you become a prima donna, you may suddenly discover that you are a *persona non grata*, a person who is no longer acceptable or in favor.

- Strive for excellence, and perhaps you will graduate with honors or *cum laude*. Colleges differ on the grade point averages that are required for different designations of distinction and high honor. At some institutions, a cumulative grade point average of 3.500–3.699 is required for *cum laude*, a 3.700–3.899 for *magna cum laude*, and a 3.900–4.000 for *summa cum laude*. Some students, however, are satisfied to graduate with a "Thank the Lordy."

REVIEW QUESTIONS

After studying the material, answer the following questions:

1. What areas are usually included in a communications department? _____ _____

2. What is ethical behavior? _____ _____

3. What is a cliché? _____

4. What is good diction? _____

5. What is a double entendre? _____ _____

6. What is a malapropism? _____ _____

7. What is plagiarism? _____

8. What is a prima donna? _____

9. What is a *persona non grata*? _____

10. What is *summa cum laude*? _____

Your instructor may choose to give a brief review of these communications and language concepts.

| SELECTION 2 | Health | MyReadingLab |

Visit Chapter 3: Organizing Textbook Information for Study in MyReadingLab to complete the Selection 2 activities and the Build Background Knowledge video activity.

PREVIEW the next selection to predict its purpose and organization and to formulate your learning plan.

Activate Schemata

What causes stress for you, and what is your response to it?
How is nutrition related to stress?

Establish a Purpose for Reading

Do you have any bad habits that sabotage your energy? What can you do to attain a higher level of performance? After recalling what you already know about keeping your body healthy, read this selection to explain the scientific impact of nutrition, exercise, and stress on the body.

Build Background Knowledge — VIDEO

Reducing Stress for College Students

To prepare for reading Selection 2, answer the questions below. Then, watch this video on managing stress in college.

What causes you the most stress in college?

Besides making changes to exercise and diet, what other ways can you reduce stress?

How has technology increased stress for college students?

This video helped me: _____

_____

_____

Increase Word Knowledge

What do you know about these words?

| correlated | perceptions | appraisal | reprimanding | cultivate |
| irrational | derogatory | suppressing | de-escalate | endorphin |

Your instructor may give a brief vocabulary review before or after reading.

Integrate Knowledge While Reading

Questions have been inserted in the margin to stimulate your thinking while reading. Remember to

| Predict | Picture | Relate | Monitor | Correct | Annotate |

SKILL DEVELOPMENT: NOTE TAKING

Annotate the selection as you read. Use an informal outline to take notes as if you were planning to use them to study for a quiz.

MANAGING STRESS IN COLLEGE

Reasons

College students thrive under a certain amount of stress, but excessive stress can overwhelm many. Studies have indicated that first-year students report not only more problems with stress, but also more emotional reactivity in the form of anger, hostility, frustration, and a greater sense of being out of control. Sophomores and juniors re5 ported fewer problems with these issues, and seniors reported the fewest problems. This may indicate students' progressive emotional growth through experience, maturity, increased awareness of support services, and more social connections.

Students generally report using health-enhancing methods to combat stress, but research has found that students sometimes resort to health-compromising 10 activities to escape the stress and anxiety of college. Numerous researchers have found stress among college students to be correlated to unhealthy behaviors such as substance abuse, lack of physical activity, poor psychological and physical health, lack of social problem solving, and infrequent use of social support networks.

Being on your own in college may pose challenges, but it also lets you take 15 control of and responsibility for your life. Although you can't eliminate all life stressors, you can train yourself to recognize the events that cause stress and to anticipate your reactions to them. **Coping** is the act of managing events or conditions to lessen the physical or psychological effects of excess stress. One of the most effective ways to combat stressors is to build coping strategies and skills, 20 known collectively as *stress-management techniques,* such as those discussed in the following sections.

PRACTICING MENTALLY TO REDUCE STRESS

Stress management isn't something that just happens. It calls for getting a handle on what is going on in your life, taking a careful look at yourself, and coming up with a personal plan of action. Because your perceptions are often part of the problem, 25 assessing your self-talk, beliefs, and actions are good first steps. Why are you so stressed? How much of it is due to perception rather than reality? What's a realistic plan of action for you? Think about your situation and map out a strategy for change. The tools in this section will help you.

Assess Your Stressors and Solve Problems

Assessing what is really going on in your life is an important first step to solving
30 problems and reducing your stress. Here's how:

- Make a list of the major
things that you are wor-
ried about right now.
35
- Examine the causes of the
problems and worries.
- Consider how big each
problem is. What are the
consequences of doing
nothing? Of taking action?
40
- List your options, including ones that you may not
like very much.
- Outline an action plan, and
then *act*. Remember that even little things can sometimes make a big difference
45   and that you shouldn't expect immediate results.
- After you act, evaluate. How did you do? Do you need to change your actions to achieve a better outcome next time? How?

> ### What's Working for You?
>
> Maybe you're already on your way to a
> less-stressed life. Below is a list of some things
> you can do to cope with stress. Which of these
> are you already incorporating into your life?
>
> ❑ I listen to relaxing music.
> ❑ I exercise regularly.
> ❑ I get 8 hours of sleep each night.
> ❑ I practice deep breathing.

One useful way of coping with your stressors, once you have identified them, is
to consciously anticipate and prepare for specific stressors, a technique known as
50 **stress inoculation.** For example, suppose speaking in front of a class scares you.
Practice in front of friends or in front of a video camera to banish panic and prevent
your freezing up on the day of the presentation.

Like a vaccine to prevent disease?

Change the Way You Think and Talk to Yourself

As noted earlier, our appraisal of a situation is what makes things stressful. Several
types of negative self-talk can make things more stressful. Among the most common
55 are *pessimism,* or focusing on the negative; *perfectionism,* or expecting superhuman
standards; *"should-ing,"* or reprimanding yourself for things that you should have
done; *blaming* yourself or others for circumstances and events; and *dichotomous
thinking,* in which everything is either black or white (good or bad) instead of somewhere in between. To combat negative self-talk, we must first become aware of it,
60 then stop it, and finally replace the negative thoughts with positive ones—a process
called as **cognitive restructuring.** Once you realize that some of your thoughts may
be negative, irrational, or overreactive, interrupt this self-talk by saying, "Stop" (under your breath or aloud), and make a conscious effort to think positively.

Related to cognitive psychology in Chapter 1?

CULTIVATING YOUR SPIRITUAL SIDE

One of the most important factors in reducing stress in your life is taking the time
65 and making the commitment to cultivate your spiritual side: finding your purpose
in life and living your days more fully.

MANAGING EMOTIONAL RESPONSES

Have you ever gotten all worked up about something, only to find that your perceptions were totally wrong? We often get upset not by realities, but by our faulty perceptions.

Spending time communicating and socializing can be an important part of building a support network and reducing your stress level.
Monkey Business/Fotolia

70   Stress management requires that you examine your emotional responses to interactions with others. With any emotional response to a stressor, you are responsible for the emotion and the resulting behaviors. Learning to tell the difference between normal emotions and emotions that are based on irrational beliefs or that are expressed and interpreted in an over the-top manner can help you stop the emo-
75 tion or express it in a healthy and appropriate way.

Fight the Anger Urge

Anger usually results when we feel we have lost control of a situation or are frustrated by a situation that we can do little about. Major sources of anger include (1) perceived *threats* to self or others we care about; (2) *reactions to injustice,* such as unfair actions, policies, or behaviors; (3) *fear,* which leads to negative responses; (4)
80 *faulty emotional reasoning,* or misinterpretation of normal events; (5) *low frustration tolerance,* often fueled by stress, drugs, lack of sleep, and other factors; (6) *unreasonable expectations* about ourselves and others; and (7) *people rating,* or applying derogatory ratings to others.

    Each of us has learned by this point in our lives that we have three main
85 approaches to dealing with anger: *expressing it, suppressing it,* or *calming it.* You may be surprised to find out that, in the long run, expressing your anger is probably the healthiest thing to do, if you express anger in an assertive rather than an aggressive way. However, it's a natural reaction to want to respond aggressively, and that is what we must learn to keep at bay. To accomplish this, there are several strategies
90 you can use:

- **Identify your anger style.** Do you express anger passively or actively? Do you hold anger in, or do you explode? Do you throw the phone, smash things, or scream at others?

- **Learn to recognize patterns in your anger responses and how to de-escalate them.** For 1 week, keep track of everything that angers you or keeps you stewing. What thoughts or feelings lead up to your boiling point? Keep a journal and listen to your anger. Try to change your self-talk. Explore how you can interrupt patterns of anger, such as counting to 10, getting a drink of water, or taking some deep breaths.

- **Find the right words to de-escalate conflict.** Communicate to de-escalate. When conflict arises, be respectful and state your needs or feelings rather than shooting zingers at the other person. Avoid "you always" or "you never" and instead say, "I feel _____ when you _____" or "I would really appreciate it if you could _____." Another approach would be to say, "I really need help understanding . . . or . . . figuring out a way to _____." If you find you are continually revved up for a battle, consider taking a class or workshop on assertiveness training or anger management.

- **Plan ahead.** Explore options to minimize your exposure to anger-provoking situations such as traffic jams. Give yourself an extra 15 minutes, and learn to "chill" when unexpected delays occur.

- **Vent to your friends.** Find a few close friends you can confide in. They can provide insight or another perspective. But, don't wear down your supporter with continual rants.

- **Develop realistic expectations of yourself and others.** Anger is often the result of unmet expectations, frustrations, resentments, and impatience. Are your expectations of yourself and others realistic? Try talking about your feelings with those involved at a time when you are calm.

- **Turn complaints into requests.** When frustrated or angry with someone, try reworking the problem into a request. Instead of screaming and pounding on the wall because your neighbors are blaring music at 2:00 A.M., talk with them. Try to reach an agreement that works for everyone. Again, think ahead about the words you will use.

- **Leave past anger in the past.** Learn to resolve issues and not bring them up over and over. Let it go. If you can't, seek the counsel of a professional to learn how.

Learn to Laugh, Be Joyful, and Cry

Have you ever noticed that you feel better after a belly laugh or a good cry? Adages such as "laughter is the best medicine" and "smile and the world smiles with you" didn't evolve out of the blue. Humans have long recognized that smiling, laughing, singing, dancing, and other actions can elevate our moods, relieve stress, make us feel good, and help us improve our relationships. Learning to take yourself less seriously and laugh at yourself is a good starting place. Crying can have similar positive physiological effects in relieving tension. Several studies have indicated that laughter and joy may increase endorphin levels, increase oxygen levels in the blood, decrease stress levels, relieve pain, enhance productivity, and reduce risks of chronic disease.

Positive ways to release emotion

HOW STRESSED ARE YOU?

Let's face it: Some periods in life, including your college years, can be especially stressful! Learning to "chill" starts with an honest examination of your life experiences and your reactions to stressful situations. Respond to each section, assigning points as directed. Total the points from each section, then add them and compare to the life-stressor scale.

SELECTION 2

1 RECENT HISTORY

In the last year, how many of the following major life events have you experienced? (Give yourself **five points** for each event you experienced; if you experienced an event more than once, give yourself **ten points**, etc.)

1. Death of a close family member of friend _____
2. Ending a relationship (whether by choice or not) _____
3. Major financial upset jeopardizing your ability to stay in college _____
4. Major move, leaving friends, family, and/or your past life behind _____
5. Serious illness (you) _____
6. Serious illness (of someone you're close with) _____
7. Marriage or entering a new relationship _____
8. Loss of a beloved pet _____
9. Involved in a legal dispute or issue _____
10. Involved in a hostile, violent, or threatening relationship _____

Total _____

2 SELF-REFLECTION

For each of the following, indicate where you are on the scale of 0 to 5.

		Strongly Disagree					Strongly Agree
1.	I have a lot of worries at home and at school.	0	1	2	3	4	5
2.	My friends and/or family put too much pressure on me.	0	1	2	3	4	5
3.	I am often distracted and have trouble focusing on schoolwork.	0	1	2	3	4	5
4.	I am highly disorganized and tend to do my schoolwork at the last minute.	0	1	2	3	4	5
5.	My life seems to have far too many crisis situations.	0	1	2	3	4	5
6.	Most of my time is spent sitting; I don't get much exercise.	0	1	2	3	4	5
7.	I don't have enough control in decisions that affect my life.	0	1	2	3	4	5
8.	I wake up most days feeling tired, like I need a lot more sleep.	0	1	2	3	4	5
9.	I often have feelings that I am alone and that I don't fit in very well.	0	1	2	3	4	5
10.	I don't have many friends or people I can share my feelings or thoughts with.	0	1	2	3	4	5
11.	I am uncomfortable in my body, and I wish I could change how I look.	0	1	2	3	4	5
12.	I am very anxious about my major and whether I will get a good job after I graduate.	0	1	2	3	4	5
13.	If I have to wait in a restaurant or in lines, I quickly become irritated and upset.	0	1	2	3	4	5

		Strongly Disagree					Strongly Agree
14.	I have to win or be the best in activities or in classes or I get upset with myself.	0	1	2	3	4	5
15.	I am bothered by world events and am cynical and angry about how people behave.	0	1	2	3	4	5
16.	I have too much to do, and there are never enough hours in the day.	0	1	2	3	4	5
17.	I feel uneasy when I am caught up on my work and am relaxing or doing nothing.	0	1	2	3	4	5
18.	I sleep with my cell phone near my bed and often check messages/tweets/texts during the night.	0	1	2	3	4	5
19.	I enjoy time alone but find that I seldom get enough alone time each day.	0	1	2	3	4	5
20.	I worry about whether or not others like me.	0	1	2	3	4	5
21.	I am struggling in my classes and worry about failing.	0	1	2	3	4	5
22.	My relationship with my family is not very loving and supportive.	0	1	2	3	4	5
23.	When I watch people, I tend to be critical and think negatively about them.	0	1	2	3	4	5
24.	I believe that people are inherently selfish and untrustworthy, and I am careful around them.	0	1	2	3	4	5
25.	Life is basically unfair, and most of the time there is little I can do to change it.	0	1	2	3	4	5
26.	I give more than I get in relationships with people.	0	1	2	3	4	5
27.	I tend to believe that what I do is often not good enough or that I should do better.	0	1	2	3	4	5
28.	My friends would describe me as highly stressed and quick to react with anger and/or frustration.	0	1	2	3	4	5
29.	My friends are always telling me I "need a vacation to relax."	0	1	2	3	4	5
30.	Overall, the quality of my life right now isn't all that great.	0	1	2	3	4	5

Total _____

Scoring

Total your points from Sections 1 and 2. _____

Although the following scores are not meant to be diagnostic, they do serve as an indicator of potential problem areas. If your scores are:

0–50, your stress levels are low, but it is worth examining areas where you did score points and taking action to reduce your stress levels.

51–100, you may need to reduce certain stresses in your life. Long term stress and pressure from your stresses can be counterproductive. Consider what you can do to change your perceptions of things, your behaviors, or your environment.

100–150, you are probably pretty stressed. Examine what your major stressors are and come up with a plan for reducing your stress levels right now. Don't delay or blow this off because it could lead to significant stress-related problems, affecting your grades, your social life, and your future!

151–200, you are carrying high stress, and if you don't make changes, you could be heading for some serious difficulties. Find a counselor on campus to talk with about some of the major issues you identified above as causing stress. Try to get more sleep and exercise, and find time to relax. Surround yourself with people who are supportive of you and make you feel safe and competent.

(1,531 words)

—From Rebecca J. Donatelle, *Health: The Basics*, 11th ed.

Recall

Review your notes. Stop to talk, write, and think about the selection.

Your instructor may choose to give a brief comprehension review.

THINK CRITICALLY ABOUT THE SELECTION

If you haven't already done so, complete the stress assessment. Notice item 7 in the "Recent History" section. Why do you think that a happy occasion like marriage or a new relationship can be stressful?

Why do you think some college students resort to unhealthy and self-defeating activities when they are stressed? What are the ultimate effects?

WRITE ABOUT THE SELECTION

Which of the strategies for coping with stress do you think would work best for you?

Response suggestion: Make a list of the strategies discussed in the selection and add other positive strategies that you have found helpful. Next to each method, write a few adjectives that describe how you would expect to feel after trying it. Create a specific plan of action for the next time that you feel highly stressed. Include some way to remind yourself of your plan so that you can easily find it.

CHECK YOUR COMPREHENSION

After reading the selection, answer the following questions with *a, b, c,* or *d*. To help you analyze your strengths and weaknesses, the question types are indicated.

Main Idea _____ 1. What is the best statement of the selection's main point?

  a. Coping strategies and skills can help ease the stress that many college students feel.
  b. Stress is a serious problem among college students.
  c. Some students resort to unhealthy ways to cope with stress.
  d. Learning to manage emotional responses, especially to anger, is key to combatting stress.

Detail _____ 2. Replacing negative thoughts with positive ones is called

  a. should-ing.
  b. appraisal.
  c. de-escalation.
  d. cognitive restructuring.

Inference _____ 3. We can infer from the passage that stress inoculation works because

  a. through exposure to small doses of a stressor, we gradually reduce the impact of a similar but formerly very stressful situation.
  b. we have recognized the situations that create the most stress for us.
  c. it involves the well-researched and safe use of anti-anxiety medications.
  d. it keeps you from freezing up when you are giving a class presentation.

Main Idea _____ 4. The main idea of the section "Managing Emotional Responses" is best stated by which of the following?

  a. Crying can provide very helpful relief of tension.
  b. Uncontrolled anger can be very dangerous.
  c. Learning to respond normally to emotional triggers is a critical part of stress management.
  d. Laughter is the best medicine.

Author's Purpose _____ 5. The primary purpose of this selection is to

  a. startle readers with statistics showing the high number of college students who suffer from excessive stress.
  b. inform readers of positive stress management strategies.
  c. convince readers to pay attention to spirituality.
  d. dramatize the importance of anger management.

SELECTION 2

Detail   _____ 6. The selection states that stress among college students has been shown to correlate with

     a. uncertainty about career choices after graduation.
     b. infrequent use of social support networks.
     c. taking very heavy course loads.
     d. maintaining a job while going to college.

Detail   _____ 7. Cognitive restructuring involves

     a. planning ahead to reduce anger-producing situations.
     b. laughing more.
     c. changing the way we think and talk to ourselves.
     d. communicating to de-escalate.

Inference   _____ 8. Based on the strategies presented in the selection, the best way to de-escalate an angry conflict with another person is to say something like

     a. "If you don't stop making me look stupid, we're finished."
     b. "This is just like the last time we were at a party together."
     c. "You always make fun of me when we're with other people."
     d. "I feel disrespected when you behave that way in front of other people."

Detail   _____ 9. Which of the following is not mentioned as a major source of anger?

     a. reactions to unfairness
     b. fear
     c. physical violence
     d. faulty emotional reasoning

Main Idea (topic)   _____ 10. This selection is mostly about

     a. strategies to reduce stress.
     b. controlling anger.
     c. stressful situations.
     d. causes of stress.

Answer the following questions with (_T_) true or (_F_) false.

Detail   _____ 11. According to the selection, laughter can reduce the risk of chronic disease.

Inference   _____ 12. The selection suggests that a reasonable amount of stress can be beneficial.

Detail   _____ 13. According to this passage, expecting oneself to be perfect is a common form of negative self-talk.

Inference   _____ 14. Because it is not mentioned in the selection, we can infer that the authors do not believe that physical exercise is a good stress management strategy.

Inference   _____ 15. The passage suggests that stress is not so much what happens to us as the way we think about what happens.

BUILD YOUR VOCABULARY

According to the way the italicized word was used in the selection, indicate *a, b, c,* or *d* for the word or phrase that gives the best definition. The number in parentheses indicates the line of the passage in which the word is located. Use a dictionary in addition to the context clues to more precisely define the terms.

_____ 1. *"correlated* to unhealthy behaviors" (11)
   a. unrelated
   b. blamed
   c. linked
   d. shifted

_____ 2. *"perceptions* are often" (24)
   a. views
   b. actions
   c. plans
   d. stressors

_____ 3. "our *appraisal* of a situation" (53)
   a. response
   b. involvement
   c. facts
   d. evaluation

_____ 4. *"reprimanding* yourself" (56)
   a. praising
   b. scolding
   c. expecting
   d. trusting

_____ 5. *"cultivate* your spiritual side" (65)
   a. plant
   b. treasure
   c. emphasize
   d. develop

_____ 6. *"irrational* beliefs" (73)
   a. unreasonable
   b. strongly held
   c. logical
   d. common

_____ 7. "applying *derogatory* ratings" (82–83)
   a. complimentary
   b. sincere
   c. insulting
   d. incorrect

_____ 8. *"suppressing* it" (85)
   a. venting
   b. approving
   c. holding back
   d. rethinking

_____ 9. "Communicate to *de-escalate"* (100)
   a. encourage
   b. reduce
   c. speak
   d. deny

_____ 10. "increase *endorphin* levels" (134)
   a. hormones that contribute to natural feelings of well being
   b. stress hormones
   c. blood chemistry
   d. natural brain chemicals that are associated with memory

Concept Prep for Health

A Sampling of Careers in Health Science

For some health science careers, a medical degree is necessary. For others, a two- or four-year degree or a technology certificate is required.

- Medical assistant
- Laboratory technician
- Community health worker
- Medical sonographer
- Health care interpreter
- Surgical technician

What is blood pressure?

Blood pressure is the measure of the pressure exerted by the blood as it flows through the arteries. Blood moves in waves and is thus measured in two phases. The *systolic pressure* is the pressure at the height of the blood wave when the left ventricle of the heart contracts to push the blood through the body. The **diastolic pressure** is the pressure when the ventricles are at rest and filling with blood. The figures are expressed as the systolic "over" the diastolic pressure. The average blood pressure of a healthy adult is **120 over 80**.

What can happen to arteries as we age?

Cholesterol—a white soapy substance that is found in the body and in foods such as animal fats—can accumulate on the inner walls of the arteries—blood vessels that carry blood away from the heart—and narrow the channels through which blood flows. Nutritionists recommend eating **unsaturated fats,** such as vegetable or olive oils, as opposed to **saturated fats** (animal fats), which are solid at room temperature.

Another condition that lessens the flow of blood through the arteries is hardening of the arteries, or **arteriosclerosis**. A surgical technique called an *angioplasty* is used to clear the arteries. A catheter with a small balloon is inserted into the arteries around the heart to compress fatty deposits and restore the flow of blood.

What are some frequently discussed medical procedures?

- A **CAT scan** (computerized axial tomography) is a painless, noninvasive procedure that uses radiation to show a three-dimensional image of the body. The diagnostic procedure is used to detect tumors and other conditions. It shows differences in the density of soft tissue, with high-density substances appearing white and low-density substances appearing dark.
- An **MRI** (magnetic resonance imaging) uses magnetic fields and radio waves to detect hidden tumors and other conditions by mapping the vibration of atoms. An MRI is painless and does not use radiation.
- **Chemotherapy** is a treatment for cancer in which the patient receives chemicals that destroy

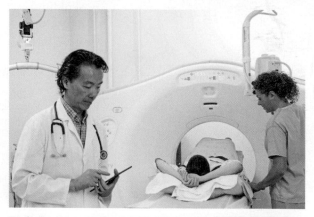

Radiologists are physicians who specialize in imaging technologies. Radiologic technologists are trained to operate equipment but not to diagnose or interpret results for medical diagnosis.

Trish23/Fotolia

cancer cells. Currently, more than 50 anticancer drugs are available for use. Temporary hair loss is a common side effect of chemotherapy.

- **Radiation** is another treatment for destroying malignant cancer cells. Unfortunately, it also destroys some healthy cells.
- A **mammogram** is an X-ray of the breast to detect tumors that are too small to be detected by other means.
- A **Pap test** is a procedure in which cells are taken from the cervical region and are tested for cancer.

- **PSA** (prostate-specific antigen) levels in the blood are measured to detect prostate cancer in men. A **prostatic ultrasound** can also be used.
- A **sonogram** or **ultrasound** test uses high-frequency sound waves to detect abnormalities. It is a noninvasive procedure that can be used to view the size, position, and sex of a fetus.
- **Amniocentesis** is a procedure for detecting abnormalities in the fetus. Fluid is drawn from the liquid surrounding the fetus by a needle through the mother's stomach. The fluid contains cells of the fetus that can be analyzed.

REVIEW QUESTIONS

After studying the material, answer the following questions:

1. What is the difference between systolic and diastolic pressure? _____
   _____
   _____

2. Which type of pressure should be higher? _____
   _____

3. How does cholesterol harm the body? _____
   _____

4. How can you distinguish saturated fats? _____
   _____

5. What does an angioplasty do? _____
   _____

6. What medical procedure uses drugs to cure cancer? _____
   _____

7. What procedure uses magnetic fields and radio waves to detect tumors and other conditions without radiation? _____

8. What test can indicate prostate cancer? _____

9. What procedure extracts fetal cells for diagnosis? _____
   _____

10. What type of X-ray is used to detect breast cancer? _____
    _____

Your instructor may choose to give a brief review of these health concepts.

SELECTION 3   Criminal Justice   MyReadingLab

Visit Chapter 3: Organizing Textbook Information for Study in MyReadingLab **to complete the Selection 3 activities and the Build Background Knowledge video activity.**

PREVIEW the next selection to predict its purpose and organization and to formulate your learning plan.

Activate Schemata

Have you seen television programs or read novels in which criminals are proven guilty by matching their DNA with evidence that is found at the crime scene? Perhaps you've wondered how in real life the police manage to get suspects' DNA if the suspects don't voluntarily give samples. Do you think it should be legal for police to use DNA that they have gathered from what most people would consider trash?

Establish a Purpose for Reading

Read to find out how police are getting DNA from suspects who refuse to give samples and the questions that this practice raises.

Build Background Knowledge — VIDEO

DNA Leads to Suspect

To prepare for reading Selection 3, answer the questions below. Then, watch this video on the role DNA played in a quadruple slaying case.

What do you know about DNA and its connection to criminal cases?

How might the improper handling of DNA evidence affect a criminal case?

Should convicted criminals be given the right to challenge their case based on a reexamination of DNA evidence? Why or why not?

This video helped me: _____

_____

_____

Increase Word Knowledge

What do you know about these words?

unique	unorthodox	scrutiny	smoking gun	utensils
reclusive	scenario	elaborate	akin	analogy

Your instructor may give a brief vocabulary review before or after reading.

Integrate Knowledge While Reading

Questions have been inserted in the margins to stimulate your thinking while reading. Remember to

Predict   Picture   Relate   Monitor   Correct   Annotate

SKILL DEVELOPMENT: NOTE TAKING

Annotate this selection and then make map-style notes of the key ideas as if you were planning to use your notes to study for a quiz.

POLICE DNA COLLECTION SPARKS QUESTIONS

I can picture this scene!

When a 60-year-old man spat on the sidewalk, his DNA became as public as if he had been advertising it across his chest.

Police officers secretly following Leon Chatt . . . collected the saliva—loaded with Chatt's unique genetic makeup—to compare with DNA evidence from the
5 scene of an old murder they believed he'd committed.

Later, Chatt was charged in one of Buffalo's oldest unsolved cases, the 1974 rape and stabbing of his wife's stepsister, Barbara Lloyd.

While secretly collecting a suspect's DNA may be an unorthodox approach to solving crimes, prosecutors say it crosses no legal boundaries—that when someone
10 leaves their DNA in a public place via flakes of skin, strands of hair or saliva, for example, they give up any expectation of privacy.

But the practice has raised questions from Washington State to Florida, where similar collections are under scrutiny.

"If we felt it wasn't proper and we didn't have a strong legal foundation, we
15 wouldn't have done it," Erie County New York District Attorney Frank Clark said, discussing another recent case involving secretly obtained DNA.

In that case, the smoking gun was tableware the suspect used during a night out with his wife. Undercover investigators had waited out Altemio Sanchez at the bar of a Buffalo restaurant one evening and moved in on his water glass and utensils
20 after he'd gone.

Two days later, the 49-year-old factory worker and father of two was charged with being the elusive "Bike Path Rapist" believed responsible for the deaths of three women and rapes of numerous others from the early 1980s through 2006.

But sometimes crime labs make mistakes

Lawyers for Sanchez and Chatt say both men continue to profess their inno-
25 cence. Both have pleaded not guilty to charges of second-degree murder and their cases are pending in the courts.

CRIME SCENE AND DATABASE DNA

DNA, which is unique to every person, has become a cold case squad's best friend. Investigators can re-examine things like hair, blood, semen and carpet fibers from

decades-old crime scenes and cross-reference the DNA with ever-expanding data-
30 bases kept by law enforcement.

"It's one of the greatest tools that law enforcement has today," said Dennis
Richards, the Buffalo Police Department's chief of detectives.

New York State last year underscored the value of DNA by tripling, to about
46%, the number of people convicted of crimes who must submit a sample to the
35 state's database.

To catch up on a backlog, Erie County in January conducted an unusual two-day
DNA "blitz." Hundreds of convicts who "owed" a sample were summoned to a downtown courthouse, where an assembly line of sorts was set up to swab their mouths.

ABANDONED DNA

But it is the so-called "abandoned" DNA like that collected from Sanchez and
40 Chatt—and suspects elsewhere arrested based on discarded cigarettes or chewing
gum—that concerns people like Elizabeth Joh. The University of California law professor believes it is time legislators consider regulating such collections out of concerns for privacy.

Right now, police rely on abandoned DNA when they lack enough evidence to
45 obtain a court-ordered sample.

"If we look at this kind of evidence as abandoned, then it really permits the
police to collect DNA from anyone—not just cold case issues—from anyone at any
time and really for no good reason or any reason at all," Joh said.

"That's something that maybe sounds like a science fiction scenario—police
50 running after people trying to get their DNA," she said, "but we really don't know
where this could lead."

Asked whether there should be boundaries on such collections, Richards said,
"That's one for the lawyers to argue in a court of law."

Chatt's attorney, John Jordan, said he would "absolutely" challenge the DNA
55 evidence in his client's case in court but declined to elaborate.

THE ISSUES

Prosecutors tend to view abandoned DNA as akin to trash, which courts have up-
held as fair game for investigators, Joh said.

She pointed to the case of *California v. Greenwood,* in which the U.S. Supreme
Court ruled in 1988 that police did not need a warrant to search a suspected drug
60 dealer's trash because he should have had no expectation of privacy when he placed
it on the curb. Trash, the judges wrote, is "readily accessible to animals, children,
scavengers, snoops, and other members of the public."

But Joh argued comparing DNA and trash is a poor analogy.

"Obviously, we might want to discard that cigarette, but do we really mean to
65 give up all kinds of privacy claims in the genetic material that might lie therein?"
she asked.

As advances in technology make DNA analysis faster and cheaper, "I think of it
really as a kind of frontier issue," she said.

Richards, meanwhile, pointed out that while abandoned DNA can confirm a
70 suspect's identity, it also works to the benefit of someone who is innocent.

"DNA rules people in, but it also rules people out," he said.

That point was not lost on the husband of murder victim Barbara Lloyd, who
was questioned for hours after he reported his wife's death from 16 stab wounds in

[handwritten margin note: Would I want my DNA taken this way?]

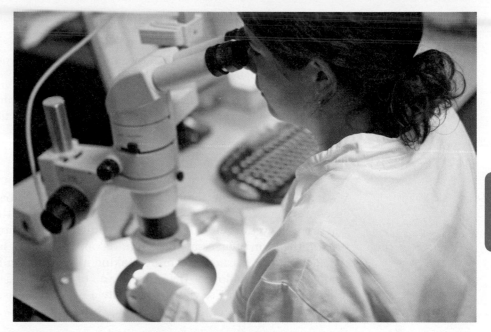

Crime labs use the latest DNA analysis to solve crimes.
Kay Ransom/Fotolia

their bedroom that March 1974 morning. Police ruled Galan Lloyd out as a suspect
75 after a few days.

Chatt's arrest, he said, proved that was the right decision.

"If there were people out there who still thought I did it, this should do it,"
Lloyd, now 59, told *The Buffalo News.*

Barbara Lloyd was killed as her then-3-year-old son, Joseph, and 14-month-old
80 daughter, Kimberly, slept. The now-grown children recently persuaded police to
take another look at the killing, leading police to close in on Chatt.

"We were very fortunate that at that time there was a detective in the evidence
collection unit who was able to secure evidence from the scene, which was later
used for comparison," Richards said. "Here we are 30 years later, able to open up a
85 box and submit some of the items that we found and to have a DNA analysis done."

Joh suggests proceeding with caution.

"My hope is there will be much greater awareness of what this means, not just
for these particular cases, but for everyone," she said. "Is DNA sampling going to be
ordinary and uncontroversial for the general population, in which case abandoned
90 DNA may not be so alarming, or does it raise a whole host of privacy questions?"

(1,042 words)

The Associated Press

Shouldn't this be routine? [annotation pointing to lines 82–83]

Recall

Review your notes. Stop to talk, write, and think about the selection.

Your instructor may choose to give you a brief comprehension review.

THINK CRITICALLY ABOUT THE SELECTION

If you were on the jury for a murder or rape case, would you convict a defendant on the basis of DNA evidence alone? Why or why not?

Do you think that collecting DNA from incarcerated criminals without their permission, as is done in New York State, is a legitimate practice?

WRITE ABOUT THE SELECTION

What are the arguments for and against the legal use of "abandoned" DNA in court cases? As the article suggests, the issue will be decided in the courts. Imagine that you are a lawyer arguing the case in the United States Supreme Court. Prepare a brief in the form of an essay that supports one side of this issue.

Response Suggestion: Begin by making a two-column list of reasons for and against using "abandoned" DNA. Include all of the reasons used in this article and add your own ideas. Use your list to write a persuasive essay defending one position or the other.

Your instructor may choose to give you a brief comprehension review.

CHECK YOUR COMPREHENSION

After reading the selection, answer the following questions with *a, b, c,* or *d*. To help you analyze your strengths and weaknesses, the question types are indicated.

Main Idea ———— 1. Which of the following statements best expresses the main idea of this selection?

  a. Abandoned DNA can be critical evidence in solving a crime, but its use also raises privacy issues.
  b. DNA is a wonderful breakthrough in criminal justice.
  c. DNA is used to solve many crimes.
  d. Police secretly collected Leon Chatt's DNA.

Detail ———— 2. What was the source of DNA used to convict Leon Chatt?

  a. saliva that he spat onto the sidewalk
  b. saliva on a drinking glass
  c. saliva on a discarded cigarette
  d. saliva left on a fork

Detail ———— 3. What was the decision in the *California v. Greenwood* case?

  a. That police must have a warrant to use DNA that has been left on a suspect's discarded cigarette.
  b. That police can use DNA evidence that is found on a glass at a crime scene.
  c. DNA from Chatt's saliva could not be used in court.
  d. It is legal to search trash for evidence.

Detail ———— 4. Who was found to be the "Bike Path Rapist?"

  a. Leon Chatt
  b. Frank Clark
  c. Altemio Sanchez
  d. John Jordan

Main Idea ———— 5. The main point of the section, "Abandoned DNA," is

  a. Dennis Richards said that the issue must be resolved in court.
  b. abandoned DNA should be allowed as evidence.
  c. some people are concerned that allowing abandoned DNA as evidence violates an individual's right to privacy.
  d. DNA is a powerful tool in a criminal investigation.

Inference ———— 6. The most likely reason that John Jordan did not want to explain his statement that he would challenge the DNA evidence in Chatt's case is

  a. he knew his client was guilty.
  b. it would be unwise to discuss a current case.
  c. he was not sure what he would do.
  d. he believed the DNA issue was not important.

SELECTION **3**

Detail _____ 7. Who is Elizabeth Joh?

    a. Leon Chatt's attorney
    b. the prosecuting attorney in *California v. Greenwood*
    c. Altemio Sanchez's attorney
    d. a law professor at the University of California

Detail _____ 8. What was the purpose of the two-day DNA blitz mentioned in the selection?

    a. to try to find Barbara Lloyd's killer
    b. to demonstrate the need for a universal DNA database
    c. to enlarge the DNA database of known criminals
    d. to enlarge the DNA database of the general public

Detail _____ 9. Elizabeth Joh suggested that collecting abandoned DNA would not be an issue

    a. if all convicted criminals' DNA were saved in a database.
    b. if DNA were collected properly at crime scenes.
    c. if the DNA of the entire population were saved in a database.
    d. if crime labs were more accurate in their analyses of DNA samples.

Inference _____ 10. From the details in the selection, we can infer that in New York State at least

    a. no one is required to submit a DNA sample for the DNA database.
    b. every convicted criminal must submit a DNA sample for the DNA database.
    c. only a percentage of convicted criminals must submit a DNA sample for the DNA database.
    d. everyone, including the general public, must submit a DNA sample for the DNA database.

Answer the following with *T* (true) or *F* (false).

Inference _____ 11. Police and prosecuting attorneys would be likely to favor the use of abandoned DNA in court cases.

Author's Purpose _____ 12. The purpose of this selection is to convince readers that collecting abandoned DNA should be illegal.

Inference _____ 13. The selection suggests that several states are collecting abandoned DNA.

Inference _____ 14. DNA evidence is used only to convict someone but not to eliminate someone as a suspect.

Inference _____ 15. From the details in the selection, we can conclude that DNA stored as evidence can last for many years for future examination.

BUILD YOUR VOCABULARY

According to the way the italicized word was used in the selection, indicate *a, b, c,* or *d* for the word or phrase that gives the best definition. The number in parentheses indicates the line of the passage in which the word is located. Use a dictionary in addition to the context clues to more precisely define the terms.

_____ 1. *"unique* genetic makeup" (4)
 a. commonly shared
 b. one-of-a-kind
 c. interesting
 d. variable

_____ 2. "an *unorthodox* approach" (8)
 a. unusual
 b. traditional
 c. incorrect
 d. formal

_____ 3. "are under *scrutiny*" (13)
 a. close examination
 b. valued
 c. brief review
 d. peeking

_____ 4. "the *smoking gun* was" (17)
 a. murder weapon
 b. fire starter
 c. clear evidence
 d. vague hint

_____ 5. "and *utensils*" (19)
 a. carpentry tools
 b. wife
 c. leftover food
 d. forks, knives, spoons

_____ 6. "the *elusive* Bike Path Rapist" (22)
 a. accessible
 b. handsome
 c. available
 d. hard to find

_____ 7. "a science fiction *scenario*" (49)
 a. fan
 b. story or situation
 c. scare
 d. character

_____ 8. "declined to *elaborate*" (55)
 a. tell
 b. deny
 c. explain
 d. confess

_____ 9. *"akin* to trash" (56)
 a. similar
 b. different
 c. unrelated
 d. opposite

_____ 10. "a poor *analogy*" (63)
 a. comparison
 b. difference
 c. test
 d. grade

VOCABULARY BOOSTER

Who's Who in Medicine?

Suffixes   *-ist, -ician:* "one who"   *-ologist:* "one who studies"

- **dermatologist**: skin doctor (*derma:* skin)

  Dermatologists remove skin cancers.

- **internist**: medical doctor for internal organs (*internus:* inside)

  The *internist* will administer a series of tests to determine the cause of Ben's mysterious pain.

- **intern**: medical school graduate serving an apprenticeship at a hospital

  The *interns* work under the close supervision of doctors on the staff.

- **gynecologist**: doctor for reproductive systems of women (*gyne:* women)

  The *gynecologist* recommended a Pap smear to check for cervical cancer.

- **obstetrician**: doctor who delivers babies (*obstetrix:* midwife)

  Many *obstetricians* are also gynecologists.

- **pediatrician**: doctor for children (*paidos:* children)

  Pediatricians sometimes use antibiotics to treat infections.

- **ophthalmologist** or **oculist**: doctor who performs eye surgery

  The *ophthalmologist* performed cataract surgery on the woman.

- **optometrist**: specialist for measuring vision

  An *optometrist* tests eyesight and fits glasses and contact lenses.

- **optician**: specialist who makes visual correction lenses for eyeglasses and contact lenses

  Opticians usually work behind the scene, often at an optometrist's office.

- **orthopedist**: doctor who corrects abnormalities in bones and joints (*orthos:* straight or correct)

  The *orthopedist* set up his practice near a ski area.

- **orthodontist**: dentist for straightening teeth

  Her braces had to be adjusted every six weeks by the *orthodontist*.

- **cardiologist**: heart doctor (*cardio:* heart)

  Cardiologists treat patients who have had heart attacks.

- **psychiatrist**: doctor for treating mental disorders (*psycho:* mind)

  The *psychiatrist* prescribed drugs for the treatment of depression.

- **psychologist**: counselor for treating mental disorders

  The *psychologist* administered tests to determine the cause of the child's behavior.

- **neurologist**: doctor for disorders of the brain, spinal cord, and nervous system (*neuron:* nerve)

  Neurologists are searching for new treatments for patients who have suffered spinal cord injuries.

- **oncologist**: doctor for treating cancer and tumors (*onkos:* mass)

  The *oncologist* recommended various methods for dealing with the cancerous tumor.

- **urologist**: doctor specializing in the urinary tract (*ouro:* urine)

  The urologist was treating several patients for impotence.

- **podiatrist**: specialist in the care and treatment of the foot (*pod:* foot)

  The *podiatrist* knew the best way to deal with blisters, corns, and bunions.

- **anesthesiologist**: doctor who administers anesthesia to patients undergoing surgery (*anesthesia:* insensibility)

  Usually, a patient will meet the *anesthesiologist* just before surgery.

- **hematologist**: doctor who studies the blood and blood-forming organs (*hemat:* blood)

  A hematoma is treated by a *hematologist*.

- **radiologist**: doctor using radiant energy for diagnostic and therapeutic purposes (*radio:* radiant waves)

  After the removal of a cancerous tumor, further treatment by a *radiologist* is usually recommended.

Review

Part I

Indicate whether the following sentences are true (*T*) or false (*F*):

_____ 1. *Radiologists* are physicians who evaluate X-rays.

_____ 2. A *psychologist* is unable to prescribe medications for patients.

_____ 3. If a mental illness is suspected, a patient may be referred to a *psychiatrist*.

_____ 4. An *internist* is a medical school graduate serving an apprenticeship at a hospital.

_____ 5. *Dermatologists* recommend the daily use of sunscreen.

_____ 6. A *neurologist* specializes in the treatment of heart attacks.

_____ 7. Medical school is required in order to become an *optician*.

_____ 8. *Pediatricians* examine babies.

_____ 9. *Oncologists* specialize in eye treatment.

_____ 10. A *hematologist* might help a patient whose blood fails to clot properly.

Part II

Choose the type of doctor from the boxed list that best fits the job description.

| anesthesiologist | podiatrist | urologist | cardiologist | orthodontist |
| orthopedist | optometrist | obstetrician | intern | ophthalmologist |

11. Performs eye surgery _____

12. Treats diseases of the foot _____

13. Delivers babies _____

14. Works with bones and joints _____

15. Treats disorders of the urinary tract _____

16. Administers anesthesia _____

17. Dispenses contact lenses _____

18. Treats heart problems _____

19. Corrects problems with teeth _____

20. Apprentice to physician or surgeon _____

Your instructor may choose to give a brief review.

4 Vocabulary

Learning Objectives

In this chapter, you will learn to:

1 Apply a variety of strategies to learn and expand your vocabulary
2 Use context clues to find meaning in new words
3 Use word structure to find meaning in new words
4 Use reference aids to clarify meanings of new words
5 Strengthen word memory with rich meaning

Vocabulary Booster: What's In, What's Out? What's Hot, What's Not?

Pedro Bigeriego/Fotolia

REMEMBERING NEW WORDS AND UNLOCKING MEANING

Have you ever made lists of unknown words that you wanted to remember? Did you dutifully write down the word, its definition, and promise to review the list at night before going to bed? Did it work? Probably not! Memorization can be an effective cramming strategy, but it does not seem to produce long-term results. Recording only the word and its definition does not establish the associations that are necessary for long-term memory. Instead, associate as much detailed meaning to a new word as you can. The richer the details, the better are your chances of remembering.

Clever memory techniques can also help to expand your vocabulary. With these methods, or **mnemonic devices**, you visualize and organize units into new relationships. You can also use rhymes to tie words together. For example, to remember the word *mnemonics*, think of Nem-on-ic as "putting a name on it." To remember that *suppression* means "to force out bad thoughts," visualize "SUPerman PRESSing" evil thoughts away. A noted speaker, John Berthoud, usually begins a speech by explaining how to pronounce his last name, which is French. He tells audiences to think, "Not one *bear*, but *two*," or "You are naked, and I am *bare, too*." The following suggestions can help you associate and organize.

Associate Words in Phrases

Never record a word in isolation. Rather, think of the word and record it in a phrase that suggests its meaning. The phrase may be part of the sentence in which you first encountered the word or one that you create yourself. Such a phrase provides a setting for the word and enriches the links to your long-term memory.

For example, the word *caravel* means "a small sailing ship." Record the word in a phrase that creates a memorable setting, such as "a caravan of gliding caravels on the horizon of the sea."

Associate Words with Rhymes or Sounds

Link the sound of a new word with a rhyming word or phrase. The brain appreciates connections and patterns. For example, the word *hoard*, which means "to accumulate or stockpile," can be linked with *stored*, as in "He stored his hoard of Halloween candy in the closet."

BRAIN BOOSTER

Use Your Senses to Make More Sense!

All information enters your brain through your senses—vision, hearing, smell, touch, and taste. When it enters through more than one channel, the effect is stronger. How can college students apply this fact about the brain? Access multiple inputs when you are studying. Draw, use a computer keyboard, make and manipulate flash cards, write notes in an organized, clear visual form, say or sing the material aloud, or watch related videos. Music that has a regular rhythm and is not distracting can be helpful. When used sparingly, even fragrances and tastes can be associated with specific information and can be remembered easily. Which senses will be involved when you make concept cards to learn new vocabulary?

Associate Words with Images

Expand the phrase that you have chosen for learning a word into a vivid mental image. Create a situation or an episode for the word. Furthermore, enrich your memory link by drawing a picture of your mental image.

For example, the word *candid* means "frank and truthful." Imagine a friend asking your opinion on an unattractive outfit. A suggestive phrase for learning the word might be, "My candid reply might have hurt her feelings."

Seek Reinforcement

Look and listen for your new words. You will probably discover that they are used more frequently than you thought. Notice them, welcome them, and congratulate yourself on your newfound word knowledge.

Create Concept Cards

Many students use index cards to record information about new words. As illustrated below, one good system is to write the word in a phrase on the front of the card, also noting where the word was encountered. On the back of the card, write an appropriate definition, use the word in a new sentence, and draw an image illustrating the word. Review the cards, quiz yourself, and watch your vocabulary grow.

Front

"birds are restrained"

from a psychology textbook

Back

held back, not allowed to move

The sheriff restrained the prisoner

with handcuffs.

EXERCISE 4.1

Creating Concept Cards to Associate Meaning

Pair up with a classmate to create your own mnemonics for the following words. For each item, use rhyme and imagery to create a word link, a playful sentence, and a cartoon on a concept card.

1. *scrutinize:* to look very carefully; to examine

2. *dormant:* asleep or inactive

3. *entreat:* to ask earnestly; to implore, plead, beg

4. Make up a mnemonic to help people remember your name.

Use Strategies to Unlock Meaning While Reading

What do you do when you come to an unfamiliar word while you are reading? Do you skip it? Do you perhaps stop to look it up in a dictionary? Some new words will be key terms that are important to the field of study. Others will be critical to understanding the material, and some can be ignored without impairing your comprehension. If the word is important, use the following three strategies to understand and remember the word.

The first strategy involves using **context clues**, the words and phrases surrounding the unfamiliar word. This strategy often provides a good idea of the word's meaning without interfering with your comprehension. Select words you want to remember and mark them consistently so that you can easily find them later. When you finish reading, make concept cards (see page 177) to set the words in memory.

The second strategy uses **word structure**. Words, like people, have families that share the same names. In the case of words, the names are called *prefixes*, *roots*, and *suffixes*. A basic knowledge of word parts can help you unlock the meaning to thousands of associated word family members. For example, the prefix *ambi-* means "both," as in the word *ambivert*, which means "being both introverted and extroverted." You can apply your knowledge of *ambi-* to new words, such as *ambidextrous*, *ambiguous*, and *ambivalence* to help determine and remember their meanings.

To clarify meaning, employ the third strategy—use word reference aids, such as a **dictionary**, a **glossary**, or a **thesaurus**.

These three strategies will help you unlock the meaning of words while you read, but truly making the new words part of your vocabulary requires some effort. Use the memory tools described at the beginning of this chapter and, lastly, add as much deep meaning to them as possible.

The rest of this chapter explains these strategies in greater detail. Use the practice exercises to help you add the methods to your word attack tool box. If you read widely, apply the strategies, and use your new words, you will soon impress yourself and others with your large vocabulary!

USING CONTEXT CLUES

Learning Objective 2

Use context clues to find meaning in new words

Using **context clues** is the most common method of unlocking the meanings of unknown words. The *context* of a word refers to the sentence or paragraph in which the word appears. Readers use several types of context clues. In some cases, words are defined directly in the sentences in which they appear; in other instances, the sentence offers clues or hints that enable the reader to arrive indirectly at the meaning of the word. The following examples show how each type of clue can be used to figure out word meanings in textbooks.

Definition or Synonym

Complex material, particularly scientific material, has a lot of specialized vocabulary. Fortunately, new words are often directly defined as they are introduced in the text. Often, **synonyms**—words with the same or a similar meaning as the unknown word—are given. Do you know the meaning of *erythrocytes* and *oxyhemoglobin*? Read the following textbook sentence in which these two words appear and then select the correct definition for each word.

EXAMPLE

When oxygen diffuses into the blood in external respiration, most of it enters the red blood cells, or erythrocytes, and unites with the hemoglobin in these cells, forming a compound called oxyhemoglobin.

—Willis H. Johnson et al.,
Essentials of Biology

_____ _Erythrocytes_ means

    a. diffused oxygen.
    b. red blood cells.
    c. the respiration process.

_____ _Oxyhemoglobin_ means

    a. hemoglobin without oxygen.
    b. dominant oxygen cells.
    c. a combination of oxygen and hemoglobin.

EXPLANATION   The answers are _b_ and _c_. Notice that the first word, _erythrocytes_, is used as a synonym. Sometimes, a signal word for a synonym is _or_. Other signal words that will help you discover meaning through the use of definition are _is, that is, in other words, for example_, and _is defined as_. The second word, _oxyhemoglobin_, is part of the explanation of the sentence. Sometimes commas or dashes indicate a definition or synonym. Did you notice that in the third sentence of this section?

Elaborating Details

Terms are not always directly defined in the text. Instead, an author may give descriptive details that illustrate meaning. In political science texts, for example, you may come across the word _confederation_. Keep reading and see if you can figure out the meaning from the hints in the following paragraph.

EXAMPLE   There is a third form of governmental structure, a _confederation_. The United States began as such, under the Articles of Confederation. In a confederation, the national government is weak and most or all the power is in the hands of its components, for example, the individual states. Today, confederations are rare except in international organizations such as the United Nations.

—Robert Lineberry,
Government in America

_____ A _confederation_ is a governmental structure with

    a. strong federal power.
    b. weak federal power.
    c. weak state power.
    d. equal federal and state power.

EXPLANATION   The answer is _b_ and can be figured out from the details in the third sentence.

Examples

At other times, examples will be given to clarify meaning. In psychology courses, for instance, you will frequently encounter a complicated word describing something that you have often thought about but have not named. Read the following paragraph to find out what *psychokinesis* means.

EXAMPLE

Another psychic phenomenon is *psychokinesis*, the ability to affect physical events without physical intervention. You can test your powers of psychokinesis by trying to influence the fall of dice from a mechanical shaker. Are you able to have the dice come up a certain number with a greater frequency than would occur by chance?

—Douglas W. Matheson,
Introductory Psychology: The Modern View

_____ *Psychokinesis* means

    a. extrasensory perception.
    b. an influence on happenings without physical tampering.
    c. physical intervention affecting physical change.

EXPLANATION The answer is *b*. The word is first directly defined in a complicated manner, and then the definition is clarified by a simple example.

Comparison

In certain cases, complex concepts are best understood when they are compared with something else. Economics texts, for example, include many concepts that are difficult to understand. The use of a familiar term in a comparison can help the reader relate to a new idea. Can you explain a *trade deficit*? The following comparison will help.

EXAMPLE

When the United States imports more than it exports, we have a *trade deficit* rather than a trade balance or a trade surplus. Similarly, a store manager who buys more than she sells will create a financial deficit for the company.

_____ A *trade deficit* means that a nation

    a. sells more than it buys.
    b. buys more than it sells.
    c. sells what it buys.

EXPLANATION The answer is *b*. The comparison explains the definition by creating a more understandable situation.

Contrast

In other cases, a contrast is made to help you read between the lines and infer word meaning. Can you explain what *transsexuals* are and how they differ from *homosexuals*? The following paragraph gives some clues.

EXAMPLE   *Transsexuals* are people (usually males) who feel that they were born into the wrong body. They are not homosexuals in the usual sense. Most homosexuals are satisfied with their anatomy and think of themselves as appropriately male or female; they simply prefer members of their own sex. Transsexuals, in contrast, think of themselves as members of the opposite sex (often from early childhood) and may be so desperately unhappy with their physical appearance that they request hormonal and surgical treatment to change their genitals and secondary sex characteristics.

—Rita Atkinson et al.,
Introduction to Psychology

_____ A *transsexual* is a person who thinks of himself or herself as a

a. homosexual.
b. heterosexual.
c. member of the opposite sex.
d. person without sex drive.

EXPLANATION   The answer is *c*. By contrasting homosexuals and transsexuals, the reader is better able to infer the difference between the two. Signal words that indicate contrast are *but, yet, however,* and *in contrast*.

Antonyms

Finally, the context clue may be an **antonym**, or a word that means the opposite of the unknown word. Antonyms are signaled by words and phrases such as *however, but, yet, in contrast,* or *on the other hand*. Using the following context, is *nonconfrontational* behavior violent?

EXAMPLE   Some passive belief systems call for *nonconfrontational* behavior; yet others call for rebellion.

—Adapted from Daniel G. Bates and Elliot M. Franklin,
Cultural Anthropology, 3rd ed.

_____ A *nonconfrontational* behavior is

a. violent.
b. rebellious.
c. not openly rebellious.
d. sympathetic.

EXPLANATION   The signal word *yet* suggests that *nonconfrontational* is the opposite of violent and rebellious, so *c* is correct. The word *passive* is also a clue to the meaning.

Limitations of Context Clues

Although the clues in the sentence in which an unknown word appears are certainly helpful in deriving the meaning of the word, these clues will not always give a complete and accurate definition. To understand totally the meaning of a word, take some time after completing your reading to look up the word in a glossary or a dictionary. Context clues operate just as the name suggests: They are hints, not necessarily definitions.

EXERCISE 4.2

The Power of Context Clues

How can context clues assist you in unlocking the meaning of unknown words? For each of the following items, make two responses. First, without reading the sentence containing the unknown word, select *a, b, c,* or *d* for the definition that you feel best fits each italicized word. Then read the material in which the word is used in context and answer again.

Compare your answers. Did reading the word in context help? Were you initially uncertain of any word but then able to figure out the meaning after reading it in a sentence?

_____ 1. *assimilationist*

      a. one who adopts the habits of a larger cultural group
      b. a machinist
      c. a typist
      d. one who files correspondence

        _____ When members of a minority group wish to give up what is distinctive about them and become just like the majority, they take an *assimilationist* position. An example is the Urban League.

—Reece McGee et al.,
Sociology: An Introduction

_____ 2. *expropriated*

      a. took from its owners
      b. industrialized
      c. approximated
      d. increased in size

        _____ Under a decree of September 1952, the government *expropriated* several hundred thousand acres from large landholders and redistributed this land among the peasants.

—Jesse H. Wheeler, Jr., et al.,
Regional Geography of the World

_____ 3. *stimulus*

      a. writing implement
      b. distinguishing mark
      c. something that incites action
      d. result

_____ While we are sleeping, for example, we are hardly aware of what is happening around us, but we are aware to some degree.

Any loud noise or other abrupt *stimulus* will almost certainly awaken us.

—Gardner Lindzey et al.,
Psychology

_____ 4. *autocratic*

a. automatic
b. democratic
c. self-starting
d. dictatorial

_____ Autocratic leadership can be extremely effective if the people wielding it have enough power to enforce their decisions and if their followers know that they have it. It is especially useful in military situations where speed of decision is critical. Among its disadvantages are the lack of objectivity and the disregard for opinions of subordinates.

—David J. Rachman and Michael Mescon,
Business Today

 **Context Clues in Academic Reading**

Use the context clues to write the meaning of the italicized words.

1. Robbery, which should not be confused with burglary, is a personal crime and involves a face-to-face confrontation between victim and *perpetrator*.

—Frank Schmalleger,
Criminal Justice Today, 8th ed.

A *perpetrator* is _____

_____ .

2. In 1727 Sir Isaac Newton became seriously ill, and on March 20 one of the greatest physicists of all time died. He was *accorded* a state funeral and interred in Westminster Abbey—a high and rare honor for a commoner.

—Adapted from Larry D. Kirkpatrick and Gregory E. Francis,
Physics: A World View, 5th ed.

Accorded means _____

_____.

3. At times, two sides cannot—or will not—agree. The speed and ease with which such an *impasse* is resolved depend in part on the nature of the contract issues.

—Adapted from Ricky W. Griffin and Ronald J. Ebert,
Business, 8th ed.

An *impasse* means _____

_____.

4. Social psychologist Robert Zajonc found that people like previously seen things better than unfamiliar ones; research shows that familiarity breeds not contempt but *affinity*.

—Adapted from Stephen M. Kosslyn and Robin S. Rosenberg,
Psychology: The Brain, the Person, the World, 2nd ed.

Affinity means _____

_____.

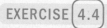 EXERCISE 4.4 ## Context Clues in Short Textbook Passages

Use context clues from each passage that follows to write the meaning of the italicized words.

Passage 1

Blocked by her family and publicly *maligned*, Florence Nightingale struggled against *prevailing norms* to carve out her occupation. She was the daughter of a wealthy *gentry* family, and from her father she received a man's classical education. Women of her *milieu* were expected to be educated only in domestic arts.

—Adapted from Mark Kishlansky et al.,
Civilization in the West, 6th ed.

1. maligned _____

_____

2. prevailing norms _____

_____

3. gentry _____

_____

4. milieu _____

_____

Passage 2

The Clean Air Act, as amended in 1990, directed the U.S. Environmental Protection Agency (EPA) to issue regulations that require the gasoline used in pollution-*prone* areas to be "*reformulated*" in order to burn cleaner (that is, to reduce ozone-forming and toxic air pollutants) and not evaporate as easily. The Reformulated Gasoline Program was *implemented* in 1995. Reformulated gasoline is blended with chemicals commonly called "oxygenates," which raise the oxygen content of gasoline. Oxygen helps gasoline burn more completely, reducing harmful tailpipe emissions. According to the EPA, reformulated gasoline produces 15 to 17 percent less pollution than *conventional* gasoline, and further improvements are expected as new formulas are developed.

—Frederick K. Lutgens and Edward J. Tarbuck,
The Atmosphere: An Introduction to Meteorology, 9th ed.

1. prone _____

_____

2. reformulated _____

_____

3. implemented _____

_____

4. conventional _____

_____

Multiple Meanings of a Word

Even when a word's meaning seems clear, many words—particularly short ones—can be confusing because they have more than one meaning. The word *bank*, for example, can be used as a noun to refer to a financial institution, the ground rising from a river, or a mass of clouds. As a verb, *bank* can mean to laterally incline an airplane, to accumulate, or to drive a billiard ball into a cushion. Thus, the meaning of the word depends on the sentence and paragraph in which the word is used. Be alert to context clues that indicate an unfamiliar use of a seemingly familiar word.

EXERCISE 4.5   **Multiple Meanings**

The boldface words in the following sentences have multiple meanings. Write the definition of each boldface word as it is used in the sentence.

1. The overcooked cauliflower emitted a **foul**, lingering odor. _____

_____

2. With April 15 looming, the woman began to **comb** the den for her missing W2 forms. _____

_____

3. What she enjoyed most about early morning was that the world seemed so **still.** _____

_____

4. Having misplaced the overdue text, the library patron now owed a **fine** nearly equal to the cost of the book. _____

_____

UNDERSTANDING THE STRUCTURE OF WORDS

Learning Objective 3

Use word structure to find meaning in new words

What is the longest word in the English language, and what does it mean? At one time, and perhaps still, the longest word in *Webster's New International Dictionary* was

pneumonoultramicroscopicsilicovolcanokoniosis

Look at the word again and notice the smaller and more familiar word parts. Do you know enough of the smaller word parts to figure out the meaning of the word? Nurnberg and Rosenblum unlock the meaning as follows:

pneumono: pertaining to the lungs, as in *pneumon*ia

ultra: beyond, as in *ultra*violet rays

micro: small, as in *micro*scope

scopic: from the root of Greek verb *skopein*, to view or look at

silico: from the element *silicon*, found in quartz, flint, and sand

volcano: the meaning of this is obvious

koni: the principal root, from a Greek word for *dust*

osis: a suffix indicating illness, such as trichin*osis*

Now, by putting the parts together again, we deduce that *pneumonoultramicroscopicsilicovolcanokoniosis* is a disease of the lungs caused by extremely small particles of volcanic ash and dust.

This dramatic example demonstrates how an extremely long and technical word can become more manageable by breaking it into smaller parts. The same is true for many of the smaller words that we use every day. A knowledge of word parts will help you unlock the meaning of literally thousands of words. One vocabulary expert identified a list of 30 prefixes, roots, and suffixes, and claims that knowing these 30 word parts will help unlock the meaning of 14,000 words.

Like people, words have families and, in some cases, an abundance of close relations. Clusters, or what might be called *word families*, are composed of words with the same base or **root**. For example, *bio* is a root meaning "life." If you know that *biology* means the study of life, it becomes easy to figure out the definition of a word like *biochemistry*. Word parts form new words as follows:

prefix + base word or root   base word or root + suffix
prefix + base word or root + suffix

Prefixes and suffixes are added to root words to change the meaning. A **prefix** is added to the beginning of a word, and a **suffix** is added to the end of a word. For example, the prefix *il-* means "not." When that prefix is added to the word *legal*, the resulting word, *illegal*, becomes the opposite of the original. Suffixes can change the meaning of a word or can change the way in which a word can be used in a sentence. The suffix *-cide* means "to kill." When added to *frater*, which means "brother," the resulting word, *fratricide*, means "to kill one's brother." Adding *-ity* or *-ize* to *frater* changes both the meaning and the way in which the word can be used grammatically in a sentence.

EXAMPLE   To demonstrate how prefixes, roots, and suffixes overlap and make families, start with the root *gamy*, meaning "marriage," and ask some questions.

1. What is the state of having only one wife called? _____
   (*mono-* means "one")

2. What is a man who has two wives called? _____
   (*bi-* means "two," and *-ist* means "one who")

4. What is a man who has many wives called? _____
   (*poly-* means "many")

5. What is a woman who has many husbands called? _____
   (*andro-* means "man")

6. What is someone who hates marriage called? _____
   (*miso-* means "hater of")

EXPLANATION   The answers are (1) monogamy, (2) bigamist, (3) polygamist, (4) polyandrist, and (5) misogamist. Notice that in several of the *gamy* examples, the letters change slightly to accommodate language sounds. Such variations of a letter or two are typical when you work with word parts. Often, you have to drop or add letters in order to maintain the rhythm of the language, but the meaning of the word part remains the same regardless of the change in spelling. For example, the prefix *con-* means "with" or "together," as in *conduct*. This same prefix is used with variations in many other words:

cooperate   *collection*   *correlate*   *communicate*   *connect*

Thus, *con-*, *co-*, *col-*, *cor-*, and *com-* are all forms of the prefix that means "with" or "together."

EXERCISE 4.6   **Word Families**

Create your own word families from the word parts that are supplied. For each of the following definitions, supply a prefix, root, or suffix to make the appropriate word.

The prefix *bi-* means "two."

1. able to speak two languages: bi _____
2. having two feet, like humans: bi _____
3. representing two political parties: bi _____
4. occurring at two-year intervals: bi _____
5. cut into two parts: bi _____
6. mathematics expression with two terms: bi _____
7. instrument with two eyes: bi _____
8. coming twice a year: bi _____

The root *vert* means "to turn."

1. to change one's beliefs: _____ vert
2. to go back to old ways again: _____ vert
3. a car with a removable top: _____ vert _____
4. activities that are intended to undermine or destroy: _____ vers _____
5. an outgoing, gregarious person: _____ vert
6. a quiet, introspective, shy person: _____ vert
7. conditions that are turned against you; misfortune: _____ vers _____
8. one who deviates from normal behavior, especially sexual: _____ vert

The suffix *-ism* means "doctrine, condition, or characteristic."

1. addiction to alcoholic drink: _____ ism
2. a brave and courageous manner of acting: _____ ism
3. prejudice against a particular gender or sex: _____ ism
4. doctrine that is concerned only with fact and reality: _____ ism
5. system that uses terror to intimidate: _____ ism
6. writing someone else's words as your own: _____ ism
7. driving out an evil spirit: _____ ism
8. purification ceremony to join a church: _____ ism

EXERCISE 4.7

Prefixes, Roots, and Suffixes

Using the prefix, root, or suffix provided, write the words that best fit the following definitions:

1. *con-* means "with"

   infectious or catching: con _____

2. *sub-* means "under"

   under the conscious level of the mind: sub _____

3. *vita* means "life"

   a pill to provide essential nutrients: vita _____

4. *thermo* means "heat"

   device for regulating furnace heat: thermo _____

5. *ven* means "come"

   a meeting for people to come together: _____ ven _____

6. *rupt* means "break or burst"

   a volcanic explosion: _____ rupt _____

7. *meter* means "measure"

   instrument to measure heat: _____ meter

8. *naut* means "voyager"

   voyager in space: _____ naut

USING WORD REFERENCE AIDS

Learning Objective 4

Use reference aids to clarify meanings of new words

A reference aid such as a dictionary, glossary, or thesaurus is indispensable for finding precise definitions and other information about new words. However, avoid interrupting your reading to look up a word unless it is essential to your understanding of the text. Instead, use the context and word structure clues, mark the word, and go to the reference aid when you finish reading. The following sections provide explanations and practice for using common word reference aids.

Using a Dictionary

Do you have an excellent collegiate dictionary, such as *Merriam-Webster's Collegiate Dictionary*? Every college student needs a large dictionary to keep at home. In class, you may use a small paperback dictionary or an online one for a quick check of spelling or word meaning.

Several online dictionaries offer easy and free access for limited use but require a yearly subscription fee for premium services. At www.Merriam-Webster.com, for example, you can type your word into the Search window and receive the definition, word origin, and pronunciation for free. The site also provides an encyclopedia link, "Word of the Day" services, word games, an online thesaurus, and a dictionary for kids. Another easy-to-use free site, www.dictionary.com, includes definitions, foreign dictionaries, translations into foreign languages, a thesaurus, games, and a word of the day. Most word-processing programs have a dictionary and thesaurus feature that is accessed by highlighting the word and right clicking. Try these sites and see how they compare with your collegiate dictionary. In evaluating the sites, consider that good dictionaries not only contain the definitions of words but also provide the following additional information for each word. It is important to note that the paperback and online/electronic versions of dictionaries are convenient but do not provide the depth of information needed for college study that is found in the larger collegiate editions.

Guide Words.   The two words at the top of each dictionary page are the first and last entries on the page. They help guide your search for a particular entry by indicating what is covered on that page.

In the sample that follows, *flagrante delicto* is the first entry on the page of the dictionary on which *flamingo* appears, and *flappy* is the last entry on that page. Note that the pronunciation of the word *flamingo* is followed by the part of speech *(n)*, plural spellings, and the origin of the word.

fla·min·go \flə-ˈmiŋ-(ˌ)gō\ *n, pl* **-gos** *also* **-goes** [obs. Sp *flamengo* (now *flamenco*), lit., Fleming, German (conventionally thought of as ruddy-complexioned)] (1565) : any of several large aquatic birds (family Phoenicopteridae) with long legs and neck, webbed feet, a broad lamellate bill resembling that of a duck but abruptly bent downward, and usu. rosy-white plumage with scarlet wing coverts and black wing quills

\ə\ abut \ᵊ\ kitten, F table \ər\ **further** \a\ ash \ā\ ace \ä\ mop, mar
\au̇\ **out** \ch\ **chin** \e\ bet \ē\ **easy** \g\ go \i\ hit \ī\ ice \j\ job
\ŋ\ **sing** \ō\ go \ȯ\ law \ȯi\ boy \th\ thin \t̲h̲\ **the** \ü\ **loot** \u̇\ **foot**
\y\ yet \zh\ vision \k̲, ⁿ, œ, ᵫ ᵞ\ *see* Guide to Pronunciation

By permission. From *Merriam-Webster's Collegiate® Dictionary*,
11th Edition © 2015 by Merriam-Webster, Inc.
(www.Merriam-Webster.com)

Pronunciation.   The boldface main entry divides the word into sounds, using a dot between each syllable. After the entry, letters and symbols show the pronunciation. A diacritical mark (ˈ) at the end of a syllable indicates stress on that syllable. A heavy mark means major stress; a lighter one indicates minor stress.

As shown in the illustration above, a key explaining the symbols and letters appears at the bottom of the dictionary page. For example, a word like *ragweed* (rag'-wêd) would be pronounced with a short *a* as in *ash* and a long *e* as in *easy*.

The *a* in *flamingo* sounds like the *a* in *abut*, and the final *o* has a long sound, as in *go*. The stress is on the first syllable.

Part of Speech.   The part of speech is indicated in an abbreviation for each meaning of a word. A single word, for example, may be a noun with one definition and a verb with another. The noun *flamingo* can be used as only one part of speech, but *sideline* can be both a noun and a verb (see the following entry).

¹side·line \-ˌlīn\ *n* (ca. 1862)   **1** : a line at right angles to a goal line or end line and marking a side of a court or field of play for athletic games   **2 a** : a line of goods sold in addition to one's principal line   **b** : a business or activity pursued in addition to one's regular occupation   **3 a** : the space immediately outside the lines along either side of an athletic field or court   **b** : a sphere of little or no participation or activity — usu. used in pl.
²sideline *vt* (1943) : to put out of action : put on the sidelines

By permission. From *Merriam-Webster's Collegiate® Dictionary*, 11th Edition © 2015 by Merriam-Webster, Inc. (www.Merriam-Webster.com)

Spellings.   Spellings are given for the plural of the word and for special forms. This is particularly useful when you are trying to determine whether letters need to be added or dropped to form the new words. The plural of *flamingo* can be spelled correctly in two different ways. Both *flamingos* and *flamingoes* are acceptable.

Origin.   For many entries, the foreign word and language from which the word was derived will appear after the pronunciation. For example, *L* stands for a Latin origin and *G* for a Greek origin. A key for the many dictionary abbreviations usually appears at the beginning of the book.

The word *flamingo* has a rich history. It comes from the Spanish *(Sp)* word *flamenco*, which derived from the older, now obsolete *(obs. Sp)* word *flamengo*. It relates to the ruddy complexion that was once thought to be typical of German or Fleming (i.e., Flemish, from a part of Belgium) people. That's a lot of information packed into an entry on a single pink bird!

Multiple Meanings.   A single word can have many shades of meaning or several completely different meanings. The various meanings are numbered.

The word *flamingo* on page 190 has only one meaning. The word *sideline*, however, has several, as shown in the previous entry.

A sideline can be a business, a product, or a designated area. In addition, it can mean to move something out of the action. To select the appropriate meaning, consider the context or the way in which the word is used in the sentence. For example, consider the intended meaning in "As a sideline to being a full-time student, I also play in a band on the weekends."

EXERCISE 4.8

Using the Dictionary

Answer the following questions, using an online entry from *Merriam-Webster's Collegiate Dictionary* that is reproduced on page 192. Write *T* (true) or *F* (false).

_____ 1. Among is a preposition.

_____ 2. Among is not used to describe and compare the opinions and feelings of a group of people.

_____ 3. Between cannot be used as a substitute for among.

_____ 4. Amongst is not a variant of among.

_____ 5. Among was first used sometime before the 12th century.

_____ 6. Amidst is a synonym for among.

An Encyclopædia Britannica Company

Join Us On

Merriam-Webster

Dictionary Thesaurus Medical Scrabble Spanish Central Browse Dictionary Browse Thesaurus

| among | SEARCH > | Get our free apps! iPhone · iPad · Android |

Games   Word of the Day   Video   Blog: Words at Play   My Faves

Dictionary

among

preposition \ə-ˈməŋ\

SAVE POPULARITY

Cite! Share G+1 Tweet

: in or through (a group of people or things)

: in the presence of (a group of people)

—used to talk about the opinions, feelings, etc., of a group of people

Full Definition of AMONG

1 : in or through the midst of : surrounded by <hidden *among* the trees>

2 : in company or association with <living *among* artists>

3 : by or through the aggregate of <discontent *among* the poor>

4 : in the number or class of <wittiest *among* poets> <*among* other things she was president of her college class>

5 : in shares to each of <divided *among* the heirs>

6 a : through the reciprocal acts of <quarrel *among* themselves>

b : through the joint action of <made a fortune *among* themselves>

See among defined for English-language learners »

See among defined for kids »

Usage Discussion of AMONG

There is a persistent but unfounded notion that *between* can be used only of two items and that *among* must be used for more than two. *Between* has been used of more than two since Old English; it is especially appropriate to denote a one-to-one relationship, regardless of the number of items. It can be used when the number is unspecified <economic cooperation *between* nations>, when more than two are enumerated <*between* you and me and the lamppost> <partitioned *between* Austria, Prussia, and Russia — Nathaniel Benchley>, and even when only one item is mentioned (but repetition is implied) <pausing *between* every sentence to rap the floor — George Eliot>. *Among* is more appropriate where the emphasis is on distribution rather than individual relationships <discontent *among* the peasants>. When *among* is automatically chosen for more than two, English idiom may be strained <a worthy book that nevertheless falls *among* many stools — John Simon> <the author alternates *among* modern slang, clichés and quotes from literary giants — A. H. Johnston>.

Variants of AMONG

among also **amongst** \-ˈmən(k)st\

Examples of AMONG

The disease spread quickly *among* the members of the community.

The house is nestled *among* the trees.

The ball was hidden *among* the leaves.

There were ducks *among* the geese.

There were several hecklers scattered *among* the crowd.

He lived *among* artists and writers.

The people of the town were frightened to think that a killer might be living *among* them.

Origin of AMONG

among from Middle English, from Old English *on gemonge*, from *on* + *gemonge*, dative of *gemong* crowd, from *ge-* (associative prefix) + *-mong* (akin to Old English *mengan* to mix); *amongst* from Middle English *amonges*, from *among* + *-es* -s — more at CO-, MINGLE

First Known Use: before 12th century

Related to AMONG

Synonyms

amid (*or* amidst), mid, midst, through, in the thick of

[+] **more**

Rhymes with AMONG

bee-stung, black lung, brown lung, far-flung, forked tongue, high-strung, iron lung, Kaifeng, low-slung, unsung, with young

Using a Glossary

Each college subject seems to have a language, or jargon, of its own. For example, words like *sociocultural* or *socioeconomic* crop up in sociology. In truth, these words are unique to the subject-matter area—they are *invented* words. The best definitions of such words can usually be found in the textbook itself rather than in a dictionary. The definitions may be displayed in the *margins* of a page or, more frequently, in a glossary of terms at the end of the book or each chapter. The glossary defines the words as they are used in the textbook. At the end of most textbooks is an index, which helps you find pages on which topics are discussed. In some large texts, the glossary and index are combined.

Consider the following examples from the glossary of a psychology textbook. These terms are part of the jargon of psychology and would probably not be found in the dictionary.

latent learning Hidden learning that is not demonstrated in performance until that performance is reinforced.

learning set An acquired strategy for learning or problem solving; learning to learn.

EXERCISE 4.9

Using Your Glossary

Turn to the glossary at the end of this book for help in defining the following terms. Write a definition for each in your own words. (Answers will vary.)

1. annotating: _____

   _____

   _____

2. mnemonic: _____

   _____

   _____

3. analogy: _____

   _____

   _____

4. denotation: _____

   _____

   _____

Using a Thesaurus

A thesaurus is a writer's tool. It provides synonyms; that is, words that are similar in meaning, for the word that you are looking up. It is not a dictionary, and it does not include all words. The first thesaurus was compiled in 1852 by Dr. Peter Mark

Roget, an English physician, who collected lists of synonyms as a hobby. The book suggested synonyms for commonly used words, but it also included antonyms. A thesaurus entitled *Roget's Thesaurus* is organized according to Roget's format. There are also other types of thesauruses available.

Use a thesaurus to add variety to your writing and to avoid repetitious wording. For example, if you find yourself repeating the word *guilt* in a research paper, consult a thesaurus for substitutes. *Merriam-Webster's Collegiate Dictionary and Thesaurus* suggests synonyms such as *contriteness, regret, remorse, repentance,* and *shame.*

> **guilt** 1 a feeling of responsibility for wrongdoing <he was wracked with *guilt* after he accidentally broke his sister's antique grandfather clock> **Synonyms** contriteness, contrition, penitence, regret, remorse, remorsefulness, repentance, rue, self-reproach, shame **Related Words** compunction, misgiving, prick, qualm, scruple; blame, culpability, fault; liability, rap, responsibility; chagrin, embarrassment; anguish, distress, grief, ruth, sadness, sorrow; bloodguilt, bloodguiltiness; apology, excuses, hand-wringing, mea culpa **Antonyms** impenitence, remorselessness 2 responsibility for wrongdoing or failure <the chief financial officer was saddled with the *guilt* for the company's failure> **Synonyms** culpability, fault, guilt, onus, rap **Related Words** blameworthiness, complicity, guiltiness, sinfulness; accusation, censure, condemnation, denunciation, finger-pointing, reproach; regret, remorse, self-reproach, shame **Antonyms** blamelessness, faultlessness, guiltlessness, innocence

By permission. From *Merriam-Webster's Collegiate®* *Dictionary*, 11th Edition © 2015 by Merriam-Webster, Inc. (www.Merriam-Webster.com)

Most word-processing programs have an electronic thesaurus. Usually, it is found with the spelling checker or in the Tools drop-down menu. Use your cursor to highlight (select) the word for which you want alternatives and then click on the thesaurus. Consider the context of your sentence as you choose from the array of words that appear. Be aware, though, that a thesaurus in book form will offer more choices.

EXERCISE 4.10

Using a Thesaurus

Use the entries for *carry* in *Merriam-Webster's Collegiate Dictionary and Thesaurus* on the next page to select an alternative word that fits the meaning of *carry* in the following sentences.

1. Pilates and yoga instructors encourage participants to *carry* themselves with good posture. _____

2. The infamous Typhoid Mary was able to *carry* her infectious disease to others through her employment as a cook. _____

3. When one of the wheels on my luggage broke, I was forced to *carry* my belongings in an expandable briefcase _____

4. Since he was running unopposed, the city councilor was able to easily *carry* the election. _____

carry 1 to support and take from one place to another <each camper must be able to *carry* his or her own backpack> **Synonyms** bear, cart, convey, ferry, haul, lug, pack, tote, transport **Related Words** deliver, hand over, transfer; forward, send, ship, transmit; bring, fetch, take; move, remove, shift 2 to wear or have on one's person <I always *carry* a camera with me so as to never miss a great shot> **Synonyms** bear, pack **Related Words** flaunt, show off, sport; display, exhibit, parade, show 3 to bring before the public in performance or exhibition <all of the television networks will *carry* the president's speech> **Synonyms** carry, give, mount, offer, stage **Related Words** display, exhibit, expose, parade, show, show off, unveil; preview; act, impersonate, perform, play, portray; depict, dramatize, enact, render, represent; extend, proffer, tender 4 to have as part of a whole <the idea of equality *carries* with it a number of other concepts> **Synonyms** carry, comprehend, contain, embrace, encompass, entail, involve, number, subsume, take in **Related Words** comprise, consist (of); bracket; have, hold, own, possess; admit, receive; compose, constitute, form, make; assimilate, embody, incorporate, integrate **Near Antonyms** ban, bar, debar, preclude, prevent, prohibit; deny, refuse, reject; eliminate, except, rule out; lose, mislay, misplace **Antonyms** exclude, leave (out), miss out [*British*], omit 5 to hold up or serve as a foundation for <erected a trellis to *carry* the vine> **Synonyms** bear, bolster, brace, buttress, carry, prop (up), shore (up), stay, sustain, undergird, underpin, uphold **Related Words** steady, truss, underlie 6 to receive as return for effort <*carried* off the award for best picture of the year> **Synonyms** acquire, attain, bag, bring in, capture, carry, come by, draw, gain, garner, get, knock down, land, make, obtain, procure, pull down, realize, reap, secure, win **Related Words** clear, gross, net; accomplish, achieve, notch (up), score; accumulate, amass, draw, rack up; catch, pick up; annex, occupy, take over; reacquire, reattain, recapture, regain, remake **Near Antonyms** accord, give, grant, pay; give up, hand over, part (with), relinquish, surrender, yield **Antonyms** forfeit, lose 7 to manage the actions of (oneself) in a particular way <during that difficult time the grieving parents *carried* themselves with unfailing grace and dignity> **Synonyms** acquit, bear, carry, comport, conduct, demean, deport, quit **Related Words** check, collect, compose, constrain, contain, control, curb, handle, inhibit, quiet, repress, restrain; moderate, modulate, temper; act, impersonate, play **Near Antonyms** act up, carry on, cut up, misbehave, misconduct

By permission. From *Merriam-Webster's Collegiate® Dictionary*, 11th Edition © 2015 by Merriam-Webster, Inc. (www.Merriam-Webster.com)

BRAIN BOOSTER

Meaning Matters!

Human brains are wired to remember meaningful information. Have you ever memorized a list of definitions and promptly forgotten them after the quiz? When you are learning new words, think of them as ideas that link to many other ideas with which you are already familiar. For example, *magma* is melted rock that is expelled from an erupting volcano. Magma > melted rock > lava > ash > fire > smoke > volcano > Mt. St. Helen's > Mt. Vesuvius > Pompeii > eruption > death > destruction. Strive for meaning and association. Then use what you have learned—often. REPEAT!

DEEPENING WORD MEANING

Learning Objective 5

Strengthen word memory with rich meaning

The more details that you can associate with a word, the greater the likelihood you will remember the word. Not only will you remember it, but you might also find that you are more interested in it. Pay attention to words, and you will find history, culture, and shades of meaning that might surprise you!

Exploring Word Origins

The study of word origins is called **etymology**. Not only is it fascinating to trace a word back to its earliest recorded appearance, but also your knowledge of the word's origin can strengthen your memory for the word. For example, the word *narcissistic* means "egotistically in love with oneself." Its origin is a Greek myth in which a beautiful youth named Narcissus falls in love with his own reflection; he is punished for his vanity by being turned into a flower. Thus, the myth creates an intriguing image that can enhance your memory link for the word.

The amount of information on word origins varies with the type of dictionary that you use. Because of its size, a small paperback dictionary, such as the *American Heritage Dictionary*, usually contains very little information on word origins, whereas a textbook-size edition of *Merriam-Webster's Collegiate Dictionary* offers more information. For the most information on word origins, visit the reference room in your college library and use an unabridged dictionary, such as *Webster's Third New International Dictionary*, the *Random House Dictionary of the English Language*, or the *American Heritage Dictionary of the English Language*.

EXERCISE 4.11

Word Origins

Read the following dictionary entries and answer the questions about the words and their origins:

> **¹bribe** \ˈbrīb\ *n* [ME, morsel given to a beggar, bribe, fr. AF, morsel] (15c)   **1** : money or favor given or promised in order to influence the judgment or conduct of a person in a position of trust   **2** : something that serves to induce or influence
> **²bribe** *vb* **bribed; brib·ing** *vt* (1528) : to induce or influence by or as if by bribery ∼ *vi* : to practice bribery — **brib·able** \ˈbrī-bə-bəl\ *adj* —
>
> By permission. From *Merriam-Webster's Collegiate® Dictionary*, 11th Edition © 2015 by Merriam-Webster, Inc. (www.Merriam-Webster.com)

1. *Bribe* means _____

   _____.

2. Explain the origin: _____

   _____

   _____.

¹**scape·goat** \'skāp-,gōt\ *n* [¹*scape;* intended as trans. of Heb *azazel* (prob. name of a demon), as if *'ēz 'ōzēl* goat that departs   Lev 16:8 (AV)] (1530) **1 :** a goat upon whose head are symbolically placed the sins of the people after which he is sent into the wilderness in the biblical ceremony for Yom Kippur **2   a :** one that bears the blame for others   **b :** one that is the object of irrational hostility
²**scapegoat** *vt* (1943) **:** to make a scapegoat of — **scape·goat·ism** \-,gō-,ti-zəm\ *n*

By permission. From *Merriam-Webster's Collegiate® Dictionary*, 11th Edition © 2015 by Merriam-Webster, Inc. (www.Merriam-Webster.com)

3. *Scapegoat* means _____

_____ .

4. Explain the origin: _____

_____ .

marathon *noun*, mar·a·thon *often attributive* \'mer-ə-,thän, 'ma-rə-\ Origin of MARATHON *marathon*, Greece, site of a victory of Greeks over Persians in 490 B.C., the news of which was carried to Athens by a long-distance runner First known use: 1896 **1   a :** a footrace run on an open course usually of 26 miles 385 yards (42.2 kilometers); *broadly*: a long-distance race **2   a :** an endurance contest **b :** something (as an event, activity, or session) characterized by great length or concentrated effort

By permission. From *Merriam-Webster's Collegiate® Dictionary*, 11th Edition © 2015 by Merriam-Webster, Inc. (www.Merriam-Webster.com)

5. *Marathon* means _____

_____ .

6. Explain the origin: _____

_____ .

van·dal \'van-dᵊl\ *n* [L *Vandalii* (pl.), of Gmc origin] (1530) **1** *cap* **:** a member of a Germanic people who lived in the area south of the Baltic Sea between the Vistula and the Oder rivers, overran Gaul, Spain, and northern Africa in the fourth and fifth centuries A.D., and in 455 sacked Rome **2 :** one who willfully or ignorantly destroys, damages, or defaces property belonging to another or to the public — **vandal** *adj, often cap*

By permission. From *Merriam-Webster's Collegiate® Dictionary*, 11th Edition © 2015 by Merriam-Webster, Inc. (www.Merriam-Webster.com)

7. *Vandal* means _____

_____ .

8. Explain the origin: _____

_____

_____ .

Solving Analogies

Analogies are comparisons that call upon not only your word knowledge but also your ability to see relationships. They can be difficult, frustrating, and challenging. Use logical thinking and problem-solving skills to pinpoint the initial relationship, and then establish a similar relationship with two other words.

Reader's TIP) Categories of Analogy Relationships

- **Synonyms:** Similar in meaning
  Find is to *locate* as *hope* is to *wish*.
- **Antonyms:** Opposite in meaning
  Accept is to *reject* as *rude* is to *polite*.
- **Function, use, or purpose:** Identifies what something does; watch for the object (noun) and then the action (verb)
  Pool is to *swim* as *blanket* is to *warm*.
- **Classification:** Identifies the larger group association
  Sandal is to *shoe* as *sourdough* is to *bread*.
- **Characteristics and descriptions:** Shows qualities or traits
  Nocturnal is to *raccoon* as *humid* is to *rainforest*.
- **Degree:** Shows variations of intensity
  Fear is to *terror* as *dislike* is to *hate*.
- **Part to whole:** Shows the larger group
  Page is to *book* as *caboose* is to *train*.
- **Cause and effect:** Shows the reason (cause) and result (effect)
  Study is to *graduation* as *caffeine* is to *insomnia*.

EXERCISE 4.12   Identifying Types of Analogies

Study the analogies that follow to establish the relationship of the first two words. Record that relationship, using the categories outlined in the Reader's Tip, "Categories of Analogy Relationships." Then choose the word that duplicates that relationship to finish the analogy.

1. *Trash* is to *garbage* as *soil* is to _____.

   Relationship _____

   a. earthworms
   b. dirt
   c. minerals
   d. growing

2. *Burdened* is to *overwhelmed* as *tired* is to _____.

   Relationship _____

   a. sleepy
   b. exhausted
   c. energetic
   d. rested

3. *Cappuccino* is to *coffee* as *jazz* is to _____.

   Relationship _____

   a. singer
   b. opera
   c. rock
   d. music

4. *Excited* is to *dull* as *fancy* is to _____.

   Relationship _____

   a. rich
   b. fortunate
   c. plain
   d. colorful

5. *Fork* is to *eat* as *television* is to _____.

   Relationship _____

   a. video
   b. actor
   c. entertain
   d. produce

6. *Sleeve* is to *shirt* as *lens* is to _____.

   Relationship _____

   a. book
   b. motor
   c. movement
   d. camera

7. *Smart* is to *genius* as *rigid* is to _____.

   Relationship _____

   a. steel
   b. comedy
   c. angle
   d. focus

8. *Recklessness* is to *accident* as *laziness* is to _____.

Relationship _____

   a. work
   b. money
   c. failure
   d. ability

Studying Easily Confused Words

Pairs or groups of words may cause confusion because they sound exactly alike, or almost alike, but are spelled and used differently. *Stationary* and *stationery* are examples of such words. You ride a stationary bike to work out, and you write a business letter on your office stationery. For a memory link, associate the *e* in *letter* with the *e* in *stationery*. Students frequently confuse *your* and *you're*: *your* shows possession, and *you're* is a contraction for *you are*. To differentiate confusing words, create associations to aid memory. **Homonyms**, words with different meanings that are spelled or sound alike, are not as confusing. They tend to be simple words, such as *bear* in "bear the burden" or "kill the bear."

EXERCISE **4.13**

Distinguishing Confusing Words

Study each set of easily confused words and then circle the one that correctly fits in each sentence.

   loose: unconfined; relaxed; not tight

   lose: misplace

1. She enjoyed the comfort of long, **(loose, lose)** clothing during the warm

summer months. _____

   hole: opening

   whole: entire object

2. His **(hole, whole)** check was insufficient to cover his monthly car payments.

_____

   there: a place

   their: belonging to them

   they're: they are

3. Over **(there, their, they're)** is the community shelter for the homeless.

_____

   who's: who is

   whose: belonging to whom

4. **(Whose, who's)** idea was it to attend that boring concert last weekend?

_____

SUMMARY POINTS

1 What strategies should I use to expand my vocabulary? (page 176)
- Associate words with phrases that reflect their meanings rather than as separate words.
- Associate words with rhymes or sounds to etch them in your memory.
- Associate words with images. Brains remember pictures.
- Associate words with word families that share a common element, such as a root or a prefix.
- Seek reinforcement. Be alert for your new words as you listen and read.
- Create concept cards to strengthen your memory. Quiz yourself regularly by going through your concept cards.
- Unlock meaning while reading by using context clues, word structure, and word reference aids.

2 How can context clues help me find meaning in new words? (page 178)
- Be alert to the clues in the phrases and sentences surrounding a new word.
- Notice the various types of context clues: definitions or synonyms, elaborating details, examples, comparisons, contrasts, and antonyms.
- Recognize that context clues, although very helpful, have limited power to provide an accurate definition. Consult a dictionary or a glossary if it is important to have a precise definition.
- Remember that many words have multiple meanings. Explore them to enlarge your vocabulary.

3 How can word structure help me find meaning in new words? (page 186)
- Prefixes, roots, and suffixes have meanings of their own that add to the meaning of words in which they are found. Recognizing common word parts and learning their meanings can help to unlock unfamiliar words.

4 How can reference aids clarify meanings of new words? (page 189)
- Dictionary pages are headed by guide words that indicate the first and last words on the page. Dictionary entries provide pronunciation, part of speech, spellings, origin, and multiple meanings.
- Glossaries are usually located at the back of textbooks. They list the specialized definitions of words as they are used in that book.
- A thesaurus is especially helpful to writers who need to vary the words that they use to express ideas. Each entry lists synonyms and antonyms for the entry word.

5 How can I develop rich meaning to strengthen my memory of new words? (page 196)
- Use a dictionary to discover the origins—the etymology—of new words.
- Practice completing analogies to sharpen your thinking about the meanings of words.
- Pay close attention to spelling to maintain quick visual recognition of words that sound the same but have different meanings (homonyms).

| SELECTION 1 | Health | MyReadingLab |

Visit Chapter 4: Vocabulary in MyReadingLab to complete the Selection 1 activities and the Build Background Knowledge video activity.

PREVIEW the next selection to predict its purpose and organization and to formulate your learning plan.

Activate Schemata

How much time do you spend in front of a computer screen, on your cell phone, or using some other form of electronic media?

How do you feel if you accidentally leave your cell phone at home?

Establish a Purpose for Reading

Is it possible that electronic devices can create stress? What are the effects of too much time spent with electronic media? Read this selection to find out what studies by health and behavior experts reveal about technology and health.

Build Background Knowledge — VIDEO

French Employees Unplug After Work

To prepare for reading Selection 1, answer the questions below. Then, watch this video about a ban on after-hours work email and texts in France.

Do you set a time each day to "unplug" from all technology? Why or why not?

What are the positive and negative health consequences of owning a smartphone?

How do you think technology—smartphones, iPads, etc.—has increased work stress?

This video helped me: _____

_____

_____

Increase Word Knowledge

What do you know about these words?

hailing	disorienting	technostress	persona	technosis
syndrome	immersed	perpetually	narcissism	iDisorders

Your instructor may give a brief vocabulary review before or after reading.

Integrate Knowledge While Reading

Read for the main idea and major details. Remember to

Predict   Picture   Relate   Monitor   Correct   Annotate

SKILL DEVELOPMENT: VOCABULARY STRATEGIES

As you read, use context clues and word structure to unlock the meaning of unfamiliar words. The vocabulary exercises will ask you to explore word meaning in greater depth.

TECHNOLOGY AND HEALTH

MOBILE DEVICES, MEDIA AND THE INTERNET: COULD YOU UNPLUG?

How hard would it be to give up your mobile devices, media, and the Internet for 24 hours? Judging from the results of a study with participants hailing from 37 different countries on six continents—extremely hard. All students in the study followed the same assignment: Give up Internet, TV, radio, phones, iPods/MP3 play-
5 ers, movies, video games, and any other form of electronic or social media for 24 hours. Findings included the following:

- Students around the world frequently used the term "addiction" to speak about their technology habits. "Media is my drug; without it I was lost," said one student from the UK. A student from Argentina observed: "Sometimes I felt
10 'dead,'" and a student from Slovakia noted feeling "sad, lonely and depressed."

As the world goes wireless, many of us are increasingly attached to our cell phones, laptops, and tablet computers.
Syda Productions/Fotolia

- Many students view mobile phones as an extension of the self. Going without a phone and easy access to media was disorienting. "It was an unpleasant surprise to realize that I am in a state of constant distraction," said a student from Mexico.

15   Despite the withdrawal symptoms, many students found benefits to unplugging. Some felt they had more time to talk and listen to others. Other students reported feeling liberated, and took time to do things they normally did not do, such as visit relatives or do other activities that involve face-to-face contact.

Have you thought about what going "unplugged" might mean for you? What
20   opportunities would you have if you did not use electronic media for 24 hours?

TAMING TECHNOSTRESS AND iDISORDERS

Are you "twittered out"? Is texting causing your thumbs to seize up in protest? If so, you're not alone. Like millions of others, you may find that the pressure for constant contact is stressing you out! Known as *technostress*, it is defined as stress created by a dependence on technology and the constant state of connection, which can include
25   a perceived obligation to respond, chat, or tweet. When does the constant anxiety over missed messages or an online persona cross the stress load limit?

An increasing number of people would rather hang out online talking to strangers than study, socialize in person, or connect in the real world. There are some clear downsides to all of that virtual interaction.

Social Distress

30   Authors Michelle Weil and Larry Rosen describe *technosis*, a very real syndrome in which people become so immersed in technology that they risk losing their own identity. Worrying about checking your e-mail or text messages, constantly switching to Facebook to see updates, perpetually posting to Twitter, and so on can keep you distracted and waste hours of every day.

Technology Dependency

35   Increasing research supports the concept that feeling the need to be "wired" 24/7 (while eating, studying, hanging out with friends, in the car, and in nearly every place imaginable) can lead to anxiety, obsessive compulsive disorder, narcissism, sleep disorders, frustration, time pressures, and guilt—some of the negative consequences known as *iDisorders*. When you are more worried about your friends list on
40   a social media site than you are about spending the time to make real friends, it may be time to rethink your social interactions.

To avoid iDisorders caused by technology overload or technostress, set time limits on your technology usage, and make sure that you devote at least as much time to face-to-face interactions with people you care about. Remember that you
45   don't always need to answer your phone or respond to a text or e-mail immediately.

Make a rule that you cannot turn on your device when out with friends or on vacation. *Tune in* to your surroundings, your loved ones and friends, your job, and your classes by shutting off your devices.

(614 words)

—From *Health: The Basics*, 11th ed.,
by Rebecca J. Donatelle

Recall

Stop to self-test, relate, and react.

Your instructor may choose to give you a brief comprehension review.

THINK CRITICALLY ABOUT THE SELECTION

What are the benefits of the electronic media discussed in this selection?

What are the problems associated with the electronic media discussed in this selection?

Can the problems be overcome so that the benefits can be enjoyed? How or why?

WRITE ABOUT THE SELECTION

Explain how you can use the information in this selection in your media use this week.

Response suggestion: Make an honest assessment of the amount of time that you spend using electronic media during a normal day and what you might have missed during that time. From the point of view of an outside observer, such as an advice columnist, write a letter to yourself. Include suggestions about the best ways to use your electronic media and the ones to avoid.

CHECK YOUR COMPREHENSION

After reading the selection, answer the following questions with *a, b, c,* or *d.* To help you analyze your strengths and weaknesses, the question types are indicated.

Main Idea _____ 1. What is the best statement of the selection's main point?

    a. Electronic media have both good and bad qualities.

    b. Some users check their e-mail and text messages constantly.

    c. Overuse and dependency on electronic media can create stress, which users can learn to control.

    d. Devote as much time to in-person interaction as you do to virtual interaction.

Detail _____ 2. Which of the following is not mentioned in the selection as a type of iDisorder?

    a. guilt

    b. anxiety

    c. sleep disorders

    d. broken relationships

Inference _____ 3. From the results of the study in which students gave up all electronic media for 24 hours, it is reasonable to conclude that

    a. all of the participants experienced negative reactions.

    b. the effects were the same for students regardless of their nationality.

    c. female students experienced more negative effects than males.

    d. some students were so negatively affected that they considered committing suicide.

Detail _____ 4. One of the positive effects of unplugging from technology for 24 hours that students mentioned was

    a. feeling liberated.

    b. having more time to do their homework.

    c. better concentration while they were driving.

    d. better performance at their jobs.

Author's Purpose _____ 5. The author's main purpose in writing this selection was to

    a. frighten students with technical terms like *social distress* and *technology dependency.*

    b. inform readers of the negative effects of overusing technology and of ways to avoid them.

    c. publicize the results of an international study.

    d. convince readers that they should nurture relationships in person rather than online.

BUILD YOUR VOCABULARY

Apply the strategies discussed in this chapter to unlock the meanings of the following words. The line in which the word first appears is given in parentheses. First, use context clues and word structure to make an educated guess. Next, use a dictionary to clarify the meaning of the word as it was used in the selection. Lastly, indicate which of the strategies was most helpful: context clues, word structure, or the dictionary. If the origin of the word is given, write it on the additional line.

1. hailing (2) _____

    Dictionary definition _____

    Most useful strategy/strategies _____

2. disorienting (12) _____

    Dictionary definition _____

    _____

    Most useful strategy/strategies _____

3. technostress (23) _____

    _____

    Dictionary definition _____

    _____

    Most useful strategy/strategies _____

4. persona (26) _____

    Dictionary definition _____

    _____

    Most useful strategy/strategies _____

5. technosis (30) _____

    _____

    _____

    Dictionary definition _____

    _____

    Most useful strategy/strategies _____

6. syndrome (30) _____

    Dictionary definition _____

    _____

    Most useful strategy/strategies _____

SELECTION

1

7. immersed (31) _____

   Dictionary definition _____

   _____

   Most useful strategy/strategies _____

8. perpetually (33) _____

   Dictionary definition _____

   Most useful strategy/strategies _____

9. narcissism (37) _____

   Dictionary definition _____

   _____

   Most useful strategy/strategies _____

   Origin _____

10. iDisorders (39) _____

    _____

    Dictionary definition _____

    _____

    Most useful strategy/strategies _____

VOCABULARY BOOSTER

What's In, What's Out? What's Hot, What's Not?

Prefixes:	*en-, em-:* "in"	*non-:* "not"	*e-, ec-, ef-, ex-:* "out"
Root:	*calor-:* "heat"		

Words with *en-, em-:* "in"

Jackson was able to *employ* several of his friends as technical representatives for his Internet software company.

- *enclave*: any small, distinct area or group within a larger one

  Before the Berlin Wall came down, West Berlin was a democratic *enclave* surrounded by Communist East Germany.

- *enmesh*: to catch in a net; entangle

  Animal rights groups are against the use of nets in tuna fishing because dolphins can become *enmeshed* in the nets and die.

- *ensemble*: all parts of a thing considered only as the whole, not separately, such as an entire costume or a group of musicians, singers, dancers, or actors.

  The cast of ABC's drama *Grey's Anatomy* is an *ensemble* of many actors.

- *embed*: to fix or place firmly in a surrounding mass; to insert, as a clause in a sentence

  The senator knew that to get her controversial proposal passed by Congress, she had to *embed* it in a more popular bill.

- *embellish*: to beautify with ornamental or elaborate details

  The speechwriter's goal was to enhance but not overly *embellish* the governor's speeches.

- *enroll*: to register or become a member of a group

  Jenny needed to *enroll* in the Psychology 101 class before it became filled.

Words with *e-, ec-, ef-, ex-:* "out"

Renew your driver's license before it *expires* so that you can avoid taking the driving test again.

- *emaciated*: abnormally thin, as if wasting away

  Tanica had lost so much weight on a fad diet that she looked *emaciated*.

- *eccentric*: peculiar or odd; not having the same center

  The neighbor on the corner is an *eccentric* man who wears pajamas to the grocery store.

- *effervescent*: bubbling; lively or enthusiastic

  The *effervescent* spring water foamed and sparkled as Juan poured it.

- *exalt*: raise or elevate in rank or character; praise highly

  In his opening remarks, the club president *exalted* the literary talent and accomplishments of the guest speaker.

- *exaggerate*: to stretch the limits of the truth or overstate

  John always *exaggerates* the size of the fish he claims he almost caught.

Words with *non-*: "not"

Military personnel who are not fighters, such as surgeons or chaplains, are considered *noncombatants*.

- *nonchalant*: coolly indifferent, unconcerned, unexcited

  Tonia's *nonchalant* way of accepting dates makes it seem that she just has nothing better to do.

- *nondescript*: undistinguished or dull, a person or thing of no specific type or kind; not easy to describe

  Students decorated the *nondescript* dorm rooms to reflect their own tastes and personalities.

- *nonpartisan*: objective; not controlled by an established political party

  It is necessary to forge *nonpartisan* politics when the government is split evenly between two parties.

- *nonconformist*: someone who refuses to act in accordance with established customs

  A *nonconformist* would not be a good candidate for a private school where uniforms are worn.

Words with *calor-*: "heat"

When capitalized, the word *Calorie* refers to a kilocalorie (1,000 small calories) and is used to measure the amount of energy produced by food when oxidized in the body.

- *calorie*: a specific unit of heat (cal.) in physics; a unit expressing the energy value of food (Cal.) in nutrition

  Judy tries to eat low-*calorie* meals, including salads, fish, lots of vegetables, and few desserts, to maintain a healthy weight.

- *scald*: to burn with hot liquid or steam; to bring to a temperature just short of the boiling point

  Some recipes require the cook to *scald* milk before adding it to the other ingredients.

- *caldera*: a basinlike depression or collapsed area caused by the explosion of the center of a volcano

The scientists were injured by hot lava when they got too close to the edge of the *caldera* of a still-active volcano.

- **cauldron**: a large kettle for boiling

Shakespeare's *Macbeth* includes a scene with witches stirring a boiling mixture in a *cauldron*.

Review Questions

Part I

Indicate whether the following sentences are true (*T*) or false (*F*):

———— 1. A person who is known to *embellish* is not a plain speaker.

———— 2. We tend to *exalt* those whom we hold in low regard.

———— 3. A *nonchalant* attitude could also be described as deeply caring.

———— 4. A chef can *scald* milk without boiling it.

———— 5. The brass instruments are a part of the band's *ensemble*.

———— 6. An *eccentric* relative likely has some unusual behaviors.

———— 7. Someone who dresses in a *nondescript* manner would stand out in a crowd.

———— 8. *Nonconformists* are likely to care a good deal about what others think of them.

———— 9. A dormitory room could be considered an *enclave* within the dorm itself.

————10. Jewelers have a talent for *embedding* precious stones in gorgeous settings.

Part II

Choose the best *antonym* from the boxed list for the words below.

criticize	compliant	chill	dislodge	fatten
interested	minimized	undecorated	untangled	usual

11. eccentric ——————

12. embellished ——————

13. exalt ——————

14. exaggerated ——————

15. emaciate ——————

16. enmeshed ——————

17. embed ——————

18. nonchalant ——————

19. scald ——————

20. nonconformist ——————

Your instructor may choose to give a brief review.

5 Main Idea and Supporting Details

Learning Objectives

In this chapter, you will learn to:

1 Distinguish topics, main ideas, and supporting details
2 Apply a strategy for finding the main idea
3 Identify stated main ideas
4 Distinguish major and minor details
5 Identify unstated main ideas
6 Identify main ideas of longer selections
7 Write a summary

Vocabulary Booster: The Sun, the Moon, and the Stars

R. Gino Santa Maria/Shutterstock

TOPICS, MAIN IDEAS, AND SUPPORTING DETAILS

In this chapter, we will discuss and practice what many experts believe is the most important reading skill and the key to comprehension—recognizing the main idea of a paragraph, passage, or selection. As you read, whether you're reading your history text, a novel, or an article in an online newspaper, it is important to understand the details that support, develop, and explain a main idea. They answer the question, "What's the point?" However, before attempting to discover the central point of a piece of writing, you must have a good sense of its topic.

What Is a Topic?

A **topic** is like the title of a book or a song. It is a word, name, or phrase that labels the subject but does not reveal the specific contents of the passage. Take a moment and flip back to the table of contents of this text. As you can see, the title of each chapter reflects its general topic. What's more, boldface heads within a chapter reflect subordinate topics, or subtopics. Similarly, individual passages beneath those heads have their own topics.

Think of the topic of a passage as a big umbrella under which specific ideas or details can be grouped. For example, consider the words *carrots, lettuce, onions,* and *potatoes*. What general term would pull together and unify these items?

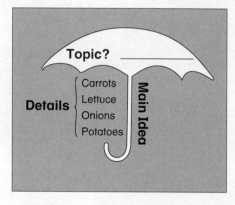

Topic: _____

Identifying Topics

Each of the following lists includes three specific items or ideas that could relate to a single topic. At the top of each list, write a general topic under which the specific ideas can be grouped.

1. _____	2. _____	3. _____
French fried	snow	triathlon
au gratin	rain	5K
scalloped	sleet	marathon

What Is a Main Idea?

While the topic is the general subject, the **main idea** of a passage is more focused and is the central message that the author is trying to convey about the material. It can be stated in a sentence that condenses thoughts and details into a general, all-inclusive statement of the author's point.

Reading specialists use various terms when they are referring to the main idea. In classroom discussions, a variety of words are used to help students understand its meaning. How many of these have you heard?

Main point	Gist	Central thought
Central focus	Controlling idea	Thesis

The last word on the list, *Thesis*, is a familiar word in English composition classes. You have probably had practice in stating a thesis sentence for English essays, but you may not have had as much practice in stating the main idea of a reading selection. Can you see the similarity between a thesis statement and a main idea statement?

How important is it to be able to find and comprehend the main idea? Experts say that it is *crucial to your comprehension of any text*. In fact, if all reading comprehension techniques were combined and reduced to one essential question, that question might be, "What is the main idea that the author is trying to get across to the reader?" Whether you read a single paragraph, a chapter, or an entire book, your most important single task is to understand the main idea of what you read.

What Are Supporting Details?

Details are statements that support, describe, develop, and explain a main idea. Specific details can include reasons, incidents, facts, examples, steps, and definitions.

There are important differences between *major details*, which are critical to the support of the main idea and your understanding of a passage, and *minor details*, which amplify the major details. One way to distinguish the two is to pay attention to signal words, which link thoughts and help you anticipate the kind of detail that is coming next. Key signal words for major supporting details are *one, first, another, furthermore, also,* and *finally*. Key signal words for minor details are *for example, to be specific, that is,* and *this means*. We will deepen our discussion of major and minor details later in this chapter.

Distinguishing Topics, Main Ideas, and Details: A Closer Look

We have seen that a topic is a general subject and that a main idea is the author's central message about the topic. Let's explore the difference between them—and the importance of supporting details—a little more closely.

The diagram that follows depicts the relationship among topics, main ideas, and major and minor details.

- The topic is the broad subject.
  ↑
- The main idea makes a point about the topic.
  ↑
- Major details develop and explain the main idea.
  ↑
- Minor details elaborate on the major details.

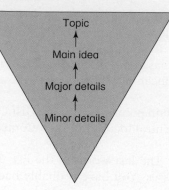

Caffeine is a general term or topic that unifies the items *coffee, tea, cola,* and *chocolate*. If those items were used as details in a paragraph, the main idea could not be expressed by simply saying "caffeine." The word *caffeine* would answer the question, "What is the passage about?" However, only your evaluation of the supporting details in the paragraph would answer the question, "What is the author's main idea?"

Think of some of the very different paragraphs about caffeine that a writer could devise using the same four details as support. If you were that writer, what would be the main idea or thesis—using the four items as supporting details—of your paragraph?

Topic: Caffeine

Main idea or thesis: _____

_____

EXAMPLE   Read the following examples of different main ideas that could be developed in a paragraph about the topic of caffeine. Explanations appear in italicized type.

1. Consumption of caffeine is not good for your health. *(Details would enumerate health hazards associated with each item.)*

2. Americans annually consume astonishing amounts of caffeine. *(Details would describe amounts of each consumed annually.)*

3. Caffeine makes money for the Starbucks empire. *(Details would show the profits and expansion of the coffee giant.)*

4. Reduce caffeine consumption with the decaffeinated version of popular caffeine-containing beverages. *(Details would promote the decaffeinated version of each item.)*

EXAMPLE   Following are examples of a topic, main idea, and supporting detail.

Topic

EARLY COGNITIVE DEVELOPMENT

Main Idea   Cognitive psychologists sometimes study young children to observe the very beginnings of cognitive activity. For example, when children first begin to utter words and
Detail   sentences, they overgeneralize what they know and make language more consistent than it actually is.

—Christopher Peterson,
Introduction to Psychology

EXPLANATION   The topic pulls your attention to a general area, and the main idea provides the focus. The detail offers elaboration and support.

EXERCISE 5.1

Differentiating Topic, Main Idea, and Supporting Details

This exercise is designed to check your ability to differentiate statements of the main idea from the topic and supporting details. Compare the items within each group and indicate whether each one is a statement of the main idea *(MI)*, a topic *(T)*, or a specific supporting detail *(SD)*.

Group 1

_____ a. For poor farm families, life on the plains meant a sod house or a dugout carved out of the hillside for protection from the winds.

_____ b. One door and usually no more than a single window provided light and air.

_____ c. Sod houses on the plains.

—James W. Davidson et al., *Nation of Nations*

Group 2

_____ a. And his personal charisma undoubtedly attracted support from many people as well.

_____ b. Barack Obama's successful bid for the U.S. presidency illustrates the two primary approaches to leadership through the eyes of followers—transformational leadership and charismatic leadership.

_____ c. Leadership through the eyes of followers.

_____ d. Barack Obama's successful bid for the U.S. presidency was fueled in part by many people's perceptions that he was both a transformational and charismatic leader.

—Ronald J. Ebert and Ricky W. Griffin, *Business Essentials*, 10th ed.

Group 3

_____ a. A new view of childhood.

_____ b. The middle-class family now became "child-centered": The care, nurture, and rearing of children was viewed as the family's main function.

_____ c. Among the well-to-do, children spent more time with servants or tutors than with their parents.

_____ d. In the nineteenth century, more than ever before, childhood was seen as a distinct state of life requiring the special and sustained attention of adults at least until the age of 13 or 14.

—H.W. Brands, et al., *American Stories: A History of the United States, Combined Volume*, 3rd ed.

STRATEGIES FOR FINDING THE MAIN IDEA

Not surprisingly, reading is easier when we know something about the topic. This illustrates the importance of schemata and should remind us to be alert to opportunities to learn about a broad range of subjects. When we are open to new experiences and read widely, we build a base of background knowledge that makes future learning easier.

Prior Knowledge and Constructing the Main Idea

How exactly do you figure out the main idea of a paragraph or a passage? Researchers have investigated the processes that readers use to construct main ideas. One researcher, Peter Afflerbach, asked graduate students and university professors to "think aloud" as they read passages on both familiar and unfamiliar topics.[1] The study concluded that expert readers use different strategies for reading familiar and unfamiliar materials.

Here is the important finding: *Already knowing something about the topic is the key* to easy reading. In other words, readers with prior knowledge of the subject do not have to struggle with information overload and can quickly recognize the author's main ideas. By contrast, readers with little prior knowledge of the subject are absorbed in trying to make meaning out of unfamiliar words and confusing sentences and have few resources for constructing a main idea. Even an expert reader in history, for example, might struggle to read chemistry books until enough knowledge is built for main idea construction to be automatic.

This research suggests that readers need different main idea strategies based on their level of background knowledge of the subject.

Strategy for Readers With Prior Knowledge.   Preview the passage and make a guess at the main idea. Read for confirmation, stopping at natural breaks to absorb the details and mentally summarize.

Strategy for Readers Without Prior Knowledge.   Preview to determine the topic. Read carefully to identify major details and, then, mentally summarize. Review to determine the relationship of the major details and the topic. Identify the main point.

What differences do you see between these approaches? Since introductory college textbooks address many topics that are new and unfamiliar, freshmen readers will frequently need to read more carefully to comprehend the main ideas of their college textbooks. Until you build up your reserves of prior knowledge through the college courses you take, constructing main ideas for course textbooks is likely to be a *conscious effort* rather than an automatic process.

Identifying Main Ideas Among Sentences

Before identifying main ideas in paragraphs, practice with a simple list of sentences. Read the sentences in the following group. They are related to a single topic, with one sentence expressing a main idea and two other sentences expressing detailed support. Circle the number of the sentence that best expresses the main idea and write the general topic for the group.

---

[1] Peter Afflerbach, "How Are Main Idea Statements Constructed? Watch the Experts!," *Journal of Reading* 30 (1987): 512–18; and "The Influence of Prior Knowledge on Expert Readers' Main Idea Construction Strategies," *Reading Research Quarterly* 25 (1990): 31–46.

EXAMPLE

1. The 1960 presidential debate between John F. Kennedy and Richard Nixon boosted Kennedy's campaign and elevated the role of television in national politics.

2. Televised presidential debates are a major feature of U.S. presidential elections.

3. Ronald Reagan's performance in the 1980 and 1984 presidential debates confirmed the public view of him as decent, warm, and dignified.

Topic: _____

—Adapted from James MacGregor Burns et al.,
Government by the People, 20th ed.

EXPLANATION   The second sentence best expresses the main idea, declaring the importance of televised presidential debates. The other two sentences are details offering specific facts in support of the topic, which is the importance of televised presidential debates.

EXERCISE 5.3

Discovering Topics and Main Ideas in Sentence Groups

Circle the number of the sentence that best expresses the general main idea and write the general topic.

Group 1

1. Dentists are trying virtual reality headsets for their patients to help reduce anxiety about dental care.

2. Gradual exposure to takeoff and landing in a virtual environment allows would-be travelers to face their phobias and prepare to take the next step, a real flight.

3. Overcoming fear is a fast-growing application of virtual reality.

4. Topic: _____

—Alan Evans et al.,
Technology in Action, 2nd ed.

Group 2

1. At present, the meaning of correlations between brain size and intelligence is not clear.

2. For example, females have about the same average intelligence as males but generally have smaller brains.

3. The Neanderthals had larger brains than we do, but there is no evidence that they were smarter.

4. Topic: _____

—Adapted from Stephen M. Kosslyn and Robin S. Rosenberg,
Psychology: The Brain, the Person, the World, 2nd ed.

Group 3

1. The smaller of the front claws moves to and from the mouth in front of the enlarged claw.

2. Unlike most animals, male fiddler crabs (genus *Uca*) are highly asymmetrical.

3. One claw grows to giant proportions, up to half the mass of the entire body.

4. Topic: _____

To determine the main idea of a paragraph, article, or book, follow the basic steps shown in the box, and ask the questions posed in the Reader's Tip, "Using Three Questions to Find the Main Idea" that follows. The order of the steps may vary, depending on your prior knowledge of the material. If you are familiar with the material, you might find that constructing the main idea is automatic and you can select significant supporting details afterward. If you are unfamiliar with the material, as may often be the case in textbook reading, you need to identify the topic and details first, and from them you will form a main idea statement.

Reader's TIP — **Using Three Questions to Find the Main Idea**

1. **Determine the topic.** *Who or what is this reading about?*
   Find a general word or phrase that names the subject. The topic should be broad enough to include all of the ideas, yet restrictive enough to focus on the direction of the details. For example, the topic of an article might be correctly identified as politics, federal politics, or corruption in federal politics, but the last might be the most descriptive of the actual contents.

2. **Identify details.** *What are the major supporting details?*
   Look at the details and key terms that seem to be significant to see if they point in a particular direction. What aspect of the topic do they address? What seems to be the common message? Details such as kickbacks to senators, overspending on congressional junkets, and lying to the voters could support the idea of corruption in federal politics.

3. **Find the main idea.** *What is the message that the author is trying to convey about the topic?*
   The statement of the main idea should be:

   - A complete sentence
   - Broad enough to include the important details
   - Focused enough to describe the author's slant

   An author's main idea about corruption in federal politics might be that voters need to ask for an investigation of seemingly corrupt practices by federal politicians.

Routes to the Main Idea

For Familiar Material

Preview ▶ ▶ ▶ Predict main idea ▶ ▶ ▶ Read ▶ ▶ ▶ Identify key details ▶ ▶ ▶ Confirm main idea

For Unfamiliar Material

Preview ▶ ▶ ▶ Determine topic ▶ ▶ ▶ Read ▶ ▶ ▶ Identify key details ▶ ▶ ▶ Find main idea

Questioning for the Main Idea

Like paragraphs, visual images also suggest main ideas. Photographers and artists compose and select images to communicate a message. Look at the picture shown below and then answer the questions that follow.

What is the general topic of the photograph? _____

_____

What details seem important? _____

_____

_____

What is the main idea the photographer is trying to convey about the topic?

_____

_____

_____

Mike Coppola/Getty

In the photo, representatives of World Wrestling Entertainment, Inc. (WWE) launch the Protein Fight Club, a campaign that spotlights the 8 grams of protein in each 8-ounce glass of milk. The details of the photo show the group holding a WWE Championship belt while standing in front of a poster with the phrases "got milk?" "#MilkWins," and "Protein Fight Club" repeated many times. The details in the photo and text plus the viewers' background knowledge about the WWE make the message persuasive: If we want to ultimately win the fight, we need the protein found in a glass of milk.

STATED MAIN IDEAS

Learning Objective 3

Identify stated main ideas

The Topic Sentence

As in the photo on the previous page, an author's main point can be directly stated in the material. When the main idea is stated in a sentence, the statement is called a **topic sentence** or **thesis statement**. Such a statement is helpful to the reader because it provides an overview of the material.

Read the following examples and answer the questions for determining the main idea using the three-question technique.

EXAMPLE

Managers can regain control over their time in several ways. One is by meeting whenever possible in someone else's office so that they can leave as soon as their business is finished. Another is to start meetings on time without waiting for late-comers. The idea is to let late-comers adjust their schedules rather than everyone else adjusting theirs. A third is to set aside a block of time to work on an important project without interruption. This may require ignoring the telephone, being protected by an aggressive assistant, or hiding out. Whatever it takes is worth it.

—Joseph Reitz and Linda Jewell,
Managing

1. Who or what is this passage about? _____

_____

2. What are the major details? _____

_____

_____

3. What is the main idea that the authors are trying to convey about the topic?

_____

_____

_____

EXPLANATION   The passage is about managers controlling their time. The major details are *meet in another office, start meetings on time,* and *block out time to* *work.* The main idea, stated in the beginning as a topic sentence, is that managers can do things to control their time.

EXAMPLE   New high-speed machines also brought danger to the workplace. If a worker succumbed to boredom, fatigue, or simple miscalculation, disaster could strike. Each year of the late nineteenth century some 35,000 wage earners were killed by industrial accidents. In Pittsburgh iron and steel mills alone, in one year 195 men died from hot metal explosions, asphyxiation, and falls, some into pits of molten metal. Men and women working in textile mills were poisoned by the thick dust and fibers in the air; similar toxic atmospheres injured those working in anything from twine-making plants to embroidery factories. Railways, with their heavy equipment and unaccustomed speed, were especially dangerous. In Philadelphia over half the railroad workers who died between 1886 and 1890 were killed by accidents. For injury or death, workers and their families could expect no payment from employers, since the idea of worker's compensation was unknown.

—James W. Davidson et al.,
Nation of Nations

1. Who or what is this passage about? _____

_____

2. What are the major details? _____

_____

_____

3. What is the main idea that the author is trying to convey about the topic? ___

_____

_____

_____

EXPLANATION   The passage is about injuries from machines. The major details are *35,000 killed, 195 died from explosions and other accidents in Pittsburgh iron and steel mills, poisoned dust killed workers in textile mills,* and *half of the rail workers who died were killed in accidents.* The main idea is that new high-speed machines brought danger to the workplace.

How Common Are Stated Main Ideas?

Research shows that students find passages easier to comprehend when the main idea is directly stated within the passage. How often do stated main ideas appear in college textbooks? Should the reader expect to find that most paragraphs have stated main ideas?

For psychology textbooks, the answer seems to be about half and half. One research study found that stated main ideas appeared in *only 58 percent* of the sampled paragraphs in introductory psychology textbooks.[2] In one of the books, the main idea was directly stated in 81 percent of the sampled paragraphs, and the researchers noted that the text was particularly easy to read.

Given these findings, we should recognize the importance of being skilled in locating and, especially, in constructing main ideas. In pulling ideas together to construct a main idea, you will be looking at the big picture and not left searching for a single suggestive sentence.

Where Are Stated Main Ideas Located?

Should college readers wish for all passages in all textbooks to begin with stated main ideas? Indeed, research indicates that when the main idea is stated at the beginning of the passage, the reader tends to comprehend the text more easily. In their research, however, Smith and Chase found that only 33 percent of the stated main ideas were positioned as the first sentence of the paragraph.

Main idea statements can be positioned at the beginning, in the middle, or at the end of a paragraph. Both the beginning and concluding sentences of a passage can be combined to form a main idea statement.

EXERCISE 5.4 ## Locating Stated Main Ideas

The following diagrams and examples demonstrate the different possible positions for stated main ideas within paragraphs. Annotate as you read the examples and then insert the main ideas and supporting details into the blank spaces provided beside the geometric diagrams.

1. **An introductory statement of the main idea is given at the beginning of the paragraph.**

EXAMPLE

Under hypnosis, people may recall things that they are unable to remember spontaneously. Some police departments employ hypnotists to probe for information that crime victims do not realize they have. In 1976, twenty-six young children were kidnapped from a school bus near Chowchilla, California. The driver of the bus caught a quick glimpse of the license plate of the van in which he and the children were driven away. However, he remembered only the first two digits. Under hypnosis, he recalled the other numbers and the van was traced to its owners.

—David Dempsey and Philip Zimbardo,
Psychology and You

---

[2]B. Smith and N. Chase, "The Frequency and Placement of Main Idea Topic Sentences in College Psychology Textbooks," *Journal of College Reading and Learning* 24 (1991): 46–54.

Main Idea: _____

Details: 1. _____
            2. _____
            3. _____
            4. _____

2. **A concluding statement of the main idea appears at the end of the paragraph.**

EXAMPLE

Research is not a once-and-for-all-times job. Even sophisticated companies often waste the value of their research. One of the most common errors is not providing a basis for comparisons. A company may research its market, find a need for a new advertising campaign, conduct the campaign, and then neglect to research the results. Another may simply feel the need for a new campaign, conduct it, and research the results. Neither is getting the full benefit of the research. When you fail to research either the results or your position *prior* to the campaign, you cannot know the effects of the campaign. For good evaluation you must have both before and after data.

—Edward Fox and Edward Wheatley,
Modern Marketing

Main Idea: _____

Details: 1. _____
            2. _____
            3. _____
            4. _____

3. **Details are placed at the beginning to arouse interest, followed by a statement of the main idea in the middle of the paragraph.**

EXAMPLE

After losing $1 billion in Euro-Disney's first year of operation, the company realized that Paris was not Anaheim or Orlando. French employees were insulted by the Disney dress code, and European customers were not accustomed to standing in line for rides or eating fast food standing up. Disney had to adjust and customize its market mix after learning that international customers are not all alike. The company ditched its controversial dress code, authorized wine with meals, lowered admission prices, hired a French investor relations firm, and changed the name to Disneyland Paris to lure the French tourist.

—Adapted from Michael Mescon et al.,
Business Today, 8th ed.

Details:

1.

2.

Main Idea:

Details:

3.

4.

4. **Both the introductory and concluding sentences state the main idea.**

EXAMPLE

You cannot avoid conflict, but you can learn to face it with a four-step conflict resolution plan. Before you bring up the issue that's upsetting you, know what you want to achieve. Have a positive outcome in mind. Then listen to what the other side says, but go beyond that to try to understand as well. Express empathy for their position. It may not be easy, but try to see the big picture. Place the conflict in context. Finally, if at all possible, end your discussion on a positive note. Set the stage for further discussion by keeping those lines of communication open. Use these four strategies for handling tensions constructively and enjoy stronger social bonds.

—Adapted from Rebecca J. Donatelle,
Access to Health, 8th ed.

Main Idea:

Details:

1.

2.

3.

4.

Main Idea:

5. **Details combine to make a point, but the main idea is not directly stated.**

EXAMPLE

This creature's career could produce but one result, and it speedily followed. Boy after boy managed to get on the river. The minister's son became an engineer. The doctor's sons became "mud clerks"; the wholesale liquor dealer's son became a bar-keeper on a boat; four sons of the chief merchant, and two sons of the county judge, became pilots. Pilot was the grandest position of all. The pilot, even in those days of trivial wages, had a princely salary—from a hundred and fifty to two hundred and fifty dollars a month, and no board to pay. Two months of his wages would pay a preacher's salary for a year. Now some of us were left disconsolate. We could not get on the river—at least our parents would not let us.

—Mark Twain,
Life on the Mississippi

Unstated Main Idea: _____

Details:
1. _____
2. _____
3. _____
4. _____

EXPLANATION   Although not directly stated, the main idea is that young boys in the area have a strong desire to leave home and get a prestigious job on the Mississippi River.

EXERCISE 5.5   ## Using Questions to Find Stated Main Ideas

Read the following passages and use the three-question system to determine the author's main idea. For each passage in this exercise, the answer to the third question will be stated somewhere within the paragraph.

Passage 1

The concept and practice of group harmony or *wa* is what most dramatically differentiates Japanese baseball from the American game. Contract holdouts for additional money, for example, are rare in Japan. A player usually takes what the club decides to give him, and that's that. Demanding more money is evidence that a player is putting his own interests before those of the team. Temper tantrums—along with practical joking, bickering, complaining, and other norms of American clubhouse life—are viewed in Japan as unwelcome intrusions into the team's collective peace of mind.

—Robert Whiting,
You Gotta Have Wa

1. Who or what is this about? _____

_____

_____

2. What are the major details? _____

_____

_____

_____

3. What is the main idea that the author is trying to convey about the topic?

_____

_____

_____

4. Underline the main idea.

Passage 2

The participants were male college students. Each student, placed in a room by himself with an intercom, was led to believe that he was communicating with one or more students in an adjacent room. During the course of a discussion about personal problems, he heard what sounded like one of the other students having an epileptic seizure and gasping for help. During the "seizure," it was impossible for the participant to talk to the other students or to find out what, if anything, they were doing about the emergency. The dependent variable was the speed with which the participant reported the emergency to the experimenter. The likelihood of intervention depended on the number of bystanders the participant thought were present. The more people he thought were present, the slower he was in reporting the seizure, if he did so at all. Everyone in a two-person situation intervened within 160 seconds, but nearly 40 percent of those who believed they were part of a larger group never bothered to inform the experimenter that another student was seriously ill.

—Richard Gerrig and Philip Zimbardo,
Psychology and Life, 17th ed.

1. Who or what is this about? _____

_____

_____

2. What are the major details? _____

_____

_____

_____

3. What is the main idea that the authors are trying to convey about the topic?

_____

_____

_____

4. Underline the main idea.

Passage 3

False childhood memories can be experimentally induced. In one classic study of false memory, researchers M. Garry and E. Loftus were able to implant a false memory of being lost in a shopping mall at 5 years of age in 25% of participants aged 18 to 53, after verification of the fictitious experience by a relative. Repeated exposure to suggestions of false memories can create those memories. Further, researchers have found that adults who claim to have recovered memories of childhood abuse or of abduction by extraterrestrials are more vulnerable to experimentally induced false memories than are adults who do not report such recovered memories.

—Samuel E. Wood, et al.,
Mastering the World of Psychology, 5th ed.

1. Who or what is this about? _____

_____

_____

2. What are the major details? _____

_____

_____

_____

_____

_____

_____

3. What is the main idea that the author is trying to convey about the topic?

_____

_____

_____

4. Underline the main idea.

WHAT ARE MAJOR AND MINOR DETAILS?

Learning Objective 4

Distinguish major and minor details

Textbooks are packed full of details, but fortunately all details are not of equal importance. Major details tend to support, explain, and describe main ideas—they are essential. Minor details, by contrast, tend to support, explain, and describe the major details. Ask the following questions to determine which details are major in importance and which are not:

1. Which details logically develop the main idea?
2. Which details help you understand the main idea?
3. Which details make you think the main idea that you have chosen is correct?

Key signal words, like those listed in the Reader's Tip that follows, form transitional links among ideas and can sometimes help you distinguish between major and minor details.

Reader's TIP Signals for Significance

- Key words for major details:

  one   first   another   furthermore   also   finally

- Key words for minor details:

  for example   to be specific   that is   this means

Develop the habit of annotating by circling major details. Later, expand your annotating by underlining minor details.

EXAMPLE

Our brains are not fully formed at birth. During infancy, synapses proliferate at a great rate. Neurons sprout new dendrites, creating new synapses and producing more complex connections among the brain's nerve cells. New learning and stimulating environments promote this increase in complexity. Then, during childhood, synaptic connections that are useful for helping the child respond to the environment survive and are strengthened whereas those that are not useful wither away, leaving behind a more efficient neural network. In this way, each brain is optimized for its environment. This plasticity, the brain's ability to change in response to new experiences, is most pronounced during infancy and early childhood, and has a resurgence in adolescence, but it continues throughout life.

—Carole Wade, Carol Tavris, and Maryanne Garry,
Psychology, 11th ed.

1. The topic of the passage is

   a. Neurons and dendrites.
   b. The brains of human infants.
   c. The plasticity of the brain.
   d. Stimulating environments.

2. Indicate whether each of the following details is major or minor in support of the author's topic:

_____ a. During infancy, synapses proliferate at a great rate.

_____ b. Neurons sprout new dendrites.

_____ c. During childhood, synaptic connections that are useful for helping the child respond to the new environment survive and are strengthened whereas those that are not useful wither away, leaving behind a more efficient neural network.

_____ d. Each brain is optimized for its environment.

_____ e. Resurgence in adolescence, but it continues throughout life.

3. Underline the sentence that best states the main idea of this passage.

EXPLANATION   For the first response, the topic of the passage is *c*. Both *a* and *d* are too broad, and *b* is a detail. For the second item, *a*, *c*, and *e* are major details because they describe important stages of human brain development. Items *b* and *d* are minor details that further explain the effects of change in each stage. The main idea is stated in both the first and the last sentences.

EXERCISE 5.6

Identifying Topics, Stated Main Ideas, and Details in Passages

Read the following passages and apply the three-question system. Select the letter of the author's topic, circle major details, identify minor ones, and underline the main idea. For each passage in this exercise, the answer to the third question will be stated somewhere within the paragraph.

Passage 1

Building and equipping the pyramids focused and transformed Egypt's material and human resources. Artisans had to be trained, engineering and transportation problems solved, quarrying and stone-working techniques perfected, and laborers recruited. In the Old Kingdom, whose population has been estimated at perhaps 1.5 million, more than 70,000 workers at a time were employed in building the great temple-tombs. No smaller work force could have built such a massive structure as the Great Pyramid of Khufu.

—Mark Kishlansky et al.,
Civilization in the West, 4th ed.

_____ 1. The topic of the passage is

a. Training Laborers for the Pyramids.
b. Resources Needed for Building Pyramids.
c. Pyramid Building Problems.
d. The Pyramids.

2. Indicate whether each of the following details is major or minor in support of the author's topic:

_____ a. The Old Kingdom had an estimated population of 1.5 million.

_____ b. More than 70,000 workers at a time were employed in building the great temple-tombs.

_____ c. Artisans had to be trained.

3. Underline the sentence that best states the main idea of this passage.

Passage 2

If you're upset or tired, you're at risk for an emotion-charged confrontation. If you ambush someone with an angry attack, don't expect her or him to be in a productive frame of mind. Instead, give yourself time to cool off before you try to resolve a conflict. In the case of the group project, you could call a meeting for later in the week. By that time, you could gain control of your feelings and think things through. Of course, sometimes issues need to be discussed on the spot; you may not have the luxury to wait. But whenever it's practical, make sure your conflict partner is ready to receive you and your message. Select a mutually acceptable time and place to discuss a conflict.

—Adapted from Steven A. Beebe, Susan J. Beebe,
and Diana K. Ivy,
Communication

_____ 1. The topic of the passage is

a. Planning for Conflict Resolution.
b. Confrontation.
c. Being Productive.
d. Solving Problems.

2. Indicate whether each of the following details is major or minor in support of the author's topic:

_____ a. Give yourself time to cool off before you try to resolve a conflict.

_____ b. If you're upset, you're at risk for a confrontation.

_____ c. Call a meeting a week later for a group project.

3. Underline the sentence that best states the main idea of this passage.

Passage 3

In a Utah case, the defendant fell asleep in his car on the shoulder of the highway. Police stopped, smelled alcohol on his breath, and arrested him for driving while intoxicated. His conviction was reversed by the Utah Supreme Court because the defendant was not in physical control of the vehicle at the time, as required by the law. In freeing the defendant, the Supreme Court judged that the legal definition of sufficiency was not established in this case because the act observed by the police was not sufficient to confirm the existence of a guilty mind. In other words, the case against him failed because he was not violating the law at the time of the arrest and because it was also possible that he drove while sober, then pulled over, drank, and fell asleep.

—Adapted from Jay S. Albanese,
Criminal Justice, Brief Edition

_____ 1. The topic of the passage is

a. Driving Drunk.
b. The Utah Supreme Court.
c. Sleeping Behind the Wheel.
d. Establishing Sufficiency for Drunken Driving.

2. Indicate whether each of the following details is major or minor in support of the author's topic:

_____ a. Police arrested the defendant for driving while intoxicated.

_____ b. The defendant was not violating a law at the time of the arrest.

_____ c. The case was tried in Utah.

3. Underline the sentence that best states the main idea of this passage.

UNSTATED MAIN IDEAS

Learning Objective 5

Identify unstated main ideas

Unfortunately, even if details are obvious, you cannot always depend on the author to provide a direct statement of a main idea. To add drama and suspense to a description or a narrative, the main idea may be hinted at or implied rather than directly stated. Main ideas are often unstated in other media as well, such as movies and photographs.

Look at the details in the photo on page 234 to decide what message the photographer is trying to communicate. Determine the topic of the picture, propose a main idea using your prior knowledge, and then list some of the significant details that support this point.

What is the topic? _____

_____

_____

What are the significant supporting details? _____

_____

_____

AP Photo/Mike Gullett

What point is the photograph trying to convey about the topic? _____
_____
_____

The topic of the photo is the devastation of homes and lives by what appears to have been a tornado. The details depict at least one home almost completely destroyed while another appears to be less damaged. Debris piled at the side of the street suggests that cleanup has begun. Viewers can infer that the people in the picture live in this neighborhood and that the man and the child in the foreground have a close connection to one of the homes. Perhaps one of the homes is where they lived. He is comforting the child. The main idea is that people's lives have been tragically disrupted by the destruction of a neighborhood, but they comfort each other and move forward. The main idea is not directly stated but is suggested by the details in the picture.

Unstated Main Ideas in Sentences

Before identifying unstated main ideas in paragraphs, practice with a simple list of sentences. First, read the related sentences in the following group. Next, create a sentence that states a general main idea for the three related thoughts.

EXAMPLE

1. Circulation of print newspapers peaked at 63.3 million in 1984, just before computers became a part of everyday life.
2. They were slow, even resistant, to moving their content to the Internet.

3. By 2009 newspaper circulation was 45.6 million, off almost one-third and slipping 7 percent a year.

—John Vivian,
The Media of Mass Communication, 11th ed.

Main idea: _____

_____

EXPLANATION   The first sentence states that the highest circulation figure for print newspapers occurred in 1984 at 63.3 million. The second sentence suggests that newspapers held back on publishing on the Internet, and the third sentence states that circulation had slipped significantly by 2009. The general main idea reflected in these sentences is that circulation of print newspapers is declining and perhaps is due to readers' preference for reading on the Internet.

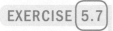

Determining Unstated Main Ideas

Read the following related sentences and state the main idea:

Group 1

1. On the positive side, children who are bilingual have a clear advantage in metalinguistic ability, the capacity to think about language.
2. In addition, most bilingual children display more advanced executive processing skills on language tasks than do monolingual children.
3. On the negative side, infants in bilingual homes reach some milestones later than those learning a single language; children growing up in bilingual homes in which the two languages vary greatly in how they are written (e.g., English and Chinese) may acquire reading skills in both languages more slowly than peers in monolingual homes.

—Denise G. Boyd and Helen L. Bee,
Lifespan Development, 7th ed.

Main idea: _____

_____

Group 2

1. President George Washington converted the paper thoughts outlined in the Constitution into an enduring, practical governing process, setting precedents that balance self-government and leadership.
2. Thomas Jefferson, a skilled organizer and a resourceful party leader and chief executive, adapted the presidency to the new realities of his day with territorial expansions and sponsorship of the Lewis and Clark expedition westward.

3. President Lincoln is remembered for saving the Union and is revered as the nation's foremost symbol of democracy and tenacious leadership in the nation's ultimate crisis.

—James MacGregor Burns,
Government by the People, 20th ed.

Main idea: _____

_____

Group 3

1. Sales prospects are much more inclined to buy from people who make them feel good and with whom they have developed a personal bond, so begin by building a rapport.
2. Ask questions to find out the prospect's real needs, and describe the product or service accordingly to focus on the buyer's benefits.
3. Go for the final close and remember to ask for the order and stop talking so the customer can make the purchase.

—Michael Mescon et al.,
Business Today, 8th ed.

Main idea: _____

_____

Unstated Main Ideas in Paragraphs

Determining the main idea of a paragraph will be easier if you use the three-step questioning strategy on page 220. The questions used to find an unstated main idea have a subtle difference, though. As you approach a passage with an implied or unstated main idea, begin by asking, "What is this about?" Reading carefully to identify key terms and major supporting details, draw a conclusion about the topic. Once you have determined the general topic of the paragraph, then ask yourself, "What do all or most of the key terms or major details suggest?" It is now up to you to figure out the author's point. Think as you read. Create an umbrella statement that brings these concepts together into a main idea statement.

EXAMPLE

Michael Harner proposes an ecological interpretation of Aztec sacrifice and cannibalism. He holds that human sacrifice was a response to certain diet deficiencies in the population. In the Aztec environment, wild game was getting scarce, and the population was growing. Although the maize–beans combination of food that was the basis of the diet was usually adequate, these crops were subject to seasonal failure. Famine was frequent in the absence of edible domesticated animals. To meet essential protein requirements, cannibalism was the only solution. Although only the upper classes were allowed to consume human flesh, a commoner who distinguished himself in a war could also have the privilege of giving a cannibalistic feast. Thus, although it was the upper strata who benefited most from ritual cannibalism, members of the commoner class could also benefit. Furthermore, as Harner explains, the social mobility and cannibalistic privileges available to the commoners through warfare provided a strong motivation for the "aggressive war machine" that was such a prominent feature of the Aztec state.

—Serena Nanda,
Cultural Anthropology, 4th ed.

1. Who or what is this about? _____

_____

_____

2. What are the major details? _____

_____

_____

3. What is the main idea the author is trying to convey about the topic? _____

_____

_____

EXPLANATION   The passage is about Aztec sacrifice and cannibalism. The major details are: Diet deficiencies occurred, animals were not available, and members of the upper class and commoners who were war heroes could eat human flesh. The main idea is that Aztec sacrifice and cannibalism met protein needs of the diet and motivated warriors to achieve.

EXERCISE 5.8

Identifying Unstated Main Ideas

Read the following passages and apply the three-question system. Select the letter of the author's topic, identify major and minor details, circle major details, identify minor details, and choose the letter of the sentence that best states the main idea.

Passage 1

Each year in the United States approximately 50,000 miscarriages are attributed to smoking during pregnancy. On average, babies born to mothers who smoke weigh less than those born to nonsmokers, and low birth weight is correlated with many developmental problems. Pregnant women who stop smoking in the first three or four months of their pregnancies give birth to higher-birth-weight babies than do women who smoke throughout their pregnancies. Infant mortality rates are also higher among babies born to smokers.

—Rebecca J. Donatelle,
Health: The Basics, 4th ed.

_____ 1. The topic of the passage is

    a. Infant Mortality.
    b. Smoking.
    c. Smoking and Pregnancy.
    d. Smoking and Miscarriages.

2. Indicate whether each of the following details is major or minor in support of the author's topic:

    _____ a. Low birth weight is correlated with many developmental problems.
    _____ b. Infant mortality rates are also higher among babies born to smokers.
    _____ c. Babies born to mothers who smoke weigh less than those born to nonsmokers.

_____ 3. Which sentence best states the main idea of this passage?

    a. Smoking during pregnancy increases the chance of miscarriages, low-weight babies, and infant mortality.
    b. Smoking during pregnancy causes many miscarriages.
    c. Ceasing smoking during pregnancy can increase infant birth weight.
    d. Smoking is a major contributor to infant mortality.

Passage 2

The young reporter with the slow Missouri drawl stamped the cold of the high Nevada desert out of his feet as he entered the offices of the Virginia City _Territorial Enterprise_. It was early in 1863. The newspaper's editor, Joseph T. Goodman, looked puzzled at seeing his Carson City correspondent in the home office, but Samuel Clemens came right to the point: "Joe, I want to sign my articles. I want to be identified to a wider audience." The editor, already impressed with his colleague of six months, readily agreed. Then came the question of a pen name, since few aspiring writers of the time used their legal names. Clemens had something in mind: "I want to sign them 'Mark Twain,'" he declared. "It is an old river term, a leadsman's call, signifying two fathoms—twelve feet. It has a richness about it; it was always a pleasant sound for a pilot to hear on a dark night; it meant safe water."

—Roderick Nash and Gregory Graves,
From These Beginnings, Vol. 2, 6th ed.

_____ 1. The topic of the passage is

    a. Becoming a Reporter.
    b. How Mark Twain Got His Name.
    c. Safe Water on the River.
    d. Working for the Virginia City _Territorial Enterprise_.

2. Indicate whether each of the following details is major or minor in support of the author's topic:

    _____ a. Clemens had worked for the newspaper for six months.

———— b. The newspaper's editor was Joseph T. Goodman.

———— c. Clemens wanted to sign his articles to be known to a wider audience.

———— 3. Which sentence best states the main idea of this passage?

    a. Samuel Clemens worked as a young reporter for the Virginia City *Territorial Enterprise.*

    b. The newspaper's editor, Joseph T. Goodman, was impressed with the young reporter, Samuel Clemens.

    c. "Mark Twain" is a river term that means two fathoms—twelve feet.

    d. The young reporter, Samuel Clemens, decided to take the pen name "Mark Twain."

Passage 3

Credit card companies entice students to apply for cards and take on debt with free T-shirts, music CDs, and promises of an easy way to pay for spring break vacations. Many students, however, can't even keep up with the minimum payment. In fact, it is estimated that in one year 150,000 people younger than 25 will declare personal bankruptcy. That means for 150,000 young people, their first significant financial event as an adult will be to declare themselves a failure. And for each one who goes into bankruptcy, there are dozens just behind them, struggling with credit card bills. In one 4-month period, for instance, a Texas A&M freshman piled up $2,500 of charges on two Visa cards and four retail credit cards. The student couldn't afford to pay the $25 minimum a month on all the cards, so she accumulated $150 in late fees and over-credit-limit fees.

—Adapted from Michael Mescon et al.,
Business Today, 8th ed.

———— 1. The topic of the passage is

    a. The Credit Card Industry.

    b. Paying Off Debt.

    c. Bankruptcy Options.

    d. Danger of Credit Cards for College Students.

2. Indicate whether each of the following details is major or minor in support of the author's topic:

———— a. Credit card companies give away music CDs.

———— b. Young people are declaring bankruptcy over credit card debt.

———— c. A Texas A&M freshman cannot pay her minimum payments.

———— 3. Which sentence best states the main idea of this passage?

    a. Credit card companies engage in illegal activities to hook students on debt.

    b. It should be illegal for credit card companies to enroll college students who have no means of payment.

c. Credit card companies entice college students into debt that can be financially disastrous.

d. Bankruptcy is an easy option for college students with overwhelming credit card debt.

EXERCISE 5.9 Writing Unstated Main Ideas

Read the following passages and use the three-question system to determine the author's main idea. Remember to annotate by circling major details. Pull the ideas together to state the main ideas in your own words.

Passage 1

On May 4, 1992, just days after a major Los Angeles riot, Oprah Winfrey took her Chicago-based nationally syndicated television program to Los Angeles for a discussion of the riot and its causes. Following the acquittal of policemen who had beaten black motorist Rodney King, the violence had taken more than fifty lives and resulted in more than $ 1 billion in property damage. "Over the last week I have, just like many of you, felt a sense of shock . . . of outrage and some tears, as people died," Winfrey explained to the Los Angeles residents invited to participate in the first of two telecasts. "What will be written into history books for our children and our grandchildren to read, the beating of Rodney King, came into our living rooms and smacked us in the face, and now we must, we must, listen to each other."

—Clayborne Carson, Emma J. Lapsansky-Werner, and Gary B. Nash
The Struggle for Freedom: A History of African Americans, Combined Volume, 2nd ed.

1. Who or what is this about? _____

_____

_____

2. What are the major details? _____

_____

_____

_____

_____

3. What is the main idea that the author is trying to convey about the topic?

_____

_____

_____

Passage 2

American executives like to get right down to business and engage in fast and tough face-to-face bargaining. However, Japanese and other Asian businesspeople often find this behavior offensive. They prefer to start with polite conversation, and they rarely say no in face-to-face conversations. As another example, South Americans like to sit or stand very close to each other when they talk business—in fact, almost nose-to-nose. The American business executive tends to keep backing away as the South American moves closer.

—Gary Armstrong and Philip Kotler,
Marketing: An Introduction, 10th ed.

1. Who or what is this about? _____

2. What are the major details? _____

_____

3. What is the main idea that the author is making about the topic? _____

_____

_____

Passage 3

In 1979 when University of Minnesota psychologist Thomas Bouchard read a newspaper account of the reuniting of 39-year-old twins who had been separated from infancy, he seized the opportunity and flew them to Minneapolis for extensive tests. Bouchard was looking for differences. What "the Jim twins," Jim Lewis and Jim Springer, presented were amazing similarities. Both had married women named Linda, divorced, and married women named Betty. One had a son James Alan, the other a son James Allan. Both had dogs named Toy, chain-smoked Salems, served as sheriff's deputies, drove Chevrolets, chewed their fingernails to the nub, enjoyed stock car racing, had basement workshops, and had built circular white benches around trees in their yards. They also had similar medical histories: Both gained 10 pounds at about the same time and then lost it; both suffered what they mistakenly believed were heart attacks, and both began having late-afternoon headaches at age 18.

Identical twins Oskar Stohr and Jack Yufe presented equally striking similarities. One was raised by his grandmother in Germany as a Catholic and a Nazi, while the other was raised by his father in the Caribbean as a Jew. Nevertheless, they share traits and habits galore. They like spicy foods and sweet liqueurs, have a habit of falling asleep in front of the television, flush the toilet before using it, store rubber bands on their wrists, and dip buttered toast in their coffee. Stohr is domineering toward women and yells at his wife, as did Yufe before he was separated.

—David G. Myers,
Psychology

1. Who or what is this about? _____

_____

_____

2. What are the major details? _____

_____

_____

3. What is the main idea that the author is trying to convey about the topic?

_____

_____

_____

DETERMINING THE MAIN IDEA OF LONGER SELECTIONS

Learning Objective 6

Identify main ideas of longer selections

Understanding the main idea of longer selections requires a little more thinking than does finding the main idea of a single paragraph. Since longer selections, such as articles or chapters, contain more material, tying the ideas together can be a challenge. Each paragraph or section of a longer selection usually represents a new supporting detail. In addition, several major ideas may contribute to developing the overall main idea. Your job is to group the many ideas under one central theme.

For longer selections, organize the paragraphs into related sections and think of a label that describes the common threads. Think of these labels as the major supporting details. Then ask, "What point do they make about the topic?"

Use the suggestions in the Reader's Tip on page 243 to determine the main idea of longer selections. The techniques are similar to those used in previewing and skimming, two skills that also focus on the overall central theme.

EXERCISE 5.10   **Determining the Main Idea of Longer Selections**

Read each passage and use the strategies in the Reader's Tip, "Getting the Main Idea of Longer Selections," on page 243 to determine the author's main idea. This time, write brief labels in the margin and underline the supporting details.

Passage 1

THE BENEFITS OF A GOOD NIGHT'S SLEEP

College students are well known for "all nighters," during which they stay up through the night to study for an exam or to finish—or even to start—a paper due in the morning. Lack of sleep is nothing to brag or laugh about. Sleep is vital to your life and can help you function at optimal levels both physically and mentally.

On the physical side, sleep helps regulate your metabolism and your body's state of equilibrium. On the mental side, it helps restore your ability to be optimistic and to have a high level of energy and self-confidence. To keep your body in balance, more sleep is needed when you are under stress, experiencing emotional fatigue, or undertaking an intense intellectual activity such as learning.

During sleep, most people experience periods of what is called rapid eye movement (REM). These movements can be observed beneath closed eyelids. In REM sleep,

> ### Reader's TIP   Getting the Main Idea of Longer Selections
>
> - **Think about the title.** What does the title suggest about the topic?
> - **Read the first paragraph or two to find a statement of the topic or thesis.** What does the selection seem to be about?
> - **Read the subheadings** and, if necessary, glance at the first sentences of some of the paragraphs. Based on these clues, what does the article seem to be about?
> - **Look for clues that indicate how the material is organized.** Is the purpose to define a term, to prove an opinion or explain a concept, to describe a situation, or to persuade the reader toward a particular point of view? Is the material organized into a list of examples, a time order or sequence, a comparison or contrast, or a cause-and-effect relationship?
> - **As you read, organize the paragraphs into subsections.** Give each subsection a title and write it in the margin. Think of it as a significant supporting detail.
> - **Determine how the overall organization and subsections relate to the whole.** What is the main idea that the author is trying to convey in the selection?

the body is quiet but the mind is active, even hyperactive. Some researchers believe that REM sleep helps you form permanent memories; others believe that this period of active brain waves serves to rid your brain of overstimulation and useless information acquired during the day. REM sleep is the time not only for dreams but also for acceleration of the heart rate and blood flow to the brain.

During non-REM sleep, in contrast, the body may be active—some people sleepwalk during this period—but the mind is not. In spite of this activity, non-REM sleep is the time when the body does its repair and maintenance work, including cell regeneration.

Although much still needs to be learned about sleep and its functions, few would disagree that sleep plays a role in the maintenance of good mental health.

—B. E. Pruitt and Jane J. Stein,
Decisions for Healthy Living

1. What does the title suggest about the topic? _____

_____

_____

2. Which sentence in the first paragraph suggests the main idea? _____

_____

_____

Brains Need the Right Amount of Sleep

As you settle into a weekly schedule that allots specific times for studying, remember that sleep is very important to learning. Scientists cannot say how much sleep is right for you, but for most people, it is between seven and eight hours. Research studies show that getting less or more sleep than your brain needs causes difficulty paying attention, thinking logically, and performing physical tasks. Schedule bedtime and wake-up time at about the same times each day to get the most from your brain.

—*Adapted from* Brain Rules: 12 Principles for
Surviving and Thriving at Home, Work and School *by John J. Medina*

3. What subtitles would you give the second, third, and fourth paragraphs?

_____

_____

4. What is the main idea of the selection? _____

_____

_____

Passage 2

SCIENTISTS DEBATE ANIMAL INTELLIGENCE

For years, any scientist who claimed that animals could think was likely to be ignored or laughed at. Today, however, the study of animal intelligence is booming, especially in the interdisciplinary field of cognitive ethology. (Ethology is the study of animal behavior, especially in natural environments.) Cognitive ethologists argue that some animals can anticipate future events, make plans, and coordinate their activities with those of their comrades.

In the 1920s, Wolfgang Kohler put chimpanzees in situations in which some tempting bananas were just out of reach and watched to see what the apes would do. Most did nothing, but a few turned out to be quite clever. If the bananas were outside the cage, the chimp might pull them in with a stick. If they were hanging overhead, and there were boxes in the cage, the chimp might pile up the boxes and climb on top of them to reach the fruit. Often the solution came after the chimp had been sitting quietly for a while. It appeared as though the animal had been thinking about the problem and was struck by a sudden insight.

When we think about animal cognition, we must be careful because even complex behavior that appears to be purposeful can be genetically prewired and automatic. The assassin bug of South America catches termites by gluing nest material on its back as camouflage, but it is hard to imagine how the bug's tiny dab of brain tissue could enable it to plan this strategy consciously. Yet explanations of animal behavior that leave out any sort of consciousness at all and that attribute animals' actions entirely to instinct do not seem to account for some of the amazing things that animals can do. Like the otter that uses a stone to crack mussel shells, many animals use objects in the natural environment as tools, and in some nonhuman primates the behavior is learned.

For example, chimpanzee mothers occasionally show their young how to use stones to open hard nuts. Orangutans in one particular Sumatran swamp have learned to use sticks as tools, held in the mouths, to pry insects from holes in tree trunks and to get seeds out of cracks in a bulblike fruit, whereas nearby groups of orangutans use only brute force to get to the delicacies. Even some nonprimates may have the capacity to learn to use tools, although the evidence remains controversial among ethologists. Female bottlenose dolphins off the coast of Australia attach sea sponges to their beaks while hunting for food, which protects them from sharp coral and stinging stonefish, and they seem to have acquired this unusual skill from their mothers.

—Carole Wade and Carol Tavris,
Psychology, 10th ed.

1. What does the title suggest about the topic? _____

_____

_____

_____

2. Which sentence in the first paragraph suggests the main idea? _____

_____

3. What subtitles would you give paragraphs one through four? _____

_____

_____

_____

4. What is the main idea of the selection? _____

_____

_____

_____

Passage 3

IMMIGRATION IN THE 1800S

What had been a trickle in the 1820s—some 128,502 foreigners came to U.S. shores during that decade—became a torrent in the 1850s, with more than 2.8 million migrants to the United States. Although families and single women emigrated, the majority of the newcomers were young European men of working age.

This vast movement of people, which began in the 1840s and continued throughout the nineteenth century, resulted from Europe's population explosion and the new farming and industrial practices that undermined or ended traditional means of livelihood. Poverty and the lack of opportunity heightened the appeal of leaving home. As one Scottish woman wrote to an American friend in 1847, "We cannot make it better here. All that we can do is if you can give us any encouragement is to immigrate to your country."

Famine uprooted the largest group of immigrants: the Irish. In 1845, a terrible blight attacked and destroyed the potato crop, the staple of the Irish diet. Years of devastating hunger followed. One million Irish starved to death between 1841 and 1851; another million and a half emigrated. Although not all came to the United States, those who did arrived almost penniless in eastern port cities without the skills needed for good jobs. With only their raw labor to sell, employers, as one observer noted, "will engage Paddy as they would a dray horse." Yet, limited as their opportunities were, immigrants saved money to send home to help their families or to pay for their passage to the United States.

German immigrants, the second largest group of newcomers during this period (1,361,506 arrived between 1840 and 1859), were not facing such drastic conditions. But as Henry Brokmeyer observed, "Hunger brought me . . . here, and hunger is the cause of European immigration to this country."

—Gary B. Nash et al.,
The American People, Vol. 1, 6th ed.

1. What does the title suggest about the topic? _____

   _____

   _____

2. What subtitles could you give paragraphs one through four? _____

   _____

   _____

   _____

3. Is there one sentence that sums up the main idea in the passage? _____

   _____

   _____

4. What is the main idea of the selection? _____

   _____

   _____

SUMMARY WRITING: A MAIN IDEA SKILL

Learning Objective 7

Write a summary

A **summary** is a series of brief, concise statements, in your own words, of the main idea and the significant supporting details. The first sentence should state the main idea or thesis; subsequent sentences should incorporate the significant details. Minor details and material that is irrelevant to the learner's purpose should be omitted. The summary should be written in paragraph form and should always be shorter than the material being summarized. It should not contain anything that is not in the original, and it must be written in your own words.

Why Summarize?

Summaries can be used for textbook study, especially when anticipating answers for essay exam questions and for condensing the plot, theme, and characters of novels and short stories. For writing research papers, summarizing is an essential skill. Using your own words to put the essence of an article into concise sentences requires a thorough understanding of the material. Doing so also prevents accusations of plagiarism—stealing someone else's work—which is a serious offense.

Writing a research paper may mean that you will have to read as many as 30 articles and four books over a period of a month or two. After each reading, you want to take enough notes so that you can write your paper without returning for another look at the original reference. Since you will be using so many different references, do your note taking carefully. The complete sentences of a summary are more explicit than underscored text or the highlighted topic-phrase format of an outline. Your summary should demonstrate a synthesis of the information. The Reader's Tip, "How to Summarize," below outlines how to write an effective summary.

Read the following excerpt on political authority as if you were doing research for a term paper and writing a summary for your notes. Mark key terms that you would include. Before reading the example provided, anticipate what you would include in your own summary.

Reader's TIP) How to Summarize

- **Keep in mind the purpose of your summary.** Your task or assignment will determine which details are important and how many details should be included.
- **Decide on the main idea that the author is trying to convey.** Make this main idea the first sentence in your summary.
- **Decide on the major ideas and details that support the author's point.** Mark the key terms and phrases. Include in your summary the major ideas and as many of the significant supporting details as your purpose demands.
- **Do not include irrelevant or repeated information.** A summary stays very focused and concise.
- **Use appropriate transitional words and phrases.** They'll show the relationship between ideas.
- **Use paragraph form.** Don't use a list or write in incomplete sentences.
- **Do not add your personal opinion.** Stick to the content of the material that you are summarizing.
- **Use your own words!** Except where specific terms from the original must be used, translate the ideas into your own words. Doing this avoids the problem of plagiarism.

Types of Authority

Where is the source of the state's authority? Weber described three possible sources of the right to command, which produced what he called traditional authority, charismatic authority, and legal authority.

Traditional Authority

In many societies, people have obeyed those in power because, in essence, "that is the way it has always been." Thus, kings, queens, feudal lords, and tribal chiefs did not need written rules in order to govern. Their authority was based on tradition, on long-standing customs, and it was handed down from parent to child, maintaining traditional authority from one generation to the next. Often, traditional authority has been justified by religious tradition. For example, medieval European kings were said to rule by divine right, and Japanese emperors were considered the embodiment of heaven.

Charismatic Authority

People may also submit to authority, not because of tradition, but because of the extraordinary attraction of an individual. Napoleon, Gandhi, Mao Tse-tung, and Ayatollah Khomeini all illustrate authority that derives its legitimacy from charisma—an exceptional personal quality popularly attributed to certain individuals. Their followers perceive charismatic leaders as persons of destiny endowed with remarkable vision, the power of a savior, or God's grace. Charismatic authority is inherently unstable. It cannot be transferred to another person.

Legal Authority

The political systems of industrial states are based largely on a third type of authority: legal authority, which Weber also called rational authority. These systems derive legitimacy from a set of explicit rules and procedures that spell out the ruler's rights and duties. Typically, the rules and procedures are put in writing. The people grant their obedience to "the law." It specifies procedures by which certain individuals hold offices of power, such as governor or president or prime minister. But the authority is vested in those offices, not in the individuals who temporarily hold the offices. Thus, a political system based on legal authority is often called a "government of laws, not of men." Individuals come and go, as American presidents have come and gone, but the office, "the presidency," remains. If individual officeholders overstep their authority, they may be forced out of office and replaced.

—Alex Thio,
Sociology, 3rd ed.

1. To begin your summary, what is the main point? _____

   _____

   _____

2. What are the major areas of support? _____

   _____

   _____

3. Should you include an example for each area? _____ _____

_____

EXPLANATION   Begin your summary with the main point, which is that Weber describes the three sources of authority as traditional, charismatic, and legal. Then define each of the three sources, but do not include examples.

Read the following summary and notice how closely it fits your own ideas.

> ### Political Authority
> Weber describes the three sources of the right to command as traditional, charismatic, and legal authority. Traditional authority is not written but based on long-standing custom such as the power of queens or tribal chiefs. Charismatic authority is based on the charm and vision of a leader such as Gandhi. Legal authority, such as that of American presidents, comes from written laws and is vested in the office rather than the person.

EXERCISE 5.11

Summarizing Passages

Read the following passages and mark the key terms and phrases. Begin your summary with a statement of the main point and add the appropriate supporting details. Use your markings to help you write the summary. Be brief but include the essential elements.

Passage 1

TECHNOLOGY ADDICTIONS

As technology becomes an ever larger part of our daily lives, the risk of overexposure to it grows for people of all ages. Some people, in fact, become addicted to new technologies, such as smartphones, video games, networking sites, and the Internet in general.

Many experts suggest that technology addiction is real and can present serious problems for those addicted. An estimated 5 to 10 percent of Internet users will likely experience Internet addiction. Younger people are also more likely to be addicted to the Internet than middle-aged users. Approximately 11 percent of college students report that Internet use and computer games have interfered with their academic performance.

Internet addicts have multiple signs and symptoms, such as general disregard for one's health, sleep deprivation, depression, neglecting family and friends, lack of physical activity, euphoria when online, lower grades in school, and poor job performance. Internet addicts may feel moody or uncomfortable when they are not online. Online addicts may be using their behavior to compensate for feelings of loneliness, marital or work problems, a poor social life, or financial problems.

—Rebecca J. Donatelle,
Access to Health, 8th ed.

Use your marked text to write a summary.

Passage 2

THE BIG BANG, EXPANSION, AND THE AGE OF THE UNIVERSE

Telescopic observations of distant galaxies show that the entire universe is *expanding*, meaning that average distances between galaxies are increasing with time. This fact implies that galaxies must have been closer together in the past, and if we go back far enough, we must reach the point at which the expansion began. We call this beginning the Big Bang, and scientists use the observed rate of expansion to calculate that it occurred about 14 billion years ago. The universe as a whole has continued to expand ever since the Big Bang, but on smaller size scales the force of gravity has drawn matter together. Structures such as galaxies and galaxy clusters occupy regions where gravity has won out against the overall expansion. That is, while the universe as a whole continues to expand, individual galaxies and galaxy clusters (and objects within them such as stars and planets) do *not* expand.

—Jeffrey Bennett, et al.
The Essential Cosmic Perspective, 7th ed.

Use your marked text to write a summary.

Passage 3

ADVANTAGES OF COMMUNITY COLLEGES

Community colleges provide a number of specific benefits. First, their low tuition cost places college courses and degrees within the reach of millions of families that could not otherwise afford them. Today, it is at community colleges that we find many students who are the first generation of their families to pursue a postsecondary degree. Compared to students who attend four-year colleges, a larger share of community college students are also paying their own way. The low cost of community colleges is especially important during periods of economic recession. Typically, when the economy slumps (and people lose their jobs), college enrollments—especially at community colleges—soar.

Second, community colleges have special importance to minorities. Currently, one-half of all African American and Hispanic undergraduates in the United States attend community colleges.

Third, although it is true that community colleges serve local populations, many two-year colleges also attract students from around the world. Many community colleges recruit students from abroad, and more than one-third of all foreign students enrolled on a U.S. campus are studying at community colleges.

Finally, while the highest priority of faculty who work at large universities typically is research, the most important job for community college faculty is teaching. Thus, although teaching loads are high (typically four or five classes each semester), community colleges appeal to faculty who find their greatest pleasure in the classroom. Community college students often get more attention from faculty than their counterparts at large universities.

—John J. Macionis,
Sociology, 10th ed.

Use your marked text to write a summary.

BRAIN BOOSTER

Chronic Stress and the Brain

Stress is an aroused physical state in which adrenaline is released to help us react quickly when we're in danger. When the danger has passed, cortisol kicks in to calm us down. Stress is designed to keep us from being eaten by predators that stalked ancient plains. The problem is that today most of us no longer face such dangers, and our stress is likely to last for extended lengths of time. It is when adrenaline levels stay high for a long time, like when we worry about how to pay for tuition and books, that stress is harmful. Chronic stress scars our blood vessels, reduces our ability to fight illness, and inhibits learning. It can actually disconnect neural networks and prevent the growth of new ones. The worst damage is done when we feel powerless. What to do? Exercise and proper amounts of sleep can help. Some people find meditation and prayer effective. Just as important, however, is to establish a can-do attitude and a plan. Analyze the situation and take control! Decide on small steps that give you power over your situation: Visit the college financial aid office, look for a part-time job that works around your class and study schedule, or apply for a federal work study job on campus. Seek help when necessary. Make chronic stress history!

—Adapted from *Brain Rules: 12 Principles for Surviving and Thriving at Home, Work, and School* by John Medina

SUMMARY POINTS

1 How do I distinguish topics, main ideas, and supporting details? (page 214)

- Topics are broad. They describe who or what a selection is about. They are usually expressed in a word or a phrase.
- Main ideas support and develop the topic. They express the point that the author is making through the details about the topic. They are expressed in a sentence, which may or may not be stated directly in the selection.
- Major supporting details develop and explain the main idea. Minor details elaborate on the major details. Supporting details are often indicated by signal words. Certain signal words are typically used to mark major details, and others typically mark minor details.

2 What strategies can I use to find the main idea? (page 218)

- The best strategy depends on whether or not you are familiar with the topic:
  If you have schemata on the topic, preview, predict the main idea, read, identify the details, and confirm the main idea.
  If you do not have schemata on the topic, preview, determine the topic, read, identify the key details, and find the main idea.
- Use the three-question strategy:
  Who or what is this reading about? (topic)
  What are the major supporting details?
  What is the message that the author is trying to convey about the topic? (main idea)

3 How can I identify stated main ideas? (page 222)

- Main ideas that are stated in a sentence within a selection are called topic sentences or thesis statements.

- Use the same three questions and strategies listed above to determine the main idea.
- Look for a sentence that reflects the main idea. It can be located at the beginning, in the middle, or at the end of a paragraph.

4 How can I distinguish major and minor supporting details? (page 230)
- Determine which details develop the main idea and which details explain the major details.
- Recognize signal words that often indicate major or minor details.

5 How can I identify unstated main ideas? (page 233)
- Use the same three questions and strategies that are used to find stated main ideas.

6 How can I identify the main ideas of longer selections? (page 242)
- Determine the topic.
- Organize the paragraphs into related sections and ask what labels could be used to describe groups of these ideas.
- Ask what point these groups of ideas are making about the topic.

7 How can I write a summary? (page 246)
- Determine the supporting details and main point. Use a paragraph form. The first sentence should state the main idea. Organize the details into the remaining sentences in the order in which they occur in the selection. Do not include anything that is not in the original selection. Use your own words.

SELECTION 1   Psychology   MyReadingLab

Visit Chapter 5: Main Idea and Supporting Details in MyReadingLab **to complete the Selection 1 activities and the Build Background Knowledge video activity.**

P REVIEW the next selection to predict its purpose and organization and to formulate your learning plan.

Activate Schemata

How many people do you think would harm another person if they were ordered to do so by an authority figure? Under what conditions might they do so or refuse to do so?

Establish a Purpose for Reading

What became known as the Milgram Obedience Study set out to determine if people would obey when they were told to harm another person. Read the selection to learn the results of this classic experiment.

Build Background Knowledge — VIDEO

Would You Fall For That?

To prepare for reading Selection 1, answer the questions below. Then, watch this video that hu morously examines human behavior.

Why do we sometimes trust authority figures rather than our own beliefs?

When have you followed instructions that you suspected were wrong? Why did you follow these instructions?

What circumstances might cause someone to ignore their personal beliefs and follow along with the crowd?

This video helped me:_____

_____

_____

Increase Word Knowledge

What do you know about these words?

ominously	confederates	sadistic	anguished	replications
compliance	subverted	softer	narcissism	barbarism

Your instructor may give a brief vocabulary review before or after reading.

Integrate Knowledge While Reading

Questions have been inserted in the margins to stimulate your thinking while reading. Remember to

Predict   Picture   Relate   Monitor   Correct   Annotate

THE OBEDIENCE STUDY

In the early 1960s, Stanley Milgram designed a study that would become world famous. Milgram wanted to know how many people would obey an authority figure when directly ordered to violate their ethical standards. Participants in the study thought they were part of an experiment on the effects of punishment on learning. Each
5 was assigned, apparently at random, to the role of "teacher." Whenever the learner, seated in an adjoining room, made an error in reciting a list of word pairs he was supposed to have memorized, the teacher had to give him an electric shock by depressing a lever on a machine (see photo). With each error, the voltage (marked from 0 to 450) was to be increased by another 15 volts. The shock levels on the machine were labeled
10 from SLIGHT SHOCK to DANGER-SEVERE SHOCK and, finally, ominously, XXX. In reality, the learners were confederates of Milgram and did not receive any shocks, but none of the teachers ever realized this during the study. The actor-victims played their parts convincingly: As the study continued, they shouted in pain and pleaded to be released, all according to a prearranged script.

15   Before doing this study, Milgram asked a number of psychiatrists, students, and other adults how many people they thought would "go all the way" to XXX on
What would you predict? → orders from the researcher. The psychiatrists predicted that most people would refuse to go beyond 150 volts, when the learner first demanded to be freed, and that only one person in a thousand, someone who was disturbed and sadistic, would
20 administer the highest voltage. The nonprofessionals agreed with this prediction, and all of them said that they personally would disobey early in the procedure.

That is not, however, the way the results turned out. Every single person administered some shock to the learner, and about two-thirds of the participants, of all ages and from all walks of life, obeyed to the fullest extent. Many protested to the

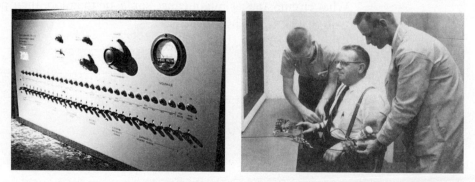

The Milgram Obedience Experiment. On the left is Milgram's original shock machine; in 1963, it looked pretty ominous. On the right, the "learner" is being strapped into his chair by the experimenter and the "teacher."
From the film "Obedience" © 1968 by Stanley Milgram.

25 experimenter, but they backed down when he calmly asserted, "The experiment requires that you continue." They obeyed no matter how much the victim shouted for them to stop and no matter how painful the shocks seemed to be. They obeyed even when they themselves were anguished about the pain they believed they were causing. As Milgram noted in 1974, participants would "sweat, tremble, stutter, bite
30 their lips, groan, and dig their fingernails into their flesh"—but still they obeyed.

Over the decades, more than 3,000 people of many different ethnicities have gone through replications of the Milgram study. Most of them, men and women equally, inflicted what they thought were dangerous amounts of shock to another person. High percentages of obedience occur all over the world, ranging to more than
35 90 percent in Spain and the Netherlands according to two studies in 1994 and 1995.

What countries scored lowest?

Milgram and his team subsequently set up several variations of the study to determine the circumstances under which people might disobey the experimenter. They found that virtually nothing the victim did or said changed the likelihood of compliance, even when the victim said he had a heart condition, screamed in agony,
40 or stopped responding entirely, as if he had collapsed. However, people *were* more likely to disobey under certain conditions:

- **When the experimenter left the room,** many people subverted authority by giving low levels of shock but reporting that they had followed orders.
- **When the victim was right there in the room,** and the teacher had to admin-
45 ister the shock directly to the victim's body, many people refused to go on.
- **When two experimenters issued conflicting demands,** with one telling participants to continue and another saying to stop at once, no one kept inflicting shock.
- **When the person ordering them to continue was an ordinary man,** appar-
50 ently another volunteer instead of the authoritative experimenter, many participants disobeyed.
- **When the participant worked with peers who refused to go further,** he or she often gained the courage to disobey.

Obedience, Milgram concluded, was more a function of the *situation* than of the
55 personalities of the participants. "The key to [their] behavior," Milgram summarized, "lies not in pent-up anger or aggression but in the nature of their relationship to authority. They have given themselves to the authority; they see themselves as instruments for the execution of his wishes; once so defined, they are unable to break free."

What do you think?

60 The Milgram study has had critics. Some consider it unethical because people were kept in the dark about what was really happening until the session was over (of course, telling them in advance would have invalidated the study) and because many suffered emotional pain (Milgram countered that they would not have felt pain if they had simply disobeyed instructions). The original study could never be
65 repeated in the United States today because of these ethical concerns. However, a "softer" version of the experiment was done in 2008, in which "teachers" who had not heard of the original Milgram study were asked to administer shocks only up to 150 volts, when they first heard the learner protest. That amount of shock had been a critical choice point in Milgram's study, and in the replication, nearly 80 percent of
70 those who went past 150 ended up going all the way to the end. Overall obedience rates were only slightly lower than Milgram's, and once again, gender, education, age, and ethnicity had no effect on the likelihood of obeying. In another, rather eerie

cyberversion replication of Milgram's study, participants had to shock a virtual woman on a computer screen. Even though they knew she wasn't real, their heart
75 rates increased and they reported feeling bad about delivering the "shocks." Yet they kept doing it.

Some psychologists have questioned Milgram's conclusion that personality traits are virtually irrelevant to whether or not people obey an authority. Certain traits, they note, especially hostility, narcissism, and rigidity, do increase obedience
80 and a willingness to inflict pain on others. Others have objected to the parallel Milgram drew between the behavior of the study's participants and the brutality of the Nazis and others who have committed acts of barbarism in the name of duty. The people in Milgram's study typically obeyed only when the experimenter was hovering right there, and many of them felt enormous discomfort. In contrast, most Nazis
85 acted without direct supervision by authorities, without external pressure, and without feelings of anguish.

Nevertheless, no one disputes that Milgram's compelling study has had a tremendous influence on public awareness of the dangers of uncritical obedience. As researcher John Darley observed in 1995, "Milgram shows us the beginning of a
90 path by means of which ordinary people, in the grip of social forces, become the origins of atrocities in the real world."

Is this a fair objection?

(1,153 words)

From Carole Wade, Carol Tavris, and Maryanne Garry,
Psychology, 11th ed.

Recall

Stop to talk, write, and think about the selection.

Your instructor may choose to give you a brief comprehension review.

THINK CRITICALLY ABOUT THE SELECTION

What parallels do you see between Nazi atrocities in the concentration camps during World War II and the results of the Milgram obedience study? Are there differences in the two situations?

If you were a participant in this experiment as a "teacher," what would you do—assuming you knew nothing about the real purpose of the study?

WRITE ABOUT THE SELECTION

Review the bulleted list of conditions under which the "teachers" were more likely to disobey the experimenter. Think of situations that can arise in everyday life—cyberbullying, intervening to stop a beating or other cruel behavior, or treatment of prisoners, for instance—and how a condition on the list might relate to it.

Response Suggestion: Select one of the conditions on the list and write a one-paragraph scenario to demonstrate how that factor might cause a person not to engage in cruel behavior or how the absence of that condition might encourage a person to be cruel.

Your instructor may choose to give you a brief comprehension review.

Summarize

Write a one-paragraph summary of this selection to serve as notes that would prepare you for a class discussion or a test.

SKILL DEVELOPMENT: FIND THE MAIN IDEA

Answer the following with *T* (true) or *F* (false):

_____ 1. The main point of the second paragraph is that psychiatrists and nonprofessionals all predicted that most people would refuse to deliver more than 150 volts to the "learner" in the experiment.

_____ 2. The main point of the third paragraph is that every participant felt guilty about the pain they believed they were causing.

_____ 3. The main point of the fourth paragraph is that, in later studies by Milgram, the results were the same regardless of ethnicity or nationality.

_____ 4. The main point of the seventh paragraph is that the original study could never be repeated in the United States.

CHECK YOUR COMPREHENSION

After reading the selection, answer the first question in your own words and answer the subsequent questions with *a, b, c,* or *d*. To help you analyze your strengths and weaknesses, the question types are indicated.

Main Idea (Topic) 1. Who or what is the topic of the selection? _____

_____

What is the main idea that the author is trying to convey about the topic?

_____

_____

_____

Detail _____ 2. In the original experiment, participants thought the study was about
   a. the extent to which people would obey orders.
   b. how much voltage the "learners" would tolerate before complaining of pain.
   c. how quickly the "teachers" would realize they were not actually administering a shock.
   d. the effects of punishment on learning.

Detail _____ 3. The maximum level of voltage that the "teachers" could administer was labelled
   a. XXX.
   b. Slight Shock.
   c. Maximum Shock.
   d. Danger—Severe Shock.

Main Idea (Topic) _____ 4. Which of the following is a good label or marginal annotation for the third paragraph?
   a. The experiment
   b. Results
   c. Further studies
   d. Conclusions

Inference _____ 5. The selection implies that
   a. most of the participants obeyed because they took secret pleasure in administering shocks to the learners.
   b. many participants felt uncomfortable and perhaps guilty about inflicting pain on the learners.
   c. all of the participants felt uncomfortable or guilty about inflicting pain.
   d. Milgram and his team felt uncomfortable about the ethics of the experiment.

Main Idea (topic) ———— 6. Which of the following is a good label or marginal annotation for the sixth paragraph?

    a. The experiment
    b. Results
    c. Further studies
    d. Conclusions

Inference ———— 7. The selection suggests that

    a. Milgram's original study violated the ethical standards for psychological experiments that were in place in the 1960s.
    b. other countries have stricter standards than the United States.
    c. the United States now has stricter ethical standards governing psychological experiments than in the 1960s.
    d. countries outside the United States have no ethical standards governing psychological experiments.

Detail ———— 8. Which of the following was not listed as a condition under which participants were more likely to disobey?

    a. When the victim was in obvious agony
    b. When participants were with others who disobeyed
    c. When the victim was in the same room with the participant
    d. When the experimenter was not in the room with the participant

Inference ———— 9. Milgram's response to criticism that participants suffered emotional pain from the experience implies that

    a. the experimenters threatened participants with punishment if they refused to obey.
    b. some potential participants refused to take part when they learned what they were expected to do.
    c. many participants chose to stop the experiment when the "learner" seemed to suffer pain.
    d. the participants were not forced to obey orders.

Author's Purpose ———— 10. The primary purpose of this selection is to

    a. criticize Milgram for conducting an unethical experiment.
    b. dramatize the conditions of the original experiment.
    c. present an informative report of a famous experiment and its results.
    d. cause readers to support strict standards regarding psychological experiments.

Answer the following with *T* (true) or *F* (false).

Inference ———— 11. Some critics of the Milgram experiment implied that Nazis in World War II concentration camps did not feel pressured to obey orders to hurt prisoners.

Inference ———— 12. In spite of criticism regarding the ethics of this experiment, it provided very valuable insights into human behavior.

Detail ———— 13. The real subjects in the experiment were the "learners."

Detail ———— 14. Milgram's obedience study has been repeated many times since the 1960s.

Detail ———— 15. A majority of the participants obeyed throughout the experiment.

BUILD YOUR VOCABULARY

According to the way the italicized word was used in the selection, indicate *a, b, c,* or *d* for the word or phrase that gives the best definition. The number in parentheses indicates the line of the passage in which the word is located. Use a dictionary in addition to the context clues to more precisely define the terms.

———— 1. "and, finally, *ominously*" (10)
a. predictably
b. worryingly
c. favorably
d. softly

———— 2. "learners were *confederates*" (11)
a. partners
b. rebels
c. students
d. victims

———— 3. "was disturbed and *sadistic*" (19)
a. crazy
b. angry
c. cruel
d. psychotic

———— 4. "*anguished* about the pain" (28)
a. unconcerned
b. contented
c. violent
d. distressed

———— 5. "gone through *replications*" (32)
a. changes
b. examinations
c. revisions
d. repetitions

———— 6. "likelihood of *compliance*" (39)
a. obedience
b. defiance
c. refusal
d. approval

———— 7. "*subverted* authority" (42)
a. obeyed
b. undermined
c. accepted
d. corrected

———— 8. "a '*softer*' version" (66)
a. less dangerous
b. easier
c. less harsh
d. more controversial

———— 9. "*narcissism*, and rigidity" (79)
a. sympathy
b. self-admiration
c. selflessness
d. self-hatred

———— 10. "acts of *barbarism*" (82)
a. brutality
b. kindness
c. selfishness
d. ingratitude

What is classical conditioning?

Classical conditioning is the learning that takes place when a subject is taught, or conditioned, to make a new response to a neutral stimulus. This is illustrated by the research of *Ivan Pavlov*, a Russian scientist in the late nineteenth century. Pavlov was studying the basic processes of digestion, focusing on salivation in dogs. Because salivation is a *reflex*, it is an unlearned, automatic response in dogs. When presented with food, dogs will automatically salivate. As his research progressed, Pavlov noticed that the dogs would salivate at the sight of the assistant who delivered the food. At this point, Pavlov decided to investigate learning.

Pavlov reasoned that no learning was involved in the dog's automatic salivation (the *unconditioned response*) when presented with food (the *unconditioned stimulus*). He wondered, however, if he could teach the dogs to salivate at the sound of a bell. To investigate this, Pavlov decided to pair the sound of a bell with the presentation of the food—sound first, food second. The bell alone was a *neutral stimulus* that had never before caused salivation. After a number of *trials* (presenting sound and food together), the dogs became conditioned to associate the sound of the bell with the food. The dogs soon would salivate at the sound, even when the food was withheld. Learning had taken place; Pavlov had taught the dogs to react to a neutral stimulus. Once learning or conditioning had taken place, the sound became a *conditioned stimulus* and the salivation became a *conditioned response*. To take this experiment a step further, if the sound is consistently presented without food, the salivation response will gradually weaken until the dogs completely stop salivating at the sound of the bell (*extinction*). Pavlov's work on animals and learning laid the groundwork for the American behaviorists of the twentieth century.

What is behaviorism?

At the beginning of the twentieth century, many American psychologists disagreed with Freud's psychoanalytical approach (see page 44). They wanted to measure behavior in the laboratory and explain personality in terms of learning theories and observable behaviors. *B. F. Skinner* was a leader in this new movement. He borrowed from Pavlov's work and conducted research on operant conditioning.

Skinner posed questions such as, "What are your beliefs about rewards and punishments?" "Do consequences affect your behaviors?" "Are you a reflection of your positive and negative experiences?" Skinner believed that consequences shape behavior and that your personality is merely a reflection of your many learned behaviors.

Two pigeons seek food in a box developed by psychologist B. F. Skinner as part of his operant conditioning research.
Bettmann/Corbis

Skinner demonstrated *operant conditioning* (behaviors used to operate something) "by putting a rat inside a small box that came to be known as a *"Skinner box."* The rat explored the box until eventually it found that it could make food appear by pressing a lever. The rat enjoyed the food and dramatically increased the lever pressings. The food was a *positive reinforcer* for the lever pressing. In other words, the food reinforced the behavior and increased it. To stop the lever-pressing behavior *(extinction)*, the rat was given a shock each time the lever was touched. The shock was a *punishment* that decreased the lever pressing. When a parent nags a child for avoiding homework (punishment) and then refrains from nagging when the child does the homework, doing homework is reinforced. Pleasant consequences (food) are *positive reinforcers*; the removal of something unpleasant (no nagging) is a *negative reinforcer*.

Behavior modification, a type of *behavior therapy*, uses the principles of classical and operant conditioning to increase desired behaviors and decrease problem behaviors. You can use these principles to train a pet, stop a smoking habit, or overcome a fear of flying. Does the desire to make a good grade (positive reinforcement) affect your studying behavior? Skinner would say yes.

REVIEW QUESTIONS

After studying the material, answer the following questions:

1. Who was Ivan Pavlov? _____

2. What is a reflex? _____

3. What is a neutral stimulus? _____

4. Why is the response to the food called unconditioned? _____

5. What is a conditioned stimulus? _____

6. What is extinction? _____

7. How did B. F. Skinner differ from Freud? _____

8. How does operant conditioning differ from classical conditioning? _____

9. What is the role of a positive reinforcer? _____

10. In behavior modification, what makes you want to change behaviors?
_____

Your instructor may choose to give a brief review of these psychology concepts.

| SELECTION 2 | Short Story | MyReadingLab |

Visit Chapter 5: Main Idea and Supporting Details in MyReadingLab to complete the Selection 2 activities and the Build Background Knowledge video activity.

P REVIEW the next selection to predict its purpose and organization and to formulate your learning plan.

Activate Schemata

What is the proper ethical response to encountering a seriously injured person?
Why do teens join street gangs?
What kind of violence is prevalent among urban street gangs?

Establish a Purpose for Reading

Why is someone on the sidewalk, bleeding? In this story, read about the fatal consequences of an act of gang violence with the intention of discovering the author's unstated message about gang culture in our society. As you read, be aware of the author's use of symbolism and note the way the rainy setting and the reactions of other characters contribute to the story's mood and the main character's realizations.

Build Background Knowledge — VIDEO

Street Gangs Menace Suburbs

To prepare for reading Selection 2, answer the questions below. Then, watch this video on street gangs reaching into the suburbs.

How have gang activities changed over the past 20 years?

Why do you think someone would join a gang?

Why is it difficult for the police to control gangs and their activities?

This video helped me: _____

_____

_____

Increase Word Knowledge

What do you know about these words?

scripted	excruciating	clutching	rumble	lurched
soothing	relentless	foraging	loathing	hysterically

Your instructor may give a brief vocabulary review before or after reading.

Integrate Knowledge While Reading

Questions have been inserted in the margins to stimulate your thinking while reading. Remember to

Predict   Picture   Relate   Monitor   Correct   Annotate

ON THE SIDEWALK, BLEEDING

The boy lay on the sidewalk bleeding in the rain. He was sixteen years old, and he wore a bright purple silk jacket, and the lettering across the back of the jacket read THE ROYALS. The boy's name was Andy, and the name was delicately scripted in black thread on the front of the jacket, just over the heart. ANDY.

5   He had been stabbed ten minutes ago. The knife entered just below his rib cage and had been drawn across his body violently, tearing a wide gap in his flesh. He lay on the sidewalk with the March rain drilling his jacket and drilling his body and washing away the blood that poured from his open wound. He had known excruciating pain when the knife had torn across his body, and then sudden comparative

10   relief when the blade was pulled away. He had heard the voice saying, "That's for you, Royal!" and then the sound of footsteps hurrying into the rain, and then he had fallen to the sidewalk, clutching his stomach, trying to stop the flow of blood.

Why would the author choose the name Royal?

He tried to yell for help, but he had no voice. He did not know why his voice had deserted him, or why the rain had become so steadily fierce, or why there was

15   an open hole in his body from which his life ran redly, steadily. It was 11:13 P.M., but he did not know the time.

There was another thing he did not know.

He did not know he was dying. He lay on the sidewalk, bleeding, and he thought only: *That was a fierce rumble. They got me good that time*, but he did not

Why are these words in italics?

20   know he was dying. He would have been frightened had he known. In his ignorance he lay bleeding and wishing he could cry out for help, but there was no voice in his throat. There was only the bubbling of blood from between his lips whenever he opened his mouth to speak. He lay in his pain, waiting, waiting for someone to find him.

25   He could hear the sound of automobile tires hushed on the rain-swept streets, far away at the other end of the long alley. He lay with his face pressed to the sidewalk, and he could see the splash of neon far away at the other end of the alley, tinting the pavement red and green, slickly brilliant in the rain.

He wondered if Laura would be angry.

Gang members flash hand signals.
Hector Mata/Getty

30   He had left the jump to get a package of cigarettes. He had told her he would be back in a few minutes, and then he had gone downstairs and found the candy store closed. He knew that Alfredo's on the next block would be open until at least two, and he had started through the alley, and that was when he had been ambushed.

He could hear the faint sound of music now, coming from a long, long way off.
35 He wondered if Laura was dancing, wondered if she had missed him yet. Maybe she thought he wasn't coming back. Maybe she thought he'd cut out for good. Maybe she had already left the jump and gone home. He thought of her face, the brown eyes and the jet-black hair, and thinking of her he forgot his pain a little, forgot that blood was rushing from his body.

40   Someday he would marry Laura. Someday he would marry her, and they would have a lot of kids, and then they would get out of the neighborhood. They would move to a clean project in the Bronx, or maybe they would move to Staten Island. When they were married, when they had kids . . .

He heard footsteps at the other end of the alley, and he lifted his cheek from the
45 sidewalk and looked into the darkness and tried to cry out, but again there was only a soft hissing bubble of blood on his mouth.

The man came down the alley. He had not seen Andy yet. He walked, and then stopped to lean against the brick of the building, and then walked again. He saw Andy then and came toward him, and he stood over him for a long time, the min-
50 utes ticking, ticking, watching him and not speaking.

Then he said, "What's a matter, buddy?"

Andy could not speak, and he could barely move. He lifted his face slightly and looked up at the man, and in the rain-swept alley he smelled the sickening odor of alcohol and realized the man was drunk. He did not know he was dying, and so he
55 felt only mild disappointment that the man who found him was drunk.

The man was smiling.

"Did you fall down, buddy?" he asked. "You mus' be as drunk as I am." He grinned, seemed to remember why he had entered the alley in the first place, and said, "Don' go 'way. I'll be ri' back."

60 The man lurched away. Andy heard his footsteps, and then the sound of the man colliding with a garbage can, and some mild swearing, and then the sound of the man urinating, lost in the steady wash of the rain. He waited for the man to come back.

It was 11:39.

When the man returned, he squatted alongside Andy. He studied him with 65 drunken dignity.

"You gonna catch cold there," he said. "What's the matter? You like layin' in the wet?"

Andy could not answer. The man tried to focus his eyes on Andy's face. The rain spattered around them.

70 "You like a drink?"

Andy shook his head.

How was the drunk compassionate? → "I gotta bottle. Here," the man said. He pulled a pint bottle from his inside jacket pocket. He uncapped it and extended it to Andy. Andy tried to move, but pain wrenched him back flat against the sidewalk.

75 "Take it," the man said. He kept watching Andy. "Take it." When Andy did not move, he said, "Nev' mind, I'll have one m'self." He tilted the bottle to his lips, and then wiped the back of his hand across his mouth. "You too young to be drinkin' anyway. Should be 'shamed of yourself, drunk and layin' in a alley, all wet. Shame on you. I gotta good mind to call a cop."

80 Andy nodded. Yes, he tried to say. Yes, call a cop. Please. Call one.

"Oh, you don' like that, huh?" the drunk said. "You don' wanna cop to fin' you all drunk an' wet in an alley, huh: Okay, buddy. This time you get off easy." He got to his feet. "This time you lucky," he said again. He waved broadly at Andy, and then almost lost his footing. "S'long, buddy," he said.

85 Wait, Andy thought. *Wait, please, I'm bleeding.*

"S'long," the drunk said again, "I see you aroun'," and then he staggered off up the alley.

Andy lay and thought: *Laura, Laura. Are you dancing?*

The couple came into the alley suddenly. They ran into the alley together, run-
90 ning from the rain, the boy holding the girl's elbow, the girl spreading a newspaper over her head to protect her hair. Andy lay crumpled on the pavement and he watched them run into the alley laughing, and then duck into the doorway not ten feet from him.

"Man, what rain!" the boy said. "You could drown out there."

95 "I have to get home," the girl said. "It's late, Freddie. I have to get home."

"We got time," Freddie said. "Your people won't raise a fuss if you're a little late. Not with this kind of weather."

"It's dark," the girl said, and she giggled.

"Yeah," the boy answered, his voice very low.

100 "Freddie? . . ."

"Um?"

"You're . . . standing very close to me."

"Um."

There was a long silence. Then the girl said, "Oh," only that single word, and
105 Andy knew she had been kissed, and he suddenly hungered for Laura's mouth. It

was then that he wondered if he would ever kiss Laura again. It was then that he wondered if he was dying.

No, he thought, *I can't be dying, not from a little street rumble, not from just being cut. Guys get cut all the time in rumbles. I can't be dying. No, that's stupid. That don't make*
110   *any sense at all.*

"You shouldn't," the girl said.

"Why not?"

"I don't know."

"Do you like it?"

115   "Yes."

"So?"

"I don't know."

"I love you, Angela," the boy said.

"I love you, too, Freddie," the girl said, and Andy listened and thought: *I love*
120 *you, Laura. Laura, I think maybe I'm dying. Laura, this is stupid but I think maybe I'm dying. Laura, I think I'm dying.*

He tried to speak. He tried to move. He tried to crawl toward the doorway where he could see two figures embrace. He tried to make a noise, a sound, and a grunt came from his lips, and then he tried again, and another grunt came, a low
125 animal grunt of pain.

"What was that?" the girl said, suddenly alarmed, breaking away from the boy.

"I don't know," he answered.

"Go look, Freddie."

"No. Wait."

130   Andy moved his lips again. Again the sound came from him.

"Freddie!"

"What?"

"I'm scared."

"I'll go see," the boy said.

135   He stepped into the alley. He walked over to where Andy lay on the ground. He stood over him, watching him.

"You all right?" he asked.

"What is it?" Angela said from the doorway.

"Somebody's hurt," Freddie said.

140   "Let's get out of here," Angela said.

"No. Wait a minute." He knelt down beside Andy. "You cut?" he asked.

Andy nodded. The boy kept looking at him. He saw the lettering on the jacket then. THE ROYALS. He turned to Angela.

"He's a Royal," he said.

145   "Let's . . . what . . . what . . . do you want to do, Freddie?"

"I don't know. I don't know. I don't want to get mixed up in this. He's a Royal. We help him, and the Guardians'll be down on our necks. I don't want to get mixed up in this, Angela."

"Is he . . . is he hurt bad?"

150   "Yeah, it looks that way."

"What shall we do?"

"I don't know."

"We can't leave him here in the rain," Angela hesitated. "Can we?"

"If we get a cop, the Guardians'll find out who," Freddie said. "I don't know,
155 Angela. I don't know."

Angela hesitated a long time before answering. Then she said, "I want to go home, Freddie. My people will begin to worry."

"Yeah," Freddie said. He looked at Andy again. "You all right?" he asked. Andy lifted his face from the sidewalk, and his eyes said: *Please, please help me*, and maybe
160 Freddie read what his eyes were saying, and maybe he didn't.

What would you have done at this point? What is ethical?

Behind him, Angela said, "Freddie, let's get out of here! Please!" There was urgency in her voice, urgency bordering on the edge of panic. Freddie stood up. He looked at Andy again, and then mumbled, "I'm sorry." He took Angela's arm and together they ran towards the neon splash at the other end of the alley.

165   *Why, they're afraid of the Guardians*, Andy thought in amazement. *But why should they be? I wasn't afraid of the Guardians. I never turkeyed out of a rumble with the Guardians. I got heart. But I'm bleeding.*

The rain was soothing somehow. It was a cold rain, but his body was hot all over, and the rain helped cool him. He had always liked rain. He could remember
170 sitting in Laura's house one time, the rain running down the windows, and just looking out over the street, watching the people running from the rain. That was when he'd first joined the Royals.

He could remember how happy he was when the Royals had taken him. The Royals and the Guardians, two of the biggest. He was a Royal. There had been
175 meaning to the title.

Now, in the alley, with the cold rain washing his hot body, he wondered about the meaning. If he died, he was Andy. He was not a Royal. He was simply Andy, and he was dead. And he wondered suddenly if the Guardians who had ambushed him and knifed him had ever once realized he was Andy. Had they known that he
180 was Andy or had they simply known that he was a Royal wearing a purple silk jacket? Had they stabbed *him*, Andy, or had they only stabbed the jacket and the title and what good was the title if you were dying?

I'm Andy, he screamed wordlessly, *For Christ's sake, I'm Andy*.

An old lady stopped at the other end of the alley. The garbage cans were stacked
185 there, beating noisily in the rain. The old lady carried an umbrella with broken ribs, carried it with all the dignity of a queen. She stepped into the mouth of the alley, shopping bag over one arm. She lifted the lids of the garbage cans delicately, and she did not hear Andy grunt because she was a little deaf and because the rain was beating a steady relentless tattoo on the cans. She had been searching and foraging
190 for the better part of the night. She collected her string and her newspapers, and an old hat with a feather on it from one of the garbage cans, and a broken footstool from another of the cans. And then delicately she replaced the lids and lifted her umbrella high and walked out of the alley mouth with a queenly dignity. She had worked quickly and soundlessly, and now she was gone.

195   The alley looked very long now. He could see people passing at the other end of it, and he wondered who the people were, and he wondered if he would ever get to know them, wondered who it was of the Guardians who had stabbed him, who had plunged the knife into his body.

"That's for you, Royal!" the voice had said, and then the footsteps, his arms
200 being released by the others, the fall to the pavement. "That's for you, Royal!" Even in his pain, even as he collapsed, there had been some sort of pride in knowing he was a Royal. Now there was no pride at all. With the rain beginning to chill him, with the blood pouring steadily between his fingers, he knew only a sort of dizziness. He could only think: *I want to be Andy*.

205   It was not very much to ask of the world.

He watched the world passing at the other end of the alley. The world didn't know he was Andy. The world didn't know he was alive. He wanted to say, "Hey, I'm alive! Hey, look at me! I'm alive! Don't you know I'm alive? Don't you know I exist?"

He felt weak and very tired. He felt alone, and wet and feverish and chilled, and 210 he knew he was going to die now, and the knowledge made him suddenly sad. He was not frightened. For some reason, he was not frightened. He was filled with an overwhelming sadness that his life would be over at sixteen. He felt all at once as if he had never done anything, never seen anything, never been anywhere. There were so many things to do, and he wondered why he'd never thought of them before, 215 wondered why the rumbles and the jumps and the purple jackets had always seemed so important to him before, and now they seemed like such small things in a world he was missing, a world that was rushing past at the other end of the alley.

I don't want to die, he thought. *I haven't lived yet.*

Does Andy deserve to die? How is his life wasted?

It seemed very important to him that he take off the purple jacket. He was very 220 close to dying, and when they found him, he did not want them to say, "Oh, it's a Royal." With great effort, he rolled over onto his back. He felt the pain tearing at his stomach when he moved, a pain he did not think was possible. But he wanted to take off the jacket. If he never did another thing, he wanted to take off the jacket. The jacket had only one meaning now, and that was a very simple meaning.

What is the author's view of gang culture?

225 If he had not been wearing the jacket, he wouldn't have been stabbed. The knife had not been plunged in hatred of Andy. The knife hated only the purple jacket. The jacket was a stupid, meaningless thing that was robbing him of his life. He wanted the jacket off his back. With an enormous loathing, he wanted the jacket off his back.

He lay struggling with the shiny wet material. His arms were heavy; pain 230 ripped fire across his body whenever he moved. But he squirmed and fought and twisted until one arm was free and then the other, and then he rolled away from the jacket and lay quite still, breathing heavily, listening to the sound of his breathing and the sounds of the rain and thinking: *Rain is sweet, I'm Andy.*

She found him in the doorway a minute past midnight. She left the dance to 235 look for him, and when she found him, she knelt beside him and said, "Andy, it's me, Laura."

He did not answer her. She backed away from him, tears springing into her eyes, and then she ran from the alley hysterically and did not stop running until she found a cop.

240 And now, standing with the cop, she looked down at him, and the cop rose and said, "He's dead," and all the crying was out of her now. She stood in the rain and said nothing, dead boy on the pavement, looking at the purple jacket that rested a foot away from his body.

The cop picked up the jacket and turned it over in his hands.

245 "A Royal, huh?" he said.

The rain seemed to beat more steadily now, more fiercely.

She looked at the cop and, very quietly, she said, "His name is Andy."

The cop slung the jacket over his arm. He took out his black pad, and he flipped it open to a blank page.

250 "A Royal," he said.

What happens next?

Then he began writing.

(3,022 words)

—Evan Hunter
Happy New Year, Herbie, and Other Stories

Recall

Stop to talk, write, and think about the selection.

Your instructor may choose to give you a brief comprehension review.

THINK CRITICALLY ABOUT THE SELECTION

Why did the author set this story late on a cold, rainy night?

In a way, Andy's jacket is a character in this story. Would "The Jacket" be a good title? Explain your thinking.

WRITE ABOUT THE SELECTION

How do Andy's thoughts of his own life evolve from the beginning to the end of the story?

Response Suggestion: Use the italicized thoughts to trace Andy's emotional journey.

SKILL DEVELOPMENT: FIND THE MAIN IDEA

Answer the following with *T* (true) or *F* (false):

———— 1. One of the central themes of this story is that Andy initially thought the jacket gave him identity, but he learned instead that it robbed him of his identity.

———— 2. The main point of the story is that Andy could have lived if others had helped him.

———— 3. The fact that the murder happened in March is a major detail.

CHECK YOUR COMPREHENSION

After reading the selection, answer the first item in your own words and answer the subsequent questions with *a, b, c,* or *d*. To help you analyze your strengths and weaknesses, the question types are indicated.

1. Who or what is the topic? _____

Main Idea   What is the main idea that the author is trying to convey about the topic?

_____

Detail   _____ 2. All of the following are true about Andy's jacket *except*

    a. it was purple.
    b. *The Royals* was written on the back.
    c. *Andy* was written on the left side of the front.
    d. it was torn in the back from the stab wounds.

Inference   _____ 3. The reader can assume that the primary reason Andy was stabbed was because

    a. he was threatening a member of the Guardian gang.
    b. he was wearing a jacket that said *The Royals*.
    c. he witnessed Guardians engaged in illegal activity in the alley.
    d. he was dating a girlfriend of the Guardians.

Inference   _____ 4. The reader can conclude that the drunk

    a. thought he was helping Andy.
    b. was afraid and did not want to help Andy.
    c. understood that Andy was dying.
    d. saw the blood and left.

Inference   _____ 5. The reader can conclude that Angela and Freddie

    a. would not have called the police if Andy did not have the jacket.
    b. recognized Andy from the dance.
    c. feared retribution from the Guardians.
    d. contacted Laura so that she could find Andy.

Inference   _____ 6. The reader can conclude all of the following about the old lady *except*

    a. she never heard Andy.
    b. she was salvaging items from trash, as if poor or homeless.
    c. the author felt she carried herself with dignity despite her actions.
    d. she saw trouble and wanted no involvement.

Inference _____ 7. The author suggests that the person who could most accurately be called a coward in the story is

    a. the drunk.
    b. the old lady.
    c. Freddie.
    d. Laura.

Inference _____ 8. The author suggests that Andy took off the jacket because

    a. he did not want Laura to find him wearing the jacket.
    b. he wanted other members of the Royals to be proud of him.
    c. he wanted to reclaim his personal identity.
    d. as a sign of honor, he wanted to avoid implicating gang members in his death.

Inference _____ 9. The author suggests all the following about the cop *except*

    a. he recognized Andy as a person.
    b. he recorded the death as a meaningless gang killing.
    c. he was familiar with the activities of the gangs.
    d. he was not surprised to find a dead boy in the alley.

Inference _____ 10. The author suggests that Andy's anger at his death was directed primarily toward

    a. the Guardians.
    b. the Royals.
    c. himself.
    d. Angela and Freddie.

Answer the following with *T* (true) or *F* (false):

Author's Purpose _____ 11. The author's main purpose is to engage the reader's emotions.

Inference _____ 12. According to the story, the time that elapsed from the stabbing until Andy was found by Laura was 58 minutes.

Detail _____ 13. Andy cut through the alley because it was the shortest way to the candy store, which was open until 2:00.

Inference _____ 14. The author suggests that there are other gangs in the area besides the Guardians and the Royals.

Inference _____ 15. As Andy got closer to death, he thought more about his wasted life and less about Laura.

BUILD YOUR VOCABULARY

According to the way the italicized word was used in the selection, select *a, b, c,* or *d* for the word or phrase that gives the best definition. The number in parentheses indicates the line of the passage in which the word is located. Use a dictionary in addition to the context clues to more precisely define the terms.

_____ 1. "*scripted* in black thread" (3)
   a. painted
   b. carved
   c. blocked
   d. handwritten

_____ 2. "known *excruciating* pain" (8–9)
   a. immediate
   b. humiliating
   c. agonizing
   d. tantalizing

_____ 3. "*clutching* his stomach" (12)
   a. tightly holding
   b. scratching
   c. tearing
   d. skinning

_____ 4. "fierce *rumble*" (19)
   a. knife
   b. gang member
   c. gang fight
   d. gang order

_____ 5. "man *lurched* away" (60)
   a. sneaked
   b. staggered
   c. ran
   d. excused himself

_____ 6. "rain was *soothing*" (168)
   a. cold
   b. endless
   c. calming
   d. irritating

_____ 7. "steady *relentless* tattoo" (189)
   a. noisy
   b. ugly
   c. rhythmical
   d. persistent

_____ 8. "*foraging* for the better part" (189)
   a. singing
   b. searching for food
   c. speaking aloud
   d. hiding

_____ 9. "enormous *loathing*" (228)
   a. hatred
   b. eagerness
   c. strain
   d. energy

_____ 10. "ran from the alley *hysterically*" (238)
   a. quickly
   b. fearfully
   c. sadly
   d. frantically

Concept Prep for Literature

What is literature?

Literature, the art form of language, is invented from the author's imagination. The purpose is to entertain an audience, to explore the human condition, and to reveal universal truths through shared experiences. As a reader, you are allowed inside the minds of characters, and you learn about life as the characters live it. After reading, you are enriched. Literature includes four categories, or *genres*: essays, fiction, poetry, and drama. Although the four genres differ in intent, they share many of the same elements.

What are literary elements?

Plot. The *plot* describes the action in a story, play, or epic poem. It is a sequence of incidents or events.

Events in the story build progressively to reveal conflict to the reader. The *conflict* is a struggle or a clash of ideas, desires, or actions. Conflicts can exist between the main character and another character, external forces, or within the character.

As the plot moves forward, the *suspense* builds. The conflict intensifies to a peak, or *climax*, which comes near the end of the story and is the turning point. The *denouement* is the outcome of conflicts. Then the action falls and leads to a *resolution*, which answers any remaining questions.

Characters. In literature, you are told what characters think and feel. Thus, by the experience of "living through" significant events with the character, you are better able to understand the complexities of human nature.

Point of View. The *point of view* in literature is not defined as bias or opinion, as it is in Chapter 8. Rather, it describes who tells the story. It can be in the *first person*, as the *I* in a diary; the *second person*, using the word *you*; or most commonly, the *third person*, in which the author is the all-knowing observer.

Tone. The *tone* is the writer's attitude toward the subject or the audience. Word clues may suggest that the author is being humorous. Cutting remarks, on the other hand, may suggest *sarcasm*. The author's emotional and intellectual attitude toward the subject also describes the *mood*, or overall feeling of the work.

Setting. All stories exist in a time and place. Details must be consistent with the setting or else they distract your attention. The *setting* is the backdrop for the story and the playground for the characters.

Figures of Speech and Symbolism. Literary writing appeals to the five senses and, unlike scientific or academic writing, uses images to convey a

Awarded the Nobel Prize for Literature in 1993, author Toni Morrison also won a Pulitzer Prize for her novel, *Beloved*.

Evan Agostini/Getty

274

figurative or symbolic meaning rather than an exact literal meaning. *Metaphors* and *similes* are the most common, and they both suggest a comparison of unlike things. For more on figurative language, see Chapter 7.

The imagery or *symbolism* in a story can be an object, action, person, place, or idea that carries a condensed and recognizable meaning. For example, an open window might represent an opportunity for a new life.

Theme. The *theme* is the main idea or the heart and soul of the work. The theme is a central insight into life or universal truth. This message is never preached but is revealed to your emotions, senses, and imagination through powerful, shared experiences. The theme should not be reduced to a one-sentence moral, such as "Honesty is the best policy" or "Crime does not pay." Instead, ask yourself, "What has the main character learned during the story?" or "What insight into life does the story reveal?"

REVIEW QUESTIONS

After studying the material, answer the following questions:

1. What is literature? _____

   _____

2. What is plot? _____

3. What is the climax of "On the Sidewalk, Bleeding"? _____

   _____

4. What is the resolution? _____

   _____

5. How do you learn about the characters in "On the Sidewalk, Bleeding"? _____

   _____

6. What is the most common point of view in a story? _____

7. How does the definition of *point of view* differ in literature and in the question, "What is your point of view on cloning?" _____

   _____

8. What do you feel is the author's attitude toward the subject in "On the Sidewalk, Bleeding"? _____

   _____

9. What is the overriding symbol in "On the Sidewalk, Bleeding"? _____

   _____

10. What is the theme of a story? _____

    _____

Your instructor may choose to give a brief review of these literary concepts.

SELECTION 3   Criminal Justice   MyReadingLab

Visit Chapter 5: Main Idea and Supporting Details in MyReadingLab to complete the
Selection 3 activities and the Build Background Knowledge video activity.

P REVIEW the next selection to predict its purpose and organization and to
formulate your learning plan.

Activate Schemata

Have you seen television programs or read novels that feature crimes solved with
mathematical models? The idea is spreading and is the subject of research that
bridges criminal justice, mathematics, sociology, and anthropology.

Establish a Purpose for Reading

The research described in this selection holds promise for determining who is
likely to have committed a crime. Read to find out how it works and why police
departments and even advertisers would be interested in it.

Build Background Knowledge — VIDEO

Mathematician Hacks OKCupid To Find True Love

To prepare for reading Selection 3, answer the
questions below. Then, watch this video that examines how a mathematical equation led to love.

What role does math play in your everyday life?

Do you enjoy math? Why or why not?

What role do you think math plays in online dating?

This video helped me: _____

_____

_____

Increase Word Knowledge

What do you know about these words?

algorithm	simulated	mimicked	perpetrator	rivalries
exploits	implications	nodes	hackers	anthropology

Your instructor may give a brief vocabulary review before or after reading.

Integrate Knowledge While Reading

Questions have been inserted in the margins to stimulate your thinking while reading. Remember to

Predict   Picture   Relate   Monitor   Correct   Annotate

SELECTION 3

FIGHTING VIOLENT GANG CRIME WITH MATH

University of California at Los Angeles (UCLA) mathematicians working with the Los Angeles Police Department to analyze crime patterns have designed a mathematical algorithm to identify street gangs involved in unsolved violent crimes. Their research is based on patterns of known criminal activity between gangs, and repre-
5 sents the first scholarly study of gang violence of its kind.

CREATION AND TESTING

What is an algorithm?

In developing their algorithm, the mathematicians analyzed more than 1,000 gang crimes and suspected gang crimes, about half of them unsolved, that occurred over a 10-year period in an East Los Angeles police district known as Hollenbeck, a small

That's a lot! 10 area in which there are some 30 gangs and nearly 70 gang rivalries.

To test the algorithm, the researchers created a set of simulated data that closely mimicked the crime patterns of the Hollenbeck gang network. They then dropped some of the key information out—the victim, the perpetrator or both—and tested how well the algorithm could calculate the missing information.

"If police believe a crime might have been committed by one of seven or eight
15 rival gangs, our method would look at recent historical events in the area and compute probabilities as to which of these gangs are most likely to have committed a crime," said the study's senior author, Andrea Bertozzi, a professor of mathematics

Applied mathematics?

and director of applied mathematics at UCLA.

RESULTS

About 80 percent of the time, the mathematicians could narrow it down to three
20 gang rivalries that were most likely involved in a crime.

"Our algorithm placed the correct gang rivalry within the top three most likely rivalries 80 percent of the time, which is significantly better than chance," said Martin Short, a UCLA adjunct assistant professor of mathematics and co-author of the study. "That narrows it down quite a bit, and that is when we don't know anything
25 about the crime victim or perpetrator."

A big improvement!

The mathematicians also found that the correct gang was ranked No. 1—rather than just among the top three—50 percent of the time, compared with just 17 percent by chance.

"We can do even better," Bertozzi said. "This is the first paper that takes this
30 new approach. We can improve on that 80 percent by developing more sophisticated methods."

Mathematical algorithms are helping to address unsolved violent gang crime.
Eric Milos/Shutterstock

APPLICATIONS

"Our algorithm exploits gang activity patterns to produce the best probability of which gang, or which three gangs, may have been responsible for the crimes," she said. Police can investigate further when the gangs are narrowed down.

35   Bertozzi and her colleagues have been working with the LAPD on a variety of classes of crime. The implications of the research go beyond fighting gangs and beyond fighting crime.

"The algorithm we devised could apply to a much broader class of problems that involve activity on social networks," Bertozzi said. "You have events—they

40 could be crimes or something else—that occur in a time series and a known network. There is activity between nodes, in this case a gang attacking another gang. With some of those activities, you know exactly who was involved and with others, you do not. The challenge is how to make the best educated judgment as to who was involved in the unknown activities. We believe there are a number of social net-

45 works that have this same kind of pattern."

Identifying hackers would be an example; helping businesses target advertising to consumers who would be most interested in their products and services in a way that would protect privacy would be another.

"An advertiser may not care who individual people are but just how they
50 behave," Bertozzi said. "Advertisers could target consumers by knowing their shopping behavior without knowing their identities."

Can I think of other uses? →

The lead author of the study is Alexey Stomakhin, a UCLA doctoral student in applied mathematics who worked for a year to design the algorithm that can fill in the missing information.

THE BEST JOB IN THE WORLD

55 Bertozzi describes her work as "the best job in the world—working with great young mathematicians and having an impact on society." She noted that UCLA is ranked No. 2 in the U.S. in applied mathematics. Bertozzi is interested in applying mathematics to address practical problems that affect peoples' lives.

"Nowhere else are they doing research like this—only at UCLA," Short said.
60 Last year Bertozzi, Short, and colleagues, including Jeffrey Brantingham in anthropology, reported a new mathematical model that allows them to analyze different types of criminal "hotspots"—areas where many crimes occur, at least for a time.

The new research is federally funded by the National Science Foundation, the U.S. Army Research Office's mathematics divisions, the U.S. Office of Naval
65 Research, and the U.S. Air Force Office of Scientific Research.

(774 words)

—Stuart Wolpert,
UCLA Newsroom

Recall

Stop to talk, write, and think about the selection.

Your instructor may choose to give you a brief comprehension review.

THINK CRITICALLY ABOUT THE SELECTION

List the ways in which the author suggests that this algorithm can be helpful.

Considering how well this algorithm appears to help solve crimes, do you think it could be helpful in preventing crime? Explain.

Mathematics has many practical uses. In what other situations is mathematics applied to everyday problems?

WRITE ABOUT THE SELECTION

Bertozzi said that she has the best job in the world. Would you enjoy work like this? Or would you like to be on the receiving end of her work, using it to identify criminals or advertising targets? What does she love about her job? What makes a job appealing to you?

Response Suggestion: In one paragraph, use the reasons Bertozzi cites and expand on them to explain why someone might love that job. In a second paragraph, describe the kind of work you aim to do and the characteristics that you believe will make it "the best job in the world."

Summarize

Write a one-paragraph summary of this selection to serve as notes that would prepare you for a class discussion or a test.

SKILL DEVELOPMENT: FIND THE MAIN IDEA

Answer the following with *T* (true) or *F* (false):

_____ 1. The main point of the section, "Creation and Testing," is that about half of the crimes used to develop this model were unsolved.

_____ 2. The main point of the "Results" section is that the algorithm worked well enough to be helpful in identifying gangs that were responsible for crimes.

_____ 3. The main point of "Applications" is that the algorithm can be useful, not only in solving crimes, but also in other areas.

_____ 4. The main point of the entire selection is that mathematician Andrea Bertozzi loves her job.

CHECK YOUR COMPREHENSION

After reading the selection, answer the following questions with *a, b, c,* or *d.* To help you analyze your strengths and weaknesses, the question types are indicated.

Main Idea   1. Who or what is the topic? _____

_____

What is the main idea that the author is trying to convey about the topic? ____

_____

_____

Detail _____ 2. What was the original purpose of this research?

    a. To identify the Los Angeles gangs responsible for crimes
    b. To help police identify computer hackers
    c. To arrest the leaders of violent gangs
    d. To make social comparisons

Inference _____ 3. It is reasonable to conclude from this article that

    a. the results of this research cannot be used in any other way than mentioned in the article.
    b. the results of research are sometimes useful for purposes other than originally intended.
    c. Bertozzi and her team will not do further research like this.
    d. research always achieves its intended purpose.

Inference _____ 4. Given information in the article, why would the researchers focus on the Hollenbeck area of East Los Angeles?

    a. It was chosen at random for research purposes.
    b. It was the only area approved by the LAPD.
    c. UCLA is located in that area.
    d. It appears to have a very heavy incidence of gang-related crime.

Inference _____ 5. The algorithm apparently could predict which gang committed a crime and

    a. the location of the crime.
    b. the time and place of the crime.
    c. the victim, or both the perpetrator and the victim.
    d. the victim.

Detail _____ 6. The algorithm was based on what information?

    a. knowledge of the Hollenbeck streets
    b. police theories and recent events in the Hollenbeck area
    c. known facts about gang members
    d. information provided by gang members

Detail _____ 7. How often was the algorithm able to correctly identify the gang that was responsible for a crime?

    a. 100 percent of the time
    b. 80 percent of the time
    c. 75 percent of the time
    d. 50 percent of the time

Detail _____ 8. How often was the algorithm able to correctly narrow the gangs that were involved down to three?

    a. 100 percent of the time
    b. 80 percent of the time
    c. 75 percent of the time
    d. 50 percent of the time

Inference _____ 9. Uses for the results of this research that were mentioned in this article include all of the following *except*

    a. naming individuals who might like to buy certain products.
    b. finding groups of consumers who are likely to be interested in certain products.
    c. identifying hackers who manipulate computer information illegally.
    d. identifying gangs that were likely to have committed a certain crime.

Detail _____ 10. Who funded this research?

    a. the Los Angeles Police Department
    b. the University of California at Los Angeles
    c. various divisions of the federal government
    d. Andrea Bertozzi, Martin Short, and Alexey Stomakhin

Answer the following with *T* (true) or *F* (false).

Inference _____ 11. The article implies that gang members assisted with this research.

Detail _____ 12. The algorithm did a better job of identifying the perpetrator than would happen by chance.

Inference _____ 13. If police use this algorithm, they do not have to do further investigation.

Author's Purpose _____ 14. The primary purpose of this selection is to inform readers.

Detail _____ 15. One reason Bertozzi enjoys her work is that it benefits society.

BUILD YOUR VOCABULARY

According to the way the italicized word was used in the selection, indicate *a, b, c,* or *d* for the word or phrase that gives the best definition. The number in parentheses indicates the line of the passage in which the word is located. Use a dictionary in addition to the context clues to more precisely define the terms.

_____ 1. "a mathematical *algorithm*" (3)
   a. a subject for study
   b. a college degree
   c. an answer to a problem
   d. procedure for solving a problem

_____ 2. "*simulated* data" (10)
   a. artificial
   b. authentic
   c. real
   d. genuine

_____ 3. "*mimicked* the crime patterns" (11)
   a. changed
   b. released
   c. imitated
   d. viewed

_____ 4. "the *perpetrator*" (12)
   a. the police
   b. one who investigates a crime
   c. the victim of a crime
   d. one who commits a crime

_____ 5. "gang *rivalries*" (20)
   a. partnerships
   b. friendships
   c. competitions
   d. networks

_____ 6. "*exploits* gang activity patterns" (32)
   a. misuses
   b. takes advantage of
   c. ignores
   d. benefits

_____ 7. "*implications* of the research" (36)
   a. dangers
   b. significance
   c. errors
   d. details

_____ 8. "activity between *nodes*" (41)
   a. swellings on a plant
   b. departments
   c. events, points of activity
   d. enlarged part of the body

_____ 9. "Identifying *hackers*" (46)
   a. manufacturers
   b. people who illegally access computer systems
   c. experts who provide computer help
   d. a beginner

_____ 10. "in *anthropology*" (60–61)
   a. the study of human beings
   b. the study of women
   c. the study of criminology
   d. the study of medicine

SELECTION 3

VOCABULARY BOOSTER

The Sun, the Moon, and the Stars

Roots	sol, helio: "sun"	luna: "moon"
	aster, astro: "star"	

Words with *sol, helio:* "sun"

A sundial is a primitive example of a *solar* chronometer, an instrument that shows the time of day by means of the sun.

- **solar**: of or pertaining to the sun; proceeding from the sun; operating on energy from the sun

  Solar panels on rooftops to heat water for homes have become a popular way to conserve energy.

- **solarium**: a glass-enclosed room that is exposed to the sun's rays

  A *solarium* in a home usually becomes the favorite spot in winter because it is naturally warmed by the sun.

- **solstice**: either of two times a year when the sun is farthest from the equator

  The summer *solstice*, the longest day in the Northern Hemisphere, occurs around June 21 or June 22, when the sun is farthest north of the equator.

- **heliotherapy**: treatment of disease by exposure to sunlight

  Heliotherapy is prescribed sunbathing for certain illnesses, such as tuberculosis or rickets.

- **heliotropic**: turning or growing toward the light or sun

  Without frequent turning, some *heliotropic* houseplants would grow only in one direction—toward the sunlight.

- **helium**: an inert gaseous element present in the sun's atmosphere and in natural gas

  Because *helium* is a chemically inactive gas, it is used as a substitute for flammable gases in dirigibles (blimps).

Words with *luna:* "moon"

The small *demilune* table was just the right size for the narrow foyer because its half-moon shape did not extend far into the room.

- **lunar**: of or pertaining to the moon; round or crescent-shaped; measured by the moon's revolutions

  A *lunar* month is equal to one revolution of the moon around the earth, approximately 29½ days.

- **lunatic**: an insane or recklessly foolish person

  The old gentleman was labeled a *lunatic* and unable to handle his legal affairs responsibly.

- ***lunatic fringe***: members on the edges of a group, such as a political or religious group, who hold extreme views

  Members of the *lunatic fringe* of some environmentalist movements have destroyed property to protest further building in certain areas.

- ***lunar eclipse***: an obscuring of the light of the moon when the earth is positioned between the moon and the sun

  During a *lunar eclipse,* the earth casts its shadow on the moon.

- ***lunar year***: a division of time that is equal to twelve lunar months

  In a *lunar year*, the moon orbits the earth 12 times.

Words with *aster, astro:* "star"

An *aster* is a daisylike flower with colored petals radiating around a yellow disk.

- ***asterisk***: a small, starlike symbol (*) used in writing and printing to refer to footnotes or omissions

  An *asterisk* can be used to refer readers to an explanation of an item in the written material.

- ***asteroid***: one of many celestial bodies orbiting the sun; most asteroid orbits are between those of Mars and Jupiter.

  Scientists believe that *asteroids* collided with Earth in the past and predict that they will do so again.

- ***astronomy***: the science that deals with the universe beyond Earth's atmosphere

  Astronomy involves studying the motion, position, and size of celestial bodies.

- ***astronomical***: pertaining to astronomy; extremely large or enormous

  Projected costs for the new hospital wing were so *astronomical* that the board decided to postpone the project.

- ***astrology***: the study that attempts to foretell the future by interpreting the influence of the stars on human lives

  Most people don't believe in *astrology;* they believe that they are responsible for what happens in their future.

- ***astronaut***: a person who is trained for space flight

  The *astronaut* went to bed early the night before his scheduled space shuttle mission.

Review

Part I

Choose the word from the list that best completes each of the sentences below.

lunatic	astronomical	astronomy	astrology
solarium	heliotropic	lunar eclipse	astronauts

1. A _____ plant might be compared to a person who is a sun worshipper.

2. The world's population appears to be growing at an alarmingly large, or _____, rate.

3. Someone who is branded a _____ would not be sought out for sound advice.

4. The competition is fierce for gaining admittance to the training program for _____ in Houston.

5. Black holes, supernovas, and constellations are all studied in the science of _____.

6. A warm _____ is the perfect place to keep plants alive during the winter months.

7. According to _____, personality traits are determined by the planetary alignments on a person's birthday.

8. In ancient times, the appearance of a _____ was mistakenly thought to be a sign that the end of the world was near.

Part II

Indicate whether the italicized words are used correctly *(C)* or incorrectly *(I)* in the following sentences:

_____ 9. *Solar* panels are becoming more popular in home design as the costs of other forms of energy continue to rise.

_____ 10. *Lunar* explorations involve spacecraft searching for proof of life on Mars.

_____ 11. Years ago native people celebrated the winter *solstice,* which is the coldest day of the year.

_____ 12. A sun worshipper would likely be happy with a prescription for *heliotherapy.*

_____ 13. An *asterisk* is on one of the keys on most cell phones.

_____ 14. *Asters* are small planets of varying sizes, often confused with meteors.

_____ 15. A person who is labeled a *lunatic* is not known for giving wise advice.

Your instructor may choose to give you a brief review.

Patterns of Organization

Learning Objectives

In this chapter, you will learn to:

1 Understand the value of knowing the pattern of organization
2 Recognize the function of transitional words
3 Recognize common patterns of organization in textbooks
4 Use clues to identify the pattern of organization
5 Recognize mixed patterns of organization

Vocabulary Booster: Can I Get That in Writing?

TEXTBOOK ORGANIZATION: THE BIG PICTURE

Learning Objective 1

Understand the value of knowing the pattern of organization

The **pattern of organization** in a textbook is the presentation plan, format, or structure for presenting the message. Why is it important to identify organizational patterns in textbooks and other types of writing? Basically, such patterns serve as the book's blueprint, showing the reader how the book was built. They signal how facts and ideas are presented. The number of details in a textbook can be overwhelming. Identifying the pattern of organization of a section or a chapter can help you master the complexities of the material. If you know the pattern of organization, you can predict the format of upcoming information.

Although key transitional words can signal a particular pattern, the most important clue to the pattern is the main idea itself because it usually dictates the organizational pattern. Your aim as a reader is to identify the main idea. To accomplish that, be alert to the signal words, anticipate the overall pattern of organization, and place the major supporting details into the outline or pattern that is used by the author.

WHAT DO TRANSITIONAL WORDS DO?

Learning Objective 2

Recognize the function of transitional words

Small words can carry a big load. A single word can signal the level of importance, a connection, or a direction of thought. For example, if a friend begins a sentence by saying, "I owe you $100," would you prefer that the next word be *and* or that it be *but*? The word *and* signals addition and would give you high hopes for the return of your money. However, the word *but* signals a change of thought, which, in this case, would be in a negative direction. If the next word were *first*, you would anticipate a sequence of events before repayment. If the next word were *consequently*, you would hope that the positive result would be the return of your $100.

Such words are **transitional words**—sometimes called *signal words*—that connect parts of sentences or whole sentences and lead you to anticipate either a continuation of or a change in thought. Transitions show the relationships of ideas within sentences, between sentences, and between paragraphs. Writers use transitions to keep their readers' comprehension on track and to guide them through the logic of the message. To avoid repetition, authors choose from a variety of signal words to indicate the transition of thought. These signal words or transitions can be categorized as shown in the following examples and in the Reader's Tip, "Transitions and Their Functions," on page 290.

Words That Signal Addition

in addition	moreover	furthermore	and	also	another

EXAMPLES

José was given a raise after six months at his job. *In addition*, he became eligible for health insurance benefits.

After causing a disturbance in the movie theater, Brian and his friends were asked to leave. *Furthermore*, they were barred from attending that theater ever again.

Words That Signal Examples or Illustrations

for example	for instance	to illustrate	such as	including

EXAMPLES   Traffic seems to be getting heavier. *For instance,* last year it took only 20 minutes to get to school, and now it takes 30 minutes.

Some experts believe that a fetus in the womb can be affected by sounds *such as* classical music or the mother's voice.

Words That Signal Time or Sequence

first	second	finally	last	afterward	after	during
while	before	then	previously	until	now	next

EXAMPLES   Apply sunscreen *while* you are walking on the beach and *before* swimming in the surf. *Afterward*, reapply the sunscreen even if it is waterproof.

To build a good financial foundation, *first* pay yourself in the form of savings and *then* pay your bills.

Words That Signal Comparison

Similarly	likewise	in the same manner	like	as	just as	as well

EXAMPLES   If you treat someone with kindness, he or she will probably treat you in kind. *Likewise,* if you treat someone with disrespect, you will probably be disrespected.

Portland is a port city in Oregon; *similarly*, it is a seaport in Maine.

Words That Signal Contrast

however	but	nevertheless	whereas
on the contrary	conversely	yet	in contrast
even though	on the other hand	although	instead

EXAMPLES   Using a knife to cut a bagel can be dangerous to the fingers. *On the other hand*, using a bagel holder keeps fingers safe from the falling blade.

Today, many families eat dinner separately and on the run, *whereas* in the past, the family dinner hour was a time for bonding and an opportunity to instill values or share dreams.

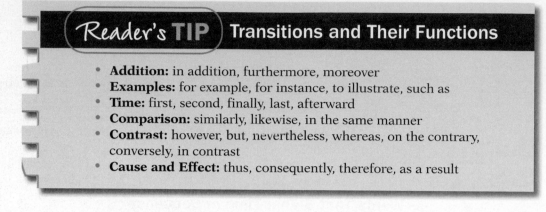

Words That Signal Cause and Effect

thus	consequently	therefore	as a result
accordingly	because	so	hence

EXAMPLES

Because of his work to end apartheid in South Africa, Nelson Mandela spent 27 years in prison. Upon his release, Mandela treated his oppressors with respect and worked to unite the country. *Consequently*, he shared a Nobel Peace Prize with then-president Frederik Willem de Klerk.

There has been a severe shortage of rainfall this year. *Therefore*, we have instituted a ban on outdoor watering.

EXERCISE 6.1

Anticipating Transitions

Choose a transitional word from the boxed lists to complete the sentences that follow.

however	for example	in addition	consequently	in the meantime

1. Forget the boring tourist narrative and turn walking around a city into a hip audio tour experience with Soundwalk podcasts. In New York, _____, you can pop in a 50-minute podcast to explore Chinatown, the Meatpacking District, or Wall Street.

2. The United States has an ever-increasing demand for oil. _____, we are researching alternative sources of energy, such as solar energy, to reduce our dependence on oil.

3. _____ to alternative energy research, we have begun drilling for oil on a small portion of our public lands to lessen our dependence on foreign sources of oil.

4. Drilling on public lands, _____, is not popular with environmentalists who believe the drilling cannot be done without spoiling the land. They have filed lawsuits in several states and await the results.

5. _____, we can strive to be more fuel-efficient to help reduce our demand for energy.

| furthermore | for example | nevertheless | finally | in contrast |

6. African American music in twentieth-century America evolved from ragtime, to jazz, to rhythm and blues, to soul, and _____, to rap and hip hop.

7. The concert tickets were outrageously priced. _____, this was a once-in-a-lifetime opportunity, and other luxuries would have to be sacrificed to compensate for the expense.

8. Mardi Gras as celebrated in New Orleans is similar to Carnival as celebrated throughout Latin America. Carnival lasts for five days; _____, Mardi Gras lasts only one day.

9. Internet car sales, rather than hurting auto dealerships, have actually helped them. _____, most customers conduct research on the Web but still visit a dealer to actually buy an automobile. A well-informed consumer who is ready to purchase makes the salesperson's job easier.

10. Since Melissa failed to notify her parents that she had backed into another vehicle in the college parking lot, they were outraged to learn of the accident through a third party. _____, due to her lack of honesty, Melissa's parents decided that she would no longer be covered under their auto insurance policy.

| first | likewise | whereas | therefore |

11. Rather than immediately train to run in a marathon, you might _____ consider entering a 5K or 10K race.

12. Couples do not always share personality traits; Tom is introverted, _____ his wife could be considered outgoing.

13. Cell phones must be turned off and put away before class; _____, your instructor expects you to do the same with all other electronic devices, except for laptops.

14. Rain seems to develop at the most inopportune moments; _____, it is wise to keep an umbrella handy.

PATTERNS OF ORGANIZATION IN TEXTBOOKS

Learning Objective 3

Recognize common patterns of organization in textbooks

As transitional words signal connections and relationships of ideas within and among sentences, they also help signal the overall organizational pattern of the message. When you write, you choose a pattern for organizing your thoughts. That organizational pattern is probably dictated by the main idea of your message. Before beginning to write, you must ask, "If this is what I want to say, what is the best logical pattern to use to organize my message?"

The next exercise contains examples of the patterns of organization that you will encounter in textbooks. Some are used much more frequently than others, and some are typical of particular disciplines. For example, history textbooks often use the patterns of time order and cause and effect. Management textbooks frequently use the simple listing pattern, whereas psychology textbooks make heavy use of the definition-and-example pattern. The Reader's Tip, "Patterns of Organization and Signal Words," following the exercise (see page 299) lists each type of organizational pattern with some related signal words.

BRAIN BOOSTER

Brains Like Patterns

Human brains are designed to notice patterns because patterns are how we make sense of the world. We learn through repeated experience that a toy pushed off the table falls to the floor, so we expect that to happen every time. When we see an incomplete circle, our brains attempt to complete it. If we miss a word in a spoken sentence, we fill in the blank with something that makes sense. Each time the pattern repeats, our neuronal network grows larger and stronger. Use this natural feature of your brain to your advantage when reading! Look for the pattern that the author used to organize the information. When you see the pattern, you can make better sense of the author's message.

—*Adapted from* 12 Brain/Mind Learning Principles in Action: Developing Executive Functions of the Human Brain, *by Caine, Caine, McClintic, and Klimek*

EXERCISE 6.2

Patterns of Organization

Notice the graphic organizer that accompanies each pattern of organization described in the following sections. After you read each example, enter the key points into the blank graphic organizer to show that you understand the pattern.

Simple Listing

With **simple listing**, items are randomly listed in a series of supporting facts or details. These supporting elements are of equal value, and the order in which they are presented is of no importance. Changing the order of the items does not change the meaning of the paragraph. Additional information about listed items might also be included to provide interest and depth.

Transitional words that are often used to link ideas in a paragraph with a pattern of simple listing include *in addition, also, another, several, for example, furthermore,* and *a number of.*

EXAMPLE   **THE BIG FIVE**

Although many theories of personality have been proposed, the most widely accepted theory today is the five-factor theory, or "the Big Five," as it is sometimes called. This theory claims that characteristics of personality can be described by how an individual rates on dimensions of extraversion, neuroticism, conscientiousness, agreeableness, and openness to experience. Research has confirmed that these five factors are present regardless of cultural background.

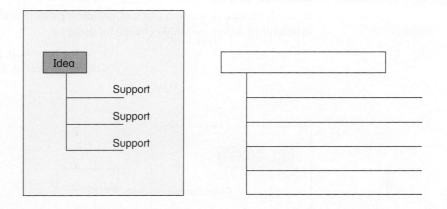

Definition

Frequently in a textbook, an entire paragraph is devoted to defining a complex term or idea. With **definition**, the concept is defined initially and then expanded with examples and restatements. In a textbook, a defined term is usually signaled by *italic* or **bold** type.

EXAMPLE   **ULTRASOUND**

Ultrasound is a technique that uses sound waves to produce an image that enables a physician to detect structural abnormalities. Useful pictures can be obtained as early as five or six weeks into pregnancy. Ultrasound is frequently used in conjunction with other techniques such as amniocentesis and fetoscopy.

—John Dacey and John Travers,
Human Development, 2nd ed.

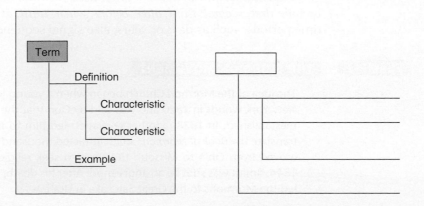

Description

Description is like listing; the characteristics that make up a description are no more than a simple list of details.

EXAMPLE   **CARIBBEAN**

Caribbean America today is a land crowded with so many people that, as a region (encompassing the Greater and Lesser Antilles), it is the most densely populated part of the Americas. It is also a place of grinding poverty and, in all too many localities, unrelenting misery with little chance for escape.

—H. J. De Blij and Peter O. Muller,
Geography: Realms, Regions, and Concepts, 7th ed.

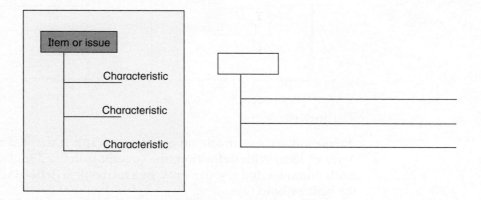

Time Order, Sequence, or Narration

Items are listed in the order in which they occurred or in a specifically planned order in which they must develop. In this case, the **chronological** or **time order**, or **sequence** is important, and changing it would change the meaning. **Narration**, writing which tells a story, is an example of writing in which time order is important.

Transitional words that are often used for time order, sequence, or narration include *first, second, third, after, before, when, until, at last, next,* and *later.* Actual time periods, such as days or years, also signal sequence and time.

EXAMPLE   **THE MORMON MOVEMENT**

The idea of the Mormon Church began when a young Joseph Smith, Jr., went into the New York woods in 1820 and was told by God that the true church of God would be reestablished. In 1823, another revelation led him to find buried golden plates and translate the *Book of Mormon.* Smith attracted thousands of followers and in the 1830s moved from Ohio to Missouri to Illinois to seek religious freedom for his group. In 1844, Smith was shot by an angry mob. After his death, a new leader, Brigham Young, led the Mormons to the Great Salt Lake in Utah.

Topic:			Topic:		
When did it happen?	What happened?		When did it happen?	What happened?	

Comparison

With **comparison**, items are presented according to similarities between or among them. Transitional words that are often used for comparison include *similar*, *in the same way*, *likewise*, and *just like*.

EXAMPLE   **JAZZ GREATS**

Jazz greats Louis Armstrong and Billie Holiday overcame similar obstacles in their struggling early years. Both were raised in the slums by working mothers, and both learned the necessary discipline for success through hard work. As a teen, Armstrong hauled coal from 7 A.M. to 5 P.M. for 75 cents a day and then practiced on his trumpet after work. Similarly, after school, Holiday scrubbed the white stone steps of neighbors' houses to earn an average of 90 cents a day, and then she came home to practice her singing.

Contrast

With **contrast**, items are presented according to differences between or among them. Transitional words that are often used for contrast include *different*, *in contrast*, *on the other hand*, *but*, *however*, and *bigger than*.

EXAMPLE   **ORANGES**

An orange grown in Florida usually has a thin and tightly fitting skin, and it is also heavy with juice. Californians say that if you want to eat a Florida orange you have to get into a bathtub first. On the other hand, California oranges are light in weight and have thick skins that break easily and come off in hunks.

—John McPhee,
Oranges

Comparison and Contrast

Some passages combine comparison and contrast into a single paragraph. This combination is called a **comparison-and-contrast** pattern and is demonstrated in the following example.

EXAMPLE   **HISPANIC AMERICANS**

The primary groups in the rising new minority are Mexican Americans and Cuban Americans. Mexican Americans are heavily concentrated in the Southwest, whereas Cuban Americans are concentrated in Florida, particularly in the Miami area. Together the groups are called Hispanic Americans or Latinos. Although their histories are different, they share several similarities. They both speak the Spanish language, and most of them, at least 85 percent, are Roman Catholic.

The graphic below is helpful for organizing the details of all three variations of the comparison-and-contrast patterns.

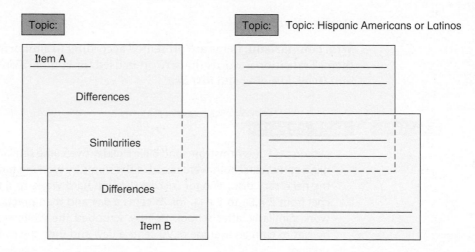

Cause and Effect

With **cause and effect**, an element is shown as producing another element. One is the *cause* or the "happening" that stimulated the particular result or *effect*. A paragraph may describe one cause or many causes, as well as one or many results. Transitional words that are often used for cause and effect include *for this reason, consequently, on that account, hence,* and *because.*

EXAMPLE   **WINTER CAMP AT VALLEY FORGE**

General George Washington's Continental Army set up camp on the frozen grounds of Valley Forge in December 1777 and experienced dire consequences. The winter was particularly cold that year, and the soldiers lacked straw and blankets. Many froze in their beds. Food was scarce, and soldiers died of malnutrition. Because of the misery and disease in the camp, many soldiers deserted the army and went home.

Topic:		Topic:	
Cause Why did it happen?	Effect What happened?	Cause Why did it happen?	Effect What happened?

Classification

To simplify a complex topic, authors frequently begin introductory paragraphs by stating that the information that follows is divided into a certain number of groups or categories. The divisions are then named, and the parts are explained. Signal words often used for **classification** include *two divisions*, *three groups*, *four elements*, *five classes*, *six levels*, *seven categories*, *eight types*, and so on.

EXAMPLE   **PREDATION**

Predation, the interaction in which one species kills and eats another, involves two groups. The predator, or consumer, must be alert and skillful to locate and capture the prey. The consumable group, or prey, constantly must adapt its behavior to defend against being eaten.

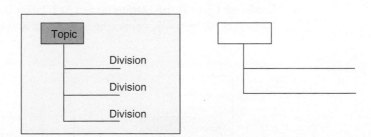

Summary

A **summary**, which usually appears at the end of an article or a chapter, condenses the main idea or thesis into a short and simple concluding statement with a few major supporting details. Transitional words are *in conclusion*, *briefly*, *to sum up*, *in short*, and *in a nutshell*.

EXAMPLE **WWII: A TOTAL WAR**

In conclusion, World War II was more of a total war than any previous war in history. Some 70 nations took part in the war, and fighting took place on the continents of Europe, Asia, and Africa. Entire societies participated, either as soldiers, war workers, or victims of occupation and mass murder.

—Adapted from James Kirby Martin et al.,
America and Its People

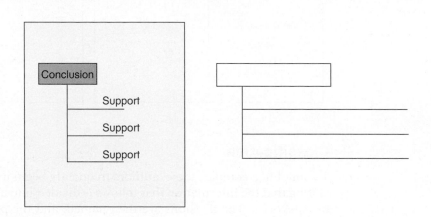

Location or Spatial Order

Location, or **spatial order**, identifies the whereabouts of a place or an object. Transitional words are *north, east, south, west, next to, near, below, above, close by, within, without, adjacent to, beside, around, to the right or left side*, and *opposite*.

EXAMPLE **EGYPT**

The Republic of Egypt is located in the northeastern corner of Africa. The northern border of Egypt is the Mediterranean Sea. Libya is the country to the west, and the Sudan lies to the south. Across the Suez Canal and to the east lies Israel.

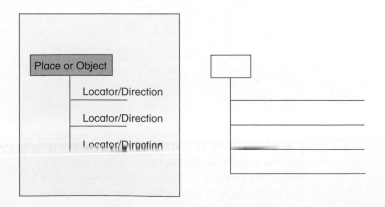

> ## Reader's TIP — Patterns of Organization and Signal Words
>
> - **Cause and Effect:** because, for this reason, consequently, hence, as a result, thus, due to, therefore
>   (shows one element as producing or causing a result or effect)
> - **Classification:** groups, categories, elements, classes, parts
>   (divides items into groups or categories)
> - **Comparison:** in a similar way, similar, parallel to, likewise, in a like manner
>   (lists similarities among items)
> - **Contrast:** on the other hand, bigger than, but, however, conversely, on the contrary, although, nevertheless
>   (lists differences among items)
> - **Definition:** can be defined, means, for example, like
>   (initially defines a concept and expands with examples and restatements)
> - **Description:** is, as, is made up of, could be described as
>   (lists characteristics or details)
> - **Generalization and Example:** to restate, that is, for example, to illustrate, for instance
>   (explains with examples to illustrate)
> - **Location or Spatial Order:** next to, near, below, above, close by, within, without, adjacent to, beside, around, to the right or left side, opposite
>   (identifies the whereabouts of objects)
> - **Simple Listing:** also, another, several, further, moreover, in addition
>   (randomly lists items in a series)
> - **Summary:** in conclusion, briefly, to sum up, in short, in a nutshell
>   (condenses major points)
> - **Time Order, Sequence, or Narration:** first, second, finally, after, before, next, later, now, at last, until, thereupon, while, during
>   (lists events in order of occurrence)

Generalization and Example

In the **generalization-and-example** pattern, a general statement or conclusion is supported with specific examples. Transitional words include *to restate that*, *that is*, *for example*, *to illustrate*, and *for instance*.

EXAMPLE   SMOKING

To restate it in simple terms, smoking kills. The American Cancer Society estimates that tobacco smoking is the cause of 30 percent of all deaths from cancer. Lung cancer is the leading cause of death from cancer in the United States, with 85 percent to 90 percent of these cases linked to smoking. Save your life by not smoking.

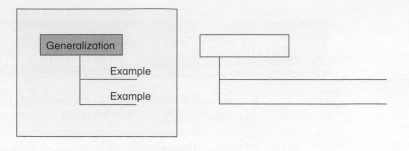

CLUES TO THE ORGANIZATIONAL PATTERN

Learning Objective 4

Use clues to identify the pattern of organization

Active readers use several clues to determine the organizational pattern of the material. The most experienced readers predict the pattern from a brief preview and confirm their predictions as they read. No one clue is enough, though. It takes all of the following elements to be sure:

1. **Transitional words:** Use the lists in this chapter to help you recognize the function of the transitional words and phrases. Remember, though, that some words may be used in more than one pattern.
2. **Graphic organizers:** If the details fit in the graphic organizer, this is additional evidence that the predicted pattern is correct.
3. **Relationship among the details and the main idea:** This is the most reliable evidence that a reader has to identify the pattern. Good readers are always most concerned about recognizing the main idea and the details that support it.

EXERCISE 6.3

Identifying Paragraph Patterns

Each of the following items presents the first two sentences of a paragraph, stating the main idea, and a major supporting detail. Select the letter that indicates the pattern of organization that you predict for each.

_____ 1. Jim Vicary coined the term *subliminal advertising,* claiming that inserting messages like "Eat popcorn" and "Drink Coca-Cola" into movies would increase consumption. According to Vicary, the messages, flashed too fast for the human eye to recognize but registered in the brain, would prompt a rush to the snack bar.

    a. summary
    b. classification
    c. definition
    d. comparison and contrast

_____ 2. Now an integral part of the recruiting strategy, companies of all sizes are finding that e-cruiting, job recruiting over the Internet, has many benefits. To begin, the Internet is a fast, convenient, and inexpensive way to find prospective job candidates.

    a. description
    b. simple listing
    c. time order
    d. classification

_____ 3. As a result of the Great Depression, Hollywood flourished. Cheap tickets, free time, and the lure of fantasy brought 60 million to 80 million Americans to the movies each week.

    a. comparison and contrast
    b. simple listing
    c. cause and effect
    d. description

_____ 4. Queens ruled England in the second half of the sixteenth century. In 1553, Mary I took the throne. She was followed in 1558 by Elizabeth I, who ruled for the next 45 years.

    a. summary
    b. contrast
    c. classification
    d. time order

_____ 5. Although both artists lived in Spain, Pablo Picasso and Salvador Dalí had styles that differed dramatically. Picasso depicted his subjects in abstract terms, whereas Dalí painted the stark reality of the image.

    a. description
    b. comparison and contrast
    c. time order
    d. simple listing

_____ 6. Michelangelo depicted the creation of Eve on a panel that is almost in the center of the ceiling of the Sistine Chapel. _The Creation of Adam,_ a larger and more famous panel, is located adjacent to it and toward the back of the chapel.

    a. simple listing
    b. time order
    c. location or spatial order
    d. definition

_____ 7. In short, the Internet can be a source of dangerous misinformation. Anyone can develop a website and fill it with distortions of the truth and inflammatory accusations.

    a. classification
    b. summary
    c. definition
    d. time order

_____ 8. In case of a sprained ankle, you should first apply ice to constrict the blood vessels and stop internal bleeding. Next, elevate your foot above the level of your heart to further control bleeding by making the blood flow away from the injured area.

    a. summary
    b. classification
    c. generalization and example
    d. sequence

EXERCISE 6.4

Patterns of Organization and Main Idea

Read the following passages and use the three-question system that you learned in Chapter 5 to determine the author's main idea. In addition, indicate the dominant pattern of organization that is used by the author. Select from the following list:

classification   definition   cause and effect   comparison and contrast

Passage 1

Also called ice pellets, sleet is formed when raindrops or melted snowflakes freeze as they pass through a subfreezing layer of air near Earth's surface. Sleet does not stick to trees and wires, and it usually bounces when it hits the ground. An accumulation of sleet sometimes has the consistency of dry sand.

—Frederick K. Lutgens and Edward J. Tarbuck,
The Atmosphere, 9th ed.

1. Who or what is this about? _____
_____

2. What are the major details? _____
_____
_____
_____
_____

3. What is the overall pattern of organization? _____

4. What is the main idea that the authors are trying to convey about the topic?
_____
_____

Passage 2

In organizational settings, there are usually five kinds of power: legitimate, reward, coercive, referent, and expert power. Legitimate power is power that is granted through the organizational hierarchy; it is the power that is defined by the organization to be accorded to people occupying a particular position. A manager can assign tasks to a subordinate, and a subordinate who refuses to do them can be reprimanded or even fired. Reward power is the power to give or withhold rewards. Rewards that a manager may control include salary increases, bonuses, promotion recommendations, praise, recognition, and interesting job assignments. Coercive power is the power to force compliance by means of psychological, emotional, or physical threat. In most organizations today, coercion is limited to verbal reprimands, written reprimands, disciplinary layoffs, fines, demotion, and termination. Referent power is abstract; it is based on identification, imitation, loyalty, or charisma. Followers may react favorably because they identify in some way with a leader. Expert power is derived from information or expertise. A manager who knows how to interact with an eccentric but important customer, a scientist who is capable of achieving an important technical breakthrough that no other company has dreamed of, and an administrative assistant who knows how to unravel bureaucratic red tape all have expert power over anyone who needs that information.

—Adapted from Ronald J. Ebert and Ricky W. Griffin,
Business Essentials, 10th ed.

1. Who or what is this about? _____

_____

2. What are the major details? _____

_____

_____

_____

_____

3. What is the overall pattern of organization? _____

4. What is the main idea that the authors are trying to convey about the topic?

_____

_____

_____

Passage 3

The law of demand states that the quantity demanded will increase as the price is lowered as long as other factors that affect demand do not change. The makers of M&M'S candy conducted an experiment in the law of demand, holding the necessary demand-affecting conditions constant. Over a 12-month test period, the price of M&M'S was held constant in 150 stores while the content weight of the candy was increased. By holding the price constant and increasing the weight, the price (per ounce) was lowered. In the stores where the price was dropped, sales rose by 20 to 30 percent almost overnight. As a result of the law of demand, a reduction in prices caused the quantity demanded to rise.

—Adapted from Paul R. Gregory,
Essentials of Economics, 6th ed.

1. Who or what is this about? _____

_____

2. What are the major details? _____

_____

_____

3. What is the overall pattern of organization? _____

4. What is the main idea that the author is trying to convey about the topic? ____

_____

_____

_____

Passage 4

Men, women, and children had different tasks on the overland trail. Men concerned themselves almost entirely with hunting, guard duty, and transportation. They rose at 4 A.M. to hitch the wagons, and after breakfast began the day's march. At noon, they stopped and set the teams to graze. After the midday meal, the march continued until sunset. Then, while the men relaxed, the women fixed dinner and the next day's lunch, and the children kindled the fires, fetched water, and searched for wood or other fuel. For women, the trail was lonely, and they worked to exhaustion. Some adjusted their clothing to the harsh conditions, adopting the new bloomer pants, shortening their skirts, or wearing "wash dresses"—so called because they had shorter hemlines that did not drag on the wet ground on washday. Other women continued to wear their long dresses, thinking bloomers "indecent." Both men and women carried firearms in case of Indian attacks, but most emigrants saw few Indians en route.

—H. W. Brands, et al., *American Stories: A History of the United States, Combined Volume,* 3rd ed.

1. Who or what is this about? _____

_____

_____

2. What are the major details? _____

_____

_____

_____

_____

3. What is the overall pattern of organization? _____

4. What is the main idea that the author is trying to convey about the topic?

_____

_____

_____

> **BRAIN BOOSTER**
>
> **Watering the Brain**
>
> Our brains are made up of about 80 percent water, and brain function depends on maintaining adequate hydration. Only water will do! The sugars in coffee, tea, and soft drinks bind to the water in them, the body processes them as foods, and the benefits of the water are lost. In fact, these drinks actually act as diuretics and dehydrate the body rather than hydrate it. If you feel listless, sleepy, or cannot concentrate, you might just need a drink of water.
>
> —*Adapted from* Brain-Based Learning: The New Paradigm of Teaching, *2nd ed., by Eric Jensen (p. 66) Corwin Press, 2008*

MIXED ORGANIZATIONAL PATTERNS

Learning Objective 5

Recognize mixed patterns of organization

Suppose you were writing an orientation article describing support services available at your own college. You could present the resources in a **simple listing** pattern, or you could discuss them in the **sequence** or **time order** in which a freshman is likely to need them or in terms of the most convenient geographic locations to students. Within your article, you might use a **description** or a **definition** pattern to identify a relatively unknown service on campus, with examples of how it has helped others. You could demonstrate **cause and effect** with facts and statistics on how using services has helped students. You might also choose to **compare and contrast** a special service with that at another college. You could supply additional information to the list of resources by presenting the qualifications of professional staff providing the services. To wrap things up, you could create an overall **summary** about the support services. Thus, one long article might have an overall **simple listing** pattern of organization yet contain individual paragraphs that follow other patterns.

In other words, a longer piece of writing can contain several secondary patterns. However, one primary pattern usually dominates and dictates the overall organization of the ideas in the passage. Recognizing the primary and secondary patterns will help you understand the author's point.

EXERCISE 6.5 Identifying Combined Organizational Patterns

Read the following textbook excerpts and answer the questions that follow. Note how combined organizational patterns may help you understand the main idea of a longer piece of writing. Signal words are set in bold type to help you identify a particular pattern.

Passage 1

Does this title suggest a pattern?

WHAT ARE DUST DEVILS?

A common phenomenon in arid regions of the world is the whirling vortex called the dust devil. Although they resemble tornadoes, dust devils are generally much smaller and less intense than their destructive cousins. Most dust devils are only a few meters in diameter and reach heights no greater than about 100 meters (300 feet). **By definition,** these whirlwinds are usually short-lived microscale phenomena. Most form and die out within minutes. In rare instances dust devils have lasted for hours.

Unlike tornadoes, which are associated with convective clouds, dust devils form on days when clear skies dominate. **In contrast,** these whirlwinds form from the ground upward, exactly the opposite of tornadoes. Because surface heating is critical to their formation, dust devils occur most frequently in the afternoon when surface temperatures are highest.

Which pattern is suggested by the boldface words in this paragraph?

When the air near the surface is considerably warmer than the air a few dozen meters overhead, the layer of air near Earth's surface becomes unstable. In this situation, warm surface air begins to rise, **causing** air near the ground to be drawn into the developing whirlwind. **As a result,** the rotating winds that are associated with dust devils are produced by the same phenomenon that causes ice skaters to spin faster as they pull their arms closer to their bodies. As the inwardly spiraling air rises, it carries sand, dust, and other loose debris dozens of meters into the air. It is this material that makes a dust devil visible. Occasionally, dust devils form above vegetated surfaces. Under these conditions, the vortices may go undetected unless they interact with objects at the surface.

—Adapted from Frederick K. Lutgens and Edward J. Tarbuck,
The Atmosphere, 9th ed.

1. Who or what is this about? _____

_____

2. What overall pattern is suggested by the title? _____

_____

3. What is the pattern of organization in the first paragraph? _____

_____

4. What is the pattern of organization in the second paragraph?_____

_____

5. What is the pattern of organization in the third paragraph? _____

_____

6. What is the main idea that the authors are trying to convey about the topic?

_____

_____

Passage 2

THE SUCCESS OF eBAY

eBay is one of the most successful e-commerce businesses. **Unlike** Amazon.com, it does not need expensive warehouses and storage facilities. eBay earns its revenues by charging a small fee to sellers who list their products on eBay for sale. **While other** dot-com companies have suffered losses in recent years, eBay, **on the other hand,** has been consistently profitable, earning almost $150 million in annual profits.

eBay exists in all major countries (eBay Germany, eBay Austria, eBay Canada, and so on). It operates a worldwide virtual auction market in which registered sellers can list products and registered buyers can enter bids for them. Participants in this virtual market can follow the progress of bids online as each auction progresses. (Usually an ending time of each auction is listed.)

Products auctioned on eBay range from the ordinary to the unique or exotic. On a given day, wooden crates of rough jade ($15.95), a Tibetan bronze Buddha ($88), a 1913 Catholic dictionary ($204), a 1725 bible ($348), and an 1895 U.S. Navy steam launch engine ($2,025) can be found on auction.

eBay deals with problems of dishonesty. **That is,** eBay maintains bulletin boards of comments submitted by eBay subscribers, organized by the identification number of eBay buyers and sellers. These ratings provide information on records of past honesty and reliability. A "cheating" buyer or seller would not be able to buy or sell on eBay after disclosure of negative comments.

eBay **offers several** enormous **advantages** to buyers and sellers. **First,** the seller can gain access to a large number of potential buyers of unusual products by paying a small fee to eBay. **Second,** buyers have the opportunity to bid on thousands of products and services without leaving the comfort of their homes. Historically, exotic products such as Rembrandt paintings and Kennedy presidential memorabilia were auctioned by prestigious auction houses such as Sotheby's, which typically collected fees of 15 percent or more. It appears to be only a matter of time until rare and expensive items will be auctioned on eBay.

—Adapted from Paul R. Gregory,
Essentials of Economics, 6th ed.

1. Who or what is this about? _____

_____

2. What overall pattern is suggested by the title? _____

_____

3. What is the pattern of organization in the first paragraph? _____

_____

4. What is the pattern of organization in the second paragraph? _____

_____

5. What is the pattern of organization in the third paragraph? _____

_____

6. What is the pattern of organization in the fourth paragraph? _____

_____

7. What is the pattern of organization in the final paragraph? _____

_____

SUMMARY POINTS

1 What is the value of knowing the pattern of organization? (page 288)
- Recognizing how an author organized the presentation of ideas helps the reader predict what is coming next.
- The pattern provides insight into the main point of the selection.

2 How can I recognize the function of transitional words? (page 288)
- Become familiar with the function of common transitional words. The term, *for example*, logically introduces an example that elaborates on a previous point. *However*, indicates a contrast to an idea that was just discussed.
- Train yourself to notice these markers. They are like road signs that guide you through the author's thinking. They can suggest the organizational pattern and ultimately help you understand the material.

3 How can I recognize common patterns of organization in textbooks? (page 292)
- Train yourself to look for these common patterns: Simple listing; definition; description; time order, sequence, or narration; comparison; contrast; comparison and contrast; cause and effect; classification; summary; location or spatial order; generalization and example.

4 What clues can I use to identify the pattern of organization? (page 300)
- Use these clues to identify the pattern:
  Transitional words
  Graphic organizers
  The relationship among the details and the main idea
- Use all of the clues; no single clue can reliably determine the pattern, although the relationship among the details and the main idea is the best indicator.

5 How can I recognize mixed patterns of organization? (page 305)
- Keep in mind that authors frequently use several patterns in a single chapter, section, or even a paragraph. Be alert to the transitional words and changes in thought.
- Determine the dominant pattern, the one that best represents the author's main point. Be aware of the patterns that help to present supporting ideas and see how they contribute to the primary pattern and main idea.

SELECTION 1 — Communications — MyReadingLab

Visit Chapter 6: Patterns of Organization in MyReadingLab to complete the Selection 1 activities and the Build Background Knowledge video activity.

PREVIEW the next selection to predict its purpose and organization and to formulate your learning plan.

Activate Schemata

What situations are likely to create conflict in your life?
What are your typical reactions in a conflict with another person?
What strategies do you try to use to resolve conflicts?

Establish a Purpose for Reading

Read the selection to learn effective strategies for dealing with conflict.

Build Background Knowledge — VIDEO

Taking a Bite Out of Anger

To prepare for reading Selection 1, answer the questions below. Then, watch this video that examines the connection between anger and hunger.

What internal factors (ex: hunger, fatigue, etc.) might contribute to anger?

What is the best way to express anger when talking to a loved one?

What is the best way for someone to address conflict in the workplace?

This video helped me: _____

_____

_____

Increase Word Knowledge

What do you know about these words?

inopportune	elusive	empathize	validate	legitimate
engendering	retaliate	aggravated	escalate	inevitably

Your instructor may give a brief vocabulary review before or after reading.

Integrate Knowledge While Reading

Questions have been inserted in the margin to stimulate your thinking while reading. Remember to

Predict   Picture   Relate   Monitor   Correct   Annotate

MANAGING CONFLICT

Before trying to manage or resolve a conflict, you need to prepare. Conflict resolution is an extremely important communication experience, and you don't want to enter it without adequate thought. Here are a few conflict management strategies to prepare you to resolve conflict.

SET THE STAGE

5   First, try to fight in private. When you air your conflicts in front of others, you create a variety of other problems. You may not be willing to be totally honest when third parties are present; you may feel you have to save face and therefore must win the fight at all costs. You run the risk of embarrassing your partner in front of others, and this embarrassment may create resentment and hostility.

10   Be sure you're each ready to fight. Although conflicts arise at the most inopportune times, you can choose the time to resolve them. Confronting your partner when she or he comes home after a hard day of work may not be the right time for resolving a conflict. Make sure you're both relatively free of other problems and ready to deal with the conflict at hand.

Is it better to wait than to deal with the problem right away?

15   Know what you're fighting about. Sometimes people in a relationship become so hurt and angry that they lash out at the other person just to vent their own frustration. The problem at the center of the conflict (for example, the uncapped toothpaste tube) is merely an excuse to express anger. Any attempt to resolve this "problem" will be doomed to failure, because the problem addressed is not what is causing the 20   conflict. Instead, the underlying hostility, anger, and frustration need to be addressed.

Fight about problems that can be solved. Fighting about past behaviors or about family members or situations over which you have no control solves nothing. Any attempt at resolution will fail, because the problems are incapable of being solved.

Now that you're prepared for the conflict resolution interaction, consider the 25   following steps to help you navigate through this process.

DEFINE THE CONFLICT

Your first and most essential step is to define the conflict. Here are several techniques to keep in mind.

- **Define both content and relationship issues**. Define the obvious content issues (who should do the dishes, who should take the kids to school) as well 30   as the underlying relationship issues (who has been avoiding household responsibilities, whose time is more valuable).

Sometimes, is it hard to pinpoint the real problem?

- **Define the problem in specific terms**. Conflict defined in the abstract is difficult to deal with and resolve. It's one thing for a husband to say that his

Gladskikh Tatiana/Shutterstock

wife is "cold and unfeeling" and quite another to say that she does not call
him at the office, kiss him when he comes home, or hold his hand when
they're at a party. These behaviors can be agreed on and dealt with, but the
abstract "cold and unfeeling" remains elusive.

- **Focus on the present**. Avoid **gunnysacking** (a term derived from the large
  burlap bag called a gunnysack)—the practice of storing up grievances so
  they may be unloaded at another time. Often, when one person gunnysacks,
  the other person gunnysacks; for example, the birthdays you forgot and the
  times you arrived late for dinner are all thrown at you. The result is two
  people dumping their stored-up grievances on each other with no real attention to the present problem.

- **Empathize**. Try to understand the nature of the conflict from the other person's point of view. Why is your partner disturbed that you're not doing
  the dishes? Why is your neighbor complaining about taking the kids to
  school? Once you have empathically understood the other person's feelings, validate those feelings when appropriate. If your partner is hurt or
  angry and you believe such feelings are legitimate and justified, say so:
  "You have a right to be angry; I shouldn't have said what I did about your
  mother. I'm sorry. But I still don't want to go on vacation with her." In expressing validation, you're not necessarily expressing agreement; you're
  merely stating that your partner has feelings that you recognize as
  legitimate.

- **Avoid mind reading**. Don't try to read the other person's mind. Ask questions to make sure you understand the problem as the other person is experiencing it. Ask directly and simply: "Why are you insisting that I take the
  dog out now, when I have to call three clients before nine o'clock?"

EXAMINE POSSIBLE SOLUTIONS

What if the other person won't cooperate in resolving the problem?

60 Most conflicts can probably be resolved through a variety of solutions. Here are a few suggestions. Brainstorm by yourself or with your partner. Try not to inhibit or censor yourself or your partner as you generate these potential solutions. Once you have proposed a variety of solutions, look especially for solutions that will enable each party to win—to get something he or she wants. Avoid win–lose solutions, in 65 which one person wins and one loses. Such outcomes will cause difficulty for the relationship by engendering frustration and resentment. Carefully weigh the costs and the rewards that each solution entails. Seek solutions in which the costs and the rewards will be evenly shared.

Using a specific example will help us work through the various steps in the 70 conflict resolution process. In this example, the conflict revolves around Pat's not wanting to socialize with Chris's friends. Chris is devoted to these friends, but Pat actively dislikes them. Chris thinks they're wonderful and exciting; Pat thinks they're unpleasant and boring.

For example, among the solutions that Pat and Chris might identify are these:

75 1. Chris should not interact with these friends anymore.
   2. Pat should interact with Chris's friends.
   3. Chris should see these friends without Pat.

Clearly solutions 1 and 2 are win–lose solutions. In solution 1, Pat wins and Chris loses; in 2, Chris wins and Pat loses. Solution 3 has some possibilities. Both 80 might win and neither must necessarily lose. This potential solution, then, needs to be looked at more closely.

TEST THE SOLUTION

First, test the solution mentally. How does it feel now? How will it feel tomorrow? Are you comfortable with it? In our example, will Pat be comfortable with Chris's socializing with these friends alone? Some of Chris's friends are attractive; will this 85 cause difficulty for Pat and Chris's relationship? Will Chris give people too much to gossip about? Will Chris feel guilty? Will Chris enjoy seeing these friends without Pat?

Second, test the solution in practice. Put the solution into operation. How does it work? If it doesn't work, then discard it and try another solution. Give each solu-90 tion a fair chance, but don't hang on to a solution when it's clear that it won't resolve the conflict.

Perhaps Chris might go out without Pat once to test this solution. Afterward, the couple can evaluate the experiment. Did the friends think there was something wrong with Chris's relationship with Pat? Did Chris feel guilty? Did Chris enjoy this 95 new experience? How did Pat feel? Did Pat feel jealous? Lonely? Abandoned?

EVALUATE THE SOLUTION

Did the solution help resolve the conflict? Is the situation better now than it was before the solution was tried? Share your feelings and evaluations of the solution.

Pat and Chris now need to share their perceptions of this possible solution. Would they be comfortable with this solution on a monthly basis? Is the solution 100 worth the costs each will pay? Are the costs and rewards evenly distributed? Might other solutions be more effective?

SELECTION
1

ACCEPT OR REJECT THE SOLUTION

If you accept the solution, you're ready to put it into more permanent operation. Let's say that Pat is actually quite happy with the solution. Pat was able to use the evening to visit college friends. The next time Chris goes out with the friends Pat doesn't like,
105 Pat intends to go out with some friends from college. Chris feels pretty good about seeing friends without Pat. Chris explains that they have both decided to see their friends separately and both are comfortable with this decision. If, however, either Pat or Chris feels unhappy with this solution, they will have to try out another solution or perhaps go back and redefine the problem and seek other ways to resolve it.

WRAP IT UP

110 Even after the conflict is resolved, there is still work to be done. Often, after one conflict is supposedly settled, another conflict will emerge—because, for example, one person feels that he or she has been harmed and needs to retaliate and take revenge in order to restore a sense of self-worth. So it's especially important that the conflict be resolved and not be allowed to generate other, perhaps more significant conflicts.
115   Learn from the conflict and from the process you went through in trying to resolve it. For example, can you identify the fight strategies that merely aggravated the situation? Do you or your partner need a cooling-off period? Can you tell when minor issues are going to escalate into major arguments? Does avoidance make matters worse? What issues are particularly disturbing and likely to cause difficul-
120 ties? Can they be avoided?
       Keep the conflict in perspective. Be careful not to blow it out of proportion to the extent that you begin to define your relationship in terms of conflict. Avoid the tendency to see disagreement as inevitably leading to major blowups. Conflicts in most relationships actually occupy a very small percentage of the couple's time, and yet in recollec-
125 tion they often loom extremely large. Also, don't allow the conflict to undermine your own or your partner's self-esteem. Don't view yourself, your partner, or your relationship as a failure just because you had an argument or even lots of arguments.
       Attack your negative feelings. Negative feelings frequently arise after an interpersonal conflict. Most often they arise because one or both parties used unfair fight
130 strategies to undermine the other person—for example, personal rejection, manipulation, or force. Resolve to avoid such unfair tactics in the future, but at the same time let go of guilt and blame toward yourself and your partner. If you think it would help, discuss these feelings with your partner or even a therapist. Apologize for anything you did wrong. Your partner should do likewise; after all, both parties
135 are usually responsible for the conflict.
       Increase the exchange of rewards and cherishing behaviors to demonstrate your positive feelings and to show you're over the conflict and want the relationship to survive and flourish.

(1,695 words)

—From Joseph A. DeVito,
The Interpersonal Communication Book, 13th ed.

Recall

Stop to self-test, relate, and react.

Your instructor may choose to give you a brief comprehension review.

SELECTION

1

THINK CRITICALLY ABOUT THE SELECTION

Which of the strategies in this selection are you are most likely to try? Why?

Conflict resolution is a critical skill in international diplomatic negotiations as well as in interpersonal conflicts. Do you think any of the ideas in this selection would be useful for foreign conflict resolution? Explain your answer.

WRITE ABOUT THE SELECTION

Imagine this scenario: It is very difficult to study at home because it is noisy and the people living with you want and need your attention. You must also do your share of the housekeeping chores. Your study time is limited, and you don't have easy transportation to a more suitable study place. If you don't resolve this problem, you are in danger of failing your classes. What will you do?

Response Suggestion: Use the strategies in this selection to devise a plan to address the problem in a way that is agreeable to everyone. Put your plan into writing in a form that is similar to the pattern used in the selection.

SKILL DEVELOPMENT: IDENTIFY ORGANIZATIONAL PATTERNS

Answer the following questions with *T* (true) or *F* (false):

_____ 1. The overall organizational pattern is time order.

_____ 2. The organizational pattern of the section "Wrap It Up" is classification.

CHECK YOUR COMPREHENSION

After reading the selection, answer the following questions with *a, b, c,* or *d*. To help you analyze your strengths and weaknesses, the question types are indicated.

Main Idea ———— 1. Which of the following best expresses the main idea of this selection?

   a. Even small disagreements can destroy relationships.
   b. Wait until both people are ready to fight to bring up conflicts.
   c. Be specific when defining the problem.
   d. Conflicts can be resolved successfully with a few strategies.

Detail ———— 2. According to the selection, *gunnysacking* is

   a. storing up complaints to unload on the other person during an argument.
   b. airing a specific grievance that has no relationship to the current conflict.
   c. fighting about family members or friends over whom you have no control.
   d. bringing up a conflict when you are both angry and hurt.

Detail ———— 3. The article specifically describes which of the following as a "relationship" issue?

   a. who should do the dishes
   b. who should take out the trash
   c. who has been avoiding household responsibilities
   d. who should do the yard work and wash the car

Inference ———— 4. Based on the explanation in the selection, which of the following would the author consider a "content" issue?

   a. who should do the grocery shopping
   b. whose time is more valuable
   c. jealousy about free time spent with others
   d. choice of religious affiliation

Main Idea ———— 5. Which statement best describes the main point of the last section, "Wrap It Up"?

   a. The section summarizes the main points in the article.
   b. Take steps to be sure the conflict is truly resolved and that feelings are healed.
   c. Keep the conflict in perspective.
   d. Increase cherishing behaviors after the conflict is resolved.

Inference ———— 6. The paragraph with the subheading "Empathize" implies that which of the following is an appropriate response to your partner's anger?

   a. Tell your partner why he or she should not feel angry.
   b. Avoid responding with anger by leaving the room.

c. Understand your partner's feelings and agree to what he or she wants regardless of your own feelings.

d. Acknowledge the angry feelings and apologize if appropriate, but stand by your own feelings about the situation.

Detail _____ 7. In the example involving Pat and Chris, which of the following statements is correct?

a. Solution 1 is a win–win solution.
b. Solution 2 is a win–win solution.
c. Solution 3 can be a win–win solution.
d. All three solutions are win–lose solutions.

Detail _____ 8. When Pat and Chris tested their solution,

a. Chris realized he didn't enjoy going out without Pat.
b. the result was not given in the article, only the possible results.
c. going out without Pat created unwanted gossip.
d. Pat felt left out and abandoned.

Inference _____ 9. From the selection, readers can infer that

a. successfully resolving a conflict means that future conflicts will not occur.
b. the best relationships are the ones in which there are no conflicts.
c. disagreements almost always escalate into major blow-ups in close personal relationships.
d. using conflict resolution strategies like these is likely to increase each person's satisfaction with the relationship.

Author's Purpose _____ 10. Which of the following is the main purpose of this selection?

a. to engage readers emotionally with interesting examples
b. to inform readers of tested strategies for managing interpersonal conflicts
c. to entertain readers with typical conflict situations that they might have experienced
d. to persuade readers to use the conflict management strategies that the selection describes

Answer the following with *T* (true) or *F* (false).

Inference _____ 11. An underlying assumption is that, for the strategies to succeed, all parties must want to work out a solution that preserves a good relationship.

Detail _____ 12. According to the selection, it is always best to resolve a conflict immediately.

Inference _____ 13. Resolving a conflict to everyone's satisfaction might require a lot of patience.

Detail _____ 14. In any conflict, one person must always win and the other must lose.

Inference _____ 15. The authors would agree with the old saying that couples should "kiss and make-up" after a fight.

BUILD YOUR VOCABULARY

According to the way the italicized word is used in the selection, indicate *a, b, c,* or *d* for the word or phrase that gives the best definition. The number in parentheses indicates the line of the passage in which the word is located. Use a dictionary in addition to the context clues to more precisely define the terms.

_____ 1. "*inopportune* times" (10–11)
    a. stressful
    b. embarrassing
    c. convenient
    d. inconvenient

_____ 2. "remains *elusive*" (37)
    a. vague
    b. clear
    c. harsh
    d. critical

_____ 3. "*Empathize.* Try to" (45)
    a. dismiss
    b. enliven
    c. relate to
    d. talk to

_____ 4. "*validate* those feelings" (49)
    a. reject
    b. recognize as true
    c. enlarge
    d. disprove

_____ 5. "feelings are *legitimate*" (50)
    a. unimportant
    b. exaggerated
    c. dramatic
    d. reasonable

_____ 6. "by *engendering* frustration" (66)
    a. creating
    b. destroying
    c. mistaking
    d. expressing

_____ 7. "needs to *retaliate*" (112)
    a. take a break
    b. heal
    c. strike back
    d. feel sorry

_____ 8. "*aggravated* the situation" (116)
    a. created
    b. angered
    c. worsened
    d. frustrated

_____ 9. "going to *escalate*" (118)
    a. flow
    b. degrade
    c. dramatize
    d. intensify

_____ 10. "as *inevitably* leading" (123)
    a. probably
    b. certainly
    c. soon
    d. later

Visit Chapter 6: Patterns of Organization in MyReadingLab to complete the Selection 2 activities and the Build Background Knowledge video activity.

Preview the next selection to predict its purpose and organization and to formulate your learning plan.

Activate Schemata

What kinds of groups are likely to go on strike?
What would it mean for students to go on strike?
For what reasons might you participate in a strike?

Establish a Purpose for Reading

Read the selection to learn about what a courageous young woman did for a cause in which she believed very strongly.

Build Background Knowledge — VIDEO

Student Protests

To prepare for reading Selection 2, answer the questions below. Then, watch this video on student protests in reaction to the killing of Trayvon Martin.

What issues would make you lead a protest?

What are some of the most well known student protests in the United States?
What were the protestors' demands?

What role does technology play in protests?

This video helped me: _____

_____

_____

Increase Word Knowledge

What do you know about these words?

ploy	facsimile	soliloquy	stoke	studious
makeshift	desegregation	defer	legacy	militant

Your instructor may give a brief vocabulary review before or after reading.

Integrate Knowledge While Reading

Questions have been inserted in the margin to stimulate your thinking while reading. Remember to

Predict   Picture   Relate   Monitor   Correct   Annotate

BARBARA JOHNS LEADS A STUDENT STRIKE

Just before 11: 00 A.M. on April 23, 1951, the phone rang in the principal's office at Robert R. Moton High School in Farmville, Virginia. In a muffled voice, the caller said that two Moton students were in trouble at the bus terminal and then hung up. The call—a ploy to lure Principal Boyd Jones away from the building—succeeded.
5 As soon as he headed to the bus station, a student delivered forged notes to the school's teachers, signed with a facsimile of the principal's characteristic J, saying that all teachers and students were to report immediately for an assembly. After Moton's 450 students filed into the central hall, which doubled as the auditorium, the stage curtain swung open, revealing a group of student leaders. At the rostrum
10 stood sixteen-year-old Barbara Rose Johns, who announced that the assembly was for students only; emphasizing her point, she rapped her shoe on a bench while shouting to the teachers, "I want you out of here!"

That's bold! Did they leave?

Then Johns began what one of the student leaders called "her soliloquy." Moton's school buildings were totally inadequate, Johns told the students. The
15 white high school in Farmville had a gymnasium, cafeteria, locker rooms, infirmary, and an auditorium with fixed seats; Moton had none of these. When Moton's student body outgrew the building's 180-student capacity, the Prince Edward County school board put up three temporary structures covered with tar paper. Some people said the "tarpaper shacks" looked like a poultry farm. Teachers had to stop
20 teaching to stoke the sometimes dangerous woodstoves that made close-by students too hot but left those farther away too cold. "We will not accept these conditions," Johns told the students. "We will do something. We will strike."

Is this an issue for which you would strike?

Johns assured the students that they would not be punished if they stuck together because the local jail was not big enough to hold them all. Exiting the
25 school, they paraded with already made placards: "We Are Tired of Tar Paper Shacks—We Want a New School." The students overwhelmingly decided not to consult their parents first but to act on their own. The next day they rode buses to school but stayed outside, protesting on the school grounds.

According to her family, Johns had been quiet and studious before she took
30 charge of the student protest. She had read widely—notably Booker T. Washington's *Up from Slavery*, Richard Wright's *Native Son,* and other books she found in the library of her uncle, Vernon Johns, an outspoken pastor who had once been president of Virginia Seminary. The Reverend Johns had inspired his young niece's rebelliousness before he left Farmville to become pastor of Dexter Avenue Baptist
35 Church in Montgomery, Alabama. "I used to admire the way he didn't care who you were if he thought that something was right," Barbara Johns said of her uncle.

SELECTION 2

Pictureguy32/Fotolia

As she became increasingly angered by Moton's makeshift facilities, a teacher challenged her to do something, and she did.

In the hectic first day of the strike, the students called the National Association
40 for the Advancement of Colored People (NAACP) office in Richmond. Johns and Carrie Stokes, president of the Moton student council, followed up with a letter to veteran NAACP lawyer Spottswood Robinson: "We hate to impose, as we are doing, but under the circumstances that we are facing, we have to ask for your help." Two days later, Robinson and his longtime NAACP associate Oliver T. Hill stopped by
45 Farmville to meet with the students, who were told to bring their parents. "I had a horror of talking to a group of these kids with no adults around," Robinson recalled. After the meeting, the two attorneys were sufficiently impressed by the students' determination to agree to help them, if they agreed to seek desegregation rather than merely better facilities. "What made us go ahead," Robinson explained later,
50 "was the feeling that someone would have to show them something before they would go back to school."

> *What would cause them to take such drastic action?* →

The strike at Moton was planned and led by students. When other students suggested they should defer to the adults who had been working for years to get the county school board to approve a new black school, Johns rejected the advice, citing
55 scripture: "A little child shall lead them." In a later interview, she said, "We knew we had to do it ourselves, and if we had asked for adult help before taking the first step, we would have been turned down." One student leader recalled Johns predicting, "We could make a move that would broadcast Prince Edward County all over the world." Events proved her right, as the strike at Moton became a lawsuit that
60 was combined with other desegregation cases to become *Brown v. Board of Education of Topeka*, the most important and successful legal effort in the NAACP's long campaign to end segregation in the nation's public schools.

But Johns was not a party to the suit she helped initiate. After threats to her and a cross burning on the school grounds, her parents feared for her safety and sent her

65 to live with her Uncle Vernon in Montgomery, where she finished high school. Her leadership, however, left a legacy of student activism that continued to grow in the following years.

Johns and the Moton students bypassed their parents to appeal directly to the NAACP, which during the early 1950s dominated African American politics at the
70 national level. Under Thurgood Marshall's leadership, the NAACP Legal Defense and Education Fund had achieved major victories, most notably the Supreme Court rulings against segregated graduate and professional schools. During a time when black leftist leaders such as W. E. B. Du Bois and Paul Robeson faced Cold War repression, the NAACP, with more than a thousand local branches, was the leading
75 force in African American activism. The NAACP's reliance on litigation and lobbying was shown to produce major legal and legislative victories.

Within the NAACP, however, some members remained dissatisfied with the slow pace of civil rights reform. Local black activism eventually posed a challenge to the NAACP at the national level, as impatient members were eager to experiment
80 with new protest tactics.

The year-long Montgomery bus boycott movement that began late in 1955 was an important turning point because it demonstrated that many African Americans were ready for more militant forms of civil rights activism. The boycott also revealed that a black community could remain united in struggle for more than a year.
85 Although Martin Luther King, Jr., was but twenty-six years old at the start of the boycott, he emerged as a nationally known civil rights leader and the head of his own organization, the Southern Christian Leadership Conference (SCLC). But still younger activists soon pushed his group as well as the NAACP toward greater militancy. The students who braved mobs to desegregate Little Rock Central High
90 School in 1957 and the black college students who launched a wave of sit-in demonstrations in 1960 inspired an upsurge in grassroots protests through the South. By the spring of 1960, when student protest leaders formed the Student Nonviolent Coordinating Committee (SNCC), it was apparent that the southern freedom struggle was beyond the control of any single leader or organization.

Marshall later became a judge on the U.S. Supreme Court.

(1,198 words)

—From Clayborne Carson, et al.
The Struggle for Freedom: A History of African Americans, Combined Volume, 2nd ed.

Recall

Stop to self-test, relate, and react.

Your instructor may choose to give you a brief comprehension review.

THINK CRITICALLY ABOUT THE SELECTION

Is there an issue about which students today feel strongly enough to take action as dramatic as Barbara Rose Johns did? Explain your response.

What methods might students use today to achieve a significant change?

WRITE ABOUT THE SELECTION

Many people believe that American students should have the option to attend two years of college for little or no cost as an extension of the current public education system. What do you think? Would this create a better prepared workforce and better educated citizens? Would the economic and social benefits balance the additional cost?

Response Suggestion: Brainstorm your thoughts about this issue and construct an argument to support your opinion. Begin with a clear statement of your position and continue with logical reasons. Your purpose is to convince readers to agree with you.

SKILL DEVELOPMENT: IDENTIFY ORGANIZATIONAL PATTERNS

Answer the following questions with *T* (true) or *F* (false):

_____ 1. The overall organizational pattern of the selection is classification.

_____ 2. The organizational pattern of the fourth paragraph, which begins "According to her family . . . ," is cause and effect.

CHECK YOUR COMPREHENSION

After reading the selection, answer the following questions with *a, b, c,* or *d.* To help you analyze your strengths and weaknesses, the question types are indicated.

Main Idea   ————   1. Which of the following best expresses the main idea of this selection?

    a. Barbara Johns insisted that all teachers leave the auditorium before she addressed the students.

    b. Segregation often meant that schools for African Americans were inferior to schools for whites.

    c. Barbara Johns led a student strike for better school conditions that inspired further student activism.

    d. Moton High School students sought help from the NAACP.

Detail   ————   2. The original intention of the Moton student strike was

    a. to improve the school's physical condition.

    b. to improve the school facilities and to desegregate the schools in Farmville.

    c. to set an example for other African Americans to fight for better schools.

    d. to demonstrate to the nation that conditions in African American and white schools were unequal.

Inference   ————   3. It is reasonable to infer that the Moton students chose not to tell their parents about their plans to strike because

    a. they thought their parents would want to join in.

    b. they thought their parents might notify school authorities.

    c. they thought the strike might not happen.

    d. they thought their parents would try to stop them.

Detail   ————   4. The NAACP agreed to help the students because

    a. the students were impassioned and determined to get better facilities.

    b. they knew nothing would come of the students' efforts if they didn't help.

    c. they wanted recognition for civil rights issues.

    d. the Moton parents saw that help was necessary to improve the condition of Moton High School.

Main Idea   ————   5. Which statement best describes the main point of the fourth paragraph, which begins "According to her family?"

    a. Barbara Johns's uncle, a pastor, encouraged her to speak out against injustice.

    b. A teacher challenged Barbara Johns to do something about the poor conditions at the school.

    c. Barbara Johns was a quiet and studious girl.

    d. Several factors influenced Barbara Johns to do something about the poor conditions at Moton High School.

Inference _____ 6. The details suggest that Barbara Johns's role in the Moton High School strike was

    a. as a loyal and passionate follower.

    b. as a convincing leader who could inspire and encourage others to follow.

    c. as a strong leader who made all the decisions.

    d. as a religious leader in her school and community.

Detail _____ 7. According to the article, Barbara Johns was strongly influenced by which of the following?

    a. the example set by Martin Luther King, Jr.

    b. the beliefs of her parents

    c. her uncle, Vernon Johns, and the writing of Booker T. Washington and Richard Wright

    d. the discontent of fellow Moton High School students

Detail _____ 8. The end result of the Moton student strike was

    a. improved school facilities for Moton students.

    b. increased racial division in Farmville.

    c. desegregation in all public Farmville schools.

    d. a lawsuit that combined with others in the *Brown v. Board of Education of Topeka* case, which finally achieved school desegregation in the United States.

Inference _____ 9. Based on the details in the selection, which is a reasonable inference about the civil rights movement?

    a. As it grew in strength, disagreements within the NAACP about tactics and results caused several new organizations to use more forceful methods to achieve their goals.

    b. After the Moton student strike, the civil rights movement lost steam but became active again after a period of quiet.

    c. Young people tended to support less bold methods to achieve racial justice.

    d. Barbara Johns and her uncle, Reverend Vernon Johns, took roles as national leaders in the ongoing civil rights movement.

Author's Purpose _____ 10. Which of the following is the main purpose of this selection?

    a. to encourage others to take action for an important cause

    b. to impress readers with the courage of Barbara Johns and the Moton students

c. to chronicle a dramatic action by a few young people that had far-reaching effects to end school desegregation

d. to inform readers of the poor conditions of African American schools in the 1950s

Answer the following with *T* (true) or *F* (false).

Inference ———— 11. Readers can logically infer that most, if not all, students at Moton High School were African American.

Detail ———— 12. Barbara Johns graduated from Moton High School.

Inference ———— 13. Although they favored different methods than the NAACP, the SCLC and SNCC remained committed to nonviolent means of achieving racial justice.

Detail ———— 14. The NAACP made significant progress toward racial justice primarily through sit-ins, boycotts, and marches.

Author's Purpose ———— 15. The quotes from Barbara Johns were included to emphasize her passion and decisive leadership.

BUILD YOUR VOCABULARY

According to the way the italicized word is used in the selection, indicate *a, b, c,* or *d* for the word or phrase that gives the best definition. The number in parentheses indicates the line of the passage in which the word is located. Use a dictionary in addition to the context clues to more precisely define the terms.

———— 1. "a *ploy* to lure" (4)
a. power play
b. rejection
c. trick
d. surprise

———— 2. "a *facsimile* of" (6)
a. signature
b. letter
c. note
d. copy

———— 3. "her *soliloquy*" (13)
a. dialogue
b. monologue
c. rant
d. complaints

———— 4. "to *stoke* the sometimes dangerous" (20)
a. put out
b. fuel
c. cool
d. heat

———— 5. "quiet and *studious*" (29)
a. scholarly
b. shy
c. unfriendly
d. conceited

———— 6. "*makeshift* facilities" (37)
a. rotting
b. permanent
c. strong
d. crude

_____ 7. "to seek *desegregation*" (48)
   a. merging of races in schools
   b. separation of races in schools
   c. peaceful resolution
   d. rebuilding

_____ 8. "*defer* to the adults" (53)
   a. apply
   b. seek advice
   c. submit
   d. disengage

_____ 9. "left a *legacy*" (66)
   a. memory
   b. inheritance
   c. bad taste
   d. factual account

_____ 10. "more *militant* forms" (83)
   a. peaceful
   b. illegal
   c. aggressive
   d. difficult

Concept Prep for Art History

A Sampling of Careers in Art History

- Museum curator
- Antiques dealer
- Educator
- Researcher for museums, galleries, auction houses, or organizations that maintain historic sites

Why study art history?

Just as written history is a verbal record of the events and people of the past, fine art is a visual interpretation of reality and a reflection of past taste and values. Art tells us about people and their culture, as illustrated in the earliest primitive cave drawings depicting animals and hunters or in the elaborate tombs in the Egyptian pyramids, built for the pharaohs. Through art, we can glimpse a likeness of Elizabeth I, feel the power of a ship battle at sea, or view the majesty of the American frontier. Artists link us to the past through beauty, creativity, and emotion.

When we say "the arts," what do we mean? The **arts** and the **fine arts** refer to creative works in painting, sculpture, literature, architecture, drama, music, opera, dance, and film. A work that is especially well crafted is said to be fine art.

Museums, a word derived from Greek to mean "places presided over by the Muses," display fine arts in paintings and sculpture. Some of the greatest museums in the world are the **Louvre** in Paris, the **Prado** in Madrid, and the **Metropolitan Museum of Art** in New York City.

Who are some of the great artists?

- One of the most extraordinary artists was **Leonardo da Vinci** (1452–1519). He was considered a **Renaissance man** because of his genius, insatiable curiosity, and wide interests in art, engineering, anatomy, and aeronautics. He painted the **Mona Lisa**, the world's most famous painting. This woman with the mysterious smile whose eyes seem to follow you is displayed in the Louvre behind several layers of bulletproof glass.
- **Michelangelo** (1475–1564) was a sculptor, painter, architect, and poet. Before he was 30 years old, he created the famous marble statue, **David**, which portrays the biblical king in his youth. Michelangelo was commissioned by the pope to paint the ceiling of the **Sistine Chapel** in the Vatican in Rome. For four years, the artist worked on his back in the chapel to complete **The Creation of Adam**, which contains more than 400 individual figures.
- The founder and leading artist of the **Impressionists** was **Claude Monet** (1840–1926). Critics said the feathery brushstrokes and play of light in his works conveyed the "impression" of a particular moment. Monet advocated getting out of the studio and painting outdoors, facing the subject. He painted many scenes of the gardens and water lily ponds surrounding his home in **Giverny** near Paris.
- **Vincent van Gogh** (1853–1890) borrowed from the Impressionists but achieved another dimension in the swirling brushstrokes of his work to convey his unique vision. His sunflower paintings and **The Starry Night** are among his most famous works, but in his lifetime, van Gogh sold only one painting. He suffered from depression and spent his last years in a mental institution. In an argument with another artist, he cut off his own ear.
- **Pablo Picasso** (1881–1973) is one of the most influential of all modern artists. Because traditional skills in painting were so easy for him, he looked for new modes of expression. He was the originator of Cubism, an abstract style of painting that displays several perspectives of an object simultaneously. One of his most acclaimed paintings is **Guernica**, a haunting visual protest against the savagery of war.
- By the twentieth century, female artists were becoming more prominent. **Mary Cassatt** (1861–1914), an Impressionist, holds a unique place in American art. She was one of the first

The Starry Night (1889), Vincent van Gogh, oil on canvas, 29 × 36 1/4" (73.7 × 92.1 cm)

Vincent Van Gogh/SuperStock

women artists to succeed professionally. Cassatt began her work in Pennsylvania but later settled in Paris. Domestic scenes became her theme, and she portrayed women and children in intimate settings.

- **Frida Kahlo** (1907–1954), a Mexican artist, is sometimes called the "portrait genie." She dramatized her life story in self-portraits, interweaving them with symbolism, myth, and surrealistic elements. Kahlo was studying to be a physician when a serious car accident hospitalized her. She took up painting and did not return to medicine. Her colorful creations reflect the endurance of life and the traditions of Mexico.
- **Georgia O'Keeffe** (1887–1986) was one of the first American artists to experiment with abstract form. She interpreted nature in beautiful geometric shapes. O'Keeffe combined the appearance of sculpture and photography in her paintings of flowers, sunbleached animal bones, clouds, and surreal desert scenes. Her clear, bright colors reflect her love of the Southwest and American independence.

REVIEW QUESTIONS

After studying the material, answer the following questions:

1. What do works included in "the arts" have in common? _____

_____

2. Where is the Louvre? _____

3. What is a Renaissance man? _____

_____

4. What is unusually engaging about Mona Lisa's face? _____

_____

5. What story is painted on the ceiling of the Sistine Chapel? _____

_____

6. How did the Impressionists get their name? _____

_____

7. What scenes did Monet paint at Giverny? _____

8. Which painter advocated painting outdoors? _____

9. How did van Gogh disfigure himself? _____

10. Why did Picasso turn to Cubism? _____

Your instructor may choose to give a brief review of these art history concepts.

SELECTION 3   Business   MyReadingLab

Visit Chapter 6: Patterns of Organization in MyReadingLab to complete the Selection 3 activities and the Build Background Knowledge video activity.

PREVIEW the next selection to predict its purpose and organization and to formulate your learning plan.

Activate Schemata

Do you prefer pizzas from Domino's, Pizza Hut, or Papa John's?
If your dream could become a reality, what small business would you start?

Establish a Purpose for Reading

Downsizing, outsourcing, women's increasing presence in the workforce, and Internet technology are now shaping the American entrepreneurial spirit. The advantages and rewards of small business ownership are great, but so are the risks. What do you expect to learn from this selection about Papa John's and small businesses? After recalling what you already know about start-up businesses, read the selection to learn what defines a small business, why people open them, and why Papa John's is successful.

Build Background Knowledge — VIDEO

Successful Business Models

To prepare for reading Selection 3, answer the questions below. Then, watch this video on strategies for starting a successful business.

If you could start a new business, what would it be?

What are the advantages and disadvantages of owning a business?

Why do you think most new businesses started by entrepreneurs fail within the first five years?

This video helped me: _____

_____

_____

Increase Word Knowledge

What do you know about these words?

void	successive	droves	dominant	titans
novice	debut	vaulted	stagnant	heritage

Your instructor may give a brief vocabulary review before or after reading.

Integrate Knowledge While Reading

Questions have been inserted in the margin to stimulate your thinking while reading. Remember to

Predict   Picture   Relate   Monitor   Correct   Annotate

WHY IS PAPA JOHN'S ROLLING IN THE DOUGH?

As a high school student working at a local pizza pub, John Schnatter liked everything about the pizza business. "I liked making the dough; I liked kneading the dough; I liked putting the sauce on; I liked putting the toppings on; I liked running the oven," recalls Schnatter. Obsessed with perfect pizza topping and bubble-free
5 melted cheese, Schnatter knew that something was missing from national pizza chains: superior-quality traditional pizza delivered to the customer's door. And his dream was to one day open a pizza restaurant that would fill that void.

Why are bubbles bad?

Schnatter worked his way through college making pizzas, honing the techniques and tastes that would someday become Papa John's trademark. Shortly after gradu-
10 ating from Ball State University with a business degree, he faced his first business challenge. His father's tavern was $64,000 in debt and failing. So Schnatter sold his car, used the money to purchase $1,600 of used restaurant equipment, knocked out a broom closet in the back of his father's tavern, and began selling pizzas to the tavern's customers. Soon the pizza became the tavern's main attraction and helped turn
15 the failing business around. In 1985 Schnatter officially opened the first Papa John's restaurant. Then he set about opening as many stores as the market would bear.

But Schnatter needed a recipe for success. With Little Caesar's promoting deep discounts and Domino's emphasizing fast delivery, Papa John's needed a fresh approach to compete successfully with the big chains. If you were John Schnatter,
20 how would you grow a small pizza operation into one that could compete with national players? Would you franchise your concept? Would you remain a private enterprise or go public? Would you expand overseas? Where would you focus your efforts?

UNDERSTANDING THE WORLD OF SMALL BUSINESS

Many small businesses start out like Papa John's: with an entrepreneur, an idea, and
25 a drive to succeed. In fact, the United States was originally founded by people involved in small business—the family farmer, the shopkeeper, the craftsperson. Successive waves of immigrants carried on the tradition, launching restaurants and laundries, providing repair and delivery services, and opening newsstands and bakeries.

What companies succeeded?

30 The 1990s were a golden decade of entrepreneurship in the United States. Entrepreneurs launched small companies in droves to fill new consumer needs. Many took advantage of Internet technologies to gain a competitive edge. Some succeeded; others failed. But the resurgence of small businesses helped turn the U.S. economy into the growth engine for the world.

35 Today, over 5.8 million small companies exist in the United States. But defining what constitutes a small business is surprisingly tricky, because *small* is a relative term.

One reliable source of information for small businesses is the Small Business Administration (SBA). This government agency serves as a resource and advocate for small firms, providing them with financial assistance, training, and a variety of
40 helpful programs. The SBA defines a small business as a firm that (a) is independently owned and operated, (b) is not dominant in its field, (c) is relatively small in terms of annual sales, and (d) has fewer than 500 employees. The SBA reports that 80 percent of all U.S. companies have annual sales of less than $1 million and that about 60 percent of the nation's employers have fewer than five workers.

FACTORS CONTRIBUTING TO THE INCREASE IN THE NUMBER OF SMALL BUSINESSES

45 Three factors are contributing to the increase in the number of small businesses today: technological advances, an increase in the number of women and minority business owners, and corporate downsizing and outsourcing.

TECHNOLOGY AND THE INTERNET

The Internet, together with e-commerce, has spawned thousands of new business ventures. ShippingSupply.com is one such firm. Karen Young, a collector of knick-
50 knacks, founded this small business when she was looking for affordable packing and shipping materials for her mail-order items. On a whim, Young decided to market bubble wrap, plastic foam, and shipping tubes she purchased directly from manufacturers to eBay sellers. Today, ShippingSupply.com has eight full-time employees, occupies 7,000 feet of warehouse space, and has over 35,500 customers in its
55 database.

Do Internet companies have low start-up costs?

RISE IN NUMBER OF WOMEN AND MINORITY SMALL-BUSINESS OWNERS

The number of women-owned small businesses has also increased sharply over the past three decades—from 5 percent to over 39 percent of all small businesses. These
60 businesses now employ more than 18.5 million people and ring up more than $3.1 trillion in annual sales. Women are starting small businesses for a number of reasons. Some choose to run their own companies so they can enjoy a more flexible work arrangement; others start their own businesses because of barriers to corporate advancement, known as the glass ceiling. Josie Natori is a perfect example of
65 such a scenario. By her late twenties, Natori was earning six figures as the first female vice president of investment banking at Merrill Lynch. But Natori knew that her chances of further advancement were slim in the male-dominated financial world. So she started her own lingerie line. Today, Natori is the owner of a multi-million-dollar fashion empire that sells elegant lingerie and evening wear.

DOWNSIZING AND OUTSOURCING

70 Contrary to popular wisdom, business start-ups soar when the economy sours. During hard times, many companies downsize or lay off talented employees, who then have little to lose by pursuing self-employment. In fact, several well-known companies were started during recessions. Tech titans William Hewlitt and David Packard joined forces in Silicon Valley in 1938 during the Great Depression. Bill Gates started

John Schnatter, founder and president of the Papa
John's Pizza chain
Mark Von Holden/Getty Images

75 Microsoft during the 1975 recession. And the founders of Sun Microsystems, Compaq Computer, Adobe Systems, Silicon Graphics, and Lotus Development started their companies in 1982—in the midst of a recession and high unemployment.

To make up for layoffs of permanent staff, some companies **outsource** or subcontract special projects and secondary business functions to experts outside the 80 organization. Others turn to outsourcing as a way to permanently eliminate entire company departments. Regardless of the reason, the increased use of outsourcing provides opportunities for smaller businesses to serve the needs of larger enterprises.

Is this a cause-and-effect relationship?

BEHIND THE SCENES: PAPA JOHN'S PIPING HOT PERFORMANCE

John Schnatter did a remarkable job of expanding from a single pizza store he started in his father's tavern. Three years after Schnatter opened his first Papa John's, he 85 expanded outside of the Louisville, Kentucky, area. He was no novice. He knew the grass roots of the pizza business, he had an intuitive grasp of what customers wanted, and he knew how to make pizzas taste a little bit better than the competition. Moreover, he had the qualities of an entrepreneur: driven, intense, willing to make things happen, visionary, and very competitive.

90 John Schnatter used franchising to grow the business. Today about 75 percent of Papa John's are franchised; the rest are company-owned. He was encouraged by Kentucky Fried Chicken, Long John Silver's, Chi-Chi's, and other Kentucky-born restaurants that had successfully taken their franchised restaurants national. Schnatter thought, "What the heck, maybe I could do it too." But to keep growth under

95 control, Papa John's didn't just move into an area and open up 200 stores. Schnatter grew the stores one at a time—spending up to six months to a year assessing an area's potential.

It wasn't long before Papa John's began grabbing business from such giants as Pizza Hut, Little Caesar's, and delivery king Domino's. Then in 1999 Papa John's

100 made its European debut by acquiring Perfect Pizza Holdings, a 205-unit delivery and carryout pizza chain in the United Kingdom. The acquisition gave Papa John's instant access to proven sites that would have been difficult to obtain. Besides the real estate, Perfect Pizza had a good management team that Schnatter could fold into his organization.

105 Today, Papa John's has vaulted past Little Caesar's to become the nation's third-largest pizza chain. The company now boasts over 2,700 stores in 47 states and 9 international markets. Annual sales have mushroomed to about $1.7 billion. In spite of its tremendous growth, Schnatter insists on maintaining the highest quality standards. He does so by keeping things simple. About 95 percent of the restaurants

Does lack of variety lower costs?

110 are takeout only. The menu is simple—just two types of pizza, thin crust or regular— no exotic toppings, no salads, no sandwiches, and no buffalo wings. Owners are trained to remake pies that rate less than 8 on the company's 10-point scale. If the cheese shows a single air bubble or the crust is not golden brown, out the offender goes. Schnatter's attention to product quality has earned the company awards. Papa

115 John's was twice voted number one in customer satisfaction among all fast-food restaurants in the American Consumer Satisfaction Index.

To keep things in order, Schnatter visits four to five stores a week, often unannounced. He also trains managers how to forecast product demand. Stores project demand one to two weeks in advance. They factor in anything from forthcoming

120 promotions to community events to the next big high school football game. If a big game is on TV, Schnatter wants to make sure the store owners are ready for the surge in deliveries.

Still, like many companies today, Papa John's faces new challenges. It's becoming increasingly difficult to grow the company's share of the pie. Although Ameri-

125 cans consume pizza at a rate of 350 slices a second, the pizza industry is stagnant and highly competitive. Growth usually comes at the expense of a competitor's existing business. Moreover, to keep profitability in line, Schnatter has scaled back company expansion plans and even closed some unprofitable outlets. But Schnatter is determined to succeed. And if one strength rises above the others in Schnatter's

130 path to success, it's his ability to recruit and retain the right people. "There's nothing special about John Schnatter except the people around me," Schnatter says. "They make me look better" and they make Papa John's what it is—committed to its heritage of making superior-quality, traditional pizza.

(1,595 words)

—Courtland L. Bovée, John V. Thrill, and Barbara E. Schatzman,
Business in Action, 2nd ed. © 2004, pp. 91, 109–110.
Reprinted by permission of Pearson Education, Inc.,
Upper Saddle River, NJ

Recall

Stop to self-test, relate, and react.

Your instructor may choose to give you a brief comprehension review.

THINK CRITICALLY ABOUT THE SELECTION

What personal qualities contribute to John Schnatter's success?

According to the selection, what business practices have made Papa John's a leader in the pizza business?

WRITE ABOUT THE SELECTION

What factors contribute to the opening of small businesses? Why did John Schnatter open his pizza business?

Response Suggestion: Discuss and explain the cause-and-effect relationship of at least five factors that prompt people to take risks and start something new.

SKILL DEVELOPMENT: IDENTIFY ORGANIZATIONAL PATTERNS

Answer the following with *T* (true) or *F* (false):

_____ 1. The first and last sections are examples with anecdotal information about a real business.

_____ 2. The section, "Understanding the World of Small Business," defines a small business.

_____ 3. The organizational pattern of the section, "Factors Contributing to the Increase in the Number of Small Businesses," is cause and effect.

_____ 4. The organizational pattern of the section, "Downsizing and Outsourcing," is comparison and contrast.

CHECK YOUR COMPREHENSION

After reading the selection, answer the following questions with *a, b, c,* or *d.* To help you analyze your strengths and weaknesses, the question types are indicated.

Main Idea ———— 1. Which is the best statement of the main idea of this selection?

    a. Through hard work, Papa John's has expanded globally and become the third largest pizza company in the world.

    b. The golden decade for entrepreneurship has peaked but is not over, as proved by Papa John's Pizza.

    c. Current factors are contributing to a rise in the number of small businesses, and Papa John's Pizza is a glowing example of one such entrepreneurial success.

    d. The highly competitive pizza business requires more than good tomato sauce to turn dough into dollars.

Detail ———— 2. When John Schnatter started his pizza business, he had all of the following *except*

    a. years of experience making pizza dough.

    b. a college degree in business.

    c. training in running the pizza ovens.

    d. restaurant equipment from his father's business.

Inference ———— 3. The author implies that John Schnatter

    a. pulled his father's business out of a $64,000 debt.

    b. closed his father's tavern to open his pizza parlor.

    c. was financed in the pizza business by his father.

    d. continued to use the formula of liquor sales with pizza.

Detail ———— 4. As defined by the Small Business Administration, a small business is all of the following *except*

    a. it has fewer than 500 employees.

    b. it is independently operated.

    c. it is owned by stockholders.

    d. it is not dominant in its field.

Inference ———— 5. The author suggests that Karen Young's ShippingSupply.com business is

    a. primarily a retail store that customers enter to buy supplies.

    b. a prime candidate for franchising.

    c. a mail-order knickknack venture.

    d. a firm that conducts business over the Internet, with supplies shipped from a warehouse.

Inference ———— 6. The author implies that a glass ceiling is

    a. a barrier to high-level corporate advancement.

    b. a more flexible work arrangement.

    c. an entry into investment banking.

    d. a barrier to male-dominated entry-level positions.

Detail _____ 7. Downsizing in a company means to

    a. fire incompetent workers.

    b. lay off valued employees.

    c. freeze hiring until profits improve.

    d. subcontract for special projects.

Inference _____ 8. An example of outsourcing done by an American company would be

    a. selling products in India.

    b. hiring experienced European workers for an American company.

    c. contracting for payroll accounting to be done by a company in Ireland.

    d. buying coffee beans from Latin America and processing them in the United States.

Inference _____ 9. The author suggests that Schnatter's success can be attributed to all of the following *except*

    a. hiring good people.

    b. adding a variety of items to the menu.

    c. insisting on high-quality standards for pizzas.

    d. personally visiting stores to keep things in order.

Inference _____ 10. The reader can conclude that of the company's 2,700 stores,

    a. most are owned by Schnatter.

    b. all but 340 stores are now franchised.

    c. the company owns about 675 of them.

    d. Perfect Pizza Holdings franchised 2,400 stores.

Answer the following with *T* (true) or *F* (false):

Detail _____ 11. During a recession and times of high unemployment, few new businesses are started.

Detail _____ 12. According to the Small Business Administration, over half of the small American businesses hire fewer than five workers.

Inference _____ 13. Schnatter bought Perfect Pizza in the United Kingdom because it was poorly managed.

Inference _____ 14. The author suggests that Papa John's plans to expand into salads and sandwiches.

Author's Purpose _____ 15. The primary purpose of this selection is to advertise Papa John's Pizza.

BUILD YOUR VOCABULARY

According to the way the italicized word was used in the selection, select *a, b, c,* or *d* for the word or phrase that gives the best definition. The number in parentheses indicates the line of the passage in which the word is located.

_____ 1. "would fill that *void*" (7)
a. goal
b. empty space
c. union
d. demand

_____ 2. "*Successive* waves of immigrants" (26–27)
a. one after another
b. eager
c. unsteady
d. overwhelming

_____ 3. "launched small companies in *droves*" (31)
a. efforts
b. desperation
c. reactions
d. large numbers

_____ 4. "not *dominant* in its field" (41)
a. growing
b. foremost
c. secure
d. competitive

_____ 5. "Tech *titans*" (73)
a. enthusiasts
b. explorers
c. giants
d. hobbyists

_____ 6. "was no *novice*" (85)
a. beginner
b. pushover
c. coward
d. follower

_____ 7. "its European *debut*" (100)
a. achievement
b. marketing ploy
c. market entry
d. diversity

_____ 8. "has *vaulted* past Little Caesar's" (105)
a. sneaked
b. crawled
c. leaped
d. slowly moved

_____ 9. "pizza industry is *stagnant*" (125)
a. nervous
a. cutthroat
b. small
c. not growing

_____ 10. "committed to its *heritage*" (132–133)
a. logo
b. brand
c. management
d. tradition

VOCABULARY BOOSTER

Can I Get That in Writing?

Roots	*graph:* "write"	*scrib, scrip:* "write"

Words with *graph:* "write"

Tests that use computer-readable answer sheets require that a no. 2 *graphite* pencil be used for marking the answers.

- *graph*: something written; a diagram or chart; a network of lines connecting points

  The calculus homework required a written solution and a corresponding *graph* for each problem.

- *graphic*: described in realistic detail; vivid; pertaining to any of the graphic arts, such as painting, drawing, and engraving

  The movie's *graphic* violence guaranteed that it would not get anything other than an R rating.

- *phonograph*: a machine for reproducing sound from records in the form of cylinders or spiral-grooved rotating disks

  The early *phonograph* had a tubalike device that transmitted sound.

- *cinematography*: the art or technique of motion-picture photography

  The movie that was named Best Picture at the Academy Awards also won the award for best *cinematography*.

- *polygraph*: a lie detector

  A *polygraph* records changes in pulse rate or respiration to determine if a person is telling the truth.

- *geography*: the science dealing with differences between areas of the Earth's surface, such as climate, population, elevation, vegetation, or land use

  Interactions between populations may be explained by *geography*, such as whether mountains or rivers separate them or whether they are in close proximity.

- *telegraph*: a system for sending distant messages or signals between two electronic devices connected by wire

  The telephone and e-mail have all but replaced the *telegraph* as a means of communicating.

Words with *scrib, scrip:* "write"

The bride and groom had an inscription engraved inside their wedding rings.

- *scribble*: to write hastily or carelessly; to cover with meaningless marks

  Before running to catch my bus, I quickly *scribbled* a note to my roommate that I would not be home for dinner.

- *transcribe*: to make a written or typed copy of spoken material; to translate into another language

  Saundra loved her job at the United Nations, where she *transcribed* multilingual meetings into English.

- *transcript*: a written, typewritten, or printed copy of something

  An official *transcript* of your college records is required when you transfer to another school.

- *ascribe*: to assign or attribute to a particular cause or source

  Stephen *ascribes* his good looks to his father's genes.

- *subscription*: a sum of money pledged as a contribution; the right to receive a magazine or other service for a sum; the act of appending one's signature to a document

  Public television relies on *subscriptions* pledged during its annual fund-raising drives.

- *prescription*: a written direction from a doctor for the preparation and use of a medicine

  Pharmacists read and fill *prescriptions* and usually warn about possible side effects of the prescribed drugs.

- *circumscribe*: to draw a circle around; to enclose within bounds or to confine

  Since Emilio had just started to drive, he had a *circumscribed* area beyond which he was not allowed to take the family car.

- *script*: handwriting; written text of a play, movie, or television program

  The *script* of the play was revised when the screenwriters started work on the movie version of the story.

- *postscript*: an addition to a concluded and signed letter; a supplement appended to a book

  I forgot to tell my mom about my promotion until after I had signed the letter, so I added a *postscript* telling her about my new position.

- *description*: a representation of something in words or pictures; a sort or variety of something

  The witness to the robbery gave the police sketch artist a good *description* of the suspect.

Review

Part I

Choose the best synonym from the boxed list for the words and phrases below.

graphic	scribble	transcript	subscription	prescription
script	postscript	transcribe	inscription	circumscribe

1. document showing dialogue _____   7. vivid _____

2. addendum _____   8. translate _____

3. scrawl _____   9. written or carved words

4. direction _____   _____

5. purchase _____   10. limit _____

6. a copy _____

Part II

From the list, choose the word that best completes each sentence below.

transcript	telegraph	geography	polygraph	cinematography
phonograph	ascribe	graphic	graph	prescription

11. You must supply the most recent copy of your college _____ when transferring to another university.

12. Cult members tend to _____ only the best qualities to their leader.

13. _____ violence in a film results in a restricted rating.

14. Findings obtained from _____ tests are not ordinarily admitted as legal evidence in court.

15. If you are a visual learner, you prefer gaining information through pictures or a _____ rather than a lecture.

16. In the 1960s, people used the _____ to listen to music, since CD players were not yet available.

17. Studies of the _____ of the Appalachian Mountains found them to be among the oldest land masses in the United States.

18. Prior to the invention of the telephone, the _____ allowed traveling news reporters to promptly transmit their breaking stories back to city newspapers.

19. The older woman's _____ for a long, healthy life included proper nutrition, adequate exercise and rest, and lots of laughter.

20. Exceptional _____ can make the viewer feel transported to another place.

Your instructor may choose to give a brief review.

7 Inference

Learning Objectives
In this chapter, you will learn to:

1 Define inference
2 Make reasonable inferences while reading
3 Recognize connotative language
4 Identify euphemisms and politically correct language
5 Recognize and interpret types of figurative language
6 Use details and schemata to make inferences
7 Draw logical conclusions while reading

Vocabulary Booster: Say What?

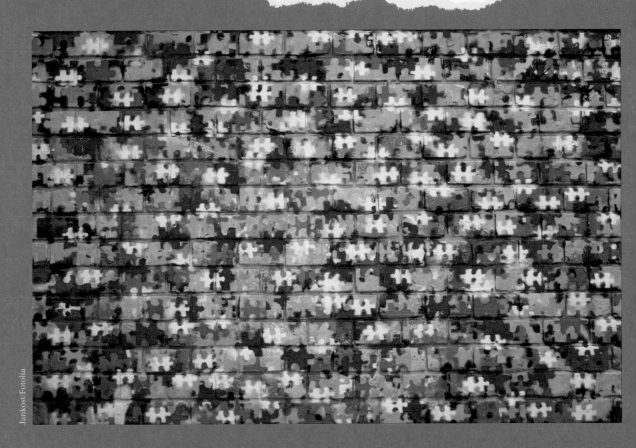

Jankost/Fotolia

WHAT IS AN INFERENCE?

At the first and most basic level of reading, the *literal level*—the level that presents the facts—you can actually point to the words on the page to answer a literal question. However, at the second and more sophisticated level of reading—the *inferential level*—you no longer can point to such an answer but, instead, must form it from clues and suggestions within the text. This is the process of making an **inference**.

EXAMPLE   In the following passage from Michael Ondaatje's novel, *The English Patient*, the author implies an activity, and the reader infers what is happening. Mark the point at which you understand the activity.

> She moves backwards a few feet and with a piece of white chalk draws more rectangles, so there is a pyramid of them, single then double then single, her left hand braced flat on the floor, her head down, serious. . . .
>
> She drops the chalk into the pocket of her dress. She stands and pulls up the looseness of her skirt and ties it around her dress. She pulls from another pocket a piece of metal and flings it out in front of her so it falls just beyond the farthest square.
>
> She leaps forward, her legs smashing down, her shadow behind her curling into the depth of the hall. She is very quick, her tennis shoes skidding on the numbers she has drawn into each rectangle, one foot landing, then two feet, then one again until she reaches the last square.[1]

EXPLANATION   How many sentences did it take for you to infer that she is playing the game of hopscotch? You may have visualized the activity as early as the author's description of drawing "single then double then single," or perhaps you caught on a bit later, when she jumps. In any case, you were able to make the inference when the clues from the text merged with your own prior knowledge.

Two different terms are used in discussing inferential thinking: The writer or speaker *implies*, and the reader or listener *infers*. This merging of suggested thought is also figuratively called **reading between the lines**. Throughout this text, many of the thought questions, or think-alouds, appearing in the margins alongside the longer reading selections ask you to read between the lines.

At the inferential level, authors not only entertain readers but also subtly manipulate them. When you read, always consider what is left unsaid. This is also true for the spoken word. For example, when asked, "How do you like your new boss?" you might answer, "She is always well dressed" rather than "I don't like her." By not volunteering information that directly answers the question, you convey your lack of approval or, certainly, your lack of enthusiasm. In some cases, this lack of information might send a damaging message. For example, when you graduate and look for that perfect position, you will need to ask professors and previous employers for job recommendations. Take care that the person you ask to recommend you is 100 percent on your team. The following exercise illustrates the power of what is left unsaid.

---

[1]As quoted in Stephanie Harvey and Anne Goudvis, *Strategies That Work* (Portland, ME: Stenhouse Publishers, 2000), p. 37.

EXERCISE **7.1**

Reading Between the Lines

Read the two recommendations and decide whom you would hire.

> **Carlos** has been working as an assistant for one year and has been a valuable member of our team. He aggressively tackles new accounts, making calls after hours to track down customers and ship needed products. He excels in sales and follows through with the details in keeping customers satisfied. We want to keep Carlos but have no openings for advanced positions. I highly recommend him for the position at your company.

> **Roger** has worked for our company for one year as an assistant. Our company sells chicken by-products, mostly thighs and legs that are not used in America, to Russia and third-world countries. Because of the international nature of our business, communication is extremely important. During his year with us, Roger has faithfully attended all meetings and has been friendly with our staff. We certainly wish him well.

Which one would you hire? Why? _____

_____

_____

_____

_____

_____

_____

Any employer is wise enough to infer the meaning of a vaguely worded reference. Similarly, inferential skills are important in interpreting persuasive reports and arguments, because facts that are detrimental to the supported position may have been omitted to manipulate a reader's opinion. Such omissions send a "Reader Beware" signal. One of the most effective tools that selectively uses words and photos to send persuasive messages is advertising.

Cigarette advertisements, for example, entice the public through suggestion, not facts, to spend millions of dollars on a product that is known to be unhealthy. They use words and photos in a sophisticated way to lure consumers. Depending on the brand, smoking offers the refreshment of a mountain stream or the sophisticated elegance of the rich and famous. Never do the ads directly praise smoking or promise pleasure; instead, the ads *imply* smoking's positive aspects. The cigarette advertisers avoid lawsuits for false advertising by never putting anything tangible into print. The emotionalism of a full-page advertisement is so overwhelming that the consumer hardly notices the cautionary note in small print at the bottom of the page: "Warning: The Surgeon General Has Determined That Cigarette Smoking Is Dangerous to Your Health."

WHAT IS REQUIRED TO MAKE A REASONABLE INFERENCE?

Learning Objective 2

Make reasonable inferences while reading

Some experts describe the process of reading as a conversation between the author and the reader. Certainly, the conversation begins with the words on the printed page, but every reader brings a different set of background knowledge and experiences, or schemata, to them. Just as we use our accumulated wisdom to understand a friend's spoken story, we also interpret an author's message through the lens of our personal experience.

To make reasonable inferences, effective readers use logic to put together the author's clues—informational details, word choice—and their own knowledge and experience. Giving too much weight to any part of the equation can cause us to misinterpret the message. The diagram below helps to visualize the elements of a valid inference.

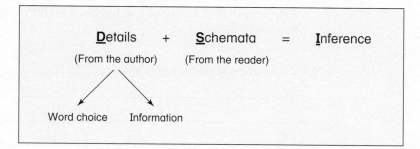

EXERCISE 7.2

Implied Meaning in Advertisements

Advertisers can directly state that a detergent cleans, but the task of advertising other products can be more complicated. Look through magazines and newspapers to locate three advertisements: one each for cigarettes, alcoholic beverages, and fragrances. Answer the following questions about each advertisement:

1. What is directly stated about the product?

2. What does the advertisement suggest about the product?

3. Who seems to be the suggested audience or customer for the product? Why?

Authors and advertisers have not invented a new comprehension skill; they are merely capitalizing on a highly developed skill of daily life. Think, for example, of the inferences that you make every day by noticing what people say or don't say, by examining what they do or don't do, and by interpreting what others say or don't say about them. In fact, if you lacked these skills, you would miss out on a lot of the humor in jokes, cartoons, and sitcoms.

Implied Meaning in Humor

Jokes and cartoons require you to read between the lines and make connections. They are funny, not so much because of what is said, but because of what has been left unsaid. When you "catch on" to a joke, it simply means that you make the connection and recognize the **inference**, the **implied meaning**. To enjoy the joke, you link prior knowledge to what is being said. If you are telling a joke and your listener lacks the background knowledge to which the joke refers, your attempt will fall flat because the listener cannot understand the implied meaning. Listeners cannot connect with something that they don't know, so be sure to choose the right joke for the right audience.

Biting humor has two levels of implied meaning. On the surface, the joke makes us laugh. At a deeper level, however, the humor ridicules our beliefs, practices, or way of life.

BRAIN BOOSTER

The Brain's Pleasure Center and Learning

One of the oldest and most important survival mechanisms we and most creatures have is pleasure. We are motivated by the reward of pleasant sensations. When we feel happy, satisfied, or fulfilled, we want to repeat the actions that made us feel that way. The pleasure centers of human brains are located deep below the frontal cortex. The frontal cortex is associated with the brain chemical, dopamine, which is thought to create the feeling of well-being. How does this fact of brain function relate to learning? When we associate learning with pleasure—satisfaction in a job well done, the joy of learning something new, having fun with a learning game or sharing humor during class, for instance—negative emotions take a back seat, and we are relaxed enough to learn some more. Take advantage of this wonderful aspect of the human brain. Have fun!

Adapted from The Art of Changing the Brain *by James E. Zull*

 **EXERCISE 7.3**

Implied Meaning in Cartoons

Explain the inferences that make the following cartoons funny.

"Oh no, we're being spammed!"

Arnie Levin/The New Yorker Collection/The Cartoon Bank

Inference: _____

_____

_____

"I drove to the garden centre for a tree to offset my carbon footprint...
so now I've got to go back for another one..."

Clive Goddard/CartoonStock

Inference: _____

_____

_____

_____

_____

_____

In cartoons, subtle expressions in the drawings, along with the words, imply meaning. In speech or writing, carefully chosen words imply attitude and manipulate the emotions of the reader.

CONNOTATIVE LANGUAGE

Learning Objective 3

Recognize connotative language

Notice the power of suggested meaning as you respond to the following questions:

1. If you read the following author's description of classmates, which student would you assume is smartest?
   a. a student annotating items on a computer printout
   b. a student with earphones listening to a CD
   c. a student talking with classmates about the newest TV show

2. Which would you find discussed in a vintage small town of the 1940s?
   a. movies
   b. cinema
   c. picture shows

3. Who probably earns the most money?
   a. a worker in a dark suit, white shirt, and tie
   b. a worker in jeans and a t-shirt
   c. a worker in a pale blue uniform with a company name on the pocket

Can you prove your answers? It's not the same as proving when the Declaration of Independence was signed, yet you still have a feeling for the way each question should be answered. Even though a right or wrong answer is difficult to explain for this type of question, certain answers can still be defended as most accurate; in the preceding questions, the answers are *a*, *c*, and *a*. The answers are based on feelings, attitudes, and knowledge that is commonly shared by members of society.

A seemingly innocent tool, word choice is the first key to implied meaning. For example, compare the following sentences:

Esmeralda is skinny.

Esmeralda is slender.

If she is skinny, she is unattractive; but if she is slender, she must be attractive. Both adjectives might refer to the same underweight person, but *skinny* communicates a negative feeling, whereas *slender* communicates a positive one. This feeling or emotionalism surrounding a word is called **connotation. Denotation**, on the other hand, is the specific meaning of a word. The connotative meaning goes beyond the denotative meaning to reflect certain attitudes and prejudices of society. Even though it may not seem premeditated, writers select words, just as advertisers select symbols and models, to manipulate the reader's opinions.

EXERCISE 7.4

Recognizing Connotation in Familiar Words

In each of the following word pairs, write the letter of the word with the more positive connotation:

_____ 1. (a) issue   (b) problem

_____ 2. (a) loneliness   (b) independence

_____ 3. (a) tolerant   (b) pushover

_____ 4. (a) difficult   (b) challenging

_____ 5. (a) pale   (b) fair

_____ 6. (a) direct   (b) rude

_____ 7. (a) cop   (b) officer

_____ 8. (a) lead   (b) dominate

_____ 9. (a) lazy   (b) easygoing

_____ 10. (a) unanswered   (b) ignored

EXERCISE 7.5 Choosing Connotative Words

For each word listed below, write a word with a similar denotative meaning that has a positive (or neutral) connotation and one that has a negative connotation. Answers will vary.

	Positive	**Negative**
eat	dine	devour
1. child	_____	_____
2. ruler	_____	_____
3. innocent	_____	_____
4. supportive	_____	_____
5. quiet	_____	_____

EXERCISE 7.6 Connotation in Textbooks

For each of the underlined words in the following sentences, indicate the meaning of the word and reasons why the connotation is positive or negative.

EXAMPLE

While the unions fought mainly for better wages and hours, they also championed various social reforms.

—Leonard Pitt,
We Americans

championed: Positive; means "supported" and suggests heroes or winners

1. The ad was part of the oil companies' program to sell their image rather than their product to the public. In the ad they boasted that they were reseeding all the disrupted areas with a newly developed grass that grows five times faster than the grass that normally occurs there.

—Robert Wallace,
Biology: The World of Life

boasted: _____

_____

2. At noon, a group of prominent bankers met. To stop the hemorrhaging of stock prices, the bankers' pool agreed to buy stocks well above the market.

—James Kirby Martin et al.,
America and Its People

hemorrhaging: _____

_____

3. The nation's capital is <u>crawling</u> with lawyers, lobbyists, registered foreign agents, public relations consultants, and others—more than 14,000 individuals representing nearly 12,000 organizations at last count—all seeking to influence Congress.

—Robert Lineberry et al.,
Government in America, Brief Version, 2nd ed.

crawling: _____

EUPHEMISMS AND POLITICALLY CORRECT LANGUAGE

Learning Objective 4

Identify euphemisms and politically correct language

A **euphemism** is a substitution of a mild, indirect, or vague term for one that is considered harsh, blunt, or offensive. It is a polite way of saying something that is embarrassing or indelicate. In the funeral business, for example, euphemisms abound. In fact, one website lists 213 terms for *death* or *dying,* such as *pass to the great beyond* or *big sleep.* Remember that the word part *eu-* means "good."

Politically correct language is a form of euphemism that is used to avoid offending a group of people or raising a politically sensitive idea. For example, *collateral damage* refers to civilian casualties. Other examples are the janitor being called the *sanitation engineer,* a handicapped person being called *differently abled,* or someone with a missing tooth being called *dentally disadvantaged.*

EXAMPLE

Euphemism: My stomach feels unsettled.

Politically correct: The troops were hit by friendly fire.

FIGURATIVE LANGUAGE

Learning Objective 5

Recognize and interpret types of figurative language

What does it mean to say, "She worked like a dog"? To most readers, it means that she worked hard, but since few dogs work, the comparison is not literally true or particularly logical. **Figurative language** is, in a sense, another language because it is a different way of using "regular" words so that they take on new meaning. For example, "It was raining buckets" and "raining cats and dogs" are lively, figurative ways of describing a heavy rain. New speakers of English, however, who comprehend on a literal level, might look up in the sky for the descending buckets or animals. The two expressions create an exaggerated, humorous effect, but on a literal level, they do not make sense.

Consider an example from a Shakespearean play. When Hamlet prepares to confront his mother, he says, "I will speak daggers to her, but use none." With an economy of expression, he vividly suggests his feelings. Much more is implied than merely saying, "I will speak sternly to her." No one expects he will use a knife on his mother, but the connotation is that the words will be sharp, piercing, and wounding. An author uses figurative language, sometimes called **imagery**, to stimulate readers' minds to imagine beyond the printed page by adding color, attitude, or wit.

Idioms

When they are first used, the phrases "works like a dog" and "raining cats and dogs" were probably very clever. Now they have lost their freshness but still convey meaning for those who are "in the know." Such phrases are called **idioms**, or expressions that do not make literal sense but have taken on a new, generally accepted meaning over many years of use.

EXAMPLE

She tried to keep a stiff upper lip during the ordeal.

His eyes were bigger than his stomach.

EXPLANATION   The first example means to maintain emotional control, and the second example means to ask for more food than you are able to eat.

EXERCISE 7.7

Understanding Idioms

What do the following idioms mean?

1. burning the candle at both ends _____

_____

2. to have the Midas touch _____

_____

3. walking on air _____

_____

4. to beef up _____

_____

5. costs an arm and a leg _____

_____

Similes

A **simile** is a comparison of two unlike things, using the word *like* or *as*.

EXAMPLE

And every soul, it passed me by,
Like the whizz of my crossbow!

—Samuel Taylor Coleridge,
The Rime of the Ancient Mariner

Metaphors

A **metaphor** is a direct comparison of two unlike things (without using *like* or *as*).

EXAMPLE

The corporate accountant is a computer from nine to five.

Your simple word of assurance was the starting gun that moved me from uncertainty to action.

Hyperbole

Hyperbole, sometimes called **overstatement**, is an exaggeration to describe something as being more than it actually is; for example, *the lights of the village were brighter than a thousand stars*. An **understatement**, on the other hand, minimizes a point, such as saying, *"I covered expenses"* after winning $3 million in Las Vegas.

EXAMPLE

Hyperbole: I could sleep for 20 days and nights and still be tired.

Understatement: His clothes have seen better days.

Personification

Personification is the process of attributing human characteristics to nonhuman things.

EXAMPLE

The birds speak from the forest.

Time marches on.

Verbal Irony

Verbal irony is the use of words to express a meaning that is the opposite of what is literally said.[2] If the intent is to hurt, the irony is called **sarcasm**.

EXAMPLE

"What a great looking corporate outfit!" (Said to someone wearing torn jeans)

"There is nothing like a sunny day for a picnic." (Said during a thunderstorm)

---

[2]The general term *irony* refers to a twist in meaning or a surprise ending; it may involve a humorous or a tragic undertone.

In *situational irony*, events occur contrary to what is expected, as if in a cruel twist of fate. For example, Juliet awakens and finds that Romeo has killed himself because he thought that she was dead.

In *dramatic irony*, the reader or audience is aware of certain details in a situation of which the characters are not aware.

EXERCISE 7.8

Discovering Figurative Language in Essays

Read the following essay, titled "The Barrio," and enjoy the figurative language. Indicate *a* or *b* for the type of figurative language used and write a response to each question.

The train, its metal wheels squealing as they spin along the silvery tracks, rolls slower now. Through the gaps between the cars blinks a streetlamp, and this pulsing light on a barrio streetlamp beats slower, like a weary heartbeat, until the train shudders to a halt, the light goes out, and the barrio is deep asleep.

Members of the barrio describe the entire area as their home. It is a home, but it is more than this. The barrio is a refuge from the harshness and the coldness of the Anglo world. It is a forced refuge. There is no want to escape, for the feeling of the barrio is known only to its inhabitants, and the material needs of life can also be found here.

The *tortilleria* [tortilla factory] fires up its machinery three times a day, producing steaming, round, flat slices of barrio bread. In the winter, the warmth of the tortilla factory is a wool *sarape* [blanket] in the chilly morning hours, but in the summer, it unbearably toasts every noontime customer.

The *panaderia* [bakery] sends its sweet messenger aroma down the dimly lit street, announcing the arrival of fresh, hot sugary *pan dulce* [sweet rolls].

The pool hall is a junior level country club where *chucos* [young men], strangers in their own land, get together to shoot pool and rap, while veterans, unaware of the cracking, popping balls on the green felt, complacently play dominoes beneath rudely hung *Playboy* foldouts.

—Robert Ramirez,
in *Models for Writers*, 8th ed.,
by Alfred Rosa and Paul Escholz

_____ 1. blinks a streetlamp: a. personification b. simile

_____ 2. like a weary heartbeat: a. metaphor b. simile

_____ 3. the barrio is deep asleep: a. personification b. simile

_____ 4. tortilla factory is a wool sarape: a. metaphor b. simile

_____ 5. toasts every noontime customer: a. metaphor b. simile

_____ 6. [the aroma] announcing the arrival: a. personification b. simile

_____ 7. pool hall is a junior level country club: a. personification b. metaphor

8. How does the figurative language add to the pleasurable reading of the essay?

_____

_____

9. Why does the author use Spanish vocabulary? _____

_____

10. What is the connotation of words like *home* and *refuge* in describing the barrio?

_____

_____

EXERCISE 7.9   **Figurative Language in Textbooks**

The figurative expressions in the following sentences are underlined. Identify the type, define each expression, and, if possible, suggest the reason for its use.

EXAMPLE   As a trained nurse working in the immigrant slums of New York, she knew that table-top abortions were common among poor women, and she had seen some of the tragic results.

—Leonard Pitt,
We Americans

EXPLANATION   table-top abortions: It is a metaphor, which may now be an idiom from repeated usage, and means "illegal." The connotation suggests the reality of where the operations probably occurred.

1. The Confederate States of America adopted a constitution and elected Jefferson Davis, a Mississippi senator and cotton planter, its provisional president. The divided house had fallen, as Lincoln had predicted.

—Adapted from Gary B. Nash et al.,
The American People: Creating a Nation and a Society,
6th ed., Vol. 1: To 1877

divided house: _____

_____

2. Henry VIII lived large. He was a bear of a man, famed for his ability to hunt all day while wearing out a pack of trained horses, for his prowess in wrestling bouts, including one with King Francis I of France, and of course, for having six wives.

—Mark Kishlansky et al.,
Civilization in the West, 6th ed.

lived large: _____

_____

a bear of a man: _____

_____

3. For some reason, I knew they were going to stop me. My heart clenched like a fist; the muscles in my back knotted up.

—Benjamin Alire Sáenz
Exile, El Paso, Texas

like a fist: _____

_____

Figurative Language in Poetry

Poets use connotations and imagery to appeal to the senses and convey striking pictures to us with great economy of words. Because much of the meaning in poetry is implied, this literary form can seem challenging. The highly condensed language of poetry makes every word valuable.

Some poems consist of short rhymes or descriptions of love or emotion, whereas others have a plot and characters. To understand a poem, read it several times and at least once out loud. Know the meanings of words and pay attention to sentence structure and line breaks. Visualize what you read and use each part of the poem to help you understand the other parts.

EXAMPLE The haiku poetic form, adapted from Japanese tradition, expresses an insight or impression in about 17 syllables and is usually arranged in three lines. What are the image and impression in the following haiku?

> life begins with roots
> grows majestically upward
> falls, feeding the earth
> —Eli Kenneth Morris

EXPLANATION The image is of a stately tree and the cycle of life. The impression can be extended to apply to a person, born with connections to generations of family, growing tall, and ultimately dying, the person's remains enriching the earth.

EXERCISE 7.10 ## Understanding Poetry

Read the following two poems and answer the questions. Remember to read the poems aloud at least once to appreciate the sound of the words. Look for figurative language and interpret its meaning.

Poem 1

THE NEGRO SPEAKS OF RIVERS (1921)

I've known rivers:
I've known rivers ancient as the world and older than the flow of human blood in human veins.
My soul has grown deep like the rivers.
I bathed in the Euphrates* when dawns were young.
I built my hut near the Congo** and it lulled me to sleep.
I looked upon the Nile and raised the pyramids above it.
I heard the singing of the Mississippi when Abe Lincoln went down to New Orleans,
and I've seen its muddy bosom turn all golden in the sunset.
I've known rivers:
Ancient, dusky rivers.
My soul has grown deep like the rivers.

Langston Hughes

*Euphrates: river flowing from Turkey to unite with the Tigris to make the Shatt-al-Arab
**Congo: Zaire river flowing from central Africa into the Atlantic

1. What is the meaning of dusky? _____

   _____

2. List the similes that the poet uses. _____

   _____

   _____

   _____

   _____

   _____

3. Write the examples of personification and their meanings. _____

   _____

   _____

   _____

   _____

4. Why does the poet refer to rivers in the Middle East, Africa, and the southern
   U.S. city of New Orleans? _____

   _____

   _____

   _____

5. What is the meaning that the poet is trying to convey? _____

   _____

   _____

   _____

Poem 2

UNTITLED (BEFORE 1891)

The nearest dream recedes, unrealized.
The heaven we chase
Like the June bee
Before the school-boy
Invites the race;
Stoops to an easy clover—
Dips—evades—teases—deploys;
Then to the royal clouds

(continued)

Lifts his light pinnace*
Heedless of the boy
Staring, bewildered, at the mocking sky.

Homesick for the steadfast honey,
Ah! the bee flies not
That brews that rare variety.

—Emily Dickinson

*pinnace: A ship's small boat

1. The entire poem is built upon a simile that likens dreams to what?

   _____

2. What figure of speech is "The heaven we chase," and what does it mean?

   _____

3. This poem presents a clear visual image. Describe the image in your own words.

   _____

   _____

4. Why is the boy "staring, bewildered, at the mocking sky. Homesick for the steadfast honey"? _____

   _____

5. In your own words, explain the meaning that the poet is trying to convey about dreams. _____

   _____

CLUES TO MAKING LOGICAL INFERENCES

Learning Objective 6

Use details and schemata to make inferences

Many types of text—not just advertising, humor, and poetry—demand that you read between the lines in order to understand the author's goals or meaning. You can make inferences based on facts, the voice of a narrator, descriptions, and actions.

Inferences Based on Facts

The way in which facts are juxtaposed can imply a certain message. For example, an author selected the following facts from issues of *Time* magazine and presented them consecutively to suggest an inference. No direct connection is stated, so the reader must thoughtfully reflect on the suggested message. This pause for thought adds power to the message.

EXAMPLE

28% Proportion of public libraries in the United States that offered Internet access in 1996

95% Proportion of libraries that offered Internet access in 2002

17% Increase in library attendance between 1996 and 2002
Inference: _____

EXPLANATION   The inference is that library attendance has improved because many more libraries have Internet access. Before libraries buy more computers, however, specific data on daily use should be collected.

EXERCISE 7.11

Making Inferences Based on Facts

1 billion   Number of birds killed by flying into glass windows in the United States each year

121 million   Number of birds killed annually by U.S. hunters

1. Inference: _____

_____

_____

_____

408   Species that could be extinct by 2050 if climate change trends continue

6.6 tons   Average amount of greenhouse gases emitted annually by each American, an increase of 3.4% since 1990

2. Inference: _____

_____

_____

_____

1   Rank of Super Bowl Sunday, among all the days of the year, in pizza sales at the major U.S. pizza chains

20%   Increase in frozen-pizza sales on Super Bowl Sunday

3. Inference: _____

_____

_____

—*Time* Magazine, March 1, 2004;
January 19, 2004; February 2, 2004.

Inferences Based on the Voice of a Speaker or Narrator

Read the following excerpt about children and see if you can guess who is complaining:

> Children now love luxury. They have bad manners, contempt for authority. They show disrespect for elders. They contradict their parents, chatter before company, cross their legs and tyrannize their teachers.[4]

Did you assume that this is a contemporary description of modern youth? Although it may sound that way, actually the Greek philosopher Plato attributed the quotation to his student and fellow philosopher, Socrates, who lived almost 2,500 years ago. Perhaps the only phrase in the excerpt that does not fit a modern speaker is the "cross their legs." The rest of the clues sound deceptively modern, leading readers to make an inappropriate assumption.

How can you tell whether an inference is valid or invalid? If an inference is appropriate or valid, it can be *supported by the clues within the passage*. The clues "add up," and the logic allows you to feel confident in making certain assumptions. On the other hand, an inappropriate or invalid inference goes beyond the evidence and may be an "off-the-wall" stab at meaning that was never suggested or intended.

Readers and listeners alike are constantly making inferences, and, as more information is revealed, self-correction is sometimes necessary. For example, as we listen to strangers talk, we make assumptions about their backgrounds, motives, and actions. Thus, dialogue is an especially fertile ground for observing how the active mind looks for hidden meaning.

EXERCISE 7.12

Inferences Based on Dialogue

Considering the facts presented in the passage, mark the inferences as *V* (valid) or *I* (invalid).

Passage 1

I'm eight years old. But I have the mind of a nineteen-year-old. Mom says it's making up for all the wrong Dad did. Today there's going to be a whole camera crew here. They're going to film different angles of me beating myself at chess. Then they want me to walk around the neighborhood in my Eagle Scout uniform. Dad doesn't want to talk to them. So I guess they'll do an exterior of the penitentiary.

—Matt Marinovich,
The Quarterly

_____ 1. A film is being shot about the child because he is so smart for his age.

_____ 2. The child is a boy.

_____ 3. The father was abusive to the mother and child.

---

[4]Suzy Platt, *Respectfully Quoted* (Washington, DC: Library of Congress, 1989), p. 42.

_____ 4. The child has been raised by his mother.

_____ 5. The father is in prison.

Passage 2

"Now how are we going to get across this monster?" Lisa asked.

"Easy," said John. "We take the rope over, get it around that big tree and use the winch to pull the Jeep across."

"But who swims the flood with the rope?"

"Well, I can't swim," he said, "but you're supposed to be so good at it."

—Anne Bernays and Pamela Painter,
What If?

_____ 1. John wants Lisa to swim with the rope across the water to attach it to the tree.

_____ 2. Water has flooded the path of the Jeep.

_____ 3. Lisa and John anticipated that they would be crossing water with the Jeep.

_____ 4. Lisa and John are driving on a mountain trail after a storm.

_____ 5. Lisa and John work together on a film crew.

Inferences Based on Action and Description

Reading would be rather dull if authors stated every idea, never giving you a chance to figure things out for yourself. For example, in a mystery novel, you carefully weigh each word, each action, each conversation, each description, and each fact in an effort to identify the villain and solve the crime before it is revealed at the end. Although textbook material may not have the Sherlock Holmes spirit of high adventure and suspense, authors use the same techniques to imply meaning.

Note the inferences in the following example.

EXAMPLE   **JOHNSON IN ACTION**

President Lyndon Johnson suffered from the inevitable comparison with his young and stylish predecessor. LBJ was acutely aware of his own lack of polish; he sought to surround himself with Kennedy advisers and insiders, hoping that their learning and sophistication would rub off on him. Johnson's assets were very real—an intimate knowledge of Congress, an incredible energy and determination to succeed, and a fierce ego. When a young marine officer tried to direct him to the proper helicopter, saying, "This one is yours," Johnson replied, "son, they are all my helicopters."

LBJ's height and intensity gave him a powerful presence; he dominated any room he entered, and he delighted in using his physical power of persuasion. One Texas politician explained why he had given in to Johnson: "Lyndon got me by the lapels and put his face on top of mine and he talked and talked and talked. I figured it was either getting drowned or joining."

—Robert A. Divine et al.,
America Past and Present

Considering the details presented in the passage, mark the inferences as *V* (valid) or *I* (invalid).

_____ 1. Johnson was haunted by the style and sophistication of John F. Kennedy.

_____ 2. Johnson could be both egotistical and arrogant about his presidential power.

_____ 3. Even if he did not mentally persuade people, Johnson could physically overwhelm them into agreement.

EXPLANATION   The answer to question 1 is *Valid*. He "suffered from the inevitable comparison," and he went so far as to retain the Kennedy advisers. Question 2 is *Valid*. The anecdote about the helicopters proves that. Question 3 is *Valid*. His delight in "using his physical powers of persuasion" and the anecdote about the Texas politician support that.

In the following exercises, you can see how authors use suggestions. From the clues given, you can deduce the facts.

EXERCISE 7.13

Inferences Based on Description of a Person

Looking back on the Revolutionary War, one cannot say enough about Washington's leadership. While his military skills proved less than brilliant and he and his generals lost many battles, George Washington was the single most important figure of the colonial war effort. His original appointment was partly political, for the rebellion that had started in Massachusetts needed a commander from the South to give geographic balance to the cause. The choice fell to Washington, a wealthy and respectable Virginia planter with military experience dating back to the French and Indian War. He had been denied a commission in the English army and had never forgiven the English for the insult. During the war he shared the physical suffering of his men, rarely wavered on important questions, and always used his officers to good advantage. His correspondence with Congress to ask for sorely needed supplies was tireless and forceful. He recruited several new armies in a row, as short-term enlistments gave out.

—Leonard Pitt,
We Americans

Mark the inferences as *V* (valid) or *I* (invalid).

_____ 1. The author regards George Washington as the most brilliant military genius in American history.

_____ 2. Washington resented the British for a past injustice.

_____ 3. The author believes that Washington's leadership was courageous and persistent even though not infallible.

EXERCISE 7.14

Inferences Based on Action

When he came to the surface he was conscious of little but the noisy water. Afterward he saw his companions in the sea. The oiler was ahead in the race. He was swimming strongly and rapidly. Off to the correspondent's left, the cook's great white and corked back bulged out of the water, and in the rear the captain was hanging with his one good hand to the keel of the overturned dinghy.

There is a certain immovable quality to a shore, and the correspondent wondered at it amid the confusion of the sea.

—Stephen Crane,
The Open Boat

Answer the following with *a, b, c,* or *d*. Draw a map indicating the shore and the positions of the four people in the water to help you visualize the scene.

_____ 1. The reason that the people are in the water is because of

      a. a swimming race.
      b. an airplane crash.
      c. a capsized boat.
      d. a group decision.

_____ 2. In relation to his companions, the correspondent is

      a. closest to the shore.
      b. the second or third closest to the shore.
      c. farthest from the shore.
      d. in a position that is impossible to determine.

_____ 3. The member of the group that had probably suffered a previous injury is the

      a. oiler.
      b. correspondent.
      c. cook.
      d. captain.

EXERCISE 7.15

Inferences Based on Description of a Place

Mexico, by many indicators, should be among the most prosperous nations on earth. It is a large country, occupying some 72 percent of the land of Middle America and containing 57 percent of the population of that area. It has benefited throughout its history from some of the richest mineral deposits on earth—first its silver in the colonial period and now its petroleum and natural gas. Mexico's proximity to the technologically advanced and wealthy United States is also a potential economic advantage of significance as are its varied agricultural landscapes, which range from irrigated deserts in the north to tropical rain forests in parts of the gulf coastal lowlands. To understand Mexico's limited economic achievement, we must evaluate the treatment of its people.

—David Clawson and Merrill Johnson,
World Regional Geography, 8th ed.

Answer the following with *T* (true) or *F* (false):

_____ 1. The author implies that Mexico has fallen short of its economic potential.

_____ 2. The author implies that Mexico's lag in economic achievement is due to the treatment of its people.

_____ 3. The author implies that profits from Mexico's silver, oil, and gas were exploited or stolen by other countries.

Inferences Based on Prior Knowledge

Just as a joke is funny only if you have the right background knowledge, college reading is easier if you have **prior knowledge** needed to grasp the details that are frequently implied rather than directly spelled out. For example, if a sentence began, "Previously wealthy investors were leaping from buildings in the financial district," you would know that the author was referring to the stock market crash of 1929 on Wall Street in New York City. The details fall into an already existing schema. Although the specifics are not directly stated, you have used prior knowledge and have "added up" the details to infer time and place.

Inferring Time and Place

EXERCISE 7.16

Read the following passages and indicate *a*, *b*, or *c* for the suggested time and place. Use your prior knowledge of "anchor dates" in history to logically think about the possible responses. If necessary, use reference materials to fill gaps in your schemata. As the Brain Booster, "Boost Brain Power Through Collaboration," below mentions, working with a small group can also help. Underline the clues that helped you arrive at your answers.

Passage 1

For disgruntled or abused women, divorce was sometimes available. Wives with grievances could sue for divorce in some colonies. For instance, although Puritan colonists preferred to keep couples together and often fined troublesome spouses or ordered them to "live happily together," they believed that some marriages could not be saved.

BRAIN BOOSTER

Boost Brain Power Through Collaboration

Instead of growing vicious claws or sharp teeth for survival, humans grew large brains. The problems associated with giving birth to babies with adult-size heads, however, necessitate long childhoods during which brains and heads can grow. Long childhoods require the protection of adults from predators and other dangers that might kill a child. Long ago, humans learned to band together for the safety of everyone. Relationships with other humans were (and are) vital to survival and learning. Living in a group resulted in the development of emotions and the ability to read the emotions of others. What does this have to do with succeeding in college? Working cooperatively with other students and your professors is advantageous to you and everyone in your class. Embrace it!

As you do exercises that require making inferences, you are likely to see the importance of background knowledge. If you find your schemata lacking, work with a partner or two to pool your knowledge for the benefit of all.

Adapted from Brain Rules: 12 Principles
for Surviving and Thriving at Work, Home, and School
by John Medina

Because Puritans viewed marriage as a legal contract rather than a religious sacrament, if one party violated the terms of a marital contract the marriage could be dissolved.

—Glenda Riley,
Inventing the American Woman: An Inclusive History,
3rd ed., Vol. 1: To 1877

_____ 1. The time period that this passage refers to is probably

    a. the 1600s to 1700s.
    b. the 1800s to 1900s.
    c. the 1900s to 2000s.

_____ 2. The part of colonial America discussed here is likely

    a. uncolonized territory in the west.
    b. the northeast.
    c. the southern colonies.

    3. Underline the clues to your answers.

Passage 2

Families at dinner were startled by the sudden gleam of bayonets in the doorway and rose up to be driven with blows and oaths along the weary miles to the stockade. Men were seized in their fields or going along the road, women were taken from their wheels and children from their play. In many cases, on turning for one last look as they crossed the ridge, they saw their homes in flames, fired by the lawless rabble that followed on the heels of the soldiers to loot and pillage. So keen were these outlaws on the scent that in some instances they were driving off the cattle and other stock of the Indians almost before the soldiers had fairly started their owners in the other direction. Systematic hunts were made by the same men for Indian graves, to rob them of the silver pendants and other valuables deposited with the dead. A volunteer, afterward a colonel in the Confederate service, said: "I fought through the Civil War and have seen men shot to pieces and slaughtered by thousands, but the Cherokee removal was the cruelest work I ever knew."

—James Mooney,
Myths of the Cherokee, 19th Annual Report,
Bureau of American Ethnology

_____ 4. The time period discussed is probably

    a. the 1600s.
    b. the 1700s.
    c. the 1800s.

_____ 5. The place is most likely

    a. the Great Lakes region of the United States.
    b. the southeastern United States.
    c. the Texas-Mexican border.

    6. Underline the clues to your answers.

Passage 3

As unskilled workers, most found employment in the low-status, manual-labor jobs in the factories, mines, needle trades, and construction. At that time, workers had no voice in working conditions, for labor unions had not yet become effective. The 84-hour workweek (14 hours per day, 6 days per week) for low wages was common. Jobs offered no paid vacations, sick pay, or pension plans. Child labor was commonplace, and entire families often worked to provide a subsistence-level family income. Lighting, ventilation, and heating were poor. In the factories, moving parts of machinery were dangerously exposed, leading to numerous horrific accidents. There was no workers' compensation, although many laborers were injured on the job. A worker who objected was likely to be fired and blacklisted. Exploited by the captains of industry, the immigrants became deeply involved in the labor-union movement, so much so that to tell the story of one without the other is virtually impossible.

—Vincent N. Parrillo,
Strangers to These Shores: Race and Ethnic Relations in the United States with Research Navigator, 8th ed. © 2006. Printed and electronically reproduced by permission of Pearson Education, Inc., Upper Saddle River, NJ.

_____ 7. The time period discussed is probably

     a. the late 1600s.
     b. the late 1700s.
     c. the late 1800s.

_____ 8. The place is probably

     a. California.
     b. New York.
     c. Mississippi.

     9. Underline the clues to your answers.

Expanding Prior Knowledge

Your responses to questions regarding the previous passages depended on your previous knowledge of history and your general knowledge. If you did not understand many of the inferences, you might ask, "How can I expand my prior knowledge?" The answer is not an easy formula or a quick fix. The answer is part of the reason that you are in college; it is a combination of broadening your horizons, reading more widely, and being an active participant in your own life. Expanding prior knowledge is a slow and steady daily process.

Reader's TIP Making Inferences

- Consider the attitude implied in the author's choice of words.
- Think about what might have been left out.
- Unravel actions.
- Interpret motives.
- Use suggested meaning and facts to make assumptions.
- Draw on prior knowledge to make connections.
- Base conclusions on stated ideas and unstated assumptions.

DRAWING CONCLUSIONS

Learning Objective 7

Draw logical conclusions while reading

To arrive at a **conclusion,** you must make a logical deduction from both stated ideas and unstated assumptions. Drawing conclusions is much like making inferences, but it extends thinking a step further. Using hints as well as facts, you rely on prior knowledge and experience to interpret motives, actions, and outcomes. You draw conclusions on the basis of perceived evidence, but because perceptions differ, conclusions can vary from reader to reader. Generally, however, authors attempt to direct readers to preconceived conclusions. Read the following example and look for a basis for the stated conclusion.

EXAMPLE   **UNDERGROUND CONDUCTOR**

Harriet Tubman was on a northbound train when she overheard her name spoken by a white passenger. He was reading aloud an ad which accused her of stealing $50,000 worth of property in slaves, and which offered a $5,000 reward for her capture. She lowered her head so that the sunbonnet she was wearing hid her face. At the next station she slipped off the train and boarded another that was headed south, reasoning that no one would pay attention to a black woman traveling in that direction. She deserted the second train near her hometown in Maryland and bought two chickens as part of her disguise. With her back hunched over in imitation of an old woman, she drove the chickens down the dusty road, calling angrily and chasing them with her stick whenever she sensed danger. In this manner Harriet Tubman was passed by her former owner who did not even notice her. The reward continued to mount until it reached $40,000.

—Leonard Pitt,
We Americans

Conclusion: Harriet Tubman was a clever woman who became a severe irritant to white slave owners.

What is the basis for this conclusion?

_____

_____

EXPLANATION   Harriet Tubman's disguise and subsequent escape from the train station provide evidence of her intelligence and resourcefulness. The escalating amount of the reward, which eventually reached $40,000, proves the severity of the sentiment against her.

EXERCISE 7.17   ## Drawing Conclusions

Read the following passages. For the first passage, indicate evidence for the conclusion that has been drawn. For the latter passages, write your own conclusion and also indicate supporting evidence. Use the suggestions in the Reader's Tip, "Making Inferences," on the previous page.

Passage 1

Albert Einstein did not begin to talk until he was three years old, and he wasn't entirely fluent even by the time he was nine. His language skills were so poor that his parents seriously worried that he might be mentally retarded! Nevertheless, he eventually learned to speak not only his native German, but also French and English. However, he mixed German with his French, and he had a strong accent. His English, learned later in life, never became fluent—as countless satirists have noted, he made grammatical mistakes and had a heavy German accent.

—Stephen M. Kosslyn and Robin S. Rosenberg,
Psychology: The Brain, the Person, the World, 2nd ed.

Conclusion: Einstein's language skills were not an accurate reflection of his true intelligence.

What is the basis for this conclusion? _____

_____

_____

_____

Passage 2

In Massachusetts, Nicola Sacco and Bartolomeo Vanzetti—an immigrant shoe-factory worker and a poor fish peddler—were charged with and convicted of robbery and murder in 1920. The prosecutor insulted immigrant Italian defense witnesses and appealed to the prejudices of a bigoted judge and jury. Despite someone else's later confession and other potentially exonerating evidence, their seven-year appeals fight failed to win them retrial or acquittal. They were executed in 1927. At his sentencing in 1927, Vanzetti addressed presiding judge Webster Thayer. At one point in his moving speech, he said,

"I would not wish to a dog or a snake, to the most low and misfortunate creature of the earth—I would not wish to any of them what I have had to suffer for the things that I am not guilty of. . . . I have suffered because I was an Italian, and indeed I am an Italian."

—Vincent N. Parrillo,
Strangers to These Shores: Race and Ethnic Relations in the United States with Research Navigator, 8th ed. © 2006. Printed and electronically reproduced by permission of Pearson Education, Inc., Upper Saddle River, NJ.

Conclusion: _____

_____

_____

What is the basis for this conclusion? _____

_____

_____

_____

_____

Passage 3

Many Irish were single women taking jobs as domestics or nannies for the native-born urban elite. In 1800, there was 1 domestic servant for every 20 families, but by 1840, the ratio had dropped to 1 servant for every 10 families. Unmarried Irish (and Scandinavian) young women often came first and worked in U.S. homes. Their daily typical workload was 16 hours of cooking, cleaning, tending to the children, and nursing the sick, six days a week. With little time to themselves, these women saved their earnings for passage money for other family members. Records from the Boston Society for the Prevention of Pauperism offer one illustration of the difficulties women had seeking jobs in a household compared to men finding work in labor gangs. Between 1845 and 1850, it received employment applications from 14,000 female foreigners in contrast to 5,034 male applications.

—Vincent N. Parrillo,
Strangers to These Shores: Race and Ethnic Relations in the United States with Research Navigator, 8th ed. © 2006. Printed and electronically reproduced by permission of Pearson Education, Inc., Upper Saddle River, NJ.

Conclusion: _____

_____

_____

What is the basis for this conclusion? _____

_____

_____

_____

EXERCISE 7.18

Building a Story Based on Inferences

The following well-known story unfolds as the reader uses the clues to predict the final outcome and make inferences about the relationships among the characters. The author never directly tells the reader how Mrs. Mallard feels about her marriage but, instead, leaves many hints. Like a mystery, the story is fun to read because the reader is actively involved. Use your inferential skills to figure it out.

THE STORY OF AN HOUR

Knowing that Mrs. Mallard was afflicted with a heart trouble, great care was taken to break to her as gently as possible the news of her husband's death.

It was her sister Josephine who told her, in broken sentences, veiled hints that revealed in half concealing. Her husband's friend Richards was there, too, near her. It was he who had been in the newspaper office when intelligence of the railroad disaster was received, with Brently Mallard's name leading the list of "killed." He had only taken the time to assure himself of its truth by a second telegram, and had hastened to forestall any less careful, less tender friend in bearing the sad message.

She did not hear the story as many women have heard the same, with a paralyzed inability to accept its significance. She wept at once, with sudden, wild abandonment, in her sister's arms. When the storm of grief had spent itself she went away to her room alone. She would have no one follow her.

There stood, facing the open window, a comfortable, roomy armchair. Into this she sank, pressed down by a physical exhaustion that haunted her body and seemed to reach into her soul.

She could see in the open square before her house the tops of trees that were all aquiver with the new spring life. The delicious breath of rain was in the air. In the street below a peddler was crying his wares. The notes of a distant song which someone was singing reached her faintly, and countless sparrows were twittering in the eaves.

There were patches of blue sky showing here and there through the clouds that had met and piled one above the other in the west facing her window.

She sat with her head thrown back upon the cushion of the chair, quite motionless, except when a sob came up into her throat and shook her, as a child who has cried itself to sleep continues to sob in its dreams.

She was young, with a fair, calm face, whose lines bespoke repression and even a certain strength. But now there was a dull stare in her eyes, whose gaze was fixed away off yonder on one of those patches of blue sky. It was not a glance of reflection, but rather indicated a suspension of intelligent thought.

There was something coming to her and she was waiting for it, fearfully. What was it? She did not know; it was too subtle and elusive to name. But she felt it, creeping out of the sky, reaching toward her through the sounds, the scents, the color that filled the air.

Now her bosom rose and fell tumultuously. She was beginning to recognize this thing that was approaching to possess her, and she was striving to beat it back with her will—as powerless as her two white slender hands would have been.

When she abandoned herself a little whispered word escaped her slightly parted lips. She said it over and over her breath: "Free, free, free!" The vacant stare and the look of terror that had followed it went from her eyes. They stayed keen and bright. Her pulses beat fast, and the coursing blood warmed and relaxed every inch of her body.

She did not stop to ask if it were not a monstrous joy that held her. A clear and exalted perception enabled her to dismiss the suggestion as trivial.

She knew that she would weep again when she saw the kind, tender hands folded in death; the face that had never looked save with love upon her, fixed and gray and dead. But she saw beyond that bitter moment a long procession of years to come that would belong to her absolutely. And she opened and spread her arms out to them in welcome.

There would be no one to live for during those coming years; she would live for herself. There would be no powerful will bending her in that blind persistence with which men and women believe they have a right to impose a private will upon a fellow creature. A kind intention or a cruel intention made the act seem no less a crime as she looked upon it in that brief moment of illumination.

And yet she had loved him—sometimes. Often she had not. What did it matter! What could love, the unsolved mystery, count for in face of this possession of self-assertion which she suddenly recognized as the strongest impulse of her being.

"Free! Body and soul free!" she kept whispering.

Josephine was kneeling before the closed door with her lips to the keyhole, imploring for admission. "Louise, open the door! I beg; open the door—you will make yourself ill. What are you doing, Louise? For heaven's sake open the door."

"Go away. I am not making myself ill." No; she was drinking in a very elixir of life through that open window.

Her fancy was running riot along those days ahead of her. Spring days, and summer days, and all sorts of days that would be her own. She breathed a quick prayer that life might be long. It was only yesterday she had thought with a shudder that life might be long.

She arose at length and opened the door to her sister's importunities. There was a feverish triumph in her eyes, and she carried herself unwittingly like a goddess of Victory. She clasped her sister's waist, and together they descended the stairs. Richards stood waiting for them at the bottom.

Someone was opening the front door with a latchkey. It was Brently Mallard who entered, a little travel-stained, composedly carrying his gripsack and umbrella. He had been far from the scene of the accident, and did not even know there had been one. He stood amazed at Josephine's piercing cry; at Richards' quick motion to screen him from the view of his wife.

But Richards was too late.

When the doctors came they said she had died of heart disease—of joy that kills.

—Kate Chopin

1. How did Mrs. Mallard's response to the news of her husband's death change during the story? _____

_____

_____

_____

_____

2. What does the author suggest about Richards's feelings for Mrs. Mallard? Underline the clues. _____

_____

_____

_____

3. Did you predict the real fate of Brently Mallard? What hints did the author provide? _____

_____

_____

4. What was the real cause of Mrs. Mallard's death? _____

_____

5. What is the irony in the use of the phrases "a heart trouble" at the beginning of the story, and "heart disease" as the cause of her death at the end of the story?

_____

_____

SUMMARY POINTS

1 What is the definition of *inference*? (page 342)
- In reading, an inference is an interpretation or understanding based on known facts or evidence. Making an inference is sometimes referred to as "reading between the lines" because inferences are not directly stated but must be deduced from details provided by the author and the prior knowledge of the reader.

2 How can I make reasonable inferences while reading? (page 344)
- Notice the clues that the author provides in details such as word choice and information. Combine the details with your own schemata to understand the author's meaning.

3 How can I recognize connotative language? (page 346)
- Connotative language communicates an attitude or an emotional overtone that can be positive or negative without actually stating it directly. Watch for emotional language. To see the contrast, think of other words that communicate a different point of view or that convey no opinions.

4 How can I recognize euphemisms and politically correct language? (page 349)
- Be alert to words or phrases that substitute a softer, more polite, or indirect term for a harsh, unpleasant, or uncomfortable one.
- When reading about controversial ideas, people, or events, notice wording that hides unpleasantness or that seeks to avoid offending any person or group.

5 How can I interpret figurative language? (page 349)
- Become familiar with the common forms of figurative language: idioms, similes, metaphors, hyperbole, personification, and verbal irony.
- Remember that figurative language is not meant to be understood literally. Instead, it provides a more interesting or subtle way of expressing an idea than a direct statement can provide.

6 How do clues and prior knowledge contribute to reasonable inferences? (page 356)
  - Details in the text, such as facts, information about a speaker or narrator, actions of a character or descriptions of a person or place, point the reader to logical inferences.
  - The reader's existing schemata lend meaning to clues in the text, and together they lead to logical inferences. Students can expand their prior knowledge by reading widely and participating in a broad range of activities.

7 How can I draw logical conclusions while reading? (page 365)
  - Drawing logical conclusions depends on using details provided by the author, one's own schemata, and recognizing assumptions made by the author. A conclusion goes a step further than an inference in that readers might arrive at different conclusions, depending on their own opinions and backgrounds. Like inferences, though, a logical conclusion must still be based on a reasonable interpretation of the author's message.

| SELECTION 1 | Short Story | MyReadingLab |

Visit Chapter 7: Inference in MyReadingLab to complete the chapter activities and the Build Background Knowledge video activity.

P REVIEW the next selection to predict its purpose and organization and to formulate your learning plan.

Activate Schemata

What do you expect from a short story?
What kind of security do hotels usually have?

Establish a Purpose for Reading

Short stories entertain, so read to enjoy and predict the outcome.

Build Background Knowledge — VIDEO

Convicted Con Artist Reveals How He Scammed Others

To prepare for reading Selection 1, answer the questions below. Then, watch this video on scam artists and their victims.

What are some scams that you have experienced or heard of from other people?

What role has technology played in modern-day scams?

Why do you think so many people fall victim to scam artists?

This video helped me: _____

_____

_____

Increase Word Knowledge

What do you know about these words?

| genteel | indigo | retreated | diffused | purity |
| cascading | insinuating | sanatorium | scurrying | swag |

Your instructor may give a brief vocabulary review before or after reading.

Integrate Knowledge While Reading

Inference questions have been inserted in the margin to stimulate your thinking and help you read between the lines. Remember to

Predict   Picture   Relate   Monitor   Correct   Annotate

A DIP IN THE POOLE

Why was the narrator watching Mr. Stuyvesant?

I was sitting in a heavy baroque chair in the Hotel Poole's genteel lobby, leafing through one of the plastic-encased magazines provided by the management, when the girl in the dark tweed suit picked Andrew J. Stuyvesant's pockets.

5 She worked it very nicely. Stuyvesant—a silver-haired old gentleman who carried a malacca walking stick and had fifteen or twenty million dollars in Texas oil—had just stepped out of one of the chrome-and-walnut elevators directly in front of me. The girl appeared from the direction of the curving marble staircase, walking rapidly and with elaborate preoccupation, and collided with him. She excused herself. Bowing in a gallant way, Stuyvesant allowed as how it was perfectly all right, 10 my dear. She got his wallet and the diamond stickpin from his tie, and he neither felt nor suspected a thing.

The girl apologized again and then hurried off across the padded indigo carpeting toward the main entrance at the lobby's opposite end, slipping the items into a tan suede bag she carried over one arm. Almost immediately, I was out of my chair and moving 15 after her. She managed to thread her way through the potted plants and the dark furnishings to within a few steps of the double-glass doors before I caught up with her.

I let my hand fall on her arm. "Excuse me just a moment," I said, smiling.

She stiffened. Then she turned and regarded me as if I had crawled out from one of the potted plants. "I beg your pardon?" she said in frosty voice.

20 "You and I had best have a little chat."

"I am not in the habit of chatting with strange men."

"I think you'll make an exception in my case."

Her brown eyes flashed angrily as she said, "I suggest you let go of my arm. If you don't, I shall call the manager."

25 I shrugged. "There's no need for that."

"I certainly hope not."

"Simply because he would only call me."

"What?"

"I'm chief of security at the Hotel Poole, you see," I told her. "What was once 30 referred to as the house detective."

She grew pale, and the light dimmed in her eyes. "Oh," she said.

I steered her toward the arched entrance to the hotel's lounge, a short distance on our left. She offered no resistance. Once inside, I sat her down in one of the leather booths and then seated myself opposite. A blue-uniformed waiter approached, but I 35 shook my head and he retreated.

I examined the girl across the polished surface of the table. The diffused orange glow from the small lantern in its center gave her classic features the impression of purity and innocence, and turned her seal-brown hair into a cascading black wave.

Trinity Mirror/Mirrorpix/Alamy

I judged her age at about twenty-five. I said, "Without a doubt, you're the most
40 beautiful dip I've ever encountered."

"I . . . don't know what you're talking about."

"Don't you?"

"Certainly not."

"A dip is underworld slang for a pickpocket."

45 She tried to affect indignation. "Are you insinuating that *I* . . .?"

"Oh come on," I said. "I saw you lift Mr. Stuyvesant's wallet and his diamond
stickpin. I was sitting directly opposite the elevator, not fifteen feet away."

She didn't say anything. Her fingers toyed with the catch on the tan suede bag.
After a moment, her eyes lifted to mine, briefly, and then dropped again to the bag.
50 She sighed in a tortured way. "You're right, of course. I stole those things."

I reached out, took the bag from her and snapped it open. Stuyvesant's wallet,
with the needle-point of the stickpin now imbedded in the leather, lay on top of the
various feminine articles inside. I removed them, glanced at her identification long
enough to memorize her name and address, reclosed the bag and returned it to her.

Why did he memorize this information?

55 She said softly, "I'm . . . not a thief, I want you to know that. Not really, I mean."
She took her lower lip between her teeth. "I have this . . . *compulsion* to steal. I'm
powerless to stop myself."

"Kleptomania?"

"Yes. I've been to three different psychiatrists during the past year, but they've
60 been unable to cure me."

I shook my head sympathetically. "It must be terrible for you."

"Terrible," she agreed. "When . . . when my father learns of this episode, he'll
have me put into a sanatorium." Her voice quavered. "He threatened to do just that
if I ever stole anything again, and he doesn't make idle threats."

65 I studied her. Presently, I said, "Your father doesn't have to know what happened here today."

"He . . . he doesn't?"

"No," I said slowly. "There was no real harm done, actually. Mr. Stuyvesant will get his wallet and stickpin back. And I see no reason for causing the hotel undue
70 embarrassment through the attendant publicity if I report the incident."

Her face brightened. "Then . . . you're going to let me go?"

I drew a long breath. "I suppose I'm too soft-hearted for the type of position that I have. Yes, I'm going to let you go. But you have to promise me that you'll never set foot inside the Hotel Poole again."

75 "Oh, I promise!"

"If I see you here in the future, I'll have to report you to the police."

"You won't!" she assured me eagerly. "I . . . have an appointment with another psychiatrist tomorrow morning. I feel sure he can help me."

I nodded. "Very well, then." I turned to stare through the arched lounge
80 entrance at the guests and uniformed bellboys scurrying back and forth in the lobby. When I turned back again, the street door to the lounge was just closing and the girl was gone.

I sat there for a short time, thinking about her. If she was a kleptomaniac, I reflected, then I was Mary, Queen of Scots. What she was, of course, was an accom-
85 plished professional pickpocket—her technique was much too polished, her hands much too skilled—and an extremely adept liar.

I smiled to myself, and stood and went out into the lobby again. But instead of resuming my position in the baroque chair before the elevator bank, or approaching the horseshoe-shaped desk, I veered left to walk casually through the entrance doors
90 and out to Powell Street.

As I made my way through the thickening late-afternoon crowds—my right hand resting on the fat leather wallet and the diamond stickpin in my coat pocket— I found myself feeling a little sorry for the girl. But only just a little.

After all, Andrew J. Stuyvesant had been *my* mark from the moment I first
95 noticed him entering the Hotel Poole that morning—and after a three-hour vigil I had been within fifteen seconds of dipping him myself when she appeared virtually out of nowhere.

Wouldn't you say I was entitled to the swag?

(1,130 words)

—Bill Pronzini

What is the significance of the story's title?

How is this ending ironic?

Recall

Stop to self-test, relate, and react.

Your instructor may choose to give you a brief comprehension review.

THINK CRITICALLY ABOUT THE SELECTION

Look back at the story for clues to the ending.

What prior knowledge might have made you suspicious of the narrator—a movie that you have seen, a book that you have read, or perhaps another short story?

What do you think is the time setting of the story? Could it take place in the present day? Explain the basis for your answers.

WRITE ABOUT THE SELECTION

When did you figure out the ending? Was the ending predictable? How did the author manipulate and entertain you?

Response Suggestion: Evaluate the craft of this short story. How is the author a master of the format? What structural factors contributed to your enjoyment?

SKILL DEVELOPMENT: IMPLIED MEANING

According to the implied meaning in the selection, answer the following items with *T* (true) or *F* (false):

_____ 1. The reader can logically conclude that *swag* is most likely loot acquired by unlawful means.

_____ 2. When the man says, "Excuse me just a moment" to the female pickpocket, she looks at him with admiration.

_____ 3. The woman admits her guilt to the thief because she wants help for her kleptomania.

_____ 4. The man lets the woman pickpocket go because he is too soft-hearted.

_____ 5. The man implies that Mary, Queen of Scots, was also a kleptomaniac.

CHECK YOUR COMPREHENSION

Answer the following items with *a, b, c,* or *d.* To help you analyze your strengths and weaknesses, the question types are indicated.

Main Idea ———— 1. Which is the best statement of the main idea of this selection?

    a. A life of crime has many risks.

    b. Lying can get you both into and out of jams.

    c. Criminals deceive by presenting themselves as law enforcement agents.

    d. A thief is cheated by another clever thief.

Inference ———— 2. The reader can conclude that the man sitting in the hotel lobby chair thinks that the woman pickpocket is

    a. somewhat inexperienced.

    b. unattractive.

    c. extremely skilled.

    d. quite polite.

Inference ———— 3. When the man catches up with the woman pickpocket at the hotel doors, he speaks to her in

    a. an evil way.

    b. an official manner.

    c. a joking voice.

    d. an icy fashion.

Inference ———— 4. The narrator does not want the woman to ever return to the hotel because

    a. he wants the territory for himself.

    b. he wants to protect the hotel.

    c. he does not want her to get caught.

    d. she is a kleptomaniac and needs treatment.

Inference ———— 5. The reader can conclude that the "light dimmed in her eyes" when the woman pickpocket realizes that

    a. the man wants the wallet she stole.

    b. the man is extremely angry with her.

    c. her father will be angry that she has stolen again.

    d. she has been caught in the act.

Inference ———— 6. The narrator would describe the actual concern experienced by the woman's father as

    a. sympathetic.

    b. nonexistent.

    c. therapeutic.

    d. threatening.

Inference _____ 7. The ending to this story indicates that when the man says earlier in the story, "It must be terrible for you," he was

    a. insincere.
    b. concerned.
    c. annoyed.
    d. troubled.

Inference _____ 8. By saying she has "an appointment with another psychiatrist tomorrow morning," the reader can conclude that the woman is

    a. finally ready to get help.
    b. following her father's orders.
    c. making up a story.
    d. planning another crime.

Inference _____ 9. The reader can infer from the phrase, "the thickening late-afternoon crowds," that people are

    a. walking too slowly.
    b. just getting off work.
    c. out enjoying the weather.
    d. arriving at the hotel.

Inference _____ 10. The narrator's description of his sitting in the hotel lobby reveals that he is very

    a. patient.
    b. brave.
    c. sincere.
    d. talkative.

Answer the following with *T* (true) or *F* (false):

Detail _____ 11. The narrator suggests that he will use physical force if the woman pickpocket will not confess to her crime.

Inference _____ 12. The woman finally realizes that the narrator is a thief.

Author's Purpose _____ 13. The author's purpose is to caution readers to be watchful for thieves.

Inference _____ 14. The reader can conclude that the narrator memorized the woman's name and address so that he can later report her to the hotel.

Inference _____ 15. The story title is a humorous play on words.

BUILD YOUR VOCABULARY

According to the way the italicized word was used in the selection, select *a*, *b*, *c*, or *d* for the word or phrase that gives the best definition. The number in parentheses indicates the line of the passage in which the word is located. Use a dictionary in addition to the context clues to more precisely define the terms.

_____ 1. *"genteel* lobby" (1)
    a. formal
    b. run-down
    c. tacky
    d. gentle

_____ 2. *"indigo* carpeting" (12)
    a. thick
    b. blue
    c. antique
    d. new

_____ 3. "he *retreated*" (35)
    a. withdrew
    b. hid
    c. sat in another booth
    d. returned to the kitchen

_____ 4. *"diffused* orange glow"
    (36)
    a. pretty
    b. bright
    c. small
    d. scattered

_____ 5. "impression of *purity*"
    (37)
    a. harshness
    b. blandness
    c. innocence
    d. dimness

_____ 6. *"cascading* black wave"
    (38)
    a. increasing
    b. swimming
    c. falling
    d. wet

_____ 7. *"insinuating* that" (45)
    a. lying
    b. flirting
    c. hoping
    d. suggesting

_____ 8. "into a *sanatorium*" (63)
    a. health spa
    b. hospital
    c. condo
    d. convent

_____ 9. *"scurrying* back" (80)
    a. rushing
    b. walking
    c. skating
    d. looking

_____ 10. "the *swag*" (98)
    a. a depression in the
       earth
    b. profits
    c. satisfaction
    d. sway

Concept Prep for Philosophy and Literature

A Sampling of Careers for Philosophy and Literature Majors

A degree in philosophy develops analytical and critical thinking skills, which are useful in many careers.

- Business
- Journalism
- Law
- Education
- Public relations
- Religion

Likewise, a degree in literature serves as the foundation needed for a variety of careers (see page 274).

The ancient Greeks laid the foundations for Western traditions in science, philosophy, literature, and the arts. They set the standards for proportion and beauty in art and architecture, and we continue to ponder their questions about the good life, the duties of a citizen, and the nature of the universe.

Who were the most notable Greek philosophers?

- One of the most notable Greek philosophers was *Socrates,* the teacher of Plato. Socrates sought an understanding of the world while other teachers of the time taught students how to get along in the world. Socrates proclaimed himself to be the wisest of all the thinkers because he knew how little he knew. He used a method of teaching that explored a subject from all sides, with questions and answers, as opposed to the lecture method. Today, this teaching technique is known as the *Socratic method.* Socrates took no pay for his teachings. As an old man, he was condemned to death by the citizens of Athens, who claimed that he denied the gods and corrupted the youth. More likely, however, Socrates was a natural target for enemies and was made the scapegoat for the city's military defeat. As ordered, Socrates drank the poison hemlock and died. He left behind no written works, but his pupil Plato later immortalized Socrates's lively discussions in his own works.

- *Plato* is often considered the most important figure in Western philosophy. Without him, the thoughts of Socrates and previous philosophers might not have been recorded. Plato used a dialogue format to explore many subjects, such as ethics and politics. He founded a school in Athens called the Academy and became the teacher of Aristotle.

In Raphael's painting, *School of Athens,* Plato and Aristotle converse.

School of Athens (Detail) (1511), Raphael. Stanza della Segnatura, Vatican Palace.

Erich Lessing/Art Resource, NY

- *Aristotle* was a disciple of Plato and then broke away to develop his own philosophy and school, called the Lyceum. He wrote on virtually every subject and laid the foundation for analytical reasoning and logic. He was the tutor of Alexander the Great. In the political unrest following Alexander's death, Aristotle remembered the fate of Socrates and fled Athens to escape prosecution.

What are literary genres?

Over hundreds of years, certain stories, essays, and poems have remained timeless in their appeal and relevance to human life. These works are considered *literature*, the art form of language. As you read a piece of literature, you are allowed inside the minds of characters, and you feel what they feel. You learn about life as the characters live it or as the poet entices you to feel it. After reading, you are enriched, as well as entertained. As defined in most college courses, literature includes four categories, or *genres*: poetry, drama, fiction, and essays.

Poetry

Poetry has its roots in the pleasure of rhythm, repetition, and sound. Before the written word, rhythm and repetition were used to help people organize and recall episodes in history. Poetry was danced, chanted, and performed with the whole body in tribal cultures as a way of keeping cultural truths alive. In the *Odyssey,* an ancient Greek epic written by *Homer* that recounts the adventures of Odysseus during his return from the war in Troy to his home on a Greek island, the rhyme format made the epic easier to remember. Thus, the poem became a vehicle for preserving the lore of the sea, warfare, and Greek mythology.

Poetry appeals to the senses, offering strong visual images and suggestive symbolism to enhance pleasure. *Lyric* poems are brief and emotional, *narrative* poems tell a story with plot and characters, *dramatic* poems use dialogue to express emotional conflict, and *epic* poems tell a long narrative with a central hero of historical significance.

Drama

The origins of *drama* lie in religious ceremonies in ancient Greece, where masters of Greek drama competed for prizes. Without movies or television, the ancient Greeks created plays for religious instruction and for entertainment. These dramatic performances eventually evolved into the categories of comedy, tragedy, and romantic tragedy.

Plays are narratives and thus contain all of the literary elements of short stories and novels. As in works of fiction, the main character in a play is sometimes called a *protagonist*, from the Greek word for "first actor." The character who is trying to move against or harm the main character is called the *antagonist* (from the prefix *anti-*).

Plays are written to be performed rather than read. The actors interpret the actions for the audience, and a single play can seem vastly different, depending on which production company performs it. After hundreds of years, the plays of *William Shakespeare* are still relevant to the human condition; they entertained audiences in England in the late 1500s, on the American frontier in the mid-1800s, and both on stages and in movie theaters in the 2000s.

Fiction

Fiction creates an illusion of reality in order to share an experience and communicate universal truths about the human condition. Each work of fiction is subject to interpretation on many different levels. Short stories and novels are written to entertain by engaging you in the life of another human being.

- A *short story* is a brief work of fiction ranging from 500 to 15,000 words. It is a narrative with a beginning, middle, and end that tells a sequence of events. The *plot* of the story involves *characters* in one or more *conflicts*. As the conflict intensifies, the *suspense* rises to a *climax,* or turning point, which is followed by the *denouement,* or unraveling. Then the action falls for a *resolution*. Because the short story is brief and carefully crafted, some literary experts recommend reading a short story three times: first to enjoy the plot, second to recognize the elements, and third to appreciate how the elements work together to support the theme. Setting, point of view, tone, and symbolism all contribute to this appreciation.

- The *novel* is an extended fictional work that has all of the elements of a short story. Because of its length, a novel usually has more characters and more conflicts than a short story.

The essay

An *essay* is a short work of nonfiction that discusses a specific topic. Much of your own college writing will follow an essay format. The *title* of an essay suggests the contents, the *thesis* is usually stated in the *introduction*, the *body* provides evidence to prove the thesis, and the *conclusion* summarizes in a manner to provoke further thought.

REVIEW QUESTIONS

After studying the material, answer the following questions:

1. What is the Socratic method of teaching? _____

    _____

2. For what underlying reason was Socrates forced to drink poison? _____

    _____

    _____

3. Why was Plato particularly important to the teachings of Socrates? _____

    _____

4. What acronym might you devise to remind you of the chronological order of the lives of the three famous philosophers? _____

    _____

5. What was a significant contribution of Aristotle? _____

    _____

6. What is a literary genre? _____

    _____

7. What was the original purpose of drama? _____

    _____

8. What was the purpose of the *Odyssey*? _____

    _____

9. Which genre is most frequently written by college students in the classroom setting? _____

10. What is the typical relationship between the protagonist and the antagonist?

    _____

    _____

Your instructor may choose to give a brief review of these philosophy and literature concepts.

Philosophy   MyReadingLab

Visit Chapter 7: Inference in MyReadingLab to complete the Selection 2 activities and the Build Background Knowledge video activity.

P REVIEW the next selection to predict its purpose and organization and to formulate your learning plan.

Activate Schemata

What is a myth?
Do you remember hearing or reading myths about Roman and Greek gods?
How do individuals and cultures make sense of things they don't understand?

Establish a Purpose for Reading

Read the selection to learn about the importance of myths and how an ancient Native American culture explained life and death.

Build Background Knowledge — VIDEO

Myth vs. Reality

To prepare for reading Selection 2, answer the questions below. Then, watch this video that covers a heated spiritual debate.

How can you tell the difference between a myth and reality?

Why do you think some people believe in myths without having scientific proof that the myth is true?

Besides scientific proof, what other ways can we prove that a myth is true?

This video helped me: _____

_____

_____

Increase Word Knowledge

What do you know about these words?

abstraction	primal	bard's	incongruities	stamp
ruses	unscrupulousness	antagonists	protagonists'	propensity

Your instructor may give a brief vocabulary review before or after reading.

Integrate Knowledge While Reading

Questions have been inserted in the margin to stimulate your thinking while reading. Remember to

Predict   Picture   Relate   Monitor   Correct   Annotate

COYOTE

OUR STORIES AS MYTHS

From the most ancient times to the modern day, people have created myths. Here, we are using the word in the positive sense, as a story that presents in narrative form the basic beliefs and values of people. Your own life-story as remembered and told by yourself, your own personal myth, does the same for you individually. When a myth,
5 then, tells about the creation of the world, the first humans, the foundation of a nation, and the lives of the gods and heroes whom it honors, what it does is tell stories that explain who we—our country, our culture, our religion, ourselves—are now. They may not be accurate in every detail—indeed, much may be read back into the story— but they speak of what is really important to us now. That is why such stories should
10 not be thought of as science or history in the modern sense, but as self-understanding.

What would your story say about your values?

Moreover, myths are not just stories for the self alone. Anyone who has been part of a body such as a school, military unit, business, or corporation knows there are certain stories that are part of the lore of that group, that help explain what and who it really is. Knowing these stories helps make one an insider instead of just a
15 newcomer. Stories of what it was like when so-and-so was here, why another person didn't fit in, this-or-that eccentric individual, the big fire or break-in. . . . These accounts are often not told officially; in fact, they may be particular to a subgroup, even subversive. There are stories students tell when the teachers aren't listening, or that employees tell out of earshot of the bosses. Nonetheless, the stories are part of
20 the lore and distinctive culture of that institution, and so are part of belonging.

Why story? Why not some more abstract scientific kind of explanation? First, we need to be able to relate personally to the narrative. We can slip our own lives more easily into a larger, more general story that gives it meaning, than into an abstraction. Our lives, after all, are not abstractions but stories. We are not just good or bad, or just
25 oxygen, carbon, and other elements, but a life-story. So this personal story might aspire to share in the greater story of a heroic or divine exemplar. I might model my life on Hercules, or see my meditations as like those of the Buddha even if less deep, or my suffering as my way of sharing in the world-saving agony of Christ.

Such tales impart certain fundamental values through the story and the way it
30 is told. It probably would not occur to primal peoples to ask whether the narratives are literally true in a modern scientific sense, even though they may deal with such ultimate questions as where the world came from, and why is there life—and death. They are just tales, and sometimes there are several alternative stories about those matters told by the same people.

Can these things be transmitted in a written story?

35 The style of the story, and the way it is told by a master storyteller, solemnly or with a wink and a chuckle, can say quite a bit about our world, how we respond to its buffeting, and how we live out own lives. The bard's voice and expression suggest an attitude one could take toward this beautiful and baffling planet. Much out there is lovely as a sunrise, yet also much makes us weep, up to the brutal cutting short of a life
40 just as it was getting well underway. Do we laugh at the incongruities of our world, or cry, or shout angry defiance, or just blank out the bad and try to see only the good?

There are myths for all these responses.

STORIES BEFORE WRITING

Second, we must remember that these stories may well go back, in their ultimate sources, to tales told even before the invention of writing. Back then, stories were the best means 45 by which a tribe's crucial information was passed on from one generation to another, because they were the form in which it was most easily remembered. Oral cultures—those without writing—think as well as tell stories differently from those with writing.

Is this true now for my family and friends' stories?

COYOTE

Let's then take as an illustration of myth that well-known trickster in Native North American mythology, Coyote, and his role in the creation of the world and the 50 setting-up of human life the way it is.

A trickster is a mythic figure—other examples are the Greek Hermes and Nordic Loki—neither wholly good nor bad, but full of jokes and the unexpected. Generally male, he tends to have extreme appetites for food, drink, and sex, and is often a thief and deceiver. Yet he can also be helpful to us humans when he feels like it. But, as 55 we will see, sometimes even his well-intended attempts at innovation get out of hand and lead to trouble.

Does his mischief make him more appealing?

The Native American Coyote is wily, cunning, ruthless, and unwilling to defer to anyone else, man, beast, or god. Coyote is out only for himself, even his sense of humor has an edge to it, and his "jokes" can be cruel. Yet like many other tricksters, 60 he can also serve as a "culture hero," a divine or semidivine figure who gives humans valuable tools such as fire or irrigation, or even helps in the creation of the world.

No less than humans of the same stamp, Coyote can be appealing in his cleverness, his disguises, and his ruses, by which he sometimes outsmarts even himself. For all his unscrupulousness and bad conduct, like some children he's cute even when 65 he's bad. His limitless energy and seemingly inexhaustible bag of tricks fascinate, and those who have made Coyote's acquaintance rarely tire of his exploits. Native Americans have enjoyed listening to his tales around the campfire for centuries.

(One can think of Coyote, and most other tricksters, as like Jack Sparrow, performed for laughs and thrills by Johnny Depp in the Pirates of the Caribbean 70 movies. Jack is clearly just playing his own game, and sees others mostly as toys or as means to get what he wants for himself. Yet he cannot help but catch every eye and steal every heart when he's on screen, with his liquid eyes, his gymnastics, and clever ploys; you can't help cheering him on even as you're appalled.)

What do Coyote and his stories say about our world? His set of tales suggest a 75 wondrous and beautiful world, but . . . something went wrong. The gods, humans, and animals running around the earth, trying to scratch a living from it or trying to improve it, are not always good or reliable, though always entertaining. They can send currents in contrary directions and go beyond what was intended. Even so, what can we do but laugh and enjoy the story?

80 Here is a Coyote story from the Maidu people of California. It includes two themes, creation and the origin of death, both common motifs in myth.

Who do you like better?

At the beginning, when nothing lay below but endless waters, two beings looked down and began talking about what they could do next to make it into a better place. They were Earthmaker and Coyote. Earthmaker, a re-85 spectable god, wanted to create a good, decent world in which pain and death were not, and spouses remained faithful to one another. But Coyote said in effect, "Why not make it a little more interesting?"

He's not exactly evil, and at first
he and Earthmaker get along; the
90   two are like good buddies talking
enthusiastically about their new
project, Earth. But clearly they are of
different temperaments. One is
straight, well meaning, but a little
95   dull and unimaginative; the other
more interested in angles and
bursting with imagination: more
than is called for, and enough to get
him into trouble. (Clearly the Maidu
100   considered the world offered plenty
of evidence for both these personalities
at work in its dramas.)

Rosario Rizzo/Fotolia

In time, Earthmaker and Coyote
had a falling out. Earthmaker wanted
105   the people he was making, when they
died, to be placed in water overnight
and then be able to rise up again the
next morning; and he wanted even married couples to be celibate, as there
was no need for procreation in a world without death. Coyote said of this:

110   "But you, Earthmaker,
          are not speaking for human contentment and joy!
          But I speak for a world where men can laugh
          and feel good and come to take delight in themselves
          and in the women they care for.
115   So then, an old man,
          flirting and playing around with a young woman,
              should feel like a lad again.
          And women should feel that way too."

Coyote obviously felt that a world without flirting, love, and sex was
120   hardly worth living in, even if the price was death, for immortal life in such
a world would be bound to get very boring. To this, Earthmaker had no
answer, so

          . . . he thought to himself:
          "You, Coyote, have overcome me in everything;
125   so then, without my saying so,
          let there be Death in the World."

But, as happened more often than not, Coyote's victory came back on
himself. Not long afterward he sent his own fine son to fetch some water.
On that simple expedition the boy was bitten by a rattlesnake, and died.

130   Then Coyote cried out to Earthmaker:
          "May I never say such things again!
          You must make my son come back to life!

But Earthmaker paid no attention, and Coyote, full of anger and remorse as he learned what death meant in personal as well as theoretical
135   terms, could only say of Earthmaker,

"I will chase him no longer. . . . I will never catch up with him."

What do we learn from this myth? First, that life is made up out of two forces, sometimes in harmony but more often pulling against each other: a serious, constructive side, and a fun, but rebellious and potentially destructive side. Most of us have both sides in ourselves. Yet they are not deadly antagonists like, say, the Christian God and Satan; rather the whole interplay is more like a game, or even a joke on the protagonists' propensity for going beyond their limits. We may as well take the world that way.

(1,703 words)

—From Robert S. Ellwood,
Introducing Religion: Religious Studies for the Twenty-First Century, 4th ed.

Recall

Stop to self-test, relate, and react.

Your instructor may choose to give you a brief comprehension review.

THINK CRITICALLY ABOUT THE SELECTION

Why are some family stories remembered and retold again and again?

What myths are part of American history? What values do they illustrate?

WRITE ABOUT THE SELECTION

Recall a story from your own family or friends that has been repeated many times. Why is it repeated? What does it say about your family or group?

Response Suggestion: Retell the story in writing. Be sure to include details that reveal the setting, characters, actions, emotions, or other characteristics that make the story memorable. You might want to ask others for their recollections. Then, add a paragraph that reflects on what the story says about your family or group. Does it reveal some of your values? Does retelling the story create a sense of belonging? Does it draw the group closer because of your shared experience?

SKILL DEVELOPMENT: INFERENCE

Answer the following questions with *T* (true) or *F* (false):

_____ 1. Myths only arise from ancient cultures.

_____ 2. It is likely that every culture creates myths.

_____ 3. The Coyote stories were probably handed down orally from generation to generation.

_____ 4. Myths are never written down.

_____ 5. Stories about historical heroes like George Washington, for example, are most likely to be entirely factual.

CHECK YOUR COMPREHENSION

After reading the selection, answer the following questions with *a, b, c,* or *d*. To help you analyze your strengths and weaknesses, the question types are indicated.

Main Idea _____ 1. Which of the following best expresses the main idea of this selection?

    a. Myths are the stories of ancient cultures.
    b. Individuals have their own myths.
    c. Myths like the Coyote story reflect the values and beliefs of a culture, group, or individual.
    d. The Coyote story explains why humans die.

Detail _____ 2. According to the selection, which is true about myths?

    a. They are created to tell historical facts.
    b. Most myths are about individual stories.
    c. It is unusual for a myth to be humorous.
    d. They are written or told in narrative form.

Inference _____ 3. Based on the details in the selection, which would be true of stories told about past experiences with a group of friends?

    a. They create a sense of belonging to the group.
    b. They could not be appropriately described as myths.
    c. They accurately relate exactly what happened.
    d. They usually are recorded as an official record of the group's history.

Inference _____ 4. Which of the following is a purpose of myths about cultural heroes?

    a. to record historical facts
    b. to inspire admirable behavior
    c. to provide inspiration for a movie
    d. to provide pure entertainment

Main Idea _____ 5. Which statement best describes the main point of the fifth paragraph, which begins, "The style of the story . . . ?"

    a. The structure of a myth must conform to certain standards to be effective.
    b. A myth can make us laugh or cry.
    c. The tone of a myth, whether it is oral or written, imparts meaning to the story.
    d. Myths rarely describe bad behavior or people who have gone wrong.

Author's Purpose _____ 6. Which of the following best expresses the main purpose of the entire selection?

    a. to entertain
    b. to inform
    c. to amuse
    d. to persuade

Detail _____ 7. According to the Coyote story,

    a. Earthmaker liked Coyote's proposal to create death.
    b. in Earthmaker's plan, there was no need for human reproduction.
    c. Earthmaker tried to reverse Coyote's mistake and erase death.
    d. Earthmaker argued against Coyote's proposal.

Main Idea _____ 8. Which of the following best expresses the main point of the Coyote story in this selection?

    a. Humans ultimately die because of Coyote's proposal to Earthmaker, for which Coyote ultimately paid a heavy price.
    b. At the beginning of the world, Earthmaker and Coyote wanted to make the world a better place.
    c. Good does not always overcome evil.
    d. Earthmaker and Coyote were buddies at first but had a falling out.

Inference _____ 9. From suggestions in the selection and prior knowledge, which of the following is most likely to be true?

    a. We are attracted to Coyote because he is imperfect like us.
    b. Coyote serves as a role model that we should strive to imitate.
    c. Earthmaker is weak and has lost control of the world.
    d. Earthmaker represents good, and Coyote represents evil.

Author's Purpose _____ 10. Why did the author include the Coyote myth in the selection?

    a. to entertain readers with an interesting story
    b. to highlight the beliefs of the ancient Maidu tribe
    c. to provide an example that illustrates the points made in the rest of the selection
    d. to convince readers that the Maidu people had a rich oral tradition

Answer the following with *T* (true) or *F* (false).

Inference _____ 11. Readers can logically infer that Earthmaker has more power than Coyote.

Inference (Drawing Conclusions) _____ 12. A logical conclusion from the Coyote story is that the Maidu people did not concern themselves with such spiritual questions as creation or the purpose of life.

Inference _____ 13. Earthmaker and Coyote represent contrasting human traits.

Inference (Drawing Conclusions) _____ 14. We can conclude from the Coyote story that the Maidu people believed in a force for good and a force for mischief and potential destruction.

Inference _____ 15. Earthmaker represents the Christian God, and Coyote represents Satan.

BUILD YOUR VOCABULARY

According to the way the italicized word is used in the selection, indicate *a, b, c,* or *d* for the word or phrase that gives the best definition. The number in parentheses indicates the line of the passage in which the word is located. Use a dictionary in addition to the context clues to more precisely define the terms.

_____ 1. "into an *abstraction*" (24)
   a. proposal
   b. argument
   c. general idea
   d. rejection

_____ 2. "to *primal* peoples" (30)
   a. primitive
   b. law-abiding
   c. literate
   d. spiritual

_____ 3. "The *bard's* voice" (37)
   a. poet's
   b. leader's
   c. teacher's
   d. person's

_____ 4. "*incongruities* of our world" (40)
   a. tragedies
   b. beauties
   c. foolishness
   d. inconsistencies

_____ 5. "of the same *stamp*" (62)
   a. evilness
   b. brilliance
   c. mold
   d. thinking

_____ 6. "and his *ruses*" (63)
   a. stupidity
   b. tricks
   c. strength
   d. masks

_____ 7. "his *unscrupulousness*" (64)
   a. good sense
   b. standards
   c. crimes
   d. deviousness

_____ 8. "deadly *antagonists*" (140)
   a. friends
   b. enemies
   c. heroes
   d. tragic figures

_____ 9. "the *protagonists*" (142)
   a. main characters'
   b. actors'
   c. gods'
   d. people's

_____ 10. "*propensity* for going" (142)
   a. desire
   b. sin
   c. objection
   d. tendency

| **SELECTION 3** | Personal Narrative | MyReadingLab |

Visit Chapter 7: Inference in MyReadingLab to complete the Selection 3 activities and the Build Background Knowledge video activity.

PREVIEW the next selection to predict its purpose and organization and to formulate your learning plan.

Activate Schemata

Do you know someone who cannot read?
How would being illiterate affect a person's life?

Establish a Purpose for Reading

Could someone who couldn't read graduate from high school and college and become a teacher? Read to find out about the experiences of John Corcoran, a teacher who couldn't read.

Build Background Knowledge — VIDEO

Reading to Children During Infancy

To prepare for reading Selection 3, answer the questions below. Then, watch this video on the role reading plays in early childhood literacy.

At what age should parents start reading to their children?

What connection do you see between reading to children and literacy?

Why do you think illiteracy continues to be a problem in the United States?

This video helped me: _____

_____

_____

Increase Word Knowledge

What do you know about these words?

| intermittently | competence | masquerade | illiterates | adept |
| covert | cunning | ploy | subterfuge | inconspicuous |

Your instructor may give a brief vocabulary review before or after reading.

Integrate Knowledge While Reading

Inference questions have been inserted in the margin to stimulate your thinking and help you read between the lines. Remember to

Predict   Picture   Relate   Monitor   Correct   Annotate

John Corcoran, author of The Teacher Who Couldn't Read, *fooled everyone except his three-year-old daughter.*

SELECTION 3

FEAR THE COLLEGE YEARS

Why was Corcoran afraid of college?

One little voice within me said, *John, you bluffed your way through high school, but college is big time. You'll never fool those guys.*

Another voice, gritty and determined, answered, *You can't give up now. Prove you have a mind. Go for it!*

5   My parents never considered that I wouldn't go to college. Mother would pepper her conversation with, "When you go to college. . . ." My dad had degrees or college credits from six different institutions of higher learning and read books like a kid eats popcorn—whole handfuls at a time. He taught school intermittently for 40 years to support his family. He insisted that we speak the King's English, which

10   meant no slang or swearing. Of course his son would go to college. Education was important to him, as was natural curiosity, athletics, and hard work.

I thought, *I can't let my family down.*

In my imagination there were two fields with a fence between them. To get to the literate side where the grass was greener, I needed a passport stamped with the

15   seal of a college diploma that wasn't blank.

Recent studies have shown that even mildly reading-disabled children from supportive homes are prone to be more anxious and less happy than their peers. Also, research indicates that social competence is lower for reading-impaired boys.

I can't say that I was an unhappy person, but certainly I lived on the edge of

20   anxiety. Would my mask be yanked off? Would I be humiliated and degraded before my family and peers? Every day I walked that tightrope, believing there was no net to keep me from certain destruction.

What do people think of illiterates?

By the time I entered college, I was well into my masquerade. All I had to do was remember what people thought of illiterates. There didn't seem to be any safe

25   harbor for us. We were the dumb ones, the no-goods.

Who could I trust to give me more than just superficial dignity? The schools had their chance to teach me to read when I was in the elementary grades. For the first six years of my schooling, no one uncovered my need. Nothing had changed, except I was more adept at learning and gaining my own education without the basic skills.

How was he able to get through elementary school undetected?"

30   I went to two junior colleges in California and plowed through like an explorer wading through mud up to his knees. Mildred went to both schools (I don't know if she followed me or I followed her), and without her I'm not sure I would have made it. She was in many of my classes and did everything she could to help me with my studies. She typed papers I dictated, summarized books for my reports, and encour-

35   aged me. She was my survival kit. They say love is blind, and I believe it, because with all the help Mildred gave me, she never knew I couldn't read.

John Corcoran, who was unable to read until age 48, is committed to fighting adult illiteracy in the United States.
Zuma/Newscom

One day an amazing offer came. I was presented with a full athletic scholarship—including board, room, and ten dollars cash a month for laundry—to Texas Western College (now the University of Texas in El Paso). A dillar, a dollar. I wasn't even a
40 ten o'clock scholar! But I was six-foot-four, could dunk a basketball, and could at least read the scoreboard.

Facing such an enticing offer, I couldn't turn it down.

From the day I registered, I began to plan my strategy. My scholastic criminal career was about to begin. I'm not proud of any of my covert actions, and it has
45 taken me many years to be able to publicly confess them. If there is no honor among thieves, there is certainly no honor among cheaters.

An illiterate person who gives the appearance of reading is always in danger of being discovered. As I began my college years, I realized I would need every ounce of cunning I could muster. I found I could get through a few courses—speech, office
50 machines, typing, and PE—with a minimal amount of cheating. I got a legitimate A in practice teaching math at Austin High School.

Why was he able to get through these classes?

Frank Laubach, the visionary leader of the volunteer literacy movement bearing his name, has said, "A literate person is not only an illiterate person who has learned to read and write; he is another person." I wanted to be another person, someone
55 who could understand the names on classroom doors. Was this room for English poetry or basic economics? Was I carrying a sociology, psychology, political science, or philosophy text? No one can understand the struggle within the soul of an illiterate unless he attempts to lead a life without being sure of words on a bottle, a menu, a street sign, a newspaper, a bill, a legal document, or a letter. It's like being blind in
60 a strange room without the benefit of touch.

Mildred became a dim chapter in my book of romance as I began to date one of the smartest girls in school, a beauty queen who was chosen as Miss El Paso. She wore my fraternity pin but never suspected it was an intentional ploy when I asked her to decide what she wanted at the local eatery. When she ordered something on
65 the menu I could easily say, "I'll take the same." I became very adept at dodging and ducking the printed word. Most of the time it was as natural as breathing.

I would do anything to pass my courses. If I could get test answers, I would go to any extreme to copy them before class. It was during that era, I believe, that the term cat burglar became a cultural idiom. I must have seen the movie *To Catch a Thief*
70 starring Cary Grant and Grace Kelly because, with a flair for drama and youthful agility, one night I climbed the fire escape at the faculty office building and crept along a three-inch wide ledge, arms outstretched, my fingers gripping the protruding decorative trim on the side of the building. When I finally reached the window, I pried it open with a butter knife and entered my business administration profes-
75 sor's office. Once inside, it was easy to get copies of the quizzes. With the answers in my pocket, I inched my way back across the ledge and climbed down to the ground.

On one occasion there was a file cabinet that I couldn't open, but I was sure it held a treasure of tests and answers. One of my buddies, who was almost as adept at subterfuge as I was, helped me enter the faculty offices at 3 A.M., carry the cabinet
80 down two flights of stairs and into an off-campus apartment. We called for a locksmith, who swallowed my story of needing to enter the file to get some valuable papers, and he opened it with his special tools. When he left, my buddy and I carried it across campus and back up to the third floor without being caught. That was an act of a desperate young man, and except for the grace of God, I could have been
85 arrested for breaking and entering.

One required course challenged my plans. It was U.S. Government, and the teacher did not have prepared tests I could pilfer. He would write three essay questions on the board and give us two hours to answer. I found my solution in Clarence, a genius-level student with a major crush on my sister Judy. Clarence and I worked
90 out a mutually beneficial exchange of favors. He desperately wanted to take Judy to the SAE formal, and I desperately needed answers to the U.S. Government final.

When the day for finals arrived, I got to class early and found a seat next to the window in the first-floor classroom. I took two blue books to class, one to copy the questions and drop out the window to Clarence, the other to pretend I was writing
95 answers. It took me a long time to laboriously copy the essay questions from the board into one blue book, but when I finished, I slipped it out the window, where Clarence was waiting to catch it. He sat under a tree and easily wrote the essays. Meanwhile, I spent the remaining two hours scribbling in my dummy book. Clarence got a blind date with Judy and I passed my final. Fair exchange.

100 *Using schemes like these John Corcoran managed to graduate from college. He married and pursued successful careers as a high school mathematics teacher, coach, and real estate investor, and he fooled everyone except his three-year-old daughter. She knew her dad wasn't really reading her new bedtime story. At the age of 48, John Corcoran finally summoned enough courage to seek help for his reading disability.*

105 One day I was in a grocery store and heard someone talking about the Carlsbad library literacy program. *Maybe someone can help me*, I thought. When I got home, I called the library and asked, "Do you have a literacy program?" Even then, I wondered if the librarian would question my inquiry. She told me where to find the Carlsbad Adult Learning Center.

110 A few weeks later, on a hot August day, I left home dressed in a suit and tie, looking for all the world like a hotshot businessman, and drove to a small, inconspicuous office in the next town. I was told the sign said, "Adult Learning Center of Carlsbad."

Why did Corcoran wear a suit and tie?

I didn't hear a voice from heaven, but as I walked in the door—48 years old, frustrated, maybe even *desperate*—it was the beginning of my new life and the birth
115 of a miracle.

Today, Corcoran is a respected spokesperson for adult literacy programs and founder of the John Corcoran Foundation, Inc.—Advocate for Literacy.

(1,620 words)

—From John Corcoran,
The Teacher Who Couldn't Read: A Memoir

Recall

Stop to self-test, relate, and react.

Your instructor may choose to give you a brief comprehension review.

THINK CRITICALLY ABOUT THE SELECTION

Corcoran uses many forms of figurative language throughout this selection. What examples can you find of idioms, similes, metaphors, literary analogies, and other types of figurative language?

How does Corcorcan's use of figurative language contribute to your reading of the narrative?

WRITE ABOUT THE SELECTION

It is hard to believe that someone could graduate from high school, earn a college degree, become a successful high school teacher, and run a profitable business without being able to read. Yet, John Corcoran did all of these things.

Response Suggestion: Why do you think no one recognized that he could not read? Do you admire Corcoran? Why or why not?

SKILL DEVELOPMENT: IMPLIED MEANING

According to the implied meaning in the selection, answer the following with *T* (true) or *F* (false):

_____ 1. When Corcoran's father used the term, "King's English," he meant correct, formal, English.

_____ 2. Corcoran found the junior college classes easy.

_____ 3. Corcoran stole test answers from a college teacher only one time.

_____ 4. Corcoran was caught and arrested for breaking into a faculty office.

_____ 5. Corcoran believed that being able to read would change his life.

CHECK YOUR COMPREHENSION

After reading the selection, answer the following questions with *a*, *b*, *c*, or *d*. To help you analyze your strengths and weaknesses, the question types are indicated.

Main Idea   ————   1. Which of the following statements best summarizes this selection?

    a. Being unable to read is a huge obstacle to success in modern society.

    b. Although he is not proud of how he did it, John Corcoran managed to graduate from college despite being unable to read; eventually, he faced his disability and sought help.

    c. John Corcoran stole tests from teachers' files and enlisted his friends to help him pass exams.

    d. John Corcoran is ashamed of what he did to cover up his reading disability and to graduate from high school and college.

Detail   ————   2. Corcoran received a scholarship to attend

    a. Texas Western College.

    b. a California college.

    c. two community colleges.

    d. the University of Texas at Austin.

Inference   ————   3. Details in the selection suggest that Corcoran's college scholarship was

    a. to play football.

    b. an academic scholarship.

    c. to play basketball.

    d. for having excellent high school grades.

Main Idea   ————   4. Which of the following best states the main idea of the third paragraph?

    a. Corcoran's father taught school off and on for 40 years.

    b. A college degree is still critical to success.

    c. Corcoran's parents believed that a college education was essential.

    d. Corcoran's mother did not attend college.

Inference   ————   5. From the article, readers can infer that

    a. Corcoran had difficulty in mathematics.

    b. Corcoran could have learned to read but didn't try.

    c. Corcoran was not disturbed by his inability to read.

    d. Corcoran was skilled in areas other than reading.

Inference   ————   6. Mildred must have been

    a. Corcoran's sister.

    b. one of Corcoran's teachers.

    c. Corcoran's future wife.

    d. a high school and college girlfriend.

Detail _____ 7. Which of the following was Clarence's reason for helping Corcoran with his U.S. Government test?

   a. He wanted a date with Corcoran's sister.
   b. He wanted to show Corcoran how smart he was.
   c. He needed the money that Corcoran was going to pay him.
   d. He wanted to help his friend.

Detail _____ 8. Where did Corcoran finally receive teaching that addressed his reading disability?

   a. at an evening class at a nearby elementary school
   b. at a public library
   c. at a community adult learning center
   d. at a class offered by a community college

Inference _____ 9. A "cat burglar" is most likely someone who

   a. steals valuable, pedigreed animals for resale.
   b. is a glamorous, "movie star" kind of thief.
   c. enters quietly, without being noticed, to take what he or she wants.
   d. specializes in stealing answers to tests and quizzes.

Detail _____ 10. To pass Corcoran's U.S. Government final, which of the following did he and Clarence do?

   a. They stole a locked file cabinet and got a locksmith to open it.
   b. They passed questions and answers through an open window.
   c. Clarence quizzed him repeatedly until he was able to memorize the answers.
   d. They climbed into a second-story window to steal the test.

Answer the following with *T* (true) or *F* (false):

Inference _____ 11. Corcoran was plagued by worry that his reading disability would be discovered.

Detail _____ 12. According to the article, even children with mild reading problems are often less happy than their peers.

Author's Purpose _____ 13. The author's primary purpose is to inspire others through his personal story.

Inference _____ 14. Corcoran dated the former Miss El Paso because he was in love with her.

Detail _____ 15. Corcoran earned an honest "A" in mathematics practice teaching.

SELECTION 3

BUILD YOUR VOCABULARY

According to the way the italicized word was used in the selection, indicate *a*, *b*, *c*, or *d* for the word or phrase that gives the best definition. The number in parentheses indicates the line of the passage in which the word is located. Use a dictionary in addition to the context clues to more precisely define the terms.

_____ 1. "taught school *intermittently*" (8)
     a. happily
     b. occasionally
     c. loyally
     d. continuously

_____ 2. "social *competence* is lower" (18)
     a. proficiency
     b. interest
     c. popularity
     d. activity

_____ 3. "well into my *masquerade*" (23)
     a. school years
     b. athletic activities
     c. studies
     d. cover-up

_____ 4. "people thought of *illiterates*" (24)
     a. people who are not truthful
     b. people who cannot read
     c. people who don't go to college
     d. people who are unpleasant

_____ 5. "more *adept* at learning" (29)
     a. clumsy
     b. resistant
     c. skilled
     d. pleased

_____ 6. "my *covert* actions" (44)
     a. secret
     b. illegal
     c. unethical
     d. daring

_____ 7. "every ounce of *cunning*" (49)
     a. stupidity
     b. strength
     c. help
     d. cleverness

_____ 8. "an intentional *ploy*" (63)
     a. insult
     b. mistake
     c. plan
     d. kindness

_____ 9. "adept at *subterfuge*" (79)
     a. crime
     b. academics
     c. trickery
     d. acting

_____ 10. "small, *inconspicuous* office" (111)
     a. well decorated
     b. not easily noticed
     c. elegant
     d. ground floor

SELECTION 3

Concept Prep for Political Science

A Sampling of Careers in Political Science

A bachelor's degree in political science provides an excellent foundation for various careers, some of which may also require specialized training or an advanced degree.

- Intelligence officer
- Attorney
- Campaign manager
- City planner

- Nonprofit organization manager
- Government official
- Teacher
- Diplomat

Did you take a literacy test to prove that you could read when you registered to vote? Instead, you probably completed a simple postcard or registered seamlessly when you applied for a driver's license, but it was not always that easy. In the past in the United States, the ability to read was commonly used as a ploy to discriminate against certain groups of people. In Southern and some Western states, literacy tests were commonly required for voter registration. This practice eliminated many African Americans from voting because they had little or no access to education. Similarly, literacy tests were also used to turn away "undesirable" immigrants in the early 1900s. Although literacy tests were ruled illegal by the Voting Rights Act of 1965 and a series of Supreme Court decisions, still today many citizens do not exercise their rights because of their inability to read. This change did not come easily. It was the result of pressure applied by people who knew the rights endowed by the U.S. Constitution and who were prepared to fight for them. In 2013, the U.S. Supreme Court struck down a key part of the Voting Rights Act. The controversial decision allows states to require voters to show a government-issued proof of identity, which poses a barrier to many legal U.S. citizens.

What is the U.S. Constitution?

The Constitution of the United States is a document that defines the structure of our government and the roles, powers, and responsibilities of public officials. It was signed in Philadelphia in 1787. Before the Constitution, the Declaration of Independence in 1776 affirmed our independence from England. The Articles of Confederation were written to govern the resulting new union of states that joined to fight for freedom and forge a new democracy. The articles created a loose union and left most of the authority with individual states. After the Revolution, as economic conflicts arose and more central control was needed, the Constitution was written to give more power to the federal government, replacing the Articles of Confederation. Our country is still governed by this same Constitution of 1787, which also guarantees our civil liberties and civil rights, including freedom of expression, due process, and equal protection.

Because no document is perfect, the writers of the Constitution allowed for amendments, and the Constitution has been amended 27 times.

What are the three branches of government?

The Constitution divides the federal government into three branches: the executive, the legislative, and the judicial branches.

- The *executive branch* consists of the president, whose powers include approving or vetoing (refusing to sign) laws passed by Congress, and the *president's cabinet*, an advisory group of 13 government department heads appointed by the president. For example, Hillary Clinton was a member of President Barack Obama's cabinet.
- The *legislative branch* of the government consists of the two houses of Congress: the Senate and the House of Representatives. The *Senate*, with 100 members (two from each state), and the *House of Representatives*, with 435 members (apportioned to each state according to population), pass federal laws and serve on

committees that investigate problems and oversee the executive branch.

- The *judicial branch* consists of a system of federal courts, the highest of which is the *U.S. Supreme Court.* It consists of a chief justice and eight associate justices who are appointed by sitting presidents. The Supreme Court ensures uniformity in the interpretation of national laws.

Each of the three branches has checks and balances over the other branches so that power is shared.

What are political parties?

- Our president, senators, and representatives are nominated for office by a political party, an organization formed to support and elect candidates who uphold the views and beliefs of the group. Over the years, political parties have changed and some have disappeared. Today, the two major parties are Republican and Democrat.
- The *Republican Party,* also called the GOP, for "Grand Old Party," began in 1854. Its symbol is the elephant, and Abraham Lincoln was the first Republican president. The party tends to be against expanding the size and responsibilities of the federal government and to support private enterprise. The party image is *conservative,* an ideology or set of beliefs that prefers the existing order and opposes change.
- The *Democratic Party* was organized by Thomas Jefferson in the late eighteenth century, and its first elected president was Andrew Jackson. The party tends to support the expansion of federal programs and a tax system that puts a greater burden on the rich and corporations. Its symbol is the donkey. The party image is *liberal,* an ideology that supports the strong role of government in economic and social issues.

Before elections, both parties pay organizations such as *Gallup* to conduct *polls,* questioning voters about the most important issues and sampling public opinion on voting preferences.

What are capitalism, Communism, and socialism?

- *Capitalism* is an economic system based on a free market for goods and services. Production centers, such as factories, seek profits and are owned by individuals as well as corporations and their stockholders, not the government.

The U.S. Capitol is home to the legislative branch of the federal government, the United States Congress.

abadesign/Shutterstock

The United States has a capitalist economy, although it is not purely capitalistic, since government does impose regulations on business.

- *Communism* is almost the opposite of capitalism. It is an economic, political, and social system in which there is no individual ownership. The government controls businesses, and goods and property are owned in common by all citizens. Goods are available to all people as they are needed. The Communist system was envisioned by Karl Marx and is associated with the former Soviet Union and China.

- *Socialism* is an economic system advocating government or collective ownership of goods, rather than private ownership. In Karl Marx's theory, it represents the transition between capitalism and Communism in which people are paid according to work done. Communists are socialists, but not all socialists are Communists.

REVIEW QUESTIONS

After studying the material, answer the following questions:

1. Why were the Articles of Confederation replaced? _____

   _____

2. How does the Declaration of Independence differ from the Constitution? ____

   _____

   _____

3. How many justices sit on the Supreme Court? _____

   _____

4. In which branch of the government do members of the cabinet serve? _____

5. Which branch of the government passes laws? _____

6. In which house of Congress does each state have the same number of representatives? _____

   _____

7. How do Republican and Democratic views on federal government expansion differ? _____

   _____

8. Would a push to reduce corporate taxes most likely be a liberal or a conservative cause? _____

   _____

9. Would a dynamic business owner prefer capitalism or socialism? _____

   _____

10. In theory, under which system—capitalism or Communism—does a worker share equally in goods, regardless of the work that he or she does? _____

Your instructor may choose to give a brief review of these political science concepts.

VOCABULARY BOOSTER

Say, What?

Roots   *dic, dict:* "say"   *locu, loqui:* "speak"   *lingu:* "tongue"

Words with *dic, dict:* "say"

When Stephen became the supervisor and began to tell his co-workers how to do their jobs, he soon discovered that they did not respond well to his *dictatorial* management style.

- **dictate**: to say or read out loud for transcription; to command with authority

  Sarena's parents *dictated* the nonnegotiable conditions of her upcoming slumber party: no boys, no alcohol.

- **dictator**: a ruler using absolute power without hereditary right or consent of the people

  Fidel Castro, who staged a coup to oust former president Fulgencio Batista of Cuba, was a *dictator* who has remained in power for many years.

- **diction**: that aspect of speaking or writing that is dependent on the correct choice of words; the voice quality of a speaker or a singer

  Listening to public speakers with fine *diction* is much easier than trying to decipher the words of those whose speech is not clear and distinct.

- **contradict**: to state the opposite of or to deny; to imply denial with actions

  Mark's wild lifestyle seems to *contradict* his claim of being the quiet, studious type.

- **indict**: to charge with a crime; to seriously criticize or blame

  The grand jury *indicted* the alleged computer hacker for breaking into banking system computers to illegally move funds electronically.

- **predict**: to declare in advance or to foretell the future

  Meteorologists *predict* the weather based on facts, experience, and the use of complex meteorological instruments.

- **dictionary**: a reference book, either digital or print, of alphabetically arranged words and their meanings

  Word-processing computer programs usually contain a *dictionary* and can run a spelling check on documents.

Words with *locu, loqui:* "speak"

The defendant's attorney was skilled in fluent, forceful, and persuasive speech, so it came as no surprise that his closing statement was *eloquent* enough to convince the jury of his client's innocence.

- **elocution**: the study and practice of public speaking; a style of speaking or reading out loud

Julianne was taking speech classes for all her electives, hoping that the *elocution* practice would help in the frequent presentations that were required in her chosen career of public relations.

- *locution*: a word or phrase as used by a particular person or group

  In the late 1960s and early 1970s, hippies used *locutions* such as "groovy" or "way out, man."

- *colloquial*: characteristic of informal speech or writing; conversational

  Choosing the word *nope* instead of *no* is an example of using a *colloquial* expression.

- *soliloquy*: the act of speaking to oneself; a speech in a drama in which a character reveals innermost thoughts

  Aspiring actors often use *soliloquies* from Shakespeare's plays as audition monologues.

- *loquacious*: tending to talk too much or too freely; garrulous

  When meeting new people, Nadia often becomes nervous and *loquacious*, and tends to chatter on and on about unimportant things.

- *circumlocution*: a roundabout or indirect way of speaking; using more words than necessary

  After all the *circumlocution* in Sydney's story, such as what she was wearing, what she had to eat, and what time they left, we finally got to hear whether or not she liked her blind date.

Words with *lingu:* "tongue"

When you visit the doctor, it is customary for the nurse to take your *sublingual* temperature and your blood pressure.

- *linguistics*: the study of language

  Phonetics is the branch of *linguistics* involving the study of the production of speech sounds and the written symbols representing them.

- *multilingual*: able to speak several languages with some ease

  Some public schools in the United States are experiencing a need for *multilingual* teachers due to the influx of immigrants who do not yet speak English.

Review

Part I

Choose the best antonym from the following list for each of the words listed below.

acquit or discharge	confirm	dialogue	directness	elected ruler
formal speech	obey	recall	silent	unconvincing

1. contradict _____
2. circumlocution _____
3. dictate _____
4. predict _____
5. loquacious _____

6. dictator _____
7. indict _____
8. eloquent _____
9. soliloquy _____
10. colloquial _____

Part II

From the following list, choose the word that best completes each of the sentences below.

locution	dictionary	indict	dictate	linguistics
diction	elocution	sublingual	dictatorial	contradict

11. His outstanding performance in the classroom seemed to _____ his rather ordinary test scores.

12. Studies indicate that multiples such as twins and triplets often communicate with their own unique words and phrases, or forms of _____.

13. To help with the study of technical vocabulary, a specialized _____ would be a useful purchase.

14. With infants, health-care professionals often opt for another means of assessing fever in lieu of a _____ temperature reading.

15. Several colleges offer a camera for _____ practice in speech labs.

16. The number of white collar criminals that courts are choosing to _____ has increased.

17. Virginia tried very hard not to give unwanted child-rearing instructions to her son and daughter-in-law because she remembered how she resented her own mother's _____ attitude.

18. A speaker with clear, distinct _____ is more easily understood than one with a regional accent.

19. Her friends are wondering how much longer she will remain in a relationship with a domineering person who seems to _____ rather than communicate.

20. Some researchers in the field of _____ specialize in the study of the development of regional dialects.

Your instructor may choose to give you a brief review.

8 Point of View

Learning Objectives

In this chapter, you will learn to:

1 Identify the author's point of view
2 Distinguish facts and opinions
3 Identify the author's purpose for writing
4 Recognize the author's tone

Vocabulary Booster: Lights, Camera, Action!

Maxim Tupikov/Shutterstock

WHAT IS THE AUTHOR'S POINT OF VIEW?

Learning Objective 1

Identify the author's point of view

An author's **point of view**—his or her opinions and theories concerning the subject matter—will influence the presentation of the material. For example, the author of a British textbook might describe American history during Revolutionary times as a colonial uprising on a distant continent, while an American author would praise the heroic struggle for personal freedom and survival. Each of the two authors would write from a different point of view and express particular opinions because each would have a different way of looking at the subject matter.

In this and other college reading textbooks, *point of view* refers to the author's views on the subject about which the author is writing. This definition differs from *literary point of view*, which refers to the narrative voice of the author: first, second, or third person.

Recognizing the author's point of view is part of understanding what you read. Sophisticated readers seek to identify the beliefs of the author to know "where he or she is coming from." When the point of view is not directly stated, the author's choice of information (facts and opinions) and choice of words (the author's tone) provide clues to the author's point of view and purpose for writing. These elements are critical to understanding the author's message.

Textbooks and the Author's Point of View

If you are like many people, you might assume that textbooks contain facts rather than opinions, that historical accounts are based on fact and do not vary from one author to another, and that textbooks are free from an author's bias. Nothing could be further from the truth. Textbooks are replete with interpretation, opinion, and slanted—rather than balanced—views. In short, they reflect the author's point of view and the "politically correct" winds of change.

For example, in a world civilization textbook, you will read about the wealthy and cosmopolitan Persian Empire, whose kings were righteous rulers believed to be elected by the gods. About 2,500 years ago, the Persian Empire was at its height, with spectacular public buildings and palaces at the capital, Persepolis, located in what is now Iran. Yes, *you* will read about the splendor of the empire, but twenty-first-century

Non Sequitur/Universal UClick

inhabitants of the region will not. Read what the following textbook authors have to say about the way historical facts about that region are treated:

> Islam denigrates the earlier cultures of its converts, just as it was noted that Christianity can. Everything before Islam was, in Arabic, *jahiliya*, "from the age of ignorance." This leaves little room in these peoples' historical consciousness for their pre-Islamic past, so they often lack interest in it. For example, despite Persia's brilliant antique history, for contemporary Iranians the glory began with the coming of Islam. Many people in Muslim countries view their own ancient cultural landscapes without interest. They may even discourage tourists from viewing pre-Islamic ruins.
>
> —Edward Bergman and William Renwick,
> *Introduction to Geography*, 2nd ed.

In other violent changes of regime, such as the Communist takeover of the Russian Empire, new leaders have also thrown out the old history books and written new ones to reflect the new political thinking. Even in American history books, you now see more about women and minorities, not because lost historical records have recently been unearthed, but in response to public demand. Thus, no rule about the purity of the content applies to textbook writing.

The slant may start with, but is not limited to, what is included in the book, and it continues with the author's interpretation. For example, the view of government in political science texts varies with liberal and conservative authors. Climate change, cloning, and stem cell replacement therapy can be opinion-laden topics in biology texts. And, although the name of the first U.S. president does not vary from one American history book to another, the emphasis on the importance of George Washington's administration may vary, depending on the author's point of view.

In short, *everything you read is affected by the author's point of view, purpose, tone, and presentation of facts and opinions.*

What Is Bias?

The terms *point of view* and *bias* are very similar and are sometimes used interchangeably. When facts are slanted, though not necessarily distorted, to reflect the author's personal beliefs, the written material is said to reflect the author's bias. Thus, a **bias** is simply an opinion or position on a subject. As commonly used, however, *bias* has a negative connotation, suggesting narrow-mindedness and prejudice, whereas *point of view* suggests thoughtfulness and openness. Perhaps you would like to refer to your own opinion as a point of view and to those of others, particularly if they disagree with you, as biases!

EXAMPLE   Read the following passage and use the choice of information and words to identify the author's point of view or bias. Underline the clues that support your answer:

> As president, Richard Nixon enjoyed the pomp and circumstance of office. He liked to listen to the presidential song, "Hail to the Chief," and to review at strict attention ranks of marching soldiers. Nixon's vaguely royal pretensions seemed harmless enough initially, but after Watergate many people began to feel that an all-too-royal president was endangering democratic practice.
>
> —Morris P. Fiorina et al.,
> *The New American Democracy*, 3rd ed.

EXPLANATION   The author feels that former President Nixon began to think that he was king of the country rather than president of a democracy. This is suggested by the passage and by phrases such as *pomp and circumstance, royal pretensions, all-too-royal*, and *endangering democratic practice*.

Reader's TIP) Questions to Uncover Bias

- What is your opinion on the subject?
- What is the author's opinion on the subject?
- What are the author's credentials for writing on the subject?
- What does the author have to gain?
- Does the author use facts or opinions to support his or her statements?
- Are the facts selected and slanted to reflect the author's bias?

EXERCISE 8.1

Recognizing an Author's Point of View

Read the following passages, and use the choice of information and words to identify the author's point of view or bias. Underline the clues that support your answers.

Passage 1

Commercial fishing vessels, which can catch massive amounts of fish using dragnets, have emptied coastal waters of fish, often with the help of government subsidies. No longer is the sea an inexhaustible source of food, as 60 percent of all fishing regions are now showing a decline in catch.

—Christian Goergen,
Politics in a Globalized World

What is the author's point of view? Underline clues that support your answer.

_____

_____

_____

Passage 2

Unless you are willing to argue that single mothers are lazier than others, it will be hard to deny that circumstances and government policies matter for poverty. Single mothers are the largest group among the poor, because they are caught between a rock and a hard place. They need to take care of their children—often without support from a father—but without support from others, they also need to work to make money. Especially if they are young and do not have a good education, it will be very hard to find a job that pays enough for childcare and a decent living. Thus, many women are forced to rely on the welfare system.

—Christian Goergen,
Politics in a Globalized World

What is the author's point of view? Underline clues that support your answer.

_____

_____

_____

EXERCISE 8.2

Comparing Points of View of Different Authors

Read the following two descriptions of Mary Stuart, queen of Scotland, from two different history books. Although both include positive and negative comments, the second author obviously finds the subject more engaging and has chosen to include more positive details.

Portrait of Mary Stuart, Queen of Scots (16th century), Anonymous.
Scala/Art Resource, New York.

Passage 1

Mary Stuart returned to Scotland in 1561 after her husband's death. She was a far more charming and romantic figure than her cousin Elizabeth, but she was no stateswoman. A convinced Catholic, she soon ran head-on into the granitelike opposition of Knox and the Kirk. In 1567 she was forced to abdicate, and in the following year she fled from Scotland and sought protection in England from Elizabeth. No visitor could have been more unwelcome.

—Joseph R. Strayer et al.,
The Mainstream of Civilization, 4th ed.

Passage 2

Mary Stuart was an altogether remarkable young woman, about whom it is almost impossible to remain objectively impartial. Even when one discounts the flattery that crept into descriptions of her, one is inclined to accept the contemporary evidence that Mary was extraordinarily beautiful, though tall for a girl—perhaps over six feet. In addition to beauty, she had almost every other attractive attribute in high degree: courage, wit, resourcefulness, loyalty, and responsiveness, in short everything needful for worldly greatness save discretion in her relations with men and a willingness to compromise, if need be, on matters of religion. She was a thoroughgoing Roman Catholic, a good lover, and a magnificent hater.

—Shepard B. Clough et al.,
A History of the Western World

1. How are the two descriptions alike? _____

   _____

2. How do the two descriptions differ? _____

   _____

3. Which clues signal that the author of the second description is more biased

   than the first? _____

   _____

4. What is the suggested meaning in the following phrases:

   a. "no stateswoman" _____

   b. "granitelike opposition" _____

   c. "more unwelcome" _____

   d. "save discretion in her relations with men" _____

   e. "thoroughgoing Roman Catholic" _____

The Importance of the Reader's Point of View

Thus far we have considered only the author's point of view. However, to recognize a point of view, a reader must know enough about the subject to realize that there is another opinion beyond the one being expressed. Therefore, having prior knowledge and a slightly suspicious nature will open the reader's mind to countless other views and alternative arguments.

On the other hand, prior knowledge can lead to a closed mind and rigid thinking. Existing opinions affect the extent to which readers accept or reject what they read. If the readers' beliefs are particularly strong, sometimes they refuse to hear what is said or they hear something that is not said. Research has shown that readers will actually "tune out" new material that expresses views drastically different from their own. For example, if you were reading that the AIDS virus need not be a concern for most Americans, would you be "tuned in" or "tuned out"?

EXAMPLE   Read the following passage on smoking from the point of view of a nonsmoker. Next, reread it from the point of view of a smoker. Finally, answer the questions.

> Smoke can permanently paralyze the tiny cilia that sweep the breathing passages clean and can cause the lining of the respiratory tract to thicken irregularly. The body's attempt to rid itself of the smoking toxins may produce a deep, hacking cough in the person next to you at the lunch counter. Console yourself with the knowledge that these hackers are only trying to rid their bodies of nicotine, "tars," formaldehyde, hydrogen sulfide, resins, and who knows what. Just enjoy your meal.
>
> —Robert Wallace,
> *Biology: The World of Life*

1. Is the author a smoker? Underline the clues suggesting your answer. _____
   _____

2. What is your view on smoking? _____
   _____

3. Reading this passage in the guise of a nonsmoker, what message is conveyed
   to you? _____
   _____

4. Assuming the role of a smoker, what message is conveyed to you? _____
   _____

5. What is the main point that the author is trying to convey? _____
   _____

EXPLANATION   Although it is possible that both the smoker and the nonsmoker would get exactly the same message, it is more likely that the nonsmoker would be disgusted by the health risks, whereas the smoker would find the author guilty of exaggeration and discrimination. The main point is that smoking causes permanent physical damage. The attitude suggests that the author is probably not a smoker.

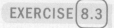

Identifying Points of View

Read the following passages and answer the questions about point of view.

Passage 1

`COLUMBUS`

On August 3, 1492, Columbus and some ninety mariners set sail from Palos, Spain, in the *Niña, Pinta,* and *Santa Maria.* Based on faulty calculations, the Admiral estimated Asia to be no more than 4,500 miles to the west (the actual distance is closer to 12,000 miles). Some 3,000 miles out, his crew became fearful and wanted to return home. But he convinced them to keep sailing west. Just two days later, on October 12, they landed on a small island in the Bahamas, which Columbus named San Salvador (holy savior).

A fearless explorer, Columbus turned out to be an ineffective administrator and a poor geographer. He ended up in debtor's prison, and to his dying day in 1506 he never admitted to locating a world unknown to Europeans. Geographers overlooked his contribution and named the Western continents after another mariner, Amerigo Vespucci, a merchant from Florence who participated in a Portuguese expedition to South America in 1501. In a widely reprinted letter, Vespucci claimed that a new world had been found, and it was his name that caught on.

—James Kirby Martin et al.,
America and Its Peoples

1. Which paragraph sounds more like the Columbus you learned about in elementary school? _____

   _____

2. What is the author's position on Columbus? Underline clues for your answer.

   _____

   _____

3. What is your view of Columbus? What has influenced your view? _____

   _____

   _____

4. What is the main point that the author is trying to convey? _____

   _____

   _____

Passage 2

`SURVIVING IN VIETNAM`

Vietnam ranks after World War II as America's second most expensive war. Between 1950 and 1975, the United States spent $123 billion on combat in Southeast Asia.

More importantly, Vietnam ranks—after our Civil War and World Wars I and II—as the nation's fourth deadliest war, with 57,661 Americans killed in action.

Yet, when the last U.S. helicopter left Saigon, Americans suffered what historian George Herring terms "collective amnesia." Everyone, even those who had fought in 'Nam, seemed to want to forget Southeast Asia. It took nearly ten years for the government to erect a national monument to honor those who died in Vietnam.

Few who served in Vietnam survived unscathed, whether psychologically or physically. One of the 303,600 Americans wounded during the long war was 101st Airborne platoon leader James Bombard, first shot and then blown up by a mortar round during the bitter Tet fighting at Hue in February 1968. He describes his traumatic experience as "feeling the bullet rip into your flesh, the shrapnel tear the flesh from your bones and the blood run down your leg. . . . To put your hand on your chest and to come away with your hand red with your own blood, and to feel it running out of your eyes and out of your mouth, and seeing it spurt out of your guts, realizing you were dying. . . . I was ripped open from the top of my head to the tip of my toes. I had forty-five holes in me." Somehow Bombard survived Vietnam.

Withdrawing U.S. forces from Vietnam ended only the combat. Returning veterans fought government disclaimers concerning the toxicity of the defoliant Agent Orange. VA hospitals across the nation still contain thousands of para- and quadriplegic Vietnam veterans, as well as the maimed from earlier wars. Throughout America the "walking wounded" find themselves still embroiled in the psychological aftermath of Vietnam.

—James Divine et al.,
America: Past and Present

1. What is the author's own view of the war? Underline clues for your answer.

   _____

   _____

2. What is your own position on the Vietnam War? _____

   _____

   _____

3. What is the purpose of Bombard's quotation? _____

   _____

   _____

4. How do you feel about war after reading this passage? _____

   _____

   _____

5. What is the main point that the author is trying to convey? _____

   _____

   _____

> **BRAIN BOOSTER**
>
> **Male and Female Brains and Their Points of View**
>
> Culture and environment obviously are important in shaping gender roles. However, neuroscience reveals that there are biological differences in male and female brains that influence thinking and behavior. Females have two X chromosomes, each containing 1,500 genes. Males have 1 X chromosome and 1 Y chromosome, which contains 100 genes. Many of the genes on the X chromosome govern verbal skills and other aspects of thinking. For this reason and others involving chemical differences, females generally tend to be better at language and seeing details, and males tend to excel at recognizing the gist of a situation.
>
> What does this mean in college or at work? Males and females might bring different points of view to a problem or an interpretation of a reading selection simply because of different brain wiring. So, working groups are often more successful at finding solutions when they are made up of both males and females. Test this in your next team project or group exercise.
>
> *—Adapted from John J. Medina,* Brain Rules.
> *© 2008 John J. Medina. Pear Press: Seattle, WA*

WHAT ARE FACTS AND OPINIONS?

Learning Objective 2

Distinguish facts and opinions

For both the reader and the writer, a point of view is a position or a belief that logically evolves over time through gained knowledge and experience and is usually based on both facts and opinions. For example, what is your position on city curfews for youth, on helping the homeless, and on abortion? Are your views on these issues supported solely by facts? Do you recognize the difference between the facts and the opinions used in your thinking?

Both facts and opinions are used persuasively to support positions. You have to determine which is which and then judge the issue accordingly. A **fact** is a statement based on actual evidence or personal observation. It can be checked objectively with empirical data and proved to be true. By contrast, an **opinion** is a statement of personal feeling or judgment. It reflects a belief or an interpretation of evidence, rather than evidence itself; it cannot be proved to be true. Look for "should" statements such as, "High school students *should* aspire to earning a college degree." Also notice other value words, such as *good, better, immoral, risky,* to name just a few. Adding the quoted opinion of a well-known authority to a few bits of evidence does not improve the data, yet this is an effective persuasive technique. Even though you may believe that an opinion is valid, it is still an opinion.

EXAMPLE

Fact: Freud developed a theory of personality.

Fact: Freud believed that the personality is divided into three parts.

Opinion: Freud constructed the most complete theory of personality development.

Opinion: The personality is divided into three parts: the id, the ego, and the superego.

Authors mix facts and opinions, sometimes in the same sentence, to win you over to a particular point of view. Persuasive tricks include quoting a source of facts who then voices an opinion or hedging a statement with "It is a fact that" and attaching a disguised opinion. Recognize that both facts and opinions are valuable but be able to distinguish between the two. The questions listed in the Reader's Tip, "Questions to Uncover Bias," on page 408 can help you.

EXERCISE 8.4

Differentiating Between Facts and Opinions

Read each statement and indicate *F* for fact and *O* for opinion. Be ready to justify your answer based on the definitions of *fact* and *opinion*.

_____ 1. Regarding the drugs that can cause death from overdose, the dangers have been blown wildly out of proportion.

—Jeffrey Reiman,
The Rich Get Richer and the Poor Get Prison:
Ideology, Class, and Criminal Justice, 7th ed.

_____ 2. A misdemeanor is a crime punishable by less than one year in prison.

—Adapted from John J. Macionis,
Social Problems

_____ 3. The most controversial tax is a general sales tax, which is levied by all but a few states on the sale of most goods, sometimes exempting food and drugs.

—Adapted from David B. Magleby et al.,
Government by the People, Teaching and
Learning Classroom Edition, 6th ed.

_____ 4. Phosphorus, found in detergents, causes an overgrowth of algae, which then consume all the available oxygen in the water, making it incapable of supporting any flora or fauna.

—Ricky W. Griffin and Ronald J. Ebert,
Business, 8th ed.

_____ 5. Witnesses who identify culprits (from photos or police lineups) within 10 seconds are 90% accurate, whereas those who take longer than 12 seconds are only 50% accurate.

—Lester A. Lefton and Linda Brannon,
Psychology, 9th ed.

_____ 6. When you feel anger, your heart rate increases and so does the temperature of your skin; and when you feel fear, your heart rate increases but your skin temperature actually decreases.

—Stephen M. Kosslyn and Robin S. Rosenberg,
Psychology: The Brain, the Person, the World, 2nd ed.

———— 7. Convicted juveniles, like adult offenders, often gain early and undeserved release from jail.

> —Judy Sheindlin,
> *Don't Pee on My Leg and Tell Me It's Raining:*
> *America's Toughest Family Court Judge Speaks Out*

———— 8. Repairing the meetinghouse, building a school, aiding a widowed neighbor—such were the proper uses of wealth.

> —Gary B. Nash et al.,
> *The American People*, 6th ed., Vol. 1

———— 9. Although there are a large number of Web browsers, some developed by Internet giants such as Microsoft, the dominant Web browser is Google, which has gained dominance by offering the most efficient search engine on the Web.

> —Paul R. Gregory,
> *Essentials of Economics*, 6th ed.

———— 10. Americans are poorly informed about politics.

> —Gary Wasserman,
> *The Basics of American Politics*, 12th ed.

EXERCISE 8.5

Discerning Facts and Opinions in Textbooks

The following passage from a history text describes Sigmund Freud. Notice the mixture of facts and opinions in developing a view of this scientist. Mark the items that follow with *F* for fact and *O* for opinion.

Passage 1

Sigmund Freud was a disciplined man, precise and punctual in his habits. In many ways, his life was typical of the life of a Viennese bourgeois professional at the end of the nineteenth century. His day was like a railway timetable, scheduled to the minute—whether seeing patients, dining with his family, or taking his daily constitutional. He even calculated his pleasures, counting as his only indulgence the 20 cigars he smoked every day.

The order in Freud's life seemed curiously at odds with his dedication to the study of disorder. He was a man of science, a medical doctor specializing in *organic* diseases of the nervous system. Early in his career, he began to question *physiological* explanations for certain nervous disorders and to search for another reason for the disorders of the mind. His exploration took him to Paris in 1885 to study with the leading French neurologist, Jean Martin Charcot (1825–1893), whose work on hysteria had won him an international reputation.

Surrounded by hysterics in Charcot's clinic, Freud wondered whether organic physical illnesses could be traced to psychological problems. Freud explored the value of hypnosis as a technique for uncovering the secret workings of the mind. He learned that emotions alone could produce physical symptoms such as blindness and paralysis. By hypnotizing patients, Freud caught glimpses of the world of the unconscious as a vast and hidden terrain. He approached the new territory as an explorer.

Freud created a new science of the unconscious, psychoanalysis, when he rejected physiological causes for nervous disorders in favor of psychological ones. He intended psychoanalysis as a theory of personality and a method of treatment or therapy. That was a dramatic break with existing theories of madness and mental disorder. On his seventieth birthday, Freud looked back over his own career and described his achievement: "The poets and philosophers before me discovered the unconscious; what I discovered was the scientific method by which the unconscious can be studied."

—Mark Kishlansky et al.,
Civilization in the West, 6th ed.

_____ 1. Freud smoked 20 cigars each day.

_____ 2. He lived the life of a typical Viennese professional of his era.

_____ 3. The order in Freud's life was at odds with his dedication to the study of disorder.

_____ 4. Freud was a medical doctor specializing in organic disorders of the nervous system.

_____ 5. Freud created the science of psychoanalysis.

The following passage from a business text discusses Winston Churchill's leadership capabilities. Notice the mixture of facts and opinions in developing a view of this former British leader. Mark the items that follow with *F* for fact and *O* for opinion.

Passage 2

Successful leaders often have the experience of prevailing in the face of adversity and learning from earlier failures. Leaders' skills also must match the circumstances. Winston Churchill's career provides a classic example.

Churchill began his remarkable political career in 1901 when he became a member of the House of Commons at the age of 26. Prior to his entry into Parliament he had seen combat as a cavalry officer in India, Cuba, and the Sudan and was awarded several medals for valor. He rose quickly in politics and governmental service, becoming the First Lord of the Admiralty (civilian head of the British Navy) in 1911. One of Churchill's decisions about deployment of naval forces in 1915 during World War I resulted in failure and marked the end of his fast-track career. Churchill returned to combat, serving as an infantry officer in 1917. After World War I Churchill returned to public office but was essentially relegated to the sidelines of politics. His calls for rearmament, warnings about the intentions of the Nazis between 1933 and 1939, and criticisms of the government's attempts to appease the Nazis were ignored. When things looked the worst in May 1940, the country turned to the 65-year-old Churchill for leadership as Prime Minister. It is said that Churchill "stood out as the one man in whom the nation could place its trust."

In June 1940 Britain had been at war with Germany for a year. British soldiers had been driven out of France and narrowly escaped capture through an evacuation from Dunkirk. France surrendered on June 22, and the United States had not yet entered World War II. The Battle of Britain, which involved heavy bombing of Britain's major cities, was about to begin, and it appeared that Germany would invade Britain. The outcome looked bleak. Churchill's hats, cigars, and two-fingered "v" for victory signs were distinctive, as well as symbolic, and endeared him to his followers. There were other qualities about Churchill as well that made him well-suited for the challenges of leadership during these difficult times. Two specific examples of his personal risk-taking are described as follows:

> Churchill as Prime Minister frequently and deliberately ran terrible personal risks. But the people admired him for it, and loved his offhand disregard for danger. Once, when a German bomb landed near his car and nearly tipped it over, he joked, "Must have been my beef that kept the car down"—a reference to his pudginess.
>
> Winston Churchill also liked to leave his underground air-raid shelter in Whitehall for the streets the moment bombs began falling. Attempts were made to stop him, because the risk of getting one's head blown off or losing a limb from shrapnel was great. . . . "I'll have you know," thundered Churchill, "that as a child my nursemaid could never prevent me from taking a walk in the Green Park when I wanted to do so. And, as a man, Adolf Hitler certainly won't."
>
> At the end of World War II in 1945, Churchill lost his bid for reelection because he was unresponsive to the needs for social change after the war. He returned to office again as Prime Minister from 1951 to 1955, but his performance was limited by age and health problems. In general, his service as a peacetime Prime Minister did not measure up to his service during war time.

—Charles R. Greer and Warren Richard Plunkett,
Supervision: Diversity and Teams in the Workplace, 10th ed.

_____ 1. Churchill began his political career at the age of 26 in the House of Commons.

_____ 2. Things looked the worst for England in May 1940.

_____ 3. France surrendered to Germany on June 22, 1940, but the United States had not yet entered the war.

_____ 4. Churchill was a frequent and deliberate risk-taker.

_____ 5. Churchill was a better leader during the war than during peacetime.

WHAT IS THE AUTHOR'S PURPOSE?

Learning Objective 3

Identify the author's purpose for writing

A textbook author can shift from an objective and factual explanation of a topic to a subjective and opinionated treatment of the facts. Recognizing the author's purpose does not mean that you will or won't accept the author's explanations; it just means that you will be a more cautious, well-informed reader.

An author always has a **purpose** in mind when putting words on paper. A textbook reader expects that the author's purpose is to inform or to explain objectively—

and, in general, this is true. At times, however, an author can slip from factual explanation to opinionated treatment of the facts, or persuasion. The sophisticated reader recognizes this shift in purpose and becomes more critical in evaluating the content. For example, a persuasive paragraph for or against more air quality control regulations should alert you to be more skeptical than you would be while reading a paragraph that only explains how air quality control works.

Just as we know that a textbook is generally intended to inform, we expect an election campaign speech to try to persuade. So, consider the context of a reading selection—the type of publication—as an important clue to its purpose. In addition, analyze the tone and the kinds of information presented, and determine the author's point of view on the topic. As always, think about the main point being made but also why the author wants to make it.

The author can have a single purpose or more than one such as the following:

inform	persuade	entertain
explain	argue	narrate
describe	condemn	shock
enlighten	ridicule	investigate

Read the following passage to determine the author's purpose.

EXAMPLE

love, *n.* A temporary insanity curable by marriage or by removal of the patient from the influences under which he incurred the disorder. This disease, like caries and many other ailments, is prevalent only among civilized races living under artificial conditions; barbarous nations breathing pure air and eating simple food enjoy immunity from its ravages. It is sometimes fatal, but more frequently to the physician than to the patient.

—Ambrose Bierce,
The Devil's Dictionary

EXPLANATION   The author defines love in a humorous and exaggerated manner for the purpose of entertaining the reader.

EXERCISE 8.6

Determining the Author's Purpose

Read the following passage and answer the questions about the author's purpose.

ISABELLA KATZ AND THE HOLOCAUST: A LIVING TESTIMONY

No statistics can adequately render the enormity of the Holocaust, and its human meaning can perhaps only be understood through the experience of a single human being who was cast into the nightmare of the Final Solution. Isabella Katz was the eldest of six children—Isabella, brother Philip, and sisters Rachel, Chicha, Cipi, and baby Potyo—from a family of Hungarian Jews. She lived in the ghetto of Kisvarda, a provincial town of 20,000 people, where hers was a typical Jewish family of the region—middle-class, attached to Orthodox traditions, and imbued with a love of learning.

In 1938 and 1939 Hitler pressured Hungary's regent, Miklós Horthy, into adopting anti-Jewish laws. By 1941 Hungary had become a German ally, and deportations and massacres were added to the restrictions. Isabella's father left for the United States, where he hoped to obtain entry papers for his family, but after Pearl Harbor, Hungary was at war with America and the family was trapped. In the spring of 1944, when Hitler occupied Hungary, the horror of the Final Solution struck Isabella. On March 19 Adolf Eichmann, as SS officer in charge of deportation, ordered the roundup of Jews in Hungary, who numbered some 650,000. On May 28, Isabella's nineteenth birthday, the Jews in Kisvarda were told to prepare for transportation to Auschwitz on the following morning. Isabella recalled:

> And now an SS man is here, spick-and-span, with a dog, a silver pistol, and a whip. And he is all of sixteen years old. On his list appears the name of every Jew in the ghetto. . . . "Teresa Katz," he calls—my mother. She steps forward. . . . Now the SS man moves toward my mother. He raises his whip and, for no apparent reason at all, lashes out at her.

En route to Auschwitz, crammed into hot, airless boxcars, Isabella's mother told her children to "stay alive":

> Out there, when it's all over, a world's waiting for you to give it all I gave you. Despite what you see here . . . believe me, there is humanity out there, there is dignity. . . . And when this is all over, you must add to it, because sometimes it is a little short, a little skimpy.

Isabella and her family were among more than 437,000 Jews sent to Auschwitz from Hungary.

When they arrived at Auschwitz, the SS and camp guards divided the prisoners into groups, often separating family members. Amid the screams and confusion, Isabella remembered:

> We had just spotted the back of my mother's head when Mengele, the notorious Dr. Josef Mengele, points to my sister and me and says, "Die Zwei" [those two]. This trim, very good-looking German, with a flick of his thumb and a whistle, is selecting who is to live and who is to die.

Isabella's mother and her baby sister perished within a few days.

> The day we arrived in Auschwitz, there were so many people to be burned that the four crematoriums couldn't handle the task. So the Germans built big open fires to throw the children in. Alive? I do not know. I saw the flames. I heard the shrieks.

Isabella was to endure the hell of Auschwitz for nine months.

The inmates were stripped, the hair on their heads and bodies was shaved, and they were herded into crude, overcrowded barracks. As if starvation, forced labor, and disease were not enough, they were subjected to unspeakable torture, humiliation, and terror, a mass of living skeletons for whom the difference between life and death could be measured only in an occasional flicker of spirit that determined to resist against impossible odds. Isabella put it this way:

> Have you ever weighed 120 pounds and gone down to 40? Something like that—not quite alive, yet not quite dead. Can anyone, can even I, picture it? . . .

Our eyes sank deeper. Our skin rotted. Our bones screamed out of our bodies. Indeed, there was barely a body to house the mind, yet the mind was still working, sending out the messages "Live! Live!"

In November, just as Isabella and her family were lined up outside a crematorium, they were suddenly moved to Birnbäumel, in eastern Germany—the Russians were getting nearer, and the Nazis were closing down their death camps and moving the human evidence of their barbarism out of reach of the enemy. In January, as the Russians and the frigid weather closed in, the prisoners were forced to march through the snows deeper into Germany, heading toward the camp at Bergen-Belsen. Those who could not endure the trial fell by the side, shot or frozen to death. On January 23, while stumbling through a blizzard with the sound of Russian guns in the distance, Isabella, Rachel, and Chicha made a successful dash from the death march and hid in an abandoned house. Two days later Russian soldiers found them. Philip had been sent to a labor camp, and Cipi made it to Bergen-Belsen, where she died.

Isabella later married and had two children of her own, making a new life in America. Yet the images of the Holocaust remain forever in her memory. "Now I am older," she says, "and I don't remember all the pain. . . . That is not happiness, only relief, and relief is blessed. . . . And children someday will plant flowers in Auschwitz, where the sun couldn't crack through the smoke of burning flesh."

—Richard L. Greaves et al.,
Civilizations of the World, 3rd ed.

1. What is the author's purpose for including this story in a history textbook?

    _____

    _____

2. What does the author mean by "its human meaning can perhaps only be understood through the experience of a single human being"? _____

    _____

    _____

    _____

3. Why does the author include Isabella's quotations? _____

    _____

    _____

4. Why does the author include Isabella's quotation about the SS man? _____

    _____

    _____

5. What is Isabella's purpose in relating her story? _____

    _____

    _____

6. Is the passage predominantly developed through facts or opinions? Give an example of each. _____

_____

_____

7. How does the passage influence your thinking about the Holocaust? _____

_____

_____

_____

WHAT IS THE AUTHOR'S TONE?

Learning Objective 4

Recognize the author's tone

The author's purpose directly affects the **tone**, the author's attitude toward the topic. If the purpose is to criticize, the tone will probably be condemning and somewhat mean-spirited. If the purpose is to entertain, the tone may be humorous, playful, or dramatic. To put it in simple terms, the tone of an author's writing is similar to the tone of a speaker's voice. For listeners, telling the difference between an angry tone and a romantic tone is easy; you simply notice the speaker's voice. Distinguishing among humor, sarcasm, and irony, however, may be more difficult. Humorous remarks are designed to be comical and amusing, whereas sarcastic remarks are designed to cut or inflict pain. As discussed in Chapter 7, ironic remarks express the opposite of the literal meaning and show the incongruity between the actual and the expected. Making such precise distinctions requires a careful evaluation of what is said. Because the sound of the voice is not heard in reading, clues to the tone must come from the writer's presentation of the message. Your job is to look for clues to answer the question, "What is the author's attitude toward the topic?" The list in the Reader's Tip, "Recognizing an Author's Tone," below shows some of the many ways a writer can express tone.

Reader's TIP   Recognizing an Author's Tone

The following words with explanations can describe an author's tone or attitude:

- **Absurd, farcical, ridiculous:** laughable or a joke
- **Apathetic, detached:** not caring
- **Ambivalent:** having contradictory attitudes or feelings
- **Angry, bitter, hateful:** feeling bad and upset about the topic
- **Arrogant, condescending:** acting conceited or above others
- **Awestruck, wondering:** filled with wonder
- **Cheerful, joyous, happy:** feeling good about the topic
- **Compassionate, sympathetic:** feeling sorrow at the distress of others
- **Congratulatory, celebratory:** honoring an achievement or festive occasion

- **Cynical:** expecting the worst from people
- **Depressed, melancholy:** sad, dejected, or having low spirits
- **Disapproving:** judging unfavorably
- **Formal:** using an official style; of a high social class, genteel
- **Frustrated:** blocked from a goal
- **Hard:** unfeeling, strict, and unrelenting
- **Humorous, jovial, comic, playful, amused:** being funny
- **Incredulous:** unbelieving
- **Indignant:** outraged
- **Intense, impassioned:** extremely involved, zealous, or agitated
- **Ironic:** stating the opposite of what is expected; having a twist at the end
- **Irreverent:** lacking respect for authority
- **Mocking, scornful, caustic, condemning:** ridiculing the topic
- **Objective, factual, straightforward, critical:** using facts without emotions
- **Optimistic:** looking on the bright side
- **Outspoken:** speaking one's mind on issues
- **Pessimistic:** looking on the negative side
- **Prayerful:** religiously thankful
- **Reverent:** showing respect
- **Righteous:** morally correct
- **Romantic, intimate, loving:** expressing love or affection
- **Sarcastic:** saying one thing and meaning another
- **Satiric:** using irony, wit, and sarcasm to discredit or ridicule
- **Sensational:** overdramatized or overhyped
- **Sentimental, nostalgic:** remembering the good old days
- **Serious, sincere, earnest, solemn:** being honest and concerned
- **Straightforward:** forthright, direct
- **Subjective, opinionated:** expressing opinions and feelings
- **Tragic:** regrettable or deplorable
- **Vindictive:** seeking revenge

Try being an author yourself. Imagine that you have been waiting a half-hour for one of your friends to show up for a meeting, and you can wait no longer. You decide to send a text. On a piece of paper, draft three different messages—one in a sympathetic tone, one in an angry tone, and one in a sarcastic tone. Notice in doing this how your tone reflects your purpose. Which one would you really send and to which friend?

EXAMPLE   Identify the tone of the following passage:

When I actually went south, and actually saw signs that said "white" and "colored" and I actually could not drink out of that water fountain, or go to that ladies' room, I had a real emotional reaction. I remember the first time it happened, was at the Tennessee State Fair. And I had a date with this, this young man. And I started to go to the ladies' room. And it said "white and colored" and I really resented that. I was outraged. So, it, it had a really emotional effect. . . . My response was, who's trying to change it, change these things. And I recall talking to a number of people in the dormitories at school and on campus, and asking them if they knew any people who were trying to—to bring about some type of change. And I remember being, getting almost depressed, because I encountered what I thought was so much apathy. At first I couldn't find anyone, and many of the students were saying, why are you concerned about that?

—Diane Nash, Interview at www.teachersdomain.org/resources
In Women and the Making of America,
Mari Jo Buhle, Teresa Murphy, and Jane Gerhard

The author's tone is _____

   a. ambivalent.
   b. congratulatory.
   c. indignant.

EXPLANATION   The author's tone is indignant (*c*). The repeated use of the word *actually,* as if she can't believe what she is experiencing, and the word *outraged,* reflect the writer's emotions. In addition, her disappointment at finding no one who shares her intense concern about this issue further conveys the continued feelings of anger and indignation.

EXERCISE 8.7

Identifying Tone

Mark the letter that identifies the tone for each of the following examples. Refer to the Reader's Tip, "Recognizing an Author's Tone," on pages 422–423 to define unfamiliar words.

_____ 1. Must I recycle everything? I don't want any more gifts of brown, "earth friendly" stationery. I want to exercise my right to burn my newspapers and throw my soda can in the trash.

     a. objective
     b. nostalgic
     c. angry

_____ 2. In the last few decades, health experts and environmentalists have looked to birth control to save us from a growing world population that already exceeds 5.5 billion. Yet, as recently as 1914, the distribution of birth control information was illegal. In that year, Margaret Higgins Sanger, founder of the magazine *The Woman Rebel*, was arrested and indicted for sending birth control information through the mail. Surprisingly, again today some factions are pressing to limit women's access to birth control.

     a. optimistic
     b. ironic
     c. sentimental

_____ 3. The Golden Age or heyday of Hollywood was in the 1930s. Americans, economically crippled by the Great Depression, went to movies for fantasy escapes into worlds created by entertainers such as Clark Gable, Greta Garbo, and the Marx Brothers.

    a. objective
    b. nostalgic
    c. bitter

_____ 4. Doublespeak hides the truth, evades the issues, and misleads. No one gets fired these days. They disappear due to downsizing, workforce adjustments, and head-count reductions. After eliminating 8,000 jobs, an automobile company called it "a volume-related production schedule adjustment." Perhaps the families of the workers called it an "involuntary lifestyle reduction."

    a. sensational
    b. impassioned
    c. bitter

_____ 5. In his early thirties, Beethoven's gradual hearing loss became total. This prevented him from playing the piano properly but not from continuing to write music. His three most complex and acclaimed symphonies were written when he was stone deaf. He never heard them played.

    a. ironic
    b. sarcastic
    c. opinionated

EXERCISE 8.8

Identifying the Author's Tone and Point of View

Read the following passages to determine the author's tone and attitude toward the subject.

Passage 1

THE FENCE

My fingers wanted to reach through the wire fence, not to touch it, not to feel it, but to break it down, with what I did not understand. The burning was not there to be understood. Something was burning, the side of me that knew I was treated different, would always be treated different because I was born on a particular side of a fence, a fence that separated me from others, that separated me from the past, that separated me from the country of my genesis and glued me to the country I did not love because it demanded something of me I could not give. Something was burning now, and if I could have grasped the source of that rage and held it in my fist, I would have melted that fence.

—Benjamin Alire Saénz,
Exile, El Paso, Texas

1. What is the author's tone? _____

_____

_____

2. Underline the words and phrases that suggest this tone.

3. What is the author's point of view? _____

_____

_____

4. What is your own point of view on the subject? _____

_____

_____

5. What is the main point that the author is trying to convey? _____

_____

_____

Passage 2

A WHOLE NEW BALLGAME

The first day of freshman basketball tryouts, I learned that coaching girls is different. I was demonstrating the correct way to set a cross screen. I positioned my legs shoulder-width apart and crossed my hands—fists clenched—over my groin to protect myself from the injury that all men fear. I paused, confused, understanding from the girls' bewildered looks that something was wrong. The other coach, a 15-year veteran of coaching girls, recognized my rookie mistake and bailed me out. He raised his arms and covered his chest, and I knew that I had entered alien territory.

—Brendan O'Shaughnessy,
"It's a Whole New Ballgame for Veteran Coach,"
Chicago Tribune, December 1, 2002

1. What is the author's tone? _____

_____

2. Underline the words and phrases that suggest this tone.

3. What is the author's point of view? _____

_____

_____

4. What is your own point of view on the subject? _____

_____

_____

5. What is the main point that the author is trying to convey? _____

_____

_____

Passage 3

WHY WOMEN SMILE

After smiling brilliantly for nearly four decades, I now find myself trying to quit. Or, at the very least, seeking to lower the wattage a bit.

Smiles are not the small and innocuous things they appear to be: Too many of us smile in lieu of showing what's really on our minds. Despite all the work we American women have done to get and maintain full legal control of our bodies, not to mention our destinies, we still don't seem to be fully in charge of a couple of small muscle groups in our faces.

Our smiles have their roots in the greetings of monkeys, who pull their lips up and back to show their fear of attack, as well as their reluctance to vie for a position of dominance. And like the opossum caught in the light by a clattering garbage can, we, too, flash toothy grimaces when we make major mistakes. By declaring ourselves non-threatening, our smiles provide an extremely versatile means of protection.

—Amy Cunningham,
"Why Women Smile"

1. What is the author's tone? _____

_____

_____

2. Underline the words and phrases that suggest this tone.

3. What is the author's point of view? _____

_____

_____

4. What is your own point of view on the subject? _____

_____

_____

5. What is the main point that the author is trying to convey? _____

_____

_____

Using Tone and Other Clues to Determine the Point of View in Editorial Cartoons

Editorial cartoons vividly illustrate how an author or an artist can effectively communicate point of view without making a direct verbal statement. Through their drawings, cartoonists have great freedom to be extremely harsh and judgmental.

For example, they take positions on local and national news events and frequently depict politicians as crooks, thieves, or even murderers. Because the accusations are implied rather than directly stated, the cartoonist communicates a point of view but is still safe from libel charges.

EXAMPLE   Study the cartoon on page 429 to determine what the cartoonist believes and is saying about the subject. Use the following steps to analyze the implied meaning and point of view:

1. Glance at the cartoon for an overview.

2. Answer the question, "What is this about?" to determine the general topic.

   _____

   _____

   _____

3. Study the details for symbolism. Who or what is represented by the images shown? _____

   _____

   _____

4. With all of the information in mind, explain the main point that the cartoonist is trying to get across. _____

   _____

   _____

5. What is the tone of the cartoon? _____

   _____

   _____

6. What is the cartoonist's purpose?

   _____

   _____

7. What is the cartoonist's point of view or position on the subject? What is your point of view? _____

   _____

   _____

   _____

EXPLANATION   Global warming is the topic of the cartoon, as suggested by the question on the back of the newspaper. The carefree polar bear sunbathes as the polar ice shelf cracks beneath the lounge chair. As the sun beams down on the polar

Cagle Cartoons, Inc.

bear and the ice melts, the bear acclimates with sun shades, suntan oil, and an iced drink from the "KOOL-R." The main point of the cartoon is that we, like the polar bear, are ignoring the reality of climate changes, and we will suffer the disastrous consequences. The question, "What global warming?" suggests that we are in as much denial as the polar bear. The tone is sarcastic and pleading. The cartoonist's purpose is to spur us into action before it is too late.

EXERCISE 8.9

Interpreting an Editorial Cartoon

Use the same steps to analyze the message and answer the questions about the cartoon shown on page 430.

1. What is the general topic of this cartoon? _____

   _____

2. What is represented by the objects, such as the circular slide, the hoop, and

   the tires? _____

   _____

   _____

   _____

   _____

   _____

3. What is the main point that the cartoonist is trying to convey? _____

_____

_____

_____

4. What is the cartoonist's purpose? _____

_____

_____

5. What is the tone of the cartoon? _____

_____

_____

6. What is the cartoonist's point of view? _____

_____

_____

_____

7. What is your point of view on the subject? _____

_____

_____

Jim Borgman/Universal Uclick.

Cartoons are fun but challenging because they require prior knowledge for interpretation. To understand current news cartoons, you have to be familiar with the latest happenings. Look on the editorial page of your newspaper to enjoy world events from a cartoonist's point of view. If you prefer viewing them online, the home pages of some Internet service providers include links to the day's best cartoons; you can also do a Google search for cartoon sites.

As stated in the beginning of the chapter, even in college textbooks, authors' attitudes and biases slip through. Your responsibility as a reader is to be alert for signs of manipulation and to be ready, by noticing not only what is said but also what is not said and to question interpretations and conclusions. Sophisticated readers draw their own conclusions based on their own interpretation of the facts.

SUMMARY POINTS

1 **How can I identify the author's point of view? (page 406)**
- In reading, *point of view* refers to the author's opinions and way of looking at the topic. The author's point of view, like the reader's point of view, can influence the presentation of facts and information in the text.
- *Bias* is similar to point of view in that it refers to the author's opinion or position on a subject. Bias usually has a negative connotation, whereas point of view generally has a more positive connotation.
- Similar to making reasonable inferences, identifying the author's point of view requires analyzing word choice and selection of details in light of your own opinions and schemata.
- Analyze the use of facts and opinions, identify the author's tone, and determine the author's purpose in writing to reveal the author's point of view on the subject.

2 **How can I distinguish between facts and opinions? (page 414)**
- Analyze details in light of the definition of fact, which is something that can be proved objectively, and of opinion, which is something representing a feeling or judgment and that cannot be proved objectively.
- Be on the lookout for emotional language, "should" statements, and value words. These usually indicate opinions.

3 **How can I identify the author's purpose for writing? (page 418)**
- Identifying the author's purpose is intertwined with analyzing tone, facts and opinions, and the author's point of view. The main point and the type of publication can be clues.

4 **How can I recognize the author's tone? (page 422)**
- *Tone* refers to the author's attitude toward the subject. It is like a speaker's tone of voice.
- Be alert to words or phrases that reflect feelings, opinions, or beliefs. Remember that the tone might also be neutral or objective and not imply any opinion on the topic.
- Editorial cartoons tend to display a tone that is satirical and critical while also being humorous. Understanding the cartoonist's point of view requires careful examination of the details and prior knowledge—schemata—on the topic.

SELECTION 1   Philosophy   MyReadingLab

Visit Chapter 8: Point of View in MyReadingLab to complete the Selection 1 activities and the Build Background Knowledge video activity.

P**REVIEW** the next selection to predict its purpose and organization and to formulate your learning plan.

Activate Schemata

Have you ever struggled with a decision?
What was your last important decision?
How did you arrive at a choice?
What is your next major decision?

Establish a Purpose for Reading

Life is about making decisions. Whether the choice is seeing a movie or going bowling, or something of greater consequence, like going to college or looking for a job, we want to make good decisions. Read to learn what causes us to hesitate and how to set standards for decision making that will last a lifetime.

Build Background Knowledge — VIDEO

The Seven Decisions

To prepare for reading Selection 1, answer the questions below. Then, watch this video on the decision-making process.

What is one of the most difficult decisions you ever made?

What role do other people's opinions have in your decision-making process?

How do you handle those times when you make a wrong decision?

This video helped me: _____

_____

_____

Increase Word Knowledge

What do you know about these words?

vacillate	alternatives	project	stymied	obstacle
obeisance	mantras	facilitate	architecture	recidivism

Your instructor may give a brief vocabulary review before or after reading.

Integrate Knowledge While Reading

Questions have been inserted in the margin to stimulate your thinking while reading. Remember to

| Predict | Picture | Relate | Monitor | Correct | Annotate |

DECISION

A Native American said he had two dogs fighting inside himself, one mean and the other good. When asked which one wins, he replied, "Whichever one I feed the most."

I can relate to this!

I will. I won't. I'll go. I'll stay. I should. I shouldn't. Yes. No. Yes. Maybe. At times we teeter on the cliff of decision. We feel stressed by indecision as we vacillate
5 through "decisions and revisions which a minute will reverse" (T. S. Eliot). If our thinking has been solid, usually the decision will follow. When it doesn't, we can assist it through a three-step process by considering the goals, alternatives, and probable outcomes of each alternative.

- • Step 1: State the goal. (What is the desired result of our decision and action?)
10 • Step 2: List the alternatives. (What are the possible plans of action—Plan A, Plan B, etc.?)
- • Step 3: Describe the probable outcome of each action plan. (Plan A, Plan B, etc.)

DIFFICULTIES IN DECIDING

Although the three-step process may appear simple, our minds do not work like machines, and other factors over which we have no control don't always work out
15 as expected. Frequently, we struggle to formulate goals, to assess the data, and to project possible outcomes. Let's look at some of the difficulties we can run into.

Do any of these apply to me?

We struggle with several common roadblocks in making decisions. There is fear: What if we are wrong? Sometimes habits are so strong or convenient that we continue our former ways even in the face of new information. Furthermore, some
20 of us are so stymied by overthinking that we never act at all. And, at times, if we want something badly enough, conflicting motives stop our thinking.

A student captures some of the feelings, tensions, insights, and results of a decision in which she had conflicting motives:

My mind screamed NO! My thoughts argued with each other repeatedly.
25 The fear had my speech and body paralyzed. Only my mind was functioning, tossing the negative messages like liquid mercury separating when put on a hard surface. I closed my eyes when I heard the Justice of the Peace say, "I now pronounce you man and wife." I started to cry! My new husband mistook those tears as joyful tears. Only I knew of the estranged feel-
30 ings that existed, knowing instantly that I had done myself a violent injustice. The vivid echoing memory of those vows creates a haunting mirage distressing all functions of my well-being.

I was a young know-it-all of seventeen. A typical sample of a teenager. I had my mind made up to disband my family. I was spiteful. I wanted to
35 prove my parents wrong! This dishonoring, ill attitude that existed is still unexplainable to this day. I know I longed for some acceptance.

Roadblocks such as fear, habits, overthinking, and conflicting motives affect decision making.

luxorphoto/Shutterstock

Fifteen years too late, the reflection is clear why I accepted those vows. I fell in love with my husband's family. His mom and dad loved me back. I had a new family that loved me just the way I was. Yeah, I really felt impor-
40 tant being a wife and daughter-in-law. These roles turned stale real fast. This was the beginning of my devastating trials in the adult world.

I've often thought of what my life would be like if I had made a different choice. This choice resulted in a brutal, costly divorce. It left me financially and emotionally distraught. An important part of my life was wasted and a long
45 recovery was ahead of me. I can't replace the precious time lost, but I've learned to balance and weigh all my choices.

HOW TO DECIDE

Face Fear

If fear is the greatest obstacle to deciding, then courage and calm help us to decide. If we can free ourselves from obeisance to others, if we can strike strongly out on our own and let the chips and opinions fall where they may, we increase our decision-
50 making power. An example of high praise given to a citizen activist was "He put his body where his words were." Courage is not bottled and sold, but it can be bought with hard work. We can change our thinking with mantras such as "I think it's right; I'll do it; others can do what they want." Easier said than done, but courage can build with practice.

Firm Our Foundation

55 When the decision is important and we have the time, the more thorough we are in our thinking preparation, the easier and better our decision will be. If we have covered our thinking bases, we have gone a long way toward deciding. We can make our thoughts objective and visible by writing them down.

A good way to capture our thoughts and facilitate decision making is to make a
60 list of pros and cons. Pick any decision issue you wish (changing jobs, asking someone out on a date, breaking up with someone, taking a certain course, and so forth).
Write it down on the chart that follows; then write all the thoughts for and against
that decision. Evaluate the items for importance by indicating a weight of 1 to 10 in
the box alongside each item, using 10 if it is extremely important and 1 if it is of
65 negligible importance. Now simply total the boxes and watch the scales of decision
begin to tip in one direction.

Decision Issue:						
PROS		**Weight**		**CONS**		**Weight**
Total				Total		

Call on Character

Sometimes, no matter what we know, the decision is hard because the results may be
hurtful to us or to those we care about, or because the decision pits our greed against
our good. When our character is in conflict, then we dig deep and decide who we are
70 and who we want to become; we reach for principles, motivation, and values; we
realize that our choices define us, that we become what we choose. To help us through
these trying decisions, we can turn to Marcus Aurelius, Roman emperor, warrior and
philosopher. He tells us to perform each action as if it were our last. Similarly, Igna-
tius of Loyola, soldier and founder of the Jesuits, tells us to imagine ourselves on our
75 deathbed and then choose as if the choice were the last event in our life.

In cases of character conflict, we can "push" the decision by focusing on the
positive side and then, when we are able, decide quickly so as not to prolong the
pain of conflicting choice.

Does character refer to moral values?

Feelings: A Boost Toward Decision

Hegel thinks that "nothing great in the world has been accomplished without pas-
80 sion." That same passion can sometimes be that extra push toward a decision. Many
of us make decisions not knowing that our feelings are driving our thoughts. If,
however, we are highly aware of our feelings, and if we give them input but not
control, we can use feelings as part of the deciding process. Antonio Domasio is
studying the emotional architecture of the brain, watching the "split-second emo-
85 tional assessments of situations that unfold so quickly that we're usually not aware
of the process. . . . Emotions turn out to be essential to our rational decision-making
processes. If we didn't have those gut responses, we'd get caught in an endless cycle
of analysis. . . . It's not that I'm saying the emotions decide things for you, it's that
the emotions help you concentrate on the right decision."

How does this relate to impulse control?

Image the Action

90 Another help in deciding is to form an image of ourselves doing the action. For instance, if we cannot decide to go to a stern school authority or a terrifying boss, we
can visualize ourselves walking down the hallway toward the person's office. When

we can do this without significant anxiety, then we can visualize ourselves knocking on the door, then walking in, and finally, saying the difficult message. It is impor-
95 tant to be relaxed at each step before we image the next one. Imaging can prepare us for difficult decisions and actions.

Role-Play into Reality
After we have imaged it, then we can act it out, or role-play it. Delancy Street, a community prison in San Francisco, used role-playing to change thinking. Male prisoners had to get haircuts, wear suits, and even walk "normally." They were asked to act as
100 if they were successful, good citizens. This acting seemed to change their thinking, for their recidivism rate was quite low. About 80 percent of the role-players entered society and stayed there; apparently, many became the citizens whom they role-played.

We too can draw upon the power of acting to help ourselves carry out a decision. When the decision demands change and we don't seem to have the power to
105 decide, we may be able to role-play the action. At first we will probably feel stiff, but repetition will make it easier; consequently, it will become easier to think about acting that way routinely. Finally, we will have the strength to do what we have been role-playing, and then our minds and our bodies will work together. By playing the role we can become the role.

How can I apply these ideas?

(1,468 words)

—From Gary R. Kirby and Jeffery R. Goodpaster,
Thinking, 4th ed., © 2007, pp. 321–327. Reproduced in
print and electronic formats by permission of Pearson
Education, Inc., Upper Saddle River, New Jersey.

Recall

Stop to self-test, relate, and react.

Your instructor may choose to give you a brief comprehension review.

THINK CRITICALLY ABOUT THE SELECTION

What is your point of view regarding the six suggestions in the "How to Decide" section?

Do the authors include facts and opinions to support their point?

What words describe the tone of the selection?

What is the primary purpose of the selection?

What is the authors' point of view on decision making?

WRITE ABOUT THE SELECTION

"It is our choices, Harry, that show what we truly are, far more than our abilities." Professor Dumbledore said this in J. K. Rowling's book, *Harry Potter and the Chamber of Secrets*. What is your point of view on this statement?

Response Suggestion: List at least five important decisions that have shaped your life, when a different choice would have made a big difference in who you are today.

SKILL DEVELOPMENT: EXPLORE POINT OF VIEW

Form a collaborative group and brainstorm a list of difficult decisions that members have made or that they are facing. Choose the thorniest one and consider the following questions:

- Which of the obstacles mentioned in the selection do you think are most likely to interfere with a decision on this issue?

- Which method mentioned in the selection do you think would be most useful?

- What decision do the members of the group think is the best? Why?

- Did group members have different points of view on these questions? Is there more than one reasonable point of view?

CHECK YOUR COMPREHENSION

After reading the selection, answer the following questions with *a, b, c,* or *d.* To help you analyze your strengths and weaknesses, the question types are indicated.

Main Idea   ————   1. Which is the best statement of the main idea of this selection?

     a. People have difficulty making decisions for several common reasons.

     b. Many people fail to think clearly about the consequences of their choices.

     c. It is important to consider our emotions but not let them control our choices.

     d. Obstacles in decision making can be overcome with practice in several areas.

Detail   ————   2. Which of the following is *not* one of the obstacles to decision making mentioned by the author?

     a. fear of making the wrong choice

     b. thinking too much and too long about the alternatives

     c. lack of confidence

     d. force of habit

Detail   ————   3. When thinking through a difficult decision, the authors recommend

     a. asking a trusted friend for advice.

     b. relying completely on our "gut" response.

     c. weighing the pros and cons by writing them down.

     d. considering the effect on our family and friends first.

Main Idea   ————   4. The main point of the section, "Call on Character," is that

     a. we should act in accordance with our most positive values.

     b. our choices should be determined by what benefits us most.

     c. consulting a religious leader for advice is helpful.

     d. we should act quickly.

Detail   ————   5. Antonio Domasio's research on emotions and the brain revealed that

     a. emotions interfere with good decision making.

     b. emotions have an important role in making good decisions.

     c. emotions tend to overshadow our thought processes.

     d. we are always aware of how our emotions inform our thinking.

Author's Purpose   ————   6. The authors include the student's story about her marriage to

     a. demonstrate how important some decisions are.

     b. show that it would have been better if she had taken her parents' advice.

     c. prove that fear can be a powerful factor in making a good decision.

     d. illustrate the point that conflicting motives may interfere with clear thinking.

Inference _____ 7. The authors might use which of the following as an example of a decision that especially involves examining character?

    a. choosing a career in either medicine or the law

    b. confronting a friend who is drinking excessively or ignoring it to preserve the friendship

    c. choosing whether to join a school club or to take a job

    d. deciding whether to live at home or to move into an apartment

Inference _____ 8. The student who made a poor decision to marry did so because

    a. she was blinded by her love for the man she married.

    b. she found acceptance and love in her husband's family that she did not experience in her own.

    c. she was too young to make a wise choice.

    d. she was pregnant and thought it would be better for the child if she married.

Inference _____ 9. You are struggling with the decision of whether to ask your boss for the promotion that you feel you've earned or to be content with your current position. Which course of action would the author most likely recommend?

    a. picturing yourself approaching your boss's office, knocking on the door, and stating your case

    b. reflecting on the emotions of frustration and resentment that you have surrounding this issue

    c. dressing as you would be expected to dress if you had the more responsible job

    d. asking coworkers what they would do in your situation

Inference _____ 10. We can infer that the Delancy Street experiment

    a. was successful with prisoners in other facilities.

    b. would only work with nonviolent inmates.

    c. changed the guards' opinions of the prisoners.

    d. made the men feel and behave like the successful citizens they were pretending to be.

Answer the following with *T* (true) or *F* (false):

Inference _____ 11. The authors believe that the three-step method will remove the problems from decision making.

Detail _____ 12. The authors believe that courage can be learned with practice.

Detail _____ 13. The authors state that feelings should have no part in decision making.

Inference _____ 14. It is reasonable to infer that the authors would not approve of researching facts in a library or on the Internet prior to making a decision.

Inference _____ 15. The authors believe that the ability to make good decisions can be learned.

BUILD YOUR VOCABULARY

According to the way the italicized word was used in the selection, indicate *a, b, c,* or *d* for the word or phrase that gives the best definition. The number in parentheses indicates the line of the passage in which the word is located. Use a dictionary in addition to the context clues to more precisely define the terms.

———— 1. "*vacillate* through decisions" (4)
 a. suffer
 b. hesitate
 c. race
 d. think

———— 2. "the goals, *alternatives*" (8)
 a. options
 b. results
 c. actions
 d. problems

———— 3. "*project* possible outcomes" (16)
 a. prefer
 b. choose
 c. criticize
 d. predict

———— 4. "*stymied* by overthinking" (20)
 a. pleased
 b. frightened
 c. blocked
 d. energized

———— 5. "the greatest *obstacle*" (47)
 a. barrier
 b. frustration
 c. emotion
 d. evil

———— 6. "*obeisance* to others" (48)
 a. respect
 b. obeying
 c. listening
 d. submission

———— 7. "*mantras* such as" (52)
 a. familiar rules
 b. repeated words or phrases
 c. figures of speech
 d. proverbs

———— 8. "*facilitate* decision making" (59)
 a. challenge
 b. block
 c. ease
 d. complete

———— 9. "*architecture* of the brain" (84)
 a. outbursts
 b. failings
 c. effects
 d. structure

———— 10. "their *recidivism* rate" (101)
 a. unhappiness
 b. success
 c. employment
 d. return to crime

Science

MyReadingLab

SELECTION 2

Visit Chapter 8: Point of View in MyReadingLab to complete the Selection 2 activities and the Build Background Knowledge video activity.

PREVIEW the next selection to predict its purpose and organization and to formulate your learning plan.

Activate Schemata

Do long-time residents in your area say that the climate has changed?
How would your area be affected by rising sea levels or a change in average temperatures?

Establish a Purpose for Reading

The issue of global climate change is being discussed by individuals and governments all around the world. Read to find out about the evidence of its existence, the causes, and the effects.

Build Background Knowledge — VIDEO

World's Top Scientists Issue Climate Warning

To prepare for reading Selection 2, answer the questions below. Then, watch this video on scientific predictions regarding climate change around the world.

What do you know about climate change and its causes?

How have you or someone you know been affected by changes to the earth's climate?

How do you think world leaders should address climate change?

This video helped me: _____

_____

_____

Increase Word Knowledge

What do you know about these words?

ecosystem	exponentially	deforestation	emissions	glaciers
terrestrial	consortium	concerted	intrinsically	vectors

Your instructor may give a brief vocabulary review before or after reading.

Integrate Knowledge While Reading

Questions have been inserted in the margin to stimulate your thinking while reading. Remember to

| Predict | Picture | Relate | Monitor | Correct | Annotate |

Earth's Changing Climate

Ancient peoples, with small populations and limited technology, had relatively little impact on Earth's physical cycles. However, as the human population grew and technology increased, people began to act more independently of natural ecosystem processes. The Industrial Revolution, which began in earnest in the mid-nineteenth century, resulted in a tremendous increase in our reliance on energy stored in fossil fuels for heat, light, transportation, industry, and agriculture. Fertilizer use on commercial farms grew exponentially. Today, human use of fossil fuels and chemical fertilizers has significantly disrupted the global nutrient cycles of nitrogen, phosphorus, sulfur, and carbon.

What fossil fuels do I use directly and indirectly?

INTERFERING WITH THE CARBON CYCLE IS CHANGING EARTH'S CLIMATE

Some of the energy from sunlight is reflected back into space by the atmosphere (particularly clouds), and by Earth's surface, especially by areas covered with snow or ice. Most sunlight, however, strikes relatively dark areas of the surface (land, vegetation, and open water) and is converted into heat that is radiated into the atmosphere. Although most of this heat continues on into space, water vapor, CO_2 and several other **greenhouse gases** trap some of the heat in the atmosphere. This is a natural process called the **greenhouse effect**, which keeps our atmosphere relatively warm and allows life on Earth as we know it.

For Earth's temperature to remain constant, the total amount of energy entering and leaving Earth's atmosphere must be equal. If atmospheric concentrations of greenhouse gases increase, more heat is retained than is radiated into space, causing Earth to warm. Greenhouse gases are in fact increasing, largely because people burn fossil fuels, releasing CO_2. Other important greenhouse gases include methane (CH_4), released by agricultural activities, landfills, and coal mining, and nitrous oxide (N_2O), released by agricultural activities and burning fossil fuels. CO_2, however, contributes by far the largest share of the greenhouse effect caused by human activities, so we will focus our discussion on this molecule.

How do we know that burning fossil fuels is a main cause?

BURNING FOSSIL FUELS IS CAUSING CLIMATE CHANGE

Since the mid-1800s, human societies have increasingly relied on energy from fossil fuels. As we burn fossil fuels in our power plants, factories, and cars, we harvest the energy of ancient sunlight and release CO_2 into the atmosphere. Burning fossil fuels accounts for about 80% to 85% of the CO_2 that human activities release into the atmosphere each year.

A second source of added atmospheric CO_2 is **deforestation**, which destroys tens of millions of forested acres annually and accounts for about 15% to 20% of humanity's CO_2 emissions. Deforestation is occurring principally in the tropics, where rain forests are rapidly being converted to agricultural land to feed growing populations and to supply the world's demand for biofuels, such as ethanol and

What are the other main sources?

biodiesel. The carbon stored in the trees returns to the atmosphere when they are cut down and burned. A third, very minor source of CO_2 is volcanic activity. Only about 1% as much CO_2 enters the atmosphere from volcanoes as from human activities.

Collectively, human activities release about 35 to 40 billion tons of CO_2 into the atmosphere each year. About half of this carbon is absorbed by oceans, plants, and soil, with the rest remaining in the atmosphere. As a result, since 1850—when people began burning large quantities of fossil fuels during the Industrial Revolution—the CO_2 content of the atmosphere has increased by about 40%—from 280 parts per million (ppm) to 392 ppm—and is growing by about 2 ppm annually (Figure a). Based on analyses of gas bubbles trapped in ancient Antarctic ice, scientists have determined that the atmospheric CO_2 content is now higher than at any time during the past 650,000 years.

What is the evidence?

A large and growing body of evidence indicates that human release of CO_2 and other greenhouse gases has amplified the natural greenhouse effect and thereby altered the global climate. Surface temperature data, recorded from thousands of weather stations around the world and from satellites that measure temperatures over the oceans, show that Earth has warmed by about 1°F (0.6°C) since 1970 (Figure b). The decade from 2001 to 2010 was the warmest ever recorded up to that time; in fact, all but 1 of the 10 warmest years on record occurred within that decade.

The overall impact of increased greenhouse gases is now usually called **climate change**, which includes both global warming and many other effects on our climate and Earth's ecosystems. Although a 1°F increase may not sound like much, our warming climate already has had widespread effects. Spring snow cover in the Northern Hemisphere is declining. Glaciers are retreating worldwide; the World Glacier Monitoring Service reports that about 90% of the world's mountain glaciers are shrinking, and that this trend seems to be accelerating. Glacier National Park, Montana, named for its spectacular abundance of glaciers, had 150 glaciers in 1910; now, only 25 remain—and the remaining glaciers are significantly smaller than they were in the recent past. The oceans are warming, which causes their water to expand

What are the effects?

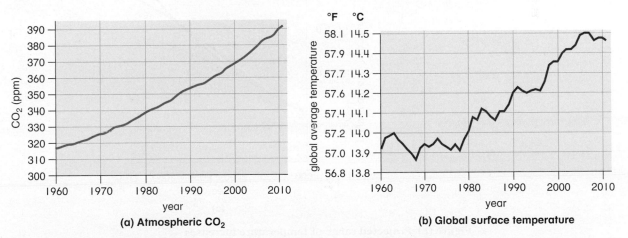

(a) Atmospheric CO_2

(b) Global surface temperature

Figures (a) & (b) Global temperature increases parallel atmospheric CO_2 increases
(a) Yearly average CO_2 concentrations in parts per million. These measurements were recorded at 11,155 feet (3,400 meters) above sea level, near the summit of Mauna Loa, Hawaii. **(b)** Global surface temperatures. Because global temperature varies considerably from year to year, this temperature graph shows trends by averaging each year with the 4 years preceding it.

Data for both graphs from the National Oceanic and Atmospheric Administration.

65 and occupy more volume; as a result, sea levels are rising. During the past 30 years, the Arctic ice cap has become almost 50% thinner and 35% smaller in area, and is shrinking by about 10% per decade. Finally, in 2011, scientists compiled the results of 53 studies that examined changes in the distribution of more than 1,000 species of terrestrial plants and animals. The species' ranges are moving toward the poles at an
70 average rate of about 10.5 miles (17 kilometers) per decade—just what would be expected if they are moving in response to a warming planet.

Climate scientists predict that a warming atmosphere will cause more severe storms, including stronger hurricanes; greater amounts of rain or snow in single storms (a phenomenon already observed in the northeastern United States during the past half-
75 century); and more frequent and more prolonged droughts. Increased CO_2 also makes the oceans more acidic, which disturbs many natural processes, including the ability of many marine animals, such as snails and corals, to make their shells and skeletons.

CONTINUED CLIMATE CHANGE WILL DISRUPT ECOSYSTEMS AND ENDANGER MANY SPECIES

How do we predict future effects?

What does the future hold? Predictions of continued climate change are based on sophisticated computer models developed and run independently by climate scien-
80 tists around the world. As the models continue to improve, they match past climate with ever-greater accuracy, providing increasing confidence in their predictions for the future. The models also provide evidence that natural causes, such as changes in the output of the sun, cannot account for the recent warming. The models match the data only when human carbon emissions are included in the calculations. The Inter-
85 governmental Panel on Climate Change (IPCC) is a consortium of hundreds of

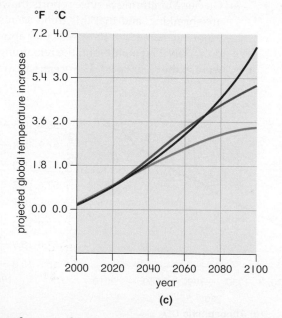

(c)

Figure (c) Projected range of temperature increases
The IPCC projections for the twenty-first century are based on three different scenarios of greenhouse gas emissions. The red, blue, and green data lines are projections based on high, moderate, and substantially reduced growth of greenhouse gas emissions, respectively. Even under the most optimistic assumptions, a continued increase in global temperatures is predicted. Global temperature change is expressed relative to the average temperature from 1980 to 1999.
Source: Data from IPCC, 2007, *Fourth Assessment Report: Summary for Policymakers.*

climate scientists and other experts from 130 nations. In their 2007 report, the IPCC predicted that even under the best-case scenario in which a concerted worldwide effort is made to reduce greenhouse gas emissions, the average global temperature will rise by at least 3.2°F (1.8°C) by the year 2100. The IPCC's high-level emissions
90 scenario projects an increase of 7.2°F (4.0°C) (Figure c). These changes in climate will be difficult to stop, let alone reverse, as we explore in "Earth Watch: Geoengineering— A Solution to Climate Change?"

Even if the more optimistic predictions are correct, the consequences for natural ecosystems will be profound. Thousands of species will change their ranges, moving
95 away from the Equator toward the poles or higher up mountainsides. Some plants and animals will find it easier to move than others will, either because they are intrinsically more mobile (such as birds) or because they can move great distances while reproducing (such as some plants that produce lightweight, wind-borne seeds). It is highly unlikely that entire communities of organisms can just pack up and move, intact. Some
100 will move farther poleward faster than others, with potentially serious consequences for certain species. For example, if a predator's main prey moves poleward faster than the predator can, then the predator may be left behind without a food supply.

Some species, particularly those on mountains or in the Arctic and Antarctic, will have nowhere to go. For example, the loss of summer sea ice is bad news for
105 polar bears and other marine mammals that rely on ice floes as nurseries for their young and as staging platforms for hunting fish or seals. As summer ice diminishes, both walrus and polar bear populations are moving onto land to give birth, putting the adults farther away from their prime hunting grounds. As the adults crowd together onto small beaches, instead of being spread out over sea ice, they some-
110 times endanger their own young; in 2009, for example, 131 walrus calves were tram-

What are the effects of increased air temperatures?

pled to death on a beach when the adults panicked and stampeded. In 2008, in response to its declining numbers and the projected contin-
115 ued loss of its habitat, the U.S. Fish and Wildlife Service designated the polar bear as a threatened species— the first species to be listed primar- ily as a result of global climate
120 change. Complete loss of sea ice, which climate models predict could occur within the next cen- tury, might cause the extinction of polar bears in the wild. Penguins in
125 the Antarctic may face similar dan- gers. Many species of penguins walk for miles across ice sheets to their breeding grounds. As the ice melts and breaks up, their journeys
130 become much more difficult. Ten of the 17 species of penguins are already on the Red List of threat- ened species developed by the International Union for Conserva-
135 tion of Nature.

Have You Ever Wondered... How Big Your Carbon Footprint Is?

Each of us affects Earth through the choices we make. A *carbon footprint* is a measure of the impact that human activities have on climate, based on the quantity of green- house gases they emit. Our personal carbon footprints give us a sense of our individual impacts. For example, each gallon of gasoline burned releases 19.6 pounds (8.9 kg) of CO_2 into the air. So, if your car gets 20 miles to the gallon, then each mile that you drive will add about a pound of CO_2 to the atmosphere.

The Web sites of the U.S. Environ- mental Protection Agency and several en- vironmental organizations provide house- hold emissions calculators that allow you to estimate your carbon footprint, and pro- vide advice on how you can reduce it. To get started, type "carbon footprint" into an Internet search engine.

Some of the movement of species may have direct impacts on human health. Many diseases, especially those carried by mosquitoes and ticks, are currently restricted to tropical or subtropical parts of the planet. Like other animals, these disease vectors will probably spread poleward as a result of warming temperatures, 140 bringing their diseases, such as malaria, dengue fever, yellow fever, and Rift Valley fever, with them. On the other hand, it may become so hot and dry in parts of the tropics that mosquitoes and some other insects may have shortened life spans, thus reducing vector-borne diseases in these regions. Although computer models can predict temperature changes, no one can confidently predict the resulting overall 145 effects on human health.

(1,919 words)

—From Teresa Audesirk, Gerald Audesirk,
and Bruce E. Byers, *Life on Earth*, 10th ed.

Recall

Stop to self-test, relate, and react.

Your instructor may choose to give you a brief comprehension review.

THINK CRITICALLY ABOUT THE SELECTION

Did you notice the general organizational pattern of cause and effect in this selection? Would you expect this to be a typical pattern for science textbooks?

In two, side-by-side columns, list the causes and effects of climate change that are discussed in the selection.

WRITE ABOUT THE SELECTION

How can the behavior of individuals reverse a problem as large as climate change?
Response Suggestion: Brainstorm the ways in which your everyday activities contribute to increased greenhouse gases and list them in one column. Next to each item, write one way you can reduce that impact on the environment.

SKILL DEVELOPMENT: EXPLORE POINT OF VIEW

Form a collaborative group to discuss the following questions:

- Some people argue that climate change is a natural phenomenon rather than the product of human activity. Is the evidence presented by the authors convincing?

- Do the members of the group agree with the view presented in the selection?

- What do the group members do to protect the environment?

- Does your college use environmentally friendly practices for paper disposal and energy use? How might students encourage environmentally friendly practices on campus?

CHECK YOUR COMPREHENSION

After reading the selection, answer the following questions with *a, b, c,* or *d.* To help you analyze your strengths and weaknesses, the question types are indicated.

Main Idea ———— 1. Which is the best statement of the main idea of this selection?

    a. If people don't act soon, climate change will destroy Earth.
    b. Greenhouse gases trap heat in the atmosphere.
    c. Climate change caused by human interference in the carbon cycle has devastating global effects.
    d. Glacial and polar ice is melting rapidly.

Detail ———— 2. According to the selection, about how much of the global carbon emissions remain in the atmosphere?

    a. three-fourths
    b. one-half
    c. one-third
    d. one-fourth

Detail ———— 3. Which human activity accounts for the largest percentage of CO_2 released into the atmosphere yearly?

    a. deforestation
    b. volcanic activity
    c. burning fossil fuels
    d. agricultural activities

Author's Purpose ———— 4. The authors use the statistics on projected increases in average air temperature to

    a. dramatize the rapid change taking place recently.
    b. alarm the reader about the melting ice caps.
    c. show that the change has been gradual and steady over time.
    d. minimize concern over the effects of greenhouse gases.

Inference ———— 5. Based on the information in the selection, which would *not* be a contributor to climate change?

    a. gasoline-powered automobiles
    b. wind-powered generators
    c. clearing of trees for farms
    d. factories

Inference ———— 6. We can infer from the line graphs on page 443 that

    a. the concentration of CO_2 in the atmosphere and air temperature are unrelated.
    b. the atmospheric CO_2 and air temperature did not rise in the years before 1960.
    c. the increase in atmospheric CO_2 and air temperature is a natural process.
    d. something has occurred in the last 50 years or so to cause a rapid rise in air temperature and atmospheric CO_2.

SELECTION 2

Detail   ———— 7. According to the selection, climate change is causing many species of animals to

    a. move toward the equator.
    b. change their eating habits.
    c. move closer to the poles.
    d. produce fewer young.

Detail   ———— 8. The carbon cycle is a natural phenomenon that ordinarily balances

    a. carbon dioxide (CO_2) and emissions from manufacturing.
    b. carbon releases from deforestation and greenhouse gases.
    c. carbon emissions and their absorption into oceans, plants, and soil.
    d. CO_2, methane, and greenhouse gases.

Inference   ———— 9. From the details presented in the selection, we can infer that

    a. the scenic views that visitors see now in national parks and other undeveloped areas are different from those that previous generations viewed.
    b. views of glaciers and rivers have changed little in the last several decades.
    c. wildlife is not seriously threatened by rising average air temperatures.
    d. there is no need for concern about the effects of climate change on agriculture.

Main Idea   ———— 10. The main point of the section, "Continued Climate Change Will Disrupt Ecosystems and Endanger Many Species," is that climate change

    a. has already caused difficulties for 10 of the 17 species of penguins.
    b. will cause many animal species to change their ranges.
    c. will negatively affect many animal and plant species.
    d. has already affected the breeding habits of walruses.

Answer the following with *T* (true) or *F* (false):

Inference   ———— 11. Climate change could introduce diseases into North America and Europe that have not usually been seen there.

Inference   ———— 12. The production of biofuels creates significant additions to CO_2 emissions.

Detail   ———— 13. Experts believe that climate change and the severity of hurricanes are unrelated.

Inference   ———— 14. Wider ranges of butterflies and birds will not affect other animal populations.

Detail   ———— 15. Experts predict that even in the best case, average global temperatures will rise at least 3.1°F (1.8°C) by the year 2100.

BUILD YOUR VOCABULARY

According to the way the italicized word is used in the selection, indicate *a*, *b*, *c*, or *d* for the word or phrase that gives the best definition. The number in parentheses indicates the line of the passage in which the word is located. Use a dictionary in addition to the context clues to more precisely define the terms.

_____ 1. "natural *ecosystem* processes" (3)
    a. interrelated communities of organisms and their nonliving environment
    b. plants in a specific area of the environment
    c. natural cycles
    d. water and air

_____ 2. "grew *exponentially*" (7)
    a. mathematically
    b. slowly
    c. very quickly
    d. in stages

_____ 3. "*deforestation*, which destroys" (31)
    a. a disease affecting trees
    b. a natural loss of forests
    c. cutting of entire forests
    d. planting of trees for fruit crops

_____ 4. "humanity's CO_2 emissions" (33)
    a. releases
    b. mistakes
    c. illnesses
    d. chemicals

_____ 5. "*Glaciers* are retreating" (59)
    a. large bodies of moving ice
    b. glass structures
    c. snowfalls
    d. ice covered mountains

_____ 6. "*terrestrial* plants and animals" (69)
    a. living
    b. land-dwelling
    c. ocean-dwelling
    d. airborne

_____ 7. "a *consortium* of hundreds" (85)
    a. meeting
    b. school or university
    c. association
    d. crowd

_____ 8. "*concerted* worldwide effort" (87)
    a. haphazard
    b. concentrated
    c. international
    d. political

_____ 9. "*intrinsically* more mobile" (96)
    a. artificially
    b. flexibly
    c. strongly
    d. naturally

_____ 10. "these disease *vectors*" (139)
    a. bacteria
    b. symptoms
    c. bugs
    d. carriers

SELECTION 3   Psychology   MyReadingLab

Visit Chapter 8: Point of View in MyReadingLab to complete the Selection 3 activities and the Build Background Knowledge video activity.

Preview the next selection to predict its purpose and organization and to formulate your learning plan.

Activate Schemata

Can you think of a criminal case in which the defendant pled "Not guilty by reason of insanity"?

Do you know someone with a mental disorder?

What should the punishment be for someone who has a mental illness and who commits a crime?

Establish a Purpose for Reading

Read to learn more about the issues surrounding mental illness and criminal and ethical responsibility.

Build Background Knowledge — VIDEO

The Insanity Defense

To prepare for reading Selection 3, answer the questions below. Then, watch this video that examines the use of the insanity defense in a murder trial.

What is an insanity defense?

Why do you think an insanity defense is controversial in criminal trials?

Do you think that criminals who are found to be unfit to stand trial due to insanity get off easier than someone who must stand trial? Why or why not?

This video helped me: _____

_____

_____

Increase Word Knowledge

What do you know about these words?

absolve	exonerate	incoherent	paranoid	ensuing
domineering	jurisdictions	provocation	delusional	reprehensibly

Your instructor may give a brief vocabulary review before or after reading.

Integrate Knowledge While Reading

Questions have been inserted in the margin to stimulate your thinking while reading. Remember to

Predict   Picture   Relate   Monitor   Correct   Annotate

MENTAL DISORDER AND PERSONAL RESPONSIBILITY

What would that problem be?

What do the authors think?

Could he have been helped?

Romance writer Janet Dailey was once caught having plagiarized whole passages from another writer's work, and in self-defense she said she was suffering from "a psychological problem that I never even suspected I had." We wonder if it was in the DSM (the Diagnostic and Statistical Manual of Mental Disorders, which is the
5 basis for diagnosing mental disorders) but would it matter if it were? What "psychological problem" would absolve a person of responsibility for cheating?

One of the great questions generated by all diagnoses of mental disorder concerns personal responsibility, a topic that requires us to ask the right questions, examine the best evidence, and sometimes live with uncertainty. In law and in
10 everyday life, many people reach for a psychological reason to exonerate themselves of responsibility for their actions. Many people—as an excuse for some habit that is immoral, illegal, or fattening—claim they are addicted to the behavior, whether it is having sex, shopping, or eating chocolate. Is their behavior really an "addiction" in the same way that drug addiction is? What about the behavior of a
15 student who spends hours on end on the Internet? Some psychologists would call this an addiction if the student constantly goes online as a way of coping with depression, anxiety, or another emotional problem. But others believe that the student is probably no different from those in previous generations, who also found plenty of ways to avoid the common problems facing students everywhere:
20 insecurity, worry about grades, a disappointing social life. This is not a mental disorder, they say, it's a normal problem, called Learning To Pass Courses and Figure Out Life.

In criminal cases, where a defendant with a severe mental disorder has committed murder, debates about appropriate penalties continue. (The insanity defense is
25 used in less than one percent of all criminal cases, and in those, nine out of ten defendants end up in mental hospitals, usually for far longer than they would have served with a criminal conviction.) In January 2011, Jared Lee Loughner went to a mall in Tucson, where he killed six people and wounded 14 more, including Congresswoman Gabrielle Giffords. His Internet postings were full of incoherent, hostile
30 themes, including paranoid distrust of the government and his college. His friends, classmates, and own writings revealed that he had been undergoing a slow downward spiral in the preceding two years. Loughner's trial was suspended while he underwent psychiatric treatment for schizophrenia, and in the ensuing year, the courts struggled to decide whether he should be forcibly medicated with antipsy-
35 chotics, which would make him seem "normal" in the courtroom, or whether he had the right to refuse.

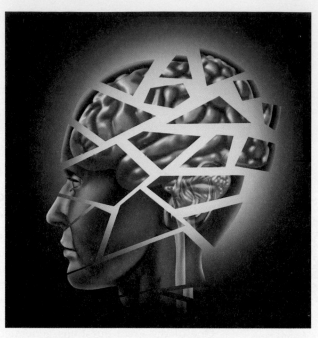

Lightspring/Shutterstock

Or consider Andrea Yates, a Texas woman who killed her five young children. Yates had suffered from clinical depression and psychotic episodes for years, and had tried to kill herself twice. Yates was overwhelmed by raising and homeschool-
40 ing all of her children by herself, with no help from her reportedly domineering husband, who permitted her two hours a week of personal time. Although she suffered a postpartum psychotic episode after the birth of their fourth child and a clinical psychologist warned against her having another baby, her husband refused to consider birth control, although not for religious reasons. Yates was
45 convicted of murder and sentenced to life in prison. On appeal four years later, another jury found her not guilty by reason of insanity and she was sent to a mental institution.

For life? What if she gets well?

Do Jared Loughner and Andrea Yates deserve our pity, along with our con-
demnation for their horrible acts of murder? Interestingly, a recent study showed
50 that many observers feel angrier and less sympathetic toward people whose mental illnesses conform to gender stereotypes: men, like Jared Loughner, who are schizophrenic or alcoholic, and women, like Andrea Yates, who are depressed. They are more sympathetic to people whose illnesses do not conform to the stereotype: alcoholic or schizophrenic women and depressed men. Appar-
55 ently, many people think that gender-typical mental disorders are less likely to be "real."

What is your opinion?

What about murderers who understand right from wrong, who are not legally insane but cannot control themselves? If we learn that their behavior might be a result of brain damage, should that affect the punishment they receive?
60 In some jurisdictions, a defendant may claim to have diminished responsibility for a crime. This claim does not exonerate the defendant, but it may result in reduced charges, perhaps from premeditated first-degree murder to manslaugh-ter, or a milder sentence if the defendant is found guilty. A diminished-capacity

defense holds that the defendant lacked the mental capacity to form a calculated
65 and malicious plan but instead was impaired by mental illness or the great provocation of the situation.

When thinking about the relationship of mental disorder to personal
responsibility, we face a dilemma, one that requires us to tolerate uncertainty.
The law recognizes, rightly, that people who are mentally incompetent,
70 delusional, or disturbed should not be judged by the same standards as mentally
healthy individuals. At the same time, society has an obligation to protect its
citizens from harm and to reject easy excuses for violations of the law. To
balance these two positions, we need to find ways to ensure that people who
commit crimes or behave reprehensibly face the consequences of their behavior,
75 and also that people who are suffering from psychological problems have the
compassionate support of society in their search for help. After all, psychological
problems of one kind or another are challenges that all of us will face at some
time in our lives.

(922 words)

—From Carole Wade, Carol Tavris, and Maryanne Garry,
Psychology, 11th ed.

Recall

Stop to self-test, relate, and react.

Your instructor may choose to give you a brief comprehension review.

THINK CRITICALLY ABOUT THE SELECTION

Do the authors include facts and opinions in this selection?

What words describe the tone of this selection?

If you were serving on a jury in a murder case in which the defendant claimed to
be innocent due to insanity, what information would you need to come to a
decision?

WRITE ABOUT THE SELECTION

This selection raises several tough questions to which there is no single right answer. According to the law, a person with a mental disorder "should not be judged
by the same standards as mentally healthy individuals." However, society has a
responsibility to protect its citizens.

Response Suggestion: Write a one-paragraph reflection on the central question
posed in this selection. In other words, state and explain your point of view on the
personal responsibility and just treatment of people who have a mental disorder
and commit a crime.

SKILL DEVELOPMENT: EXPLORE POINT OF VIEW

Form a collaborative group and discuss the members' points of view on the issues raised in this selection.

- Do you think that an author who plagiarizes another person's work can legitimately claim a psychological problem? What basis might be used to determine this?

- What is your point of view on whether people who claim they are addicted to the Internet or social media have a legitimate addiction? (You might want to refer to "Technology Addictions" in Chapter 2, page 82, and the reading selection, "Technology and Health," in Chapter 4, page 203.)

- If a person who commits a crime has a diagnosed mental illness, how should that person be treated by the criminal justice system?

CHECK YOUR COMPREHENSION

After reading the selection, answer the following questions with *a, b, c,* or *d.* To help you analyze your strengths and weaknesses, the question types are indicated.

Main Idea _____ 1. Which of the following statements best expresses the main idea of this selection?

    a. People with mental disorders should be given treatment rather than punishment.

    b. The issue of personal responsibility and mental disorder raises difficult questions for society and the criminal justice system.

    c. If you do the crime, you have to serve the time.

    d. Society needs to understand that mental illness requires treatment just like any other physical illness.

Detail _____ 2. According to this selection,

    a. psychologists agree that students who constantly go online do so to deal with the normal problems of their age group.

    b. eating too much chocolate is an addiction just like a drug addiction.

    c. previous generations did not suffer from addictions to the same degree as today.

    d. psychologists disagree as to whether spending inordinate amounts of time on the Internet is an actual addiction.

Detail _____ 3. According to this selection, how often is an insanity defense used in criminal cases?

    a. in 90% of cases

    b. in 14% of cases

    c. in less than 1% of cases

    d. in more than 5% of cases

Inference _____ 4. This selection implies that

    a. Andrea Yates might not have killed her children if the conditions of her marriage had been different.

    b. Andrea Yates received no mental health care before she murdered her children.

    c. Andrea Yates should have remained in prison.

    d. Andrea Yates is now mentally healthy due to the treatment that she received after her appeal.

Inference _____ 5. Information in this selection suggests that which person is likely to receive more sympathy?

    a. Jared Lee Loughner

    b. Andrea Yates

    c. a male defendant who is clinically depressed

    d. a female defendant who is clinically depressed

SELECTION
3

SELECTION
3

Author's Purpose _____ 6. Why did the authors include the information about Jared Lee Loughner and Andrea Yates?

a. to criticize the handling of those cases
b. to illustrate the kinds of situations that complicate such cases
c. to shock the reader with the horrible crimes that they committed
d. to cause the reader not to feel sympathy for them

Detail _____ 7. Andrea Yates

a. refused to use birth control.
b. enjoyed the challenge of homeschooling her children.
c. had not received psychological evaluation or treatment before she killed her children.
d. suffered a psychotic episode after the birth of her fourth child.

Main Idea _____ 8. Which statement best describes the main point of the last paragraph?

a. Everyone faces psychological problems at some time or another.
b. Society must protect citizens from harm.
c. People with mental disorders need appropriate care.
d. Determining the just responsibility of mentally disordered individuals while protecting society is a challenge with no single solution.

Inference _____ 9. The selection suggests that

a. the charge and punishment can be less severe for a person who has brain damage.
b. a person with brain damage will be treated the same by the courts as a person who has a mental disorder.
c. the handling of defendants with brain damage and mental disorders will be the same regardless of where they are tried.
d. charges against a person with brain damage are likely to be dismissed.

Author's Purpose _____ 10. The authors' main purpose is to

a. make a case for reduced sentences for people with mental disorders.
b. stir the emotions of the reader with specific cases.
c. present the issues surrounding the question of mental disorder and responsibility.
d. come to a conclusion about the personal responsibilities of people with mental disorders.

Answer the following with *T* (true) or *F* (false).

Detail _____ 11. The basis for psychological diagnoses is a document called the DSM.

Inference (Drawing Conclusions) _____ 12. A logical conclusion is that mentally ill defendants often spend more time in a treatment facility than healthy defendants spend in prison because they are not cured and still pose a real threat to others.

Inference _____ 13. The authors' point of view is that people with mental disorders should be treated differently by the courts than mentally healthy people.

Detail _____ 14. Jared Lee Loughner's trial was delayed because he had been forced to take antipsychotic drugs.

Inference _____ 15. The authors believe that students who use the Internet or other electronic media to avoid their problems have a mental disorder.

BUILD YOUR VOCABULARY

According to the way the italicized word is used in the selection, indicate *a, b, c,* or *d* for the word or phrase that gives the best definition. The number in parentheses indicates the line of the passage in which the word is located. Use a dictionary in addition to the context clues to more precisely define the terms.

_____ 1. "would *absolve* a person" (6)
a. accuse
b. blame
c. excuse
d. explain

_____ 2. "reason to *exonerate*" (10)
a. prosecute
b. pardon
c. protect
d. rationalize

_____ 3. "*incoherent*, hostile themes" (29)
a. dangerous
b. frightening
c. rambling
d. violent

_____ 4. "*paranoid* distrust" (30)
a. logical
b. abundant
c. foolish
d. suspicious

_____ 5. "the *ensuing* year" (33)
a. following
b. previous
c. whole
d. difficult

_____ 6. "*domineering* husband" (40)
a. understanding
b. overbearing
c. professional
d. religious

_____ 7. "In some *jurisdictions*" (60)
a. federal courts
b. counties
c. state courts
d. areas of legal authority

_____ 8. "the great *provocation*" (65–66)
a. joy
b. aggravation
c. seriousness
d. excitement

_____ 9. "*delusional*, or disturbed" (70)
a. holding a false belief
b. self-confident
c. sick
d. having a strong faith

_____ 10. "behave *reprehensibly*" (74)
a. positively
b. negatively
c. violently
d. shamefully

VOCABULARY BOOSTER

Lights, Camera, Action!

| **Roots** | *luc, lum:* "light" | *photo:* "light" |
| | *act, ag:* "to do" | |

Words with *luc, lum:* "light"

Mexican Christmas lanterns, called *luminarias*—bags with sand and a lit candle inside—line streets and driveways not only in the Southwest but also throughout America at Christmas.

- *lucid*: clear; glowing with light; easily understood; sane

  The patient's statements were not *lucid* when she was brought into the psychiatric treatment center.

- *luminescence*: the giving off of light without heat

  A fluorescent lightbulb or tube is a *luminescent* fixture that gives off light but remains cool when the mercury vapor inside the tube is acted upon by electrons.

- *luminous*: radiating or reflecting light; well lighted; shining; enlightened

  Due to the neon lighting on most of its buildings, Las Vegas is one of the most *luminous* cities in the United States at night.

- *luminary*: a celestial body; a person who is a shining example in a profession

  Muhammad Ali is still a *luminary* in the boxing world.

- *illuminate*: to supply with light; light up; to make lucid or clarify

  Let me *illuminate* the facts for you before you take misinformed action.

- *elucidate*: to make lucid or clear; explain

  Mario had to successfully *elucidate* details about his new invention to investors in order to get funding.

- *translucent*: allowing light to pass through without being transparent

  The Martinez family chose a *translucent* frosted glass that would provide privacy for the renovated bathroom.

Words with *photo:* "light"

The wrinkles and discolored skin on Brooke's face and hands were signs of *photo-aging* from spending years in the sun without sunscreen protection.

- *photogenic*: having features that look attractive in a photograph

  The supermodel was extremely *photogenic*, and she could also act.

- *photography*: a process of producing images on sensitized surfaces by the chemical action of light or other forms of radiant energy

Sensitized film in a camera receiving sunlight or flash lighting by opening the camera's aperture or eye is a form of *photography*.

- *photogrammetry*: the process of making surveys and maps through the use of aerial photographs

  The surveying firm had its own small airplane for taking aerial photos to use in the *photogrammetry* project for the National Park Service.

- *photosensitivity*: quality of being photosensitive; abnormal sensitivity of the skin to ultraviolet light

  Some prescription drugs can cause *photosensitivity*, requiring avoidance of the sun or use of a sunscreen.

- *telephoto lens*: a camera lens that produces a large image of distant or small objects

  George's *telephoto lens* made it possible to get close-up pictures of the inaccessible waterfall.

- *photocopy*: a duplicate of a document or print made on specialized copying equipment

  Xerox, the name of the first and most well-known *photocopy* machine manufacturer, is the word commonly used to mean "copy."

Words with *act, ag:* "to do"

The *actors* and *actresses* were waiting offstage for their cues to go onstage during Act Three of the play.

- *act*: anything done, being done, or to be done; a formal decision, law, or statute; a main division of a play

  A clown performing a magic *act* entertained the children at the six-year-old's birthday party.

- *activate*: to make active; to place a military unit on active status

  Before using her new credit card, Sheila *activated* it by calling a telephone number to notify the lender that she had received the card.

- *activism*: the practice of achieving political or other goals through actions of protest or demonstration

  During the 1960s, *activism* was used to protest the Vietnam War and civil rights injustices in the United States.

- *agent*: a representative working on behalf of another

  Toby's *agent* promised to get him a film role before the end of the year.

- *agency*: an organization that provides a particular service; the place of business of an agent

  The FBI is an *agency* of the U.S. government.

- **agenda**: a list or outline of things to be done or matters to be acted or voted upon

  A vote for a new accounting firm to represent the company was on the *agenda* for the annual stockholders' meeting.

- **acting**: serving as a temporary substitute during another's absence; the art of performing in plays, films, and so on.

  While the city mayor was out on maternity leave, one of the council members served as *acting* mayor.

Review

Part I

Indicate whether the following statements are true *(T)* or false *(F)*:

_____ 1. If you enjoy working with figures, a position as an Internal Revenue *agent* might be a job to consider.

_____ 2. When she began to date another man, her boyfriend considered her behavior an *act* of betrayal.

_____ 3. Some home security systems are *activated* by movement.

_____ 4. Your local township surely has an *agency* devoted to helping the homeless find shelter.

_____ 5. *Photogenic* students do not look attractive in most pictures.

_____ 6. A *telephoto lens* is used to reduce the size of the object being photographed.

_____ 7. When high-ranking executives leave their positions, companies ordinarily appoint someone to serve as an *acting* authority until a suitable replacement can be found.

_____ 8. The word *photocopy* is a synonym for the word *plagiarize*.

_____ 9. Someone who has just experienced a trauma might not be totally *lucid*.

_____ 10. People in the business of nature *photography* probably have little interest in the outdoors.

Part II

Choose an antonym from the list for each of the words below.

activism	photoaging	illuminate	photosensitivity
agent	luminous	activate	luminary

11. unknown _____   15. apathy _____

12. reacting to dark _____   16. turn off _____

13. positive effects of sun on skin _____   17. dull _____

14. adversary _____   18. to darken _____

9 Graphic Illustrations

Learning Objectives

In this chapter, you will learn to:

1 Make use of graphics to enhance reading
2 Apply specific strategies to interpret diagrams, tables, maps, graphs, and flowcharts

Vocabulary Booster: Play It Again, Sam

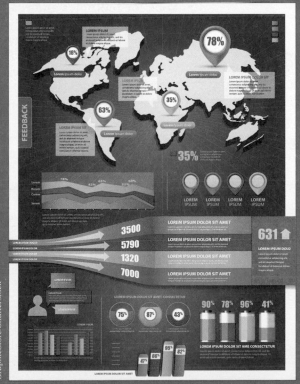

GraphicStore/Shutterstock

WHAT GRAPHICS DO

Learning Objective 1

Make use of graphics to enhance reading

If a picture is worth 1,000 words, a graphic illustration is worth at least several pages of facts and figures. Graphics express complex interrelationships in simplified form. Instead of plodding through repetitious data, you can glance at a chart, a map, or a graph and immediately see how everything fits together as well as how one part compares with another. Instead of reading several lengthy paragraphs and trying to visualize comparisons, you can study an organized design. The graphic illustration is a logically constructed aid for understanding many small bits of information.

Graphic illustrations are generally used for the following reasons:

1. **To condense.** Pages of repetitious, detailed information can be organized into one explanatory design.
2. **To clarify.** Processes and interrelationships can be more clearly defined through visual representations.
3. **To convince.** Developing trends and gross inequities can be forcefully dramatized.

Reader's TIP   How to Read Graphic Material

- **Read the title to get an overview.** What is it about?
- **Look for footnotes and read the introductory material.**
  Identify who, where, and how.
  How and when were the data collected?
  Who collected the data?
  How many persons were included in the survey or study?
  Do the researchers seem to have been objective or biased?
  Taking all of this information into account, does the study seem valid?
- **Read the labels.**
  What do the vertical columns and the horizontal rows represent?
  Are the numbers in thousands, millions, or billions?
  What does the legend represent?
- **Notice the trends and find the extremes.**
  What are the highest and lowest rates?
  What is the average rate?
  How do the extremes compare with the total?
  What is the percentage of increase or decrease?
- **Draw conclusions and formulate future exam questions.**
  What does the information mean?
  What purpose does the information serve?
  What wasn't included?
  What else is there to know about the subject?

TYPES OF GRAPHIC ILLUSTRATIONS

There are five basic kinds of graphic illustrations: (1) diagrams, (2) tables, (3) maps, (4) graphs, and (5) flowcharts. All are used in textbooks, and the choice of which is best to use depends on the type of material presented. This chapter contains explanations and exercises for the five types of graphic illustrations. Read the explanations, study the illustrations, and respond to the questions as instructed. The Reader's Tip, "How to Read Graphic Material," gets you started by summarizing how to read graphics in order to get the most information from them.

Diagrams

A **diagram** is an outline drawing or a picture of an object or a process. It shows the labeled parts of a complicated form, such as the muscles of the human body, the organizational makeup of a company's management and production teams, or the flow of nutrients in a natural ecological system. Notice the relative size and position of items in the diagram. Learn the names of the parts of the diagram and how they relate to each other.

EXERCISE 9.1

Interpreting Diagrams

The diagram on page 464 displays the components of the human respiratory system. Refer to the diagram to respond to the following statements with *T* (true), *F* (false), or *CT* (can't tell):

_____   1. The nose, sinuses, pharynx, and trachea are part of the upper respiratory system.

_____   2. The branches of the trachea, the bronchus, allow air to be conducted into both lungs.

_____   3. One way to remember the boundary between the upper and lower respiratory systems is the first letters of *larynx* and *lower*.

_____   4. One function of the respiratory system is to protect internal surfaces from temperature changes.

_____   5. The pharynx is positioned behind the mouth.

_____   6. Mucous cells line the structures of the entire upper respiratory system.

_____   7. Air intake through the nose and mouth proceeds to the lungs through the sinuses.

_____   8. It is logical to infer from the diagram that a person suffering from bronchitis has an infection that could enter the lungs if left untreated.

_____   9. The pharynx connects to both the esophagus and the larynx.

             10. The purpose of the diagram is _____

                  _____

                  _____

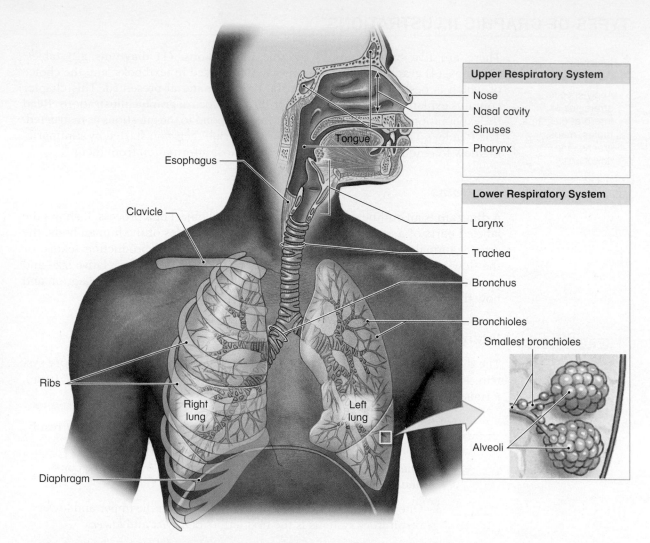

The Structures of the Respiratory System. Only the conducting portion of the respiratory tract is shown; the smaller bronchioles and alveoli have been omitted.

From Martini, Frederic H.; Nath, Judi L; Bartholomew, Edwin F., *Fundamentals of Anatomy & Physiology*, 9th Ed., © 2012, p. 815 Reprinted and Electronically reproduced by permission of Pearson Education, Inc., Upper Saddle River, New Jersey.

Tables

A **table** is a listing of facts and figures in columns and rows for quick and easy reference. The information in the columns and rows is usually labeled in two different directions. First read the title for the topic and then read the footnotes to judge the source. Determine what each column represents and how they interact. Notice totals; make comparisons.

EXERCISE 9.2

Interpreting Tables

Refer to the table, "The Nutritional Content of Combination Foods," shown on the next page to respond to the following statements with *T* (true), *F* (false), or *CT* (can't tell):

_____ 1. A one-cup serving of macaroni and cheese has fewer calories than a one-cup serving of chicken fried rice.

THE NUTRITIONAL CONTENT OF COMBINATION FOODS

Many of the foods that you eat are probably mixed dishes that contain servings from multiple food groups. The following table should help you estimate the servings from each food group for some popular food items. Because the preparation process can vary greatly among recipes, these are only estimates.

Food and Sample Portion	Grains Group (oz eq)	Vegetable Group (cups)	Fruit Group (cups)	Milk Group (cups)	Meat and Beans Group (oz eq)	Estimated Total Calories
Cheese pizza, thin crust (one slice from medium pizza)	1	1/8	0	1/2	0	215
Macaroni and cheese (1 cup, made from packaged mix)	2	0	0	1/2	0	260
Bean and cheese burrito (one)	2½	1/8	0	1	2	445
Chicken fried rice (1 cup)	1½	½	0	0	1	270
Large cheeseburger	2	0	0	1/3	3	500
Turkey sub sandwich (6" sub)	2	½	0	¼	2	320
Peanut butter and jelly sandwich (one)	2	0	0	0	2	375
Apple pie (one slice)	2	0	¼	0	0	280

Data from: U.S. Department of Agriculture, Mixed Dishes in MyPyramid. www.mypyramid.gov. Accessed March 2009.

_____ 2. A peanut butter and jelly sandwich provides as much protein as a bean and cheese burrito.

_____ 3. The large cheeseburger used for this analysis probably contained lettuce and tomato.

_____ 4. The turkey sub sandwich probably contained cheese.

_____ 5. Two slices of pizza contain more servings from the milk group than one bean and cheese burrito.

_____ 6. To obtain the largest serving of vegetables, select the bean and cheese burrito.

_____ 7. A person could have two slices of thin crust, cheese pizza and still eat fewer calories than in one large cheeseburger.

_____ 8. A serving of macaroni and cheese, a bean and cheese burrito, a cheeseburger, a turkey sub sandwich, a peanut butter and jelly sandwich, and a slice of apple pie all contain the same ounce-equivalent servings from the grains group.

_____ 9. Other than small differences in fruit and milk servings, a slice of apple pie and one cup of macaroni and cheese differ only by 20 calories.

10. The purpose of the table is to show _____

_____

Maps

Traditional **maps**, such as road maps and atlas maps, show the location of cities, waterways, sites, and roads, as well as the differences in the physical terrain of specified areas. A modern use of the map as a visual aid is to highlight special characteristics or population distributions of a particular area. For example, a map of the United States might highlight all states that voted for the Republican presidential candidate in red and all states that voted for the Democratic candidate in blue.

Begin reading a map by noting the title and source. The legend of a map, which usually appears in a corner box, explains the meanings of symbols and shading. Notice the position of the parts of the map and think how the positions might influence other factors highlighted on the map.

EXERCISE 9.3

Interpreting Maps

Use the legend on the map on the next page to help you respond to the subsequent statements with *T* (true), *F* (false), or *CT* (can't tell).

_____ 1. The average U.S. household income is $41,217.

_____ 2. Montana is the only state that has no counties showing Jabove average or high median household income.

_____ 3. Nevada shows no counties with below average median income.

_____ 4. The greatest number of counties with below and low average median income is in the southern half of the United States.

_____ 5. Arizona is the only state that has no counties with high median household income.

_____ 6. For the most part, counties with large cities tend to have above average to high median incomes.

_____ 7. All counties along the U.S.–Mexican border have below average or low median incomes.

_____ 8. The information in this map is from the U.S. Census Bureau.

_____ 9. In Alaska, there are fewer people in the high-income bracket than there are in the low-income bracket.

10. The purpose of the map is to show _____

_____

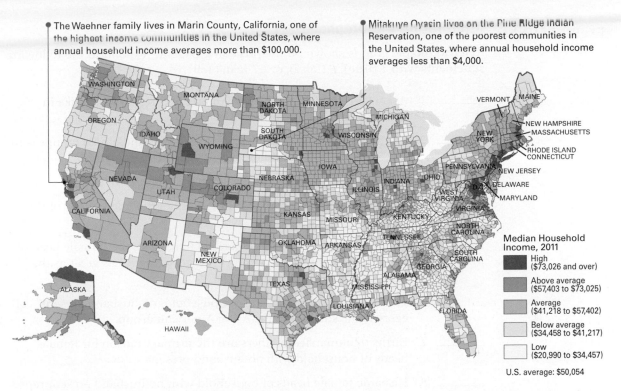

This map shows the median household income (i.e., how much money, on average, a household earned) in the more than 3,000 counties in the United States during the year 2011.

Source: U.S. Census Bureau (2012).

Pie Graphs

A **pie graph** is a circle divided into wedge-shaped slices. The complete pie or circle represents a total, or 100 percent. Each slice is a percentage or fraction of that whole. Budgets, such as the annual expenditure of federal or state governments, are frequently illustrated by pie graphs. Examine the size of the parts that make up the whole graph.

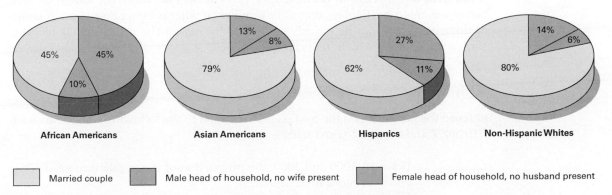

Diversity Snapshot. All racial and ethnic categories show variations in family form.

Source: U.S. Census Bureau (2012).

EXERCISE 9.4

Interpreting Pie Graphs

Refer to the pie graphs shown on the preceding page to respond to the following statements with T (true), F (false), or CT (can't tell).

————— 1. Asian and non-Hispanic white Americans are the most alike in terms of their family form.

————— 2. The smallest group in each of the four racial and ethnic groups is in the "male head of household, no wife present" category.

————— 3. Married couples represent the largest percentage in all four groups.

————— 4. Unmarried partners living together are not included in any of the family forms.

————— 5. The percentage of African American females in the "female head of household, no husband present" category is twice as great as the same category for Hispanics.

————— 6. The size of the "female head of household, no husband present" category is the smallest in the Asian American group.

————— 7. Births to unmarried mothers are the primary reason for female heads of household with no husband present.

————— 8. Hispanic female heads of household with no husband present represent a little more than double the percentage in that same category for Asian Americans.

————— 9. The largest percentage of married couples is in the non-Hispanic white population.

           10. The purpose of the pie graphs is to show ———————————

————————————————————————————

————————————————————————————

Bar Graphs

A **bar graph** is a series of horizontal or vertical bars in which the length of each bar represents a particular amount or number of what is being discussed. A series of different items can be quickly compared by noting the different bar lengths. Notice the scale on which items are measured.

EXERCISE 9.5

Interpreting Bar Graphs

Refer to the bar graph on the next page to respond to the following statements with T (true), F (false), or CT (can't tell):

————— 1. Between 1900 and 2000, the proportion of the population aged 65 and over more than tripled.

————— 2. The dip in median age in 1970 was due to the large number of young immigrants entering the United States at that time.

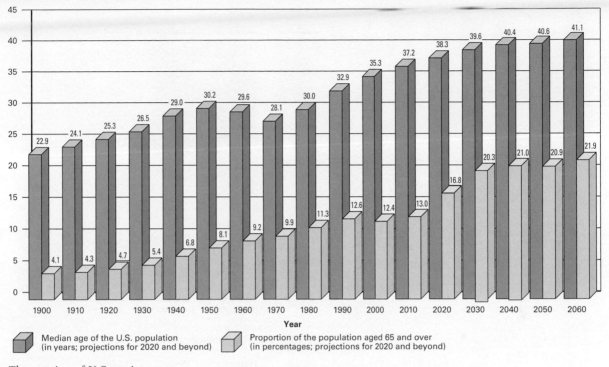

The graying of U.S. society.
Source: U.S. Census Bureau (2012).

_____ 3. The proportion of the population aged 65 and over is expected to double between 2010 and 2060.

_____ 4. The median age rose by 12.4 years between 1900 and 2000.

_____ 5. The data given for 2020–2060 are actual population figures based on U.S. Census information.

_____ 6. In each instance shown, the proportion of the population aged 65 and over changed in accordance with the median age of the population.

_____ 7. In 1950, the portion of the population under age 65 was 91.9 percent.

_____ 8. The increase in the percentage of older people is due to advances in health care.

_____ 9. The projected change in median age from 2020 to 2060 is expected to increase at the same rate as it did in the 50 years immediately before 2020.

10. The purpose of the bar graph is to show _____

_____

_____

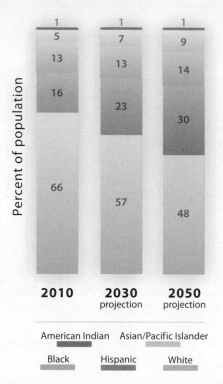

Projected U.S. Ethnic Composition, 2010–2050

Cumulative Bar Graphs

Both bar graphs and line graphs can be designed to show cumulative effects in which all of the lines or segments add up to the top line or total amount. Rather than having multiple bars or lines, the groups are stacked on top of each other to dramatically show differences. The **cumulative bar graph** above illustrates a cumulative effect.

EXERCISE 9.6

Interpreting Cumulative Bar Graphs

Refer to the cumulative bar graph above to respond to the following statements with *T* (true), *F* (false), or *CT* (can't tell):

_____ 1. From 2010 to 2050, the percentage of the population of American Indians is expected to shrink.

_____ 2. In each year shown, the percentage of the population that is white decreases.

_____ 3. From 2010 to 2050, the percentage of Hispanics in the population is expected to more than triple.

_____ 4. The percentage of black Americans is expected to decrease between 2010 and 2050.

_____ 5. The actual number of Asian/Pacific Islanders in the population is projected to increase from 2010 to 2050.

6. The purpose of the bar graph is _____

_____

_____

Line Graphs

A **line graph** is a continuous curve or frequency distribution in which numbers are plotted in an unbroken line. The horizontal scale measures one aspect of the data (usually time) and the vertical line measures another aspect (usually amount). As the data fluctuate, the line will change direction and, if there are extreme differences, will become very jagged. Closely examine the scale of measurement on the two axes. The fluctuations will appear more or less dramatic depending on the scale sizes.

EXERCISE 9.7

Interpreting Line Graphs

Refer to the line graphs on the next page to respond to the following statements with *T* (true), *F* (false), or *CT* (can't tell). Notice that the scales on the vertical axes differ.

_____ 1. The rate of all property crimes is greater than the rate of all violent crimes.

_____ 2. The rates of violent crime and property crime consistently peaked and fell during the same years.

_____ 3. Murder and nonnegligent manslaughter have historically been the least frequent types of violent crime.

_____ 4. Crime rates rise and fall with similar changes in the U.S. economy.

_____ 5. The rate of all property crimes in 2011 was about 2,900 per 100,000 people in the United States.

_____ 6. The rate of all violent crimes in 2010 was 3,000 per 100,000 people in the United States.

_____ 7. The rate of forcible rape has not been higher than about 25 per 100,000 people since 1960.

_____ 8. The trends in violent and property crimes over the last ten years have been downward.

_____ 9. The rates of aggravated assault and robbery were at their highest at about the same time.

10. The purpose of the line graph is to show _____

_____

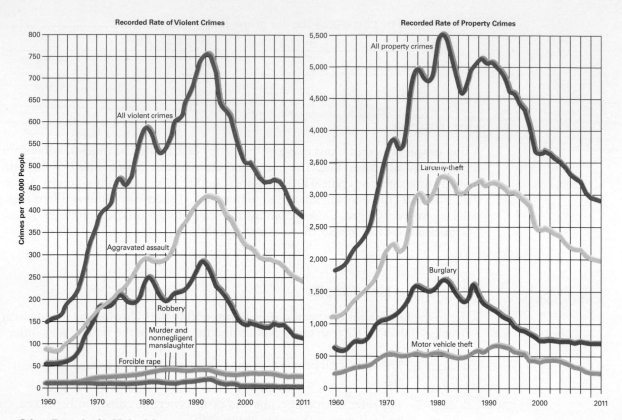

Crime Rates in the United States, 1960–2011.
The graphs show the rates for various violent crimes and property crimes during recent decades.
Source: Federal Bureau of Investigation (2012).

Flowcharts

A **flowchart** shows the sequence of a set of elements and the relationships among them. Flowcharts were first used in computer programming. Key ideas are stated in boxes, and supporting ideas are linked by arrows. Notice the progression, or "flow," from one step to another and the branching that leads to different outcomes. In the flowchart shown on page 473, arrows point toward a progression of steps that are required for a bill to become a law in the United States.

EXERCISE 9.8

Interpreting Flowcharts

A bill introduced in the U.S. House of Representatives or the U.S. Senate follows a specific path before it is passed into law. Refer to the flowchart on the next page to respond to the following statements with *T* (true), *F* (false), or *CT* (can't tell):

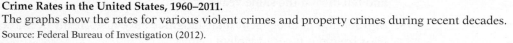

_____ 1. If a bill is introduced in the Senate, the flowchart indicates that it can be debated in the House before it is passed in the Senate.

_____ 2. After both the House and the Senate vote on a bill, it goes to the Conference Committee.

_____ 3. The president can veto and override a bill that has been passed and approved by both the House and the Senate.

_____ 4. Full Senate debate on a bill occurs before the full committee report.

_____ 5. If a bill has solid support from both the House and the Senate, the president usually signs the bill into law.

6. The purpose of the flowchart is _____

_____

How a Bill Becomes Law

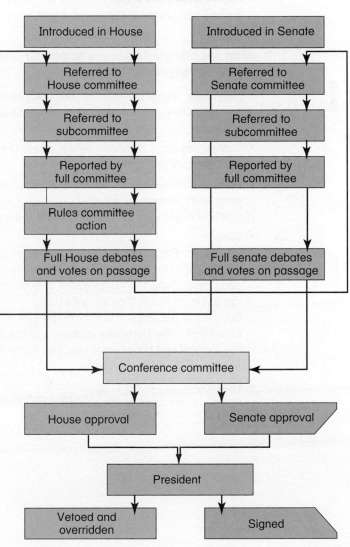

How a bill becomes law.

Source: Morris Fiorina, Paul Peterson, and Bertram Johnson, *The New American Democracy*, 3rd ed.

SUMMARY POINTS

1 How can I make use of graphics while reading? (page 462)

- Graphic illustrations condense detailed information into a more easily understood form that can also display trends and relationships. Graphic illustrations can be designed to inform as well as to convince.
- Read the title or caption that describes the entire graphic.
- Look for footnotes that indicate the source and date, as well as other information about the details in the graphic.
- Read the labels that identify the details that are presented.
- Notice the trends: highs and lows, averages, comparisons, increases or decreases over time, and so on.
- Draw conclusions about the meaning, importance, and application of the information. Think of questions about the information that might appear on a test.

2 What specific strategies are helpful for reading the different types of graphics? (pages 463–473)

- **Diagrams:** Notice the relative size and position of the details in the diagram and how the parts relate to each other. Learn the names of the parts in the diagram.
- **Tables:** Pay close attention to the labels that describe the columns and rows. Notice totals and make comparisons.
- **Maps:** Read the legend, or key, that explains the symbols and shading that were used. Notice the relative position of the parts on the map. Think how position might influence other factors described on the map.
- **Graphs:**
  Pie graphs: Pay attention to the relative size of the parts that make up the entire graph. Remember that the entire circle represents a total or 100%.
  Bar graphs: Note the relative size or strength of the items being compared and the scale on which they are measured.
  Cumulative bar graphs: Compare the size of the segments in each bar.
  Line graphs: Pay particular attention to the scale of measurement used on the vertical and horizontal axes. The scale size can be used to make a trend appear more or less dramatic.
- **Flowcharts:** Study the progression from one detail to another, especially when there are branches leading to different outcomes.

Personal Narrative

MyReadingLab

SELECTION 1

Visit Chapter 9: Graphic Illustrations in MyReadingLab to complete the Selection 1 activities and the Build Background Knowledge video activity.

PREVIEW the next selection to predict its purpose and organization and to formulate your learning plan.

Activate Schemata

What kinds of debt trouble college students?
How might debt acquired in college affect life after college?

Establish a Purpose for Reading

Read to learn how one former student's experiences and advice can help you avoid financial trouble.

Build Background Knowledge — VIDEO

Using Your Phone To Help Pay Off Debt

To prepare for reading Selection 1, answer the questions below. Then, watch this video that offers helpful tips on using your smartphone to get out of debt.

How much debt (credit cards, school loans, etc.) do you have?

What is your plan for paying off your debts?

How do you think technology might help you pay off debt?

This video helped me: _____

_____

_____

Increase Word Knowledge

What do you know about these words?

hindsight	apprentice	undermine	résumé	preclude
superficially	teeming	golden	minimize	grabbing them by the horns

Your instructor may give a brief vocabulary review before or after reading.

Integrate Knowledge While Reading

Questions have been inserted in the margin to stimulate your thinking while reading. Remember to

Predict   Picture   Relate   Monitor   Correct   Annotate

LITTLE INCOME, BIG DEBT: MANAGING MONEY IN COLLEGE

Did he really need more money?

When I was in college, I used my student loans to finance my lifestyle.

    I worked at a decent-paying job ($9 an hour for a job related to my major), but that wasn't enough. I needed more. So I took out student loans, even though scholarships covered most of my tuition and housing expenses. Even worse, I didn't 5 really understand the value of the college education I was getting. I completed a major, decided it wasn't for me, completed a different major, and took enough classes for some minors along the way. When I finally graduated after six years, I had accumulated about $35,000 in student loan debt. Including interest, I've paid about $32,000 so far, and I've got about $16,000 left to go.

College students can easily get into debt due to student loans and other expenses.
ARENA Creative/Shutterstock

WHAT DID I LEARN FROM THIS DISASTER, AND HOW CAN COLLEGE STUDENTS USE WHAT I LEARNED?

10 A lot of students entering college take out student loans to pay for it. The money they're spending, in the form of loans, far exceeds the money they're taking in. I know all about it. I was doing this very thing just a handful of years ago. I made some incredibly stupid mistakes along the way, and it takes a lot of hindsight to see the things I could have and should have done. If I had it to do all over again—if I were a college student today with
15 a big pile of student loans building up and not much income—here's what I would do.

Take the Studies Seriously
The cost of college is tremendous. During your years there, not only are you investing the cost of tuition, but you're also investing the income you might have made doing something else, like becoming an electrician's apprentice or starting your own business. If you're paying $10,000 for your tuition and other expenses and you're
20 giving up $20,000 in income, that's $30,000 each year in college is costing you. That's more than $500 every week.

What's the best way to undermine that investment? To flunk out. To fail a class, causing you to stay in school longer. Even a poor GPA undermines that investment. You reduce the value of the degree by reducing your opportunities right after college if you
25 have a low GPA. Hit the books. If it's a choice between a side job and the books, choose the books every time. If you need to borrow more money because of it, borrow that money. Don't undermine the value of your big investment just to save a little bit of money.

A different way of looking at grades

Take Advantage of the Other Opportunities, Too
College isn't just about hitting the books and partying. There are *tons* of opportunities on a college campus to start building your career and résumé, which *will* im-
30 prove your opportunities and salary when you leave school (further improving the value of your student loan investment). That's not to say the experience should preclude fun, but you should put effort into joining groups—and spending social time with those groups—that build leadership skills or match the topics you're studying.

You're also better off getting strongly involved in a small number of activities
35 than getting superficially involved in a lot of activities. Try out a lot of things at first, find the ones that click for you, then get involved with those. Take on responsibilities with those groups and work toward leadership positions. You'll build valuable relationships with people, learn new things about your areas of interest and about yourself, and build up your future résumé.

How can this improve my job chances?

You're a College Student—Live as Poor as You Can
40 Don't spend your money dressing exceptionally well. There'll be plenty of time for that later on. Instead, do most of your clothes shopping at Goodwill and thrift stores. Don't think you're above it. Look at your checkbook and realize you're a person with a *negative* income—the exact person who should be utilizing such resources.

Also, the typical college campus is teeming with free entertainment. Check the
45 campus newspaper for ideas instead of spending money to have fun. Take advantage of the cheap food opportunities, too. For a while, I had a "one meal a day" meal plan in dining services. I'd eat a big meal, then snack the rest of the day on whatever was available. Realize that each time you spend money in college, you're costing your future, especially when you're surrounded by opportunities for the most inex-
50 pensive living you'll have in your adult life.

Where could I cut expenses?

Use a Credit Card Only to Buy Books—Pay the Bill Immediately
Don't listen to salespeople who insist you get their credit card. Research a good one, then use it only once a semester to buy your textbooks. Put that credit card

somewhere safe, then pay off the entire bill as soon as it comes in. *Never* use the
card for anything else. This simple plan gives you the benefits that you can get from
55 credit card use in college (mostly building credit) without the dangerous drawbacks
of building high-interest debt that you'll have trouble paying off.

Seek a Job (or Other Experiences) Related to Your Major, Even for Lower Pay

If you're going to get a job in college (most people do), look for a part-time job that's
related to your major, even if it means sacrificing pay. A job that matches well with
your studies is *golden* on your résumé when you graduate. If you already have some
60 years of experience working with this material, then you look a lot better than most
people coming out of school.

If you don't know where to begin, the first place to stop is at your departmental
office. Ask around for job opportunities within the major—research work, paperwork,
whatever's available. If you can't find anything there, look for industries near the col-
65 lege that might relate to what you're doing. Make the effort to make a personal appearance, as it shows that you're serious. Anyone can pick up the phone and dial.

I hadn't thought of this.

Minimize Your Debt

If none of the above applies to a decision, make the choice that results in the lowest
debt when you graduate. You're in college to build your future. Don't sacrifice that
future by piling on debt *without* improving your post-graduation opportunities.
70 In a nutshell, maximize the value of what you're paying for, and minimize the
level of debt. You're surrounded by valuable opportunities in college. Only by grabbing them by the horns can you really maximize the value of your college education.

(1,026 words)

—Trent Hamm, *The Simple Dollar*, February 19, 2008.
www.thesimpledollar.com.

Recall

Stop to self-test, relate, and react.

Your instructor may choose to give you a brief comprehension review.

THINK CRITICALLY ABOUT THE SELECTION

The author makes some assumptions about college students and paying for
college that don't apply to all college students.

- In what ways might college students' situations differ from the author's?
- What are some ways to help pay college costs that the author does not include?

WRITE ABOUT THE SELECTION

From what point of view does this author write? What is your perspective on the
points that he makes?

Response Suggestion: List the points on which you agree with the author and
those with which you disagree. Which advice will you follow? Explain.

SKILL DEVELOPMENT: GRAPHICS

Refer to the chart and pie graph below and answer the following items with *T* (true), *F* (false), or *CT* (can't tell):

_____ 1. As shown in the chart, after six monthly payments, the balance decreased by less than half the amount actually paid.

_____ 2. When the debt is completely paid on the payment schedule shown in the chart, the total amount paid will be about twice the original debt.

_____ 3. According to the chart, the remaining balance decreases by a greater amount with each monthly payment.

_____ 4. In the pie graph below, more than half of the budget is allotted for food and rent.

_____ 5. In the budget shown in the pie graph, the best area to reduce spending is rent.

Payment Schedule on a $500 Debt When Submitting a Fixed Minimum Monthly Payment at 18% Interest Rate*				
Month	**Minimum Payment**	**Interest Paid**	**Principal Paid**	**Remaining Balance**
January	10.00	6.25	3.75	496.25
February	10.00	6.20	3.80	491.45
March	10.00	6.16	3.84	488.61
April	10.00	6.11	3.89	484.72
May	10.00	6.06	3.99	480.78
June	10.00	6.01	4.04	476.79

*On this schedule, it would take 79 months to pay the entire debt. The interest paid would be $289.59.

Sample Expense Plan

Entertainment   Education   Rent

Transportation   Meals

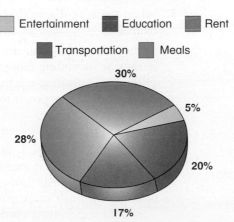

30%

5%

28%

20%

17%

CHECK YOUR COMPREHENSION

After reading the selection, answer the following questions with *a, b, c,* or *d*. To help you analyze your strengths and weaknesses, the question types are indicated.

Main Idea _____ 1. Which is the best statement of the main idea of this selection?

    a. Students should take their studies seriously.

    b. The author regrets accumulating $35,000 in student loans.

    c. To get the most out of college financially, spend more time and energy on your studies and extracurricular activities, and spend less money.

    d. Too many college students spend time on activities that do not contribute to the long-term value of their education.

Detail _____ 2. The author states that

    a. college students should use credit cards only when necessary.

    b. it is wise to invest in quality clothing for job interviews.

    c. his student loans and scholarships covered only half of his expenses.

    d. students should avoid taking a job if working would mean studying less.

Detail _____ 3. Which of the following is *not* mentioned as a benefit of being involved in campus activities?

    a. You may make connections that lead to an on-campus job.

    b. It is a way to build a more impressive résumé.

    c. You will learn about yourself and your interests.

    d. It will provide opportunities for building leadership skills.

Inference _____ 4. We can infer from the selection that the author

    a. wasted time and money by making poor choices in college.

    b. settled on his career goals early in his college years.

    c. did not take his own advice about getting a job related to his major.

    d. has had no trouble paying his student loans.

Inference _____ 5. When the author says that college students have a negative income, he means

    a. they are building wealth for the future.

    b. they are spending more than they earn.

    c. they are spending too much and should cut back.

    d. they should use credit to pay living expenses.

Main Idea _____ 6. The main point of the section, "Take the Studies Seriously," is that

    a. students should study all the time and avoid socializing.

    b. a poor grade point average limits later job opportunities.

    c. flunking out costs money.

    d. to get the most value out of their investment in college, students should concentrate on doing well in their studies.

Main Idea _____ 7. The main point of the section, "Take Advantage of the Other Opportunities, Too," is

    a. college is the time to have fun and meet people.

    b. stay involved in lots of activities instead of just a few.

    c. focus on studying during the week and save the weekends for social activities.

    d. get involved in campus activities that provide opportunities to build employment-related skills as well as to have fun.

Detail _____ 8. In calculating the cost of college, the author

    a. tallies the cost of tuition, books, fees, and entertainment.

    b. considers the cost of tuition, living expenses, and the amount that the student could be earning if the student were not going to college.

    c. totals the amount spent on food, rent, and tuition.

    d. concludes that college is not worth the immense cost.

Detail _____ 9. Which of the following does the author *not* advise doing to save money?

    a. Eat only one big meal a day.

    b. Take advantage of free entertainment on campus.

    c. Get the best paying part-time job possible.

    d. Pay credit card bills in full immediately.

Inference _____ 10. The author believes that

    a. going into debt in college should be avoided.

    b. getting a job in your major is best as long as it pays well.

    c. students should wait until later to establish a solid credit rating.

    d. going into debt in college is okay as long as it provides greater opportunities after graduation.

Answer the following with *T* (true) or *F* (false):

Inference _____ 11. The author's student loans ultimately cost him about $48,000.

Detail _____ 12. The author states that students should get jobs to avoid borrowing more money for college.

Inference _____ 13. The author believes that he made the most of his college education.

Detail _____ 14. The author argues that a poor GPA reduces the value of your degree.

Author's Purpose _____ 15. The author's intention is to help students to manage college expenses wisely.

BUILD YOUR VOCABULARY

According to the way the italicized word was used in the selection, indicate *a, b, c,* or *d* for the word or phrase that gives the best definition. The number in parentheses indicates the line of the passage in which the word is located. Use a dictionary in addition to the context clues to more precisely define the terms.

_____ 1. "takes a lot of *hindsight*" (13)
   a. wisdom after an event
   b. forethought
   c. intelligence
   d. maturity

_____ 2. "an electrician's *apprentice*" (18)
   a. helper
   b. tool carrier
   c. employer
   d. trainee

_____ 3. "*undermines* that investment" (23)
   a. maximizes
   b. selects
   c. increases
   d. weakens

_____ 4. "your career and *résumé*" (29)
   a. begin again
   b. history of work and qualifications
   c. employment evaluation
   d. college transcript

_____ 5. "should *preclude* fun" (31–32)
   a. prevent
   b. include
   c. involve
   d. be

_____ 6. "*superficially* involved" (35)
   a. greatly
   b. energetically
   c. shallowly
   d. sadly

_____ 7. "campus is *teeming*" (44)
   a. full of
   b. well known for
   c. on fire
   d. getting together

_____ 8. "*golden* on your résumé" (59)
   a. shining
   b. beautiful
   c. precious
   d. complete

_____ 9. "*minimize* the level" (70)
   a. add to
   b. equalize
   c. examine
   d. reduce

_____ 10. "*grabbing them by the horns*" (71–72)
   a. paying for
   b. fighting for
   c. submitting to
   d. taking advantage of

Science

MyReadingLab

SELECTION 2

Visit Chapter 9: Graphic Illustrations in MyReadingLab to complete the Selection 2 activities and the Build Background Knowledge video activity.

PREVIEW the next selection to predict its purpose and organization and to formulate your learning plan.

Activate Schemata

Increasingly, more Americans are desperate to lose weight. It seems there is no one who hasn't attempted a diet at one time or another. Can you name a celebrity who has a diet to promote? Do you know someone who has had weight loss surgery? Do you have personal experience with a weight loss plan? How successful are the current, popular methods?

Establish a Purpose for Reading

Read to learn the benefits and possible harmful effects of several popular weight loss methods. Read what scientific research has to say about the factors that lead to successful weight loss.

Build Background Knowledge — VIDEO

How Your Insurance Could Pay To Lose Weight

To prepare for reading Selection 2, answer the questions below. Then, watch this video on recent governmental legislation that directly impacts weight loss programs.

Why do you think it is so difficult to lose weight and keep it off?

Given the obesity epidemic in the United States, should the federal government offer financial assistance to support weight loss programs?

What do you think is a better way to lose weight—diet and exercise or weight loss surgery? Why?

This video helped me: _____

_____

_____

Increase Word Knowledge

What do you know about these words?

sedentary	high-fructose	igniting	unseated	kilocalories
gastric	laparoscopic	invasive	sustainability	silver bullet

Your instructor may give a brief vocabulary review before or after reading.

Integrate Knowledge While Reading

Questions have been inserted in the margins to stimulate your thinking while reading. Remember to

Predict	Picture	Relate	Monitor	Correct	Annotate

THE RISKS AND BENEFITS OF WEIGHT LOSS PLANS

Where am I on the graph?

Who profits from our focus on food?

How have food producers influenced American eating habits?

Is it our evolutionary past or our sedentary lifestyle? Is it super-sized fast food or the addition of high-fructose corn syrup (HFCS) to processed foods? Why are so many people overweight, and how do you know if you are one of them? A standard method of determining healthy weight is body mass index (BMI), a ratio of weight to height
5 (see figure, page 485). A BMI of 25–29 is considered overweight, and above 30 is obese.

Whatever is fueling the dramatic increases in overweight citizens is also igniting our interest in ways to shed body fat. According to some estimates, the U.S. market for weight loss products and services, worth about $30 billion in 1992, has expanded to more than $60 billion a year. But has this huge increase in expenditures
10 bought us thinner, healthier bodies? Not yet.

Thousands of diet books have been written. Magazines, the Internet, even several weight loss reality TV shows bombard us with advice and promises. How can we know which diet plan is fastest, safest, most long-lasting?

In recent years, many popular weight loss schemes have focused on reduced intake
15 of carbohydrates. People following "low-carb" diets often drop sugar, bread, fruits, and potatoes from their diet, swapping in cheese, nuts, and meat instead. Because of the success stories of people who have lost weight and the fatty foods these diets allow, this approach surged in popularity. Americans spend as much as $15 billion a year on "low-carb" diet aids and foods. Although some studies have found these diets to be effective,
20 others have found that they offer only short-lived benefits. The fatty foods encouraged in such diets may contribute to health problems, and reductions in fruits and vegetables cut a person's intake of vitamins, minerals, and fiber. As a result, few doctors recommend low-carbohydrate diets as a healthy way to long-term weight loss.

Low-carb diets unseated low-fat diets, an earlier dieting trend with its own
25 flood of low-fat (but often high-sugar) processed foods and attendant health concerns about inadequate fatty acids or protein. Among the many other types of diets are prepackaged meal plans and group programs where dieters attend meetings or join online chats for diet and exercise plans and support.

Losing weight is certainly big business, with some plans costing thousands of
30 dollars. However, an online program from the USDA, called MyPyramid Tracker, is free. It asks you to enter your food intake and physical activity daily. The program then analyzes your nutrient and energy intake as well as kilocalories expended by your activities. An energy balance summary indicates the weight gain or loss you can expect from your data.

35 Some severely obese individuals may be candidates for weight loss surgery. Gastric bypass surgery, which reduces the size of the stomach and the length of the small intestine, is an increasingly popular weight loss solution, with about 150,000

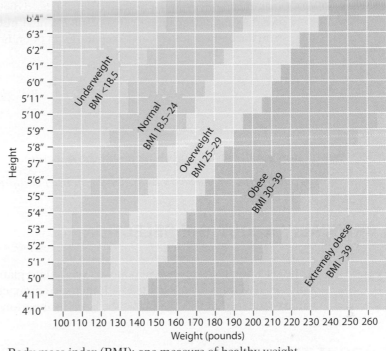

Body mass index (BMI): one measure of healthy weight

operations performed a year. This surgery limits food intake capacity and nutrient absorption. Although it has documented risks, studies show that gastric bypass
40 surgery reduces some obesity-related health risks. Lap band surgery involves an adjustable ring placed around the upper part of the stomach, which restricts the amount of food that can be eaten at one time. This laparoscopic procedure is less invasive and reversible, and its use is increasing.

Scientific studies of weight loss diets indicate that sustainability is the major
45 shortcoming of all diets. There appears to be no silver bullet for losing weight and keeping it off without lifestyle changes. These changes involve a combination of

What is the key to losing weight?

If Americans spend billions of dollars each year on weight loss products and programs, why does obesity continue to be a problem?

travellight/Shutterstock

increased exercise and a restricted but balanced diet that provides at least 1,200 kcal per day and adequate amounts of all essential nutrients. Such a combination can trim the body gradually and keep the extra pounds off.

(645 words)

—Jane B. Reece et al.,
Biology: Concepts & Connections, 7th ed.

Recall

Stop to talk, write, and think about the selection.

Your instructor may choose to give you a brief comprehension review.

THINK CRITICALLY ABOUT THE SELECTION

The selection looks at several popular weight loss plans and briefly discusses the plusses and minuses associated with them. To more clearly display the information, make a chart that lists the plans, the benefits mentioned, and the disadvantages.

WRITE ABOUT THE SELECTION

Scientists report the results of their research in specialized journals. An abstract—a brief summary—is almost always included at the beginning of a journal article to help researchers decide if they want to read the entire report. Write a one-paragraph abstract that could be used to preview this article as if it were a scientific research report.

Response Suggestion: Prepare by constructing the chart described in the "Think Critically About the Selection" section above. Begin the abstract with a sentence describing the main idea. Use your list to summarize the details and end with the article's conclusion about what works. Use your own words but include only material that is in the article.

SKILL DEVELOPMENT: GRAPHICS

Refer to the graph on page 485 and answer the following items with *T* (true) or *F* (false):

_____ 1. BMI refers to Body Measurement Index.

_____ 2. This graph shows that BMI measures a person's body fat in relation to muscle.

_____ 3. According to this graph, a person with a BMI score of 27 is categorized as overweight.

_____ 4. This graph shows that any person who weighs 200 pounds falls in the "Extremely obese" category.

_____ 5. According to this graph, normal weight ranges from just under 100 pounds to 200 pounds or possibly more for persons taller than 6'5".

CHECK YOUR COMPREHENSION

After reading the selection, answer the following questions with *a*, *b*, *c*, or *d*. To help you analyze your strengths and weaknesses, the question types are indicated.

Main Idea _____ 1. Which of the following statements best expresses the main idea of this selection?

    a. Popular weight loss methods have both risks and benefits.
    b. Obesity has become all too common among Americans.
    c. Americans spend huge amounts of money on weight loss.
    d. Gastric bypass surgery has some risks.

Detail _____ 2. Which weight loss method costs Americans as much as $15 billion a year?

    a. low-carbohydrate diets
    b. low-fat diets
    c. gastric bypass surgery
    d. lap band surgery

Detail _____ 3. Which of the following is mentioned as a negative aspect of low-carb diets?

    a. They do not emphasize the importance of exercise.
    b. They do not contain enough of the essential nutritional oils.
    c. They contain too much sugar.
    d. They lack the necessary amounts of vitamins and minerals.

Detail _____ 4. According to the selection, how much do Americans currently spend on weight loss programs?

    a. $15 billion
    b. $30 billion
    c. more than $60 billion
    d. More than $90 billion

Main Idea _____ 5. Which statement expresses the main point of the last paragraph?

    a. Good nutrition is essential to good health.
    b. Studies show that any weight loss program is better than doing nothing.
    c. Losing and keeping weight off requires exercising and restricting food intake.
    d. Everyone needs at least 1,200 kcal per day.

Inference _____ 6. The selection implies that one reason low-carb diets gained popularity is that

    a. they allow participants to eat a variety of foods with high sugar content.
    b. they allow participants to eat many satisfying foods that are high in fat.
    c. they have been shown to have long-lasting effects.
    d. there are few risks involved in a low-carb diet.

Detail _____ 7. Which of the following is mentioned as a negative aspect of low-fat diets?

    a. online diet and exercise support
    b. group meetings
    c. not enough sugar
    d. not enough protein

Detail _____ 8. Which of the following is mentioned as a positive feature of lap band surgery?

    a. It allows the patient to eat as much as he or she wishes.
    b. It is successful in all cases.
    c. It is reversible.
    d. It is performed about 150,000 times a year.

Inference _____ 9. Which of the following best sums up this selection's conclusion regarding weight loss diets?

    a. Gastric surgery has been successful for many obese individuals.
    b. To lose weight, dieters must eat less and exercise more.
    c. For good health, Americans must lose weight.
    d. Of the diets mentioned, the low-carb diet is the best choice.

Inference _____ 10. Based on the information in this selection, readers can predict that any diet they might use for weight loss would have which negative factor?

    a. The dieter would have to supplement food intake with vitamin tablets.
    b. It is likely that the dieter would feel hungry.
    c. It would not guarantee that the dieter could maintain the weight loss.
    d. The diet would require special foods that would be expensive.

Answer the following with *T* (true) or *F* (false).

Author's Purpose _____ 11. This selection is promoting MyPyramidTracker for sales and profit.

Detail _____ 12. Low-carbohydrate diets were popular before low-fat diets became popular.

Inference _____ 13. The article implies that gastric bypass surgery would not be recommended for someone in the "Overweight" category described in the graph.

Inference _____ 14. Keeping weight off after losing it is difficult.

Inference _____ 15. A person with a BMI greater than 39 is most likely to be a good candidate for gastric bypass surgery.

BUILD YOUR VOCABULARY

According to the way the italicized word was used in the selection, indicate *a, b, c,* or *d* for the word or phrase that gives the best definition. The number in parentheses indicates the line of the passage in which the word is located. Use a dictionary in addition to the context clues to more precisely define the terms.

_____ 1. "our *sedentary* lifestyle" (1)
   a. spoiled
   b. physically inactive
   c. expensive
   d. very busy

_____ 2. "*high-fructose* corn syrup" (2)
   a. very sweet form of sugar
   b. very nutritious
   c. very pleasant tasting
   d. readily available

_____ 3. "*igniting* our interest" (6–7)
   a. exciting
   b. suffocating
   c. profiting from
   d. protecting

_____ 4. "*unseated* low-fat diets" (24)
   a. started
   b. elected
   c. moved aside
   d. approved

_____ 5. "*kilocalories* expended" (32)
   a. more than the usual energy
   b. less than the usual energy
   c. amount of food
   d. scientifically accurate term for "calorie"

_____ 6. "*gastric* bypass" (36)
   a. intestinal
   b. gas-producing
   c. medical
   d. relating to the stomach

_____ 7. "*laparoscopic* procedure" (42)
   a. dangerous
   b. involving a small medical scope
   c. involving excessive cutting
   d. popular

_____ 8. "is less *invasive*" (43)
   a. expensive
   b. exciting
   c. possibly harmful
   d. successful

_____ 9. "*sustainability* is the major shortcoming" (44)
   a. ability to continue
   b. inability to be proven
   c. expense
   d. pleasantness

_____ 10. "no *silver bullet*" (45)
   a. magic weapon
   b. gun
   c. diet
   d. ammunition

SELECTION

2

SELECTION 3   Sociology   MyReadingLab

Visit Chapter 9: Graphic Illustrations in MyReadingLab to complete the Selection 3 activities and the Build Background Knowledge video activity.

Preview the next selection to predict its purpose and organization and to formulate your learning plan.

Activate Schemata

How does increasing world population affect the environment?
Do poor countries or wealthy countries cause more environmental harm?
In what ways does technology affect the natural environment?

Establish a Purpose for Reading

Humans are damaging nature with waste and overconsumption, as well as depleting natural resources. Read to learn how humans are changing the planet and why this is a topic for sociologists.

Build Background Knowledge — VIDEO

Beijing Air Pollution Forces 20 Million Indoors

To prepare for reading Selection 3, answer the questions below. Then, watch this video that examines the relationship between overpopulation and pollution in Beijing, China.

Who (or what) do you think is most responsible for damage to the environment?

What should world governments do to address damage to the environment?

What can individuals do to address damage to the environment?

This video helped me: _____

_____

_____

Increase Word Knowledge

What do you know about these words?

| material | curious | consume | materialistic | productivity |
| affluence | abundance | migration | agrarian | deficit |

Your instructor may give a brief vocabulary review before or after reading.

Integrate Knowledge While Reading

Questions have been inserted in the margin to stimulate your thinking while reading. Remember to

Predict   Picture   Relate   Monitor   Correct   Annotate

PEOPLE, TECHNOLOGY, AND THE ENVIRONMENT

Why did the author include this section?

Grandma Macionis was a beautiful and loving woman who never threw anything away. Born in Lithuania—which she called the "old country"—Lillian Macionis grew up in a small village in which everyone was poor. Even after she came to the United States as a young woman, this social world shaped her entire life.

5   Each year, the family gathered together to celebrate her birthday. The occasion brought great amusement because, after opening each present, she would carefully put aside the box, refold the wrapping paper, and roll up the ribbon so that all these things could be used again. The packaging meant as much to her as the gift itself—possibly even more because, as far as we could tell, Grandma never wore any new

10   clothes we gave her. Grandma Macionis lived a simple life guided by the belief that there was nothing wrong with what she already had. So, although she appreciated gifts as a symbol of her family's love, she viewed anything new in the material world as unnecessary and wasteful.

As curious as Grandma Macionis often seemed to her grandchildren, she was a

15   product of her culture. The social world in which she grew up produced little "trash." If socks wore thin, people mended them, again and again. When clothes became worn beyond repair, people used them as cleaning rags or sewed them together to make a quilt. For people like Grandma, everything had value, if not in one way, then in another.

Grandma Macionis never thought of herself as an environmentalist. But she

20   was: She used few resources and created almost no solid waste. Living this way may seem strange or old-fashioned to most people in the United States today. After all, most of us seem to measure social standing by how much we consume. And our modern way of life also favors "convenience," a value that leads us to buy our morning coffee in throw-away cups, to bundle our groceries in throw-away plastic bags,

25   and to rely on private cars rather than public transit. Most of us hold a materialistic, fast-paced view of the "good life." But living this way also places a great strain on our natural environment.

THE ROLE OF SOCIOLOGY

Problems related to the environment include vast amounts of solid waste, various types of pollution, the effects of acid rain, the process of global warming, and the

30   declining number of living species. None of these problems results from the natural world operating on its own. They are all products of the way humans organize their lives within societies. For this reason, environmental issues are *social* problems.

Sociologists examine how people consume natural resources and track the amount of waste and pollution that people produce. Sociologists track public

35 opinion on issues ranging from natural gas "fracking" to global warming and identify what categories of people support one side or the other of various environmental issues. But the most important contribution sociologists make is in demonstrating how our society's technology, cultural patterns, and specific political and economic arrangements affect the natural environment.

POPULATION INCREASE

40 Sociologists point to a simple formula: I = PAT, where environmental impact (*I*) reflects a society's population (*P*), its level of affluence (*A*), and its level of technology (*T*). In short, the more people in a society, the richer their way of life, and the more complex their technology, the bigger the impact on the natural environment.

Let's look first at population. Some 2,000 years ago, the world had about 300 45 million people—less than the population of the United States today (Population Reference Bureau, 2014).

In the nineteenth century, as a number of nations developed industrial technology and the medical science that goes along with it, living standards rose and death rates fell sharply. The predictable result was a sharp upward spike in world popula- 50 tion. By 1800, global population had soared to 1 billion.

In the decades that followed, population increased ever more quickly, with the planet's population reaching 2 billion by 1930, 3 billion by 1962, 4 billion by 1974, 5 billion by 1987, and 6 billion by 1999. By the beginning of 2014, more than 7.1 billion people lived on the planet. Although the rate of increase has now slowed, we con- 55 tinue to add 87 million people to the world's total each year (more than 237,000 every day) (Population Reference Bureau, 2013).

A well-known riddle illustrates how runaway growth can suddenly overwhelm the natural environment:

60 A pond has a single water lily growing on it. The lily doubles in size each day. In thirty days, it covers the entire pond. On which day did the lily cover half the pound?

The answer that come readily to mind—the fifteenth day—is wrong. The lily was not increasing in size by the same amount every day; it was *doubling* in size each day. The correct answer, then, is that the lily covered half the pond on the twenty-ninth day, 65 just one day earlier. The point is that for almost the entire month, the size of the growing lily seems manageable. Only on the twenty-ninth day, when the lily covers half the pond, are people likely to see the problem, but by then it is too late to do anything about it and the very next day, the lily chokes the life out of the entire pond.

Most experts predict that the world population will increase to about 9.6 billion 70 people by 2050 (United Nations, 2013). The most rapid population growth is occurring in the poorest regions of the world. Taken together, the nations of Africa are adding to their population at an annual rate of 2.6 percent, which will more than double Africa's population by 2050 (Population Reference Bureau, 2013).

POVERTY AND AFFLUENCE

Rapid population increase makes the problem of poverty worse. This is because 75 a surging population can offset increases in productivity so that living standards stay the same. If a society's population doubles, doubling economic productivity amounts to no gain at all in standard of living.

But poverty also makes environmental problems worse. Preoccupied with survival, poor people have little choice but to consume the resources they have, without
80 thinking about long-term environmental consequences. But the long-term trend for
the world is toward greater affluence. What are the environmental consequences of
rising population and greater affluence taking place *together*? One way to answer
this question is to consider the consequences of increasing affluence in India and
China, which together contain 2.6 billion people. China is already the world's largest
85 market for automobiles. Now that India is a middle-income nation, an ever-
increasing share of its people own motor vehicles. In 2014, a year in which about 15
million automobiles were sold in the United States, sales reached 20 million vehicles
in China. What effect will this trend toward greater auto production and use have
on the world's oil reserves? What about global air quality?

90   Simply put, if people all around the world were to live at the level of material
abundance that most people in the United States take for granted, the natural environment would rapidly collapse. From an environmentalist point of view, our planet
may suffer from economic underdevelopment in some places, but it also suffers
from economic overdevelopment in others.

THE INCREASING EFFECTS OF TECHNOLOGY

95 We gain additional insight from considering the historical development of technology. Our earliest ancestors lived by hunting animals and gathering plants. With this
simple technology, these people had little effect on the environment. They adapted
their lives to the rhythms of nature, moving from place to place with the migration

The most important lesson sociology offers about environmental issues is that the state of
our planet reflects how societies operate. What facts about U.S. society can you "read" in
this photograph?

Huguette Roe/Shutterstock

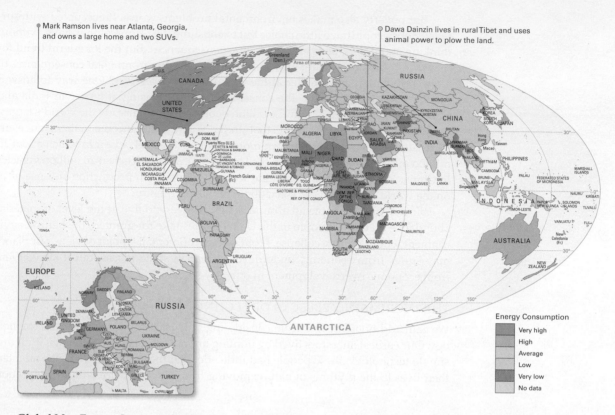

Global Map Energy Consumption in Global Perspective

People in high-income nations consume far more energy than those living in poor countries. The typical U.S. resident uses the same amount of energy in a year as 108 people in Ethiopia or 88 people in the Central African Republic. In general, the most economically productive nations are those that put the greatest burden on the natural environment. In fact, in recent years, the demand for energy in the United States has exceeded the available supply.

Source: Central Intelligence Agency (2014).

100 of animals and the changing seasons and in response to natural events such as fires, floods, and droughts.

People living in societies that gain the use of horticulture (small-scale farming), pastoralism (the herding of animals), or agriculture (with animal-drawn plows) have a greater capacity to affect the environment. But limited by the use of muscle power for energy, the environmental impact of these technologies is still 105 quite small.

The Industrial Revolution changed everything by replacing muscles with vastly more powerful combustion engines that burn fossil fuels such as coal and oil. Using industrial technology, humans are capable of bending nature to their will, tunneling through mountains, damming rivers, irrigating deserts, and 110 drilling for oil beneath the ocean floor. In the process, we consume more energy resources and also release more pollutants into the atmosphere. The overall result of new technology is that humans have brought more change to the planet's environment in the last two centuries than our ancestors did in all of human history before then.

115   The Global Map on the preceding page shows that high income, high-technology countries consume a great deal of the world's energy. Although these nations account for just 23 percent of humanity, they represent about 40 percent of the world's energy consumption. From another angle, the typical adult in the United States uses about fifty times as much energy as the average
120   person in the world, and fifty times as much as a person living in a low-income nation such as Eritrea.

Equally important, members of industrial and postindustrial societies produce 100 times more goods than people working in agrarian societies. Much of what we produce (such as packaging) is never consumed at all and is simply thrown away,
125   creating vast amounts of solid waste.

The Environment Deficit

This short look at human history teaches an important lesson: The increase in human population, the rising level of affluence around the globe, and the development of more powerful technology have positive consequences, but they also put the lives of future generations at risk. The evidence is mounting that we are running up an
130   **environmental deficit**, *serious, long-term harm to the environment caused by humanity's focus on short-term material affluence* (Bormann, 1990).

Facing up to the environmental deficit is important for three reasons. First, it reminds us that environmental quality is a *social issue*, reflecting choices people make about what technology to use, how many children to have, and how much to
135   consume. Second, it suggests that much environmental damage may be *unintended*. By focusing on the short-term benefits of, say, cutting down forests or using throwaway packaging, we satisfy our desire for material goods and convenience. At the same time, however, we fail to see that such behavior has long-term, harmful environmental effects. Third, in some respects the environmental deficit is *reversible*. If
140   members of modern societies make different choices, they can undo many (but not all) environmental problems.

(1,832 words)

—From John J. Macionis,
Social Problems, 6th ed. © 2015.
Printed and electronically
reproduced by permission of
Pearson Education, Inc., Upper Saddle River, NJ.

Recall

Stop to self-test, relate, and react.
Your instructor may choose to give you a brief comprehension review.

THINK CRITICALLY ABOUT THE SELECTION

Explain why environmental issues are an appropriate subject for sociologists.

What specific environmental issues arise from overpopulation and modern technology?

WRITE ABOUT THE SELECTION

How are humans changing the planet, and what are the consequences?

Response Suggestion: Focus on one major change, such as population growth, sophisticated technology, or a specific environmental problem. How does it affect us now? How might it affect us 50 years from now?

SKILL DEVELOPMENT: GRAPHICS

Refer to the global map on page 494 and answer the following items with *T* (true) or *F* (false):

_____ 1. In general, Western and northern European countries use more energy than central and eastern European countries.

_____ 2. All of the Central and South American countries use an average amount of energy.

_____ 3. All of the highest energy-consuming nations lie north of the equator.

_____ 4. We can infer from the global map that Mark Ramson uses more energy than Dawa Dainzin.

_____ 5. The demand for energy in the United States has exceeded the supply in recent years.

CHECK YOUR COMPREHENSION

After reading the selection, answer the following questions with *a, b, c,* or *d.* To help you analyze your strengths and weaknesses, the question types are indicated.

Main Idea ———— 1. Which is the best statement of the main idea of this selection?

a. Social problems cause poverty and suffering around the world today.
b. Advances in technology are destined to worsen rather than solve environmental problems.
c. The environment is suffering from overpopulation and poverty.
d. Several factors contribute to the environmental problems that we face today.

Author's Purpose ———— 2. The reader can conclude that the story about Grandma Macionis is used to introduce this selection because the author

a. feels that Grandma Macionis was ecologically aware.
b. needs to provide an example of how social problems originate.
c. sees Grandma Macionis as someone from whom humans today could learn.
d. feels Grandma Macionis was careful in spending her money.

Detail ———— 3. The author indicates that our very earliest ancestors did not appreciably alter their environment because they

a. rejected the use of technology.
b. lived simply in cooperation with nature.
c. were affected by fires, floods, and droughts.
d. migrated during the seasons.

Inference ———— 4. The author implies that the world's environmental deficit is in direct proportion to

a. the material demands of humanity and population growth.
b. technological research.
c. the dreams of future generations.
d. the toxicity of pollutants.

Detail ———— 5. The author says that the "spike in world population" in the years leading up to 1800 was predictable partly because

a. there were great advances in medicine.
b. the world's population was fairly small.
c. there were no major wars taking place.
d. productivity was growing rapidly.

Detail ———— 6. The author claims that those who live in poverty

a. seek to destroy the environment.
b. damage the environment out of necessity.
c. take little from the environment.
d. consider long-term consequences.

Inference _____ 7. The author indicates that from an environmentalist perspective, world economic development is not

    a. fair.
    b. efficient.
    c. balanced.
    d. obvious.

Detail _____ 8. Which statement best reflects the main idea of the section, "Poverty and Affluence?"

    a. Rapid population growth makes the problems of poverty worse.
    b. Poverty makes environmental problems worse.
    c. China is already the world's largest market for automobiles.
    d. While poverty has a negative effect on the environment, increasing affluence is a more devastating concern.

Inference _____ 9. The environmental effects of increasing affluence in India and China will likely include

    a. greater employment opportunities.
    b. increased air pollution and depletion of oil reserves.
    c. more nuclear waste.
    d. clogged waterways and reduced recreational land.

Inference _____ 10. Which of the following is a logical reason that the rate of population growth has slowed in recent years?

    a. the need for children to support elderly parents
    b. fewer people of child-bearing age
    c. successful education efforts and increased availability of effective birth control
    d. greater employment opportunities

Answer the following with *T* (true) or *F* (false):

Detail _____ 11. Forty percent of the world's energy consumption occurs in 23 percent of the world's population.

Detail _____ 12. An average adult in the United States uses four times as much energy as the average person in the entire world.

Inference (Point of View) _____ 13. The author is writing from an environmentalist's point of view.

Detail _____ 14. The world population is growing by about 237,000 people every day.

Detail _____ 15. The author believes that it is possible to reverse some global environmental problems.

BUILD YOUR VOCABULARY

According to the way the italicized word was used in the selection, indicate *a, b, c,* or *d* for the word or phrase that gives the best definition. The number in parentheses indicates the line of the passage in which the word is located. Use a dictionary in addition to the context clues to more precisely define the terms.

_____ 1. "In the *material* world" (12)
a. good
b. spiritual
c. physical
d. real

_____ 2. "As *curious* as" (14)
a. peculiar
b. sweet
c. wonderful
d. frugal

_____ 3. "much we *consume*" (22)
a. eat
b. use up
c. earn
d. save

_____ 4. "hold a *materialistic*" (25)
a. poverty-stricken
b. lively
c. money- or possession-oriented
d. religious

_____ 5. "increases in *productivity*" (75)
a. population
b. wealth
c. technology
d. output

_____ 6. "toward greater *affluence*" (82)
a. wealth
b. growth
c. poverty
d. happiness

_____ 7. "material *abundance*" (91)
a. prosperity
b. misfortune
c. consequence
d. development

_____ 8. "*migration* of animals" (98)
a. reproduction
b. movement
c. breeding
d. destruction

_____ 9. "*agrarian* societies" (123)
a. undeveloped
b. mountainous
c. industrial
d. agricultural

_____ 10. "environmental *deficit*" (130)
a. condition
b. shortage
c. technology
d. design

VOCABULARY BOOSTER

Play It Again, Sam

Prefix	**Root**
re-: "back, again"	*lud, lus:* "to play"

Words with *re-:* "back, again"

Although Humphrey Bogart never said the line, "Play it again, Sam," in the movie *Casablanca*, it has been *repeatedly* attributed to his character, Rick.

- *reconcile*: to cause to become friendly or peaceable again; to cause one to accept something not desired

  The purpose of the peace conference was to get the opposing sides to *reconcile* their differences and find a way to coexist in the region.

- *reconstruct*: to build again; to create again in the mind from available information

  The witness to the auto accident was asked by the police officer to *reconstruct* from memory the events leading up to the crash.

- *recriminate*: to bring a countercharge against an accuser

  Melissa feared that legally accusing her ex-husband of being an unfit father would cause him to *recriminate* against her as an unfit mother.

- *refrain*: to keep oneself from doing something

  I had to *refrain* from laughing when the professor walked into class wearing bedroom slippers.

- *regress*: to revert to an earlier or less advanced state

  The paralyzed patient had been making progress in physical therapy, but suddenly she *regressed* to being unable to walk a single step.

- *reiterate*: to say or do repeatedly

  The infomercial *reiterated* the cleaning product's claims until I became annoyed at hearing over and over how white my shirts could be.

- *rejuvenate*: to make young again; to make new again

  The facial product line was promoted as being able to *rejuvenate* a user's skin by reducing wrinkles and uneven skin tones within two weeks with a money-back guarantee.

- *renege*: to go back on one's word

  Daniel had to *renege* on his promise to drive his friends to the football game after his father refused to lend him the car.

- *repel*: to push away by force; to fail to mix with; to resist absorption; to cause distaste in

  Oil and water do not mix; rather, they *repel* each other.

- **repercussion**: an effect of some previous action, recoil after impact; reverberation

  Excessive running on pavement can have serious *repercussions* on your health, such as wearing out knee joints from the constant impact.

- **retract**: to withdraw a statement or opinion as inaccurate; to withdraw a promise

  Celebrities often sue magazines or newspapers, asking for *retractions* of inaccurate statements printed about them.

- **revenge**: to inflict pain or harm in return for a wrong received; to get even or get satisfaction

  Cindy's *revenge* for Sonia's lies was not inviting Sonia to the best party of the year.

Words with *lud, lus:* "to play"

The *prelude* or introductory piece of music to an opera is called an overture.

- **ludicrous**: causing laughter because of absurdity; ridiculous

  Darren looked *ludicrous* in the extremely short haircut that made his ears stick out.

- **allude**: to casually or indirectly refer to

  He will *allude* to his days as a football star whenever the guys start discussing sports.

- **allusion**: a casual or passing reference to something, either direct or implied

  A casual *allusion* to Shakespeare would be to call him the bard.

- **interlude**: any intermediate performance or entertainment, such as between the acts of a play

  The instrumental *interlude* between the verses of the song had a melancholy sound.

- **delude**: to mislead the mind or judgment of

  Jonathan felt silly when he realized that the two con artists who had tricked him out of his money had *deluded* him.

- **elude**: to avoid capture; to escape perception or comprehension of

  The reason for her popularity *eludes* me; I just don't get it.

- **illusion**: an unreal or misleading appearance or image

  Faux finishes like marbleizing a column with paint create an inexpensive *illusion* in home decorating.

Review

Part I

Indicate whether the italicized words are used correctly (*C*) or incorrectly (*I*) in the following sentences:

 1. Realizing that he had provided inaccurate information during his testimony, the defendant wished to *retract* his statement.

_C_ 2. The host continued to *repel* the guests and thus strengthen their friendship.

_C_ 3. A brief *interlude* was held before the concert began.

_I_ 4. Detectives attempt to *reconstruct* the scene of a crime in order to solve it.

_C_ 5. Self-tanning skin products create the *illusion* of a natural glow, without the accompanying sun damage.

_I_ 6. The couple planned a month in the sun together in order to *rejuvenate* their relationship.

_C_ 7. Her carefully chosen, tasteful outfit allowed the woman to *elude* others that she was an upstanding member of society.

_C_ 8. The persistent toddler *repeatedly* asked his mother for items at his eye level in the grocery store.

_I_ 9. The test monitor had to *reiterate* directions that had already been given.

_C_ 10. Some say that the best form of *revenge* is a life well lived.

Part II

Indicate whether the following statements are true (*T*) or false (*F*):

_F_ 11. People sometimes *delude* themselves into believing things that are not true.

_T_ 12. A sign of growing up is learning that all actions have *repercussions*, whether positive or negative.

_T_ 13. To discourage the young man from asking her out, she could *allude* to the fact that her boyfriend would be visiting during the upcoming weekend.

_F_ 14. The orchestra played a brief *prelude* at the concert's conclusion.

_T_ 15. Her father's attempts to dance were made all the more *ludicrous* by his total lack of rhythm.

_F_ 16. The boys knew their mother would not *renege* on her threat to withdraw privileges in exchange for poor behavior.

_T_ 17. By remaining silent, she thought she could avoid *recriminating* herself.

_T_ 18. Prior to offering counsel for divorce, family law attorneys are trained to encourage a couple to *reconcile*, if at all possible.

_F_ 19. Knowing her nephew might be sensitive about his appearance, she encouraged his cousins to *refrain* from commenting.

_T_ 20. To *regress* could be considered the opposite of making progress.

Critical Thinking

Learning Objectives

In this chapter, you will learn to:

1 Distinguish analytical thinking and critical thinking
2 Recognize arguments
3 Analyze and evaluate arguments
4 Define inductive and deductive reasoning
5 Practice thinking critically
6 Define creative thinking

Vocabulary Booster: Foreign Terms

Andrey Kuzmin/Shutterstock

WHAT IS THINKING?

Learning Objective 1

Distinguish analytical thinking and critical thinking

Thinking is an organized and controlled mental activity that helps you solve problems, make decisions, and understand ideas. Benjamin Bloom's well-known taxonomy of thinking skills describes what we know intuitively—that some kinds of thinking are harder than others. Bloom's research produced a hierarchy that defines the different kinds of thinking and puts them in order according to the amount of mental energy and attention they demand: (1) Knowledge, (2) Comprehension, (3) Application, (4) Analysis, (5) Synthesis, and (6) Evaluation. The first two or three types are generally considered lower-level thinking, and the second three or four types are considered higher-level thinking.

As college students, you are expected to use all six levels. In other words, you cannot stop with memorizing and understanding what you read or hear. You must also be able to apply it, examine its parts, combine it with your existing schemata, and assess its value.

What Is Analytical Thinking?

Analytical thinking involves separating and examining parts to identify reasons, causes, and support. To think analytically is not simply to ponder; it is demanding, challenging, and rewarding work requiring skill and confidence. Analytical thinking is what you do when you recognize the major and minor supporting details in an essay or a textbook passage. It is what you do when you determine the main point that an author is making through the details presented. As you will see in this chapter, analysis is the part of the critical thinking process that involves recognizing the details that support an author's position on an issue. After analysis comes evaluating the strength of the support and the strength of the argument.

All thinkers experience confusion, mental blocks, and failure at times. When faced with such adversity, poor thinkers get frustrated. They initially have trouble knowing where to begin and tend to jump haphazardly from one part of the problem to another. Lacking confidence, they eventually give up. Good thinkers, on the other hand, are strategic. They form a plan and systematically try different solutions. They work with confidence, persistently stick with the task, and find solutions.

EXERCISE 10.1

Problem Solving

Experience the thinking processes of good thinkers by solving the following problem. Warm up your thinking skills, formulate a plan, believe that you can do it (I did it, so can you!), be persistent, and solve this problem. Have fun with it!

Record your solution patterns as you "pour water" into empty glasses. If one approach fails, try another. This is not a trick but a problem that can be systematically solved—without throwing water away or estimating amounts. Use the illustration shown below to stimulate your thinking.

> Rowena has three unmarked glasses of different sizes: 3 ounces, 5 ounces, and 8 ounces. The largest glass is full, and the other two glasses are empty. What can Rowena do to get 4 ounces of liquid into each of the two larger glasses?

—Adapted from Vincent Ryan Ruggiero,
The Art of Thinking, 7th ed.

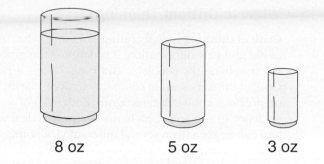

8 oz   5 oz   3 oz

There are several ways to solve this problem.

1. _____
   _____
   _____
   _____

2. _____
   _____
   _____
   _____

3. _____
   _____
   _____
   _____

If you worked on the exercise at length, you have experienced the rigors of earnest analytical thinking. Did you work strategically? What was your plan? What were the frustrations? Were you persistent? Did you believe in your ability to find a solution? Did you enjoy using analytical thinking for problem solving?

Problems in real life are usually expressed as questions that need an action plan. For example, how would you respond if company managers decided that your job required you to solve the following problems?

- How can workers be enticed to carpool?
- How can awards be distributed to employees to mark each five years of service?
- How can a dead elephant be removed from the parking lot after an unfortunate media event?

You would, of course, work systematically to find solutions to the stated problems.

What does all of this have to do with critical thinking? Assuming it was your managers who identified the bigger issues regarding the need for carpooling, five-year service awards, and elephant removal, they were the ones who did the critical thinking, and you were the one who got to do the problem solving.

What Is Critical Thinking?

Critical thinking is deliberating in a purposeful, organized manner to assess the value of old and new information; it is defining the problems to be solved. Analytical thinking is solving the problem, and it also plays a part in the critical thinking process. Critical thinkers search, compare, analyze, clarify, evaluate, and conclude. They build on previous knowledge, recognize both sides of an issue, and evaluate the reasons and evidence in support of each. And they often deal with issues that can be controversial and can be seen from several different viewpoints. The words *how can* usually begin a problem-solving question, whereas *should* begins a critical thinking question.

For example, imagine the critical thinking that is needed to answer the controversial question, "Should state legislators vote to take away the driver's licenses of students aged 16 through 18 who drop out of school?" Supporters would say that such a law would reduce the number of high school dropouts; detractors would contend that the law would violate the rights of students; and others would dismiss the idea on the basis that government should not be in the parenting business. After forming a position, each side would line up evidence to build a persuasive argument to use in lobbying legislators. Both the developers of the arguments and the legislators would be critical thinkers. For the 16- to 18-year-old dropouts, the stakes would be high. The diagram below illustrates the parts and possibilities of the critical thinking process.

Some professors speak of critical thinking as if it were a special discipline rather than an application of many known skills. However, critical thinking

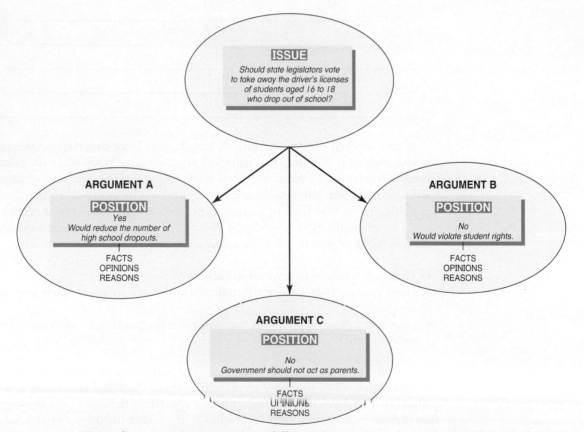

Depending on your position, many different arguments can be constructed for a single issue.

> ### Reader's TIP — Four Habits of Effective Critical Thinkers
>
> - **Be willing to plan.** Think first and write later. Don't be impulsive. Develop a habit of planning.
> - **Be flexible.** Be open to new ideas. Consider new solutions for old problems.
> - **Be persistent.** Continue to work even when you are tired and discouraged. Good thinking is hard work.
> - **Be willing to self-correct.** Don't be defensive about errors. Figure out what went wrong and learn from your mistakes.

actually uses the many skills covered in the preceding chapters of this textbook. Continue reading to discover how "old friends" like *topic, main idea, details,* and *point of view* can connect with new terminology to become powerful vehicles of persuasion. In this chapter, we discuss a few new techniques for identifying and evaluating the support in an argument.

Critical Thinking Skills and College Goals

Many colleges cite the ability to think critically as one of the essential academic outcomes of a college education. An educated person is expected to think systematically, to evaluate, and to draw conclusions based on logic. At your college, an emphasis on critical thinking probably crosses the curriculum and thus becomes a part of every college course. When an instructor returns a paper to you with comments like "good logic" or "not enough support" written on it, the comments are referring to critical thinking. The same is true if you make a class presentation and are told either that your thesis is very convincing or that you are missing vital supporting information. See the Reader's Tip, "Four Habits of Effective Critical Thinkers."

Critical thinking instruction has its own specialized vocabulary, often using seemingly complex terms for simple ideas. As you work through this chapter, you will become familiar with the critical thinking application of the following terminology:

analogy	argument	assertion	believability	conclusion	consistency
deduction	fallacy	induction	premise	relevance	reliability

Barriers to Critical Thinking

Some people are mired in their own belief systems and do not want to rethink, change, or be challenged. They may be gullible and thus easily persuaded by a slick presentation or an illogical argument. For many people, the following barriers interfere with critical thinking:

1. **Frame of reference.** Each of us has an existing belief system that influences the way we deal with incoming information. We interpret new experiences according to what we already believe. We are culturally conditioned to resist

change and feel that our own way is best. We refuse to look at the merits of something that our belief system rejects, such as the advantages of legalizing drugs, for example.

2. **Wishful thinking.** We talk ourselves into believing things that we know are not true because we want them to be true. We irrationally deceive ourselves and engage in self-denial. For example, we might refuse to believe well-founded claims of moral corruption leveled at our favorite relative or a politician for whom we voted.

3. **Hasty moral judgments.** We tend to evaluate someone or something as good or bad, right or wrong, and remain fixed in this thinking. Such judgments are often prejudiced, intolerant, emotional, and self-righteous. An example of this type of barrier to thinking critically would be the statement, "Abortion should never be legal."

4. **Reliance on authority.** An authority such as a clergy member, a doctor, or a teacher is an expert source of information. We give authorities and institutions, such as churches or governments, the power to think for us and thus block our own abilities to question and reason.

5. **Labels.** Labels ignore individual differences and lump people and things into categories. Labels oversimplify, distort the truth, and usually incite anger and rejection. For example, to say, "People who love America and people who do not" forces others to take sides as a knee-jerk reaction. Stereotyping is a kind of labeling.

EXERCISE 10.2

Identifying Types of Barriers

Read the numbered statements below and identify each statement with *a, b, c,* or *d* for the type of barrier that the statement best represents:

a. Wishful thinking
b. Frame of reference or hasty moral judgment
c. Reliance on authority
d. Labels

EXAMPLE

The new drug will not be helpful because the Federal Drug Administration (FDA) has not yet approved it.

EXPLANATION   The answer is c, reliance on authority, which in this case is a government agency. A critical thinker might argue that the FDA is slow to test and respond to new drugs, and that many drugs are used safely and successfully in other countries before the FDA grants approval for Americans.

_____ 1. Since attendance is not taken for each class session, unlimited absences are acceptable for the course.

_____ 2. According to the director of writing assistance, students are more likely to feel comfortable with peer tutors than with college instructors.

_____ 3. City dwellers are an impatient lot; they are rude and in a hurry.

_____ 4. Offering financial assistance to people who have fallen on hard times keeps them from learning to be independent.

RECOGNIZING AN ARGUMENT

Learning Objective 2

Recognize arguments

Just as we may realize that we have barriers to critical thinking, we also need to recognize that not every statement is an argument. An **assertion** such as "I like soy milk" or "We had a huge overnight snowfall, and my car is covered" is a nonargumentative statement that is intended to inform or explain. An **argument**, on the other hand, is an assertion that supports a conclusion and is intended to persuade. The difference is intent and purpose. For example, the statement, "The grass is wet because it rained last night," is an explanation, not an argument. To say, however, "You should water the grass tonight because rain is not predicted for several days" constitutes an argument. In the latter case, the conclusion of watering the grass is based on a "fact," the forecast, and the intent is to persuade by appealing to reason. To identify arguments, use inferential skills and recognize the underlying purpose or intent of the author.

EXERCISE 10.3

Identifying Arguments

Practice recognizing arguments by identifying each of the following statements with *A* (argument) or *N* (nonargumentative statement of information).

EXAMPLE

The foods in salad bars sometimes contain preservatives to keep them looking fresh and appealing.

> **EXPLANATION**   This is not an argument. It is not intended to move you to action. It is a statement of fact similar to "It sometimes snows at night."

_____ 1. Brown eyes and brown hair are genetically dominant over blue eyes and blond hair.

_____ 2. Since summer enrollment is low, the college should initiate a parking fee to offset lost income.

_____ 3. Student employment should first be offered to those who have demonstrated the most significant financial need.

_____ 4. Americans own more radios than they do television sets.

_____ 5. College students should date people their own age.

STEPS IN ANALYZING AND EVALUATING AN ARGUMENT

Learning Objective 3

Analyze and evaluate arguments

Analyzing an argument through critical thinking and evaluation combines the use of most of the skills that have been taught in this text. The amount of analysis depends on the complexity of the argument. Some arguments are simple; others are lengthy and complicated. The following is a four-step procedure that you can use to guide your critical thinking:

1. Identify the position on the issue.
2. Identify the support in the argument.
3. Evaluate the support.
4. Evaluate the argument.

Step 1: Identify the Position on the Issue

To identify the position on an issue or the conclusion in persuasive writing, use your main-idea reading skills. First, determine the topic that is the issue by asking yourself, "What is the passage primarily about?" Then ask, "What is the author trying to convey about the issue?" If you're not sure, examine the details and determine what point they support. Your answer will be a statement of the position that is being argued—in other words, the main point, thesis, or conclusion. For example, on the topic or issue of searching school lockers for weapons, one position or main point might be that it can prevent violence and a contrasting position or main point might be that it is an invasion of privacy.

In a college course on critical thinking or logic, the parts of an argument that you would be asked to identify would probably be called the **conclusion** and the **premises**. The conclusion is the position on the issue or the main point, and the premises are the supporting points. For example, an argument now exists on the death of Alexander the Great more than 2,300 years ago. The conclusion that some epidemiologists have reached is that he died of West Nile virus rather than typhoid or malaria. One premise states that he became paralyzed before he died, and paralysis is a symptom of the brain infection that marks West Nile virus. Another premise holds that Alexander saw ravens pecking one another, and some fell dead in front of him; ravens are among the types of birds that are particularly susceptible to West Nile virus.

When reading an argument, be aware of the author's bias and your own biases. Do not allow your own beliefs to cloud your thinking. Guard against falling for the

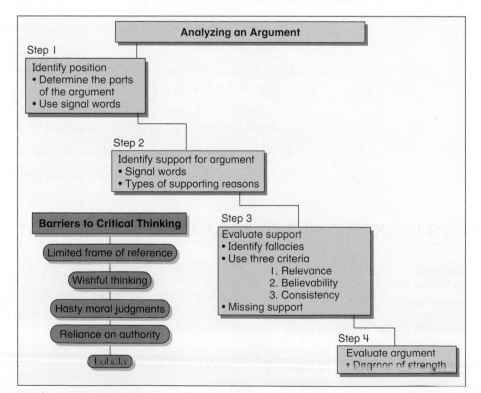

Use four sequential steps to analyze an argument. Be cautious of barriers that inhibit critical thinking.

barriers to critical thinking that include limited frame of reference, wishful thinking, hasty moral judgments, reliance on authority, and labeling. Be sensitive to emotional language and the connotation of words. Cut through the rhetoric and get to the heart of the matter.

EXAMPLE   Read the following passage and identify the position on the issue that is being argued:

> The technology for television has far exceeded the programming. Viewers are recipients of crystal clear junk. Network programming appeals to the masses for ratings and advertising money and thus offers little creative or stimulating entertainment.

EXPLANATION   Several debatable issues about television are suggested by this passage. They include the abundance of technological advancement, the power of ratings, and the importance of advertising money. The topic or issue, however, concerns the quality of network programming. Although it is not directly stated, the argument or central issue is "Network television programming offers little creative or stimulating entertainment."

Signal Words   We have said that the position on the issue may be stated as the thesis or main point. However, it does not necessarily appear at the beginning of an argument. Instead, it might be embedded within the passage or stated at the end as a conclusion. Look for the following key words that may be used to signal the central issue:

as a result	finally	in summary	therefore
consequently	for these reasons	it follows that	thus, should

EXAMPLE   What is the position on the issue that is being argued in the following passage?

> Although spending a year in a U.S. prison costs more than attending college for a year at Harvard, almost no one leaves prison rehabilitated. Prisoners meet and share information with other hardened criminals to refine their "skills." It seems reasonable, therefore, to conclude that prisons in the United States are societal failures.

EXPLANATION   The position on the issue of prison rehabilitation in this argument is directly stated in the last sentence. Note the inclusion of the signal word *therefore*.

EXERCISE 10.4

Identifying the Position on the Issue

Read the following sentence groups and indicate the number of the sentence that states the position on the issue.

1. (1)Ten is the new twenty. (2)In modern America, the stage of late childhood has all but disappeared. (3)Parents allow their under-thirteens to play video games that are rated for mature audiences and to view movies that are intended for teens or adults.

Position on issue: _____

2. [1]Online courses are often a time-saver for students who live far from campus. [2]The majority of institutions offering these classes are accredited and have experienced faculty. [3]Consider taking courses online because of the many advantages that come with this option for learning.

   Position on issue: _____

3. [1]The amount of time a doctor spends with a patient has declined over the past few decades. [2]Managed care has led to quantity over quality when it comes to patient appointments. [3]Doctors see a prescribed number of patients within an allotted time period, regardless of the medical issues involved.

   Position on issue: _____

4. [1]We are fast becoming a nation of perfectionists. [2]We trim our body fat, color our hair, and pump our muscles. [3]Our teeth are whitened, our bodies dieted and exercised, and, in some cases, "perfection" is even attempted via surgery.

   Position on issue: _____

5. [1]Some parts of the country encourage recycling by providing curbside collection of recyclables at no cost to the consumer. [2]Other places charge the same amount to collect recycled products as they do to collect general refuse. [3]If policies that entice consumers to recycle were implemented nationwide, our country's rate of recycling would certainly increase greatly.

   Position on issue: _____

Step 2: Identify the Support in the Argument

In a college logic course, after identifying the position on the issue of an argument, you would be asked to identify and number the premises, or supporting statements. For example, in an argument about searching high school lockers, a proponent's first premise or supporting statement might be that *guns and knives are always found in searches*. Other premises, such as *the school owns the lockers* and *metal detectors at the school's entrance miss harmful, illegal drugs*, would have added further supporting evidence. In short, to identify the premises, simply identify significant supporting details for the main point.

Signal Words   Supporting statements, or premises, may be directly stated or may be signaled. The key words that signal support for an argument are in some cases the same as those that signal significant supporting details. They include the following:

because	if	assuming that
since	first, second, finally	given that

EXAMPLE   What happens when the passage about U.S. prisons (see page 511) is rewritten so that signal words introduce supporting details? Read the following:

One can conclude that prisons in the United States are societal failures. First, almost no one leaves prison rehabilitated. Second, prisoners meet and share information with other hardened criminals to refine their "skills." Furthermore, taxpayers should consider that a year in prison costs more than a year at Harvard.

EXPLANATION The argument is the same with or without the signal words. In a longer passage, the signal words usually make it easier to identify the significant supporting details or premises.

EXERCISE 10.5

Identifying Support for the Argument

Read the following sentence groups. Record the number of the sentence that states the position on the issue that is being argued and the numbers of the supporting statements.

1. (1)Radar detectors on cars warn drivers of police surveillance. (2)At the beep, drivers slow down to avoid tickets. (3)Such devices should be banned because they promote driving beyond the legal speed limit.

    Position on issue: _____ Support: _____

2. (1)Major game reserves in Africa, such as the Ngorongoro Crater, are in protected areas, but many lie adjacent to large tracts of land with no conservation status. (2)Animals that migrate off the reserves compete with humans for food and are therefore endangered. (3)Thus, clear boundaries between areas for animals and people would minimize friction.

    Position on issue: _____ Support: _____

3. (1)Some state laws prohibit the sale of obscene material to minors. (2)Consequently, in those states, musicians who sell CDs with obscene lyrics should be prosecuted. (3)Such lyrics brutalize women and are audio pornography.

    Position on issue: _____ Support: _____

4. (1)Doctors should try to make a patient's visit to the office less humiliating. (2)First, you see a receptionist who tells you to fill out forms and wait your turn. (3)Next, the nurse takes your blood pressure and extracts blood while you look at the diplomas on the wall. (4)Finally, you are led into a cold room to strip down and wait still longer for the doctor to appear for a few expensive minutes of consultation.

    Position on issue: _____ Support: _____

5. (1)In most companies, college graduates get higher-paying jobs than those who do not attend college. (2)As the years go by in a company, promotions and their accompanying raises tend to go primarily to the college graduates. (3)Thus, it can be concluded that a college degree is worth money.

    Position on issue: _____ Support: _____

Reader's TIP — Types of Support for Arguments

- **Facts:** objective truths
  Ask: How were the facts gathered? Are they true?

- **Examples:** anecdotes to demonstrate the truth
  Ask: Are the examples true and relevant?

- **Analogies:** comparisons to similar cases
  Ask: Are the analogies accurate and relevant?

- **Expert opinions:** words from a recognized expert
  Ask: What are the credentials and biases of the expert?

- **Causal relationship:** saying that one thing caused another
  Ask: Is it an actual cause or merely an association?

- **Common knowledge claim:** assertion of wide acceptance
  Ask: Is it relevant? Does everyone really believe it?

- **Statistics:** numerical data
  Ask: Do the numbers accurately describe the phenomenon?

- **Personal experiences:** personal anecdotes
  Ask: Is the experience applicable to other situations?

Types of Support Readers would probably prefer support for an argument to be in the simple form of a smoking gun with fingerprints on it, but such conclusive evidence is usually hard to find. Evidence comes in many different forms and may be tainted with opinion. The Reader's Tip, "Types of Support for Arguments," contains some categories of "evidence" that typically are used as supporting reasons in an argument. Each type, however, has its pitfalls and should be immediately tested with an evaluative question.

Step 3: Evaluate the Support

As a reader, you will decide to accept or reject the author's conclusion based on the strength and acceptability of the reasons and evidence. Keep in mind that, although strong arguments are logically supported by valid reasons and evidence, weak, invalid arguments also may be supported by the crafty use of reason and evidence. Your job is to assess the validity of the support.

Teachers of logic warn students to beware of fallacies when they evaluate the support for an argument. A **fallacy** is an inference that appears to be reasonable at first glance, but closer inspection proves it to be unrelated, unreliable, or illogical. For example, to say that something is right because everybody is doing it is not a convincing reason for accepting an idea. Such "reasoning," however, can be compelling and is used so frequently that it is labeled a *bandwagon fallacy*.

Logicians have categorized, labeled, and defined more than 200 types of fallacies or tricks of persuasion. For critical thinkers, however, the emphasis should be less on memorizing a long list of types of fallacies and more on understanding how such irrelevant reasoning techniques can manipulate logical thinking. Fallacies are tools employed in constructing a weak argument that critical thinkers should spot. In a court of law, the opposing attorney would shout "Irrelevant, Your Honor!" to alert the jury to the introduction of fallacious evidence.

Evaluate the support for an argument according to three criteria: (1) **relevance**, (2) **believability**, and (3) **consistency**. The following list of fallacies that are common to each area can sensitize you to the "tools" of constructing a weak argument.

1. **Relevance fallacies: Is the support related to the conclusion?**

   - *Ad hominem.* An attack on the person rather than the issue is used in the hope that the idea will be opposed if the person is opposed.
     Example: Do not listen to Mr. Hite's views on education because he didn't even finish high school.
   - *Bandwagon.* Everybody is doing it, and you will be left out if you do not quickly join the crowd.
     Example: Everybody around the world is drinking Coke, so you should, too.
   - *Misleading analogy.* Two things are compared, suggesting that they are similar when they are, in fact, distinctly different.
     Example: College students are just like elementary school students; they need to be taught self-discipline.
   - *Straw person.* A distorted or exaggerated form of the opponent's argument is introduced and dismissed as ridiculous.
     Example: When a teenage daughter is told that she cannot go out on a weeknight before a test, she replies, "It's unreasonable to say that I can never go out on a weeknight."
   - *Testimonials.* Respected celebrities make strong, convincing claims, although they are not actually experts.
     Example: A famous actor endorses a medication to treat headaches.
   - *Transfer.* An association with a positively or negatively regarded person or thing lends the same association to the argument (also called guilt or virtue by association).
     Example: A local politician quotes President Lincoln in a speech as if to imply that Lincoln would have agreed with and voted for the candidate.

2. **Believability fallacies: Is the support believable or highly suspicious?**

   - *Incomplete facts* or *card stacking.* Factual details are omitted to misrepresent reality.
     Example: Buy stock in this restaurant chain because it is under new management and people eat out a lot.
   - *Misinterpreted statistics.* Numerical data are applied to unrelated populations that the numbers were never intended to represent.
     Example: More than 20 percent of people exercise daily and thus do not need fitness training.

Signe Wilkinson Editorial Cartoon used with the permission of Signe Wilkinson and the Cartoonist Group. All rights reserved.

- *Overgeneralizations.* Examples and anecdotes are asserted as if they apply to all cases rather than to a select few.
  Example: High school students do little work during their senior year and thus are overwhelmed at college.
- *Questionable authority.* A testimonial suggests that people who are not experts actually do have authority in a certain area.
  Example: Dr. Lee, a university sociology professor, testified that the DNA reports were 100 percent accurate.

3. **Consistency fallacies: Does the support hold together, or does it fall apart and contradict itself?**

- *Appeals to emotions.* Highly charged language is used for emotional manipulation.
  Example: Give money to our organization to help these children—starving orphans—who are in desperate need of medical attention.
- *Appeals to pity.* Pleas to support the underdog are made on behalf of a person or an issue.
  Example: Please give me an A for the course because I need it to get into law school.
- *Circular reasoning* or *begging the question.* Support for the conclusion merely restates the conclusion.
  Example: Drugs should not be legalized because it should be against the law to take illegal drugs.
- *Oversimplification.* An issue is reduced to two simple choices—either this way or that way—without consideration of other alternatives or "gray areas" in between.
  Example: The choices are very simple in supporting our foreign-policy decision to send troops. You are either for America or against it.
- *Slippery slope.* Objections to an issue are raised because unless the issue is dealt with, it will lead to greater evil and disastrous consequences.
  Example: Support for assisting the suicide of a terminally ill patient will lead to the ultimate disposal of the marginally sick and elderly.

EXERCISE 10.6

Identifying Fallacies

Identify the type of fallacy in each of the following statements by indicating *a*, *b*, or *c*:

_____ 1. Celebrities are not experts on the environment and should not speak out on environmental policy.

    a. testimonial
    b. *ad hominem*
    c. bandwagon

_____ 2. Prayer in school is like cereal for breakfast. They both get the morning off to a good start.

    a. circular reasoning
    b. appeal to emotions
    c. misleading analogy

_____ 3. The advocate for rezoning of the property concluded by saying, "George Washington was also concerned about land and freedom."

    a. transfer
    b. *ad hominem*
    c. straw person

_____ 4. The explanation for the distribution of grades is simple. College students either study or they do not study.

    a. misinterpreted statistics
    b. oversimplification
    c. appeal to pity

_____ 5. Your written statement agreeing with my position will enable me to keep my job.

    a. misinterpreted statistics
    b. appeal to pity
    c. card stacking

_____ 6. Everyone in the neighborhood has worked on the new park design and agreed to it. Now we need your signature of support.

    a. bandwagon
    b. appeal to emotions
    c. begging the question

_____ 7. Democrats go to Washington to spend money with no regard for the hardworking taxpayer.

    a. circular reasoning
    b. bandwagon
    c. overgeneralization

———— 8. The suicide rate is highest over the Christmas holidays, which means that Thanksgiving is a safe and happy holiday.

    a. misinterpreted statistics
    b. card stacking
    c. questionable authority

———— 9. The workers' fingers were swollen and infected, insects walked on their exposed skin, and their red eyes begged for mercy and relief. We all must join their effort.

    a. oversimplification
    b. appeal to emotions
    c. overgeneralization

———— 10. Our minister, Dr. Johnson, assured the family that our cousin's cancer was a slow-growing one so that a brief delay in treatment would not be detrimental.

    a. transfer
    b. straw person
    c. questionable authority

Determine Missing Support   Arguments are written to persuade and thus include the proponent's version of the convincing reasons. Therefore, writers might leave out or gloss over evidence that would contradict their points. In analyzing an argument, remember to ask yourself, "What is left out?" Be an advocate for the opposing point of view and guess at the evidence that would be presented. Decide if evidence was consciously omitted because of its adverse effect on the conclusion. For example, a businessperson arguing for an increased monthly service fee might neglect to mention how much of the cost reflects administrative raises and profit.

Step 4: Evaluate the Argument

Important decisions are rarely made quickly or easily. A period of incubation is often needed for deliberating among alternatives. Allow yourself time to go over arguments, weighing the support and looking at the issues from different perspectives. Good critical thinkers are persistent in seeking solutions.

One researcher, Diane Halpern, expresses the difficulty of decision making by saying, "There is never just one war fought. Each side has its own version, and rarely do they agree."[1] As a reader, you are obligated to consider all factors carefully in seeking the truth. Halpern uses a picture of a table that represents the position on an issue and compares the legs of the table to four different degrees of support. Use them to evaluate the strength of an argument.

---

[1]Diane Halpern, *Thought and Knowledge*, 2nd ed. (Hillsdale, NJ: Lawrence Erlbaum, 1989), p. 191.

The Strength of an Argument

Strong Argument

- Strong, related reasons provide support.
- Many weak reasons can provide support.
- A few weak reasons do not adequately support.
- Unrelated reasons give no support.

Weak Argument

Remember, in critical thinking, there is no "I'm right, and you're wrong." There are, however, strong and weak arguments. For instance, you might agree with the author's conclusion but find the support insufficient to make a strong argument. On the other hand, you might disagree with the author's position but acknowledge that he or she has constructed a strong argument. Strong, relevant, believable, and consistent reasons build a good argument.

EXERCISE 10.7

Evaluating Your Own Decision Making

Now that you are familiar with the critical thinking process, analyze your own thinking in making the important recent decision of where to attend college. No college is perfect; many factors must be considered. The issue or conclusion is that you have decided to attend the college where you are now enrolled. List relevant reasons and/or evidence that support your decision. Evaluate the strength of your reasoning. Are any of your reasons based on fallacies?

Position: My decision to attend this college was based on the following:

1. _____

_____

2. _____

_____

3. _____

_____

4. _____

_____

5. _____

_____

How would you evaluate your own critical thinking in making a choice among colleges? Perhaps you relied heavily on information from others. Were those sources credible?

INDUCTIVE AND DEDUCTIVE REASONING

Learning Objective 4

Define inductive and deductive reasoning

In choosing a college, did you follow an inductive or deductive reasoning process? Did you collect extensive information on several colleges and then weigh the advantages and disadvantages of each? Those who follow an **inductive reasoning** process start by gathering data, and then, after considering all available material, they formulate a conclusion. Textbooks based on this plan give details first and then lead you into the main idea or conclusion. They strive to put the parts into a logical whole and thus reason "up" from particular details to a broad generalization. This is sometimes called "bottom-up" reasoning.

Deductive reasoning, on the other hand, follows the opposite pattern. With this type of reasoning, you start with the conclusion derived from a previous experience and apply it to a new situation. Perhaps your college choice is a family tradition; your parents are alumni, and you have always expected to attend that school. Perhaps you are attending the college closest to where you live. Although your thinking may have begun with the conclusion, you probably have since discovered many reasons why the college is right for you. When writers use a deductive type of reasoning, they first give a general statement and then enumerate the reasons. This is also known as "top-down" thinking.

Despite the formal distinction between inductive and deductive reasoning, in real life we switch back and forth between them as we think. Our everyday observations lead to conclusions that we then reuse and modify to form new conclusions.

Inductive Reasoning	**Deductive Reasoning**
(2) Conclusion	(1) CONCLUSION
⬆	⬇
(1) DATA, REASONS, EVIDENCE	(2) Data, Reasons, Evidence

APPLYING THE FOUR STEPS OF CRITICAL THINKING

Learning Objective 5

Practice thinking critically

The following is an example of how the four-step process of critical thinking can be used to evaluate an argument. Read the argument, analyze it according to the directions for each step, and then read the explanation of how the critical thinking process was applied. Remember that critical thinking takes time, concentrated effort, and persistence.

THE ARGUMENT: EXTRATERRESTRIAL LIFE

(1)Surely life exists elsewhere in the universe. (2)After all, most space scientists today admit the possibility that life has evolved on other planets. (3)Besides, other planets in and out of our solar system are strikingly like Earth. (4)They revolve around their sun, they borrow light from the sun, and several are known to revolve on their axes, and to be subject to the same laws of gravitation as Earth. (5)What's more, aren't those who make light of extraterrestrial life soft-headed fundamentalists clinging to the foolish notion that life is unique to their planet?

—Joel Rudinow and Vincent Barry,
Invitation to Critical Thinking, 3rd ed.

- **Step 1.** *Identify the position on the issue.* What is the topic of this argument, and what is the main point that the writer is trying to convey? Although many ideas may be included, what is the central idea being discussed and supported? Record the number of the sentence that states the position on the issue.

  _____

- **Step 2.** *Identify the support in the argument.* What are the significant details that support the position that is being argued? Record the numbers of the sentences that are supporting statements.

  _____

- **Step 3.** *Evaluate the support.* Examine each supporting assertion separately for relevance, believability, and consistency. Can you identify any as fallacies that are intended to sell a weak argument? List each sentence that expresses a fallacy and identify the type of fallacy. Then identify the type of supporting information that you feel is missing.

  Evaluation: _____

  _____

  _____

  Missing support: _____

  _____

  _____

- **Step 4.** *Evaluate the argument.* What is your overall evaluation of the argument? Is the argument convincing? Does the argument provide good reasons and/or evidence for believing the thesis?

Explanation of the Four Steps

- **Step 1.** *Identify the position on the issue.* The position, assertion, thesis, main point, or conclusion is directly stated in the first sentence. Good critical thinkers would note, however, that "life" is not clearly defined as plant, animal, or human.
- **Step 2.** *Identify the support in the argument.* This argument contains three main premises, or significant supporting details, in the following sentences:
    Sentence 2: Space scientists admit the possibility that life has evolved on other planets.
    Sentence 3: Other planets in and outside our solar system are strikingly like Earth.
    Sentence 5: Those who make light of extraterrestrial life are soft-headed fundamentalists clinging to the foolish notion that life is unique to this planet.

- **Step 3.** *Evaluate the support.* The first supporting detail, Sentence 2: This is a vague appeal to authority that does not reveal who "most space scientists" are. Do the scientists work for NASA? Sentence 3: This is also vague and is presented as a misleading comparison. Other planets may be round, but they have different temperatures and different atmospheres. Sentence 5: This is an oversimplified, personal attack on those who may not agree with the argument. Missing support: Scientific support for this argument seems to be missing. The support is weak in all three areas: relevance, believability, and consistency.

- **Step 4.** *Evaluate the argument.* This is a weak argument. There may be good reasons to believe that life exists on other planets, but this argument fails to provide them. The possibility of extraterrestrial life might be argued through statistics from astronomy and a specific definition of "life."

EXERCISE 10.8

Applying the Four Steps to Different Arguments

Read the following five arguments and apply the four-step process of critical thinking for evaluating each argument. Using the sentence numbers, identify the position on the issue and the supporting details. Then evaluate the argument.

Argument 1

CHILD CRIMINAL OFFENDERS

(1)Centuries ago, when there was little or no distinction between children and adults in daily life, children who committed crimes were treated exactly as adult offenders were treated. (2)More recently, they have been treated quite differently; they are given special consideration for first offenses, receive lighter sentences for second and subsequent offenses, and are placed in special reform schools and rehabilitation centers rather than in prisons. (3)But many people have begun to question the wisdom of that special consideration. (4)They reason that the crime in question, and not the criminal's age, should dictate the punishment. (5)Children who kill are either guilty of murder or not guilty.

—Adapted from Vincent Ryan Ruggiero,
The Art of Thinking, 7th ed. pp. 18, 237, 229. Published by
Longman. © 2004 by Pearson Education, Inc., Glenview, IL.

- **Step 1.** Identify the position on the issue. _____

- **Step 2.** Identify the supporting statements in the argument. _____

- **Step 3.** Evaluate the supporting statements. Examine each supporting statement for relevance, believability, and consistency. List each sentence that expresses a fallacy and identify the type of fallacy. Then identify the type of supporting information that you feel is missing.

Evaluation: _____

_____

_____

Missing support: _____ _____

_____

- **Step 4.** Evaluate the argument. What is your overall evaluation and why?

_____

_____

Argument 2

INVASION OF PRIVACY

(1)When you call 911 in an emergency, some police departments have a way of telling your telephone number and address without your saying a word. (2)The chief value of this, say the police, is that if the caller is unable to communicate for any reason, the dispatcher knows where to send help. (3)But don't be duped by such paternalistic explanations. (4)This technology is a despicable invasion of privacy, for callers may be unaware of the insidious device. (5)Even if they are, some persons who wish anonymity may be reluctant to call for emergency help. (6)Remember that the names of complainants and witnesses are recorded in many communities' criminal justice systems. (7)A fairer and more effective system seemingly would include an auxiliary number for 911 callers who wish anonymity.

—Joel Rudinow and Vincent E. Barry,
Invitation to Critical Thinking, 3rd ed.

- **Step 1.** Identify the position on the issue. _____
- **Step 2.** Identify the supporting statements in the argument. _____
- **Step 3.** Evaluate the supporting statements. Examine each supporting statement for relevance, believability, and consistency. List each sentence that expresses a fallacy and identify the type of fallacy. Then identify the type of supporting information that you feel is missing.

Evaluation: _____

_____

_____

_____

Missing support: _____

_____

_____

- **Step 4.** Evaluate the argument. What is your overall evaluation and why?

_____

_____

_____

Argument 3

BAN BOXING

[1]As a practicing physician, I am convinced that boxing should be banned. [2]First, boxing is a very visible example that violence is accepted behavior in our society—outside the ring as well as inside. [3]This sends the wrong message to America's youth. [4]Second, boxing is the only sport where the sole object is to injure the opponent. [5]Boxing, then, is morally offensive because its intent is to inflict brain injuries on another person. [6]Third, medical science can't take someone who has suffered repeated blows to the head and restore that person to normal function. [7]This causes many physicians to conclude that our society should ban boxing. [8]Boxing is morally and medically offensive. [9]So as a physician, I believe boxing should be banned.

—From Robert E. McAfee,
"Regulation Won't Work: Ban Boxing," as appeared in *USA Today*.
December 20, 1990. Reprinted by permission of the author.

- **Step 1.** Identify the position on the issue. _____

- **Step 2.** Identify the supporting statements in the argument. _____

- **Step 3.** Evaluate the supporting statements. Examine each supporting statement for relevance, believability, and consistency. List each sentence that expresses a fallacy and identify the type of fallacy. Then identify the type of supporting information that you feel is missing.

  Evaluation: _____
  _____
  _____

  Missing support: _____
  _____
  _____

- **Step 4.** Evaluate the argument. What is your overall evaluation and why?
  _____
  _____
  _____

Argument 4

DETECT ONLINE ROMANCE

[1]The following story is proof that surveillance software should be considered ethically correct. [2]The software is cheap. [3]Its legality has not been questioned. [4]It is available from a host of companies. [5]Computer spying woke me up to reality, as the story explains.

[6]"I'm not doing anything wrong, believe me," she'd said for weeks. But he didn't buy it. He'd read her e-mail, listened in on her phone conversations. He watched the

chats, too. Fifty bucks bought him software to slip into the family computer and secretly record his wife's every move.

So it's 5 A.M., she's sleeping upstairs, he ventures onto the computer. He starts up the software and finds a series of black-and-white snapshots taken of the screen while she was online. She calls herself "rita_neb" and her every come-on, every flirtation, every misspelling, is saved. The correspondent is some guy in Nebraska, and the talk is not just flirting but, you know, graphic—and Greg Young begins to cry. His 22-year marriage is over.

—Bill Hancock, "Spying at Home:
A New Pastime to Detect Online Romance,"
Computers and Security, October 1, 2000

- **Step 1.** Identify the position on the issue. _____

- **Step 2.** Identify the supporting statements in the argument. _____

- **Step 3.** Evaluate the supporting statements. Examine each supporting statement for relevance, believability, and consistency. List each sentence that expresses a fallacy and identify the type of fallacy. Then identify the type of supporting information that you feel is missing.

Evaluation: _____

_____

_____

Missing support: _____

_____

_____

- **Step 4.** Evaluate the argument. What is your overall evaluation and why?

_____

_____

_____

_____

Argument 5

FILM VIOLENCE

(1)I walked out of the movie after a half hour. (2)It was either leave or throw up. (3)In an early scene, a wolf attacks two young men, killing one and badly slashing the other. (4)No gory detail is left to the imagination. (5)Yet, somehow, many people around me in the theater found the visual assault enjoyable as they laughed and laughed.

(6)Chicago film critic Roger Ebert reported that in viewing another film on two separate occasions, he observed both audiences laughing in scenes showing a woman beaten, raped, and cut up. (7)One respectable-looking man next to him kept murmuring, (8) "That'll teach her." (9)Ebert found that reaction frightening. Like any powerful experience, film viewing has the capacity to brutalize us. (10)No one should be permitted to poison the air the rest of us breathe. [11]Neither should a filmmaker have the right to poison the social climate.

—Adapted from Vincent Ryan Ruggiero,
The Art of Thinking, 7th ed.

- **Step 1.** Identify the position on the issue. _____

- **Step 2.** Identify the supporting statements in the argument. _____

- **Step 3.** Evaluate the supporting statements. Examine each supporting statement for relevance, believability, and consistency. List each sentence that expresses a fallacy and identify the type of fallacy. Then identify the type of supporting information that you feel is missing.

Evaluation: _____
_____
_____
_____
_____

Missing support: _____
_____

- **Step 4.** Evaluate the argument. What is your overall evaluation and why?
_____
_____
_____

CREATIVE AND CRITICAL THINKING

Learning Objective 6

Define creative thinking

A chapter on critical thinking would not be complete without an appeal for creative thinking. You might wonder, "Are critical thinking and creative thinking different?" **Creative thinking** refers to the ability to generate many possible solutions to a problem, whereas critical thinking refers to the examination of those solutions for the selection of the best of all possibilities. Both ways of thinking are essential for good problem solving.

Diane Halpern uses the following story to illustrate creative thinking:

Many years ago when a person who owed money could be thrown into jail, a merchant in London had the misfortune to owe a huge sum to a money-lender. The money-lender, who was old and ugly, fancied the merchant's beautiful teenage daughter. He proposed a bargain. He said he would cancel the merchant's debt if he could have the girl instead.

Both the merchant and his daughter were horrified at the proposal. So the cunning money-lender proposed that they let Providence decide the matter. He told them that he would put a black pebble and a white pebble into an empty money-bag and then the girl would have to pick out one of the pebbles. If she chose the black pebble, she would become his wife and her father's debt would be canceled. If she chose the white pebble, she would stay with her father and the debt would still be canceled. But if she refused to pick out a pebble, her father would be thrown into jail and she would starve.

Reluctantly the merchant agreed. They were standing on a pebble-strewn path in the merchant's garden as they talked, and the money-lender stooped down to pick up two pebbles. As he picked up the pebbles the girl, sharp-eyed with fright, noticed that he picked up two black pebbles and put them into the money-bag. He then asked the girl to pick out the pebble that was to decide her fate and that of her father.

—Diane Halpern,
Thought and Knowledge, 2nd ed.

If you were the girl, what would you do? Think creatively, and, without evaluating your thoughts, list at least five possible solutions. Next, think critically to evaluate your list and then circle your final choice.

1. _____

2. _____

3. _____

4. _____

5. _____

In discussing the possible solutions to the problem, Halpern talks about two kinds of creative thinking: vertical thinking and lateral thinking. **Vertical thinking** is a straightforward and logical way of thinking that would typically result in a solution like, "Call his hand and expose the money-lender as a crook." The disadvantage of this solution is that the merchant is still in debt, so the original problem has not been solved. **Lateral thinking**, on the other hand, is a way of thinking *around* a problem or even redefining the problem. A lateral thinker might redefine the problem from "What happens when I get the black pebble?"[2] to "How can I avoid the black pebble?" Using this new definition of the problem and other seemingly irrelevant information, a lateral thinker could come up with a winning solution. When the girl reaches into the bag, she could fumble and drop the stone that she selects on the "pebble-strewn path." The color of the pebble that she dropped could then be determined by looking at the one left in the bag. Since the remaining pebble is black, the dropped one that is now mingled in the path must have been white. Any other admission would expose the money-lender as a crook. Probably, the heroine thought of many alternatives, but thanks to her ability to generate a novel solution and evaluate its effectiveness, the daughter and the merchant lived happily free of debt.

Creative and critical thinking enable us to see new possibilities and approaches to solving problems. For example, after many years of researching a cure for

---

[2]Edward DeBono, *New Think: The Use of Lateral Thinking in the Generation of New Ideas* (New York: Basic Books, 1968), p. 195.

> **BRAIN BOOSTER**
>
> **The Creative Brain**
>
> Studies in neuroscience demonstrate that creativity involves both conscious and unconscious brain activity. Many groundbreaking inventions have started with dreams or *seemingly* "out-of-nowhere" ideas. The key word here is *seemingly* because creative insights begin with conscious attention to a problem and a desire to solve it. When the background work of identifying a problem and gathering information has been done, our brains can work behind the scenes, unconsciously, to uncover a solution.
>
> To pave the way for creative insights, first identify a problem and collect as much information about it as possible from many sources. Try to look at the problem from many points of view. Then—this step is key—let the whole thing incubate. Do something else that takes your mind completely to another focus. When you're least expecting it, your unconscious mind just might give birth to a surprise, maybe in a dream, in the hazy period before becoming fully awake, in the shower, while exercising, or driving to school or work. As soon as possible, write it down. Examine the idea, refine it, and test it. You might have a great way to approach your term paper or even a new invention.
>
> —*Adapted from* 12 Brain/Mind Learning Principles in Action: Developing Executive Functions of the Human Brain, *2nd ed.*
> *Renate Caine, et al.*

smallpox, Dr. Edward Jenner stopped focusing on patients who were sick with the disease and instead began studying groups of people who never seemed to get smallpox. Shortly thereafter, using this different perspective, Dr. Jenner discovered the clues that led him to the smallpox vaccine.

SUMMARY POINTS

1 What are the definitions of analytical thinking and critical thinking? (page 504)

- Analytical thinking involves separating and examining parts to identify reasons, causes, and support. It is used to solve problems and is part of the critical thinking process. Good analytical thinkers are strategic, systematic, and persistent.
- Critical thinking is thinking in a purposeful, organized manner to assess the value of old and new information. Critical thinking involves defining problems to be solved, comparing, analyzing, evaluating, and concluding, often regarding controversial issues.
- *Should* often begins a critical thinking question; *how can* usually begins the next step, problem solving.
- Common barriers to critical thinking include wishful thinking, hasty moral judgments, reliance on authority, and labels.

2 How can I recognize an argument? (page 509)

- An argument contains a conclusion that is intended to persuade the reader or listener.
- An assertion, on the other hand, is a nondebatable statement that is intended to inform or explain.

3 **What are the steps to analyzing and evaluating an argument? (page 509)**
   - Identify the issue (called the *conclusion*), the author's position on the topic, using main idea skills. Look for common signal words that indicate the conclusion.
   - Identify the supporting evidence. These details are called *premises*. Use common signal words to help locate them. Typical supporting evidence includes facts, examples, analogies, expert opinions, causal relationships, common knowledge claims, statistics, and personal experiences.
   - Evaluate the supporting evidence by questioning the evidence provided. Ask, "Is it relevant to the conclusion?" "Is it believable?" and "Does it consistently support the same conclusion?" Be alert to common logical fallacies and consider what evidence is missing that might contradict the conclusion or further support it.
   - Evaluate the entire argument. Consider the strength of the argument on the basis of the evidence provided. Unrelated reasons make a very weak argument. A few weak reasons also provide inadequate support. Many weak reasons can constitute a relatively strong argument. Strong, related reasons create a very strong, solid argument. Remember that you are evaluating the strength of the argument, not whether you agree with the conclusion.

4 **What are inductive and deductive reasoning? (page 520)**
   - Inductive reasoning begins by examining the details, the evidence, and from them arriving at a logical conclusion.
   - Deductive reasoning begins with a given conclusion and then provides evidence to support it.

5 **How should I practice critical thinking? (page 520)**
   - Critical thinking requires time, systematic concentrated effort, rereading, and reexamination of the argument presented.
   - Avoid the barriers to critical thinking.
   - Follow the four steps.
   - Be persistent even when the thinking is difficult!

6 **What is the definition of creative thinking? (page 526)**
   - Creative thinking is the generation of many possible solutions to a problem.
   - It is sometimes called *lateral thinking* as opposed to *vertical thinking,* which relies on logic.

Themed Readings

The readings in this section explore the intricately woven connections among technology and the criminal and ethical issues that its capabilities raise. The purpose is twofold. The first intent is to explore a subject with which most, if not all of us, have direct or indirect experience. Two readings from criminal justice textbooks examine the ways in which criminals exploit computer technology to break the law and the ways in which police use computer technology to thwart the criminals. The third reading, an essay written by a professional online writer, focuses on the anonymity of the Internet and the harm that can be done when ethical boundaries are breached. These different perspectives create both a basis and a catalyst for thinking about the issues surrounding technology, crime, and ethics.

The second purpose of this themed collection is for you to practice analytical and critical reading with only gentle guidance. There are no multiple choice or true–false questions. Instead, you will be asked to demonstrate your thinking about what you have read, much like the expectations in your college classes. By approximating the real reading tasks that you will encounter throughout college, you will be better prepared to manage your college reading with confidence and skill.

College reading requires both analytical and critical thinking skills. As you read the following selections, use those skills. Put the reading techniques that you have practiced throughout this book—deciphering unfamiliar vocabulary, using the three stages of reading, organizing material for study, identifying main ideas and supporting details, recognizing patterns of organization, making reasonable inferences, and being alert to the author's point of view—to work as you read. Make connections among the selections, consider your prior knowledge, and examine your own opinions. If you read to understand and to question, you will be ready to analyze and evaluate the material.

Technology, Crime, and Ethics

Perhaps you remember a movie that features a character who uses explosives to break into bank vaults. Or maybe you are familiar with a television show that dramatizes the forensic work of detectives and scientists who probe DNA to identify a murderer. Have you read or heard accounts of a stalker who uses a telephone to frighten or embarrass a victim? In all these scenarios, we see the threads of technology, crime, and ethics. The technology of the twenty-first century raises the stakes when it comes to what a criminal, a law enforcement official, or a hateful person can do with technology.

Where does the line between criminal behavior and ethical misconduct lie? How and when should society intervene? Read the following true stories to set the stage for your thinking about these questions.

A decade or so ago, if a college student used a camera to spy on his gay roommate and passed the pictures around, hardly anyone would have made a fuss—least of all the criminal justice system. It might have been passed off as a youthful prank. The perpetrator would probably not have been arrested and prosecuted, much less convicted and sentenced to jail. But in 2010, just such a case set off a firestorm focusing national attention on cyber-bullying faced by gay and lesbian teens.

Tyler Clementi was an eighteen-year old student at Rutgers University in Piscataway, New Jersey, who jumped to his death from the George Washington Bridge on September 22, 2010. Without Clementi's knowledge, on September 19 his roommate, Dharun Ravi, and a fellow student, Molly Wei, used a webcam on Ravi's computer and a computer in Wei's dorm room to view Clementi kissing another man. On September 21, the day prior to the suicide, Ravi notified friends and followers on Twitter to watch via his webcam a second encounter between Clementi and his friend.

Ravi and Wei were indicted for their roles in the webcam incidents, though they were not charged with involvement in the suicide itself. Wei accepted a plea agreement on May 6, 2011, allowing her to avoid prosecution. On March 16, 2012, Ravi was found guilty of 15 counts involving crimes of invasion of privacy, attempted invasion of privacy, bias intimidation, tampering with evidence, and witness tampering. He was given a sentence including a 30-day jail term.

***

The death of Tyler Clementi followed another computer-related "cyber-bullying" case involving Megan Meier. Meier was a thirteen-year-old from Dardenne Prairie, Missouri. Soon after opening an account on MySpace, Meier received a message from Lori Drew, who had assumed a false identity of a 16-year-old boy, Josh Evans. Meier and Josh became online friends but never met in person or spoke. Meier thought he was attractive and began to exchange messages with the fabricated Josh Evans. She was described by family as having had her "spirits lifted."

On October 15, 2006, the tone of the messages changed, with Drew saying (via the account), "I don't know if I want to be friends with you anymore because I've heard that you are not very nice to your friends." Similar messages were sent; some of Megan's messages were shared with others; and bulletins were posted about her. After telling her mother, Tina Meier, about the increasing number of hurtful messages, the two got into an argument over the vulgar language Meier used in response to the messages and the fact that she did not log off when her mother told her to.

After the argument, Meier ran upstairs to her room. According to Meier's father, Ronald Meier, and a neighbor who had discussed the hoax with Drew, the last message sent by the Evans account read: "Everybody in O'Fallon knows how you are. You are a bad person and everybody hates you. Have a shitty rest of your life. The world would be a better place without you." Meier responded with a message reading: "You're the kind of boy a girl would kill herself over." The last few correspondences were made via AOL Messenger instead of MySpace. She was found 20 minutes later, hanging by the neck in a closet. Despite attempts to revive her, she was pronounced dead the next day.

Both the Tyler Clementi and Megan Meier cases are sobering reminders that modern-day computer crime is not limited to criminals with a profit motive. Rather, they are evidence that cyber criminals out for revenge or other motives are keenly aware of potential victims who are young and impressionable. Worse yet, such criminals are often able to hide behind false identities while prowling the Internet and avoiding detection by the police.

With the personal computer now in many households and mainframe computers acting as the epicenter of almost all Fortune 500 companies, the problem of computer crime, or cybercrime, is now a mainstream social problem.

—From Michael D. Lyman, *Criminal Investigation,* 7th ed.

Criminal Justice

MyReadingLab

Visit Chapter 10: Critical Thinking in MyReadingLab to complete the Selection 1 activities and the Build Background Knowledge video activity.

PREVIEW the next selection to predict its purpose and organization and to formulate your learning plan.

Activate Schemata

Have you or someone you know been a victim of identity theft?
Have you used a credit card or debit card at a store whose database of card information has been stolen by hackers?
What do you know about pirated music or videos?

Establish a Purpose for Reading

Think of the various ways in which you or others have been harmed by people who have misused computer technology.

Build Background Knowledge — VIDEO

How To Protect Yourself Against Cybercrime

To prepare for reading Selection 1, answer the questions below. Then, watch this video that offers strategies to protect yourself against cybercrime.

How has technology helped to increase criminal activity?

How have you (or someone you know) been affected by cybercrime?

How do you protect yourself from cybercrime?

This video helped me: _____

_____

_____

Integrate Knowledge While Reading

Questions have been inserted in the margin to stimulate your thinking while reading. Remember to

Predict   Picture   Relate   Monitor   Correct   Annotate

High Technology and Criminal Opportunity

cybercrime: Any crime that involves the use of computers or the manipulation of digital data as well as any violation of a federal or state cybercrime statute.

On January 20, 2012, New Zealand police broke into the megamansion of ex-German
5 national Kim Dotcom. Dotcom, 38, whose given name is Kim Schmitz, is founder of the Internet piracy Web site Megaupload.com—a site that U.S. officials estimate cost legal copyright holders in this country at least $500 million in lost revenues. Megaupload, which is registered in Hong Kong, was reported to have 150 million registered users and 50 million daily visitors. The site, which accounted for 4% of all
10 daily traffic on the Web, illegally made music, videos, PDFs, and other copyrighted files available to anyone willing to pay a small fee. Those fees, however, along with money spent on advertisements posted to the site, added up, and authorities estimate that Dotcom earned hundreds of millions of dollars from his illegal operations, including $42 million in 2010 alone.

15   When police arrived at his $30 million mansion, one of the largest private homes
in New Zealand, the 6-foot, 7-inch 300-pound Dotcom locked them out using high-tech electronic security devices and fled to a safe room stocked with weapons. More than 100 officers, many with special equipment, were needed to extract him and to place him under arrest.

Is Dotcom's size relevant?

THE ADVANCE OF TECHNOLOGY

20 Technology and crime have always been closely linked. The con artist who uses a
telephone in a financial scam, the robber who uses a firearm and drives a getaway car, even the murderer who wields a knife—all employ at least rudimentary forms of technology in the crimes they commit. Technology can be employed by both crime fighters and lawbreakers. Early forms of technology, including the telegraph,
25 telephone, and automobile, were embraced by agents of law enforcement as soon as they became available. Evidence derived from fingerprint and ballistics analysis is routinely employed by prosecutors; and emerging technologies promise to keep criminologists and law enforcement agents in step with high-tech offenders.

What forms of today's technology will be this commonplace in the future?

As technology advances, it facilitates new forms of behavior, so we can be certain
30 that tomorrow's crimes will differ from those of today. Personal crimes of violence and traditional property crimes will continue to occur, but advancing technology will create new and as-yet-unimaginable opportunities for criminals and other international actors positioned to take advantage of it and of the power it will afford.

A frightening preview of such possibilities was seen during the collapse of the
35 Soviet Union when the resulting social disorganization made the acquisition of fissionable materials, stolen from Soviet stockpiles, simple for even relatively small outlaw organizations. In what is a nightmare for authorities throughout the world, Middle Eastern terrorist groups are making forceful efforts to acquire former Soviet nuclear weapons and the raw materials necessary to manufacture their own bombs,
40 and some evidence suggests that nuclear weapons parts may have already been sold to wealthy international drug cartels and organized criminal groups, who could hoard them to use as bargaining chips against possible government prosecution.

More recently, in 2012 and 2013, the Obama administration identified the Chinese military as the source of cyber intrusions into public and private Web sites throughout the United States, and the 2013 Verizon Data Breach Investigations Report found that "state-affiliated actors tied to China are the biggest movers in 2012. Their efforts to steal IP" addresses, the report said, "comprise about one-fifth of all breaches" covered by the report. About the same time, U.S. defense officials announced that hackers linked to China's government broke into an American computer system used to send commands to nuclear weapons. In response, the Obama administration began efforts in 2013 to combat the persistent Chinese cyberespionage campaign.

CYBERCRIME

What is cybercrime? →

The twenty-first century has been termed the postindustrial information age. Information is vital to the success of any endeavor, and certain forms of information hold nearly incalculable value for those who possess it. Patents on new products, pharmaceutical formulations, corporate strategies, and the financial resources of corporations all represent competitive and corporate trade secrets. Government databases, if infiltrated, can offer terrorists easy paths to destruction and mayhem.

Some criminal perpetrators intend simply to destroy or alter data without otherwise accessing or copying the information. Disgruntled employees, mischievous computer **hackers**, business competitors, and others may have varied degrees of interest in destroying the records or computer capabilities of others.

High-tech criminals seeking illegitimate access to computerized information take a number of routes. One is the path of direct access, wherein office workers or corporate spies, planted as seemingly innocuous employees, use otherwise legitimate work-related entry to a company's computer resources to acquire wanted information.

Another path of illegal access, called computer trespass, involves remote access to targeted machines. Anyone equipped with a computer and Internet access has potential access to numerous computer systems. Many such systems have few, if any, security procedures in place. Similarly, electromagnetic field (EMF) decoders can scan radio frequency emanations generated by all types of computers. Keystroke activity, internal chip-processed computations, and disk reads, for example, can be detected and interpreted at a distance by such sophisticated devices. Computers secured against such passively invasive practices are rarely found in the commercial marketplace, although the military had adopted them for many applications. Within the last decade, wireless networking has heightened fears of data theft, and cell phones, handheld devices, and other forms of radio communication offer opportunities for data interception.

The realities of today's digital world have led to a relatively new form of crime, called cybercrime, and to new laws intended to combat it. Simply put, cybercrime, or computer crime, is any violation of a federal or state computer-crime statute. Many argue that only those crimes that use computer technology as central to their commission may properly be called "cybercrimes." However, a number of other kinds of offenses can also be described as cybercrimes.

A Federal Bureau of Investigation (FBI) typology distinguishes between five types of cybercrime:

1. internal cybercrimes, such as viruses
2. Internet and telecommunications crimes, including illegal hacking

90   3. support of criminal enterprises, such as databases supporting drug distribution
4. computer-manipulation crimes, such as embezzlement
5. hardware, software, and information theft.

Table 1 lists these five categories, with additional examples of each.

TABLE 1   CATEGORIES OF CYBERCRIME

Internal Cybercrimes (Malware)
Trojan horses
Logic bombs
Trap doors
Viruses
Internet and Telecommunications Crimes
Phone phreaking
Hacking
Denial of service attacks
Illegal websites
Dissemination of illegal material (for example, child pornography)
Misuse of telecommunications systems
Theft of telecommunications services
Illegal eavesdropping
Illegal Internet-based gambling
Support of Criminal Enterprises
Databases to support drug distribution
Databases to support loan-sharking
Databases to support illegal gambling
Databases to keep records of illegal client transactions
Electronic money laundering
Communications of furtherance of criminal conspiracies
Computer-Manipulation Crimes
Embezzlement
Electronic fund transfer fraud
Other fraud/phishing
Extortion threats/electronic terrorism
Hardware, Software, and Information Theft
Software piracy (warez)
Thefts of computers
Thefts of microprocessor chips
Thefts of trade secrets and proprietary information
Identity theft

95 When discussing cybercrime, it is important to realize that a huge number of today's financial transactions are computerized. Although most people probably think of money as bills and coins, money today is really just information—information stored in a computer network, possibly located within the physical confines of a bank, but more likely existing as bits and bytes of data on service providers' ma-
100 chines. Typical financial customers give little thought to the fact that very little "real" money is held by their bank, brokerage house, mutual fund, or commodities dealer. Nor do they often consider the threats to their financial well-being by activities such as electronic theft or the sabotage of existing accounts. Unfortunately, however, the threat is very real. Computer criminals equipped with enough information
105 (or able to find the data they need) can quickly and easily locate, steal, and send vast amounts of money anywhere in the world.

No reliable estimates exist as to the losses suffered in such transactions due to the activities of technologically adept criminal perpetrators. Accurate estimates are lacking largely because sophisticated high-tech thieves are so effective at eluding
110 apprehension.

THE EXTENT OF CYBERCRIME

What are the costs of cybercrime? → A recent estimate by the U.S. Secret Service in conjunction with the CERT Cyber-security Center puts the annual cost of cybercrime in the United States at around $666 million. The 2011 CSO (Chief Security Officer) Cyber Security Watch Survey, a cooperative effort between the U.S. Secret Service, Deloitte & Touche, Carnegie
115 Mellon's Software Engineering Institute (CERT), and CSO magazine, found that a sophisticated cybercrime-fueled underground economy exists in America and that its members continue to develop a sophisticated arsenal of damaging software tools with which most companies cannot keep pace while remaining focused on their core businesses. At about the same time, a white paper entitled Cyber Crime: A Clear and

Lisa S./Shutterstock

120 Present Danger was released by Deloitte & Touche's Center for Security & Privacy Solutions. The paper pointed out the following facts:

- Cybercrime is now serious, widespread, aggressive, growing, and increasingly sophisticated, and it poses major implications for national and economic security.
125
- Many industries and institutions and public- and private-sector organizations (particularly those within the critical infrastructure) are at significant risk.
- Relatively few organizations have recognized organized cybercriminal networks (instead of hackers) as their greatest potential cybersecurity threat;
130 even fewer are prepared to address this threat.
- Cyberattacks and security breaches are increasing in frequency and sophistication, with discovery usually occurring only after the fact, if at all.
- Current perimeter-intrusion detection, signature-based malware, and antivirus solutions are providing little defense and are rapidly becoming
135 obsolete.
- Effective deterrents to cybercrime are not known, available, or accessible to many practitioners, many of whom underestimate the scope and severity of the problem.
- There is a likely nexus between cybercrime and a variety of other
140 threats, including terrorism, industrial espionage, and foreign intelligence services.

Another industry group, the Computer Security Institute (CSI), surveyed 351 business organizations and found that computer crime cost most companies an average of less than $100,000 in 2010; although two companies lost much more than
145 that—$20 million in one case and more than $25 million in another.

(1,471 words)

—From Frank J. Schmalleger,
Criminology Today: An Integrative Introduction, 7th ed.

Recall

Stop to self-test, relate, and react.

Your instructor may choose to give you a brief comprehension review.

THINK ANALYTICALLY ABOUT THE SELECTION

Like most textbook selections, this excerpt from a criminology textbook presents information but does not put forward an arguable position. To digest a reading selection like this, use analytical skills. Take it apart, look at the details that make up the parts, and make sense of them to determine the main point and its significance. The questions below will guide you through the process.

1. List unfamiliar words that are important to understanding the selection and write brief definitions of them. Use context and structure clues first, and then verify your thinking with a dictionary.

Words	Definitions
_____	_____
_____	_____
_____	_____
_____	_____
_____	

2. Use your annotations to respond to the following questions about the selection.

Introduction:

Who is Kim Dotcom? _____

_____

What is important about his story? _____

_____

_____

_____

The Advance of Technology:

List the examples of the changing criminal use of technology. _____

_____

_____

_____

_____

What is the main point of this section? _____

_____

Cybercrime:

Why is the twenty-first century called the postindustrial information age?

_____

_____

For what reasons do criminals intrude into computer networks? _____

_____

SELECTION 1

What methods do they use? _____
_____
_____

List the FBI's five types of cybercrimes _____
_____
_____

The Extent of Cybercrime:

What is the point of this section? _____
_____
_____

What is the main idea of the entire selection? _____
_____

THINK CRITICALLY ABOUT THE SELECTION

Before reading this selection, you thought of some ways in which you or others have been harmed by the misuse of computer technology. Do your examples fit into one of the FBI's five types of cybercrimes described in Table 1? If so, explain which type. If not, describe your example and why it was harmful. Should it be included in the table?

Why is information so valuable in the twenty-first century?

WRITE ABOUT THE SELECTION

A student of criminal justice would need to remember the major points of this selection. An outline, a map, Cornell notes, or a summary would help to consolidate the material in memory when studying for a test.

Response Suggestion: Use your answers to the "Skill Development" questions above to write a one-paragraph summary of the information needed for test preparation.

SELECTION 2   Criminal Justice   MyReadingLab

Visit Chapter 10: Critical Thinking in MyReadingLab to complete the Selection 2 activities and the Build Background Knowledge video activity.

P REVIEW the next selection to predict its purpose and organization and to formulate your learning plan.

Activate Schemata

What high-tech equipment have you seen police using in television shows and movies?
Are you familiar with auto dashboard radar detectors?
What do you know about the use of DNA evidence in convicting criminals and freeing innocent prisoners?

Establish a Purpose for Reading

Read to learn about the technology that police are using and developing to catch and convict criminals.

Build Background Knowledge — VIDEO

Crime Fighting Chemical Spray

To prepare for reading Selection 2, answer the questions below. Then, watch this video on a newly developed chemical spray designed to catch criminals.

How has technology helped to decrease crime?

Name three technological advances in the fight against crime.

If you could design crime-fighting technology, what would you invent? Why?

This video helped me: _____

_____

_____

Integrate Knowledge While Reading

Questions have been inserted in the margin to stimulate your thinking while reading. Remember to

| Predict | Picture | Relate | Monitor | Correct | Annotate |

FIGHTING CRIME WITH TECHNOLOGY

Technology is a double-edged sword: It arms evildoers with potent new weapons of crime commission, yet it provides police agencies and criminal justice personnel with powerful tools useful in the battle against crime. Criminally useful or evasive technologies and law enforcement capabilities commonly leapfrog one another.
5 Consider traffic radar, which has gone from early always-on units through trigger-operated radar devices to today's sophisticated laser-based speed-measuring apparatus—each change being an attempt by enforcement agencies to keep a step ahead of increasingly sophisticated radar-detection devices marketed to drivers. Radar-jamming devices and laser jammers are also now used by people apparently
10 intent on breaking speed-limit laws. Not to be outdone, suppliers to law enforcement agencies have created radar detector detectors, which are used by authorities in states where radar detectors have been outlawed.

INTO THE FUTURE: "SPIDERMAN SNARES," STROBE LIGHTS, AND VEHICLE IMMOBILIZERS

Examples of future devices?

More innovative crime-fighting technologies are becoming available. The Spider-man snare, being tested for its usefulness in incapacitating fleeing suspects, is a
15 16-foot-wide net that is compressed into a small shotgun-like shell. The net has small weights at its circumference and wraps itself around its target after being fired. The snare's impact is harmless, and test subjects report being able to watch with open eyes as the net wraps around them. Another example is a special-frequency disco-like strobe light which quickly disorients human targets by causing intense diz-
20 ziness, leaving subjects unable to resist cuffing and arrest (operators wear special glasses designed to counter the influence of the light). Because high-speed chases pose a substantial danger to the public, scientists have developed an electromagnetic pulsing device that can be used to temporarily disable a vehicle's electrical system, causing the engine to stall. The prototype is said to be safe enough to use on
25 vehicles driven by those wearing pacemakers.

As new technologies are developed, their potential usefulness in law enforcement activities is evaluated by the FBI, the National Institute of Justice (NIJ), and other agencies. The NIJ's Technology Assessment Program (TAP) focuses on four areas of advancing technology: protective equipment, such as bulletproof vests and other body
30 armor; forensic sciences, including advances in DNA technology; transportation and weapons, such as electronic stun guns and other less-lethal weapons; and communications and electronics, including computer security and electronic eavesdropping.

Recently, the U.S. Department of Justice's National Law Enforcement and Corrections Technology Center (NLECTC) began testing a high-power compact micro-
35 wave source designed for vehicle immobilization. The microwave beam emitted by the device can interfere with an automobile's computer circuitry, effectively shutting down a car's engine from up to 35 feet away. As the technology is improved, the device will likely become operable over longer distances, and it may soon become a routine tool in police work.

DNA TECHNOLOGY

40 On January 16, 2001, Christopher Ochoa, age 34, was released from a Texas prison after serving 13 years for a murder he did not commit. Ochoa had confessed to the

rape and murder of 20-year-old Nancy DePriest at a Pizza Hut in Austin in 1988; although Ochoa later said he had been coerced by homicide detectives into confessing, no one believed him. A decade after he began serving a life sentence, law students at the Wisconsin Innocence Project at the University of Wisconsin-Madison took an interest in his case, studied surviving information, and concluded that DNA evidence conclusively proved that someone else had killed DePriest. The students and their law professor took the evidence to District Judge Bob Perkins, who called the case "a fundamental miscarriage of justice" and ordered Ochoa set free. According to authorities, evidence of DePriest's murder now points to Texas inmate Achim Joseph Marino, who confessed to her murder in 1996 following a religious conversion. Marino, currently serving three life sentences for other crimes, has provided investigators with the gun and handcuffs used to commit the crime.

Would you like to do this work?

DNA ANALYSIS

How is DNA collected and used?

The law students involved in the case used **DNA profiling,** matching DNA samples taken from mouth swabs of Marino with the DNA found in semen taken from the victim's body. Without DNA profiling, Ochoa would still be in prison, and DePriest's real killer would be unknown.

A person's genetic code is contained in his or her DNA, whose composition is unique to each individual (except in the case of identical twins). DNA samples can be taken from blood, hair, semen, saliva, or even small flakes of skin left at the scene of a crime. After processing, DNA profiles appear like bar codes on film negatives, codes that can exonerate a suspect or provide nearly irrefutable evidence of guilt.

Although DNA analysis is theoretically possible using only a single cell, most reputable DNA laboratories require a considerably greater quantity of material to conduct an effective analysis, but that could change. Using a Nobel Prizewinning

DNA profiling involves the scientific analysis of DNA that is taken from samples of body tissues or fluids in order to identify individuals.
Alexander Raths/Shutterstock

technique called "polymerase chain-reaction technology," minute strands of DNA can be effectively amplified so that even the identity of a person taking a single puff from a cigarette can be accurately established from the trace DNA left on the cigarette. Although the cost and complexity are prohibitive, these technological advances
70 are expected to be available to a range of forensic analysts.

DNA DATABASES

Why are they useful?

As DNA evidence is accepted throughout jurisdictions nationwide and worldwide, digitized forensic DNA databases (similar to widely used fingerprint archives) are useful at the state and national levels, and most of the states and the federal government (through the FBI laboratory) already have them. In 1998, the FBI announced
75 that its National DNA Index System (NDIS)—which enables U.S. forensic laboratories to exchange and compare DNA profiles electronically, thereby linking unsolved serial violent crimes to each other and to known offenders—had begun operation. Shortly thereafter, all 50 states had passed legislation requiring convicted offenders to provide samples for DNA databases, and all states have been invited to par-
80 ticipate in NDIS. The federal DNA Identification Act of 1994 authorized the FBI to establish DNA indexes for (1) offenders convicted of crimes, (2) samples recovered from crime scenes, and (3) samples recovered from unidentified human remains. There is the potential for coordination between the federally funded multibillion-dollar Human Genome Project and forensic DNA programs, which could lead to
85 explosive growth in the use of DNA in criminal case processing.

In 1995, the British police, operating under a new nationwide crime bill, became the first national police force in the world to begin routine collection of DNA samples from anyone involved in a "recordable" offense (a serious crime). It appears that genetic profiling will become one of the most significant crime-fighting tech-
90 nologies of the twenty-first century. "Genetic profiling—the use of biotechnology to identify the unique characteristics of an individual's DNA—is about to become as prevalent as the Breathalyzer and more important than the fingerprint."

In 1996, the NIJ released a comprehensive report, titled *Convicted by Juries, Exonerated by Science,* on the applicability of DNA testing to criminal case processing,
95 calling DNA testing "the most important technological breakthrough of twentieth century forensic science" and providing a detailed review of 28 cases in which post-conviction DNA evidence exonerated defendants who had been sentenced to lengthy prison terms. The men in the study had served, on average, seven years in prison, and most had been tried and sentenced prior to the widespread availability
100 of reliable DNA testing.

Is this an invasion of privacy?

Finally, it is important to note that a growing number of jurisdictions are requiring the gathering of DNA information from arrestees; and in 2013, the U.S. Supreme Court held, in the case of *Maryland* v. *King,* that "When officers make an arrest supported by probable cause . . . and bring the suspect to the station to be detained in
105 custody, taking and analyzing a cheek swab of the arrestee's DNA is, like fingerprinting and photographing, a legitimate police booking procedure that is reasonable under the Fourth Amendment."

KEVIN MITNICK—HACKER TURNED SECURITY EXPERT

At the time of his arrest in February 1995, Kevin Mitnick was the most-wanted computer criminal in U.S. history. His crimes included wire fraud, computer fraud, and
110 wire communication interception, and the cost to his victims included millions of

dollars in lost licensing fees, marketing delays, lost research and development, and the costs of repairing compromised computer systems.

Cloned cellular telephones, hacker software programs, "sniffer" devices, and so-called social engineering were the tools Mitnick used to conduct the computer
115 crime spree that launched a lengthy investigation beginning in 1992. The evidence amassed by the FBI during its three-year probe was sufficient to force Mitnick to accept a plea bargain rather than risk more severe penalties by going to trial. His corporate victims included a number of Fortune 500 companies, and he used University of Southern California computer systems to hide software code and obscure
120 his identity.

Born August 6, 1963, and a product of a blue-collar upbringing in California's San Fernando Valley, Mitnick's 1981 juvenile arrest for stealing computer manuals led to his being placed on probation. The experience had little deterrent effect, however, as evidenced by his subsequent arrests in 1989 (for possession of unauthorized
125 access devices) and in 1992 (for allegedly hacking into California Department of Motor Vehicles computers).

An intriguing element of Mitnick's case was the manner in which he was finally caught. Computer expert Tsutomu Shimomura, infuriated after Mitnick hacked into and stole information from his home computer, employed a dramatic cybersleuth-
130 ing effort to track Mitnick down, resulting in Mitnick's arrest by the FBI in a Raleigh, North Carolina, apartment complex.

Are there others like Mitnick? →

As a result of his 1995 arrest, Mitnick spent more than five years in prison, with more than eight months of it in solitary confinement. Now, at 50 years old a significantly matured Mitnick has done a 180-degree turnaround in his approach
135 to computer security. On March 1, 2000, he testified before the U.S. Senate's Governmental Affairs Committee, during which he suggested that the millions of dollars corporations spend on firewalls and secure access devices are negated by "the weakest link in the security chain: the people who use, administer and operate computer systems." Mitnick regaled the committee with tales of his use
140 of "social engineering" (what he defines as "using manipulation, influence, and deception to get a trusted insider to release information and to perform some sort of action item") that enables a hacker to successfully attack the insider's own computer system.

Mitnick now heads up a highly successful computer consulting firm that spe-
145 cializes in advising on computer security issues. He suggests that it is easier to hack today than it was years ago, citing social engineering as still an extraordinarily effective technique for computer exploit. Mitnick's message is clear: Notwithstanding tremendous advances in both hardware and software security measures, the weak link is still the human element.

(1,750 words)

—From Frank J. Schmalleger,
Criminology Today: An Integrative Introduction, 7th ed.

Recall

Stop to self-test, relate, and react.

Your instructor may choose to give you a brief comprehension review.

THINK ANALYTICALLY ABOUT THE SELECTION

In Selection 2, as in Selection 1, the author presents information. In addition, though, he also touches on a controversial legal and ethical issue. He does not take a stand on the issue, but perhaps you have an opinion. Analyze the structure of the selection to understand how the details contribute to each major part and how the parts develop the subject of the entire selection. Use the questions below as a guide.

1. List unfamiliar words that are important to understanding the selection and write brief definitions of them. Use context and structure clues first, and then verify your thinking with a dictionary.

   Words   Definitions

   _____   _____

   _____   _____

   _____   _____

   _____   _____

   _____   _____

2. Use your annotations to respond to the following questions about the selection.

Introduction:

Why did the author begin by discussing radar detectors? _____

_____

_____

_____

Into the Future:

Which of the developing technologies best captures your interest? Why?

_____

_____

_____

DNA Technology:

DNA Analysis. How is DNA collected, and how much is enough? _____

_____

_____

_____

DNA Databases. What U.S. governmental entities have DNA databases in use now? _____

How are they used? _____

_____

_____

What legal decisions allow the collection and sharing of DNA? _____

_____

_____

_____

_____

Kevin Mitnick:

How does this true story contribute to the selection? _____

_____

_____

_____

What is the main point of this selection? _____

_____

_____

THINK CRITICALLY ABOUT THE SELECTION

The United States federal and state governments have established laws allowing and, in some cases, requiring the collection of DNA for the purpose of criminal detection. Some people feel that this violates citizens' rights to privacy. At the same time, governments have the responsibility to protect citizens and keep the peace. What points can be made on each side of the issue? Do the benefits outweigh the drawbacks? What is your position?

WRITE ABOUT THE SELECTION

Imagine that you were arrested for a robbery that you did not commit, but a sample of your DNA was taken as a matter of normal procedure. You were released when the real perpetrator was found. However, your DNA sample, which is now in the national database, revealed a genetic abnormality that guarantees that you will suffer a rare disease. You are unable to find a company to provide affordable health insurance due to the potentially large costs of your future care.

Response Suggestion: Draft a letter to your congressional representative that makes a case against the current DNA collection laws and suggests an alternative that protects innocent people yet recognizes the need for protection against criminals.

Visit Chapter 10: Critical Thinking in MyReadingLab to complete the Selection 3 activities and Build Background Knowledge video activity.

P REVIEW the next selection to predict its purpose and organization and to formulate your learning plan.

Activate Schemata

Have you been hurt by harsh comments made about you on social media?
Do you think that people write things on Internet sites that they wouldn't say face-to-face?
Have you heard news stories about people who committed suicide after enduring hateful, malicious verbal attacks on social media sites?

Establish a Purpose for Reading

How should we respond to online abuse? Read to find out how this professional writer was hurt by anonymous Internet posts, her response, and the surprising result.

Build Background Knowledge — VIDEO

Principal Fights Against Cyberbullying
To prepare for reading Selection 3, answer the questions below. Then, watch this video on drastic steps taken by a school principal to address cyberbullying.

What is the best way for schools to protect students from cyberbullying?

How can individuals protect themselves from cyberbullying?

Besides school, name three other environments where cyberbullying takes place.

This video helped me: _____

_____

_____

Integrate Knowledge While Reading

Questions have been inserted in the margin to stimulate your thinking while reading. Remember to

Predict   Picture   Relate   Monitor   Correct   Annotate

THE WRITER AND THE TROLL

For the past three years or so, at least one stranger has sought me out pretty much every day to call me a fat bitch (or some pithy variation thereof). I'm a writer and a woman and a feminist, and I write about big, fat, bitchy things that make people uncomfortable. And because I choose to do that as a career, I'm told, a constant barrage
5 of abuse is just part of my job. Shrug. Nothing we can do. I'm asking for it, apparently.

Do you find it surprising?

Being harassed on the Internet is such a normal, common part of my life that I'm always surprised when other people find it surprising. You're telling me you don't have hundreds of men popping into your cubicle in the accounting department of your mid-sized, regional dry-goods distributor to inform you that—hmm—you're
10 too fat to rape, but perhaps they'll saw you up with an electric knife? No? Just me? People who don't spend much time on the Internet are invariably shocked to discover the barbarism—the eager abandonment of the social contract—that so many of us face simply for doing our jobs.

Sometimes the hate trickles in slowly, just one or two messages a day. But other
15 times, when I've written something particularly controversial (i.e., feminist)—like, say, my critique of men feeling entitled to women's time and attention, or literally anything about rape—the harassment comes in a deluge. It floods my Twitter feed, my Facebook page, my email, so fast that I can't even keep up (not that I want to).

What?!

It was in the middle of one of these deluges two summers ago when my dead
20 father contacted me on Twitter.

Hatred of women?

At the time, I'd been writing a lot about the problem of misogyny (specifically jokes about rape) in the comedy world. My central point—which has been gleefully misconstrued as "pro-censorship" ever since—was that what we say affects the world we live in, that words are both a reflection of and a catalyst for the way our
25 society operates. When you talk about rape, I said, you get to decide where you aim: are you making fun of rapists? Or their victims? Are you making the world better?

Does she support censorship?

Or worse? It's not about censorship, it's not about obligation, it's not about forcibly limiting anyone's speech—it's about choice. Who are you? Choose.

The backlash from comedy fans was immediate and intense: "That broad doesn't
30 have to worry about rape." "She won't ever have to worry about rape." "No one would want to rape that fat, disgusting mess." "People like you make me want to commit rape out of anger." It went on and on, to the point that it was almost white noise. After a week

How might a more vulnerable person react?

or so, I was feeling weather-beaten but fortified. Nothing could touch me anymore.

But then there was my dad's dear face twinkling out at me from my Twitter
35 feed. Someone—bored, apparently, with the usual angles of harassment—had made a fake Twitter account purporting to be my dead dad, featuring a stolen, beloved photo of him, for no reason other than to hurt me. The name on the account was "PawWestDonezo," because my father's name was Paul West, and a difficult battle with prostate cancer had rendered him "donezo" (goofy slang for "done") just
40 18 months earlier. "Embarrassed father of an idiot," the bio read. "Other two kids are fine, though." His location was "Dirt hole in Seattle."

My dad was special. The only thing he valued more than wit was kindness. He was a writer and an ad man and a magnificent baritone (he could write you a jingle and record it on the same day)—a lost breed of lounge pianist who skipped dizzy-
45 ingly from jazz standards to Flanders and Swann to Lord Buckley and back again—and I can genuinely say that I've never met anyone else so universally beloved, nor do I expect to again. I loved him so, so much.

Del.

There's a term for this brand of gratuitous online cruelty: we call it Internet trolling. Trolling is recreational abuse—usually anonymous—intended to waste the
50 subject's time or get a rise out of them or frustrate or frighten them into silence. Sometimes it's relatively innocuous (like asking contrarian questions just to start an argument) or juvenile (like making fun of my weight or my intelligence), but, par-

Is this illegal?

ticularly when the subject is a young woman, it frequently crosses the line into bona fide, dangerous stalking and harassment.
55   And even "innocuous" harassment, when it's coming at you en masse from hundreds or even thousands of users a day, stops feeling innocuous very quickly.

Should there be consequences for abuse like this?

It's a silencing tactic. The message is: you are outnumbered. The message is: we'll stop when you're gone. The volume and intensity of harassment is vastly magnified for women of colour and trans women and disabled women and fat women and sex
60 workers and other intersecting identities. Who gets trolled has a direct impact on who gets to talk; in my personal experience, the fiercest trolling has come from tra- ditionally white, male-dominated communities (comedy, video games, atheism) whose members would like to keep it that way.

I feel the pull all the time: I should change careers; I should shut down my social
65 media; maybe I can get a job in print somewhere; it's just too exhausting. I hear the same refrains from my colleagues. Sure, we've all built up significant armour at this point, but, you know, armour is heavy. Internet trolling might seem like an issue that only affects a certain subset of people, but that's only true if you believe that living in a world devoid of diverse voices wouldn't profoundly affect your life.
70   Sitting at my computer, staring at PawWestDonezo, I had precious few options. All I could do, really, was ignore it: hit "block" and move on, knowing that that ac- count was still out there, hidden behind a few gossamer lines of code, still putting words in my dad's mouth, still using his image to mock, abuse and silence people. After all, it's not illegal to reach elbow-deep into someone's memories and touch
75 them and twist them and weaponise them. Nor should it be, of course. But that doesn't mean we have to tolerate it without dissent.

Over and over, those of us who work on the Internet are told, "Don't feed the trolls. Don't talk back. It's what they want." But is that true? Does ignoring trolls actually stop trolling? Can somebody show me concrete numbers on that? Anecdotally,

Internet trolling often crosses the line to more dangerous stalking and harassment.
Valua Vitaly/Shutterstock

80   I've ignored far more trolls than I've "fed," and my inbox hasn't become any quieter. When I speak my mind and receive a howling hurricane of abuse in return, it doesn't feel like a plea for my attention—it feels like a demand for my silence.

And some trolls are explicit about it. "If you can't handle it, get off the Internet." That's a persistent refrain my colleagues and I hear when we confront our harassers. But 85 why? Why don't YOU get off the Internet? Why should I have to rearrange my life—and change careers, essentially—because you wet your pants every time a woman talks?

When does verbal abuse become illegal? My friends say, "Just don't read the comments." But just the other day, for instance, I got a tweet that said, "May your bloodied head rest on the edge of an Isis blade." Colleagues and friends of mine have had their phone numbers and addresses 90 published online (a harassment tactic known as "doxing") and had trolls show up at their public events or threaten mass shootings. So if we don't keep an eye on what people are saying, how do we know when a line has been crossed and law enforcement should be involved? (Not that the police have any clue how to deal with online harassment anyway—or much interest in trying.)

How do media companies respond? 95 Social media companies say, "Just report any abuse and move on. We're handling it." So I do that. But reporting abuse is a tedious, labor-intensive process that can eat up half my working day. In any case, most of my reports are rejected. And once any troll is blocked (or even if they're suspended), they can just make a new account and start all over again.

100   I'm aware that Twitter is well within its rights to let its platform be used as a vehicle for sexist and racist harassment. But, as a private company—just like a comedian mulling over a rape joke, or a troll looking for a target for his anger—it could choose not to. As a collective of human beings, it could choose to be better.

Her decision So, when it came to the case of PawWestDonezo, I went off script: I stopped 105 obsessing over what *he* wanted and just did what felt best to me that day. I wrote about it publicly, online. I made myself vulnerable. I didn't hide the fact it hurt. The next morning, I woke up to an email:

His response   *Hey Lindy, I don't know why or even when I started trolling you. It wasn't because of your stance on rape jokes. I don't find them funny either.*
110   *I think my anger towards you stems from your happiness with your own being. It offended me because it served to highlight my unhappiness with my own self.*
I have e-mailed you through two other gmail accounts just to send you idiotic insults. I apologize for that.
I created the PaulWestDunzo@gmail.com account & Twitter account. (I have 115 *deleted both.)*
I can't say sorry enough.
It was the lowest thing I had ever done. When you included it in your latest Jezebel article it finally hit me. There is a living, breathing human being who is reading this shit. I am attacking someone who never harmed me in any way. And for no reason 120 *whatsoever.*
I'm done being a troll.
Again I apologize.
I made donation in memory to your dad.
I wish you the best.

125   He had donated $50 to Seattle Cancer Care Alliance, where my dad was treated.

That email still unhinges my jaw every time I read it. A reformed troll? An admission of weakness and self-loathing? An apology? I wrote back once, expressed my disbelief

and said thank you—and that was that. I returned to my regular routine of daily hate mail, scrolling through the same options over and over—Ignore? Block? Report?
130 Engage?—but every time I faced that choice, I thought briefly of my remorseful troll.

Last summer, when a segment of video game fans began a massive harassment campaign against female critics and developers, my thoughts wandered back to him more and more. I wondered if I could learn anything from him. And then it struck me: why not find out?

135 We only had made that one, brief exchange, in the summer of 2013, but I still had his email address. I asked the popular United States radio program "This American Life" to help me reach out to him. They said yes. They emailed him. After a few months of gruelling silence, he finally wrote back. "I'd be happy to help you out in any way possible," he said.

140 And then, there I was in a studio with a phone—and the troll on the other end.

We talked for two-and-a-half hours. He was shockingly self-aware. He told me that he didn't hate me because of rape jokes—the timing was just a coincidence—he hated me because, to put it simply, I don't hate myself. Hearing him explain his choices in his own words, in his own voice, was heart breaking and fascinating. He
145 said that, at the time, he felt fat, unloved, "passionless" and purposeless. For some reason, he found it "easy" to take that out on women online.

I asked why. What made women easy targets? Why was it so satisfying to hurt us? Why didn't he automatically see us as human beings? For all his self-reflection, that's the one thing he never managed to articulate—how anger at one woman
150 translated into hatred of women in general. Why, when men hate themselves, it's women who take the beatings.

But he did explain how he changed. He started taking care of his health, he found a new girlfriend and, most importantly, he went back to school to become a teacher. He told me   in all seriousness—that, as a volunteer at a school, he just gets
155 so many hugs now. "Seeing how their feelings get hurt by their peers," he said, "on purpose or not, it derails them for the rest of the day. They'll have their head on their desk and refuse to talk. As I'm watching this happen, I can't help but think about the feelings that I hurt." He was so sorry, he said.

I didn't mean to forgive him, but I did.
160 This story isn't prescriptive. It doesn't mean that anyone is obliged to forgive people who abuse them, or even that I plan on being cordial and compassionate to every teenage boy who tells me I'm too fat to get raped (sorry in advance, boys: I still bite). But, for me, it's changed the timbre of my online interactions—with, for instance, the guy who responded to my radio story by calling my dad a "faggot." It's
165 hard to feel hurt or frightened when you're flooded with pity. And that, in turn, has made it easier for me to keep talking in the face of a mob roaring for my silence. Keep screaming, trolls. I see you.

Change of attitude (annotation pointing to line 160)

(2,254 words)

—From Lindy West
The Guardian, February 2, 2015

Recall

Stop to self-test, relate, and react.

Your instructor may choose to give you a brief comprehension review.

THINK ANALYTICALLY ABOUT THE SELECTION

1. List unfamiliar words that are important to understanding the selection and write brief definitions. Use context and structure clues first, and then verify your thinking with a dictionary.

Words   Definitions

_____   _____

_____   _____

_____   _____

_____   _____

_____   _____

THINK CRITICALLY ABOUT THE SELECTION

Apply the four-step format for evaluating the argument.

- **Step 1.** Identify the position on the issue. State the main point that the author is making.

  _____

  _____

Step 2. Identify the support in the argument. Make lettered lists of the major assertions of support. Use the categories provided to organize the details that the author includes to support her point.

I. People post comments that abandon "the social contract" and sometimes threaten physical harm.

  A. _____

  _____

  B. _____

  _____

  C. _____

  _____

  D. _____

  _____

  E. _____

  _____

  F. _____

  _____

G. _____
_____

H. _____
_____

I. _____
_____

J. _____
_____

II. Online harassment is harmful.

A. _____
_____

B. _____
_____

C. _____
_____
_____

D. _____
_____
_____
_____

E. _____
_____

F. _____
_____

III. Other options to control online harassment aren't effective.

A. _____
_____

B. _____
_____

C. _____
_____

D. _____
_____

E. _____

_____

F. _____

_____

IV. What should be done?

A. _____

_____

_____

B. _____

_____

C. _____

_____

_____

_____

D. _____

_____

• **Step 3.** Evaluate the support using the letters that you listed in Step 2. Comment on relevance, believability, and consistency for the assertions that you listed in Step 2. Label any fallacies. What supporting information do you feel is missing?

_____

_____

_____

_____

_____

_____

_____

_____

_____

_____

_____

_____

_____
_____
_____
_____
_____
_____
_____
_____
_____
_____
_____

Step 4. Evaluate the argument. What is your overall evaluation and why?

_____
_____
_____
_____
_____
_____
_____
_____
_____
_____
_____
_____

What is your opinion on the issue?

_____
_____

WRITE ABOUT THE SELECTION

What are appropriate standards for social media and other Internet communications? What is a fitting response to harsh or damaging comments? Who should be responsible for keeping the standards?

Response Suggestion: Write your own essay in which you defend your position on Internet communication. What are the appropriate standards?

VOCABULARY BOOSTER

Foreign Terms

- **bon vivant**: a lover of good living; a gourmet

  While living in Paris with plenty of money, he enjoyed the lifestyle of a *bon vivant*.

- **avant-garde**: advance guard, pioneers, offbeat

  The radical ideas of the sociology professor may be too *avant-garde* for the conservative freshmen.

- **carte blanche**: "white paper," unlimited authority, blanket permission

  The new company gave her *carte blanche* to entertain the top three customers at the convention.

- **magnum opus**: great work

  After seven years of work, the novel was recognized as the author's *magnum opus*.

- **de rigueur**: strict etiquette, very formal, in good taste at the moment

  A jacket and necktie are *de rigueur* for the occasion.

- **déjà vu**: already seen

  The feeling of *déjà vu* became more intense as the same people seemed to be saying the same things as in 1997.

- **double entendre**: allowing two interpretations, with one usually being off-color

  As soon as the sentence was uttered, the speaker realized the *double entendre* and laughed knowingly.

- **faux pas**: "false step," or mistake

  I realized the *faux pas* when I saw my friends giggling in the background.

- **joie de vivre**: "joy for living"

  The guide's *joie de vivre* was contagious, making the trip enjoyable for us all.

- **esprit de corps**: group spirit of pride

  Through shared experiences, the marines build a strong *esprit de corps*.

- **coup d'état**: sudden stroke that overturns a government

  The foreign diplomats sought to leave before the predicted *coup d'état*.

- **raison d'être**: "reason for being," justification

  For the last three years, raising my child has been my *raison d'être*.

- **potpourri**: mixture

  A *potpourri* of ideas was presented for the group to consider.

- *nouveau riche*: newly rich, suggesting poor taste

   Have you seen the pillow that says, "Better to be *nouveau riche* than not rich at all"?

- *nom de plume*: pen name, pseudonym

   Samuel Clemens used Mark Twain as his *nom de plume*.

- *junta*: group of political plotters

   By gaining control of the military, the *junta* overthrew the existing government.

- *sotto voce*: "under the voice," in a whisper

   The criticism was overheard, even though it was said *sotto voce*.

- *vendetta*: blood feud

   Because of the assault, the gang continued the *vendetta*.

- *alfresco*: "in the fresh air," outdoors

   During the summer months, the restaurant offered *alfresco* dining.

- *fait accompli*: finished action

   Submit your comments to the dean before the decision becomes a *fait accompli*.

Review

Part I

Indicate whether the following sentences are true *(T)* or false *(F)*:

_____ 1. If you fail to discuss grades with your instructor before final conferences, the mark you receive is most likely a *fait accompli*.

_____ 2. During the cold winter months, many restaurant patrons enjoy dining *alfresco*.

_____ 3. *Avant-garde* forms of art are considered old-fashioned.

_____ 4. One who is a *bon vivant* could be said to enjoy the good life.

_____ 5. Being color-blind, her boyfriend failed to realize that combining red shorts with an orange shirt could be a serious fashion *faux pas*.

_____ 6. His *raison d'être* for failing to notify us of his late arrival was that his cell phone had no remaining minutes.

_____ 7. A person with great *joie de vivre* would likely be an unpleasant companion.

_____ 8. A *coup d'état* is not likely to occur in a country with an unstable government.

_____ 9. The graduate student considered her doctoral thesis to be her *magnum opus*.

_____ 10. A novelist may write books using a *nom de plume*.

———— 11. Tourists in Italy may observe the sights and scenes of Venice while riding in a *vendetta*.

———— 12. A *junta* does not desire political power.

Part II

Choose the word from the list that means the opposite of the words below.

nouveau riche	sotto voce	de rigueur	déjà vu
esprit de corps	double entendre	carte blanche	potpourri

13. casual ————————

14. low morale ————————

15. restricted power ————————

16. not seen before ————————

17. single meaning ————————

18. loudly ————————

19. one variety ————————

20. chronically poor ————————

GLOSSARY

active academic reading The purposeful use of attention, effort, strategies, and resources to learn through reading.

ad hominem An argument in which the person rather than the issue is attacked.

analogy A comparison showing connections with, and similarities to, previous experiences.

analytical thinking Thinking that involves separating and examining parts to identify reasons, causes, and supporting information; it is part of the critical thinking process.

annotating Marking textbook material for future study; one of the thinking strategies that good readers use during reading.

antonym A word that means the opposite of another word.

appeals to emotions A critical thinking fallacy that uses highly charged language for emotional manipulation.

appeals to pity A critical thinking fallacy that pleads for you to support the underdog, the person, or the issue that needs your help.

argument Assertions that support a conclusion with the intention of persuading.

assertion A nondebatable statement that is intended to inform or explain.

attention Uninterrupted mental focus.

bandwagon A critical thinking fallacy that gives the idea that everybody is doing it and that you will be left out if you do not quickly join the crowd.

bar graph An arrangement of horizontal or vertical bars in which the length of each bar represents an amount or number.

believability Support for a topic or conclusion that is not suspicious but is believable; a criterion for evaluating support for an argument that judges the degree to which support is logical and reasonable.

bias An opinion or position on a subject, recognized through facts that are slanted toward an author's personal beliefs.

card stacking See **incomplete facts**.

cause and effect A pattern of organization in which one item is shown as having produced another.

chronological order A pattern of organization in which items are listed in time order or sequence.

circular reasoning, begging the question A critical thinking fallacy that gives support for the conclusion that is merely a restatement of the conclusion.

classification A pattern of organization dividing information into groups or categories. The divisions are then named, and the parts are explained.

cognitive psychology A body of knowledge that describes how the mind works or is believed to work.

comparison A pattern of organization that presents items according to similarities between or among them.

comparison and contrast A pattern of organization in which similarities and differences are presented.

concentration The focusing of your full attention on a task.

conclusion Interpretation based on evidence and suggested meaning. In logic, the position on an issue or the main point.

connotation The feeling associated with the definition of a word.

consistency The degree to which support for a conclusion holds together and does not contradict itself; a criterion for judging the strength of support for an argument.

content test A test designed to measure understanding, retention, and the ability to apply what was learned in a course.

context clues Hints within a sentence that help unlock the meaning of an unknown word.

contrast A pattern of organization that presents items according to differences between or among them.

Cornell Method A system of note taking that involves writing phrases or sentence summaries on the right side of the page, with key words and topics written on the left side of the page.

correct One of the six strategies that good readers use during reading; refers to correcting gaps in comprehension.

creative thinking The ability to generate many possible solutions to a problem.

critical thinking Deliberating in a purposeful, organized manner to assess the value of information or arguments.

cumulative bar graph A bar graph in which all of the bar's lines or segments add up to a total. Rather than having multiple bars or lines, the groups are stacked on top of each other to dramatically show differences.

deductive reasoning Thinking that starts with a conclusion and then finds evidence to support it.

definition A pattern of organization that is devoted to defining an idea and further explaining it with examples.

denotation The dictionary definition of a word.

description A pattern of organization listing characteristics of a person, place, or thing.

details Statements that support, describe, develop, and explain a main idea.

diagram A drawing of an object showing labeled parts.

dictionary A word reference that lists words alphabetically and includes definitions, the pronunciation, and additional information about each entry.

distractor A response on a multiple-choice test that diverts the reader from the correct response.

etymology The study of word origins, involving the tracing of words back to their earliest recorded appearance.

euphemism A substitution of a mild, indirect, or vague term for one that is considered harsh, blunt, or offensive.

external distractions Temptations of the physical world that divert attention from a task.

fact A statement based on evidence or personal observation that can be proved true.

fallacy A statement that first appears reasonable but on closer inspection proves to be unrelated, unreliable, or illogical.

figurative language Words used to create images that take on a new meaning.

fixation A stop that your eyes make while reading.

flowchart A diagram showing how ideas are related, with boxes and arrows indicating levels of importance and movement.

generalization and example A pattern of organization in which a general statement or conclusion is supported with specific examples.

glossary An alphabetical listing of words and definitions as they are used in a book. It usually appears at the end of a book.

graphic organizer A diagram that presents the major and minor details of a text passage in visual form.

habit A repetitious act that is performed almost unconsciously.

homonyms Words with different meanings that are spelled or sound alike, such as *bear* in "bear the burden" or "kill the bear."

hyperbole Exaggeration using figurative language to describe something as being more than it actually is. See **overstatement**.

idiom A figurative expression that does not make literal sense but communicates a generally accepted meaning.

imagery Mental pictures created by figurative language.

implied meaning See **inference**

incomplete facts or **card stacking** A critical thinking fallacy that gives or leaves out factual details in order to misrepresent reality.

inductive reasoning Thinking that begins with the collection of data and then formulates a conclusion based on those data.

inference Meaning that is suggested rather than directly stated. (See **implied meaning**.)

integrating knowledge The process of connecting new and existing knowledge.

internal distractions Concerns that come repeatedly to mind and disturb your concentration.

lateral thinking A way of creatively thinking around a problem or redefining it to seek new solutions.

line graph A continuous curve or frequency distribution in which numbers are plotted in an unbroken line; the horizontal scale measures time, and the vertical scale measures amount.

location See **spatial order**.

locus of control A person's belief about control over personal success or failure; an individual with an external locus of control blames external factors, whereas a person with an internal locus of control attributes results to his or her own behavior.

main idea The primary point about the topic of a passage.

map A graphic display that shows the location or characteristics of a particular area.

mapping A method of graphically displaying material to show relationships and importance for later study.

metacognition Awareness and understanding of your thinking process as well as the ability to regulate and direct it.

metaphor A figure of speech that directly compares two unlike things without using the words *like* or *as*.

misinterpreted statistics A critical thinking fallacy that improperly applies numerical data to unrelated populations that they were never intended to represent.

misleading analogy A critical thinking fallacy that compares two things, suggesting that they are similar when they are, in fact, distinctly different.

mnemonic device A technique using images, numbers, rhymes, or letters to improve your memory.

monitor One of the six strategies that good readers use during reading; requires awareness of ongoing comprehension.

multiple meanings The defining of a word in several ways. For example, the dictionary lists over 30 meanings for the word *run*.

narration A pattern of organization in which details are presented, usually in time order, to tell a story.

narrative A form of writing that tells a story, usually in time order.

neuroscience The scientific study of the molecular and cellular levels of the brain and nervous system, and the study of behavior produced by the brain.

note taking A method of writing down short phrases and summaries to record textbook material for future study.

opinion A statement of a personal view, judgment, or belief; it cannot be proved true.

outlining A method of using indentations, Roman numerals, numbers, and letters to organize a topic for future study.

overgeneralizations A critical thinking fallacy involving examples and anecdotes that are asserted to apply to all situations rather than to a select few. *Example:* High school students do little work during their senior year and thus are overwhelmed at college.

oversimplification A critical thinking fallacy that reduces an issue to two simple choices, without consideration of other alternatives or "gray areas" in between.

overstatement See **hyperbole**.

pattern of organization The plan, format, or structure for presenting the details in a passage.

personification Attributing human characteristics to nonhuman things.

pie graph A circular graph that is divided into wedge-shaped segments to show portions totaling 100 percent.

point of view An author's position or opinion on a subject.

politically correct language A form of euphemism that is used to avoid offending a group of people or raising a politically sensitive idea.

predict One of the six strategies that good readers use during reading; refers to developing an expectation of the ideas that may come next.

prefix A group of letters added to the beginning of a word and causing a change of meaning.

premise A point in support of a conclusion.

previewing A method of glancing over a reading passage to predict the topic and organization of the passage and thus assess your prior knowledge and needed skills.

prior knowledge Previous learning about a subject. See **schema**.

purpose A writer's underlying reason or intent for writing.

questionable authority A critical thinking fallacy that gives a testimonial suggesting authority from people who are not experts.

rate The reading pace that is calculated according to the number of words read in one minute.

reading between the lines The figurative phrase for an inference by the reader or listener.

reading efficiency Adjusting reading rate to fit the material and purpose for reading.

recall Reviewing what was included and learned after reading a passage.

recall diagram An informal outline that is used to record the main idea, major details, and personal responses to reading material.

regression Rereading material because of a lack of understanding or concentration.

relate One of the six strategies that good readers use during reading; refers to comparing the reader's knowledge and experience to the ideas that are presented.

relevance The degree to which supporting material is related to the conclusion; a criterion for judging the strength of support for an argument.

root The stem or basic part of a word; in English, roots are derived primarily from Latin and Greek.

sarcasm A tone or language that expresses biting humor, usually meaning the opposite of what is literally said, with the purpose of hurting or ridiculing someone. A harsh form of verbal irony.

scanning Searching reading material quickly to locate specific points of information.

schema A skeleton or network of knowledge about a subject.

sequence A pattern of organization in which the details are placed in the order in which they must occur, as in the steps in a recipe or process. See **chronological order** and **time order**.

signal words See **transitional words**.

simile A form of figurative language that compares two things using the words *like* or *as*.

simple listing A pattern of organization that randomly lists items in a series.

skimming A technique for selectively reading to get the gist or main idea.

slippery slope A critical thinking fallacy that objects to something by assuming that it will lead to greater evil and disastrous consequences.

spatial order, location order A pattern of organization that identifies the location of a place or object.

standardized reading test A test that is designed to measure reading comprehension and that is given to very large populations. It is carefully constructed, tested, administered, and scored in a consistent or "standard" manner.

straw person A critical thinking fallacy that gives a setup in which a distorted or exaggerated form of the opponent's argument is introduced and knocked down as if to represent a totally weak opposition.

study process See **study system**.

study reading A technique for thorough reading of material for the purpose of deep comprehension and long-term memory.

study system A plan for working through stages to read and learn textbook material.

subvocalization The inaudible inner voice that is used as part of the reading process.

suffix A group of letters added to the end of a word and causing a change in meaning as well as the way the word can be used in the sentence.

summary A concise statement of the main idea and significant supporting details. Also, a pattern of organization in which already stated information is reviewed.

synonym A word with the same meaning as another word.

table A listing of facts and figures in columns and rows for quick and easy reference.

testimonials A critical thinking fallacy that gives opinions of agreement from respected celebrities who are not actually experts.

thesaurus A word reference that provides synonyms for words in an alphabetical listing.

thesis statement A sentence that states the author's main point; usually refers to a longer piece of writing such as an essay. (See **topic sentence**.)

thinking An organized and controlled mental activity that helps you solve problems, make decisions, and understand ideas.

time order A pattern of organization that presents items in the chronological order or sequence in which they occurred.

To Do List A reminder list of activities that you need to accomplish.

tone A writer's attitude toward a subject.

topic A word or phrase that labels the subject of a paragraph, reading passage, article, or book.

topic sentence A sentence that condenses the main thoughts and details of a passage into a general, all-inclusive statement of the author's message; usually refers to a short piece of writing such as a paragraph. (See **thesis statement**.)

transfer A critical thinking fallacy that gives an association with a positively or negatively regarded person or thing in order to lend the same association to the argument.

transitional words, or **signal words** Connecting words that signal the direction of the writer's thought or the pattern of organization.

understatement Figurative language that minimizes a point.

verbal irony The use of words to express a meaning that is the opposite of what is literally said.

vertical thinking A straightforward and logical way of thinking that searches for a solution to the stated problem.

visualize One of the six strategies that good readers use during reading; refers to forming mental pictures of the content that is presented in print.

vocalization An immature habit in which readers move their lips while reading.

word structure Word parts, such as prefixes, roots, and suffixes, which lend meaning to many English words.

CREDITS

p. 4: Adapted from Patricia Wolfe: *Brain Matters*. ©2001 Association for Supervision and Curriculum Development: Alexandria, VA. **p. 11:** Medina, John: *Brain Rules: 12 Principles for Surviving and Thriving at Work, Home, and School*, Pear Press, 2008, 2014. www.brainrules.net. Reprinted with permission. **p. 15–16:** Wade, Carole; Tavris, Carol: *Psychology*, 10th Ed. ©2011. Printed and Electronically reproduced by permission of Pearson Education, Inc., Upper Saddle River, New Jersey. **p. 21:** Goldfield, David: *The American Journey*, 3rd Ed. ©2004. Pearson Education, Inc. **p. 23:** Adapted from James E. Zull: *The Art of Changing the Brain*. ©2002 Stylus Publishing, LLC. Sterling, VA. **p. 26:** Walbank, Walter T.: *Civilization Past and Present*, 8th Ed. ©1996. Pearson Education, Inc. **pp. 37–38:** Wood, Samuel; Wood, Ellen Green; Boyd, Denise: *Mastering the World of Psychology*, 5th Ed. ©2014, p. 162. Reprinted and Electronically reproduced by permission of Pearson Education, Inc., New York, NY. **pp. 47–50:** Jones, Jacqueline A.; Wood, Peter H.; Borstermann, Thomas; May, Elaine Tyler; Ruiz, Vicki L.: *Created Equal: A History of the United States, Volume 2 (From 1865)*, 3rd Ed. ©2009. Printed and Electronically reproduced by permission of Pearson Education, Inc., Upper Saddle River, New Jersey. **pp. 59–61:** Audesirk, Teresa; Audesirk, Gerald; Byers, Bruce E.: *Life on Earth*, 5th Ed. ©2009. Printed and Electronically reproduced by permission of Pearson Education, Inc., Upper Saddle River, New Jersey. **p. 77:** Wallace, Robert: *Biology: The Science of Life*, 4th Ed. ©1996. Pearson Education, Inc. **p. 77:** Adapted from *Learning and Memory: The Brain in Action*, by Marilee Sprenger. ©1999 Association for Supervision and Curriculum Development. **p. 81:** Wallace, Robert; Gerald P. Sanders; Robert J. Ferl: *Biology: The Science of Life*, 4th Ed. ©1996. Pearson Education, Inc. **p. 82:** Donatelle, Rebecca, et al.: *Health: The Basics*, 11th Ed. ©2015. Pearson Education, Inc. **pp. 83–84:** Wallace, Robert; Gerald P. Sanders; Robert J. Ferl: *Biology: The Science of Life*, 4th Ed. ©1996. Pearson Education, Inc. **p. 85:** Cunningham, John: *Human Biology*, 2nd Ed. ©1989. Pearson Education, Inc. **p. 86:** Adapted from *Learning and Memory: The Brain in Action*, by Marilee Sprenger. ©1999 Association for Supervision and Curriculum Development. **pp. 86–87:** Kishlansky, Mark, et al.: *Civilization in the West*, 6th Ed. ©2006. Pearson Education, Inc. **p. 87:** Lutgens, Frederick K.; Edward J. Tarbuck: *The Atmosphere: An Introduction to Meteorology*, 9th Ed. ©2004. Pearson Education, Inc. **pp. 90–93:** From America.gov Archive, March 1, 2010, Bureau of International Information Programs, U.S. Department of State by A'Lelia Bundles. **pp. 99–102:** Donatelle, Rebecca J.; Ketcham, Patricia: *Access to Health*, 12th Ed. ©2012. Printed and Electronically reproduced by permission of Pearson Education, Inc., Upper Saddle River, New Jersey.* Requested material is data collected from Sources: –American College Health Assoc, American College Health National College Assessment–Reference Group Data Fall 2009 Baltimore: American College Health Assoc 2010. **pp. 109–111:** Armstrong, Gary; Kotler, Philip: *Marketing: An Introduction*, 10th Ed. ©2011. Printed and Electronically reproduced by permission of Pearson Education, Inc., Upper Saddle River, New Jersey. **p. 124:** Medina, John: *Brain Rules: 12 Principles for Surviving and Thriving at Work, Home, and School*, Pear Press, 2008, 2014. www.brainrules.net. Reprinted with permission. **pp. 128–129:** Greer, Charles R.; Plunkett, Richard Warren: *Supervision: Diversity and Teams in the Workplace*, 10th Ed. ©2003, pp. 24–25. Reprinted and Electronically reproduced by permission of Pearson Education, Inc., New York, NY. **p. 133:** Thompson, Janice; Manore, Melinda: *Nutrition: An Applied Approach*, 1st Ed. ©2005, p. 60. Reprinted and Electronically reproduced by permission of Pearson Education, Inc., New York, NY. **pp. 136–138:** Gerow, Josh: *Psychology: Introduction*, 1st Ed. ©1988, pp. 393–395. Reprinted and Electronically reproduced by permission of Pearson Education, Inc., New York, NY. **p. 138:** Medina, John: *Brain Rules: 12 Principles for Surviving and Thriving at Work, Home, and School*, Pear Press, 2008, 2014. www.brainrules.net. Reprinted with permission. **pp. 143–144:** Armstrong, Gary; Kotler, Philip, *Marketing: An Introduction*, 10th Ed. ©2011. Printed and Electronically reproduced by permission of Pearson Education, Inc., Upper Saddle River, New Jersey. **pp. 165–167:** Thompson, Carolyn: "Police DNA Collection Sparks Questions," Associated Press, March 17, 2007. Reprinted with permission. **p. 178:** Johnson, Willis H. Johnson, et al.: *Essentials of Biology*, 2nd Ed. ©1976. Holt, Rinehart and Winston. **p. 179:** Lineberry, Robert: *Government in America*, 15th Ed. ©2011. Pearson Education, Inc. **p. 180:** Matheson, Douglas W.: *Introductory Psychology: The Modern View*, 2nd Ed. ©1982. Harlan Davidson. **p. 181:** Atkinson, Rita, et al.: *Introduction to Psychology*, 16th Ed. ©2014. Thomson Learning. **p. 181:** Bates, Daniel G.; Elliot M. Franklin: *Cultural Anthropology*, 3rd Ed. ©2003. Pearson Education, Inc. **p. 182:** McGee, Reece, et al.: *Sociology: An Introduction*, 2nd Ed. ©1980. Holt, Rinehart and Winston. **p. 182:** Wheeler, Jr., Jesse H., et al.: *Regional Geography of the World*, 3rd Ed. ©1970. Holt, Rinehart & Winston. **p. 183:** Lindzey, Gardner, et al.: *Psychology*, 3rd Ed. ©1988. Worth Publishing. **p. 183:** Rachman/Mescon/Bovee/Thill: *Business Today*, 8th Ed. ©1997. Reprinted and Electronically reproduced by permission of Pearson Education, Inc., New York, NY. **p. 183:** Schmalleger, Frank: *Criminal Justice Today*, 8th Ed. ©2005. Pearson Education, Inc. **p. 183:** Kirkpatrick, Larry; Gregory Francis: *Physics: A World View*, 6th Ed. ©2007. Cengage. **p. 184:** Griffin, Ricky W.; Ronald J. Ebert: *Business*, 8th Ed. ©2006. Pearson Education, Inc. **p. 184:** Kosslyn, Stephen M.; Robin S. Rosenberg: *Psychology: The Brain, the Person, the World*, 2nd Ed. ©2004. Pearson Education, Inc. **p. 184:** Kishlansky, Mark, et al.: *Civilization in the West*, 6th Ed. ©2006. Pearson Education, Inc. **p. 185:** Lutgens, Frederick K.; Edward J. Tarbuck: *The Atmosphere: An Introduction to Meteorology*, 9th Ed. ©2004. Pearson Education, Inc. **p. 190:** By permission from *Merriam-Webster's Collegiate® Dictionary*, 11th Edition ©2015 by Merriam-Webster, Inc (www.Merriam-Webster.com). **p. 191:** By permission from *Merriam-Webster's Collegiate® Dictionary*, 11th Edition ©2015 by Merriam-Webster, Inc (www.Merriam-Webster.com). **p. 192:** By permission from *Merriam-Webster's Collegiate® Dictionary*, 11th Edition ©2015 by Merriam-Webster, Inc (www.Merriam-Webster.com). **p. 194:** By permission from *Merriam-Webster's Collegiate® Dictionary*, 11th Edition ©2015 by Merriam-Webster, Inc (www.Merriam-Webster.com). **p. 195:** By permission from *Merriam-Webster's Collegiate® Dictionary*, 11th Edition ©2015 by Merriam-Webster, Inc (www.Merriam-Webster.com). **p. 196:** By permission from *Merriam-Webster's Collegiate® Dictionary*, 11th Edition ©2015 by Merriam-Webster, Inc (www.Merriam-Webster.com). **p. 197:** By permission from *Merriam-Webster's Collegiate® Dictionary*, 11th Edition ©2015 by Merriam-Webster, Inc (www.Merriam-Webster.com). **p. 197:** By permission from *Merriam-Webster's Collegiate® Dictionary*, 11th Edition ©2015 by Merriam-Webster, Inc (www.Merriam-Webster.com). **p. 197:** By permission from *Merriam-Webster's Collegiate® Dictionary*, 11th Edition ©2015 by Merriam-Webster, Inc (www.Merriam-Webster.com). **pp. 203–204:** Donatelle, Rebecca J., *Health: The Basics*, 11th Ed. ©2015, 79, 203. Reprinted and Electronically reproduced by permission of Pearson Education, Inc., New York, NY. **p. 216:** Peterson, Christopher: *Introduction to Psychology*. ©1991. HarperCollins. **p. 217:** Davidson, James W., et al.: *Nation of Nations*, 6th Ed. ©2008. McGraw-Hill. **p. 217:** Griffin, Ricky W.; Ronald J. Ebert: *Business*, 10th Ed. ©2015. Pearson Education, Inc. **p. 217:** Brands, HW, et al.: *American Stories: A History of the United States, Combined Volume*, 3rd Ed. ©2015. Pearson Education, Inc. **p. 219:** Burns, James MacGregor, et al.: *Government by the People*, 20th Ed. ©2004. Pearson Education, Inc. **p. 219:** Evans, Alan, et al.: *Technology in Action*, 2nd Ed. ©2006. Pearson Education, Inc. **p. 219:** Kosslyn, Stephen M.; Robin S. Rosenberg: *Psychology: The Brain, the Person, the World*, 2nd Ed. ©2004. Pearson Education, Inc. **p. 222:** Reitz, Joseph; Linda Jewell: *Managing*. ©1993. Pearson Education, Inc. **p. 223:** Davidson, James W., et al.: *Nation of Nations*, 6th Ed. ©2008. McGraw-Hill. **p. 224:** Dempsey, David; Philip Zimbardo: *Psychology and You*, 1st Ed. ©1978. Pearson Education, Inc. **p. 225:** Fox, Edward; Edward Wheatley: *Modern Marketing*. ©1978. Pearson Education, Inc. **pp. 225–226:** Mescon, Michael, et al.: *Business Today*, 8th Ed. ©1997. Pearson Education, Inc. **p. 226:** Donatelle, Rebecca J.: *Access to Health*, 8th Ed. ©2004. Pearson Education, Inc. **p. 227:** Twain, Mark: *Life on the Mississippi*, 1883. **p. 227:** Whiting, Robert: *You Gotta Have What it Takes*. ©2009. Vintage, Random House. **p. 228:** Gerrig, Richard; Philip Zimbardo: *Psychology and Life*, 17th Ed. ©2005. Pearson Education, Inc. **p. 229:** Wood, Samuel; Wood, Ellen Green; Boyd, Denise: *Mastering the World of Psychology*, 5th Ed. (c) 2014. Reprinted and Electronically reproduced by permission of Pearson Education, Inc., New York, NY. **p. 230:** Wade, Carole; Carol Tavris; Maryanne Garry: *Psychology*, 11th Ed. ©2014. Pearson Education, Inc. **p. 231:** Kishlansky, Mark, et al.: *Civilization in the West*, 4th Ed. ©2001. Pearson Education, Inc. **p. 232:** Beebe, Steven A.; Susan J. Beebe; Diana K. Ivy: *Communication*, 5th Ed. ©2013. Pearson Education, Inc. **pp. 232–233:** Albanese, Jay S.: *Criminal Justice, Brief Edition*. ©2011. Pearson Education, Inc. **pp. 234–235:** Vivian, John: *The Media of Mass Communication*, 11th Ed. ©2013. Pearson Education, Inc. **p. 235:** Boyd, Denise G.; Helen L. Bee: *Lifespan Development*, 7th Ed. ©2015. Pearson Education, Inc. **pp. 235–236:** Burns, James MacGregor, et al.: *Government by the People*, 20th Ed. ©2004. Pearson Education, Inc. **p. 236:** Mescon, Michael, et al.: *Business Today*, 8th Ed. ©1997. Pearson Education, Inc. **pp. 236–237:** Nanda, Serena: *Cultural Anthropology*, 4th Ed. ©1991. Cengage. **p. 237:** Donatelle, Rebecca J.: *Health: The Basics*, 4th Ed. ©2001. Pearson Education, Inc. **p. 238:** Nash, Roderick; Gregory Graves: *From These Beginnings, Vol. 2*, 6th Ed. ©2000. Pearson Education, Inc. **p. 239:** Mescon, Michael, et al.: *Business Today*, 8th Ed. ©1997. Pearson Education, Inc. **p. 240:** Carson, Clayborne; Emma J. Lapsansky-Werner, and Gary B. Nash: *The Struggle for Freedom: A History of African Americans, Combined Volume*, 2nd Ed. ©2011. Pearson Education, Inc. **pp. 240–241:** Armstrong Gary; Kotler, Philip: *Marketing: An Introduction*, 10th Ed. ©2011. Printed and Electronically reproduced by permission of Pearson Education, Inc., Upper Saddle River, New Jersey. **p. 241:** Myers, David: *Psychology*, 10th Ed. ©2014. Cengage Learning. **pp. 242–243:** Pruitt, BE; Jane J. Stein: *Decisions for Healthy Living*. ©2004. Pearson Education, Inc. **p. 244:** Medina, John: *Brain Rules: 12 Principles for Surviving and Thriving at Work, Home, and School*, Pear Press, 2008, 2014. www.brainrules.net. Reprinted with permission. **pp. 244–245:** Wade, Carole; Tavris, Carol: *Psychology*, 10th Ed. ©2011. Printed and Electronically reproduced by permission of Pearson Education, Inc., Upper Saddle River, New Jersey. **pp. 245–246:** Nash, Gary B., et al.: *The American People, Vol 1*, 6th Ed. ©2008. Pearson Education, Inc. **p. 248:** Thio, Alex: *Sociology*, 3rd Ed. ©1992. Pearson Education, Inc. **p. 249:** Donatelle, Rebecca J.: *Access to Health*, 8th Ed. ©2004. Pearson Education, Inc. **p. 250:** Bennett, Jeffrey, et al.: *The Essential Cosmic Perspective*, 7th Ed. ©2015. Pearson Education, Inc. **p. 250:** Macionis, John J.: *Sociology*, 10th Ed. ©2005. Pearson Education, Inc. **p. 251:** Medina, John: *Brain Rules: 12 Principles* *for Surviving and Thriving at Work, Home, and School*, Pear Press, 2008, 2014. www.brainrules.net. Reprinted with permission. **pp. 254–256:** Wade, Carole; Tavris, Carol; Garry, Maryanne: *Psychology*, 11th Ed. ©2014, pp. 578–579. Reprinted and Electronically reproduced by permission of Pearson Education, Inc., New York, NY. **pp. 264–269:** Hunter, Evan: "On the Sidewalk, Bleeding," *Happy New Year, Herbie and Other Stories*. Copyright ©1963, 1991 by Evan Hunter. Reprinted by permission of Gelfman Schneider Literary Agents, Inc. All rights reserved. **pp. 277–279:** Wolpert, Stuart: "Fighting Violent Gang Crime with Math," UCLA Newsroom. Reprinted with permission. **p. 292:** Caine, Caine, McClintic, and Klimek: *12 Brain Mind Learning Principles in Action: Developing Executive Function of the Human Brain*, ©2008. Corwin. **p. 293:** Dacey, John; John Travers: *Human Development*, 2nd Ed. ©1994. McGraw-Hill. **p. 294:** De Blij, H.J.; Peter O. Muller: *Geography: Realms, Regions, and Concepts*, 7th Ed. ©1994. John Wiley. **p. 295:** McPhee, John: *Oranges*. ©1975. Farrar, Straus and Giroux. **p. 298:** Martin, James Kirby, et al.: *America and Its People*. ©1989. Pearson Education, Inc. **p. 302:** Lutgens, Frederick K.; Tarbuck, Edward J.; Tada, Dennis G: *The Atmosphere: An Introduction to Meteorology*, 9th Ed., ©2004, p. 147. Reprinted and Electronically reproduced by permission of Pearson Education, Inc., New York, NY. **pp. 302–303:** Ebert, Ronald; Ricky W. Griffin: *Business Essentials*, 10th Ed. ©2015. Pearson Education, Inc. **p. 303:** Adapted from Paul R. Gregory, *Essentials of Economics*, 6th Ed. ©2005. Pearson Education, Inc. **p. 304:** Brands, H.W., et al.: *American Stories: A History of the United States,* Combined Volume, 3rd Ed. ©2015. Pearson Education, Inc. **p. 305:** Adapted from *Brain-Based Learning: The New Paradigm of Teaching*, 2nd ed., by Eric Jensen (p. 66) Corwin Press, 2008 **pp. 305–306:** Lutgens, Frederick K.; Tarbuck, Edward J.; Tasa, Dennis G, *The Atmosphere: An Introduction to Meteorology*, 9th Ed., ©2004, p. 195. Reprinted and Electronically reproduced by permission of Pearson Education, Inc., New York, NY. **pp. 306–307:** Adapted from Paul R. Gregory, *Essentials of Economics*, 6th Ed. ©2005. Pearson Education, Inc. **pp. 310–313:** DeVito, Joseph A.: *The Interpersonal Communication Book*, 13th Ed. ©2013, pp. 298–303. Reprinted and Electronically reproduced by permission of Pearson Education, Inc., New York, NY. **pp. 319–321:** Carson, Clayborne; Emma J. Lapsansky-Werner, and Gary B. Nash; *The Struggle for Freedom: A History of African Americans*, Combined Volume, 2nd Ed. ©2011. Pearson Education, Inc. **pp. 330–333:** Bovee, Courtland L.; Thill, John V.; Schatzman, Barbara E.: *Business in Action*, 2nd Ed. ©2004. Printed and Electronically reproduced by permission of Pearson Education, Inc., Upper Saddle River, New Jersey. **p. 345:** Zull, James E.: *The Art of Changing the Brain*. ©2002 Stylus Publishing, LLC. Sterling, VA. **p. 348:** Pitt, Leonard: *We Americans*, 3rd Ed. ©1987. Kendall Hunt. **p. 348:** Wallace, Robert: *Biology: The Science of Life*, 4th Ed. ©1996. Pearson Education, Inc. **p. 348:** Martin, James Kirby, et al.: *America and Its People*. ©1989. Pearson Education, Inc. **p. 349:** Lineberry, Robert: *Government in America,* Brief Version, 2nd Ed. ©1995. HarperCollins. **p. 350:** Samuel Taylor Colderidge, *The Rime of the Ancient Mariner*, 1798. **p. 352:** Ramirez, Robert: "The Barrio" in *Models for Writers: Short Essays for Composition*, 8th Edition, by Alfred Rosa and Paul Eschholz. New York: Bedford/St. Martin's, 2003. Reprinted by permission of Robert Ramirez. **p. 353:** Pitt, Leonard: *We Americans*, 3rd Ed. ©1987. Kendall Hunt. **p. 353:** Nash, Gary B., et al.: *The American People: Creating a Nation and a Society*, 6th Ed., Vol, 1: to 1877. ©2008. Pearson Education, Inc. **p. 353:** Kishlansky, Mark, et al.: *Civilization in the West*, 6th Ed. ©2006. Pearson Education, Inc. **p. 353:** Saenz, Benjamin Alire: "Exile, El Paso, Texas," *The Late Great Mexican Border*. ©1996. Cinco Puntos Press. **p. 354:** Morris, Eli: "Life Begins With Roots." Used by permission of the author. **p. 354:** Hughes, Langston: "The Negro Speaks of Rivers," 1921. **pp. 355–356:** Dickinson, Emily: "The nearest dream recedes, unrealized," from *Poems: Second Series*. Edited by T. W. Higginson and Mabel Loomis Todd. Published by Roberts Brothers of Boston, 1921. **p. 357:** *Time Magazine*, March 1, 2004-January 19, 2004; February 2, 2004. **p. 358:** Marinovich, Matt: "Intelligence," *The Quarterly*, Issue 24, Winter 1992. **p. 359:** Bernays, Anne and Pamela Painter: *What If? Writing Exercises for Fiction Writers*. ©1990. William Morrow. **p. 359:** Devine, Robert A., et al: *America: Past and Present*, 10th Ed. ©2010. Pearson Education, Inc. **p. 360:** Pitt, Leonard: *We Americans*, 3rd Ed. ©1987. Kendall Hunt. **pp. 360–361:** Crane, Stephen: "The Open Boat," 1897. **p. 361:** Clawson, David and Merrill Johnson: *World Regional Geography*, 8th Ed. ©2004. Pearson Education, Inc. **p. 362:** Medina, John: *Brain Rules: 12 Principles for Surviving and Thriving at Work, Home, and School*, Pear Press, 2008, 2014. www.brainrules.net. Reprinted with permission. **p. 363:** Riley, Glenda: *Inventing the American Woman: An Inclusive History*, 3rd Ed., Vol 1 to 1877. ©1987. Harlan Davidson. **p. 363:** Mooney, James: *Myths of the Cherokee*, 19th Annual Report, Bureau of American Ethnology. **p. 364:** Parrillo, Vincent N.: *Strangers to These Shores: Race and Ethnic Relations in the United Stated with Research Navigator,* 8th Ed. ©2006. Printed and Electronically reproduced by permission of Pearson Education, Inc., Upper Saddle River, New Jersey. **p. 365:** Pitt, Leonard: *We Americans*, 3rd Ed. ©1987. Kendall Hunt. **p. 366:** Parrillo, Vincent N.: *Strangers to These Shores: Race and Ethnic Relations in the United States with Research Navigator*, 8th Ed. ©2006. Printed and Electronically reproduced by permission of Pearson Education, Inc., Upper Saddle River, New Jersey. **p. 366:** Kosslyn, Stephen M. and Robin S. Rosenberg: *Psychology: The Brain, the Person, the World*, 2nd Ed. ©2004. Pearson Education, Inc. **p. 367:** Parrillo, Vincent N.: *Strangers to These Shores: Race and Ethnic Relations in the United States with Research Navigator*, 8th Ed. ©2006. Printed and Electronically reproduced by permission of Pearson Education, Inc., Upper Saddle River, New Jersey. **pp. 368–369:** Chopin, Kate: "The Story of an Hour," 1894. **pp. 373–375:** Pronzini, Bill: "A Dip in the Poole." Copyright ©1970 by H.S.D. Publications, Inc. First published in *Alfred Hitchcock's Mystery Magazine*. Reprinted by permission of the author. **pp. 384–387:** Shipley, William: "Coyote Story," *The Maidu Indian Myths and Stories of Hancibyjim*, Heyday Books, 1991. Reprinted courtesy of Heyday, www.heydaybooks.com. **pp. 392–395:** Corcoran, John: "The Teacher Who Couldn't Read." Reprinted with permission of John Corcoran. **p. 407:** Bergman, Edward and William Renwick: *Introduction to Geography*, 2nd Ed. ©2002. Pearson Education, Inc. **p. 407:** Fiorina, Morris P., et al.: *The New American Democracy*, 3rd Ed. ©2003. Pearson Education, Inc. **p. 408:** Goergen, Christian: *Politics in a Globalized World* ©2007. Kendall Hunt Publishing Company. **pp. 408–409:** Goergen, Christian: *Politics in a Globalized World* ©2007. Kendall Hunt Publishing Company. **p. 410:** Strayer, Joseph R., et al.: *The Mainstream of Civilization*, 4th Ed. ©1984. Harcourt. **p. 410:** Clough, Shepard B., et al.: *A History of the Western World*. ©1967. D.C. Heath. **p. 411:** Wallace, Robert: *Biology: The World of Life*, 6th Ed. ©1992. HarperCollins. **p. 412:** Martin, James Kirby, et al.: *America and Its People*. ©2011. Pearson Education, Inc. **pp. 412–413:** Devine, Robert A., et al: *America: Past and Present*, 10th Ed. ©2010. Pearson Education, Inc. **p. 414:** Medina, John: *Brain Rules: 12 Principles for Surviving and Thriving at Work, Home, and School*, Pear Press, 2008, 2014. www.brainrules.net. Reprinted with permission. **p. 415:** Reiman, Jeffrey: *The Rich Get Richer and the Poor Get Prison*, 7th Ed. ©2004. Pearson Education, Inc. **p. 415:** Macionis, John: *Social Problems*, 5th Ed. ©2013. Pearson Education. **p. 415:** Magleby, David B.: *Government by the People, Teaching and Learning Classroom Edition*, 6th Ed. ©2006. Pearson Education, Inc. **p. 415:** Griffin, Ricky W.; Ronald J. Ebert: *Business*, 8th Ed. ©2006. Pearson Education, Inc. **p. 415:** Lefton, Lester A.; Linda Brannon: *Psychology*, 9th Ed. ©2006. Pearson Education, Inc. **p. 415:** Kosslyn, Stephen M.; Robin S. Rosenberg: *Psychology: The Brain, the Person, the World*, 2nd Ed. ©2004. Pearson Education, Inc. **p. 416:** Sheindlin, Judy: *Don't Pee on My Leg and Tell Me It's Raining*. ©1996. HarperCollins. **p. 416:** Nash, Gary B., et al.: *The American People, Vol I*, 6th Ed. ©2008. Pearson Education, Inc. **p. 416:** Gregory, Paul R.: *Essentials of Economics*, 6th Ed. ©2005. Pearson Education, Inc. **p. 416:** Wasserman, Gary: *The Basics of American Politics*, 12th Ed. ©2006. Pearson Education, Inc. **pp. 416–417:** Kishlansky, Mark, et al.: *Civilization in the West*, 6th Ed. ©2006. Pearson Education, Inc. **pp. 417–418:** Greer, Charles R.; Plunkett Richard Warren: *Supervision: Diversity and Teams in the Workplace*, 10th Ed. ©2003. Pearson Education, Inc. **p. 419:** Bierce, Ambrose: "The Devil's Dictionary," 1911. **pp. 420–421:** Greaves, Richard L.; Zaller, Robert; Cannistraro, Philip V.; Murphey, Rhoads: *Civilizations of the World: The Human Adventure*, 3rd Ed. ©1997. Reprinted and Electronically reproduced by permission of Pearson Education, Inc., New York, NY. **pp. 423–424:** Buhle, Mary Jo; Teresa Murphy; Jane Gerhard: *Women and the Making of America*. ©2009. Pearson Education, Inc. **p. 425:** Saénz, Benjamin Alire: "Exile," El Paso, Texas. ©2006. Cinco Puntos Press. **p. 426:** O'Shaughnessy, Brendan: "It's a Whole New Ballgame for Veteran Coach," *Chicago Tribune*, December 1, 2002. **p. 427:** Cunningham, Amy: "Why Women Smile," Lear's Magazine, March 1993. **pp. 433–436:** Kirby, Gary R.; Goodpaster,, Jeffrey R., *Thinking*, 4th Ed. ©2007, pp. 321–327. Reprinted and Electronically reproduced by permission of Pearson Education, Inc., New York, NY. **p. 443:** Audesirk, Gerald; Audesirk, Teresa; Byers, Bruce E.: *Biology: Life on Earth*, 10th Ed. ©2014, pp. 544, 545. Reprinted and Electronically reproduced by permission of Pearson Education, Inc., New York, NY. **p. 444:** Audesirk, Gerald; Audesirk, Teresa; Byers, Bruce E., *Biology: Life on Earth*, 10th Ed. ©2014, pp. 544, 545. Reprinted and Electronically reproduced by permission of Pearson Education, Inc., New York, NY **pp. 443–446:** Audesirk, Gerald; Audesirk, Teresa; Byers, Bruce E., *Biology: Life on Earth*, 10th Ed. ©2014, pp. 541–545. Reprinted and Electronically reproduced by permission of Pearson Education, Inc., New York, NY. **pp. 451–453:** Wade, Carole; Tavris, Carol; Garry, Maryanne: *Psychology*, 11th Ed. ©2014, pp. 578–579. Reprinted and Electronically reproduced by permission of Pearson Education, Inc., New York, NY. **p. 464:** Martini, Frederic H.; Nath, Judi L; Bartholomew, Edwin F.: *Fundamentals of Anatomy & Physiology*, 9th Ed. ©2012, p. 815. Reprinted and Electronically reproduced by permission of Pearson Education, Inc., Upper Saddle River, New Jersey. **p. 465:** U.S. Department of Agriculture, Mixed Dishes in MyPyramid. www.mypyramid.gov. Accessed March 2009. **p. 467:** US Census Bureau (2012). **p. 468:** US Census Bureau (2012). **p. 469:** US Census Bureau (2012). **p. 470:** Rowntree, Lester; Lewis, Martin; Price, Marie; Wyckoff, William, *Diversity Amid Globalization*: *World Regions, Environment, Development*, 3rd Ed. ©2006, p. 98. Reprinted and Electronically reproduced by permission of Pearson Education, Inc., New York, NY. **p. 472:** Crime Rates in the US, 1960-2011, FBI, 2012. **p. 473:** Fiorina, Morris P.; Peterson, Paul E: *The New American Democracy*, 3rd Ed. ©2003, p. 369. Reprinted and Electronically reproduced by permission of Pearson Education, Inc., New York, NY. **pp. 4[illegible]:** [illegible]: "Little Income, Big Debt: Managing Money in College," *The Simple Dollar*, February 19, 2008. Reprinted with permission. **pp. 484–486:** Reece, Jane B.; Taylor, Martha R.; Simon, Eric J.; Dickey, Jean L., Campbell. *Biology: Concepts &* *Connections*, 7th Ed. ©2012. Printed and Electronically reproduced by permission of Pearson Education, Inc., Upper Saddle River, New Jersey. **pp. 491–495:** Macionis, John J.: *Social Problems*, 2nd Ed. ©2005. Printed and Electronically reproduced by permission of Pearson Education, Inc., Upper Saddle

INDEX

Note: *n* following a page number refers to a footnote.